THE YOUNG
TURKS' CRIME
AGAINST
HUMANITY

HUMAN RIGHTS AND CRIMES AGAINST HUMANITY
Eric D. Weitz, Series Editor

Echoes of Violence: Letters from a War Reporter by Carolin Emcke

Cannibal Island: Death in a Siberian Gulag by Nicolas Werth. Translated by Steven Rendall with a foreword by Jan T. Gross

Torture and the Twilight of Empire from Algiers to Baghdad by Marnia Lazreg

Terror in Chechnya: Russia and the Tragedy of Civilians in War by Emma Gilligan

"If You Leave Us Here, We Will Die": How Genocide Was Stopped in East Timor by Geoffrey Robinson

Stalin's Genocides by Norman Naimark

Against Massacre: Humanitarian Intervention in the Ottoman Empire, 1815–1914 by Davide Rodogno

All the Missing Souls: A Personal History of the War Crimes Tribunals by David Scheffer

The Young Turks' Crime against Humanity: The Armenian Genocide and Ethnic Cleansing in the Ottoman Empire by Taner Akçam

THE YOUNG TURKS' CRIME AGAINST HUMANITY

The Armenian Genocide and Ethnic Cleansing in the Ottoman Empire

TANER AKÇAM

Lee Hazell, 08/12/2021
London, England

PRINCETON UNIVERSITY PRESS

PRINCETON AND OXFORD

Library of Congress Cataloging-in-Publication Data

Akçam, Taner, 1953–

    The Young Turks' crime against humanity : the Armenian
genocide and ethnic cleansing in the Ottoman Empire / Taner
Akçam.

        p. cm. — (Human rights and crimes against humanity)
    Includes bibliographical references and index.
    ISBN 978-0-691-15333-9 (alk. paper)
    1. Armenian massacres, 1915–1923. 2. Armenian
question. 3. Genocide—Turkey. 4. Ittihat ve Terakki
Cemiyeti. 5. Armenians—Turkey—History—20th century.
6. Turkey—Ethnic relations—History—20th century.
  I. Title.
    DS195.5.A4189 2012
    956.6′2023–dc23   2011049301

British Library Cataloging-in-Publication Data is available

This book has been composed in Arno Pro and Helvetica Neue Lt

Printed on acid-free paper. ∞

Printed in the United States of America

10 9 8 7 6 5 4 3 2 1

In memory of Hrant Dink, whose dream
of bringing our two peoples together
lives on in my heart and soul,
and in honor of Vahakn N. Dadrian, with
my deepest gratitude and respect

CONTENTS

PREFACE

The demise of the Ottoman state was a one-act drama that lasted a century, with a changing cast of players reenacting the same scenes over and over. As the great empire crumbled, a succession of ethnic and religious groups played out their struggles for independence on its shrinking stage against a backdrop of forced population exchanges, deportations, massacres, and ethnic cleansing.

As the last of the great early modern empires, the Ottoman state entered its long nineteenth century trailing the heritage of Byzantium but lacking the means of modernization.[1] Without the requisite political and social structures and public consensus of a nation-state, "the Muslim Third Rome" could no longer bind together the diverse groups that peopled its vast territory.[2]

"First one encounters the question of borders," wrote the French historian Fernand Braudel. "Everything else is derived from this. In order to draw a border, it is necessary to define it, to understand it, and reconstruct what that border means."[3] The nineteenth and twentieth centuries of the Ottoman Empire were the centuries in which answers to these questions were sought—and the answers were bloody.

The reason is not difficult to understand. The logic of the nation-state utterly contradicts that of empire. Whereas an empire, by definition, encompasses a number of territories and diverse peoples, a nation-state is circumscribed by two clearly defined boundaries: geographical and social. Whereas geographical borders demarcate a physical territory, social boundaries delimit a collective identity, ideally homogeneous, that binds together all inhabitants within the geographical border. Thus the era of the nation-state ushered in a new period of defining the "other."

---

[1] İlber Ortaylı, *İmparatorluğun En Uzun Yüzyılı* (Istanbul: Hil Publications, 1983).

[2] İlber Ortaylı, *Son-İmparatorluk Osmanlı*, 2nd ed. (Istanbul: Timas Publications, 2006), 44.

[3] Quoted from Hagen Schulze, *Gibt es überhaupt eine deutsche Geschichte?* (Berlin: Corso, bei Siedler, 1989), 20.

Christen Benutzt

As the Ottoman Empire devolved into nation-states, ethnic and religious groups, which until then had been living not only within the same territory but even side by side in the same villages, struggled to define themselves against the Ottoman state and their own neighbors, purging the designated "outsiders" from villages, towns, and regions from the Balkans eastward. The mass violence that accompanied the formation of nation-states in the nineteenth century erupted in the first two decades of the twentieth. The succession of wars and revolutions, brutally suppressed rebellions, forced population exchanges, deportations and ethnic cleansing, massacres and genocide—human destructiveness on a previously unimaginable scale—only concluded in 1923 with the Treaty of Lausanne, which provided for the independence of modern Turkey.

Yet it was not enough to have redrawn the boundaries of territorial and collective identity, for the developing nation-state requires a third factor, collective memory, which combines the other two. To create this common memory, the history of the former Ottoman lands as experienced by the peoples of the Balkans, Middle East, and Caucasia in all their ethnic, religious, and national variety was written anew. Strikingly, however, these divergent accounts of the immediate past can be boiled down to one of two seemingly contradictory narrative themes: one in which the Great powers dismantled and destroyed the Ottoman Empire by using its Christian subjects; the other, an account of persecution and massacre by the Ottoman authorities. These two narratives were developed and persist today as competing and mutually exclusive historiographies.

The first narrative is associated with the Muslim Turkish communities that gradually, over time, identified with their otherwise cosmopolitan and multiethnic Ottoman rulers. Muslim Turks came to believe that they founded their republic after a life-or-death struggle against the Great powers and their treacherous collaborators, the Ottoman Christians, whose sole aim was to wipe the Ottoman state and Muslim Turks from the face of the earth. For this reason, in the early years of the century, the imperative to protect their (Ottoman) state from dissolution became firmly established among Muslim Turks, especially the authorities and intellectuals: "Their greatest objective and greatest concern, the beginning and end of their thoughts, was to save the state."[4] As for the powers' expressed rationale for intervening on behalf of the Christians, it was said at the time that "Europe's humanitarianism and justice consist of pure hypocrisy [*hiyakârlık*]."[5]

This notion of an encircling threat not only helped to motivate the massacre and annihilation of Christians, especially Armenians, but it was also invoked to justify, in retrospect, the policies of destruction as legitimate, national self-defense. "It's one thing to say that the Turks killed the Armenians spontaneously," wrote the doyen of Turkish historians, Yusuf Hikmet Bayur, in his monumental work, *The History of the Turkish Revolution*, "and another to say that, when the Armenians revolted, the Turks, who were locked in a life or death struggle, used excessive force and killed a good many people."[6]

"This deportation business, as you know, has put the whole world in an uproar, and has branded us all as murderers," declared a Muslim Turkish deputy to the new parliament in 1920. "We knew even before this was done that the Christian world would not stand for it, and that they would turn their fury and hatred on us because of it. But why should we call ourselves murderers? These things that were done were to secure the future of our homeland, which we hold more sacred and dear than our very lives."[7]

The existential imperative to preserve the state at all costs was adopted as the basis of official Turkish policy and historiography. "National security" not only explained and justified the traumatic events of the past but would also support the construction of genocide denial in the future. Thereafter, an open and frank discussion of history would be perceived as a subversive act aimed at partitioning the state. Well into the new millennium, Turkish citizens who demanded an honest historical accounting were still being treated as national security risks, branded as traitors to the homeland or dupes of hostile foreign powers, and targeted with threats.

In February 2009, during a raid against the ultranationalist terror organization Ergenekon, the personnel of which were believed to be deeply

---

[4] Şerif Mardin, *Jön Türkler ve Siyasi Fikirleri* (Istanbul: İletişim Publications, 1983), 14.

[5] Quoted from a Unionist journal in ibid., 117.

[6] Yusuf Hikmet Bayur, *Türk İnkilabı Tarihi*, vol. 3, part 3 (Ankara: Türk Tarih Kurumu, 1983), 35.

[7] From a speech by Hasan Fehmi Bey in the secret session of Parliament, 17 October 1920, in *TBMM Gizli Celse Zabıtları*, vol. 1 (Ankara: Türkiye İş Bankası Yayınları, 1985), 177.

the theory (philosophy) of law

embedded in the military and state bureaucracy, the police seized a file of "Traitors to National Security." Included on this "hit list" were Hrant Dink, the Istanbul Armenian journalist who was assassinated in 2007; Nobel laureate Orhan Pamuk; and this writer.[8]

Rationalizing the Armenian annihilation and its denial in terms of "national security" has not been limited to political circles or ultranationalist criminal organizations, but has also underpinned Turkish jurisprudence. In 2007, two Turkish Armenian journalists, Sarkis Seropyan and Arat Dink, the son of assassinated journalist Hrant Dink, received suspended sentences of a year's imprisonment for using the term "genocide" in connection with the events of 1915. "Talk about genocide, both in Turkey and in other countries, unfavorably affects national security and the national interest," declared the court. "The claim of genocide . . . has become part of and the means of special plans aiming to change the geographic political boundaries of Turkey . . . and a campaign to demolish its physical and legal structure." Observing that the Republic of Turkey is under "a hostile diplomatic siege consisting of genocide resolutions," the ruling warned that "[t]he acceptance of this claim may lead in future centuries to a questioning of the sovereignty rights of the Republic of Turkey over the lands on which it is claimed these events occurred." The assertion that genocide was committed in 1915 is not protected speech, said the court, noting that "the use of these freedoms can be limited in accordance with aims such as the protection of national security, of public order, of public security."[9]

In summary, given this mind-set, one would be hard-pressed to find a reference in Turkish historiography to forced deportations, massacres, and genocide during the late nineteenth and early twentieth centuries. Instead, the Ottoman Christian communities are painted as the seditious agents of the imperialist Great powers, continually conspiring against the state.

The second narrative is associated with the ethnic and religious minority groups that were systematically, though differentially, subjected to abuses during that same period. This historiography foregrounds the minorities' quest for social and political rights throughout the nineteenth

---

[8] *Radikal,* 11 February 2009. For more detailed information about Ergenekon, see http://www.turkishgladio.com/.

[9] Court Decree, Second Penal Court of First Instance for the District of Şişli, File Number 2006/1208, Decree Number 2007/1106, Prosecution No. 2006/8617.

century and is bolstered from time to time by the interventions of the Great powers. The demise of the empire is viewed as a positive development of the national liberation struggle against the oppressive Ottomans, that is, the "Turks."

The contrasts between the official Muslim Turkish historiography and that of the other ethnic religious groups, whether or not they established a nation-state, could not be clearer. The first laments the unjust end of the great empire, while the second celebrates its partition and demise; the former criticizes the Great powers for intervening *too much*, while the latter faults them for not having intervened *enough*. The fierce partisans of either side remain convinced that the other version of events is inaccurate or irrelevant. In fact, however, a close review of the literature on the last Ottoman century reveals the opposing historical theses as two sides of a coin: they describe the same events, but from different viewpoints. The official Muslim Turkish historiography identifies itself with the decline of the state, whereas the versions of other ethnic religious groups tend to focus on the suffering of their own group in that process. What is needed, therefore, is a history that incorporates both perspectives into a single, unified account. In this way the massacres and genocide can be understood in their full historical significance.

This book does just that by building on the discourse introduced by its predecessor, *A Shameful Act*.[10] With greatly extended and unpublished documentation from the Ottoman archives, especially dating from January 1913 onward, I hope to shed new light on the increasingly radical decisions that set in motion the ethnic cleansing of Anatolia and the Armenian Genocide in particular.

The Ottoman records from August 1914 and beyond are crucial to understanding the decision-making process. They reveal that the Ottoman authorities, convinced that the Armenian reform agreement signed by the Russians in February 1914 would lead to the dissolution of the empire, were determined to prevent this outcome at any cost. The outbreak of war heightened this existential fear and the corresponding imperative to save the state, setting in motion a chain of increasingly radical policies that culminated in the campaign to extirpate the Armenians from Anatolia. As the

[10] Taner Akçam, *A Shameful Act: The Armenian Genocide and the Question of Turkish Responsibility* (New York: Metropolitan Books, 2006).

hundred-year drama drew to a close, national security concerns, among other factors, set the stage for genocide.

—

The scene opened just after the Balkan Wars of 1912–13, as the empire—having been forced to cede more than 60 percent of its territory over the entire nineteenth century—was confronting its greatest loss: more than 80 percent of its European lands (and nearly 70 percent of its European population) in less than one disastrous month. The worst defeat in Ottoman history had also displaced a huge wave of Balkan Muslim refugees southeast toward Anatolia, the home of a large Christian population and the new focus of both Great power and Ottoman concern.[11] The ruling party, the Committee of Union and Progress (hereafter CUP or Unionists),[12] was beginning to believe that collapse was imminent. "It is impossible to save Anatolia from the destiny awaiting Rumelia,"[13] headlined the newspaper *Tanin*, the CUP party organ. Kuşçubaşı Eşref, an active member of the Special Organization (Teşkilat-ı Mahsusa; hereafter SO) recounted his conversation with defense minister Enver Pasha, a triumvir of the CUP, on 23 February 1914.[14] Painting a picture of national collapse, Enver claimed that the "non-Turkish elements" within the country (read: Christians) had shown themselves to be opposed to the empire's continued existence. The salvation of the state therefore depended on taking measures against them. In the words of Kuşçubaşı Eşref, the "non-Turkish elements"

[11] Anatolia was not of central importance in Ottoman and Great power policy until the Balkan Wars. The region first became important for the Russian policy after 1905. For more detail on Russian and Great power policies and the Armenian reform issue, see Roderic H. Davison, "The Armenian Crisis, 1912–1914," *American Historical Review* 53, no. 3 (April 1948): 481–505.

[12] Whether the organization should be called committee or party is a complicated question. It was founded as the Committee for Union and Progress, but after the 1908 revolution, when it obtained a majority in Parliament, the CUP was also organized as a political party in order to carry out its parliamentary activities. Until 1913, the party in Parliament acted as the legal arm of the committee, and the relations between the party and the committee were regulated through a special statute. According to this arrangment, the committee was the upper and the party the lower organ. At the 1913 Congress, the committee organized itself as a party, and ended the party-committee duality. For more detailed information, see Tarık Zafer Tunaya, *Türkiye'de Siyasal Partiler*, vol. 3, *İttihat ve Terakki: Bir Çağın, Bir Kuşağın, Bir Partinin Tarihi* (Istanbul: Hürriyet Vakfı Yayınları, 1989), 200–204.

[13] Aram Andonian, *Balkan Savaşı* (Istanbul: Aras Yayıncılık, 1999), 227; Rumelia is used to define the territories approximating the Balkans today.

[14] For more detailed treatment of the *Teşkilat-ı Mahsusa*, see chapter 10.

were "an internal tumor," the "purging" of which was a "matter of national importance."[15]

In the wake of their devastating defeat in the Balkan Wars of 1912–13, the Unionist leaders, increasingly convinced that tolerating the Ottoman Christians would lead to national collapse, made a series of policy decisions aimed at the ethnoreligious homogenization of Anatolia. The CUP's rationale was rather simple and straightforward. Assuming a direct relationship between governability and demographics, party leaders reasoned that the Ottoman state could retain control of its remaining territories only if most of the inhabitants were Muslim Turks. This concept of *governability* can be considered as a kind of surveillance policy to collect information about the population in order to conceptualize it as a discrete, aggregate object. Governability may also be understood as "a shift in the goal of ruling, a shift from a territorial concept to a governmental one. A governmental state seeks to manage the populations, not just to rule the territories."[16] To achieve this administrative goal, therefore, the population of Anatolia would have to be reconfigured. The Christian population was to be reduced; that is, removed, and the non-Turkish Muslim groups were to be assimilated.

Faith in science held a central place in CUP philosophy. Like physicians, the Unionists would cure society's ills through the proper application of science.[17] In keeping with this orientation, their demographic policy has been characterized as "social engineering."[18] The result of this approach was the implementation, after 1913, of what I call a *demographic policy* aimed at the radical restructuring of Anatolia's population. Christians were not the sole focus of this policy, which also targeted non-Turkish Muslim communities; however, it was implemented in a differential manner, according to religion. Christians were to be eliminated by expulsion or massacre. Non-Turkish Muslims, such as the Kurds,

---

[15] From the memoirs of Kuşçubaşı Eşref, quoted in Celal Bayar, *Ben de Yazdım*, vol. 5 (Istanbul: Baha Matbaası, 1967), 1578.

[16] Peter Holquist, "'Information Is the Alpha and Omega of Our Work': Bolshevik Surveillance in Its Pan-European Context," *Journal of Modern History* 69, no. 3 (September 1997): 419.

[17] For further background on the CUP, see Taner Akçam, *A Shameful Act*, 47–67.

[18] Nesim Şeker, "Demographic Engineering in the Late Ottoman Empire and the Armenians," *Middle Eastern Studies* 43, no. 3 (2007): 46–474; Uğur Ümit Üngör, "Geographies of Nationalism and Violence: Rethinking Young Turk 'Social Engineering,'" *European Journal of Turkish Studies* 7 (2008), http://ejts.revues.org/index2583.html.

Arabs, and Balkan migrants (refugees from Christian persecution), were relocated and dispersed among the Turkish majority to be assimilated into the dominant culture. This book reconstructs in detail the implementation of this policy.

A central theme of the present study is the significance of the "5 to 10 percent principle." This rule was fundamental to the implementation of the demographic policies, in particular, the destruction of the Armenians in 1915. For example, Christians (especially the Armenians) were deported and resettled in other regions so as to constitute no more than 5 to 10 percent of the local population. In like manner, non-Turkish Muslims were relocated and redistributed among the Turkish Muslim majority in conformity with the 5 to 10 percent principle.[19]

How did the Unionists come up with this "magic" proportion? It seems to have been mentioned initially during the reform agreement talks of the 1890s and an early draft report by British colonel William Everett in 1895. The report was intended to serve as the basis for an administrative reform that would allow Armenians to hold positions in departments of government, such as the gendarmerie and police.[20] In 1913, the parties to a later round of Armenian reform talks agreed to use the Everett report as a starting point for negotiations.

In accordance with Unionist demographic policy, the ethnic character of Anatolia was thoroughly transformed. The prewar population (estimated at approximately 17.5 million in 1914) was so completely disrupted over the next six years that almost a third of the inhabitants were internally displaced, expelled, or annihilated.

—

This demographic policy was not implemented, nor was it experienced, in a linear, detailed, uniform manner. Zigzag changes of course and methods of implementation were tried at various points throughout the course of the war. Of particular significance was the differential enforce-

[19] This information suggests that the relationship between Armenian reform plans (including those of the 1890s) and genocide was stronger than has been assumed in Armenian Genocide scholarship. I am studying the reform plans of 1895 and 1914 and their impact on the genocide.

[20] For the full text of the report, see Fuat Dündar, *Crime of Numbers: The Role of Statistics in the Armenian Question (1878–1918)* (New Brunswick, NJ: Transactions, 2010), appendix 3, 178–81.

ment of the policy as it applied to two Christian populations, the Greeks and the Armenians.

Especially in 1913 and 1914, the Ottoman Greek inhabitants of the Thrace and the Aegean coast were subjected to a campaign of massacre and expulsion to Greece. This "ethnic cleansing," in modern terminology, would be suspended after November 1914 under pressure from Germany, in particular. During the war years, the policy toward the Ottoman Greeks was limited to relocation from the coastal areas into the interior out of military necessity. The later removal of the Greek population from Anatolia, especially the genocidal massacres of the Pontic Greeks and the forced population exchange with Greece in 1923, took place during the republican era in Turkey.

In contrast to the Ottoman Greeks, the Armenians were targeted by a wartime policy of total destruction. Those who survived deportation were forcibly resettled in the deserts of what are now Syria and Iraq, which left the six historically Armenian provinces of eastern Anatolia completely emptied of Armenians. By no coincidence, the targeted provinces were those in which Armenians were allowed to participate in local government, according to the Armenian Reform Agreement of February 1914.

Likewise, most of the Armenians were deported from western Anatolia to the deserts of present-day Syria and Iraq, but here again, the policy was implemented in a differential manner. Armenians were allowed to remain within the boundaries of certain provinces as long as their numbers did not exceed 5 percent of the Muslim population. As for the Armenians who were resettled in Syria and Iraq, great care was taken to ensure that they numbered no more than 10 percent of the local Muslims.

What was the relationship between demographic policy and genocidal intention? Why did the policy toward Armenians take on the form of genocide? This entire work is dedicated to answering these crucial questions. For now it is enough to say that the mass murder of Armenians was not the automatic result of the demographic policy toward the Greeks from 1913 onward. During the First World War the Ottoman authorities, having sustained a punishing sequence of military defeats, came to fear the imminent loss of the empire's entire territory, with the horrendous possibility that the reform agreement of February 1914 would be implemented. Their concern for national security was what gave the policy toward

Armenians its genocidal character. According to this reform agreement, the Armenians were to participate on an equal basis in the local administration of what now constitute the eastern provinces of Turkey (an area that is also known as historic or Western Armenia), where the Armenians were living in dense concentrations. All parties participating in the negotiations of the reform agreement knew that this was the beginning of an independent Armenian state.

Two major themes were intertwined in the Ottoman policy of extermination: the demographic restructuring of Anatolia, which was already in progress against the Greeks, and the fear of the 1914 Armenian reforms, an existential issue for the Unionists. The relationship between demographic policy and genocide is a linchpin of this book. In the Ottoman case, the demographic restructuring, and especially its 5 to 10 percent regulation, may be said to have laid the groundwork from which the Armenian Genocide would be launched. Dikran Kelegian (Diran Kelekian), an Armenian intellectual who knew the Unionists well and maintained friendships with them, foretold what was to come with this telling statement after his arrest on 24 April 1915: "They were going to implement the Armenian massacres with mathematical accuracy."[21] It is as if the 5 to 10 percent principle embodied this mathematical accuracy.

Abdullahad Nuri, in charge of the resettlement office in Aleppo, boldly summarizes the main argument of this book in a telegram he sent on 10 January 1916 to the central government: "Enquiries having been made, it is understood that hardly 10 percent of the Armenians subjected to the general deportations have reached the places destined for them; the rest have died from natural causes, such as hunger and sickness. We inform you that we are working to bring about the same result with regard to those who are still alive, by using severe measures."[22] The second great

---

[21] Aram Andonian, *Exile, Trauma and Death: On the Road to Chankiri with Komitas Vartabed*, trans. and ed. Rita Soulahian Kuyumjian (London: Gomidas Institute & Tekeyan Cultural Association, 2010), 160.

[22] Aram Andonian, *The Memoirs of Naim Bey* (1920; 2nd repr., Newton Square, PA: Armenian Historical Research Association, 1965), 57–58. Aram Andonian was an Armenian journalist and intellectual who was deported. In 1920 he obtained some telegrams from a Turkish official named Naim Bey (who worked in an office in Aleppo on issues connected with the settlement of Armenians) that included orders concerning the killing of Armenians. They were published in Adonian's book. It has been claimed that the telegrams are forgeries (Şinasi Orel and Süreyya Yuca, *The Talat Pasha Telegrams: Historical Fact or Armenian Fiction?* [Nicosia: K. Rustem & Brother, 1986]). For a discussion as

wave of massacres in Der Zor, Syria, during the summer of 1916, seems to have been motivated primarily by demographic anxieties, along with security concerns.

The wartime policies of the Ottoman government toward the Armenians were never, as has been frequently claimed, the result of military exigencies. While planning their measures against the Armenians, the authorities knew very well that the problem they wished to resolve was not simply a result of war. Rather, the policy toward the Armenians was conceived, planned, and put into effect with the clear intent of eliminating the so-called Armenian reform problem, a *gaile* (burden, trouble, worry) of civil administration in the Armenian provinces. Even before the war, stated interior minister and Unionist triumvir Talat Pasha, the Ottoman authorities had conceived of an approach "to eliminate [this problem] in a comprehensive and absolute manner" and had made several projections and considerations in this direction.[23] In this book, I will show how demographic policy and national security were intertwined in a manner that made genocide a possibility.

—

Among the Ottoman archival sources on which this study is based, great weight has been given to the records of the Ministry of the Interior's Office of the General Directorate of Security and its component units, as well as an independent unit, the Cipher Office. Although these documents do not reveal the government's plans for Christian populations other than the Greeks and Armenians, some documents do indicate that the Ottoman authorities were gathering information on the social, political, and economic conditions of these other Christian groups.[24] For example, according to a

---

to whether these documents are authentic, see Vahakn N. Dadrian, "The Naim-Andonian Documents on the World War I Destruction of Ottoman Armenians: The Anatomy of a Genocide," *International Journal of Middle East Studies* 18, no. 3 (August 1986): 311–36. Many telegrams similar to the above-mentioned one of Abdullahad Nuri are found in this book. I therefore consider it necessary to reopen the discussion concerning the authenticity of the documents published by Andonian.

[23] "the complete removal of this worry by solving and settling it in a fundamental way." Communiqué from Talat Pasha to the Office of the Grand Vizier, dated 26 May 1915, in *Ati*, 24 February 1920.

[24] "Assyrian," "Chaldean," "Nestorian," "Syriac," and "Syrian" are alternative historical names for a Christian group that mainly inhabited the southeast Anatolian provinces of Mardin, Hakkâri, and Diyarbekır.

telegram of July 1914, when the outbreak of war and the empire's participation in it were not yet certain, the Interior Ministry requested a detailed report from the regional office in Mosul on the Nestorians of the province, including their numbers and distribution, their present political and social conditions, and the propaganda to which they were being subjected, as well as the provincial government's views on appropriate measures toward them in the future.[25]

Similar messages were cabled to a great number of provincial offices of the ministry in the succeeding war years. A telegram of 10 September 1916 orders: "Report with additional comments regarding the Syriacs' stance towards the government since the beginning of the war, the regions and districts in which they are found, as well as their numbers, and whether or not they travel to other parts of the Ottoman realm for the purpose of trade and commerce."[26] It is possible to observe this situation through a document from May 1919, in which the government asks about "the number of the population of Syriacs in the province and how many of them were deported together with the Armenians, and their circumstances and situation there."[27] As this document shows, the government appears to be unaware of how many Syriacs were deported together with Armenians. The main question, though, is whether or not the Syriacs and other Christians in eastern Anatolia were treated differently than the Armenians. As can be discerned from an order sent to the eastern provinces in December 1915 that stated that "instead of deporting all the Syriac people found within the subdivision/province," they should be detained "in their present locations," one can argue that these Christian groups were treated somewhat differently than the Armenians.[28] Nevertheless, they were subjected

[25] BOA/DH.ŞFR, no. 42/263, Coded telegram from the Interior Ministry's General Directorate of Security (Emniyet-i Umumiye Müdürlüğü; hereafter EUM) to the Province of Mosul, dated 12 July 1914.

[26] BOA/DH.ŞFR, no. 68/98, Coded telegram from interior minister Talat to the Provincial District of Urfa, and to the Provinces of Mamuretülaziz (Elazığ), Diyarbekır, Bitlis, and Mosul, dated 23 September 1916.

[27] BOA/DH.ŞFR, no. 87/40, Coded telegram from the Interior Ministry's General Security Directorate to the Provinces of Aleppo, Diyarbekır, Mosul, Mamuretülaziz, and Bitlis, and to the Provincial District of Urfa, dated 1 May 1919.

[28] BOA/DH.ŞFR, no. 57/112. Coded telegram from the Interior Ministry's General Security Directorate to the Provinces of Diyarbekır, Bitlis, Mamuretülaziz (Elazığ), and Aleppo, and to the Provincial District of Urfa, dated 25 December 1915.

to similar policies and were often eliminated alongside the Armenians in spite of frequent orders to the contrary.[29]

Finally, not all of the population movements that were observed throughout the period were well defined and well planned from the start. During the war, in particular, populations were moved for a variety of ad hoc reasons. Examples include the resettlement in western and central Anatolia of nearly a million Muslim refugees who had escaped from advancing Russian units in 1915; the relocation, as required by the military, of Christians, particularly Greeks, from strategic areas along the seacoast into the interior regions of Anatolia beginning in late 1916; and the deportations of Arab families in Syria and Lebanon for political reasons. Detailed information on these events is included in this book. I thereby hope to radically restructure the present framework of debate on the 1913–18 period of Ottoman history and the "ethnic cleansing" policies that the Unionists put into place throughout Anatolia.

—

This book could be considered a "first" in another way because it explains the demographic policy and genocidal character of the actions against the Armenians on the basis of Ottoman archival records. Most of the approximately six hundred Ottoman documents presented here are seeing the light of day for the first time. By demonstrating that the policies toward the Armenians, in particular, were intended to bring about their annihilation, and supporting this argument entirely on the basis of Ottoman archival records, I hope to have made a significant contribution to the existing literature.

Because of the importance of the subject and the examination of an unprecedented number of Ottoman records at one time, I have chosen a somewhat unusual method of presentation. Unlike classic accounts of history, which analyze a given narrative chronology in light of various archival sources, this study gives central place to a single source, the Ottoman archives, as the basis for reconstructing a sequence of events as viewed

[29] For a recent and very important work that does cover the policies toward these Christian groups, see David Gaunt, *Massacres, Resistance, Protectors: Muslim-Christian Relations in Eastern Anatolia during World War I* (Piscataway, NJ: Gorgias Press, 2006).

and recorded by the central authorities. German and American records, as well as Armenian accounts, are also introduced for comparison, as appropriate, to demonstrate the consistency one finds across all sources. Examining this period from the government's perspective raises questions that I have attempted to address in chronological order; however, my approach has been thematic rather than strictly narrative.

Second, in order to nail down the correctness of a point, and at the risk of being repetitive, a superabundance of evidential records is presented throughout the study. Particularly when it pertains to "proving or disproving the genocide," one is frequently tempted to declare, "Eureka! I've found the missing document that will end all debate." Nevertheless, it should be obvious that no social policy, including genocide, can be proven with a single document. If in fact there was a policy, then it should be evident from dozens, if not hundreds or thousands of documents, and a discernible pattern should emerge from the totality of documents of the era. By introducing such a large number, I have attempted to ascertain the existence of particular policies and the pattern of their implementation.

Third, with this work, one can declare that a taboo among researchers of the Armenian Genocide has finally been broken. Until recently there have been two opposing assessments of the Ottoman and Turkish state archives. According to the "official Turkish position," what happened to the Armenians was a tragic but unintended by-product of the war, and there is no reliable evidence of a deliberate policy of systematic killing. In this view, the only source of reliable evidence on the topic is the Prime Ministerial Ottoman Archive in Istanbul. Foreign archives—American, British, German, and Austrian—as well as the domestic proceedings of the Istanbul Court-Martial, are dismissed as politically motivated distortions of the events.

Conversely, those who maintain that the policies toward the Armenians constituted genocide dismiss the Ottoman archives as an unreliable source of information. According to this view, the Ottoman records were falsified in order to cover up the genocide, and therefore the intent of the Ottoman authorities can be demonstrated only through the use of Western archives. The underlying logic common to both arguments is that the Ottoman and Western sources are mutually exclusive; that is, these documents contain irreconcilable contradictions. Each camp insists that its own particular favorite archival sources are the canonical ones, while the other side's documentation is wrong and unreliable.

In this work I hope to have demonstrated, for the first time, the falseness of this apparent contradiction. Far from conflicting with one another, the sources are in fact complementary: they tell the same story but from different points of view. In this respect, the quarrel over archival sources parallels the conflict between Muslim Turkish and minority historiographies.

Taken in their entirety, Ottoman and Western archives jointly confirm that the ruling party CUP did deliberately implement a policy of ethnoreligious homogenization of Anatolia that aimed to destroy the Armenian population. As a demonstration of the consistency among the various archives, I have incorporated German and American documents as appropriate to show that Ottoman records confirm and support those found within foreign archives.

A final word of caution on the character of the Ottoman documents presented here and their relation to the actual developments on the ground: although these "secret" and "top secret" telegrams from Istanbul provide extraordinarily important evidence of the true purpose and mentality of the ruling party and central government officials, there are few replies to indicate how and under what conditions these telegraphed orders were implemented in the various regions. More regional studies are needed in order to answer these questions.

—

When documents are published describing how the Christians were forced out of Anatolia and subjected to deportations and massacres, one further point must be emphasized. As described in this book, the CUP developed a "dual-track" mechanism for deporting the Ottoman Greeks to Greece between 1913 and 1914, as well as for deporting and killing the Armenians.

One track was the legal framework that had been created in order to execute the deportation. This encompassed official acts of state, such as the agreements with Serbia, Bulgaria, and Greece, regarding the population exchanges of 1913–14. An example of the legal track is a 27 May 1915 decree that authorizes the deportation of Armenians and that cites another government decision on the proper procedure. The official dimensions of the deportations, such as the disposition of Armenian property and the problems of resettlement, were discussed exclusively through government channels of communication.

The unofficial track consists of extralegal acts of violence, such as forced evacuations, killing orders, and massacres. For example, between 1913 and 1914, the evacuation of Ottoman Greek villages, the massacres, and the forced shipping of Ottoman Greeks out to sea were all performed and probably discussed and communicated outside government channels. Maximum effort was expended to create the impression that none of these actions by agents of the CUP were ever connected to the state. Similarly, orders to annihilate the Armenian deportees were sent to the provinces via private channels, chief among them the CUP's so-called responsible secretaries. In addition, the planners of these massacres were meticulous in ensuring that no documentation of the crimes would be left behind.

Many witnesses attested that Talat Pasha, in particular, directed the deportations from outside official channels by sending personal orders to the regional offices from a private telegraph in his home. Those witnesses included not only contemporary political figures such as Ottoman Parliament leader Halil Menteşe and American ambassador Henry Morgenthau, but also the pasha's own wife. In an interview given in October 1982, and first published in 2008, Hayriye Talat (Bafralı) acknowledged that this private line had allowed her husband to send information about the deportations to the regional offices all night long.[30]

The CUP created an organizational structure well suited to this dual-track mechanism. In the main indictment of the CUP Central Committee members during their 1919 trial in the Istanbul Court-Martial, the prosecution stated that, in line with the Unionist Party's structure and working conditions, a "secret network" (*şebeke-yi hafiye*) had been formed in order to carry out its illegal actions. The CUP itself, the indictment said, "possessed two contradictory natures (*iki mâhiyet-i mütezâdde*): the first, a visible and public [one] based on a [public] program and internal code of

[30] Murat Bardakçı, *Talat Paşa'nın Evrak-ı Metrukesi: Sadrazam Talat Paşa'nın Özle Arşivinde Bulunan Ermeni Tehciri Konusundaki Belgeler ve Hususi Yazışmalar* (Istanbul: Everest, 2008), 211.

regulations (*nizâmnâme-i dâhilîye*), the other based on secrecy and [oper-ating according to unwritten] oral instructions."[31]

As a result of this penchant for secrecy, there is practically no chance of finding records of the plans for annihilation, the "smoking gun," if you will, among the Ottoman state documents in the Prime Ministerial Ottoman Archive. Add to this the fact that from time to time, archival documents were purged, as I describe in detail below. Nevertheless, even though the CUP made every effort to disguise its crimes, the state's full resources were required to execute an operation of historic immensity, which impacted the lives of millions. Inevitably, such an enormous crime left traces among official state documents. The ethnic cleansing of the Ottoman Greeks and the genocidal policy against the Armenians can be demonstrated through these documents alone, and this book endeavors to do just that.

—

This work may also be read as a critical reflection on the silences in Otto-man historiography as practiced both in Europe and in the United States until recently. Most historians of the late Ottoman period have elided the internal deportations, expulsions, massacres, and genocide that took place during the demise of the empire. These events have been "nonexistent" in their works.[32] What is more, broaching this subject has generally been dismissed as a disturbing expression of narrow-minded ethnocentrism by members of the targeted ethnic groups. Not so long ago, it was common practice to shun anyone who tried to open the topic at the annual meet-ings of the Middle East Studies Association, the umbrella organization for scholars in this field. It was as if ignoring mass deportations and annihila-tion were an academic virtue and noble act.

The resultant damage to scholarship has not been limited to the failure to illuminate this period of history. By refusing to investigate mass annihi-lations, traditional Ottoman historians have failed to confront the mental-ity of those who perpetrate these convulsively destructive episodes. They

[31] *Takvim-i Vekayi* (hereafter *TV*), no. 3540, 5 May 1919. The first session of the trial was held on 27 April 1919.

[32] Şükrü Hanioğlu, *A Brief History of the Late Ottoman Empire* (Princeton and Oxford: Princeton University Press, 2008), is a more recent example of this kind of work.

have squandered opportunities to understand and thereby help to prevent mass violence as a means of resolving social and political problems, and to bring about that universal respect for humanistic and democratic values that makes free intellectual inquiry possible. Nowhere are the consequences of this failure more apparent than in Turkey, where a veritable industry of Armenian Genocide denial prevails in public discourse, intimidating scholars and rationalizing the violent persecution of religious and ethnic minorities.

Philosopher Jürgen Habermas's concept of "secret violence," which is built into the fabric and institutions of society, illustrates what I am trying to say. Habermas explains that this "secret violence" effectively legitimizes the tacit restrictions and exclusion of certain topics from public discourse.[33] Topics that society wishes to avoid by general consensus cannot only be relegated to the past but also forgotten. Freud describes this social-psychological process as very normal and observes that "what the society finds to be unpleasant is made wrong."[34] "Disturbing" episodes from the past disappear down the black hole of collective memory. One may speak here of a "communicative reality" in society.[35] This communicative reality determines the systems of belief and the network of social relations within which people describe their existence, their feelings, and their way of thinking. It can be described as a shared secret of society that is based on a silent consensus.

This is what happened to the Armenian Genocide and all the other instances of mass violence in that region at the turn of the century. In Turkey, since the establishment of the republic, national identity has been constructed on a communicative reality that includes a shared social secret carried by a coalition. Ottoman historiography has emerged as an important part of this social coalition. Consequently, society has lost its moral sensitivity to past genocide as well as to current and possibly future episodes of mass violence. With the disappearance of the Armenian

---

[33] Jürgen Habermas, "Die Ütopie des guten Herrschers," in *Kultur und Kritik*, ed. Jürgen Habermas (Frankfurt am Main: Suhrkamp, 1973), 386–87.

[34] Sigmund Freud, *Vorlesungen zur Einführung in die Psychoanalyse*, vol. 11, *Gesammelte Werke* (Frankfurt am Main: Fischer Verlag, 1999), 16.

[35] I borrowed "die kommunikativen Wirklichkeit" from Elias Siberski, who uses this term as one of the characteristics of underground organizations (Elias Siberski, *Untergrund und Offene Geselschaft, Zur Fragen der strukturellen Deutung des sozialen Phaenomens* [Stuttgart: F. Enke, 1967], 51).

Genocide and other mass violence from public discourse, a prevailing mind-set that makes future mass crimes possible has also been granted tacit support.

Today, Turkish society is confronting the source of all its democracy and human rights issues, including, to name some of the major ones, the Kurdish problem, the military domination of political life, and four military coups, three of which were violent. That source is this coalition of silence and the communicative reality that has made it possible. Everything—institutions, mentalities, belief systems, creeds, culture, and even communication—is open to question. The time has come—in fact, it is passing—for the social sciences to contribute to the development of democracy and civic culture in Turkey.

——

It is known that Raphael Lemkin, who coined the term "genocide," wanted to define a phenomenon that differed from the concept that found its way into the Convention on the Prevention and Punishment of the Crime of Genocide (1948). This difference was not limited to the cultural aspect of genocide, as is commonly thought. No doubt "cultural genocide" was important to Lemkin, but it was sacrificed in order to gain acceptance for a concept of genocide within criminal law.

As important as this difference is, however, another difference in Lemkin's approach should be noted. Lemkin understood genocide not only as a single act, but alternatively as a series of connected acts, a process that unfolded over time. "Generally speaking," Lemkin wrote in *Axis Rule in Occupied Europe*, the work that introduced the concept, "genocide does not necessarily mean the immediate destruction of a nation."[36] In contrast, the Genocide Convention of 1948 enshrined a narrower concept of genocide as a unitary event or act that resulted in the immediate destruction of a "national, ethnical, racial or religious group." After the broader concept of genocide as a prolonged process slipped into oblivion, all subsequent debate revolved around whether a given episode of mass violence conformed to the United Nations definition of genocide and therefore could

[36] See Raphael Lemkin, *Axis Rule in Occupied Europe* (New York: Carnegie Endowment for International Peace, 1944), 79.

be qualified as such. This was an unfortunate consequence of the adoption of genocide as a concept of criminal law.

A further consequence of the legal definition was the conceptualization of genocide solely as an act of physical destruction. For the inventor of the term, however, physical destruction was only one aspect of the genocidal process. Lemkin understood that genocide, as a social reality, constructs as much as it destroys. To quote Lemkin again: "Genocide has two phases: one, destruction of the national pattern of the oppressed group; the other, the imposition of the national pattern of the oppressor."[37] While this second phase can take many different forms, in the end the targeted group is compelled to adopt the lifestyle, culture, and institutions of the dominant group. Without doubt, assimilation is among the most effective ways to achieve this result. Scholarly debates on genocide have neglected the constructive phase of genocide for far too long.

It should not come as a surprise if I argue that Lemkin, despite having fought very hard for the acceptance of genocide as a legal concept, conceived of genocide in much broader terms as a social and political practice. It was as if he considered genocide, in this larger sense, as the comprehensive enactment of an underlying philosophy about how to construct a society. For Lemkin, genocide was a dynamic, not static, concept, and his own use of the term appears to describe the process unleashed by this philosophy.

"To what extent is it legitimate to adopt an international legal norm resulting from a political compromise between states as a basis for historical, sociological or anthropological inquiry?" asks genocide scholar Jacques Semelin.[38] The 1948 definition gave rise not only to this problem but also to a series of other equally important and interrelated conundrums that plagued the relatively new academic discipline of genocide studies:

> Genocide was regarded as a single event, and the event in question (which was generally physical annihilation) was examined from

---

[37] Ibid.

[38] Jacques Semelin, *Purify and Destroy: The Political Uses of Massacre and Genocide* (New York: Columbia University Press, 2007), 321.

the perspective of whether or not it conformed to the 1948 Genocide Convention;

Those social scientists who did not agree with the United Nations
definition (whether justified or not) began proposing their own.
Nearly every genocide scholar had her or his own definition,
and therefore most debates were focused on classification and
labeling;[39]

The Holocaust occupied the central place in these debates as a sine
qua non.

Similarity to the Holocaust became the yardstick against which an event
might or might not measure up as genocide. Every researcher of mass violence other than the Holocaust spent enormous amounts of energy trying to prove that the event they were studying shared similarities with the
Holocaust, so as to strengthen the case for genocide.[40]

Instead of developing models and trying to explain a dynamic process,
genocide scholars were working with a static concept that was delimited
by definition as a single act. It is not too much to say that this definitional-
ism has damaged the field to the point of methodological suicide. Genocide scholars have constructed their individual definitions of genocide like
the Procrustean bed of Greek mythology. They analyzed social events according to the definition they chose, stretching some points, shortening
others, and in general "cutting and pasting" the narrative to match their
"bed." To understand a dynamic historical process over a period of time
was less important than whether or not a given sequence of events met the
definition of the concept they were proposing.

Fortunately, this state of affairs is beginning to change as scholars
abandon the Procrustean model for a rather flexible concept of genocide,
which, like the term "art," is in common use without general agreement

[39] For different definitions and their relationship to one another, see Scott Strauss, "Contested
Meanings and Conflicting Imperatives: A Conceptual Analysis of Genocide," *Journal of Genocide Research* 3, no. 3 (2001): 349–75; Henry R. Huttenbach, "Towards a Conceptual Definition of Genocide," *Journal of Genocide Research* 4, no. 2 (2002): 167–76.

[40] The relationship between the Holocaust and other genocides is such a highly debated topic today
that there exists a wide range of literature on it; for an overview, see Dirk Moses, "The Holocaust
and Genocide," in *The Historiography of the Holocaust*, ed. Dan Stone (New York: Palgrave Macmillan,
2004), 533–55.

as to its meaning. In place of the endless definitionalist wrangling, new debates have arisen over structures, mentalities, continuities, and ruptures in a long genocidal process. At the head of these topics is the idea that mass annihilation must be understood and explained as a dynamic flow of events. How to identify the states of mind and institutional structures that lend themselves to mass violence, how these structures and states of mind function, and where the breaks and continuities in the process are: such are the leading questions today.

Debates on the Armenian Genocide within genocide studies have also suffered from the general weaknesses of the emerging field and have had to contend with similar issues, especially given the Turkish Republic's preferred stance of denial regarding mass annihilation. The question of whether or not the 1948 definition of genocide—or other definitions—could appropriately be applied to the events of 1915 became the touchstone for all debate. The fear that the events of 1915 would not be considered genocide if they did not resemble the Holocaust obstructed serious analysis along the lines of dynamic social processes and redirected it toward proving just how similar the Armenian Genocide was to the Holocaust. Meanwhile, a concerted effort was made to ignore all the differences that would naturally arise between two discrete events of mass violence.

At times the struggle to prove similarities reached such ludicrous lengths that some of the most significant structural components of the Armenian Genocide, such as religious conversion or the assimilation of Armenian children into Muslim households, were almost completely omitted from analyses of the events of 1915 because such elements played no role in the annihilation of the Jews in Europe. The chaotic, unorganized, and oftentimes unsystematic structure and variation at the local level was explained away as part of the Ottomans' sinister master plan.

The documents presented in this book show that prior to the physical destruction of Armenian communities, the decision was made to gather Armenian children into city orphanages and force them to abandon their religion, language, and culture. As long as genocide was understood and explained solely as a people's physical destruction, all these structural components of the Armenian Genocide were essentially ignored: permission for religious conversions in some of the regions during the early months of deportation and the resulting exemptions from deportation; the suspension and reinstatement of conversion procedures in the locations to which the Armenians had been deported; the selective granting, in those locations, of permission to convert, and the means by which the converts managed to survive; and finally, the creation of Armenian settlements in Aleppo and Der Zor between August 1915 and January 1916, together with consideration of how to implement the assimilation of the Armenians there. While this study does not aim to address each of these questions and issues, I mean to provide a snapshot, a status report, on the state of Armenian Genocide studies.

That the situation developed in this way is undoubtedly because, on one hand, the Prime Ministerial Ottoman Archive in Istanbul, which contains official records of the Ottoman government, have been underutilized as a basis for arguments about the events of 1915; and, on the other hand, because Armenian survivor narratives have been poorly integrated into the research and debates. Nevertheless, what can be said for genocide research in general is also true for Armenian Genocide studies: a new era has dawned, and we are reading by its earliest light. I would like to think of the approximately six hundred Ottoman documents and related information provided in this book as a harbinger of this new era. Even if other researchers of this topic do not fully agree with the ideas set forth here, I hope that this new source of records will help to illuminate their own analyses and opinions.

"Now this is not the end," said Winston Churchill during World War II. "It is not even the beginning of the end," Churchill continued. "But it is, perhaps, the end of the beginning."

The position of Armenian Genocide research at this very moment could not be better described than this. Our field of study has completed its first phase of solid academic production. We have, indeed, reached "the end of the beginning."[41] May this book serve as a sign that the debate on the Armenian Genocide is moving beyond the "end of the beginning" to-

---

[41] Stephan H. Astourian, "The Road Ahead for Armenian Genocide Studies," paper presented at the workshop "The State of the Art of Armenian Genocide Research: Historiography, Sources, and Future Directions," Clark University, April 2010. I thank Stephan Astourian for allowing me to use this quote, which he introduced in his paper.

ward a new horizon of understanding the Ottoman policies of 1913–18 that were directed at the empire's Christian subjects.

—

Some final words of acknowledgment: this book was first published in Turkish with the title *"Ermeni Meselesi Hallolunmuştur": Osmanlı Belgelerine Göre Savaş Yıllarında Ermenilere Yönelik Politikalar* (Istanbul: İletişim Yayınları, 2008). However, the book in your hands differs substantially from the Turkish version. Some sections have been removed, others have been completely revised and rearranged, and still others have been entirely rewritten. Moreover, several entirely new chapters and sections have been added.

Your encounter with this book was made possible through the contributions of many individuals and institutions. First, I would like to thank the Jerair Nishanian Foundation from the bottom of my heart for its contributions toward the translation and editing. Were it not for their generous contributions, this book would not have come into being. Paul Bessemer masterfully translated the original Turkish text, just as he did for my prior book, *A Shameful Act*. Fatima Sakarya was always available for any document or paragraph that required retranslation. As the editors of the book, Aram Arkun and Lou Ann Matossian accomplished a very difficult task. Not only did they transform the work into a single, unified text, they helped shape my thoughts through their ideas. I am indebted to each of these individuals, and to the Cafesjian Family Foundation for in-kind support. I owe Eric Weitz special thanks, as his guidance was important for the changes made to the book. It should, however, go without saying that the responsibility for all the ideas in the book is mine. I would also like to extend my heartfelt thanks to editorial assistant Sarah Wolf, who assisted me in preparing the manuscript for the editorial stage and who coordinated the illustrations and the redrawing of the maps, and to Princeton University Press copy editor Cathy Slovensky for her careful editing, her eye for detail, and her helpful collaboration during the manuscript review process.

I chose to use English equivalents for the names of Ottoman Turkish administrative units, regions, and people. In cases where this was impossible, the meanings of some terms used, as well as a glossary of abbreviations, may be found in the appended lists.

Worcester, Massachusetts, February 2011

Map 1. Ottoman Empire 1914 and the deportation roads. Source: *Osmanlı Belgelerinde Ermenilerin Sevk ve İskanı (1878–1920)*. Ankara: Başbakanlık Devlet Arşivleri Genel Müdürlüğü, 2007.

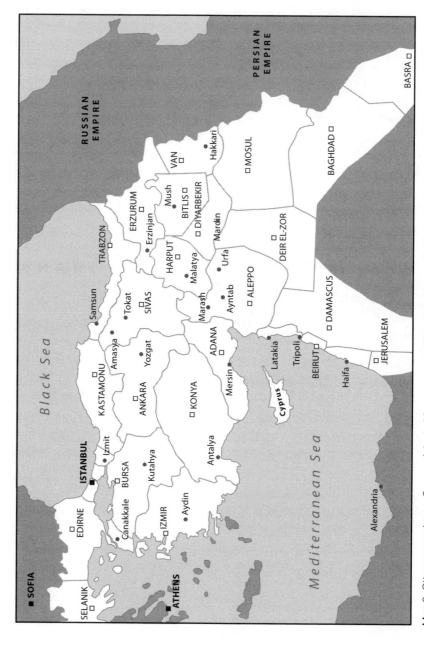

Map 2. Ottoman provinces. *Source:* Adapted from a map by Silvina Der Meguerditchian.

GUIDE TO OTTOMAN TURKISH
WORDS AND NAMES

Key to Transcription and Pronunciation

Letter	English Transcription and Pronunciation
c	*j*, as in *jan*, or *just*, or *jargon*
ç	*ch*, as in *church*
ğ	*gh*, as in *though*, or w, as in *flow* or *sowing*
ı	short *e*, as in *often*, or *o*, as in *second*
j	*zh*, as in *gendarme*
ö	*oe*, as in *Goethe*, or *i*, as in *girl*; in French it corresponds to *eu*, as in *seul*, or in German *ö*, as in *Öl* or *öffentlich*
ş	*sh*, as in *sugar*, or *shut*, or *she*
ü	high *u*, as in *fortune*, or *du* in French, or *ü* in German, as in *Lüge*
v	*w*, as in *weary* or *worry*
y	*y*, as in *young*, or *youth*, or *year*

The Ottoman Provincial Hierarchy of Governors

Rank in Turkish	Rank in English	Jurisdiction in Turkish	Jurisdiction in English
Vali	Governor-General	Vilayet	Province
Mutasarrıf	District Governor	sancak, liva	Provincial district
		Mutasarrıflık	Provincial district
Kaymakam	County Executive	Kaza	County
Müdür	Administrator	Nahiye	Township
Muhtar	Headman	Karye	Village

The Command Structure and the Ranks of Ottoman Commanders

The ranks in hierarchial order		The corresponding military units		
Ottoman Titles	English Counterparts	Modern Turkish	In Ottoman	In English
Müşir	Field Marshal	Mareşal	Ordular Grubu	Army Groups
General	Field General	Orgeneral	Ordu	Army
Birinci Ferik	Lieutenant General	Korgeneral	Kolordu	Army Corps
Ferik	Major General	Tümgeneral	Fırka	Division
Mirliva	Brigadier General	Tuğgeneral	Liva, Tugay	Brigade
Miralay	Colonel	Albay (assisted by Kaymakam, Yarbay)	Alay	Regiment
Binbaşı	Major (assisted by Adjutant Major)	Binbaşı (assisted by Kolağası)	Tabur, Müfreze	Battalion, Detachment
Yüzbaşı	Captain (assisted by First or Second Lieutenant)	Yüzbaşı (assisted by mülazım evvel or mülazımi sani), or Üsteğmen or Teğmen	Bölük (piyade, süvari)	Company (foot or mounted)
Teğmen	First Lieutenant	Teğmen	Takım, Müfreze	Squad, Platoon
Başçavuş	Sergeant Major	Başçavuş		
Çavuş	Sergeant	Çavuş		
Onbaşı	Corporal	Onbaşı		

ABBREVIATIONS

MAJOR ABBREVIATIONS IN THE BOOK

AGUS   *The Armenian Genocide in the U.S. Archives, 1915–1918* (Alexandria, VA: Chadwyck-Healey, 1991–1994), ed. Rouben Paul Adalian

AMMU   Aşair ve Muhacirin Müdiriyeti Umumiyesi (General Directorate of Tribal and Immigrant Settlement)

CUP   Ittihad ve Terakki (Committee of Union and Progress; members are Unionists)

EUM   Emniyet Umum Müdürlüğü (General Security Directorate)

IAMM   Dahiliye Nezareti İskan-ı Aşair ve Muhacir'in Müdüriyeti (Interior Ministry's Office of Tribal and Immigrant Settlement)

SO   Teşkilâtı Mahsusa (Special Organization)

TV   *Takvim-i Vekayi* (Official organ of the Ottoman government, which also published some documents of the Turkish Military Tribunal)

MINUTES OF OTTOMAN CHAMBER OF DEPUTIES AND CHAMBER OF NOTABLES

MAZC   *Meclis-i Ayan Zabıt Ceridesi* (Minutes of the Ottoman Chamber of Notables)

MMZC   *Meclis-i Mebusan Zabıt Ceridesi* (Minutes of the Ottoman Chamber of Deputies)

ARCHIVES

JERUSALEM ARMENIAN PATRIARCHATE

AAPJ   Archive of the Armenian Patriarchate in Jerusalem

PRIME MINISTERIAL OTTOMAN ARCHIVE (BAŞBAKANLIK OSMANLI ARŞIVI)

MINISTRY OF INTERIOR (DAHILIYE NEZARETI)

DH.EUM.AYŞ	Dahiliye Nezareti Emniyet-i Umumiye Asayiş Kalemi (Public Order Secretariat of General Security of the Interior Ministry)
DH.EUM.EMN	Dahiliye Nezareti Emniyet-i Umumiye Emniyet Şubesi Evrakı (Record Office of the Security Branch of General Security of the Interior Ministry)
DH.EUM.KLU	Dahiliye Nezareti Emniyet-i Umumiye Kalemi Umumi (General Secretariat of General Security of the Interior Ministry)
DH.EUM.MEM	Dahiliye Nezareti Emniyet-i Umumiye Memurin Kalemi Evrakı (Record Office of the General Security Officials of the Interior Ministry)
DH.EUM.MH	Dahiliye Nezareti Emniyet-i Umumiye Muhasebe Kalemi Evrakı (Office of Accounting of General Security of the Interior Ministry)
DH.EUM.VRK	Dahiliye Nezareti Emniyet-i Umumiye Evrak Odası Kalemi Evrakı (Record Chamber of the Documents Office of General Security of the Interior Ministry)
DH.EUM, 1. Şube	Dahiliye Nezareti Emniyet-i Umumiye Birinci Şube (First Department of General Security of the Interior Ministry)
DH.EUM, 2. Şube	Dahiliye Nezareti Emniyet-i Umumiye İkinci Şube (Second Department of General Security of the Interior Ministry)
DH.EUM, 3. Şube	Dahiliye Nezareti Emniyet-i Umumiye Üçüncü Şube (Third Department of General Security of the Interior Ministry)
DH.EUM, 5. Şube	Dahiliye Nezareti Emniyet-i Umumiye Beşinci Şube (Fifth Department of General Security of the Interior Ministry)

DH.KMS   Dahiliye Nezareti Dahiliye Kalem-i Mahsus Evrakı (Record Office of the Interior Ministry Private Secretariat)

DH.ŞFR   Dahiliye Nezareti Şifre Kalemi (Cipher Office of the Interior Ministry)

DH.SN.THR   Dahiliye Nezareti Sicill-i Nüfus Tahrirat Kalemi (Secretariat of the Registration of Population of the Interior Ministry)

MINISTRY OF FOREIGN AFFAIRS (HARICIYE NEZARETI)

HR.HMŞ.İŞO   Harciye Hukuk Müşavirliği Odası (Foreign Affairs Office of Legal Counsel)

HR.SYS   Hariciye Nezareti Siyasî Kısım (Ministry of Foreign Affairs Political Division)

GERMAN ARCHIVE

DE/PA-AA/Bo.Kons./   Politisches Archiv des Auswärtiges Amt/ Botschaft Konstantinopel (Political Archive of the Foreign Office, Constantinople Embassy files)

DE/PA-AA/R   Politisches Archiv des Auswärtiges Amt (Political Archive of the Foreign Office) (R: Reich; General Files)

BRITISH ARCHIVE (PUBLIC RECORD OFFICE, KEW)

FO 371   Foreign Office, General Correspondence Turkey

AUSTRIAN ARCHIVE (ÖSTERREICHISCHES STAATSARCHIV, VIENNA)

HHStA PA   Haus- Hof- und Staatsarchiv, Politisches Archiv (Austrian State Archive, Archives of the House, Court, and State Political Archive)

UNITED STATES ARCHIVE (WASHINGTON, D.C.)

NA/RG   National Archives and Records Administration, Record Group

THE YOUNG
TURKS' CRIME
AGAINST
HUMANITY

ONE OTTOMAN SOURCES AND THE QUESTION OF THEIR BEING PURGED

EXISTING SOURCES

One of the issues at the center of the debates about 1915 concerns which documents are available and to what degree they can be trusted. Among these sources, the official papers belonging to the Ottoman government of that time, which are found in the Ottoman Archive of the General Directorate of the Prime Ministerial State Archive of the Turkish Republic (T.C. Başbakanlık Devlet Arşivleri Genel Müdürlüğü Osmanlı Arşivi; hereafter Prime Ministerial Ottoman Archive), hold a special place, and various views have been proposed on their value. Powerful evidence that the documents in this archive have been "cleansed" in a deliberate manner casts serious doubt on the reliability of the remaining documents. In order to have an opinion about this, it is first necessary to have some general knowledge of what these sources are. Below, such a list is presented in order to bring some clarity, in particular as to when and how the archival materials were purged. It is only possible to develop a correct idea about how to evaulate the available materials by relying in this way on background information. For a general overview, it is appropriate to assemble these sources into seven separate groups.

Prime Ministerial Ottoman Archive: The first is the collection of Ottoman-language documents found in the Prime Ministerial Ottoman Archive in Istanbul. Among its holdings are the Interior Ministry Papers (Dahiliye Nezareti Evrakı), within which is found a great deal of information directly relevant to the subject. Papers from the Interior Ministry's Cipher Office, as well as papers from various branches of the General Security Directorate (Emniyet-i Umumiye Müdürlüğü; hereafter EUM), were used extensively in the preparation of this work.

The official website of the Turkish State Archives provides the following information regarding the Cipher Office:

> Among the bureaus connected to the Interior Ministry in the year 1914, one encounters the Cipher Office, which functioned as a separate office. . . . In the communications between the central Ottoman administration and its various provincial functionaries, telegraphic communication and its introduction [as a means of inter- and intraministerial communication] in particular, the "Cipher Office" gained ever increasing importance. . . . It is clear that the Cipher Office was generally the means by which communications between the Interior Ministry and its affiliated departments and offices on the one hand, and the various provinces and provincial districts on the other [took place]. But in addition to these functions, the office also acted as an intermediary bureau by means of which other ministries and state offices would occasionally encode their urgent or confidential communications. There are 20,640 documents that comprise the papers of the Cipher Office. In general these are comprised of the original "encoded" telegrams that were sent to the Interior Ministry. At present a 10-volume catalogue of the Cipher Office [documents] has been prepared and made available to researchers.[1]

In a telegram sent to all of the regional offices on 9 February 1914 are instructions for dispatching certain communications through the Cipher Office. This telegram, which was sent to all of the regional offices under the heading "Issues Requiring Care Regarding Coded Messages," states the following with respect to secret communication:

> in instances of high security and confidentiality of communication and in order to ensure good flow of information, approval was reached regarding the precautions necessary in all future matters. . . . [I]n matters pertaining to state political or military secrets and their communication, coded messages with content that gives rise to a need for restriction in its communication shall have the words (highly confidential, to be handled personally) written at the top.

---

[1] Başbakanlık Devlet Arşivleri Genel Müdürlüğü, *Başbakanlık Osmanlı Arşivi Rehberi* (Istanbul: Başbakanlık Basımevi, 2010), 375.

... [T]he instructions sent in telegrams using this language must be handled by you personally. The language will not be placed on coded messages containing ordinary confidentiality.[2]

The Cipher Office documents, which are largely comprised of short cables sent from the imperial capital to its branches in the provinces, unfortunately do not contain replies to these cables from the provinces. Some of the latter can be found scattered throughout the First, Second, and Third Departments of the General Security Directorate, but generally the great bulk of the answers from the provinces are missing.

It should be mentioned that among these provincial responses, direct information on the Armenian deportations is as good as nonexistent. Nevertheless, as will be shown below, in his function as interior minister, Talat demanded constant reports from his underlings in the provinces on subjects such as the social, economic, and political situation of the Armenian population, their actual numbers, and their relations with the empire's other ethnoreligious groups. Moreover, throughout the course of the Armenian deportation, special notebooks and registries, which reported how many Armenians had been deported, how many still remained, and so on, were sent to the capital. The fate of the documents that contained such information remains one of the great outstanding questions on this subject.[3]

Apart from the Interior Ministry documents already mentioned here, the General Directorate of the State Archive has published a large selection of documents from the other Ottoman government offices, such as the Foreign Ministry, on the Internet. A virtual visit to the official website of the State Archive shows that more than fifteen hundred such documents are now accessible online.[4] Although they were no doubt specially selected for the purpose of bolstering the official Turkish government line

[2] BOA/DH.ŞFR, no. 49/243, Coded telegram from the Interior Ministry to the Provinces of Edirne, Erzurum, Adana, Ankara, Aydın, Bitlis, Basra, Baghdad, Beirut, Hicaz, Aleppo, Hüdâvendigâr (Bursa), Diyarbekır, Damascus, Sivas, Trebizond, Kastamonu, Konya, Mamuretülaziz, Mosul, Van, and Yemen; to the Provincial Districts of Urfa, Karahisâr-ı Sahib (Afyon Karahisar), İzmit, Bolu, Canik, Çatalca, (Der) Zor, Karesi (Balıkesir), Jerusalem, Kale-i Sultaniye (Çanakkale), Menteşe, Teke, and Kayseri; and to the commander of enlightened Medina, dated 9 February 1915.

[3] While working in the archives during the summer of 2006, I received no answer to my question of where the provincial replies to the ministry's cables might now be located.

[4] See http://www.devletarsivleri.gov.tr.

on the question of the Armenian deportations, the placing of so many original archival documents on the Internet for public view must nevertheless be recognized as the very significant and laudable step that it is.

In this work I have made extensive use of both the online documents and others in the Prime Ministerial Ottoman Archive. Despite the inevitable gaps in its holdings, this repository can be considered an extremely rich resource for illuminating the period under review—so rich, in fact, that by no means can it be said to have been fully exploited by researchers (for a variety of reasons), and its value, acknowledged as well as undiscovered, must not be underestimated.[5]

Records of the Post-War Court-Martial Trials: The second important source for this period is the group of documents dated from 1919 to 1921 of the Istanbul Court-Martial (Divan-ı Harb-i Örfi), where the leaders of the CUP and their provincial representatives were tried for various crimes committed between 1908 and 1918. The principal source of information for these trials, about sixty-three cases in all, is the daily report of the sessions and official court documents (indictments, convictions, etc.) that were published in the Ottoman gazette *Takvim-i Vekayi*. This information is far from comprehensive, however, as the published accounts are incomplete and cover just twelve of the sixty-three cases. Nevertheless, the available documents are of crucial importance and cover such topics as the indictments and witness testimonies in the cases against the members of the Unionist cabinet and members of the CUP Central Committee (Merkez-i Umumi), as well as its semisecret Special Organization (Teşkilat-ı Mahsusa; hereafter SO).[6] At first these groups were tried in one

---

[5] One reason why scholars have so far been unable to fully exploit this archive—particularly on the topic at hand—is that the cataloging of its vast holdings has yet to be completed; that being said, what share of the blame must go to technical difficulties, and what share to conscious government policies, remains unclear. Scholars wishing to work in the archives have occasionally been subjected to such indignities as interrogation about their intentions and research topics, denial of access to documents, and even ejection from the archives themselves. For one example, see Ara Sarafian, "The Ottoman Archives Debate and the Armenian Genocide," *Armenian Forum* 2, no. 1 (Spring 1999): 35–44. In recent years, however, significant changes have been made. New catalogs have been made available to researchers, and an end has been put to the aforementioned indignities. During my 2006 visit, I experienced nothing but courtesy and an effort to facilitate my work, and I would like to express my debt of gratitude to the entire archival staff and, in particular, to Mustafa Budak.

[6] While there are different opinions as to when this organization, which played an increasingly central role in the Armenian Genocide, was founded, according to one document in the ATASE archives, the SO was officially established by the order of Enver Pasha on 30 November 1913. The document is

large process, but later they were prosecuted in two separate cases—one for the government officials, another for the CUP members and functionaries—although they would both conclude with a single joint ruling for all defendants. All told, the two trials were conducted in fourteen separate sessions, and the minutes of these sessions appeared in full, along with the two indictments and the joint verdict, in the following day's editions of *Takvim-i Vekayi*.

Another trial, that of the so-called responsible secretaries (*kâtib-i mesuller*) who were sent to the provinces in a quasi-official capacity in order to ensure the proper execution of the committee's actual policies, also took place at this time, but only reports of the first three sessions (out of a total of thirteen) and the final verdict appeared in *Takvim-i Vekayi*. Of the remaining ten trials for which some written record is available, only incomplete records remain, such as the verdicts in the case against officials from the provincial district of Yozgat and the province of Trebizond, or the sultan's approval of the verdicts in the Erzincan and Bayburt (provincial district) trials.[7]

Istanbul Press Accounts, 1918–22: A third important source of documentation for this period is the Istanbul press between 1918 and 1922. The newspapers of this period—in particular, those published after November 1918, in light of the partial freedom enjoyed by the press during the Allied occupation of the city—contain highly detailed reports about contemporary events, above all on Ottoman government policies toward the Armenians. Among the topics taken up by the dailies were the various trials then taking place in the capital and throughout the empire. A great many documents about these cases, such as the texts of the verdicts in the aforementioned Erzincan and Bayburt trials, which do not appear in the

reproduced in Polat Safi, "The Ottoman Special Organization—Teşkilat-ı Mahsusa: A Historical Assessment with Particular Reference to Its Operations Against British Occupied Egypt (1914–1916)," unpublished MA thesis, Institute of Economics and Social Sciences of Bilkent University, September 2006. Based on memoirs and testimonies of defendants in the military tribunal that were held in Istanbul, one may confidently assert that the SO was reorganized on 2 August 1914 in order to make Muslims in the Caucasus, Iran, India, and Africa rise up against the English and Russians, and work in Anatolia against a probable "Armenian danger." For more information on the SO, see Akçam, *A Shameful Act*, 93–97, 130–40.

[7] For the minutes and transcripts, which were originally published in *TV*, see V. N. Dadrian and Taner Akçam, *"Tehcir ve Taktil": Divan-ı Harb-i Örfi Zabıtları, İttihat ve Terakki'nin Yargılanması* (Istanbul: Bilgi Üniversitesi Yayınları, 2009).

pages of *Takvim-i Vekayi*, are a valuable supplement. Apart from these, the Istanbul press contained reports and transcriptions of trial testimony and recollections by individuals who were either directly involved in, or first-hand witnesses to, the events surrounding the Armenian deportations. Some of the better-known examples are those of Third Army commander Vehip Pasha, Aleppo governor Celal, and Circassian Uncle Hasan (Çerkes Hasan Amca).[8]

Archive of the Armenian Patriarchate of Jerusalem: The fourth source of information on the events in question is the Archive of the Armenian Patriarchate in Jerusalem. This repository is notable for its holdings of a number of documents from the Commission for the Investigation of Crimes (Tedkik-i Seyyiat Komisyonu), which was established after the Armistice on 24 November 1918 for the purpose of assembling evidence and prosecuting the crimes of deportation and massacre against the Armenians.[9] Unfortunately, the original documents and case files, both of this commission and of the courts-martial that operated between 1919 and 1922, have been lost or destroyed. Some Armenian officials who worked in the courts-martial during these years made handwritten copies of some of the documents from these files, and these copies have survived in the Armenian Patriarchate Archive.[10]

Although the status of these copies as primary-source documents has been disputed, due to the impossibility of determining their faithfulness to the now-lost originals, the authenticity of the material they contain can in many cases be corroborated and confirmed from various other sources. To give a few examples, a 26 May 1915 document from Talat Pasha, which is found in many Turkish sources, exists here in both the original Ottoman

---

[8] The memoirs of Aleppo governor Celal Bey were published in three parts in the daily *Vakit* between 10 and 13 December, while the account of Vehip Pasha would appear in the same newspaper on 31 March 1919. A series of articles by Çerkes Hasan Amca, titled "The True Story of the Deportations" [Tehcirin İç Yüzü], appeared in *Alemdar* between 19 and 28 June 1919; although the end of the eighth and last installment states "To be continued," no further installments were published.

[9] *Vakit*, 24 November 1918.

[10] The archive is unfortunately not open to all researchers. For this reason it is difficult to state with any authority the extent of its holdings. There is no need to emphasize the wrongness of such an indefensible policy as the denial of access to such a potentially valuable source. I wish to thank V. N. Dadrian, who has been allowed to work in the Armenian Patriarchate Archive, for graciously providing me with copies of some of the documents.

and an accompanying Armenian translation.[11] Also held by the Patriarchate is the copy of a 23 May 1915 cable from Talat Pasha to the provincial
offices in Erzurum, Van, and Bitlis, which informs them of the regions
from which the Armenians were to be removed and those to which they
would be relocated; the original is held by the Prime Ministerial Ottoman
Archive in Istanbul.[12] Also found in the Jerusalem Patriarchate are copies of the communications sent by the Interior Ministry's Office of Tribal
and Immigrant Settlement (Dahiliye Nezareti İskan-ı Aşair ve Muhacir'in
Müdüriyeti; hereafter IAMM or Tribal Settlement Office) to a great number of locations in Anatolia on 5 July 1915.[13] The purpose of these particular communications was to inform provincial and district officials that the
areas of Armenian resettlement had been expanded and that the Armenians should be resettled in these places in accordance with the 10 percent
principle; that is, that the resettled deportees should not exceed 10 percent of the total population.[14]

Yet another example is a copy of the 26 August 1915 telegram that
was used in the principal indictment against the Unionist leaders; it was
sent from the provincial governor of Mamuretülaziz to his counterpart
in Malatya and concerns orders to remove the numerous corpses that
had accumulated along the routes of deportation.[15] Last, there is the

[11] For other citations/reproductions of this document in Turkish sources, see Kamuran Gürün,
Ermeni Dosyası (Ankara: Türk Tarih Kurumu, 1983), 228; and Muammer Demirel, *Birinci Dünya Harbinde Erzurum ve Çevresinde Ermeni Hareketleri (1914–1918)* (Ankara: Generlkurmay, 1996), 52. Its
classification number in the Archive of the Armenian Patriarchate of Jerusalem (hereafter AAPJ) is
Carton 17, File H, Doc. no. 571–72.

[12] AAPJ, Carton 17, File H, Doc. no. 571–72; in the Prime Ministerial Ottoman Archive in Istanbul,
BOA/DH.ŞFR, no. 53/93.

[13] Originally, the IAMM had been established in December 1913 as an office within the Ministry
of the Interior. Later this office was transformed by a law on 14 March 1916. The new office, called
the Ministry of the Interior's Directorate of Tribes and Immigrants (Aşair ve Muhacirin Müdüriyet
Umumiyesi; hereafter AMMU), had expanded authority and was comprised of many suboffices. It
would grow in power and influence as the years wore on. More information is found later in this
volume.

[14] BOA/DH.ŞFR, no. 54/315, Coded cable from the IAMM to the governors of the Provinces of
Adana, Erzurum, Bitlis, Aleppo, Diyarbekır, Damascus, Sivas, Trebizond, Mamuretülaziz (Elazığ), and
Mosul; to the president of the Commission on Abandoned Property in Adana and Aleppo; and to the
heads of the Provincial Districts (*Mutasarrılık*) of (Der) Zor, Marash, Canik, Kayseri, and İzmit, dated
5 July 1915; AAPJ, Carton 17, File H, Doc. no. 585.

[15] AAPJ, Carton 7, File H, Doc. no. 635; for its appearance in *TV*, see issue no. 3540, 5 May 1919.
The indictment was read at the trial's first session, which was held on 27 April 1919.

aforementioned testimony of Ottoman Third Army commander Vehip Pasha, which was subsequently published in the Ottoman daily *Vakit*. A copy of the original Ottoman text is also found at the Patriarchate.[16]

Another group of documents, which through comparison with other original documents can be shown to contain firsthand information, is the collection of cabled correspondence between various military functionaries, such as a copy of the 23 July 1915 cable from Colonel Halil Recai, the acting commander of the Fifth Army, to the Office of the (Ottoman) Chiefs of Staff (Başkumandanlık Vekaleti), regarding Armenian activities in Boğazlıyan and environs.[17] Also found there are copies of messages that would play a central role in the conviction and execution of Kemal, the county head (*kaymakam*) of Boğazlıyan. Various documents found in the Prime Ministerial Ottoman Archive in Istanbul either mention the content of or make reference to these telegraphic communications: many of these were read at various sessions of the Yozgat trials, and copies of them are housed in the Patriarchate's Archive in Jerusalem. That the same reference number of these telegrams is found on all three of these sources must be seen as important corroborating evidence that the contents of the Jerusalem copies are authentic.[18]

Minutes of the Fifth Department: The fifth source comprises the minutes of the Ottoman Parliament's Fifth Department (5. Şube), which was formed by the Chamber of Deputies in November 1918 in order to investigate the wartime crimes of Ottoman government members.[19]

---

[16] The entire text of the testimony was published in *Vakit* on 31 March 1919. Location number in AAPJ: Carton 17, File H, Doc. no. 171–82.

[17] For the original document, see *Askeri Tarih Belgeleri Dergisi* 31, no. 81 (December 1982): 171, Doc. no. 1835. The location of the copy in the AAPJ is Carton 17, File H, Doc. no. 1794.

[18] For a detailed discussion of these cables and their contents, see V. N. Dadrian, "Ermeni Soykırımı Faillerinin Türk Askeri Mahkemesinde Yargılanması: Başlıca Dört Divan-ı Harb-i Örfi Davası," in *Ermeni Soykırımında Kurumsal Roller: Toplu Makaleler*, vol. 1 (Istanbul: Belge Yayınları, 2004), 275–319.

[19] The interrogatory proceedings of the Fifth Department were transcribed by Necmettin Sahir (Sılan) Bey and published in book form under the lengthy title *Said Halim ve Mehmed Talat Pashalar Kabinelerinin Divanı Ali'ye sevkleri hakkında Divaniye Mebusu Fuat Bey merhum tarafından verilen takrir üzerine berayı tahkikat kura isabet eden Beşinci Şube tarafından icra olunan tahkikat ve zabt edilen ifadatı muhtevidir* [The Contents of the Investigations and Recorded Testimonies that Were Undertaken by the Fifth Department, Which Was Chosen by Lots to Determine the Truth of the Depositions Given by the Late Deputy for Divaniye, Fuat Bey, in Connection with the Delivering of the {Members of the} Cabinets of Said Halim Pasha and Mehmed Talat Pasha to the {Ottoman} Supreme Court] (Chamber of Deputies, No. 521, Third Electoral Term, Fifth Session) (Istanbul: Istanbul Meclis-i Mebusan

Minutes of the Ottoman Parliament: The sixth source comprises the minutes of the Ottoman Chamber of Deputies, which in November and December 1918 was the scene of numerous debates on the subject of the Armenian deportations and killings. These have been romanized and published by the Turkish Grand National Assembly.

Memoirs: The seventh and final source comprises the various recollections and memoirs that have appeared recently in Turkey's daily press or that are still awaiting publication.

THE QUESTION OF THE DESTRUCTION OF INCRIMINATING DOCUMENTS

Among the various groups of documents listed above, those relating to the trials in the Istanbul Court-Martial and the Commission to Investigate (Wartime) Crimes, which was established in November 1918, have disappeared without a trace, and there is no solid information as to their possible fate. In light of the fact that Istanbul came under the control of the Ankara government after November 1922, it is not unreasonable to suppose that all documents and files belonging to the city's Martial Law Command (Sıkıyönetim Komutanlığı) would have been transferred to the offices of the Turkish General Staff (Genelkurmay Başkanlığı). But again, there is no information whether or not these documents are now to be found in the General Staff's Directorate for Military History and Strategic Studies (Genelkurmay Askeri Tarih ve Stratejik Etüt ve Denetleme Başkanlığı, or ATASE). Due to the tight restrictions that have been put in place, the ATASE archives are as good as closed to most civilian or foreign researchers.[20]

Matbaası, [1334] 1918). For a more recent publication in Latin letters, see Osman Selim Kocahanoğlu, *İttihat ve Terakki'nin Sorgulanması ve Yargılanması* (Istanbul: Temel Yayınları), 1998. The fact that the investigatory proceedings were held in the Fifth Department was not due to any special characteristic that it possessed. Instead, the Ottoman Parliament had a number of "departments," and lots would be drawn to determine which one would perform the function.

[20] My choice of the term "closed" in regard to the ATASE archives derives from the fact that there is very tight control and review of who is allowed to work there. A prime example of this inaccessibility is the lack of so much as a standard request form specific to this archive; those researchers who wish to work there must fill out the form used by the General Staff for hiring nonmilitary personnel. Applicant scholars then find themselves forced to answer dozens of questions entirely unrelated to scholarly research, such as whether or not anyone among their relatives has ever committed a crime— a curious procedure indeed! Furthermore, even after a researcher is granted permission to work in

The figures given below concerning some of the documents contained in the ATASE archives are sufficient to show what a great misfortune it is that these archives remain closed: "The ATASE collections include 41,591 documents on [the] Tripolitanian War of 1911, 902,800 on the Balkan War[s] of 1912–1913, and 3,671,470 on World War I, all of which have a substantial amount of files on military intelligence, in particular on the Teşkilat [SO] agents and its organization. World War I catalogues where a large number of the Teşkilat's official documents can be found (about 40,000) are arranged according to their departmental files and each file is shortly explained according to their subject."[21]

Apart from the question marks surrounding the ATASE, there is also some compelling evidence that a number of the documents from this period—including some that would otherwise belong in the Prime Ministerial Ottoman Archive—have been stolen or destroyed. The frankest accounts regarding this matter are found in the indictment against the leaders of the CUP in the Istanbul Court-Martial. The prosecutor stated that three separate groups of documents had either been destroyed or "carried off" (*aşırılmış*). The first group, which was composed of the documents belonging to the SO, was destroyed. In the indictment during the main trial of the CUP leaders, the prosecution stated that "after investigating the case [it has been determined that] a significant portion of the papers belonging to the Special Organization . . . has been taken."[22]

The second group consists of the papers belonging to the CUP Central Committee. In the same indictment the prosecution again stated that, "It has been understood that all of the documents and notebooks of the Central Committee [have been] stolen." Similarly, in various sessions of the trial, witnesses Midhat Şükrü, Küçük Talat, and Ziya Gökalp all testified that the papers of the CUP Central Committee were taken by Central Committee member Dr. Nâzım:

> Chief Judge (Reis): Since the Committee of Union and Progress was transformed into the Renewal Party (Teceddüd Fırkası) . . .

---

the archives—and few are—the tight supervision and control continues throughout his or her time in the archives.

[21] Safi, "The Ottoman Special Organization," 33.

[22] "Tedkîkât-ı vâkıadan bu dâireye [Teşkîlât-ı Mahsûsa'ya] âid evrâkdan bir kısm-ı mühimminin . . . aşırılmış," *TV*, no. 3540, 5 May 1919; the trial's first session was held on 27 April 1919.

had the documents and other papers previously belonging to the Union and Progress [C]entr[al Committee] also been turned over to the Renewal Party?[23]

Midhat Şükrü: Of course, Your Honor. But I unfortunately learned later on that they were taken away by Dr. Nâzım Bey. I heard this from the explanations of [various] functionaries (*memur*).

Chief Judge: Had the Renewal Party itself ever looked into this matter?

Midhat Şükrü: No, Your Honor. I was questioned about this when the Renewal Party was [first] formed; they called me to the Central Committee, and questions were asked regarding the documents, and there I learned from the functionaries that they had all been taken away by Dr. Nâzım.[24]

Another Central Committee member, Ziya Gökalp, would tell a similar story during his testimony:

Chief Justice: Are the things that are said such as this reliable, that the important documents were smuggled out by Dr. Nâzım?

Ziyâ Gökalp: I received news from the [party's] General Secretariat that Dr. Nâzım had wanted the documents concerning the history of the committee; I brought them from Europe, and he said that we should preserve them. Take the good ones, he said. Afterward I heard about this from Midhat Şükrü Bey. Later on, when they were brought into custody, I learned that no one was able to sort out the other papers from among them. I later learned that they had brought the documents in a chest, and that they had been taken away in this manner.[25]

[23] The last congress of the CUP opened on 1 November 1918 with a speech by Talat Pasha. On 5 November, the congress declared that the party itself had now come to an end and declared itself defunct, but the creation of a new party, the Renewal Party, was announced at the congress. The organizational structure and property of the CUP was transferred to the new party. At the point of the testimony cited earlier, the presiding judge was interrogating Midhat Şükrü on the question of this transfer. Zeki Sarıhan, *Kurtuluş Savaşı Günlüğü: Mondros'tan Erzurum Kongresine*, vol. 1 (Ankara: Öğretmen Yayınları, 1986), 19, 25. For more detailed information on the Renewal Party, see Tarık Zafer Tunaya, *Türkiye'de Siyasal Partiler*, vol. 2, *Mütareke Dönemi* (Istanbul: Hürriyet Vakfı Yayınları, 1986), 92–138.

[24] *TV*, no. 3543, 8 May 1919.

[25] Ibid.

The third group is comprised of some of the papers belonging to the Interior Ministry. In the aforementioned indictment, the following information is given: "It has been proven from the content of the memo of the Esteemed Interior Minister and of his recorded testimony that the former Director of General Security Azîz, who took the files containing important information and reports [from the Interior Ministry] before the resignation of Talât Bey [from the Interior Ministry], did not return them after [the latter's] retirement."[26] Further corroboration is found in a number of memoirs from the period that claim that before his flight abroad, Talat Pasha "first [went] to the seaside mansion of a friend . . . on the shores of Arnavutköy. . . . It was reported that these documents were incinerated in the mansion's basement furnace."[27]

The Unionists were not the only ones to carry off documents. German officers also took a great many documents with them. On departing to Germany, Hans F. L. von Seekt, who had served in the Ottoman High Command during the war, removed many important records concerning the Ottoman High Command, despite having promised "that he wouldn't take a single document with him." In a letter dated 6 November 1918, Grand Vizier İzzet Pasha complained about this situation and demanded the return of the documents, as well as the former Unionist officials then in Germany, chief among them Talat, Enver, and Cemal. Berlin promised—but failed—to repatriate the documents.[28]

In addition, a number of government officials in the provinces were ordered to burn the documents in their possession. For instance, according to the above-mentioned indictment against the CUP leaders, Ali Suat, governor (*mutasarrıf*) of the provincial district of Der Zor, was in-

---

[26] "Emniyet-i Umûmîye Müdîr-i esbakı Azîz Bey'in Talat Bey'in istifâsından evvel dâireden aldığı malûmât ve muhâberât-ı mühimmeye dâir dosyaları infisâlinden sonra iâde etmediği Dâhilîye Nezâret-i celîlesinin tezkeresi mündericâtı ve şahâdât-ı mazbûta delâletiyle sübût bulunmakda(dır)," *TV*, no. 3540, 5 May 1919.

[27] Şevket Süreyya Aydemir, *Makedonya'dan Ortaasya'ya Enver Pasha, 1914–1922*, vol. 3 (Istanbul: Remzi Kitabevi, 1978), 468.

[28] DE/PA-AA/Türkei 158/21, A48179, Cable from Ahmed İzzet Pasha to the government of Germany (submitted by the Ottoman ambassador in Berlin on 11 November 1918). The German military archive was located in Berlin during World War II. Allied bombings destroyed many of these documents. Regarding the documents taken by Seecks, see also V. N. Dadrian, *German Responsibility in the Armenian Genocide: A Review of the Historical Evidence of German Complicity* (Cambridge, MA: Blue Crane Books, 1996), 159–60.

structed by cable to burn the telegram after reading it.[29] During the Yozgat trial (third session, 10 February 1919), the judge read out the testimony given by the defendant, Boğazlıyan county head (*kaymakam*) Kemal, to the commission of inquiry during his time in custody. Kemal stated that telegrams sent to him had to be destroyed after reading.[30] At a subsequent session on 24 March the presiding judge recalled that Kemal, "in the testimony he gave before the Commission to Investigate [Wartime] Crimes," said "that he had been given the order to burn some of the documents concerning the deportations after reading them."[31]

Another bit of information about the annihilation of Armenian deportees upon arrival at their destinations was given by Ahmed Esat (later known as Esat Uras). Esat, who during the war headed the Second Department of the Security Directorate (Emniyeti Umumiye II. Şubesi Müdürü) and was later arrested by the British, said that orders regarding the killing of the deportees were sent via courier to the various provincial governors, and that after being read, the original message was to be given back to the courier.[32]

Ahmed Esat's account was corroborated by Cemal, the provincial district governor of Yozgat. In his written statement to the aforementioned commission of inquiry, 12 December 1918, Cemal gave the following account: "[CUP Party secretary] Necati Bey came to Yozgat . . . he read out the contents of a letter that he was clutching, written and signed by the provincial governor Atıf Bey . . . When I asked for the aforementioned letter from this Necati Bey he would not give it to me."[33] Cemal would repeat this testimony at the Yozgat trial's eleventh session, 5 March 1919.[34]

OFFICIAL DOCUMENTS: "DESTROY AFTER READING"

The evidence of incineration and other methods of destroying documents is not, however, limited to extractions from Istanbul courtroom interrogations and commissions of inquiry. The Prime Ministerial Ottoman Archive

---

[29] *TV*, no. 3540, 5 May 1919; report of the opening session (27 April 1919).
[30] *İkdam*, 11 February 1919.
[31] *Alemdar*, 25 March 1919.
[32] FO 371/4172/31307, report dated 10 February 1919.
[33] AAPJ, Carton 21, File M, Doc. no. 494.
[34] *Renaissance*, 6–7 March 1919.

also holds a number of Interior Ministry communications that recipients were instructed to burn after reading. A coded cable of 22 June 1915, signed by Talat Pasha and sent from the Directorate General of Security to several provincial governors (*vali*), provincial district governors (*mutasarrıf*), and other functionaries, gives a number of orders for the treatment of religious converts among the deportee convoys. The telegram concludes, "inform those who will be executing [the orders] of our communication; take the copy of this cable from the telegraph office and destroy it."[35]

Another example is the Interior Ministry telegram of 23 June 1915 that instructed the Ottoman officials in Mosul and Der Zor to "resolve this matter personally." This communication includes several extremely significant directives regarding the resettlement of deported Armenians:

> Great care must be taken that in resettling the [arriving] Armenian population they are [broken up] and placed in completely separate locations among the district's [local] population, that they are not allowed to open Armenian schools in their areas of settlement, but instead that their children are forced to continue to study at government schools, that there be [at least] a five hours' journey between the various towns and villages that will be established [for them], and that they not be put at [strategic] locations that allow them control [over the surrounding area] or [the possibility of self-]defense.

In conclusion, the local officials are instructed to "destroy the telegram after informing those [who will carry out these tasks]."[36]

As a third and final example, a telegram of 12 July 1915 orders that the "children who most likely, during the transportation and dispatch of those Armenians who were sent to a great many [different] regions, are now without adult guardianship be distributed among the more prominent and honorable people of these towns and areas who are neither Armenians

[35] BOA/DH.ŞFR, no. 54/100, Cipher telegram from interior minister Talat to Cevded Bey, governor of the Province of Van; Cemal Azmi Bey, governor of the Province of Trebizond; Tahsin Bey, governor of the Province of Erzurum; Mustafa Bey, governor of the Province of Bitlis; Sâbit Bey, governor of the Province of Mamuretülaziz; Reşid Bey, governor of the Province of Diyarbekır; Muammer Bey, governor of the Province of Sivas; and Necmi Bey, governor of the Provincial District of Canik, dated 22 June 1915.

[36] BOA/DH.ŞFR, no. 54/122, Cipher telegram from the IAMM to the Province of Mosul and the Provincial District of (Der) Zor, dated 23 June 1915.

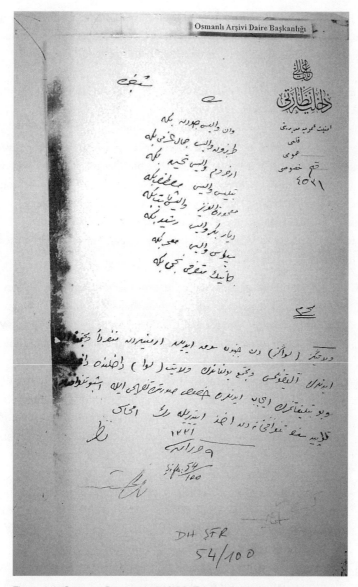

Figure 1.1. Ottoman Document 54/100. Talat's telegram on 22 June 1915 to several provincial governors (*vali*), provincial district governors (*mutasarrıf*), and other functionaries on the issue of religious conversion. It concludes, "Take the copy of this cable from the telegraph office and destroy it."

nor foreigners, for the purposes [of] their upbringing and education," and concludes, "it has been ordered that, after having been shown to the necessary persons, this cipher is to be completely destroyed."[37]

THE DESTRUCTION OF DOCUMENTS CONTINUES AFTER THE WAR

Attempts to destroy potentially incriminating documents took on a greater intensity once it became clear that the Central powers, including the Ottoman Empire, would lose the war. At the 3 June 1919 session of the court-martial trial of the wartime government ministers, former postal minister Hüseyin Haşim attested to the destruction of documents belonging to the Ministry of War. The exchange between Haşim and the presiding judge went as follows:

> *Chief Judge*: In light of the defense testimonies during the questioning of officials in Çatalca to the effect that there had been a general directive while you were in the Postal and Telegraph Ministry regarding the burning or destruction of the original telegraphic communications: do you recall why this order was given?
>
> *Hâşim Bey*: I cannot remember at all. But there was a communiqué from the General Staff Office (Karârgâh-ı Umumî), Your Honor, with the instructions (*tebliğ*) that military communications not fall into enemy hands, and they acted upon it. This [action] then would have been a part of this [overall effort]. One portion, some cables they didn't burn, but tore up instead, or sold [for scrap]. I had only been appointed minister two or three days earlier. The ministry had surrendered all of the accounting officials (*muhâsebe memûrîni*), and they felt that they absolutely had to be burnt. It's likely that this is connected to it, but I cannot remember.
>
> *Chief Judge*: It was only [documents] pertaining to military communication [that were ordered destroyed], is that correct, sir?

[37] BOA/DH.ŞFR, no. 54/411, Cipher telegram from the IAMM to the Provinces of Adana, Aleppo, Diyarbekır, Erzurum, Bitlis, Van, Trebizond, Sivas, Hüdavendigâr (Bursa), Edirne, and Mosul, and to the Provincial Districts of İzmit, Canik, Kayseri, Marash, (Der) Zor, and Urfa, dated 12 July 1915.

Hâşim Bey: Yes, sir, [only] those pertaining to military communications and nothing else. Communications both within the military and the General Staff Office.[38]

The trial at which the aforementioned exchange took place opened on 4 August 1919 and was actually against the former director of the Post and Telegraph Office Osman Nuri Effendi in Çatalca (one of the "Çatalca officials" mentioned above) for burning documents. In his testimony, the defendant stated: "I burned some papers in accordance with the order that had been given. My superiors, acting on their own authority, said to burn the papers, some from this year, others from that, and therefore so I did so." There is no information on the ultimate outcome of the trial.[39] According to the Istanbul-based Armenian daily *Zhoghovourt*, Osman Bey admitted that the documents that had been destroyed were connected to the deportations and massacres of Armenians.[40]

The destruction of documents would continue after the Ottoman defeat and into the Armistice period. The resignation of the Talat Pasha government was followed on 14 October 1918 by the formation of a new government under Ahmed İzzet Pasha, who served as grand vizier and minister of war. In one of his first executive acts, İzzet Pasha instructed the Directorate of the SO (in the Ministry of War it was actually given the deceptive name "Office of Eastern Affairs") to "immediately cease its activities and destroy its archives."[41] The aforementioned Ahmed Esat gave a similar account to his British interrogators, claiming that "shortly before the armistice agreement [government] functionaries went on various nights into the archival department and cleaned out most of the documents."[42]

The same process went on outside the imperial capital, as provincial officials were ordered to destroy the documents in their possession. Refik

[38] *TV*, no. 3573, 12 June 1919. The report is of the 3 June session.

[39] *Alemdar*, 5–6 August 1919.

[40] *Zhoghovourt*, 6 August 1919, cited by V. N. Dadrian, "Documentation of the Armenian Genocide in Turkish Sources," in *Genocide: A Critical Bibliographic Review*, vol. 2, ed. Israel W. Charny (London: Mansell; New York: Facts on File, 1991), 105.

[41] Hüsamettin Ertürk, "Milli Mücadele Senelerinde Teşkilat-ı Mahsusa" (manuscript) (Ankara: Stratejik Araştırmalar ve Askerlik Tarihi Enstitüsü, n.d.), 14, cited in Bilge Criss, *İşgal Altında Istanbul* (Istanbul: İletişim, 1983), 147.

[42] FO 371/4172/31307, folio 385, report by Heathcote-Smith, dated 4 February 1919.

Halid Karay, who served as director-general of the Post and Telegraph Office during the Armistice period, would years later (1948) publish his memoirs in the journal *Aydede*, where he recalled receiving a lengthy letter from H. Sadık Duran, an official who had served for years in the Post, Telegraph, and Telephone Administration. One section of the letter, which would later appear in the separately published book of his memoirs, says the following:

> I wish to recall to Your Eminence an event that I witnessed in this administration during the Armistice period. As you are well aware, following the Mondros Agreement the Entente Powers began to occupy our homeland one at a time by sending their armies into enter our lands from various locations. Since it was feared that during this occupation all of the correspondence and existing documents then housed in the P.T.T. central administrative building and in its provincial provinces might be confiscated, Mehmed Emin Bey sent instructions via telegraph and in the name of the ministry to all of the [provincial and departmental] centers regarding the need to completely destroy all existing official documents, as well as both the originals of telegraph cables and any copies [that had been made].[43]

It appears that some of the aforementioned cables to the provinces that ordered the burning of documents had already fallen into British hands. For instance, on 24 January 1919, the British forces managed to obtain the original of a cable from the Interior Ministry to the province of Antep that requested that the provincial official destroy all original official cables sent to the region from the general mobilization (August 1914) to the present.[44] On 17 June 1919, foreign minister Safa Bey filed a protest of the incident with the Office of the British High Commissioner, in which he acknowledged that a circular from the Diyarbekır Telegraph Administration had instructed the province's district and county centers to destroy the originals of all documents received between 1914 and 1918.[45]

[43] R. H. Karay, *Minelbab İlelmihrab (Mütareke Devri Anıları)* (Istanbul: İnkılap Kitabevi, 1992), 271–72.

[44] FO 371/4174/15450, folio 182, as referenced by Dadrian, "Documentation in Turkish Sources," 105.

[45] FO 371/4174/102551, folios 108–11, cited in Dadrian, "Documentation in Turkish Sources," 105.

INDIVIDUALS INVOLVED IN DESTROYING DOCUMENTS

Although the destruction of documents was for the most part carried out or directed by government institutions, there were also certain individuals, especially those who had been directly or indirectly involved in the Armenian deportations and massacres, who occasionally took the initiative to "hide the evidence." CUP Central Committee member from Istanbul Kör Ali İhsan Bey, while on trial at the Ankara Independence Tribunal (İstiklal Mahkemesi) for allegedly attempting to assassinate Mustafa Kemal in İzmir in 1926, admitted during questioning that he had burned all of the documents in his possession.[46] Such frankness was not uncommon, and in succeeding years many people who had acted similarly would recall the fact in their memoirs. To give two examples:

"In response to the encouragements and urgings of members of the rival İtilaf party,[47] both those suspected of crimes during wartime and all the high-level Unionist politicians and functionaries were arrested and tried," recalled prominent CUP member Ali Münif Bey (later Ali Münif Çetinkaya), the last Unionist minister of public works and a former provincial governor, county head, and provincial administrator. Sought for his role in the deportation operations in Adana Province, he would be turned over to the British for imprisonment on the island of Malta.

But Ali Münif had been warned of his imminent arrest: "They informed me that my house would be searched. Even though I didn't think that I had left anything important, our house was raided and [I] was arrested on account of a few correspondence papers that they found there." Regarding these incriminating documents, Ali Münif had the following to say: "In the criminal case that was brought against me regarding the Armenian deportations they attempted to show that I had [been guilty of] incitement in the matter . . . they found in the side pocket of a suitcase the drafts of some telegrams that I had sent from Adana to the

---

[46] Copy of the unpublished text of the indictment and defense testimonies in the trial of the "İzmir Conspirators" at the Ankara Independence Tribunal, 1926.

[47] Ali Münif is referring here to the Liberty and Concord Party (Hürriyet ve İtilaf Fırkası), which had been outlawed under the Unionists but reemerged in the Armistice period (after October 1918).

Interior Ministry. . . . Although I had in fact destroyed the more important papers in time, I had forgotten this one in the little pocket of the
suitcase . . . This document that I had failed to destroy was used against
me as proof of my guilt."[48]

The memoirs of Ahmet Rifat Çalıka, the Nationalist government's
minister of justice in Ankara during Turkey's War of Independence, were
published by his eldest son, Hurşit Çalıka, who observed a striking characteristic of his father:

> One aspect that differentiated him from most of the other Turkish
> intellectuals of his time was that he took daily notes about the events
> he witnessed and wrote his personal opinions and assessments of
> them. He did not hesitate to store away some of the documents that
> came into his possession so that they might be used by the genera-
> tions that came after him. . . . What a shame that, for reasons that he
> explains in the introduction of his memoirs that follow, he was later
> forced to get rid of them or burn them.[49]

The reasons are very clear. Ahmet Rifat had earlier received word
that he was being sought by the Istanbul Court-Martial. Furthermore,
he had been taken into the special protection of the prosecuting attorney and judge who had questioned him, and the commander of the
gendarme regiment commander who would make the arrest. As Rifat
Bey recalled:

> One day the prosecutor informed me . . . that a cipher telegram ar-
> rived at the Provinc[ial Governor's Office stating] that a joint com-
> mission would be coming to Kayseri to investigate the deportation
> [operations of 1915], and that they would be conducting interroga-
> tions and criminal investigations of those who appeared suspect, as
> well as searching houses. We went together to the home of one of
> my friends from school, where I burned [various] documents and
> my memoirs.[50]

---

[48] Taha Toros, *Ali Münif Bey'in Hatıraları* (Istanbul: İsis Yayınları, 1996), 96–97.

[49] Hurşit Çalıka, ed., *Kurtuluş Savaşında Adalet Bakanı Ahmet Rifat Çalıka'nın Anıları* (Istanbul: Printed by editor, 1992), 7.

[50] Ibid., 7, 15–16.

LIMITED SOURCES OF INFORMATION ABOUT THE REPUBLICAN ERA

In light of the information presented above, it would be wrong to con-clude with certainty either that Turkish archival documents have been meticulously preserved up to now or that only "sensitive" or incriminating records have been systematically removed and destroyed. Archival preser-vation in Turkey presents serious and fundamental problems that extend far beyond this relatively straightforward issue. Reflecting a largely negli-gent and complacent attitude toward history, the conscious destruction of historical material reveals the existence of a culture, a mind-set, that fails to see the importance of preserving historical artifacts of any kind, docu-ments perhaps least among them.[51]

The journalist Murat Bardakçı, who is known for his works of popular history, has claimed "that of the millions of documents found in the Prime Minister's Ottoman Archives today, there is not a single useful political doc-ument concerning [the last and deposed Ottoman] Sultan Vahideddin," and added, "[t]he various events [of his life] that are found are the correspon-dence between the fifth or even tenth degree [keepers of] palace protocol, things such as bestowal of medals and honors, congratulations received on the anniversary of his ascendance to the Ottoman throne or his birthday . . . but the gravest aspect of the whole affair [is] that no one today has any idea where the political documents are that should be in the archives."[52]

A similar example of apathy and complacency can be seen in the fate of the Trebizond provincial archive, which during World War I was sent for

---

[51] In the 19 December 2004 edition of the daily *Radikal,* there is a very important piece by Ayşe Hür titled "Another Archive Has Been Destroyed: How Many Is That?" [Bu İmha Edilen Kaçıncı Arşiv], in which she gives a number of striking examples of how the documents of various archives in Turkey have been unconsciously destroyed or how officials have simply stood by passively and al-lowed them to be destroyed. In her article Hür does not cite her sources due to the limitations of space and the journalistic format, but the examples that she gives are nevertheless worth repeating from the standpoint of showing just how serious the dimensions of this problem are. I would like to thank Ayşe Hür for providing me with her sources for this information and for sharing this and other information with me.

[52] Quoted in Mustafa İslamoğlu, "Şahbabanın Kemikleri Sızlamaz mı?," *Yeni Şafak,* 10 February 1999.

safekeeping to Samsun in the interior. Having survived the Russian occupation of Trebizond, it was returned to Trebizond after the Armistice, but in 1982 this five-hundred-year-old archive was "accidentally" dumped at sea![53] In Konya, the provincial seat of central Anatolia since early Ottoman times, there is unfortunately no longer a provincial archive that stretches back into the Ottoman period because in 1987, seventy-six truckloads of archival documents were removed without any attempt at a scholarly or methodical inventory and then sent to SEKA, a state-owned cellulose and paper manufacturing enterprise.[54]

Likewise, in 1931 the Registry Office of Istanbul sold some fifty tons of Ottoman-era records from the Finance Ministry Archives to Bulgaria for "three kuruş [or kurush], ten para per *okka.*"[55] The documents were transferred by open-bed truck to the Sirkeci train station, leaving in their wake a long, steady stream of paper blowing across Sultan Ahmed (Gülhane) Park. The debris was collected by garbagemen and dumped into the ocean off the shore of Istanbul's Kumkapı district.[56]

In 2000, Turkish newspapers reported that Ottoman-era documents, as well as the papers of various religious and charitable trusts and pious foundations (*evkaf*)—including the Haremeyn Foundation established by Sultan Beyazid II—had been retrieved by individual citizens from the trash heaps of SEKA.[57] Exactly who ordered these papers sent to SEKA remains a mystery, for not a single inquiry or investigation was undertaken in response to the affair, although it may be fairly assumed that their preservation was the responsibility of the Istanbul Regional Directorate for Charitable Foundations (Istanbul Vakıflar Bölge Müdürlüğü).

[53] Dr. Yusuf Küçükdağ, faculty member at Selçuk University's Turkish Research Center, quoted in Enis Berberoğlu, "Dünü unutma yoksa soyulursun," *Hürriyet*, 26 June 1998.

[54] Ibid. SEKA (Selüloz ve Kâğit Fabrikalari, or Cellulose and Paper Factories) was privatized in the 1990s and 2000s. See A. Erinç Yeldan, "Assessing the Privatization Process in Turkey: Implementation, Politics and Performance Results," *Global Policy Network*, 12 April 2006, http://www.gpn.org/research/privatization/priv_turkey_en.pdf/.

[55] One *okka* is 1.2 kilograms; one ton is 1,000 kilograms. In 1930 one American dollar was worth 2 liras 12 kurush. In the end the Turkish government gained about one hundred thousand dollars from this sale.

[56] *Bulgaristan'a satılan evrak ve cumhuriyet dönemi arşiv çalışmaları* (Ankara: Devlet Arşivleri Genel Müdürlüğü, 1993); Necati Aktaş and Seyit Ali Kahraman, *Bulgaristan'daki Osmanlı Evrakı* (Ankara: n.p., 1994), xvii; Also see Doç. Dr. Fethi Gedikli, "Osmanlı Devletinin kuruluşunun 700. yılında Osmanlı Arşivlerinin Durumu," www.osmanli.org.tr/web/makaleler/017.asp-43k.

[57] "Osmanlı Arşivi'nin Belgeleri Kâğıt Yapılsın Diye SEKA'ya Gönderildi," *Yeni Şafak*, 17 June 2000.

This disregard of the nation's own history has at times reached such proportions as to become state policy. In 1934 a regulation, "On the Destruction of Papers and Documents Whose Preservation is Unnecessary,"[58] foresaw the destruction of all government documents more than ten years old. After a seemingly endless correspondence between the central state organizations and their provincial branches over the method of destruction (which had not been specified in the regulation), it was decided that those documents that had once been confidential but had since lost any relevance or importance would be sold to paper merchants.[59] In 1939 this process was suspended due to the chaotic manner of its implementation, and in 1957 a new "Destruction Law" superseded the old regulation. Yet here again the administration and implementation of the new law were so uneven and chaotic as to render enforcement impossible, and in 1959 it was revoked on the grounds that the Finance Ministry was unable to allocate payments for the destruction of the papers. The number of governmental and quasi-governmental units that eliminated their own archives, as well as the number of documents scrapped in the process, are literally countless, for there are no surviving records to bear witness to the scope, let alone the content, of such wholesale destruction.[60]

Anecdotally, it has been claimed that in the period between the revocation of the Destruction Law (1959) and the 1980s, some seventeen governmental or government-affiliated institutions destroyed their own documents with the permission of the Turkish Grand National Assembly.[61] Orhan Koloğlu, the former director of Printing and Publications (1974, 1978–79), recalled on a television talk show that while in office, he had requested archival research in the repositories of all speeches, official statements, and proclamations made since the War of Independence, but he

[58] "Muhafazasına Lüzum Kalmayan Evrak ve Vesaitin İmhasına Dair," *Resmi Gazete,* no. 2820, 4 October 1934.

[59] "Resmi dairelerde lüzumsuz kâğıtların ne suretle yok edileceğine dair olan 1282 sayılı nizamnamenin tefsirine dair kararname," *Resmi Gazete,* no. 2913, 26 January 1935.

[60] Prof. Dr. Oğuz İçimsoy, "Özelleştirme uygulamaları ve özelleştirilen kamu kuruluşlarının arşivleri," paper given at the panel on "Privatization and Institutional Archives" [Özelleştirme ve Kurum Arşivleri] hosted by the Foundation for the Economic and Social History of Turkey [Türkiye Ekonomik ve Toplumsal Tarih Vakfı], October 1998.

[61] Atilla Çetin, "TBMM Hükümeti'nin, Osmanlı Devlet Arşivi ve Mülga Sadâret Evrakının Muhafazası Hakkında Aldığı Kararlara Ait Bazı Belgeler," *Tarih Enstitüsü Dergisi* (Special Issue in Memory of Professor Tayyib Gökbilgin) 12 (1981–82): 593–610.

was told that all such documents had been transferred from the archives to SEKA "when they had changed buildings."[62]

After the 1980 military coup, another thorough "housecleaning" was undertaken, ostensibly to help meet the state's need for paper, as well as to free more space in the institutions that held archival documents. Even so, it has become painfully apparent that this cleansing was carried out first and foremost with an eye toward the ideological concerns of the country's new leaders. Purged during this period, according to former Turkish Grand National Assembly speaker Hüsamettin Cindoruk, were all of the archives of the Republican Peoples' Party (Cumhuriyet Halk Partisi), which had single-handedly ruled and laid its imprint on Turkey for the first quarter century of the republic's existence (1923–50); a significant portion of the archives of its rival and ruling successor parties for much of the 1960s and 1970s, the Democrat (Demokrat) and Justice (Adalet) parties; all of the minutes of the Turkish Senate, the upper house in existence from 1960 to 1980; and a portion of the minutes of the Independence Tribunals that operated from the War of Independence through the 1920s. All had been shipped off to SEKA.[63]

Likewise, the archives of the Office of the General Staff's Directorate for Military History and Strategic Studies underwent a major cleanup after the 1980 coup. A historian who knew Arabic and Ottoman Turkish was summoned to the Turkish General Staff to help sort through the papers. "We read the documents in the General Staff Headquarters and the officer who was directing us would then, on the basis of our translations, classify the documents as either 'harmful' or 'harmless,'" the historian confided to me. "Those documents classified as 'harmful' were subsequently destroyed. I rescued a great many documents from destruction during this time by managing to have them classified as 'harmless.'"

This pattern of wholesale disregard for its own posterity is characteristic of an authoritarian institutional culture that tends to evaluate history and historical documents as potential "threats" that may, in some cases, need to be destroyed. Finding no inherent value in preserving its own past, Turkish officialdom prefers to get rid of it. No wonder, then, that an

---

[62] I originally heard Koloğlu make this statement on television, and he later confirmed it during a phone conversation with me on 28 January 2005.

[63] "Devlet arşivi imha ediliyor; Cumhuriyet tarihi yazılamayacak," *Zaman*, 17 June 2002.

Office for the Administration of the Archives of the Republic was established as late as 1976, that professional education in the art of archiving
was begun only at the university level, and that a professional association
of archivists was established as late as 1988. To this day in Turkey, no legislation authorizes the creation of a national archive, the obstacles to the
institutionalization of the country's archives have yet to be resolved, and
the directors of existing archives are forced to operate according to the re-
strictive regulations of the Prime Minister's Office.[64]

HOW SHOULD THE DOCUMENTS FOUND IN THE ARCHIVES BE EVALUATED?

In the wake of successive archival housecleanings and the wholesale destruction of documents, there is little reason to hope that either the Prime
Ministry's State Archives or those of ATASE will yield much more illuminating information on the events of 1915. As if the wholesale destruction of
documents were not enough to dampen the researcher's ardor, the publication by the General Directorate of the Prime Ministerial Ottoman Archive
of a series of well-ordered collections containing "all" of the documents
and records on the Armenian question—and, coincidentally enough, *all*
that would appear to reinforce the Turkish government's official version of
Ottoman and Turkish history—is reason enough to view the Ottoman archives and their administration with a wary eye.[65] Indeed, some scholars of
the period have concluded that supposedly Ottoman documents have been
fabricated in order to obscure what happened. In the words of Vahakn N.
Dadrian, "a closer scrutiny of the facts suggests, however, that the material
thus made available is not only suspect but unreliable."[66]

[64] Fahrettin Özdemirci, "Arşivlerimizin Kurumsal Yapılanma Gereksinimleri," http://80.251.40.59/humanity.ankara.edu.tr/odemirci/diger_sayfa_metinleri/fo/arsivmekanlari.pdf.

[65] Some examples of the collections published by the Prime Minister's State Archives are T. C. Başbakanlık Devlet Arşivleri Genel Müdürlüğü, *Osmanlı Belgelerinde Ermeniler (1915–1920)* (Ankara: Başbakanlık Basımevi, 1995); *Arşiv Belgelerine Göre Kafkaslar'da ve Anadolu'da Ermeni Mezâlimi [Armenian Violence and Massacre in the Caucasus and Anatolia based on Archives]*, 4 vols. (1: 1906–1918; 2: 1919; 3: 1919–1920; 4: 1920–1922) (Ankara: Başbakanlık Basımevi, 1995–1998); *Ermeniler Tarafından Yapılan Katliam Belgeleri [Documents on Massacre Perpetrated by Armenians]*, 2 vols. (1: 1914–1919; 2: 1919–1921) (Ankara: Başbakanlık Basımevi, 2001).

[66] V. N. Dadrian, "Ottoman Archives and Denial of the Armenian Genocide," in *The Armenian Genocide: History, Politics, Ethics*, ed. Richard Hovannisian (New York: St. Martin's Press, 1992), 280. It should be stressed here that the reason for the suspicion and mistrust expressed by Dadrian and

Over time two main camps have formed with regard to the reliability of the Ottoman archives, and especially the Prime Ministerial Ottoman Archive in Istanbul. Not surprisingly, these two camps have largely mirrored the two main positions on the events of 1915: those who believe in the Turkish official version of the Armenian deportations tend to view the documents in the Ottoman archives as the only reliable source, while dismissing foreign archival material, such as that from Germany, Austria, and the United States, as inherently biased and untrustworthy. In contrast, a significant group among those academics who claim that the events of 1915 constitute a genocide look upon the foreign archival material as far more reliable, given the problems of strict government control, the many cases of destroyed and missing documents, and limited access to the Ottoman archives. I maintain that this latter position is sorely lacking, and that the issue ought to be reconsidered; in fact, a complete reassessment of the Ottoman documents now available is sorely needed. It is utterly wrongheaded to view all available Ottoman documents as having been fabricated to cover up the crimes of 1915. On the contrary, even after the various housecleanings and, quite possibly, deliberate sterilizations of the Ottoman archives, the material remaining therein nevertheless contains ample information that fundamentally contradicts the official version of events long proffered by the Turkish government and its allies.

In the first place, a complete purge of all potentially "damaging" archival materials is virtually inconceivable. Certainly, for an institution such as the CUP Central Committee, the destruction of party archives is not difficult to achieve, but for a vast, multibranched, and far more complex organization like the Ottoman Interior Ministry, with its constant, voluminous correspondence among the myriad divisions and departments of its central apparatus, as well as between the center and its dozens of provincial and subprovincial representatives, such a task would be well-nigh impossible. The redundancy inherent in bureaucratic government ensures a vast amount of duplication, copies, and returned and attached correspondence, all of which greatly decrease the likelihood that the simple removal of specific papers and documents from a single branch would solve the problem.

---

other scholars is not unfounded. For more on the question of suspicious "manufactured" documents, see "The Defeat at Sarıkamış: A Turning Point," in chapter 6 in this volume.

Second, it should be stated that the decision or decisions to carry out the deportations and massacres of the Armenian population of the empire were fundamentally made by the CUP Central Committee. As will be shown below, the Committee (later Party) of Union and Progress developed the dual-track mechanism that it used during the deportations, whereby government channels were employed only for correspondence on the "official" dimensions of the deportations (i.e., deportation orders, dates of assembling and setting out, destinations, etc.). Orders concerning the annihilation of the deportees were sent to the relevant provinces by private channels, chief among them the Unionists' so-called responsible secretaries. In addition, the planners of these massacres meticulously ensured that no written documentation of the crimes would be left behind.

When this fact is added to the aforementioned instances of document destruction, it becomes necessary to conclude that the likelihood of discovering clear, unambiguously incriminating documents in the Prime Ministerial Ottoman Archive is small indeed. Nevertheless, it must also be remembered that while the orders for annihilation and their execution may have taken place within the confines of the Unionist Party apparatus, the deportation itself was official Ottoman policy, and all the wheels of government were put into gear in order to carry it out. During the course of such a massive operation, thousands of pieces of written correspondence were exchanged between the highest offices and their provincial functionaries, and between these provincial branches and the very smallest subdistricts and townships within their jurisdiction. It is completely reasonable to assume that at least some of this written correspondence is still in existence somewhere and contains clear "inside" information about the details and manner of the deportations and massacres. This, in fact, is one of this book's central claims, and I will attempt to show that the information in the Prime Ministerial Ottoman Archive clearly points in the direction of a deliberate Ottoman government policy to annihilate its Armenian population.

TWO THE PLAN FOR THE HOMOGENIZATION OF ANATOLIA

Although the Ottoman Empire possessed a lengthy history of devising and implementing population and resettlement policies, by the second half of the nineteenth century it was forced to contend with a totally new problem.[1] Large numbers of Muslims—migrants from recently lost Ottoman territories as well as expellees from other countries—began to flood into the shrinking Ottoman state, many continuing well into the imperial hinterlands. The 1912–13 Balkan Wars represented the peak of this migration and an important turning point.

Up to this time, the Ottoman authorities had always solved the problem of immigration and resettlement on a reactive, ad hoc basis; now, however, the issue would be addressed and resolved in a systematic fashion, as a part of the overall plan for the "homogenization" of Anatolia. Having initially devised and implemented a plan before the First World War to, in their own words, "free [themselves] of non-Turkish elements" in the Aegean region, the CUP then, under the cover of war, expanded this plan to include all of Anatolia. The primary goal of this project, which can be described as an "ethnoreligious homogenization" of Anatolia, was a conscious reshaping of the region's demographic character on the basis of its Muslim Turkish population. The two main pillars of this policy, which can be characterized as the government's "population and resettlement policy," were as follows: the first entailed the "cleansing" of Anatolia's non-Muslim (which basically meant Christian) population, who were considered a mortal threat to the state and even described as a "cancer" in the body of the empire; the second was the assimilation (read: Turkification) of all of Anatolia's non-Turkish Muslim communities. In this chapter

[1] For Ottoman settlement policies before the nineteenth century, see Cengiz Orhonlu, *Osmanlı İmparatorluğunda Aşiretlerin İskânı* (Istanbul: Eren, 1987); Yusuf Halaçoğlu, *XVIII. Yüzyılda Osmanlı İmparatorluğu'nun İskân Siyaseti ve Aşiretlerin Yerleştirilmesi* (Ankara: Türk Tarih Kurumu, 1988); and Kemal Karpat, *Osmanlı Nüfusu (1830–1914): Demografik ve Sosyal Özellikleri* (Istanbul: Tarih Vakfı Yayınları, 2003), 1–36, 102–21, 300–11.

I would like to introduce some basic characteristics of this demographic policy.

THE CUP POPULATION AND RESETTLEMENT POLICY: SOME PRINCIPAL CHARACTERISTICS

The ethnoreligious homogenization of Anatolia was a special population and resettlement policy and began to be implemented after the losses of the Balkan Wars. This policy was enacted through dual-track mechanism of parallel official and unofficial tracks, of which I will give various examples below. On the official track, expulsion and forced emigration were implemented either bilaterally within the framework of official "population exchange" agreements, as with Greece, Serbia, and Bulgaria as expulsion, or unilaterally as internal deportation, as with the Armenians. On the unofficial track, covert, extralegal but state-sponsored acts of terror were committed under the protective umbrella provided by the official state policies.

The CUP created an organizational structure well suited to this dual mechanism. In the main indictment of the CUP Central Committee members in their 1919 trial in Istanbul's Court-Martial, the prosecution stated that, in line with the party's structure and working conditions, a "secret network" (*şebeke-yi hafiye*) had been formed in order to carry out its illegal actions. The CUP itself, said the indictment, "possessed two contradictory natures (*iki mâhiyet-i mütezâdde*): the first, a visible and public [one] based on a [public] program and internal code of regulations (*nizâmnâme-i dâhilîye*), the other based on secrecy and [operating according to unwritten] verbal instructions."[2]

The population and resettlement policy, as implemented through the dual-track mechanism between 1913 and 1918, thoroughly transformed Anatolia's ethnic character. Over those six years, the population of Anatolia,[3] numbering approximately 17.5 million as of 1914, was so

---

[2] *TV*, no. 3540, 5 May 1919. The first session of the trial was held on 27 April 1919.

[3] According to the 1914 Ottoman census, the population of the empire, including the Arab provinces, was around 18.5 million. Excluding the latter, the population of Anatolia would have been somewhere between 15 and 17.5 million. In his studies of the empire's population, Kemal Karpat estimates the Anatolian population at about 15 million (*Ottoman Population, 1830–1914: Demographic and Social Characteristics* [Madison: University of Wisconsin Press, 1985], 190). On the basis of several

completely disrupted that almost a third of the inhabitants were internally displaced, expelled, or annihilated. Some principal characteristics of the population and resettlement policy are listed below.[4]

POPULATION COUNTS AND MAPS BASED ON THE ETHNIC CONSTRUCTION OF ANATOLIA

In order to carry out the population and resettlement policy, it was first of all necessary to restructure the Ottoman bureaucracy, in particular, the Interior Ministry. This ministry was responsible for implementing the Code of Regulations for the Settlement of Emigrants (İskân-ı Muhacirin Nizamnamesi) issued by the Ottoman government on 13 May 1913 in response to the forced migrations that followed the Balkan Wars. In December, the Interior Ministry's new IAMM was established and, according to its initial internal regulations, tasked with "meeting all of the needs of the tribes and the providing of transport (sevk), assistance and [means and areas for the] resettlement of immigrants coming from abroad, and of preventing emigration from Ottoman lands."[5] Certain reorderings and reforms were made to these regulations in 1916 with the aim of facilitating a more systematic immigration and resettlement procedure. On 10 February of that year a General Directorate of Development (İsti'mar Müdüriyeti Umumiyesi)

---

upward corrections of these figures, Justin McCarthy puts the figure for Anatolia alone at 17.5 million (*Muslim and Minorities: The Population of Ottoman Anatolia and the End of the Empire* [New York: New York University Press, 1983], 110).

[4] I would like to stress that I have approached this subject within the framework of the 1915 deportation and annihilation operations against the Armenians, not as a general discussion of Ottoman expulsion, migration, and settlement policies. The subject of Ottoman population and (Muslim) resettlement policies in the period after 1913 have been covered in two comprehensive works: Fuat Dündar, *İttihat ve Terakki'nin Müslümanları İskân Politikası (1913–1918)* (Istanbul: İletişim Yayınları, 2001); and the same author's doctoral thesis: "L'ingénierie ethnique du Comité Union et Progrès et la turcisation de l'Anatolie (1913–1918)," EHESS, Paris, 2006. For other works on the question of resettling emigrants and refugees before and after the Balkan Wars, see Karpat, *Ottoman Population*; Bilal Şimşir, *Rumeli'den Türk Göçleri*, 3 vols. (Ankara: Türk Tarih Kurumu, 1988; in the second of these volumes, which covers the period 1877–85, there is a detailed preface written by the author); Bedri Habiçoğlu, *Kafkasya'dan Anadolu'ya Göçler* (Istanbul: Nart Yayıncılık, 1993); Abdullah Saydam, *Kırım ve Kafkas Göçleri (1856–1876)* (Ankara: Türk Tarih Kurumu, 1997); Arsen Avagyan, *Osmanlı İmparatorluğu ve Kemalist Türkiye'nin Devlet-İktidar Sisteminde Çerkezler* (Istanbul: Belge Yayınları, 2004); Nedim İpek, *Rumeli'den Anadolu'ya Türk Göçleri* (Ankara: Türk Tarih Kurumu 1994); Ahmet Halaçoğlu, *Balkan Harbi Sırasında Rumeli'den Türk Göçleri (1912–1913)* (Ankara: Türk Tarih Kurumu, 1994).

[5] Reproduced in Fuat Dündar, *İttihat ve Terakki'nin*, 60.

was established within the Interior Ministry building through a decision by the Council of Ministers. This was followed five weeks later (14 March) by a law establishing a General Directorate of Tribal and Immigrant Settlement (Aşair ve Muhacirin Müdiriyeti Umumiyesi; hereafter AMMU). The latter agency would expand over the next few years, and more offices were made available to it within the Interior Ministry building.[6]

Along with these greater organizational developments, censuses were taken in order to map the ethnic and social makeup of Anatolia. Traditionally, as is well known, the fundamental demographic classification in the Ottoman census was religion; as a result, the empire's Muslim population was enumerated as a single group. Although no official census was taken during the Unionist period (1908–18), the Muslim population was subdivided on the basis of previous counts (1882, 1895, and 1905) and reclassified by ethnicity. Census takers were sent out to the provinces to record the numbers supplied by neighborhood and regional elders and religious leaders. These officials had to send reports every three months concerning changes in the population of their areas.

Population counts were generally regulated quarterly. The accountings of officials were usually sent to the central government with a message like the following: "In accordance with the decisions of the population regulation, as every province is required to prepare statistics about incidents that occur on its territory on a quarterly basis and send it to the central administration, I present the tabulated list of events occuring in the months of March, April, [and] May 1919 in this illustrious province in order to be sent to the illustrious Interior Ministry according to the requirement of the law."[7] However, as the same note revealed, the system was not working well, and there were many shortcomings. While the presentation "at the end of each month by the spiritual leaders of the non-Muslim *millets* [ethnoreligious communities] of a notebook on marriages that took place," and the reporting of all kinds of purchases and sales of real estate were required, "many people have not been registered because until now, not one of these procedures were able to be completely conformed to." The Ministry of War complained the most about this situation because of

    [6] Ibid., 60–61.

    [7] BOA/DH.SN.THR, no. 49/41, Istanbul Provincial Secretariat to Interior Ministry, dated 1 August 1911.

the disruption to its recruiting work. It wanted "mobile secretaries" to be entrusted with the work of census counting.[8] Another important issue was the ignorance of local officials, which formed an obstacle to the orderly collection of demographic information.[9]

Changes in the Muslim and non-Muslim population counts were recorded even at the county level. Births, deaths, migrations in and out, and other such statistics were listed and tabulated in quarterly reports to the Interior Ministry's Office of Population Registry (Sicill-i Nüfus İdaresi), which adjusted its information accordingly and forwarded it to the central government.[10]

Despite the noticeable increase in such activities in the wake of the Balkan debacle, Unionist efforts to obtain accurate counts of the ethnoreligious groups in Anatolia were already in progress before the war. As early as 1910, "it was asked of the population administration offices of Sındırgı, Bilecik and İnegöl that the population [figures] from the years 1884 and 1905 [1300 ve 1321] for the Armenian, Muslim and [other] non-Muslim communities be compiled separately and sent in two separate lists."[11] Moreover, even in the prewar period these efforts were undertaken with meticulous thoroughness, as is apparent from the detailed correspondence between the Office of the Population Registry and its Bitlis branch concerning the enumeration procedure in that province in February 1912,[12] as well as from a June 1913 Interior Ministry directive that "the errors in the lists of Armenian and Greek [populations] in Nallıhan and İncesu be corrected without delay."[13] Such efforts ensured that even "[b]efore the First World War the nationality-based population distribution had been determined in all areas of settlement."[14]

In addition, the prewar movements of non-Muslims, Greeks, and Armenians, in particular, were being tightly controlled and monitored. The

[8] BOA/DH.SN.THR, no. 49/41, Communication from the War Minister and Directorate of the General Staff Harbiye, dated 26 January 1914.

[9] BOA/DH.SN.THR, no. 49/19, Communication about the work of organization in the Population Department of the Province of Istanbul, dated 13 January 1914.

[10] For more information, see Fuat Dündar, İttihat ve Terakki'nin, 84–85.

[11] BOA/DH.SN.THR, 68/676 (200/1-A/90/1328.RA.9/1), Communication from the Interior Ministry to the counties of Sındırgı, Bilecik, and İnegöl, dated 14 September 1910.

[12] BOA/DH.SN.THR, 48/75, 564–71.

[13] BOA/DH.SN.THR, 42/58.

[14] Fuat Dündar, İttihat ve Terakki'nin, 85.

communities' religious authorities, as well as local secular officials, were made responsible for "reporting to the [office of] population registry . . . [all] weddings and divorces of non-Muslims . . . [all] births, deaths and changes of locale."[15]

Authorities who failed to perform their entrusted duties were to be punished. For example, in a 16 February 1914 communication from the Office of the Provincial District of İzmit (Mutasarrıflık) to the Interior Ministry, local officials reported that "the village head [*muhtar*] and priest of Kızderbendi, a small settlement attached to the town of Karamürsel, failed to report 70 births, 17 betrothals and 40 deaths to said office"; it is understood from the wording that the officials are asking what penalties should be meted out to the offending individuals. The ministry replied that the privileges of non-Muslim religious functionaries were limited according to the oaths that they had sworn, and that on the subject in question neither their religious nor communal affiliation brought them any special privilege; thus, it was advised that the offending individuals be fined, and, in the event that they failed to pay, they should be brought before the court.[16]

The statistical profiling of Anatolia's ethnoreligious communities also involved the gathering of socioeconomic data. In top secret cables to the provinces, the Interior Ministry directed local officials to compile lists "in a highly secret manner" of the wealth, education, and social status of the Christians, as well as the prominent or influential members of their communities, and forward this information to the ministry.[17] Prominent place was to be given to documentation of businesses and movable and immovable property.

The information compiled through these efforts would become the basis for both prewar and wartime policies of forcible removal and annihilation of Anatolia's Christians and the settlement of Muslims in their place. The peninsula's constantly changing demographics remained under tight con-

---

[15] BOA/DH.SN.THR, 2517/55/23, Request by the Armenian patriarch for instructions on how to put the relevant statutes into practice, dated 6 September 1914.

[16] BOA/DH.SN.THR, 49/39, Written reply (dated 19 February 1914) of the Interior Ministry's legal advisor to the telegram (dated 16 February 1914) from the Office of the District Governor of İzmit to the Interior Ministry.

[17] BOA/DH.ŞFR, no. 58/42, Coded telegram from the Interior Ministry's General Directorate of Security to the Office of the District Governor of Teke, dated 17 November 1915.

trol during the First World War. As will be shown below, what was required of provincial functionaries was a close and constant recording of changes in population makeup in regular reports to the central government. Even during the tumultuous periods of forced expulsion and internal deportations, the government expected daily reports on the changing demographics of various regions. In numerous surviving documents, the Interior Ministry's Cipher Office requests such things as "the reporting by this evening of the requested reports regarding the Greek villages,"[18] and "the sending, within the next twenty-four hours at the latest, of the reply to the cable of 23 December 1915 regarding the number of Armenians."[19]

Based on these local reports, overall population changes were recorded and ethnographic maps of the empire's remaining provinces were prepared. An example of this policy in practice can be seen in the telegram sent on 20 July 1915 by interior minister Talat Pasha to all provincial and district governors. The officials were instructed to "send, within one month, without exception, a complete and comprehensive map showing [all of] the administrative units and divisions within the province, even down to the village level, including two compiled lists containing the figures for existing [population], both earlier and currently, on the basis of the [respective] nationalities of the population in the various towns and villages."[20] As can be seen from the cable, the "two lists" were designed to help authorities track the changing demographics at the provincial and district levels, and thereby monitor and control the overall process of ethnic restructuring.

Even after the Armenian deportations were concluded, the Ottoman government continued to track internal population movements throughout the course of the war. In an "urgent and secret" cable of August 1916,

[18] BOA/DH.ŞFR, no. 63/73, Coded telegram from the Interior Ministry's General Directorate of Security to the Office of the District Governor of Karesi (Balıkesir), dated 18 April 1916.

[19] BOA/DH.ŞFR, no. 60/32, Coded telegram from the Interior Ministry's General Directorate of Security to the Province of Beirut and the Provincial District of (Der) Zor, dated 16 January 1916.

[20] BOA/DH.ŞFR, no. 54-A/51, Coded telegram from the Interior Ministry's General Directorate of Security to the governors of the Provinces of Edirne, Erzurum, Adana, Ankara, Aydın, Bitlis, Basra, Baghdad, Beirut, Hicaz, Aleppo, Hüdâvendigâr (Bursa), Diyarbekir, Damascus, Sivas, Trebizond, Kastamonu, Mamuretülaziz, Mosul, Van, Yemen, and to the Provincial District governors of Urfa, İzmit, İçel, Niğde, Marash, Bolu, Canik, Çatalca, (Der) Zor, Asir, Jerusalem, Kale-i Sultaniye (Çanakkale), Menteşe, Teke, enlightened Medina, Eskişehir, Kütahya, and Karahisâr-ı Sahib (Afyon Karahisar), dated 20 July 1915.

with instructions to "resolve this matter personally," Talat Pasha ordered officials in several regions to "quickly prepare and send a list showing separately the population figures [of] existing Greek[s] in each and every village and town within the province."[21] As will be shown below, similar inquiries and requests were constantly being made in regard to the Armenian population.

REGISTRIES REGARDING THE ETHNIC, SOCIAL, AND CULTURAL COMPOSITION OF THE POPULATION

It must be pointed out that these population reports and registries that were prepared by local officials contained much more than population figures and ratios. They also provided information on the socioeconomic construction of each and every major ethnic group, the character of their language and culture, the manner and level of their education, and their relations with the other groups. In an April 1916 cable, the IAMM asked the province of Trebizond to report "how many Kurds were living in the province, where they were residing, the status of their relations with the Turkish population, and whether or not they were preserving their own traditions and language."[22] In another cable on the same day, the IAMM questioned Sivas: "to what extent do the Kurds have mutual relations and a sense of solidarity with the population of the neighboring Turkish towns and villages? What language do they speak among themselves? Are they conversant in Turkish?"[23]

A cable from the Ministry of the Interior to the governor's office in Baghdad on 1 May 1916 provides some insight into the sort of information being gathered. After stressing that as a matter of government policy it was essential to have sound and accurate information "regarding the number and social condition of those Turks who are considered to be among the

[21] BOA/DH.ŞFR, no. 52/188, Coded telegram from interior minister Talat to the governors of the Provinces of Edirne, Diyarbekır, Adana, Sivas, Konya, Ankara, Trebizond, Aydın, Kastamonu, Mamuretülaziz, and Hüdâvendigâr (Bursa), and to the governors of the Provincial Districts of Bolu, Canik, Çatalca, Jerusalem, Kale-i Sultaniye (Çanakkale), Menteşe, Teke, Kayseri, Marash, İzmit, Niğde, Eskişehir, İçel, Kütahya, and Karahisâr-ı Sahib (Afyon Karahisar), dated 9 August 1915.

[22] BOA/DH.ŞFR, no. 62/188, Coded telegram from the Interior Ministry's IAMM to the Province of Trebizond, dated 1 April 1916.

[23] BOA/DH.ŞFR, no. 62/187, Coded telegram from the Interior Ministry's IAMM to the Province of Sivas, dated 1 April 1916.

long-settled population in Iraq," the telegram interrogates the provincial officials:

[H]ow many Turks are there in the other areas of the province? . . . [H]ow many Turks are there [total], in which provinces, districts and counties are they registered? Are they in a comfortable majority in relation to the Arab and Kurdish population of the areas in which they live? Have they been at all influenced by the languages and customs, and if so, to what extent? What language is spoken within the family and, in regard to the local elements, to what extent are their relations with the government related to their economic status? In what sort of institutions and in what language do they provide primary education to their children? Are there [Turkish] families who, in their inner workings, have either come to resemble those of the Arabs or Kurds or who lean in this direction?[24]

REGISTRIES REGARDING THE ECONOMIC CONDITIONS OF THE CHRISTIAN POPULATIONS

The central government's requests for information also gave priority to data on the economic status and situation of the Christian communities, including reports on the occupations, workplaces, and immovable property of individuals. From the documents now available, it can be seen that especially before the First World War, detailed information on the property and possessions in Christian hands was gathered into orderly reports and registries. In a cable of 5 September 1914 to Aydın and Trebizond Provinces and the provincial district of Canik (Samsun)—all areas with sizable Greek communities—the Interior Ministry requested "the preparation and sending of a report clarifying the value and owners, including type and quantity, of all property and covered buildings [such as houses, business centers, shops, etc.] belonging to the Greek community."[25] A similar request was issued ten days later to nearly all provinces of the empire.

[24] BOA/DH./ŞFR, 63/151, Coded telegram from the Interior Ministry's IAMM to the governor of Baghdad Province, dated 1 May 1916.
[25] BOA/DH.ŞFR, no. 45/200, Coded telegram from the Interior Ministry's General Directorate of Security to the Provinces of Aydın and Trebizond and to the Provincial District of Canik, dated 5 September 1914.

The recipients were to "conduct a detailed investigation of the number and value of farms and agricultural estates belonging to Greeks that were found in the province and to send it [to the capital] with due haste."[26] Again, on 6 October, the request to Aydın and Trebizond (and İzmir) was sent out again, but this time as an order, demanding that a report be prepared at once "stating the type, number and owners of all property and covered structures belonging to [members of the] Greek community in the towns and villages [of the province]."[27]

It is clear that these directives from the central government were indeed followed in the various provinces, and that the requested reports were prepared and submitted to Istanbul. A few examples of such compliance include: (1) a coded reply telegram to the capital from the head of Bergama County on 16–17 September 1914 reports that "from the tax registry it is understood that within the county there are seventy farms comprising 61,345 *dunams* belonging to Greeks and that their value stands at 10,259,635 kurush; it has been requested that the registries that contain the names and other [personal] details of the persons who own the places in which these are found, will be sent out [to you] tomorrow by the post"; and (2) a coded reply telegram to Istanbul from the governor's office in Aydın Province on 26 September 1914, states that "There are 169 farms belonging to Greeks in the province. Of these 81 are larger than 1,000 *dunams* in size, and the other 88 are less than 1,000. All told, they amount to 542,978 *dunams*, with a value of 36,535,700 kurush. Seven or eight of these farms belong to Greeks with Russian, British, American or Italian citizenship," and concludes with a report that "the list containing details [would be sent] by post."[28] From subsequent documents it is clear that such reports would continue to be prepared and submitted in later months.[29]

[26] BOA/DH.EUM, 3. Şube, 2/24, Cable from the Interior Ministry to the Provinces of Edirne, Adana, Aydın, Trebizond, and Kastamonu, and to the Provincial Districts of İzmit, Bolu, Canik, Karesi (Balıkesir), Antalya, and Menteşe, dated 15 September 1914.

[27] BOA/DH.EUM, 3. Şube, 2/31, Coded telegram from the Interior Ministry's General Directorate of Security to the Provinces of İzmir and Trebizond and to the Provincial District of Canik, dated 6 October 1914.

[28] BOA/DH.EUM, 3. Şube, 2/24.

[29] Reports prepared in the Trebizond and Aydın Provinces, for example, where there were sizable Greek populations, were sent to Istanbul on 24 December 1914. In his reply cable sent on the same day, the governor of Trebizond claims that it is "a reply to the [Interior Ministry]'s cipher telegram no.

The previously mentioned top secret cable sent to the provincial district of Teke in November 1915 asks that information on the "communal and religious institutions of the Greeks in the region, as well as on those currently employed there," be compiled in a highly secretive manner and sent to the capital along with an investigation of "the prominent and influential persons with the Greek [community] in regard to their wealth, education and social position."[30] In another cable, sent to Adana on 22 December 1915, the Interior Ministry's Security Directorate asks for a complete list of Greek-owned factories in the region, as well as an investigation and report on the economic condition and political inclinations of Greek employees in local and foreign-owned firms; additionally, information is requested on the prominent members of the Greek community and on its schools.[31]

Parenthetically, it should be noted that the gathering of this detailed information, particularly regarding the Greeks, was being undertaken in parallel with the ongoing work of a commission that was investigating the possibility of a Turkish-Greek population exchange. Indeed, there is a strong possibility that these lists were being prepared for just such a contingency. In a similar vein, detailed sixteen-point "Instructions for Completing the Lists Regarding the Exchange of Immigrants" were sent to all the provinces.[32]

Similar lists were prepared for the Armenians. During the deportations, the central government requested detailed reports on commercial and real property controlled or administered by Armenians, or belonging to Istanbul Armenians or foreigners: "[Please] report speedily, clearly and explicitly (*muvazzahen*) whether or not in Istanbul and the provinces

---

45, received on 23 Eylül [1]330 [7 October 1914]" and reports that "the three separate notebooks that are enclosed contain the number, type, monetary value and names of the owners of the properties and covered structures owned by [members of] the Greek community in the towns of Trebizond, Ordu and Giresun" (BOA/EUM, 3. Şube, 2/31).

[30] BOA/DH.ŞFR, no. 58/42, Coded telegram from the Interior Ministry's General Directorate of Security to the Provincial District of Teke, dated 17 November 1915.

[31] BOA/DH.ŞFR, no. 59/62, Coded telegram from the Interior Ministry's General Directorate of Security to the Province of Adana, dated 22 December 1915. "In light of the fact that some of the Greeks in the province of Adana own factories, it is necessary for a thorough investigation [of this matter] to be carried out and for a report [to be prepared] on the political and economic condition of those Greeks who work both in foreign firms and in privately-owned commercial houses, as well as the prominent [members of the community] and the number and location of their schools."

[32] For the full text of the instructions, see BOA/DH.EUM, 3. Şube, 2/26-A.

from which the Armenians have yet to be transported there still exist Armenians merchants, or houses of commerce, real estate, factories and such that are run by Armenians, either or as local representatives of or partners in institutions owned by other Ottoman citizens or by foreigners; if so, then [also provide] the names of those who have been deported from there, as well as the names of the owners and businesses both here and abroad."[33]

The detailed recording of Christian property and possessions continued even after the Armenian deportations. A coded telegram of 2 July 1916 from the IAMM's Bureau of Statistics to provinces and districts in the Aegean region, calls for "an investigation to be conducted and information gathered on the number of farms and large land tracts in the province [/district] in the hands of non-Muslims, along with their estimated size and value and the names and reputations of those with the right to them; upon the completion [of this task] and the writing of [this information] in a detailed report for each and every county, it should be sent with all haste [to the bureau]."[34]

THE DESIRE TO ASSIMILATE ALL THE EMPIRE'S MUSLIMS

As I will attempt to explicate below, many of the empire's Muslims were also uprooted and forced to relocate. Regardless of what drove them from their former homes, the main and ultimate goal of the Unionist government's population and settlement policies vis-à-vis the empire's non-Turkish Muslim communities was assimilation. In order to fully meld into the Turkish majority, the logic went, these groups would first have to abandon their own languages and cultures. Unlike the efforts regarding the Christian communities, the government's assimilationist motive for gathering detailed social and cultural information on the Muslims was

[33] BOA/DH.ŞFR, no. 57/24, Coded telegram from the Interior Ministry's IAMM to the president of the Commissions on Abandoned Property for the Provinces of Adana, Erzurum, Bitlis, Aleppo, Marash, Hüdâvendigâr (Bursa), Diyarbekır, Sivas, Trebizond, Canik, Mamuretülaziz, and Konya, and to the Provincial Districts of İzmit, Eskişehir, Niğde, Kayseri, and Karahisâr-ı Sahib (Afyon Karahisar), dated 1 November 1915.

[34] BOA/DH.ŞFR, no. 65/140, Coded telegram from the Bureau of Statistics of the Interior Ministry's IAMM to the Provinces of Hüdâvendigâr (Bursa), Aydın, Adana, Edirne, and to the Provincial Districts of Menteşe, Antalya, İçel, Karesi (Balıkesir), and İzmit, dated 2 July 1916.

openly and clearly stated. In the event that Muslim refugees could not be assimilated into their new communities, it was explained, an alternative location would have to be found. Those who were Turkish, however, were to preserve their language and culture.

As I will show in other documents below, the frequent use of the terms *temsil* and *temessül*, meaning to "come to resemble" or "assimilate," make it clear that this was indeed the primary aim of the government's Muslim settlement policy. In a coded telegram dated 23 January 1916 to the province of Damascus,[35] for instance,

> As it has been communicated to the Province of Damascus that it is seen as appropriate to resettle in widely disperse manner and assimilate the Tripolitanian and Algerian immigrants who were sent to and now reside in Syria, information should be provided regarding the heretofore-taken necessary steps for the resettlement of the aforementioned immigrants to the greatest possible extent, the undertaking of communication with the aforementioned province, the securing of their [re-]settlement and its results.[36]

In order to meet its settlement policy objectives, the government had to enumerate the Muslim refugees from the combat regions and classify them by social and cultural background. Requests for such information were frequently cabled to the provinces. On 17 May 1915, for instance, the IAMM requested that its provincial functionaries "report without delay the number of refugees who have been forced to relocate on account of the war and who are present there [in your respective locales] and the level of expenditure that will be necessary for the housing and assistance of those among them who are truly in need."[37] Throughout the war, similar cables would request "the establishment of a consistent and regular routine of sending information to the [Interior] Ministry regarding the

[35] This province encompasses today's capital of Syria—Damascus—and the Provincial Districts of Hama, Havrân, and Kerek.

[36] BOA/DH.ŞFR, no. 60/93, Coded telegram from the Interior Ministry's IAMM to the Province of Damascus, dated 23 January 1916.

[37] BOA/DH.ŞFR, no. 53/26, Coded telegram from the Interior Ministry's IAMM to the Provinces of Erzurum, Van, Bitlis, Trebizond, Sivas, Ankara, Kastamonu, Edirne, and Hüdâvendigâr (Bursa), and to the Provincial Districts of Canik, Karesi (Balıkesir), and Kale-i Sultaniye (Çanakkale), dated 17 May 1915.

number, manner and place of expulsion and [re-]settlement of refugees and future refugees from the war zones." In fact, it was largely on the basis of this information that the government's resettlement efforts would be planned and carried out.[38]

Investigations and inspections were conducted regarding the ethnic identities of those Muslims who were fleeing the war zones, and frequent queries were sent: "What is the number of Kurdish refugees fleeing the war zones? What are the names of the tribes to which they belong? How many youths or orphans are there traveling among them? Please report";[39] or "Of those refugees coming into the province from the war zones, which cities or tribes are they Turkish, Kurdish or Iranian, and as for the Iranians: what city or tribe do they come from? Are they Shi'ite or Sunni [Muslims]? What language [do they speak]? To what tribe do the Kurds belong? Where [are they from], how many are they, and to where have they been sent?"[40]

In order to determine whether or not the Turkish and non-Turkish Muslims could be resettled separately, specific questions were directed to each of the potential locations. It was hoped, for example, to send Turkish refugees to the Baghdad region, and to this effect a cable asking whether or not Turkish refugees, if sent to the area, would be able to preserve their own language and national identity was sent to the provincial administration in June 1916: "[Please] report your assessment as to whether or not it would be appropriate to send Turkish refugees to the townships (*nahiye*) of Şehirban and Deli Abbas and to other areas which are partially inhabited by Turks, as well as the question of what would be necessary for those Turks sent to the area to be able to preserve their language and national identity and maintain their [Turkish] way of life."[41]

[38] BOA/DH.ŞFR, no. 62/268, Coded telegram from the Interior Ministry's General Directorate of Tribal and Immigrant Affairs to the director of the Committee of Inspection (Hey'et-i Teftişiye Müdüriyeti) in the Provinces of Sivas, Diyarbekır, and Trebizond, and to the Provincial District of Tokat, dated 7 April 1916.

[39] BOA/DH.ŞFR, no. 60/136, Coded telegram from the Interior Ministry's IAMM to the Provinces of Bitlis, Diyarbekır, Mosul, Mamuretülaziz, and Erzurum, dated 26 January 1916.

[40] BOA/DH.ŞFR, no. 63/224, Coded telegram from the Interior Ministry's IAMM to the Province of Mosul, dated 6 May 1916.

[41] BOA/DH.ŞFR, no. 65/30, Coded telegram from interior minister Talat to the Province of Baghdad, dated 18 June 1916.

The principles underlying the government's assimilation policies toward non-Turkish Muslims are revealed by its actions concerning the Kurds. On the basis of their detailed ethnic and cultural profile of central and western Anatolia, the authorities viewed these areas as suitable for resettling some of the indigenous Kurds in order to facilitate their assimilation. According to its January 1916 cable to the empire's western provinces, the IAMM had been considering "the moving (*sevk*) of those Kurds who have fled to the interior due to the wartime conditions to the western provinces of Anatolia." After reporting the need for "information regarding the Kurds and Kurdish villages who are now in the [respective] inner province[s as a result of] earlier orders," the telegram asks "where the Kurdish villages are [and] how many there are; how many persons there are. Do they preserve their original language and customs? What are their relations like with the Turkish villagers and villages with whom they associate? Commence immediately with an investigation and provide a detailed report, including [personal] assessment."[42]

Once an area of settlement was identified as amenable to the assimilation of certain Muslim refugees, care was taken not to send different ethnic groups to the same location. For example, "The provinces of Konya, Ankara, Kastamonu and provincial districts of Niğde, Kayseri, Kütahya, Eskişehir, Amasya and Tokat" were chosen for the displaced Kurds.[43] Should the number of refugees have exceeded the predetermined absorptive capacity of a given province or district, the excess souls were to be sent to other regions, not randomly but according to set criteria as to the respective ethnic makeup of the refugees and their assigned destinations. In a 21 May 1916 cable to the province of Mamuretülaziz, for instance, the IAMM instructs the local authorities that "the Turkish refugees who exceed the province's absorptive capacity will be sent to the areas of Urfa, Zor [Der Zor], Marash and Ayıntab via the Ergani-Diyarbekır-Siverek

---

[42] BOA/DH.ŞFR, no. 60/140, Coded telegram from the Interior Ministry's Office of Tribal and Immigrant Resettlement to the Provinces of Konya, Kastamonu, Adana, Ankara, Sivas, Aydın, and others, and to the Provincial Districts of Kayseri, Canik, Eskişehir, Karahisarı, and Niğde, dated 26 January 1916.

[43] BOA/DH.ŞFR, no. 63/215, Coded telegram from the Interior Ministry's Office of Tribal and Immigrant Resettlement to the Province of Mosul, dated 6 May 1916.

route, while the Kurdish refugees will be sent to Kayseri, Yozgat, Ankara and Canik by way of Malatya-Sivas-Tokat, and then via the route Malatya-Darende-Şarız-Aziziye."[44]

Another telegram was sent to the province of Konya regarding the dispatch of Turkish refugees to that region, which had been set aside for Kurdish resettlement. After reporting that "word has been received that 185 of the Turkish refugees from Trebizond would be sent to Konya," the AMMU asked that the "Turks not be sent to Konya because it was where, according to previous instructions, the Kurdish refugees were to be resettled."[45] Sending Kurdish groups into areas of Arab or Kurdish predominance was prohibited since it was understood that their assimilation into broader Turkish society would be nearly impossible in such a milieu. Where such resettlement had already taken place or was still under way, it was ordered that the process cease immediately. The AMMU even notified war minister Enver Pasha in a 3 May 1916 cable that "it did not appear suitable to resettle those displaced Kurds from the eastern provinces in districts in which there were already Kurds and Arabs present," and that the decision had therefore been made to "send them from the war zone into the Anatolian interior."[46] Another telegram, sent two days earlier to the governor of Diyarbekır, first mentions that the decision to send Kurdish refugees to places in the empire's southern and southeastern provinces, such as Urfa and Der Zor, had been a wrong one, and that "it would not produce the desired result, since they would remain an uncontrolled element there, by either becoming Arabicized or by preserving their [separate] immigrant status"; therefore, the Kurds were instead to be immediately rerouted to the areas that had earlier been designated for them. Additionally, the cable listed five separate points that had to be heeded in the resettlement of the Kurds.[47]

[44] BOA/DH.ŞFR, no. 64/93, Coded telegram from the Interior Ministry's Office of Tribal and Immigrant Resettlement to the Province of Mamuretülaziz, dated 21 May 1916.

[45] BOA/DH.ŞFR, no. 67/49, Coded telegram from the Interior Ministry's General Directorate of Tribal and Immigrant Affairs to the Provincial District of Kayseri, dated 19 August 1916.

[46] BOA/DH.ŞFR, no. 63/190, Coded telegram from the Interior Ministry's General Directorate of Tribal and Immigrant Affairs to minister of war Enver Pasha, dated 3 May 1916.

[47] BOA/DH.ŞFR, no. 63/172, Coded telegram from interior minister Talat to the Province of Diyarbekır, dated 2 May 1916.

A similar cable explaining the new decision and the reasons that the Kurds should not be settled in the provincial districts of Der Zor, Marash, and Antep was sent to Urfa on 6 May. It read as follows:

> [Please] provide information regarding the forcible dispersal and resettlement of the Kurds among the Turkish population in the Anatolian interior in order to persuade [the former] to abandon their tribal way of life, backward values and customs and to bring them to a beneficial state through assimilation; likewise, provide information regarding the Kurdish refugees sent to [Der] Zor and the southern parts of Marash and Antep who are arriving there and who should absolutely not be sent there but instead to those parts of the district that are settled by Turks: how many [were sent], where were they sent and on what dates [?].[48]

Although Marash was declared to be a region in which displaced Kurds should not be settled, when they were in fact sent to the district the various surrounding provinces were put on notice, as in the following cable of 1 November 1916 to the provinces of Diyarbekır and Mamuretül-aziz: "Although it is clearly stated in the ninth point of the list of instructions that the provincial district of Marash is not one of the areas of resettlement for Kurdish refugees, it has been learned through local reports that thousands of displaced Kurds have been sent to the aforementioned district and that some of these have presented false documents [allowing them to settle here] . . . [Such a situation] should not be allowed to be repeated."[49]

Another area off-limits to Kurdish resettlement was the province of Diyarbekır. According to a November 1916 cable from interior minister Talat to the provincial governor, reports had been received that "[s]ome of the tribal leaders who, in accordance with their own wishes, were separated from their tribes, had demanded to be resettled in Diyarbekır along with their families," but that such demands are seen as unacceptable. The

[48] BOA/DH.ŞFR, no. 63/222, Coded telegram from the Interior Ministry's Office for Tribal and Immigrant Settlement to the Provincial District of Urfa, dated 6 May 1916.

[49] BOA/DH.ŞFR, no. 69/141ve 144, Coded telegram from the Interior Ministry's Office for Tribal and Immigrant Settlement to the Provinces of Diyarbekır and Mamuretülaziz, dated 1 November 1916.

reason for this rejection is clear: "It is not appropriate to settle Kurds in Diyarbekır, which is an area of Turkish resettlement."[50]

So that they would fully abandon their nomadic lifestyles, language, and customs, great importance was placed on ensuring that those displaced people who were slated for assimilation would not be settled together in large groups. The Kurdish refugees in particular were targeted for broad dispersal—and their traditional leaders, both religious and secular, were separated from and settled apart from their communities. In fact, this policy of "separating the nomads' leaders (sheikhs, beys, aghas) from the main group of nomads and then settling them in cities and towns"— "detaching the head from the body," as Kemal Karpat has characterized it—dated from the nineteenth century.[51]

The principal lines of the government's Kurdish resettlement policy were stated openly in cables to the provinces in May 1916. As the provincial districts of Urfa, Marash, and Antep were informed on 4 May,

> it is absolutely necessary that if there are Kurdish refugees who were previously sent[,] the members of these tribes should be separated from their leaders, with the leaders being settled in the towns and the [other] individual [member]s being dispersed in the Turkish villages that are scattered throughout the southern part of the district, two or three households per village, so that they will not all be resettled together as a group in one place; this, in order that they abandon the nomadic lifestyle that they have lived [until now], as well as their language and customs.

It is then requested that "the sheikhs and imams be settled separately from the [other] members of the tribe, and that other members of the tribe should likewise be resettled in a dispersed manner and that relations between the tribal leaders, the sheikhs and the individual members should not be allowed to continue."[52]

Another telegram, bearing similar contents and sent on the same day to the provinces of Sivas, Mamuretülaziz, and Erzurum, informed the

[50] BOA/DH.ŞFR, no. 70/111, Coded telegram from interior minister Talat to the Province of Diyarbekır, dated 26 November 1916.

[51] Karpat, Osmanlı Nüfusu, 19.

[52] BOA/DH.ŞFR, no. 63/187, Coded telegram from interior minister Talat to the Provincial Districts of Urfa, Marash, and Antep, dated 4 May 1916.

local officials that displaced Kurds should not be sent to areas inhabited by Arabs and other Kurds. Rather than allowing the Kurds "the possibility there of preserving their customs and national identity, and thereby continuing to exist as an unregistered entity," the telegram repeated that "it will be necessary to separate [the ordinary members of] the tribe from its prominent members," and that the Kurds should be settled "among Turkish refugees and the population of Turkified towns, and within the province or other appropriate environs . . . so that they will be unable to continue their tribal existence and preserve their national identity in the places to which they are sent."[53]

Another telegram of 6 May 1916 to the province of Mosul went so far as to list each step of this policy:

> (1) In order to reform the Kurdish element and transform it into a constructive entity it is necessary to immediately displace and send then to the assigned places in Anatolia mentioned below; (2) The areas of resettlement are: the provinces of Konya, Ankara, and Kastamonu,and the provincial districts of Niğde, Kayseri, Kütahya, Eskişehir, Amasya, and Tokat; (3) In the place of resettlements the sheikhs, leaders and mullahs will be separated from the rest of the tribe and sent to different districts, either before or after the [other] members [of the tribe], in other words, to places from which they will be unable to maintain relations with the other members.[54]

Ensuring that the displaced Kurds be sent to western and central Anatolia rather than the eastern and southeastern provinces—and that the religious and secular Kurdish leaders be separated from their tribes and settled elsewhere—were perhaps the two main pillars of this policy, but there was another, perhaps equally important consideration: taking care that the Kurds constituted no more than 5 percent of the total population in their new places of settlement. This concern is expressed in many of the pertinent communications from the central government to the provinces, and is stated openly and repeatedly in the procedural instructions:

---

[53] BOA/DH.ŞFR, no. 63/189, Coded telegram from the Interior Ministry's IAMM to the Provinces of Sivas, Mamuretülaziz, and Erzurum, dated 4 May 1916.

[54] BOA/DH.ŞFR, no. 63/215, Coded telegram from the Interior Ministry's IAMM to the Provinces of Mosul, dated 6 May 1916.

Because it does not appear appropriate for those Kurdish refugees who are coming into the province from the war zone to be settled either in the southern provinces or in places in which the Kurds constitute a majority, the [appropriate] locales have been notified that those displaced persons who are presently found in the provinces of Diyarbekır, Sivas, Erzurum and Mamûretü'l-Aziz should be sent to the interior of Anatolia so that they can be persuaded to abandon their tribal way of life and be transformed from an unregistered and unmonitored into a "grounded" and settled community. Upon their arrival to [the designated] place[,] their settlement [should proceed] as follows: (1) The leaders of the tribe will be separated from the other members and the prominent and influential members will be settled in the provincial, district or county centers according to need, while the others will be widely dispersed to the towns and villages and settled there in a manner so that their numbers will nowhere exceed five percent of the total local population; (2) the sheikhs and imams will be separated from the other members of the tribe and settled separately in a [text illegible] manner; (3) the leaders and sheikhs will not be allowed to continue to communicate with the other members of the tribe.[55]

IMPLEMENTING THE 5 TO 10 PERCENT RULE

As can be seen from the previous documents, one of the main considerations of the government's population and settlement policy was to ensure that the number of people of any group being resettled in a given area not exceed 5 to 10 percent of the total population. The questions of how this numeric range was arrived at, and its historical background, constitute a separate discussion that I will not go into here, except to state that it was applied not only to the Kurds but to all non-Turkish groups regardless of religion.[56]

[55] BOA/DH.ŞFR, no. 63/188, Coded telegram from the Interior Ministry's General Directorate of Tribal and Immigrant Affairs to the Provinces of Ankara, Konya, Hüdâvendigâr (Bursa), and Kastamonu, and to the Provincial Districts of Kütahya, Kayseri, and Niğde, dated 2 May 1916.

[56] The 5 to 10 percent principle is an important topic for research. I will restrict myself here to raising one suspicion. It is possible that the 1913–14 Armenian reform discussions played an extremely important role in making this principle so significant: the provinces to which the reforms were to

A coded telegram from the IAMM to the province of Ankara on 5 October 1915 shows that the Settlement Office had sent out a communiqué three days earlier "concerning the treatment of the Muslim refugees" who were arriving in the Ankara region. Among other points, the earlier cable emphasized that "the Albanians and Bosnians [being sent to the region] be placed in a dispersed fashion among the Turkish population at ratio of 1:10."[57]

Similar actions are understood to have been carried out concerning the Greek population of Bursa (Hüdâvendigâr) and its environs in the summer of 1916. In July the governor of Bursa ordered that Greek immigrants should be dispersed to the Turkish villages at a rate not to exceed 10 percent of the total population. A subsequent report by the Greek Orthodox Church claims that "[t]he governor was simply following out an organised plan by the C.U.P, having as an object to convert them to Mohammedanism."[58]

Although the exact ratio of immigrants to locals is not reported, it appears that a similar process was implemented in regard to the Nestorian Christians. In September 1914, for example, for military reasons the decision was made to deport Nestorian Christians thought to be "susceptible to foreign incitements" to interior destinations such as Ankara and Konya. The deportees were forbidden to resettle in large groups; concern was shown to disperse them widely, with no more than twenty Nestorian households per location.[59]

The 5 to 10 percent criterion was also applied to the Armenians, but in two ways. In some western provinces the Armenians were redistributed within the same province so as not to exceed 5 percent of the population.

---

be applied were the ones where the ratio of the Armenian population to the general population was taken as determinative. According to the reform agreement of 1914, "an accurate population census under the supervision of the inspector-general was going to be carried out at the latest within one year, [and] the proportions of ethno-religious groups and the languages they speak . . . were going to be determined" (Ramazan Yıldız, "Vilayat-ı Sitte'de Ermenilerle İlgili Reformlar," *Ermeni Araştırmaları* 25 [2007]), http://www.eraren.org/index.php?Lisan=tr&Page=DergiIcerik&IcerikNo=497/.

[57] BOA/DH.ŞFR, no. 56/290, Coded telegram from the Interior Ministry's IAMM to the Province of Ankara, dated 5 October 1916.

[58] Greek Patriarchate, *Persecution of the Greeks in Turkey, 1914–1918* (Constantinople and London: Hesperia Press, 1919), 56.

[59] BOA/DH.ŞFR, no. 46/78, Coded telegram from interior minister Talat to the Province of Van, dated 26 October 1914.

As for the Armenians who were to be resettled in the Syrian and Iraqi deserts, strict orders were given to distribute Armenian arrivals among the Muslims so as not to exceed 10 percent of the population. This regulation can be taken as a clear sign of the genocidal policy of the Ottoman authorities, a policy that deserves special treatment. It will be discussed in chapter 3 in relation to the Armenians.

MUSLIM REFUGEES DENIED PERMISSION TO SETTLE WHERE THEY WISH

One of the most significant pieces of evidence that deportees and refugees were resettled according to a prearranged plan is the simple fact that they were not allowed to settle wherever they wished but were instead forced to migrate to the destinations selected for them. The steps to be followed in the resettlement process were set forth in a detailed communiqué to all of the relevant provinces and provincial districts on 25 August 1915. From this circular it is clear that some of the refugees, rather than migrating to the places to which they had been directed, fled elsewhere. The communiqué further orders that those displaced people who did not go to their preassigned destinations were to be forcibly sent there,

> Although it was necessary to remove those refugees from these areas as soon as possible and to resettle them in the areas from which the Armenians have been deported, the aforementioned refugees have shown no desire to go there. It has been learned that as some of them have, once under way, jumped at every means and opportunity to disperse here and there, it is necessary that these displaced persons be sent there without delay and for those who have yet to be resettled and are still here to be forcibly deported without regard for their consent in the matter.

For this reason, it was stated, they were to be sent off "to their designated place of resettlement without any opportunity whatsoever being given for them to run off or flee elsewhere."[60]

---

[60] BOA/DH.ŞFR, no. 55/256, Coded telegram from the Interior Ministry's General Directorate of Security to the Provinces of Erzurum, Bitlis, Diyarbekır, Kastamonu, Adana, Ankara, Aleppo, Sivas,

Despite these clear instructions, many of the deportees are known to have moved to the places of their own choosing: efforts to prevent this would occupy a large part of the government's concerns and efforts. Numerous telegrams to the provinces testify to this fact. A message to Urfa on 15 April 1916 complains that "it is entirely unacceptible that the deportees should go to other destinations instead of to their [designated] places of resettlement" and demands that "the deportees not be allowed to sneak off and that measures be taken to prevent this."[61] In another cable sent in May 1916 to the province of Mamuretülaziz, the Settlement Office states that it had received reports that "some of the deportees have not gone to the places appointed for them but have instead run off and hidden in the environs of Diyarbekır"; "it is advised with all urgency that the deportees not be allowed to go to any place other than those areas to which they have been directed."[62] Likewise, a cable to Trebizond the following month acknowledges that "some of the deportees from Trebizond who were sent to Merzifon ended up going to the Provincial District of İzmit" and demands that such an event not be repeated; district officials are reminded that "those fleeing the war zones must be sent off to the areas of resettlement."[63]

When further such events were reported, another cable was sent on 26 June 1916, this time to the province of Kastamonu and the provincial district of Bolu, demanding that, "since it is necessary that those displaced persons fleeing the war zones be sent to the areas of resettlement listed in the special list of instructions, absolutely no opportunity whatsoever should be given for them to go any place other than the one appointed for them."[64] When it was observed that many of the deportees had acted contrary to the central government's instructions, an order was sent to

Mamuretülaziz, Hüdâvendigâr (Bursa), Trebizond, and Van, and to the Provincial Districts of Urfa, İzmit, Karesi (Balıkesir), Kütahya, Eskişehir, Canik, Kayseri, and Marash, dated 25 August 1915.

[61] BOA/DH.ŞFR, no. 63/9, Coded telegram from the Interior Ministry's General Directorate of Tribal and Immigrant Affairs to the Provincial District of Urfa, dated 15 April 1916.

[62] BOA/DH.ŞFR, no. 63/283, Coded telegram from the Interior Ministry's IAMM to the Province of Mamuretülaziz, dated 11 May 1916.

[63] BOA/DH.ŞFR, no. 65/64, Coded telegram from the Interior Ministry's General Directorate of Tribal and Immigrant Affairs to the Province of Trebizond, dated 22 June 1916.

[64] BOA/DH.ŞFR, no. 65/78, Coded telegram from the Interior Ministry's General Directorate of Tribal and Immigrant Affairs to the Province of Kastamonu and the Provincial District of Bolu, dated 24 June 1916.

undertake an investigation regarding the deportees who "report that they have lost their documents and then, hiding their nationality, deceive the officials and have themselves sent off somewhere other than the places designated for them."[65]

In some regions, even after being resettled, the refugees continued to flee from their new homes; in response, the government imposed harsh measures to prevent this. The Interior Ministry cabled to Bursa (Hüdâvendigâr) on 31 December 1917, that "[r]eports have been received from the province of Hüdâvendigâr [Bursa] that a large number of deportees from Batum has arrived in Bursa, and that many of these ran off or disappeared over the course of the journey. Although they claim that this province was not, in fact, their [correct] area for resettlement . . . absolutely no deportee should be allowed to escape in such a fashion . . . [and] any [official] who shows complacence or negligence [in this matter] will be severely punished."[66]

This prohibition and strict enforcement also covered the Turkish refugees. A telegram of January 1918 from the Interior Ministry to the province of Adana gives some idea of just how close the monitoring was in this matter:

> Of those [Muslim] refugees who fled Rumelia after the Balkan War[s] and those Turkish and Kurdish refugees that left the provinces of Van, Bitlis and Erzurum for Adana, the Kurds have been registered to be resettled in certain areas and absolutely no permission whatsoever will be given for them to go to any other place, whereas with the Turks, when the registries will be sent to the province's office of immigration they will have to be registered in the registry of "foreigners" and their registration in the basic registries will be marked and papers drawn up.[67]

---

[65] BOA/DH.ŞFR, no. 65/93, Coded telegram from the Interior Ministry's IAMM to the Provinces of Erzurum, Adana, Ankara, Aydın, Bitlis, Beirut, Aleppo, Konya, Mamuretülaziz, Mosul, and Van, and to the Provincial Districts of Urfa, İzmit, İçel, Eskişehir, Bolu, Teke, Canik, Cebel-i Lübnan, (Der) Zor, Karesi (Balıkesir), Kale-i Sultaniye (Çanakkale), Kayseri, Karahisâr-ı Sahib (Afyon Karahisar), Kütahya, Menteşe, Marash, and Niğde, dated 26 June 1916.

[66] BOA/DH.ŞFR, no. 72/131, Coded telegram from the Interior Ministry's General Directorate of Tribal and Immigrant Affairs to the Provinces of Sivas and Kastamonu, dated 31 December 2005.

[67] BOA/DH.SN.THR, no. 1857/77/47, Cable from the Interior Ministry to the Province of Adana, dated 7 January 1918.

Displaced people who resettled themselves without the direction and control of the government were ordered to evacuate their new homes immediately. A cable to the provincial district of İzmit, dated 2 July 1914, states that "reports have been received that Muslim immigrants have been settled in the Greek villages within the county of Yalova" and orders that "these persons must under no circumstances be allowed to settle [there]."[68] This firm—even harsh—attitude toward all Muslim immigrants, Turks, and non-Turks alike is another clear indication that the government's population and settlement policies were being undertaken according to a comprehensive plan that possessed clearly defined criteria for resettlement.

THE "TURKIFICATION" OF PLACE-NAMES

With the forcible emptying out of literally hundreds of Christian localities in Anatolia, the peninsula's geographic nomenclature began to be systematically transformed. A document from 1916 shows that the process of changing the names of non-Turkish settlements had been under way already for some time. Mention is made of a list that had been prepared that "shows all of the towns and villages whose names have been changed since the year 1910."[69]

One article dealing with the subject of place-names appeared in the government's 1913 Regulations on Immigrants; it mentions "the need for 'suitable names' to be given to the villages that will be constructed for the immigrants." But the changing of place-names was not limited to newly constructed settlements; rather, it covered all settlements with non-Turkish names. Initially, however, there was no overall system in place, and these efforts were done on a local level, according to the administrative rules of the specific provinces.

The first steps toward systematizing the process coincided with the Ottoman entry into World War I and were likewise accelerated by the war itself. This attempt at greater systematization can be seen in an Interior

---

[68] BOA/DH.ŞFR, no. 42/176, Coded telegram from the Interior Ministry's Private Secretariat to the Provincial District of İzmit, dated 2 July 1914.

[69] Cited in Erdal Aydoğan, *İttihat ve Terakki'nin Doğu Politikası, 1908–1918* (Istanbul: Ötüken Neşriyat, 2005), 68.

Ministry cable on 12 January 1916 to the province of Mamuretülaziz that mentions that a previous message on this subject had been sent to the provinces several months before on 17 October 1915. In the earlier communication, the ministry had requested that local officials prepare lists of the names of "cities, towns and villages that are not connected with Ottomanism [i.e., the Ottoman Turkish language]."[70]

A new book of regulations from the central government, issued on 5 January 1916, would transform the practice of renaming the human settlements and geography of Anatolia into a central aspect of government policy. The first article in this document states that "it has been decided that all of the provinces, provincial districts, villages, towns, mountains, rivers . . . etc. within the Ottoman domains which have been given non-Islamic names, such as Armenian, Greek and Bulgarian, shall be changed to Turkish."[71] Taking advantage of the favorable circumstances that the war had provided for such a move, the new regulations not only called for the rapid change of such names, but also gave information and advice on how this was to be done, including guidelines and even examples of new names. The provincial administrations were to carry out the "preliminary work of compiling lists . . . of the existing names of all the towns, villages and townships in the provinces and determining the new names to which they will be changed." The regional governments set to work on this task and regularly reported back to the central government. A document of 27 January 1916 shows that the documents gathered by the Interior Ministry were regularly forwarded to the Office of the High Command.[72]

Despite these attempts, the government's desire for a rapid conclusion of the naming process created chaos on the ground, a situation that even threatened to seriously disrupt the war effort, as the interunit correspondence within the military sank to new levels of incomprehensibility and confusion. Finally, on 15 June 1916, a decree was issued to halt the process.[73] But the halt proved to be only a hiatus, and the Turkification of place-names and geographic features would continue up to and throughout the period of the Turkish Republic, eventually eliminating not only

---

[70] Erdal Aydoğan, *İttihat ve Terakki'nin Doğu Politikası*, 68.

[71] Dündar, *İttihat ve Terakki'nin*, 82.

[72] Aydoğan, *İttihat ve Terakki'nin Doğu Politikası*, 68.

[73] Ibid., 83.

Christian or European names, but also those of Arabic, Persian, Kurdish, Laz, Georgian, and Circassian origin.[74]

THE DEPORTATION AND RESETTLEMENT POLICIES WERE BORN OUT OF DIVERGENT NEEDS

In order to prevent any misunderstandings, it should be mentioned here that not all of the deportations and relocations that are claimed to have taken place between 1913 and 1918 were the result of a centrally planned population and settlement policy for which all the details had been worked out in advance. The documents from the Interior Ministry's Cipher Office reveal that there were five main reasons for the movement of populations during this period, which I will describe in detail below.

PERCEIVED THREATS

Christian groups whose presence was deemed to be a threat (in particular, the Greeks in the Aegean coastal regions, the Syriac Christians in the Mardin-Diyarbekır area, and all Armenians) were to be removed from Anatolia through forced emigration or expulsion, and Muslims were to be resettled in these areas in their place. In the case of the Aegean Greeks, this removal was partially accomplished in the spring and summer of 1914 through expulsion to Greece, but in greater measure through a campaign of threats, intimidation, looting, and a limited number of killings. The Armenians, on the other hand, were deported beginning in May 1915, and many were massacred on the way or left to die in the desert wastes. In addition to the Armenians, a significant number of the Syriac Christians were also massacred.

The Muslim arrivals from the Balkans and Caucasus regions were systematically resettled in the Christian villages that had been emptied out. These resettlement efforts, which began in the Aegean region in 1913, would reach a new level with the wholesale evacuation of the Armenian villages in 1915 and continue throughout much of the war. The Prime Ministerial Ottoman Archive in Istanbul is replete with documents describing

[74] For a general overview of the subject, see Harun Tunçel, "Türkiye'de İsmi Değiştirilen Köyler," *Fırat Üniversitesi Sosyal Bilimler Dergisi* 10, no. 2 (2000): 23–34.

plans for relocating populations, such as the cipher to the governor of Konya ordering that "the 64 Albanian and 181 Bosnian families inside the province in the districts of Ereğli, Karaağaç, Ilgın, Akşehir, Saideli and Karaman where they are temporarily being housed shall be sent off, with their belongings, to be resettled in the abandoned villages in the provinces of Diyarbekır and Sivas; the 78 Turkish families in the aforementioned districts are to be sent to the province of Adana."[75] In general, attempts were made to ensure that the material needs of the new immigrants would be met through the "abandoned property, existing provisions, clothing and other possessions" left behind by the departing Armenians and Greeks; in fact, the Property Liquidation Commissions that were originally formed in order to monitor abandoned Armenian properties were eventually entrusted with the task of providing for the immigrants' needs.[76]

In certain regions the brief interval between the emptying of the Armenian towns and villages of their inhabitants and their repopulation with Muslim refugees may be seen as another indication that preparations had already been under way before the actual deportations. The best and most important example of this phenomenon is perhaps the Armenian deportation from Zeytun. The process of removing the Armenian inhabitants began between 8 and 10 April 1915,[77] and the process of resettling people brought from the area around Antep began less than two weeks later on 20 April 1915.[78] If one keeps in mind that the initial "emptying out"

[75] BOA/DH.ŞFR, no. 54/246, Coded telegram from the Interior Ministry's IAMM to the Province of Konya, dated 30 June 1915.

[76] BOA/DH.ŞFR, no. 61/120 and 61/122, Coded telegrams from the Interior Ministry's IAMM to the Provinces of Bitlis, Trebizond, and Sivas, dated 26 February 1916. These telegrams are examples of how the commissions functioned.

[77] Concerning the initial removal of families from Zeytun on 8–10 April, see James Bryce and Arnold Toynbee, *The Treatment of Armenians in the Ottoman Empire, 1915–16: Documents Presented to Viscount Grey of Fallodon, Secretary of State for Foreign Affairs by Viscount Bryce*, ed. Ara Sarafian (Princeton and London: Gomidas Institute, 2005), 491, footnote (by Ara Sarafian). For the events of 9 April, see NA/RG 59, 867.00/761, Report from the consul in Aleppo, J. B. Jackson, to Ambassador Morgenthau, dated 21 April 1915, reproduced in *United States Official Records on the Armenian Genocide, 1915–1917*, ed. Ara Sarafian (Princeton and London: Gomidas Institute, 2004), 10; and Aram Arkun, "Zeytun and the Commencement of the Armenian Genocide," in *A Question of Genocide: Armenians and Turks at the End of the Ottoman Empire*, ed. Ronald Grigor Suny, Fatma Müge Göçek, and Norman Naimark (Oxford and New York: Oxford University Press, 2011).

[78] BOA/DH.ŞFR, no. 52/51, Coded telegram from the Interior Ministry's IAMM to Fourth Army commander Cemal Pasha, dated 20 April 1915.

of Zeytun removed a limited number of families and that the wholesale deportation of the Armenian community of Zeytun was carried out only in response to a coded message containing the order, which was sent to the provincial district governor of Marash on 4 May, then it becomes clear that resettlement of new Muslim immigrants began long before the deportations were complete.[79]

Another telling example is the Settlement Office telegram to the province of Damascus on 22 June 1915. This cable, sent at a time when the Armenians of Aleppo and Urfa had yet to be deported, informs the local governor that the immigrants then present within the province "would be sent at a later time to resettle the areas of Aleppo, Adana and Urfa that were left devoid of Armenians" and therefore there was no need "to construct their own homes by themselves."[80] As the documents make clear, months before the actual deportations took place, decisions had already been made as to which immigrants would be settled where.

In similar fashion, a telegram of 17 May 1915 to the provincial district of Marash shows that a government functionary had already begun to resettle immigrants in the emptied Armenian villages around Marash.[81] Another cable, sent to the province of Mamuretülaziz on 25 May, demands that "those immigrants who have not yet been able to be resettled shall be sent to Adana at a later time in order to be settled in the towns that have been emptied out."[82] Another message, sent to Adana on the same date, requests that local officials provide the names of the towns currently lying empty, as well as the number of Armenians who have been deported up to that time.[83]

On 28 May the American consul in Mersin, Edward Nathan, sent a report back to the embassy on the situation in the region, in which he

[79] BOA/DH.ŞFR, no. 52/286, Coded telegram from the Interior Ministry's General Directorate of Security to the Provincial District of Marash, dated 5 May 1915.

[80] BOA/DH.ŞFR, no. 54/95, Coded telegram from the Interior Ministry's IAMM to the Province of Damascus, dated 22 June 1915.

[81] BOA/DH.ŞFR, no. 53/21, Coded telegram from the Interior Ministry's IAMM to the Provincial District of Marash, dated 17 May 1915.

[82] BOA/DH.ŞFR, no. 53/115, Coded telegram from the Interior Ministry's IAMM to the Province of Mamuretülaziz, dated 25 May 1915.

[83] BOA/DH.ŞFR, no. 53/113, Coded telegram from the Interior Ministry's IAMM to the Provinces of Adana, Aleppo, Erzurum, Van, and Bitlis, dated 25 May 1915.

mentioned that Muslims were being settled in Dörtyol in the houses of deported Armenians.[84] On 22 May the German consul in Erzurum reported to his superiors that a similar process was under way in the environs of Erzurum.[85] Once again, the relatively brief period between the emptying out and resettling of Armenian and other places of habitation would seem to attest to preparations for such actions having been made well in advance.

MILITARY REASONS

A great many more Ottoman Christian subjects were deported or otherwise forcibly displaced at various times for military reasons, as when the decision was made in October 1914 to remove those "Nestorian [Christian]s who were susceptible to foreign incitements" from the area of the Iranian border and to resettle them in central Anatolian locations such as Ankara and Konya.[86] That the forcible removal of Greek Orthodox Christians—especially the inhabitants of the Black Sea and Aegean coasts—and their relocation in the Anatolian hinterlands (a process that will be examined in greater detail in later chapters) grew considerably in scale at the end of 1916 and into 1917 is another example of the Ottomans' policy of directed population transfers.

POLITICAL CONCERNS

In large measure, the forcible deportations/resettlement actions resulted from political concerns. Into this category can be placed the first deportations that were directed at the Armenian community, which took place in the Çukurova region between the months of February and April 1915. Since it was feared that the Armenians of the region would receive military assistance from abroad and revolt, they were first deported from the

---

[84] NA/RG 59, 867.00/768, Report from Mersin consul Edward I. Nathan to Ambassador Morgenthau, dated 28 May 1915, in *United States Official Records*, ed. Sarafian, 48.

[85] DE/PA-AA/Bo.Kons., vol. 168, Report from Erzurum consul Scheubner to the German Embassy, Istanbul, dated 22 May, 1915.

[86] BOA/DH.ŞFR, no. 46/78, Coded telegram from interior minister Talat to the Province of Van, dated 26 October 1914.

İskenderun and Dörtyol areas and resettled in Adana,[87] and later on, at the beginning of April, Armenians from the Zeytun area were deported and resettled in Konya.

In similar fashion—and for similar reasons—some prominent Arab leaders and families in Syria who were thought capable of leading a revolt against the Ottoman regime were deported by Fourth Army commander and Unionist triumvir Cemal Pasha to the Anatolian interior. Documents dealing with the subject openly state that the action was taken "for political reasons."[88] Another such politically motivated deportation targeted many of the members of the new Jewish Yishuv in Palestine. In August 1915, for example, the interior minister sent a message to the Fourth Army commander and demanded that "those Jewish citizens of the enemy states who are in the lands of Palestine and who are hostile to the Ottomans be deported to Çorum."[89] One may even add to this list the deportation to the middle of Anatolia of some of the more problematic Kurdish tribes that the state had had difficulty controlling.[90]

REFUGEE RESETTLEMENT

The forcible resettlement of Muslim refugees from the war zones in the Anatolian interior was not planned in advance, but was rather an exigency born of war. In particular, the attempts to resettle the massive and unexpected wave of refugees who arrived in the wake of military setbacks on the Caucasian front can be considered as falling under this category. The

[87] More detailed information will be given on this subject in the later sections. Additionally, for a broader discussion of the February 1915 deportations from Dörtyol, İskenderun, and the later ones from Zeytun and Marash that occured in March and April, see Taner Akçam, *A Shameful Act*, 146–47, 159–61.

[88] BOA/DH.ŞFR, no. 72/66, Coded telegram from interior minister Talat to the Provinces of Edirne, Adana, Ankara, Aydın, Hüdâvendigâr (Bursa), Sivas, Kastamonu, Konya, İzmit, Eskişehir, Bolu, Karesi (Balıkesir), Menteşe, Teke, Kayseri, Karahisâr-ı Sahib (Afyon Karahisar), Kütahya, Marash, and Niğde, dated 22 January 1917.

[89] BOA/DH.ŞFR, no. 55/235, Coded telegram from interior minister Talat to the Fourth Army Command, dated 25 August 1915.

[90] The deportation to Konya of the Ciranlı tribe, which had "destroyed and looted crops, seeds, and goods" in Urfa in July 1917 and "attacked the detachment of gendarmes sent [to the scene], causing the deaths of four gendarmes" is an example of this type of action (BOA/DH.ŞFR, no. 79-A/173, Coded telegram from the Interior Ministry's General Directorate of Tribal and Immigrant Affairs to the Provincial District of Urfa, dated 27 September 1917).

Muslim refugees were also settled in the vacated Armenian and Greek towns and villages and thus took part in the government's planned population and settlement policies.

As has been shown in regard to the efforts to assimilate the Kurds, there is much documentary evidence of unaccounted for deportations and resettlement "of those refugees forced to relocate on account of the war," in particular as a result of the military reversals in the struggle against Russia.[91] A series of cables asking for information on the numbers and needs of people who had been forced to leave their home areas was sent to the provinces throughout the first years of the war.[92] A great many of these war refugees were resettled in the abandoned houses and settlements of the Armenians.[93] According to some sources, there were approximately 702,900 Muslims who fled before the advancing Russian armies in 1915 and 1916 alone; these refugees were largely resettled in central and western Anatolia.[94]

DEPORTATIONS UNKNOWN TO THE CENTRAL GOVERNMENT

Some deportations were carried out by local authorities without consulting or notifying the central government. From a December 1914 telegram to Jerusalem, it can be understood that such "evictions" were already being carried out long before any wide-ranging deportation operations were under way. The telegram, sent by interior minister Talat to the provincial governor, complained of "reports that the government had not been no-

[91] One example can be seen in BOA/DH.ŞFR, no. 61/120, Coded telegram from the Interior Ministry's IAMM to the Province of Bitlis, dated 26 February 1916.

[92] To give two examples: BOA/DH.ŞFR, no. 53/26, Coded telegram from the Interior Ministry's IAMM to the Provinces of Erzurum, Van, Bitlis, Trebizond, Sivas, Ankara, Kastamonu, Edirne, and Hüdâvendigâr (Bursa), and to the Provincial Districts of Canik, Karesi (Balıkesir), and Kale-i Sultaniye (Çanakkale), dated 17 May 1915; and BOA/DH.ŞFR, no. 62/268, Coded telegram from the Interior Ministry's General Directorate for Tribal and Immigrant Affairs to the Provinces of Sivas, Diyarbekır, and Trebizond, and to the Committee of Inspection in Tokat, dated 7 April 1916.

[93] BOA/DH.ŞFR, no. 63/261, Coded telegram from the Interior Ministry's IAMM to the Provinces of Ankara, Adana, Aleppo, Hüdâvendigâr (Bursa), Diyarbekır, Kastamonu, Mamuretülaziz, Sivas, and Trebizond, and to the Provincial Districts of İzmit, Eskişehir, Urfa, Canik, Karesi (Balıkesir), Kayseri, and Niğde, dated 6 May 1916.

[94] One document in which the Interior Ministry explains the current migration and immigration situation is published in *Askeri Tarih Belgeleri Dergisi* 31, no. 81 (December 1982): 223–34, Doc. no. 1845.

tified in advance that 500 Russian Jews living in Jaffa had been expelled [from the country]."[95] It is clear from the documentation that the expulsion of these Jews had created a hostile attitude toward the Ottoman government. Likewise, in another cable from Talat to the provincial district of Jerusalem on 6 February 1915, the interior minister complains about this situation and demands that no more people be deported without prior permission: "These cables, which a great many Jews who were expelled from Jaffa have sent to the entire world from Port Said and İskenderiye, have produced a mood of hostility toward us among American public opinion. . . . More gentle treatment must be accorded in this regard and in any case, absolutely no Jews should be deported without first asking [permission from] here."[96]

Deportations of which the central government was unaware took place in great number within the area controlled by Cemal Pasha's Fourth Army. Without informing Istanbul, the army commander ordered a number of expulsions that he saw as necessary on the basis of political and/or military necessity. On 23 August an irritated Talat cabled the general that "it has been learned that in this time some 1,700 Jews are to be expelled from there. Inform us in detail of the identity of these persons and the reasons for their expulsion."[97]

Another cable from the Security Directorate in Istanbul to Cemal Pasha, this time on 16 March 1916, states that "no reason can be understood as to why and upon whose order or from whence" certain Druze families have been deported from Havran and sent to Osmaniye County (in Adana), and demands that he "send [clarifying] information in this matter."[98] Talat would also learn after the fact of the deportation of the region's Italian citizens from Jerusalem. In a cable to the district governor of Jerusalem, he states, "It has been reported that some of the Italian citizens living in Jerusalem who have not accepted Ottoman citizenship have been

[95] BOA/DH.ŞFR, no. 48/110, Coded telegram from interior minister Talat to the Provincial District of Jerusalem, dated 22 December 1914.

[96] BOA/DH.ŞFR. no. 49/216, Coded telegram from interior minister Talat to the Provincial District governor of Jerusalem, Midhat Bey Effendi, dated 6 February 1915.

[97] BOA/DH.ŞFR, no. 55/182, Coded telegram from interior minister Talat to the Provincial District of Jerusalem, dated 23 August 1915.

[98] BOA/DH.ŞFR, no. 56/237, Coded telegram from the Interior Ministry's General Directorate of Security to the Fourth Army Command, dated 30 September 1915.

deported to the interior. Is there indeed such a decision? Please report as to whether or not it will be possible to make exceptions for women and children."[99] The needs of those sent by Cemal Pasha to the interior regions were to be met through the property and real estate left by the departing Armenians.[100]

Similar actions were witnessed in the Aegean region. In a telegram to the financial inspector in Kütahya on 26 September 1915, Talat asks, "for what reason and on whose order have the Greeks [of the area] been deported, and to where?"[101] Istanbul had found out about the action in the first place only because of a complaint lodged by the Greek Patriarchate in the city.[102]

Of course, not all of the reasons for forced deportations and resettlement efforts may be classified neatly into as discrete categories as these. In many cases military and political needs dovetailed, or at least overlapped. Moreover, great emphasis was placed on ensuring that unforeseen or undirected movements of refugees and other displaced people would be quickly corralled and brought into line with government plans for population movement and resettlement.

[99] BOA/DH.ŞFR, no. 62/28, Coded telegram from the Interior Ministry's General Directorate of Security to the Provincial District of Jerusalem, dated 16 March 1916.

[100] BOA/DH.ŞFR, no. 62/307, Coded telegram from the Interior Ministry's General Directorate of Tribal and Immigrant Affairs to the Provinces and Provincial Districts of Kütahya, Yozgad, Ankara, Çorum, Sivas, Amasya, Tokat, Konya, Isparta, Bolu, Kastamonu, Hüdâvendigâr (Bursa), and Ertuğrul, dated 13 April 1916. Cemal Pasha is appraised of the situation a little later in a cable addressed to him personally (see BOA/DH.ŞFR, no. 62/308).

[101] BOA/DH.ŞFR, no. 56/204, Coded telegram from interior minister Talat to the financial inspector in Kütahya, Muhtar Bey, dated 26 September 1915.

[102] BOA/DH.ŞFR, no. 56/253, Coded telegram from the Interior Ministry's General Directorate of Security to the financial inspector in Eskişehir, Muhtar Bey, dated 2 October 1915.

THREE   THE AFTERMATH OF THE BALKAN WARS AND THE "EMPTYING" OF EASTERN THRACE AND THE AEGEAN LITTORAL IN 1913–14

Throughout the years of 1913 and 1914 until its entry into the war, the Ottoman government carried out a basic ethnic-cleansing operation, particularly against the Greeks in Thrace and the Aegean littoral. They used a dual-track mechanism extensively. On one hand, they signed separate "population exchange" agreements with the governments of the Balkan states; on the other hand, they terrorized Ottoman Greek subjects, including with massacres, to force them to move to Greece. The number of Greeks who had to flee or had been forcefully expelled was roughly three hundred thousand. This wide-scale suppressive policy brought the Ottomans to the brink of war with Greece in the summer of 1914. The policy of forceful expulsion of ethnic groups was not, of course, unique to the Ottomans, as other Balkan countries also commonly employed it against Muslims.

OFFICIAL AGREEMENTS ON POPULATION EXCHANGE

With the reciprocal agreements that were reached with Bulgaria and Greece in the wake of the Balkan Wars, the Ottoman policies of forcible relocation and settlement that began with the mutual exchange of border populations would eventually be transformed—most pronouncedly after Enver Pasha became minister of war in January 1914—into a broader plan that would cover all of Anatolia and Thrace.

Because the other states of the Balkans were simultaneously following similar policies, after 1912 the region witnessed a number of large-scale population migrations and exchanges. The example of Macedonia can perhaps give the reader a grasp of the scale of the period's demographic shifts: between 1912 and 1925 there were at least seventeen population dislocations, some forced and unilateral affairs, while others were mutually agreed upon by two or more of the region's states.[1]

A significant number of these shifts resulted from reciprocal population exchanges between two or more countries, beginning with the accord of Turkey and Bulgaria in Istanbul on 29 September 1913, in the wake of the Second Balkan War. The treaty's relevant passage reads as follows:

> An alliance has been produced between the two governments in regard to the facilitating of the voluntary, reciprocal exchange of Bulgar[ian Orthodox] and Muslim populations from both sides as well as properties within an area that extends 15 kilometers along the [two countries'] entire shared border. The exchange will take place as an exchange of entire villages. The exchange of property by means of a voluntary drawing of lots will be carried out under the protection of the two governments, and the villages [whose populations] are to switch places will be exchanged in conjunction with the villages' council of elders. The mixed commission that will be appointed by both governments will immediately set itself to the task of effecting the exchange of said villages and the individuals from their populations, and, should it be necessary, the correcting of any imbalances [in alloted assets] that may arise from this exchange.[2]

A joint body, the Mixed Commission on Population Exchange, was established to carry out the population swap.[3] On 15 November 1913, the commissioners gathered in Edirne to sign an agreement on the mutual transfer of populations and on subsequent transactions. The chairman of the Turkish delegation, Şükrü Kaya, would "in 1914 be sent to oversee the expulsion of the Greeks of İzmir."[4]

The joint Turkish-Bulgarian Commission reconvened on 23 May 1914, at which time two subcommissions were established that would continue

[1] Stephen Lades, *The Exchange of Minorities, Bulgaria, Greece and Turkey* (New York: Macmillan, 1932), 15–16.

[2] Bayur, *Türk İnkılabı Tarihi*, vol. 2, part 2, 486. For the original French, see Stephen Lades, *The Exchange of Minorities*, 18.

[3] Kazım Öztürk, *Türk Parlamento Tarihi: TBMM-II: Dönem, 1923–1927*, vol. 3 (Ankara: TBMM Vakfı Yayınları, 1995), 616.

[4] Ibid. The experience that Şükrü Kaya gained in the Bulgarian and Greek population exchanges as the head of the IAMM at the time would again be put to use in 1915, when he would play a special role in the deportation and massacres of Armenians.

their labors until October. Although the outbreak of the First World War forced the commissions to disband, by that time they had laid the foundations of an agreement on the appraisal of the lands and properties of the 9,714 Muslim families (48,570 people) leaving Bulgaria for the Ottoman state, and the 9,472 Bulgar families (46,764 people) going in the opposite direction. Because of the war, however, the agreement was never put into action.

From the very first, the commission struggled with the results of the large migration, whether voluntary or forced, that had begun during the Balkan Wars and continued in their aftermath.[5] A 31 March 1914 cable to the district governor of Balıkesir shows that villages were being emptied of their inhabitants even as the commissioners were meeting, and that the Ottoman regime had begun moving Muslim refugees into the abandoned settlements: "It is suitable that the new immigrants coming from the occupied [Balkan] cities be settled in the houses left empty by those who have immigrated to Bulgaria, but no value has yet been placed on these houses and one of the two copies of the certified registry that is to be put together for this purpose must be sent here."[6]

The agreement with Bulgaria was soon followed by accords with Serbia (14 October 1913) and Greece (14 November 1913), with similar stipulations for the exchange of populations. All of these agreements recognized the right of anyone (which at that time meant only males)—within a certain designated period—to change nationality and emigrate to the country of their own ethnoreligious community.[7]

A further series of bilateral meetings over the spring and summer of 1914 resulted in several new agreements for the purpose of better coordinating the population exchanges. In May, for instance, the Ottoman ambassador in Athens, Galib Kemali Bey (Söylemezoğlu), proposed to exchange the Greeks of Aydın for the Muslims of Macedonia.[8] Follow-up

[5] Lades, The Exchange of Minorities, 18–20.

[6] BOA/DH.ŞFR, no. 39/133, Coded telegram from the Interior Ministry's IAMM to the Provincial District of Karesi (Balıkesir), dated 31 March 1914.

[7] Ahmet Halaçoğlu, Balkan Harbı, 23–24. For the full text of the agreement in Turkish, see Canlı Tarihler: Galip Kemali Söylemezoğlu Hatıraları; Atina Sefareti (1913–1916) (Istanbul: Türkiye Yayınevi, 1946), 56–66.

[8] In his memoirs, Galib Kemali Bey claims that the first proposal in this regard was made by him personally to the Greek prime minister Venizelos, and that the matter only became official upon Venizelos's acceptance. Naturally, it is impossible to verify his claims, but Ottoman sources do corroborate

correspondence and face-to-face meetings concluded 1 July with an agreement "On the mutual, voluntary exchange of Turks in Macedonia for Greeks in the provinces of Eastern Thrace and Macedonia";[9] a commission was then formed to coordinate the reciprocal migrations. In the correspondence between the two countries (and between their respective capitals and the affected provinces) discussing the formation of this commission, both sides explicitly clarified their understanding that "the basis of the exchange of the Muslims emigrating from Macedonia and the Greek emigrants [from Aydın and Western Thrace] was voluntary emigration."[10]

Among the commission's first tasks was to provide for the direct exchange of privately held real estate. Thus, in a 16 November 1914 cable from the Security Directorate to the province of Aydın, the district governor's office is asked "that permission be given that the farms of those Greeks who own such holdings in the Ottoman domains and the Muslims who own farms on lands that were annexed to Greece be allowed to be exchanged on a private [person-to-person] basis, [so that] the Greek properties in the Ottoman domains are sold or given away by the owners or otherwise lost to the state.[11] Because of the war, however, the various commissions established in August 1914 in provinces such as İzmir and

---

the fact that the official proposals both for the population exchange and for the forming of a commission to handle this were first made by the Ottoman government, and that the Greek government subsequently agreed to both. See, for instance, the telegram from the Interior Ministry to the Provincial District of Karesi (Balıkesir), dated 28 June 1914, which states: "Greece yesterday delivered a diplomatic note in reply to the Sublime Porte. The note is very mild [in tone] and expresses appreciation for the actions of our government . . . and accepts the [notion of] the population exchange on a voluntary basis. . . . Additionally, in the cable received [the Greek side has agreed to the formation] of a mixed commission [to be established] in İzmir in order to oversee the details of the exchange, as per the suggestion previously made by our side" (BOA/DH.ŞFR, no. 42/136). In his report of 27 May 1914, the British ambassador to the Porte, Sir Louis Mallet, states that Sait Halim Pasha told him that "he had proposed to Mr. Venizelos a few days previously that a mixed commission should be set up for arranging and regulating the exchange of population between Thrace and Macedonia" (quoted in Constantinos Emm. Fotiadis, *The Genocide of the Pontus Greeks by the Turks,* vol. 13, *Archive Documents of the Ministeries of Foreign Affairs of Britain, France, the League of Nations and S.H.A.T.* (Thessaloniki: Herodotus, 2004), 48.

[9] Ahmet Halaçoğlu, *Balkan Harbi,* 27.

[10] BOA/DH.ŞFR, no. 42/136, Coded telegram from the Interior Ministy's General Directorate of Security to the Provincial District of Karesi (Balıkesir), dated 28 June 1914.

[11] BOA/DH.ŞFR, no. 47/44, Coded telegram from the Interior Ministry's General Directorate of Security to the Province of Aydın, dated 16 November 1914.

Edirne ceased their activities in December, and as a result, none of their decisions and plans were ever implemented.[12]

THE DUAL-TRACK MECHANISM AS EMPLOYED IN THE AEGEAN REGION

The forcible removals and resettlements of entire communities were not all carried out on the basis of official bilateral agreements. For instance, migrations were often forced in the immediate aftermath of war and territorial loss long before any official discussions between the belligerents, and such talks were often simply an attempt to rationalize and organize the movements already under way.

Also during this period—and simultaneously with but independent from high-level bilateral negotiations—many of the wars gave rise to another informal demographic policy: one in which a locally dominant population would, in an unspoken but seemingly reciprocal understanding, expel the subordinated ethnoreligious groups through violence and terror.[13] For this reason, when speaking of these migrations one must be mindful of the existence and functioning of this dual-track mechanism.

While making serious attempts to impose an official and legal framework on these expulsions and migrations, the Ottoman authorities drove the Christians from their remaining territories through terror and even—when deemed necessary—massacres. These "unofficial" tactics continued

[12] Bayur, *Türk İnkılap Tarihi*, vol. 2, part 3, 262; for a detailed account of the works of the commissions over the course of their existence on the basis of Greek documents, see Yannis G. Mourelos, "The 1914 Persecutions and the First Attempt at an Exchange of Minorities Between Greece and Turkey," *Balkan Studies* 26, no. 2 (1985): 389–413.

[13] In three cables sent to Paris on the successive days of 26, 27, and 28 April, the French ambassador to the Porte at the time, Monsieur Bompard, gave examples of how all of the Balkan states resorted to almost identical methods in carrying out ethnic cleansing within their borders. For the text of the ambassador's telegrams, see Bayur, *Türk İnkılap Tarihi*, vol. 2, part 3, 256–58. In fact, the phenomenon of reciprocal ethnic cleansing in the Balkans has been the subject of many books, but the principal problem in most of these works remains their highly partisan character; the authors generally tend to exaggerate the injustices perpetrated by other groups against their own. Probably the most objective work on the events of the Balkan Wars is the report published by the Carnegie Commission soon after the events in question. It has been republished as: George F. Kennan, *The Other Balkan Wars: A 1913 Carnegie Endowment Inquiry in Retrospect with a New Introduction and Reflection on the Present Conflict* (Washington, DC: Carnegie Endowment for International Peace; Brookings Institution Publications), 1993. In this work I will not be delving into the subject of reciprocal ethnic cleansing in the Balkans, since my focus will be limited to the Armenian experience.

in parallel with, but unrestrained by and without reference to, ongoing bilateral negotiations. First used against the Greeks of the empire's Aegean region, the dual-track mechanism would be redeployed during the Armenian deportations and massacres. The memoirs of Kuşçubaşı Eşref, Halil Menteşe, Celal Bayar, and other key players provide ample information on the main outlines of the covert, parallel plan of forced migration that was implemented before the adoption of official agreements.[14] The government's primary policy objective, particularly in the Aegean and eastern Thrace, was to significantly reduce the numbers of Christians who were deemed a threat to national security. Recalling the policies put in place in the Aegean region during the spring of 1914, Halil Menteşe states that "[Interior minister] Talat Bey suggested that the country be cleansed of those elements that were seen as capable of betraying the state."[15]

Contemporary German documents confirm that the interior minister addressed German diplomats with equal frankness: "Talat Bey . . . explained without hesitation that the government wished to use the World War as a pretext [so as not to allow foreign countries to intervene] in order to cleanse the country of its internal enemies—meaning the Christians of all denominations."[16] In the words of Kuşçubaşı Eşref, a central figure in the ethnic cleansing operations, the non-Muslims were "internal tumors" in the body of the Ottoman state and had to be "cleaned out"; to do so, he claimed, was "a national cause."[17]

The main objective was to get the Christian villagers to leave, either through persuasion or, if necessary, by intimidation. Among the principal methods used to achieve this were "monitoring, humiliation, killings, preventing them from working their lands, oppressively heavy taxation, seizure of property [and] forcible conscription";[18] and when faced with

---

[14] For more detailed information on this topic, see Taner Akçam, *A Shameful Act,* 102–8.

[15] Halil Menteşe, *Osmanlı Mebusan Meclisi Reisi Halil Menteşe'nin Anıları* (Istanbul: Hürriyet Vakfı Yayınları, 1986), 165.

[16] DE/PA-AA/Bo.Kons. 169, Note added by German consul general in Constantinople and expert on Armenian affairs, Johannes Mordtmann, to the report by the consul in Aleppo, Rössler, to the German Embassy in Constantinople, dated 6 June 1915.

[17] From the memoirs of Kuşçubaşı Eşref, one of the key members of the SO, which was responsible for "cleansing" Anatolia of its non-Muslim population; quoted in Bayar, *Ben de Yazdım,* vol. 5, 1967.

[18] Elisabeth Kontogiorgi, "Forced Migration, Repatriation, Exodus: The Case of Ganos-Chora and Myriophyto-Peristaris Orthodox Communities in Eastern Thrace," *Balkan Studies* 35, no. 1 (1995): 22–24.

protests by the Greek government and other foreign powers, the Ottoman government, by virtue of the dual-track mechanism, could disclaim any involvement in these events.

The expulsions and forcible migrations from eastern Thrace began in the spring and summer of 1913. Attacks against the local Christians continued throughout the year, but after March 1914, these removals began to take on a more systematic form. As will be seen below, they were interrupted for political reasons, by the outbreak of the world war. During the war, however, the remaining Greek inhabitants of western Anatolia were moved to the interior for reasons of military and political expediency. These temporary removals, particularly those from Thrace, were prompted by the temporary presence of the Entente powers in the Dardanelles (Gallipoli): by virtue of this geographic proximity, they seem to have encouraged some nearby villages to demand "autonomy."[19] After the Armistice was signed at Mondros at the end of 1918, some of the Greek villagers who had been expelled either to Macedonia or to the Anatolian interior returned to their former places of residence, only to be forced out again after the Mudanya Armistice of 11 October 1921.[20]

What transpired in the Tekirdağ region of eastern Thrace would again be witnessed on the eastern shores of the Aegean. Beginning in the spring of 1913 and increasingly throughout 1914, the Greek villagers of western Anatolia, through intimidation and violence, were forced out and replaced with Muslim refugees—and this amid ongoing bilateral discussions of population exchanges. Characteristically, the unofficial policy was implemented through: (1) attacks on Greek villages and villagers by Special Organization (SO) units, with the central government claiming and acting as if it were not involved in the matter; (2) terror and killings to force individuals and communities from their homes; (3) the emptying of entire villages and conscription into labor brigades of all military-age male inhabitants; and (4) the seizure and redistribution of Greek-owned businesses to Muslims.[21] In an endless stream of letters to the Porte throughout March

---

[19] Ibid., 25–26. All told, almost ten thousand Greeks were forcibly resettled in the interior between June and August 1915.

[20] Ibid., 28–29.

[21] A detailed account of the attacks against Greek villages in the Aegean region can be found in Archimandrite Alexander Papadopoulos, *Persecution of the Greeks in Turkey before the European War* (New York: Oxford University Press, 1919).

and April 1913, the Greek Patriachate in Istanbul objected to the ongoing attacks on Aegean Greek villages, the looting of houses, seizures and arrests without cause, and expulsions.[22]

As previously mentioned, one of the richest sources of detailed information on the workings of the government's dual-track system are the memoirs of SO functionaries. Halil Menteşe, for instance, writes that "Provincial governors and other officials would not appear to be intervening on behalf of the government; the [Union and Progress] Committee's organization would take care of the matter."[23] To ensure that the correct people would oversee the events and ensure that they went according to plan, appointments were made at the highest levels. Eşref Kuşçubaşı writes,

> The operation to "clean out" the Aegean littoral [of its Christian population] was to be carried out by: Cafer Tayyar Bey (the late General Cafer Tayyar Eğilmez), Chief of the General Staff of the Fourth Army Corps, who was under the command of Pertev Pasha (Perteve Demirhan), who would be acting on behalf of the army, (the late) Governor of İzmir Rahmi Bey as civilian in charge and Mahmud Celâl Bey (former Republican President Celâl Bayar), who was the responsible representative of the CUP acting on their behalf. All of the forces of the state would act in accordance with the orders given by the Ministry of War and the High Command to put this plan into effect.[24]

A great share of the responsibility for implementing the plan fell to Kuşçubaşı. "The Greeks were harassed by various means, and were forced to emigrate by means of the assaults and oppressions against them. The armed gangs under the command of Special Forces commander Kuşçubaşı Eşref Bey . . . conducted raids against the Greek villages . . . Those Greek youth that could hold guns were rounded up for the purpose of [placing them in] labor battalions, and they were set to work in building roads, forestry and construction."[25]

[22] Ibid., 27–29.

[23] Halil Menteşe, Osmanlı Mebusan Meclisi Reisi, 166.

[24] Cemal Kutay, Birinci Dünya Harbinde Teşkilat-ı Mahsusa ve Hayber'de Türk Cengi (Istanbul: Ercan, 1962), 62.

[25] Nurdoğan Taçalan, Ege'de Kurtuluş Savaşı Başlarken (Istanbul: Milliyet Yayınları, 1970), 71–73.

THE DUAL-TRACK MECHANISM AS SEEN IN THE PRIME MINISTERIAL OTTOMAN ARCHIVE

Documents found in the Prime Ministerial Ottoman Archive in Istanbul show that the government created a dual-track mechanism. By this means it could create the impression that it was not fully aware of the emptying of Christian villages, although it was constantly and systematically gathering information on these same villages with the full intent of resettling Muslims there. Indeed, the close monitoring and supervision of these villages is a key piece of evidence that the government had full knowledge of the expulsions.

By far the most important document in this regard is the "extremely urgent and top secret" cable from Talat Pasha to the district governor of Tekirdağ on 14 April 1914. Talat reports that a large number of Greek villagers had assembled on the coast and requests that it be "ensured that they emigrate by boarding steamships but without any indication being given that [the process] is the result of a [government] directive."[26]

Precisely because of this dual track, some of the available documents give the impression that the government was unaware of the attacks against Christian villagers and their forcible expulsion, or, alternately, that they became aware of these occurrences only because of the complaints of the Greek Orthodox Church. For instance, in a cable sent on 22 April 1914 to the provincial governor in Edirne, the General Directorate of Security requests that "in light of a cable sent from [the village of] Mürfete to the Patriarchate [in Istanbul] in which it is reported that [the village of Kostanpolis] has been besieged by the neighboring Muslim villages and the Christians have had their property and possessions looted, please provide an immediate report on what happened and the circumstances surrounding the events."[27]

In another cable to Bolu in August 1914, the Security Directorate describes a recent attack against a Greek place of business. The Greek

[26] BOA/DH.ŞFR, no. 40/11, Coded telegram from interior minister Talat to the Provincial District of Tekfurdağı, dated 14 April 1915.

[27] BOA/DH.ŞFR, no. 40/71, Coded telegram from the Interior Ministry's General Directorate of Security to the Province of Edirne, dated 22 April 1914.

business owner was threatened with murder and the destruction of his shop if he did not quit the city within a few days. The security forces, although informed of the threats against his life and livelihood, took no preventive measures, and the Greek, an Ottoman citizen, was forced to close up shop. The Interior Ministry went no further than to dispatch a request that the shop owner not be prevented from running his business free from interruption.[28]

Of course, it is difficult to claim with any confidence that this entire process was being conducted under full government supervision and that spontaneous attacks of Muslim immigrants did not also occur without any government involvement. From some ministry telegrams one can understand that it was the Muslim refugees from the Balkan countries who instigated this type of attack and looting on their own. In response to various complaints from the provinces, the Interior Ministry demanded a halt to the "attacks that the immigrants are alleged to have committed."[29] A cable of April 1914 to the provincial district of Çatalca stated that "a group of unknown persons who call themselves a gang have been attacking villages and taking the villagers' animals" and committing "looting and theft," yet the same communiqué took pains to emphasize that the government had no connection whatsoever to these gangs. It was directed that "a declaration must be made to the effect that no one whatsoever has either come or been sent from Istanbul with the knowledge of the government, and that these persons [committing these acts] are at best individuals or gangs that have been formed for the purpose [of] taking advantage of the emigrations of the Greeks to cheaply purchase or otherwise acquire their property and possessions." It was also noted that a "mobile brigade" (kuvve-i seyyâre) must be organized to bring about the capture and arrest of these people.[30]

Today, the most telling aspect of these messages is the government's show of keen interest in preventing the abandoned villages from being

[28] BOA/DH.EUM, 3. Şube, 1/25, Coded telegram from the Interior Ministry's General Directorate of Security to the Provincial District of Bolu, dated 19 August 1914.

[29] BOA/DH.ŞFR, no. 40/38, Coded telegram from the Interior Ministry's General Directorate of Security to the Province of Edirne, dated 18 April 1914.

[30] BOA/DH.ŞFR, no. 40/63, Coded telegram from the Interior Ministry's General Directorate of Security to the Provincial District of Çatalca, dated 21 April 1914. An identical telegram was also sent to the Province of Edirne (40/64).

looted; this concern derived from the fact that Muslim immigrants were to be resettled there. To that end, explicit orders were given and the need to protect the empty villages was made clear, along with the warning that officials who failed to do so would be punished. This can be seen in a Security Directorate cable of 27 May 1914 to the provincial governor of Edirne, among others:

> Regardless of the circumstances of attacks or intimidation directed against Greek villages, the guilty parties must be arrested immediately and sent here so that they may be delivered to the Court-Martial for punishment, while the villages themselves must be put under [our] protection. In the event that the[se] villages do not receive protection and that such events continue to occur or that the perpetrators are not apprehended, local village guards and gendarmes, lower level officers and enlisted men [will be punished] by being sent off to serve in Yemen, while higher ranking officers [will be] severely [punished] by being dismissed from the military.[31]

Yet other cables sent to these very same regions—predating the communiqués cited above—amply demonstrate that the terror and "forced removal" operations against these villages were well known to the central government. Numerous telegrams directed the provinces that no difficulties should be put in the way of villagers who wished to emigrate, that the émigrés should be shown leniency in their tax obligations and other outstanding debts, that no exemption fee should be demanded from émigrés of conscription age, that they should be assisted in selling any possessions with which they wished to part, and that care should be taken to ensure their safety after they voluntarily left their villages.

Suffice it to give but a few examples: (1) a cable sent to Edirne on 1 April 1914 by the Interior Ministry's Private Secretariat mentions "that if there is nothing to be said against those who are emigrating, then certainly it cannot be acceptable that they would be attacked on their journey," and demands the appropriate measures to ensure that this does not

---

[31] BOA/DH.ŞFR, no. 41/91, Coded telegram from the Interior Ministry's General Directorate of Security to the Province of Edirne and to the Provincial Districts of Çatalca and Kale-i Sultaniye (Çanakkale), dated 27 May 1914.

happen;[32] (2) in another cable to Balıkesir the following day, the secretariat acknowledges reports that "some difficulties have been placed in the way of emigrating Bulgarians that would prevent them from doing so, such as demanding a monetary exemption fee from those who are of [military] age and preventing them from selling their property and goods." It goes on to demand that these practices be halted and that those potential émigrés "should be afforded every assistance and facilitation in order to ensure their speedy departure," adding that those who create these problems should immediately be reported to the authorities.[33]

A cable from the Settlement Office to the province of İzmit, sent on 13 April 1914, demands that "those wishing to leave be permitted to depart."[34] A message to Balıkesir ten days later says that the lands left behind by those Bulgarians leaving for Bulgaria is sufficient to cover their debts to the Agricultural Bank (Ziraat Bankası) and orders that after these debts are covered, no obstacles should be put in the way of those wishing to leave: "the allowance and facilitation of their departure is in the better interest of the state."[35] Additionally, it is ordered that when the Christians quit their villages, others should not be allowed to exploit the emigrants' constraints in order to acquire their property more cheaply or to engage in looting. The underlying reason was that Muslim immigrants were to have use of such things.[36]

An open admission that the forcible emptying out of Greek villages had been a central pillar of government policy up to that point would be indirectly made in November 1914, when the government officially ended the policy. On 2 November Talat Pasha sent out a general missive to the prov-

[32] BOA/DH.ŞFR, no. 39/138, Coded telegram from the Interior Ministry's Private Secretariat to the Province of Edirne, dated 1 April 1914.

[33] BOA/DH.ŞFR, no. 39/152, Coded telegram from the Interior Ministry's Private Secretariat to the Provincial District of Karesi (Balıkesir), dated 2 April 1914.

[34] BOA/DH.ŞFR, no. 39/223, Coded telegram from the Interior Ministry's IAMM to the Provincial District of İzmit, dated 13 April 1914.

[35] BOA/DH.ŞFR, no. 40/89, Coded telegram from the Interior Ministry's Private Secretariat to the Provincial District of Karesi (Balıkesir), dated 23 April 1914.

[36] BOA/DH.ŞFR, no. 40/160, Coded telegram from the Interior Ministry's IAMM to the Provincial District of Çatalca, dated 7 May 1914. The communication contains the following passage: "It has been reported that the Greeks who are emigrating have sold their animals for very low prices and that these have fallen into the hands of speculators (*muhtekir*). Taking the pressing needs of the Muslim immigrants into account this speculation must be prevented and the animals should preferably be sold to the immigrants."

inces in response to an understanding that he had reached with the Germans and in line with a promise he had given them. The cable instructed provincial officials that "in light of the state's current political situation, no attacks on or oppression of Greeks shall be allowed as such acts of oppression against them would not be appropriate."[37]

In a steady stream of communication with the provinces, the Interior Ministry demanded the number, location, condition, and habitational capacity of the emptied villages, and asked provincial officials whether they thought Muslims could be resettled there. For example, a 13 April 1914 cable to Balıkesir ordered that "those immigrants arriving from Salonica be settled in the homes left vacant by emigrating Greeks and Bulgarians," and that to this end, provincial officials should report on "their [housing] capacity."[38] Data on emigration, immigration, and resettlement were not, however, limited to population count. Often enough, detailed information was also requested on the social and economic character of the areas in question, such as the location and condition of abandoned lands, the trades of those leaving and arriving, and the character of their businesses. Indeed, many of the ultimate decisions on resettlement were made on the basis of this information.

On 30 June 1915, a cable was sent to several Aegean provinces and districts, including Aydın, from which it is possible to get a more detailed picture of the nature of the information being requested:

> [Please] report on how many Greeks have emigrated from [your] province up to now: from how many townships and villages, and [from] how many specific dwellings? What are the names of the villages and townships, the number of dwellings, the type and size of the fields that they have left, the [amount of] communal and private agriculture, and the type of industry and agricultural production in which they were engaged; and if [Muslim] immigrants have been

[37] BOA/DH.ŞFR, no. 46/133, Coded telegram from the Interior Ministry's General Directorate of Security to the Provinces of Edirne, Adana, Ankara, Aydın, Aleppo, Hüdâvendigâr (Bursa), Diyarbekır, Trebizond, Kastamonu, and Konya, and to the Provincial Districts of İzmit, Bolu, Canik, Çatalaca, Karesi (Balıkesir), Jerusalem, Kale-i Sultaniye (Çanakkale), Menteşe, Antalya, and Kayseri, dated 2 November 1914.

[38] BOA/DH.ŞFR, no. 39/222, Coded telegram from the Interior Ministry's IAMM to the Provincial District of Karesi (Balıkesir), dated 13 April 1914.

partially resettled in these places following the [original owners']
emigration, how many of these will be left where they are?[39]

What is significant here is that all of these actions were being undertaken
at a time in which no official understanding whatsoever had been reached
with Greece.

The monitoring and control of both the emigration and resettlement
processes were so tight that in some provinces, when new immigrants were
resettled either without or in contravention of the central government's orders, the directive would subsequently be given to remove the Muslim settlers. As in the example above, when it was learned that Muslim immigrants
had been settled in the abandoned Greek villages near Yalova, a cable to the
district governor of İzmit in early July 1914 demanded that "absolutely no
permission whatsoever be given for them to settle [there]."[40]

At other times, the government sent direct and explicit orders concerning the enterprises from which certain types of Christian employees should
be dismissed or expelled. For example, at one point the government intervened to halt the expulsion of Bulgarians working for a French company in
the county of Terkos (in the provincial district of Çatalca), since there was
a danger that Istanbul would be cut off from its water supply:

> The French Embassy, which in stating that any attempt to remove
> and expel the team of Bulgarian machinists from the township of
> Terkos who are employed there by the company, and to resettle
> in their place immigrants who are not knowledgeable and capable
> of operating machines, will undoubtedly cause these machines to
> cease functioning, and as a result will result not only in damage to
> the company, which is French, but will also deny water to Istanbul,
> has requested that the aforementioned Bulgarian labor [force] not
> be disturbed. In response to this request the Foreign Ministry has
> acceded to this demand. It is strongly recommended that either you
> yourself go or that you dispatch a special functionary [in order to
> ensure] that the process of dismissing and expelling [these employ-

[39] BOA/DH.ŞFR, no. 42/158, Coded telegram from the Interior Ministry's IAMM to the Province
of Aydın and to the Provincial Districts of Kale-i Sultaniye (Çanakkale) and Karesi (Balıkesir), dated
30 June 1914.

[40] BOA/DH.ŞFR, no. 42/176, Coded telegram from the Interior Ministry's Private Secretariat to
the Provincial District of İzmit, dated 2 June 1914.

ees] be summarily and permanently halted and that the continued employment of the current workforce of machinists be ensured.[41]

Additionally, the Ottoman government supplied the steamships and paid for the passage of Greek Christian émigrés to Greece. In a cable to the provincial district of Tekirdağ on 20 April 1914, the IAMM makes the following request: "the Greek-flagged steamship *Karmala*, which has been hired in order to bring the Greek emigrants from there to Salonica, will depart tomorrow morning. Please have the passengers ready [to embark], since compensation will have to be paid if it remains [in dock] for more than three days."[42] Above all, the government placed officials from the AMMU, which had the overall authority to organize all deportations, on board the ships as crew members, thereby ensuring that the emigration process would remain firmly under their control. In a cable to Çanakkale from 26 May 1914, the IAMM reports that "a Greek-flagged steamship has been sent in order to pick up the Greek emigrants," adding that Adil Bey from the IAMM would be "on the ship posing as one of the company's agents."[43] If they were seen to have the financial means available, the fare for the passage would generally be demanded and received from the departing Greek passengers, although it was understood that even those without the necessary funds would not be denied passage. A cable to the province of Trebizond, sent on 15 April 1914, reports that a "10-kurush fare" had been demanded of Greeks traveling to Salonica and asks for "the number of persons among the passengers who were allowed to embark even if they did not have the necessary fare." Additionally, the cable inquires whether the number of emigrants is large enough to merit sending another ship.[44]

As has been shown earlier, the state could, by means of this dual system, begin to empty out Greek villages in western Anatolia and resettle them with Muslim immigrants without waiting for international discussions

[41] BOA/DH.ŞFR, no. 40/85, Coded telegram from the Interior Ministry's Private Secretariat to the Provincial District of Çatalca, dated 25 April 1915.

[42] BOA/DH.ŞFR, no. 40/58, Coded telegram from the Interior Ministry's IAMM to the Provincial District of Tekfurdağı, dated 20 April 1914.

[43] BOA/DH.ŞFR, no. 41/80, Coded telegram from the Interior Ministry's IAMM to the Provincial District of Kale-i Sultaniye (Çanakkale), dated 26 May 1914.

[44] BOA/DH.ŞFR, no. 40/13, Coded telegram from the Interior Ministry's IAMM to the Province of Trebizond, dated 15 April 1914.

and agreements. In a cable to the province of Aydın on 21 May 1914, Talat Pasha states that "if, on the basis of Venizelos' proposal, the principle of the migration and exchange [of] . . . the Muslim population of Macedonia with the Greeks of the Aydın province," since it would take a long time to establish a commission to deal with the population exchange, "the Muslim immigrants from Macedonia who have come here by foot should be housed in the Greek villages, beginning with [those on] the coast and working inward."[45] In another telegram to Edirne on 30 June, the IAMM urgently requests information on the number of Bulgarians and Greeks who have recently left the area, and on the condition of the lands that were abandoned by the émigrés. Two earlier cables (19 May and 20 June) appear to be asking for similar information.[46]

Another IAMM cable sent on 27 July 1914 to the provincial district of Balıkesir requests information on the number of immigrants who have been settled in the abandoned villages: "How many immigrants have been settled in the houses abandoned by the Greeks and Bulgarians? How many empty [houses] are there? Please report immediately."[47] The office sent a similar cable to Bursa (Hüdâvendigâr) on 24 August 1914, reminding the governor that "there are as many as 1,500 families of non-agricultural Albanians who have yet to be resettled in your province; these must be sent, by way of Tekfurdağı, to the areas in the province of Edirne in which there are still empty houses and fields."[48]

Not only was the Ottoman government unwilling to wait for an agreement before implementing the population exchange but it was not even going to wait for discussions toward the same. On 20 May 1914, the regime had orally conveyed its aforementioned suggestion for an official

[45] BOA/DH.ŞFR, no. 41/37, Coded telegram from interior minister Talat to the Province of Aydın, dated 21 May 1914.

[46] BOA/DH.ŞFR, no. 42/163, Coded telegram from the Interior Ministry's IAMM to the Province of Edirne, dated 30 June 1914. The cable demands "the immediate providing of information and descriptions that were requested via the written correspondances [of 19 May and 20 June 1914] regarding the number of Greeks and Bulgarians who have left the province and the lands that they have left."

[47] BOA/DH.ŞFR, no. 43/116, Coded telegram from the Interior Ministry's IAMM to the Provincial District of Karesi (Balıkesir), dated 27 July 1914.

[48] BOA/DH.ŞFR, no. 45/181, Coded telegram from the Interior Ministry's IAMM to the Province of Hüdavendigâr (Bursa), dated 24 August 1914.

agreement on population exchange to Greek prime minister Venizelos. The proposal was again delivered, this time in written form, on the following day, and on 22 May, Venizelos wrote a letter stating that he adopted the suggestion in principle. The next day, the Greek Foreign Ministry replied orally that this was their position, as well,[49] but not until 27 June did Athens make its official response, stating that Greece had "accepted, by the will of the people, the principle of [population] exchange."[50] As seen above, the idea of establishing an international commission for managing the large movements of population was raised; it was adopted in July 1914, and subcommissions were established for, among others, the regions of İzmir and Edirne the following month. But it is clear that the Ottoman government did not wait for international sanction to press ahead with its own resettlement policies.

This fact was not lost on others. In his meeting in October 1914 with the Ottoman ambassador to Athens, Galib Kemali Bey, Venizelos complained of the same and requested that the Porte put an end to its expulsion of Greek Christians until some sort of agreement could be reached. In his subsequent account of their discussion, Kemali Bey claims that an exasperated Venizelos stated, "What will I do with these poor souls? If I resettle them on the lands belonging to Muslim immigrants you will cite this as proof that I have not kept the promise that I recently made," and he requested of the Ottoman representative that "no possibility be given for such situations to be repeated," personally asking instead that "[the sultan] order the creation of a mixed commission [to ensure this]."[51] In addition to this personal communication, on 22 October (and before the discussions on the formation of the commission had ended) the Greek Embassy in Istanbul delivered an official letter of protest from its government to the Porte regarding the ongoing expulsion of its Greek citizens. Among other

[49] Mourelos, "The 1914 Persecutions," 393–94 (Venizelos's reply is found in the appendix, 413–14). Ambassador Kemali Bey claims that the first official proposal was put forth on 18 May 1914 (*Canlı Tarihler: Galip Kemali Söylemezoğlu Hatıraları*, 102–3 [the work includes a Turkish translation of Venizelos's letter]).

[50] BOA/DH.ŞFR, no. 42/136, Coded telegram from interior minister Talat to the Provincial District of Karesi (Balıkesir), dated 28 June 1914.

[51] BOA/DH.EUM, 3. Şube, 2/25, Message from the Ottoman Foreign Ministry to interior minister Talat Bey, dated 18 October 1914.

things, the message stated that these forcible removals had created "great indignation . . . within Greek public opinion" and "had disturbed the good relations [between] the[ir] two countries."[52]

COMING TO THE BRINK OF WAR WITH GREECE

The Ottoman policy of forcibly emptying villages and transferring populations was, however, not without its difficulties, and it met with serious resistance both at home and abroad, at one point even bringing the empire to the brink of war with Greece. While the Porte continued to disclaim any connection to these events, many of the European states—Greece foremost among them—were not convinced. Through their ambassadors, the European governments persistently lodged protests in response to consular reports of anti-Greek violence and terror in Thrace and the Aegean regions.

In their reports to the ambassadors, the consuls of the Great powers frequently stated—in contradiction to the official Ottoman position— that the attacks, murders, looting, and forcible expulsions of villagers were taking place within the framework of a state-planned campaign.[53] One reason for this assertion was the fact that at least in some regions, the actions were plainly being organized by local functionaries of the Ottoman government and executed by the gendarmerie.[54] The Greek Embassy in

[52] BOA/DH.EUM, 3. Şube, 2/35, Message from the Greek government to the Ottoman Grand Vizierate, delivered by the Greek Embassy in Constantinople, via the Private Secretariat of the Ottoman Interior Ministry, on 22 October 1914.

[53] NA/RG 59, 867.700/630. The report by the American consul in İzmir, George Horton, sent on 9 June 1914, can be given as one example of this. Rouben Adalian, *The Armenian Genocide in the U.S. Archives, 1915–1918* (Alexandria, VA: Chadwyck-Healey, 1991–94), microfiche no. 5. This source will hereafter be referred to as *AGUS*. For other similar information in the American archives, see Rouben Paul Adalian, "Comparative Policy and Differential Practice in the Treatment of Minorities in Wartime: The United States Archival Evidence on the Armenians and Greeks in the Ottoman Empire," *Journal of Genocide Research* 3, no. 1 (2001): 31–48.

[54] In Çanakkale (Kale-i Sultaniye), for instance, in May 1914, the clearing out of some of the towns along the coast was carried out under the direct supervision of the provincial governor. Likewise, similar attacks and village evacuations were organized in the same month by Talat Bey, the gendarmerie commander of Menemen (Greek Patriarchate, *Persecution of the Greeks in Turkey, 1914–1918*, 61–62; 70–71). The name of this "Talat Bey" appears in a number of the consular reports from this region. In the American reports, it is said of him that "Death and destruction follow wherever Talaat Bey goes"; see NA/RG 59, 867.700/630, Report by American consul in İzmir,

particular complained tirelessly to the Ottoman Foreign Ministry about the abuses in the provinces; in some cases, their reports were so specific that they identified and enumerated the gendarmes involved.

An example of the specific character of these reports is this undated complaint from the Greek Embassy in Istanbul:

> On the twenty-fifth of the month some 29 gendarmes, accompanied by a number of irregular troops (*başıbozuk*), came to the town of "Sanduki," which is attached to [the provincial district of] Malkara [in Tekirdağ Province], and after seizing the inhabitants' property they beat some of them, afterward sitting on them and forcing them to sing folksongs until they wanted to go. A great many of the inhabitants were injured as a result of this treatment. . . . In Mürefte a 16-year-old girl by the name of "Mitro Konstandino" was kidnapped by the head official in the county (*kaymakam*) for the purpose of converting her to Islam. In the town of Abidin an old man by the name of "Yorgi Çelosi" disappeared. It is thought that he was killed. . . . In Urla [two] Greeks called Yani and Vangeli were killed in the middle of Anadere Square. The murderers' names are Mustafa and Hasan İsmail.[55]

In fact, even without other countries' complaints the Porte was well aware of what was being done in the provinces by their military and civil functionaries. A cable from the Security Directorate to the province of Edirne on 26 October 1914 gives a detailed list of the physical assaults, looting, and brutalizing of Christian villagers mentioned in the Greek Embassy complaints above, and requests that the events be investigated.[56] In another telegram from the Interior Ministry to the province of Aydın, a litany of further disturbances and criminal acts is followed by the statement that reports had reached the capital to the effect that these abuses had been carried out by soldiers; the telegram requests more detailed

---

George Horton, to the American Embassy in Constantinople, dated 15 June 1914, in *AGUS*, Adalian, microfiche no. 5.

[55] BOA/DH.EUM, 3. Şube, 2/35, Message from the Greek Embassy in Istanbul to the Interior Ministry's Private Secretariat (not dated).

[56] BOA/DH.EUM, 3. Şube, 2/35, Telegram from the Interior Ministry's General Directorate of Security to the Province of Edirne, dated 26 October 1914.

information about the events and directs the local officials to restore peace by appropriate measures.[57]

In the end, the foreign powers' stream of angry reactions to the campaign of anti-Greek violence and intimidation embarrassed the Ottoman government—especially the Foreign Ministry—in front of Europe. In a letter to the Interior Ministry, advisor Reşad Hikmet, writing on behalf of the Foreign Ministry, mentions a report of 7 June 1914 from the Ottoman Embassy in Paris in which the embassy informs that reports deriving from Greek sources about the massacres of Greek Christians in Anatolia and the looting of their settlements had been circulating widely in Europe. Furthermore, he bemoans the fact that these reports had placed the Ottoman regime in an awkward public position: "There is no need to emphasize the [deletrious] effect that reports such as those published regarding the Christian population within the Ottoman domains will have on the more conservative sectors of European public opinion." Additionally, the official requests that these reports, if false, should be immediately refuted, whereas if there is a measure of truth to them, then measures to prevent further abuses should be taken at once.[58]

Beyond the effect of such reports on the European public, within the empire itself the Greek community was up in arms. Greek churches in the troubled areas regularly informed the Patriarchate in Istanbul that the campaign of violence was either being organized by the government or that government functionaries observed the abuses but did not intervene to prevent them. The Patriarchate forwarded these reports to the government. For example, a cable sent by the Interior Ministry to the province of Çanakkale on 31 May 1914, refers to a telegram that had been "sent to the Patriarchate from

---

[57] BOA/DH.EUM, 3, Şube, no. 1/19, Telegram from the Interior Ministry to the Province of Aydın, dated 12 August 1914. The cable mainly states that "[i]t has been reported that in Urla two Greeks were shot in Helvacılar Square and that one of them was mortally wounded; that on the evening of the twenty-second of the current month a number of armed individuals attacked the Hıristo Karandreas family, at their farm in Yeni Efes, wounding the aforementioned and his wife and three children, and two thirteen-year-old boys were strangled to death on the twentieth of the month an individual by the name of Sampos was attacked by soldiers on his farm, which is in the area of Miresi, about one hour from İzmir, and only escaped with great difficulty; in the same place, and on the same day a Greek citizen by the name of Crisnoti was killed by soldiers. In light of these reports, it is requested that a report of the truth of these claims be submitted and that effective measures be adopted in order to restore law and order."

[58] BOA/DH.EUM, 3. Şube, no. 2/1, Coded telegram from the Foreign Ministry's General Directorate of Political Affairs to the Foreign Ministry (not dated).

Çanakkale, signed by the Metropolitan of Gallipoli," which told of attacks against the villages and reported that armed gangs were "threatening those Greek peasants who are attempting to emigrate."[59]

Throughout 1914 the Patriarchate continued lodging protests like the ones of the previous years. On 25 February 1914, it submitted a note of protest to the Porte; the following month a delegation was formed to visit members of the Ottoman government.[60] Over the course of these visits, the delegation was repeatedly informed that: (1) the government was not involved in this matter; (2) public morals had been disturbed as a result of the Balkan Wars, and (3) the Greek population was in any case voluntarily emigrating for its own reasons.[61] When these meetings produced no results, the Patriarchate decided in June "to close the Greek churches and schools in mourning and as a symbol of protest. Greek village elders also ceased work and even organized a number of strikes."[62]

In fact, there was one other reason for the Greek protests and strikes. Since 1913 there had been an organized, ongoing economic boycott against Greek products and businesses. This so-called Muslim boycott (1913–14) began in the wake of the Balkan Wars and was organized and overseen by the CUP.[63] Frequent cables were sent to the provinces by the Interior Ministry calling for boycott campaigns directed exclusively at the Greek population of the empire. To give one of these communications as an example, on 14 June 1914, the Interior Ministry's Private Secretariat issued a cable to a number of provinces and demanded that "[despite the fact that] it was announced that the boycott against the Greeks would also include the Bulgarian merchants who are few in number there, in response to the [Bulgarian] Embassy's pressure the Grand Vizier has thus ordered

[59] BOA/DH.ŞFR, no. 41/122, Coded telegram from the Interior Ministry's General Directorate of Security to the Provincial District of Kale-i Sultaniye (Çanakkale), dated 31 May 1914.

[60] During this visit the delegation asked to submit a note of protest, but when the justice minister refused to accept it, a separate letter of complaint was subsequently delivered to the grand vizier. Archimandrite Alexander Papadopoulos, *Persecution of the Greeks in Turkey*, 77–81.

[61] Hasan Babacan, *Mehmet Talat Pasha* (Ankara: Türk Tarih Kurumu, 2005), 92.

[62] Bayur, *Türk İnkılabı Tarihi*, vol. 2, part 3, 254.

[63] Zafer Toprak claims that the primary reason for the boycott was the Greek destroyer *Averof*. During the Balkan conflict the Ottoman navy had been prevented from entering the Aegean Sea because of this ship and was thus unable to come to the defense of the empire's various island possessions or the port of Salonica. During the war Ottoman Greeks had also provided significant amounts of material support to Greece. For more information, see Zafer Toprak, *Türkiye'de Ekonomi ve Toplum (1908–1950): Milli İktisat-Milli Burjuvazi* (Istanbul: Tarih Vakfı Yurt Yayınları, 1995), 107–11.

that the boycott not be conducted against them; please report the results [of this action]."[64]

In addition to its formal protests to the Porte, the Greek Patriarchate organized and sent a delegation to Europe to request the various powers to exert pressure on the empire. The Ottoman government countered by exploiting its own diplomatic channels to persuade the foreign powers not to receive the delegation. From a "secret" communication from the Ottoman Foreign Ministry to the Interior Ministry on 4 August, one can glean that as a result of the lobbying of the Ottoman Embassy in Rome, the Italian government had promised not to receive the Patriarchate's emissaries.[65]

Even beforehand, as a result of internal and external pressure, Talat Pasha had toured the Thrace region in April 1914 and prepared a report of his findings.[66] Later on, as the complaints mounted, the government was forced to send another delegation, again headed by Talat Pasha and accompanied by an official from each of the various embassies, to the Aegean region for the purpose of investigating the reports of anti-Greek actions. In his report to the Ottoman cabinet on 1 July 1914, Talat Pasha admits that acts of terror and violence have been carried out against the Greek population: "The [departing] Greeks are leaving a great many [of their] transportable possessions behind, not just beds and such; there are instances of looting, and there have been both fights and killings."[67] In light of the available evidence, Talat's description of "some killings" is a bit of an understatement: according to both American and German documents, in a June 1914 massacre that took place only in Foça, some fifty people were killed.[68] A report from the American Consulate in Salonica dated 25 June

---

[64] BOA/DH.ŞFR, no. 42/8, Coded telegram from the Interior Ministry's Private Secretariat to the Provinces of Aydın and Hüdâvendigâr (Bursa) and to the Provincial Districts of Çanakkale and Karesi (Balıkesir), dated 14 June 1914. Similar cables exist; see BOA/DH.ŞFR, nos. 42/7, 42/30, 42/32, and 42/35.

[65] BOA/DH.EUM, 3. Şube, 1/6, Communication from the Foreign Ministry's director-general of political affairs, Ahmed Reşid Bey, to the Interior Ministry, dated 4 August 1914.

[66] Papadopoulos, *Persecution of the Greeks*, 95–98. For the report sent by interior minister Talat Pasha to Grand Vizier Sait Halim Pasha, see *Canlı Tarihler, Galip Kemali Söylemezoğlu Hatıraları*, 101.

[67] Bayur, *Türk İnkılabı Tarihi*, vol. 2, part 3, 255.

[68] NA/RG 59, 867.00/630, Report by American ambassador Morgenthau, dated 19 June 1914, in *AGUS*, Adalian, microfiche no. 5. For information on these events from German sources, see DE/PA-AA/R 13925, Report by German ambassador Wangenheim, dated 30 June 1914.

puts the number of people killed during this period in İzmir and its environs at somewhere between five hundred and six hundred.[69]

Talat Pasha's effort to portray both the Ottoman government and himself as having no knowledge of the evictions and killings—a claim later belied in the memoirs of numerous Turks directly involved in the events—must be seen as simply another example of the dual-track mechanism policies outlined above. Kuşçubaşı Eşref, one of the chief actors in these "cleaning" actions, relates that during Talat's tour of the Aegean region, he secretly met with Talat in Manisa and that Talat told him, "Try not to be too visible right now, at least until I return [to Istanbul] . . . Don't even come to İzmir for two or three days. Avoid being observed by seditious elements in the coastal areas such as foreign embassies and consulates—even those of our allies."[70]

This dual-track mechanism can also be seen in the boycott actions. Subjected to so much pressure both at home and abroad, the Ottoman government sent cables to the provinces ordering that an end be put to such actions and, purporting not to have any connection to them, even demanded that a number of punishments be meted out for appearances' sake. Another cable sent in July to Rahmi Bey, then governor of Aydın Province, reads as follows, "during that time in which the political discussions are continuing it is necessary to lift the boycott.You should communicate these warnings to the necessary parties, and if you feel it is necessary, punish some of the more prominent among those who disregard these warnings. In short, use all appropriate measures to prevent the continuation of the boycott for now. Instructions to this effect have been sent to all of the provinces."[71]

As the telegram states, instructions had been sent to the empire's provinces, and they declared, "During those periods in which the government is engaged in political negotiations, the necessary measures must be taken to lift the boycott being carried out against the Greek population, since it will naturally produce adverse results; additionally, the appropriate warnings

[69] NA/RG 59, 867.00/632, Report from the American Consulate in Salonica, dated 25 June 1914, cited in Adalian, *AGUS*, microfiche no. 5.

[70] Cemal Kutay, *Etniki Etarya'dan Günümüze, Ege'nin Türk Kalma Savaşı* (Istanbul: Boğaziçi Yayınları, 1980), 226.

[71] BOA/DH.ŞFR, no. 42/198, Coded telegram from the Interior Ministry's General Directorate of Security to the governor of the Province of Aydın, Rahmi Beyefendi, dated 5 July 1914.

should be communicated to the necessary parties and those who resist and continue to impose the boycott are to be punished without exception."[72]

The reason for these new governmental measures was that the massacres of Greeks, particularly in the İzmir region, had achieved such dimensions as to bring the Ottoman government and Greece to the brink of war. Thus, the real reason for Talat's visit to the area was to help ease bilateral tensions.[73] In a meeting with the British consul in İzmir, he admitted as much. "I came here on the order of the Grand Vizier," Talat said. "His Excellency the Pasha [Prince Said Halim] does not want to go to war against the Greeks. I will do everything in my power to forestall such an event and to stabilize the situation."[74]

On the other side of the Aegean, however, Athens had long since resolved to go to war but had been unable to garner sufficient support from Serbia or Romania.[75] The archives of the European powers are replete with information both on the direct involvement of the Ottoman regime in the anti-Greek campaigns of terror and violence, and discussion of the need to resolve the crisis and avert the outbreak of hostilities between Istanbul and Athens by forming a delegation and holding direct talks.[76]

FIGURES

Various figures have been given regarding the number of Muslim refugees who either fled or voluntarily left the peninsula and came to Anatolia in the wake of the Balkan Wars. The variation—often quite wide—in the fig-

[72] BOA/DH.ŞFR, no. 42/199, Coded telegram from the Interior Ministry's Office of General Communication (Muhâberât-ı Umumiye Dairesi), Fourth Department, to the Provinces of Edirne, Adana, Aydın, Hüdâvendigâr (Bursa), and Trebizond, and to the Provincial Districts of İzmit, Bolu, Menteşe, Teke, Canik, Çatalca, Karesi (Balıkesir), and Kale-i Sultaniye (Çanakkale), dated 5 July 1914.

[73] The German and American diplomatic reports in particular devote a great deal of space and discussion to the questions of the Ottoman Greek crisis and the danger of war. For a few examples, see DE/PA-AA/R 7356, Reports of German consul in Salonica, Dr. Schwörbel, dated 26 April and 4 May 1914; DE/PA-AA/R 7464 and DE/PA-AA/R 13924, Reports of German ambassador in Athens, Count Albert von Quadt, dated 11 June 1914; and DE/PA-AA/R 13875, dated 23 June 1914. In his 11 June report Quadt states that "the situation is grave indeed, and that if the deportations and massacres continue at this pace, the Greeks may well take it upon themselves to occupy [western] Anatolia."

[74] Bayar, Ben de Yazdım, vol. 5, 1967.

[75] For Greek proposals for war against the Ottomans and the replies of the other Balkan states, see Mourelos, "The 1914 Persecutions," 396–99.

[76] For a discussion of the manner in which the issue is taken up in the American sources, see Adalian, "Comparative Policy and Differential Practice in the Treatment of Minorities in Wartime."

ures arrived at is due in part to the different timespans used by researchers and the fact that due to the paucity of exact lists and "hard" evidence, all such conclusions are ultimately based on a series of guesses and estimates. Some sources that rely on official Ottoman figures arrive at the conclusion that approximately 113,000 Muslims fled the Balkans during the wars, while the total number of Muslim immigrants to the empire during this period is 413,922.[77]

In other Turkish sources the figure of 640,000 refugees is given.[78] Greek sources claim that approximately 143,189 Muslims left Greece between the years 1912 and 1920.[79] German sources, relying on the statistical figures they received from local authorities, claim that some 430,000 Muslims left the peninsula between the Balkan Wars and April 1914.[80] A British consular report from 16 October 1914 states that from the beginning of the Balkan conflict until the time of the report, the number of Muslims immigrating to Anatolia via the port of Salonica was around 250,000.[81] For his part, Toynbee gives more precise figures, which he claims to have taken from the AMMU, and he breaks down these numbers by year. According to his classification, 177,352 immigrants came from the Balkans between 1912 and 1913; 120,566 between 1914 and 1915; and altogether, some 413, 922 arrived in the empire between 1912 and 1920.[82]

For the same reasons, the figures for the number of Greek Orthodox Christians who left the Ottoman Empire for Greece also vary greatly. For example, for the year 1914 some sources estimate that 115,000 Greeks left eastern Thrace for Greece, while another 85,000 are claimed to have been

[77] Lades, *The Exchange of Minorities*, 15–16 and note 11. These figures are identical to those given by Toynbee.

[78] A great number of Turkish sources give the figure of 1.5 million Balkan immigrants from the year 1878 until the outbreak of the First World War, but in a speech before the Chamber of Notables (i.e., the Ottoman Senate) on 7 March 1916, Şükrü Kaya, the director of the IAMM, said that the state did not have exact data on the number of immigrants since 1878. He also claimed that some 250,000 people had immigrated into the empire. A discussion and evaluation of Kaya's explanation and the figures he provides can be found in Dündar, *İttihat ve Terakki'nin*, 56–57, 215–17, and 262.

[79] Mourelos, "The 1914 Persecutions," 392n15.

[80] DE/PA-AA/R 13923, Telegram from German consul in Salonica, Dr. Schwörbel, to German chancellor Bethmann-Hollweg, dated 4 April 1914.

[81] FO 371/1999, 48-3202, Report by James Morgan, dated 16 October 1914.

[82] Arnold Toynbee, *The Western Question in Greece and Turkey: A Study in the Contact of Civilization* (New York: Howard Fertig, 1970), 138.

deported into the Anatolian interior.[83] According to the official figures of the Greek government, in the first six months of 1914, approximately 15,572 families (60,926 people) were expelled to Greece from eastern Thrace.[84] According to these same figures, the number of Greeks leaving western Anatolia for Greece is approximately 150,000 for the entire year.[85] A later report (1930) by the American ambassador in Athens claims that approximately 150,000 to 200,000 Greeks immigrated to Greece before the world war,[86] although this figure appears relatively conservative. A report at the time by the American ambassador to the Porte, Henry Morgenthau, which is based on investigations by the various foreign consuls in İzmir, determines that in 1914 between 28 May and 12 June alone, some 117,000 Greeks left the region.[87]

Théotakas, the Greek representative of the joint Armenian Greek Office, which was set up in the building of the British Occupation Forces Command in Istanbul during the Armistice period, compiled a report that put the number of Greeks expelled during the war solely from Thrace at 240,000.[88] At one point during the Armistice, the Turkish daily *Alemdar* reprinted a Greek press report that a study of the refugee question had been carried out and that this study contained a number of statistics on the Greek refugees. According to these reports in the Greek-language dailies, said the Turkish paper, a large tome had been recently published on *The Calamities that the Greeks of Turkey Have Faced.* After briefly recounting the oppression and persecutions suffered by the Greeks, starting with the conquest of Istanbul, the book provides a number of docu-

[83] Lades, *The Exchange of Minorities,* 15–16.

[84] Mourelos, "The 1914 Persecutions," 391–92.

[85] Lades, *The Exchange of Minorities,* 16n11.

[86] Note from Ambassador Skinner, dated 20 June 1930, cited in Ayhan Aktar, "Homogenizing the Nation; Turkifying the Economy: Turkish Experience of Population Exchange Reconsidered," in *Crossing the Aegean: An Appraisal of the 1923 Compulsory Exchange between Greece and Turkey,* ed. Renée Hirschon (New York and Oxford: Berghahn Books, 2003), 79–95.

[87] NA/RG 59, 867.00/634, Letter from American ambassador in Constantinople, Morgenthau, to the State Department, dated 16 July 1914, in *AGUS,* Adalian, microfiche no. 5 (final document) and no. 6 (first two documents).

[88] *British Reports on Ethnic Cleansing in Anatolia, 1919–1922: The Armenian-Greek Section,* comp. Vartkes Yeghiayan (Glendale, CA: Center for Armenian Remembrance, 2007), 13. For further information on this office and its activities, see Akçam, *İnsan Hakları,* 444–46, and *A Shameful Act,* 290–91.

ments and statistics on the oppressive actions taken against Greeks since the beginning of the Ottoman Second Constitutional Period (1908). It concludes that 274,614 Greeks were forced to leave their homes since the Balkan Wars alone, and of these, 116,438 were from Thrace, while the rest were from Anatolia—especially the areas of Çeşme and Kuşadası. During the First World War another 481,109 were deported: 129,727 from Thrace, the remainder from Anatolia. In sum, the number of Greeks deported by the Unionist regime over the last five years of its existence comes to 755,823.[89]

The Turkish sources provide wildly varying figures that range from little more than gross exaggerations to vast underestimates. Celal Bayar, for example, states that as a result of "the elimination of concentrations of non-Turk[ish people] . . . who were clustered at strategic points, before the war approximately 130,000 Greeks were deported to Greece from İzmir and its surroundings alone."[90] For the same region, however, Halil Menteşe puts the number of deportees at 200,000.[91] While these two sources concern themselves only with the Aegean region, Greek migrations from Thrace were discussed by the Ottoman Chamber of Deputies in 1919. Their estimates of the number of Greeks who emigrated voluntarily or were expelled from Thrace between 1913 to 1918 ranged between 300,000 to 500,000.[92] Eşref Kuşçubaşı claimed that in 1914, during the first months of the war alone, the number of deportees from among the "Greek and Armenian population that was concentrated in the Aegean region—particularly along the coast" was 1,150,000 souls.[93] During the Paris Peace Conference after World War I, Greek prime minister Venizelos claimed that some 300,000 Greeks had been killed over the course of the war, while another 450,000 sought refuge in Greece.[94]

[89] *Alemdar*, 15 February 1919.

[90] Bayar, *Ben de Yazdım*, vol. 5, 1967.

[91] Menteşe, *Osmanlı Mebusan Meclisi Reisi*, 166.

[92] *Meclis-i Mebusan Zabıt Ceridesi* (hereafter *MMZC*), Period 3, Assembly Year 5, vol. 1 (Ankara: TMMM Basımevi, 1992), 285, 287.

[93] Kutay, *Birinci Dünya Harbinde*, 6. Celal Bayar, who quotes Kuşçubaşı's memoirs in detail, provides figures for each and every city. The figures cited earlier are simply the sum of the individual totals he provides (Bayar, *Ben de Yazdım*, vol. 5, 1967).

[94] Cited in Doğan Avcıoğlu, *Milli Kurtuluş Tarihi*, vol. 3 (Istanbul: Tekin Yayınevi, 1987), 1138.

AN IMPORTANT DETAIL

A minor, but significant, shared characteristic of Turkish and Greek scholarship on the population movements of this period is perhaps worth mentioning. The relevant research from both sides tends to identify those leaving their own country as voluntary emigrants, whereas their coreligionists in the other country are depicted as having been forcibly expelled. Greek scholars speak of extensive Ottoman propaganda campaigns urging the Balkan Muslims to immigrate to Anatolia. It is as a direct result of this propaganda, the researchers claim, that large numbers of Greek Muslims willingly departed for the Ottoman Empire.[95]

In a March 1914 report from Athens, the German ambassador to Greece, Count Albert von Quadt, tells his superiors that the Greek foreign minister Repoulis (who was simultaneously serving as the governor-general of Macedonia) informed him that the Muslims of that region desired to leave, and that despite having taken a great many steps to prevent this, the Greek government ultimately failed to persude them to stay.[96] Various German consuls in the region included in their reports the oft-repeated claims found in the Greek press that the country's Muslims were leaving voluntarily, but made sure to add that these reports were completely false. A 25 arch 1914 report from Salonica, for instance, states that "all of the Turkish civil servants are issuing propaganda to discourage [their fellow Muslims from] emigrating," and reports that the newly appointed Turkish consul had spoken to him in this regard.[97] According to the consul, the only reason that Turks wanted to leave the region was because of the Greek government's policy toward them. Moreover, the Greeks arriving from Anatolia had been inciting the local population against the Turks.[98]

A similar situation is evident in Turkish works. In these one frequently encounters the claims that both Athens and the Greek Patriarchate in

[95] Lades, *The Exchange of Minorities*, 15–16; Kontogiorgi, "Forced Migration," 21.

[96] DE/PA-AA/R 7356, Report by German ambassador in Athens, A. Quadt, dated 20 March 1914.

[97] DE/PA-AA/R 7442, Report by German consul in Salonica, Dr. Schwörbel, dated 25 March 1914.

[98] DE/PA-AA/R 7336, Report by German consul in Salonica, Dr. Schwörbel, dated 30 March 1914.

Istanbul were conducting large-scale propaganda campaigns among the Ottoman Greeks, and that the latter were voluntarily leaving for Greece in large numbers. The reality, however, was quite the contrary. Greek officials were calling for Ottoman Greeks "not to leave their motherland" and encouraging them to remain where they were.[99] The Patriarchate even went so far as to establish a special commission to deal with the problem.[100]

Evidence from the Ottoman Cipher Office amply corroborates this claim. Orthodox churchmen petitioned the local Ottoman officials to prevent the expulsion of the Greeks, explaining that these subjects had no desire to leave the empire but had been ordered out by any means necessary. For their part, the Ottoman officials forwarded to the Porte such requests as: "the petition sent from the provincial district of Gallipoli, signed by Yanaki, the son of Haralambo, on behalf of the population of the village of Uçmakdere in the county of Mürefte, which attempts, by admonition and instruction, to discourage those who have not yet emigrated from doing so, although they have long since expressed the wish to immigrate to Greece" or "the cable sent to the [Office of the] Provinc[ial Governor] and signed by Timotio, the Metropolitan of Ganozhora, [in which it is stated] that no one has been given permission of late to grant requests to emigrate in the name of the village of Uçmakdere, and in any case there is not a single person from this village who is thinking about emigrating."[101] A telegram of 31 May 1914, from the qadi, or religious judge, of Edirne, Süleyman Effendi, to the provincial governor (then in Istanbul) can be given as another example. In this communiqué, the qadi reports on the propaganda efforts of the regional Patriarchate's functionaries to convince the Greek inhabitants to remain in place.[102]

In similar fashion, the Security Directorate's Third Department claimed that those Anatolian Greeks who were forced to flee to the Aegean islands

[99] Kontogiorgi, "Forced Migration," 23.

[100] Archimandrite Alexander Papadopoulos, *Persecution of the Greeks in Turkey*, 91.

[101] BOA/DH.EUM, 3. Şube, 1/14, Telegram from Edirne governor Adil Bey to the Interior Ministry, dated 2 August 1914.

[102] BOA/DH.ŞFR, 41/125, Telegram from qadi of the Province of Edirne, Süleyman, to the provincial governor of Edirne (then in Istanbul), dated 31 May 1914.

had sent a memorandum from the island of Midilli (Mytilene, Lesbos) to the Greek Chamber of Deputies in which the refugees claim that "the emptying out of Thrace and Anatolia of its Greek population by the Young Turk Government is an unbearable and irreparable insult to Greek history" and demand protection for the Greeks of Anatolia.[103]

Some people among the Greeks did advocate for the voluntary abandonment of Anatolia and Thrace, but most of these appear to have been Albanians who knew Greek and were sent by the Unionist government in Istanbul to areas of Greek settlement. Upon arrival, they would pretend to have been sent from Greece and attempt to convince the locals to emigrate there.[104] Moreover, the Ottoman authorities supported the various foreign embassies' extensive efforts to encourage Ottoman subjects of their own ethnicity or religion to immigrate to their "homelands." A March 1914 cable to Balıkesir reports that a certain Nezlako Çolakof Effendi, an official of the Bulgarian Embassy in Istanbul, had arrived in the region in order to convince the Bulgars of Bandırma, Balya, and certain other portions of Karesi (Balıkesir) to move to Bulgaria. A document had been handed to this embassy functionary "by the Civil Service staff in order to facilitate this effort." The cable goes on to request that his every movement and activity "be investigated and closely monitored—without his knowledge— and if something is observed that is contrary to the interests of the state and nation, it is to be immediately [reported]."[105]

Another undertaking at the time was the production of affidavits—to be signed by the expellees—that stated that they had left voluntarily and were donating their property to various Ottoman institutions.[106] In some areas, the Greek inhabitants wrote directly to the king of Greece and complained about this situation.[107] After the 1918 Armistice, this topic was

---

[103] BOA/DH.EUM, 3. Şube, 2/21 (not dated; from similar documents in the same file one can surmise that this is a note from the Foreign Ministry to the Interior Ministry's Third Department, possibly dated 30 October 1914).

[104] Archimandrite Alexander Papadopoulos, *Persecution of the Greeks in Turkey*, 83.

[105] BOA/DH.ŞFR, 39/31, Coded telegram from the Interior Ministry's Private Secretariat to the Provincial District of Karesi (Balıkesir), dated 19 March 1914.

[106] It is generally assumed that these practices were carried out in the same manner in all regions in which they took place (Archimandrite Alexander Papadopoulos, *Persecution of the Greeks in Turkey*, 86, 90, 95).

[107] For a document dealing with the Greek complaints over such actions in the İzmir region, which were forwarded by the king of Greece to the Porte via the Ottoman Foreign Ministry, see BOA/

raised in the Ottoman Parliament, where a number of Greek deputies gave information and recounted their own experiences. Efkalidis Effendi, for instance, testified about the forced emigration policy, which he described as "a policy of destruction and annihilation": "it was alleged that some branches had been established here by agents of Venizelos, and some persons were taken in by the words of these agents and . . . documents of release were received from these persons stating that they were unhappy with the misadministration, and expressing the desire to go to Greece; then they went to places that they did not know, on their own volition and with full cognizance."[108] Efkalidis Effendi also recounted that when he appealed to Talat Pasha, the interior minister showed him telegrams containing statements such as, "We are thoroughly unhappy with Turkey; we are members of Venizelos' party. We will go to Greece . . . why don't you give us permission?"[109]

As can be understood from these sources, the truth of the matter is that both Muslims in Christian lands and Ottoman Christians largely wished to remain in place, and that this desire was largely supported by both the Ottoman and Christian governments of the states to which these prospective immigrants would be going. In fact, this must be understood as a highly rational choice on the part of these populations, but their very presence as religious minorities within two mutually hostile and mistrustful polities caused their respective governments to view them as permanent pretexts for the other country to intervene in their internal affairs and to demand certain rights and protections.[110]

DH.ŞFR, 42/57, Coded telegram from the Interior Ministry's Cipher Office to the Provincial District of Karesi (Balıkesir), dated 17 June 1914.

[108] MMZC, 1991, Period 3, Assembly Year 5, vol. 1, 24 December 1918, Session 24, 288.

[109] Ibid.

[110] In his work on the Ottoman (and later, Turkish) government's decades-long Turkification policies, Ayhan Aktar uses the memoirs of Hilmi Uran, who served as county executive (kaymakam) in Çeşme during the First World War, as the basis for his claim that the emigration of Greeks from Çeşme and its environs was largely voluntary. According to Aktar, "since their legal status was unclear, the Greek government encouraged the Greek inhabitants of Anatolia to [leave the mainland and] settle the [Greek Aegean] islands" (Varlık Vergisi ve Türkleştirme Politikaları [Istanbul: İletişim Yayınları, 2000], 28). However, no archival document has come to light that would corroborate the claim that the Greek government encouraged the Greeks of the Çeşme region to leave voluntarily. On the contrary, there is, as has been shown, evidence to the effect that the outmigration was largely forced, and that those Greeks fleeing to the islands ardently protested their expulsion. In light of this fact, the information provided by Hilmi Uran must be approached with caution.

THE GREEK EXPULSIONS OF 1913–14: A TRIAL RUN
FOR THE ARMENIAN DEPORTATIONS OF 1915–17?

The "cleansing operations" that began in the spring of 1914 against the non-Muslims of western Anatolia—primarily the expulsion of the Otto- man Greeks—had a great deal in common with the subsequent "cleans- ing" of the Anatolian Armenians during World War I. Although there is as yet no direct proof that these separate cleansing operations reflected a single, all-encompassing plan, one can at the very least confidently point to a clear continuity between the two, both in regard to their general lines of organization and the people involved. The policies that were set in mo- tion against the Greeks between 1913 and 1914 appear to foreshadow the subsequent wartime deportations of the Armenians.[111]

In his memoirs of the period, United States ambassador Henry Mor- genthau relates that Istanbul police commissioner Bedri Bey told one of his (Morgenthau's) secretaries that "the Turks had expelled the Greeks so successfully that they had decided to apply the same method to all the other races in the empire."[112] Morgenthau draws a similar parallel in his embassy report of 18 November 1915, which emphasizes that the smooth deportation of 100,000 to 150,000 people before the eyes of the Great powers in May and June 1914 was a great encouragement for the wartime deportation of the Armenians.[113]

Regarding the continuity of operational cadres between the two cleans- ing campaigns, the figure of Şükrü Kaya comes to the fore as a prime exam- ple. As seen earlier, Kaya had served on the commission that oversaw the Turkish-Bulgarian population exchange after the Balkan Wars. Thereafter, he served on the Turkish-Greek Commission, which performed a similar task, and then, as director-general of the Interior Ministry's IAMM, he be- came a principal organizer of the Armenian deportations.

---

[111] Here I will only make several limited observations on the subject. In fact, the degree of continu- ity in the personnel involved in the Ottoman government's anti-Greek and anti-Armenian policies is an important topic that deserves its own study.

[112] Henry Morgenthau, *Ambassador Morgenthau's Story* (Garden City, NY: Doubleday, Page, 1918), 323.

[113] NA/RG 59, 867.00/798.5, Report by Ambassador Morgenthau, dated 18 November 1915, in *United States Official Records*, ed. Sarafian, 372.

Another important personality in this affair was Dr. Nâzım of the CUP Central Committee. As a leading member of the SO, Dr. Nâzım was among the central planners of the Armenian deportations and killings. Earlier, however, he had helped to devise the blueprint for anti-Greek operations in the İzmir region in the summer of 1914. American consular reports from İzmir refer to him as an "agitator" in the region.[114] According to Alfred van der Zee, the Danish consul in İzmir at the time, "large-scale, systematic and violently punishing" actions against the "peaceful and industrious" Greeks had been ordered by the government and directed by Dr. Nâzım.[115]

A third point of connection between these two operations is Dr. Reşid, the governor of Diyerbekır Province at the time of the Armenian deportations. Having come to prominence for helping to organize the deportation and expulsion of Greeks from the Balıkesir region in the spring and summer of 1914, Dr. Reşid was appointed governor of Mosul Province, then transferred to Diyarbekır, to which he brought a detachment of Circassian gendarmes who worked closely with him during the deportations.[116]

In both the Greek and Armenian cases, expulsions and deportations were carried out ostensibly under the legal umbrella of Ottoman population policy, but in keeping with the dual-track mechanism, an unofficial plan was implemented by a shadow organization that attacked and terrorized the Ottoman Christians. Among the most striking parallels between the Greek and Armenian operations were the formation of Special Operations units and the conscription of military-age men into labor battalions.

These similarities did not escape the notice of either Morgenthau or Toynbee. Throughout this entire period, the American ambassador drew attention in his reports to the similarity in the methods used by the Ottoman government in driving out the Greek populations in 1913 and 1914 with those used against the Armenians the following year:

[114] NA/RG 59, 867.00/636, 3-4, Report by American deputy consul in İzmir, W. H. Anderson, dated 18 July 1914, in *AGUS*, Adalian, microfiche no. 6.

[115] Matthias Bjørnlund, "The 1914 Cleansing of Aegean Greeks as a Case of Violent Turkification," *Journal of Genocide Research* 1, no. 2 (2006): 43

[116] "During the time that Dr. Reşid Bey was the governor of the provincial district of Karesi [Balıkesir], where he was stationed until 23 July, he placed great importance on forcing the Greeks of the region to emigrate, and on public works services," Nejdet Bilgi, *Dr. Mehmed Reşid Şahingiray Hayatı ve Hatıraları* (İzmir: Akademi Kitabevi, 1997), 21–22, 87–89.

The Turks adopted almost identically the same procedure against the Greeks as that which they had adopted against the Armenians. They began by incorporating the Greeks into the Ottoman army and then transferring them into labour battalions, using them to build roads in the Caucasus and other scenes of action. These Greek soldiers, just like the Armenians, died by the thousands from cold, hunger, and other privations. . . . Everywhere the Greeks were gathered in groups and, under the so-called protection of the Turkish gendarmes, they were transported, the larger part on foot, into the interior.[117]

For his part, Arnold Toynbee would make similar observations regarding the systematic and organized character of both actions: "and so the Balkan War[s] had two harvests of victims: first, the Rumili Turks on the one side, and . . . the Anatolian Greeks on the other." He added,

entire Greek communities were driven from their homes by terrorism, their houses and land and often their movable property were seized, and individuals were killed in the process. . . . The procedure bore evidence of being systematic. The terror attacked one district after another, and was carried on by "chetté" bands, enrolled from the Rumili refugees as well as from local populations and nominally attached as reinforcements to the regular Ottoman gendarmerie. . . . Turkish "political" chettés made their début in 1914 on the Western littoral . . . they carried out the designs of the Union and Progress Government against the Armenians.[118]

[117] Morgenthau, *Ambassador Morgenthau's Story*, 324–25. Morgenthau also noted that, unlike the Armenians, the Greeks had not been subjected to a general massacre.

[118] Toynbee, *The Western Question in Greece and Turkey*, 139, 280.

FOUR   THE TRANSFORMATION
OF OTTOMAN POLICIES
TOWARD THE OTTOMAN
GREEKS DURING THE FIRST
WORLD WAR

In studying the available documents from the Interior Ministry's Cipher Office, one can observe that the policy followed against the Ottoman Greeks underwent an important change in November 1914, when the use of widespread violence against the Greeks and their forcible expulsion to Greece were halted. Policies concerning the Greeks during the war years were restricted henceforth to sending some of those living in coastal areas to interior provinces for military reasons. This procedure, connected with Russian military victories at the end of 1916 and throughout 1917, was carried out in a systematic manner, particularly in the Black Sea region. In some areas, massacres of Greeks were observed, but in general the Greek population remained exempt from the policy of deportation and annihilation applied to the Armenians.

RESTRICTING THE ENTRY OF MUSLIMS FROM
   THE BALKANS

The forcible expulsion of Greeks to Greece was not the only thing that changed with the start of the war. The Ottoman government also tried to limit the flow of Muslims from the Balkans by outlawing immigration. One example of this was the case of Muslim emigrants from Bulgaria. In 1916 the governor of Edirne was warned by cable that "immigrants who have been sent by the Bulgarian government shall not be accepted without [prior] approval of the Ottoman government,"[1] and ten days later was

---

[1] BOA/DH.ŞFR, no. 66/15, Coded telegram from the Interior Ministry's General Directorate of Tribal and Immigrant Affairs to the Province of Edirne, dated 18 July 1916.

instructed that such prospective immigrants were to "be cast [back] over the Bulgarian border."[2]

Several more cables sent to the border province indicate that exceptions were occasionally made. A telegram of 30 July 1916 speaks of "the need, for the sake of the state's reputation, to again accept as before the Muslim immigrants who, for certain long-standing political and local reasons, have sought refuge [here]," and, while permitting a specific group of refugees to enter the country, clearly states that certain immigrants are not desired: "It is necessary that those fleeing refugees who have not been given permission by the government to pass through the border gates not be allowed to enter." Similarly, a telegram from 3 August clarifies even more strongly that authorized immigrants with documents in hand may be admitted, while those without such documents be barred: "It is ordered that, although it is permissible to accept those immigrants who have left Bulgaria carrying documents signed by either the Ottoman consul or other bureaucrats, those who are not bearing said documents shall in all instances be denied entry into the Ottoman domains."[3]

The main criterion for the admission of Muslim immigrants was whether they were ethnic Turks. As ordered by another cable to Edirne on 6 August, "Those [prospective] immigrants waiting at the border shall not be allowed in any circumstances to enter the country; but among those who fled [across], the ones who are Turks should not be returned, whereas no Gypsies whatseover shall be allowed in[to the country]."[4] Another message sent on the same day, however, adds that exceptions are to be made only with great difficulty, even for Turks. It is further requested that "regarding the treatment to be given to the aforementioned refugees that was stated in yesterday's cable, of those who manage to sneak into the country without permission, only Turks may be allowed in, and then, only with great difficulty; none of the others shall be permitted entry in any manner."[5] Yet an-

[2] BOA/DH.ŞFR, no. 66/104, Coded telegram from the Interior Ministry's General Directorate of Tribal and Immigrant Affairs to the Province of Edirne, dated 28 July 1916.

[3] BOA/DH.ŞFR, no. 66/130, Coded telegram from the Interior Ministry's General Directorate of Tribal and Immigrant Affairs to the Province of Edirne, dated 3 August 1916.

[4] BOA/DH.ŞFR, no. 66/147, Coded telegram from the Interior Ministry's General Directorate of Tribal and Immigrant Affairs to the Province of Edirne, dated 6 August 1916.

[5] BOA/DH.ŞFR, no. 66/157, Coded telegram from the Interior Ministry's General Directorate of Tribal and Immigrant Affairs to the Province of Edirne, dated 6 August 1916.

other cable on 10 August 1916 reiterates that this acceptance is specific only for one exceptional instance, not as a general policy: "the acceptance of all of the immigrants was done . . . on the condition that the Bulgar officials be told that no further immigrants would be accepted after this."[6]

In some situations, specific parties of immigrants were accepted. A 23 September 1916 telegram to Edirne requested that "since it has been reported by the Sofia Embassy that 129 refugees would be accepted from Gevgili and Poroy, which were occupied by the French and British, per-mission be given only to these persons to cross the border."[7] In short, the government largely stopped accepting refugees from Thrace; when per-mission was given, exceptions were made only for those of Turkish origin, and even then, only in special cases.

THE REASONS FOR THE CHANGE IN GOVERNMENT POLICY TOWARD THE GREEKS

Just as the flood of refugees from the Balkans eventually slowed to a trickle, the Ottoman government in turn abandoned its policy of deporting Greek Orthodox Christians to Greece. This change of direction was conditioned by two major factors. The first was that Athens, instead of joining the En-tente powers, had decided to remain neutral in the war. Anticipating the possibility of an alliance with the Central powers, Berlin demanded that the Ottoman government alter its policies accordingly. The second factor was that Greece had largely refrained from undertaking similar actions against its Muslim population.

While attempting to woo Greece to the side of the Central powers, Germany did not wish to be undermined by its Turkish ally's mistreat-ment of the Ottoman Greek population. Thus, from the very first days of the war, discussions on this very topic were held between Berlin and the Unionist leaders, and certain promises were given.

On 1 November 1914, Lieutenant Commander Hans Humann, the German marine attaché of the German embassy in Istanbul and a close

---

[6] BOA/DH.ŞFR, no. 66/168, Coded telegram from the Interior Ministry's General Directorate of Tribal and Immigrant Affairs to the Province of Edirne, dated 10 August 1916.

[7] BOA/DH.ŞFR, no. 68/92, Coded telegram from the Interior Ministry's General Directorate of Tribal and Immigrant Affairs to the Province of Edirne, dated 23 September 1916.

friend of war minister Enver, reported that Venizelos had promised the German ambassador in Athens that in the event of war between Turkey and the Entente powers, Greece would without question "remain neutral." The Greek prime minister's vow entailed only two conditions: Turkey was to make no provocative moves toward Greece's islands off Turkey's Aegean coast, and the deportation of Ottoman Greeks was to be halted.[8] In a subsequent report written sixteen days later, Humann relates that Talat Pasha had promised him personally that the Ottoman Greeks were henceforth to be treated with the utmost tolerance and restraint, and that he had ordered all state offices and departments to desist from any and all mistreatment of them; Humann adds that "influential Greek circles are speaking of the government's approach in highly positive terms."[9]

A final reason for the change in Ottoman policy concerning its Greek population was the threat by Venizelos that, should such actions not cease, Greece would reciprocate by carrying out a similar campaign against its own Muslim population. This threat was made in the presence of the Austrian and German ambassadors in Athens, who then relayed it to their own capitals, where it reached the Porte.[10] Some contemporary observers made mention of the fact that the visible change in the Ottoman government's policies appeared to have been made not out of a change of heart but out of diplomatic necessity. In *The Western Question in Greece and Turkey*, Toynbee also mentions that from the outbreak of the First World War until the middle of the summer of 1916, the Anatolian Greek population did not suffer undue hardship relative to the overall situation.[11]

The change in policy noted by Humann can also be traced in the Ottoman documents themselves. A general circular from Talat Pasha to all Ottoman provinces on 2 November 1914 informs the provincial authorities of the government's change of policy regarding the Greek population. "Since, in light of the state's current political situation, it would not be ap-

[8] Ernst Jäckh Papers, Manuscript and Archival Collection, Yale University Library Papers, Group no. 467, Box 1, File 17, Report by Hans Humann, military attaché at the Istanbul Embassy, dated 1 November 1914.

[9] Ibid., File 18, Report by Humann, dated 17 November 1914.

[10] FO 371/2480/2622, "Secret" Doc. no. 281, folio 252, Report sent by the British Embassy in Athens to the Foreign Ministry, cited in V. N. Dadrian, *German Responsibility*, appendix C, 230 (Dadrian does not provide the exact date of the document, but says that it was written "as much as two months after the outbreak of the war").

[11] Toynbee, *The Western Question*, 142.

propriate to exert pressure on the Greeks," he begins, "no allowance shall be given for attacks and oppressions against them."[12] Another cable sent three days later, this time to the province of Edirne, reiterates this shift and warns of sanctions on those who act in opposition to the new policy. "It is reported that the Greek population in the townships of Nadirli and Kara-halil in the county of Babaeski have been subjected to abuse and forced to emigrate. Those officials and functionaries are to be reminded one more time that in the current situation, oppressive treatment like this is not per-mitted; so that an end will be put to such behavior and those perpetrating it are to be punished."[13]

Yet despite the central government's change of direction, in some areas the Greek inhabitants continued to suffer attacks, even murders. A tele-gram sent by the Security Directorate to Muğla in February 1915, for in-stance, states that "reports have been arriving one after the other in recent days that three Greeks from the county of Muğla and six Greeks from Milas along with a miller have been killed, and that others have had their properties burned." It then reiterates that conditions have changed and re-quests that, "as a result of the current political situation, the government has urgently demanded that these attacks against the Greek community be prevented from occurring, and on the basis of this need, those who have committed the aforementioned crimes are to be zealously pursued and harshly punished."[14]

From another cable to Balıkesir, dated 4 March, one learns of the Greek government's complaints of continued violence against the Greeks of Anatolia and that, at least in some cases, the central government's change of policy has not been implemented everywhere: "The Greek government has reported by telegram that the situation in Ayvalık has grown serious, and that sealed envelopes whose contents are unknown have been de-livered to the Muslim population of the area, that the transport of grain

[12] BOA/DH.ŞFR, no. 46/133, Coded telegram from the Interior Ministry's General Director-ate of Security to the Provinces of Edirne, Adana, Ankara, Aydın, Aleppo, Hüdâvendigâr (Bursa), Diyarbekır, Trebizond, Kastamonu, and Konya, and to the Provincial Districts of İzmit, Bolu, Canik, Çatalaca, Karesi (Balıkesir), Jerusalem, Kale-i Sultaniye (Çanakkale), Menteşe, Antalya, and Kayseri, dated 2 November 1914.

[13] BOA/DH.ŞFR, no. 46/190, Coded telegram from the Interior Ministry's General Directorate of Security to the Province of Edirne, dated 5 November 1914.

[14] BOA/DH.ŞFR, no. 50/39, Coded telegram from the Interior Ministry's General Directorate of Security to the Provincial District of Menteşe, dated 18 February 1915.

and foodstuffs into the town has been prevented by the government, that after five Greeks were killed in the area near the town it was beseiged by armed gangs and finally, that there is fear of an impending attack against the Greek [population]." The cable states that "the crucial importance of the current political situation during this period demands that careful attention be paid to the necessity of not allowing any event to occur that would give cause for complaint, as well as of carrying out a serious investigation [of the incidents in question] and the adopting of decisive measures; please report the results [of these actions]."[15]

The extortion of money and materials ostensibly on behalf of the war effort and enforced through the seige of villages and towns, arbitrary arrests and murders, confiscations of houses and lands, animal rustling, and other similar actions directed against the Greek population became ever more frequent events. Just as the case in the aforementioned April 1915 attack in the area around Lüleburgaz, in some instances the perpetrators acted under the government's direct orders. Even when government functionaries were not directly involved, local officials often simply looked the other way.[16] Such abuses would become so frequent that by 1919, in its detailed enumeration of the various crimes against the Ottoman Greek community during the war, the Istanbul Patriarchate frequently used the phrase "normal oppressions arose."[17]

From available documents one also learns that the Ottomans' mistreatment of their Greek population became a cause célèbre in the domestic politics of Greece. For its part, the Ottoman government approached the matter from the standpoint of not wishing to provide Venizelos, who was now out of office, any ammunition to be used against the government in Athens, and issued warnings to the provinces in this regard. In a July 1915 cable to Balıkesir, for instance, the Interior Ministry notifies the district governor of a report from the embassy in Athens that "the supporters of Venizelos have seized upon the attacks and oppressions against the Greeks in Ayvalık [as a means of] attacking the present government," and orders

---

[15] BOA/DH.ŞFR, no. 50/164, Coded telegram from the Interior Ministry's General Directorate of Security to the Provincial District of Karesi (Balıkesir), 4 March 1915.

[16] Greek Patriarchate, *Persecution of the Greeks*. This entire work is replete with examples of this type of action: for instances of villages being surrounded and money forcibly collected, 10; for attacks, lootings, and rapes by bandits, 35; for instances of gendarmes assisting in these attacks, 35–36, 52.

[17] Ibid., 6–7.

that, in light of the Porte's relations with Berlin and the promises it has made in this regard, Ottoman officials utterly refrain from actions that would put the current Greek government in a difficult position.[18]

At the end of July another cable—this one in cipher and marked "top secret"—was sent to nearly all of the empire's provinces and districts inhabited by Greeks. The message was repeated: avoid all actions against the Greek population that might give cause for complaint. In all of these messages, what is most interesting is the justification given for refraining from anti-Greek actions. Above all, it is clear that Berlin's insistence is a central factor in the government's decision:

> as we have heard from our ambassador in Athens that Venizelos' supporters have used the various oppressions and assaults on the Greeks in certain areas as means by which to attack the current government, and since our ally, the German government, has suggested that circumstances not be created that will make it more difficult for the Gonaris Cabinet to govern, accordingly, [it is requested that] only permissible behavior toward the Greeks be engaged in, and [that] no opportunity should be given for situations [to arise] that might give cause for complaint.[19]

This warning would be repeated in a cable to Adana on 29 July 1915 concerning a group of Greek citizens whose lands had been forcibly taken. "During this period, when our relations with the government of Greece have taken on a certain delicacy," the communiqué emphasizes that "no situations should be allowed to arise regarding [our] Greek citizens that would give cause for complaint."[20]

Again and again one sees this clear change in central government policy reflected in the Interior Ministry cables to the various Ottoman provinces, as well as sensitivity to the fact that violence against the Ottoman Greeks

[18] BOA/DH.ŞFR, no. 54-A/68, Coded telegram from the Interior Ministry to the Provincial District of Karesi (Balıkesir), dated 22 July 1915.

[19] BOA/DH.ŞFR, no. 54-A/109, Coded telegram from the Interior Ministry to the Provinces of Edirne, Erzurum, Adana, Ankara, Aydın, Beirut, Aleppo, Hüdâvendigâr (Bursa), Diyarbekır, Sivas, Trebizond, Kastamonu, and Konya, and to the Provincial Districts of İzmit, Bolu Canik, Çatalca, Jerusalem, Kale-i Sultaniye (Çanakkale), Menteşe, Teke, Karahisâr-ı Sahib (Afyon Karahisar), Kütahya, Marash, Kayseri, Eskişehir, and Niğde, dated 26 July 1915.

[20] BOA/DH.ŞFR, no. 54-A/165, Coded telegram from the Interior Ministry to the Province of Adana, dated 29 July 1915.

was being used by Greek politicians for both internal and external purposes. A cable to most of the provinces sent on 9 November 1915 makes these concerns explicit:

> it has become known that the supporters of Venizelos, by exaggerating certain special measures that have been taken in regard to the Greeks in Ottoman domains, have been inciting Greek [public] opinion to war and expending great effort to thereby force the [present] Greek cabinet to resign. As it is in the political and military interest of both the Ottoman State and its allies that the present cabinet remain in power for the present, it has been decided by the state that for now a friendly and tolerant policy shall be followed toward the Greek [population of the empire], and situations shall not be allowed to arise that would give any party cause for complaint. Accordingly, instructions must be given in an appropriate manner to those who will see that the necessary measures be adopted; moreoever, it is to be communicated that those acting in defiance of these instructions will be punished.[21]

On the same date a cipher telegram to the province of Bursa (Hüdâvendigâr) reminded local officials of the need to show "Greece that the [Ottoman] Greeks are being well treated" and that "a general communiqué should be issued that the Greeks should from that day forward no longer be [forcibly] sent away."[22] When complaints of mistreatment continued to arrive at the Porte, another general memorandum was sent out to most of the empire's local administrative centers on 22 December. "Despite the tolerant and benign policy that has been adopted toward the [Ottoman] Greeks," it begins, "a section of the Greek press is continuing to publish claims that Greeks in the Ottoman domains are still, right now, being subjected to oppression." It then requests that letters of praise concerning the

[21] BOA/DH.ŞFR, no. 57/366, Coded telegram from interior minister Talat Bey to the Provinces of Edirne, Erzurum, Adana, Ankara, Aydın, Beirut, Aleppo, Hüdâvendigâr (Bursa), Diyarbekır, Damascus, Sivas, Trebizond, Kastamonu, and Konya, and to the Provincial Districts of Urfa, İzmit, Bolu, Canik, Karesi (Balıkesir), Jerusalem, Kale-i Sultaniye (Çanakkale), Menteşe, Teke, Kayseri, Karahisâr-ı Sahib (Afyon Karahisar), İçel, Eskişehir, and Kütahya, dated 9 November 1915.

[22] BOA/DH.ŞFR, no. 57/358, Coded telegram from the Interior Ministry's General Directorate of Security to the Province of Hüdâvendigâr (Bursa), dated 9 November 1915.

Ottoman government's current policy and treatment of their community be provided by Greek religious figures and notables in the regions in question and that these should be forwarded to the Istanbul press.[23] A cable to the provincial district of Çanakkale in early 1916 reemphasizes the need to "follow at present a tolerant and benign policy toward the Greeks."[24]

THE "EVACUATION" OF SOME TOWNS AND VILLAGES FOR MILITARY REASONS

Despite the Ottoman government's clear policy shift in regard to its Greek population, the emptying of Greek settlements continued after the outbreak of the war, albeit on a more limited scale; moreover, these "evacuations" were carried out largely on the basis of future military and security concerns, and were restricted to specific regions. A cable to the provincial governor of Konya on 25 April 1915 reveals that on 23 January the Ottoman High Command had already decided that those Greek inhabitants of the coastal regions who were deemed as somehow "unreliable" were to be removed and relocated. Another cable sent on the same day, this time to Konya, states that the aforementioned decision was not to be implemented in regard to the Greeks in the interior and orders that some thirty Greeks who had been deported from İsparta without the approval of the central government be returned to their homes.[25]

The aforementioned 1919 report by the Greek Patriarchate in Istanbul dates the earliest of these military evacuations to February 1915, which would seem to agree with the evidence for the High Command decision having been made on 23 January and the subsequent empire-wide memorandum to that effect.

---

[23] BOA/DH.ŞFR, no. 59/85, Coded telegram from the Interior Ministry's General Directorate of Security to the Provinces of Edirne, Erzurum, Adana, Ankara, Aydın, Aleppo, Hüdâvendigâr (Bursa), Diyarbekır, Damascus, Sivas, Trebizond, Kastamonu, Konya, and Mamuretülaziz, and to the Provincial Districts of İzmit, Karahisâr-ı Sahib (Afyon Karahisar), Niğde, İçel, Bolu Canik, Çatalca, Karesi (Balıkesir), Jerusalem, Kale-i Sultaniye (Çanakkale), Menteşe, Teke, Kayseri, Eskişehir, and Kütahya, dated 22 December 1915.

[24] BOA/DH.ŞFR, no. 59/260, Coded telegram from the Interior Ministry's General Directorate of Security to the Provincial District of Kale-i Sultaniye (Çanakkale), dated 10 January 1916.

[25] BOA/DH.ŞFR, no. 52/104, Coded telegram from the Interior Ministry's General Directorate of Security to the Province of Konya, dated 25 April 1915.

The report also mentions instances of attacks against these villages during the evacuations, including lootings and killings.[26] It recounts that in a great many cases the villagers were given but a few hours' notice, and were often forbidden to take anything with them. As a result, many died on the journey for lack of a means of transport and provisions, as well as due to the uninhabitable character of many of the places to which they were moved.[27]

In the Ottoman documents from this period, it becomes strikingly clear that the underlying reasons for the population transfers were military and security concerns, not an overarching policy toward the Greek population as a whole. A May 1916 telegram to Trebizond, for instance, reminds the local officials that "a benign and tolerant policy toward Greece was being followed," and that it was not appropriate "to remove all of the Greeks in the coastal regions into the interior"; rather, only those who were to be found in areas that were thought disadvantageous out of military considerations were to be transferred inland.[28]

The instructions to the provinces reflect a conscious and area-specific policy toward the Greeks; those in regions of perceived military vulnerability were removed to the interior, while others were left in place, although in some cases the deportees were allowed to return home. A "secret and very urgent" order of 27 July 1915 to a number of provinces requests that, "as was communicated in the coded circular of 23 June due to the needs of the current political situation, the necessary instructions are to be immediately reported and delivered to the relevant parties that the Greek population inhabiting the towns and villages of the Marmara basin be left in place."[29]

A similar operation can be seen in Antalya and the surrounding region, where Greek deportees were permitted to return to their villages or re-

---

[26] For instances of looting, robbery, and murder during the course of the forced expulsions from Edirne and its environs, see Greek Patriarchate, *Persecution of the Greeks in Turkey*, 23–24.

[27] Ibid., 23, 42, 44, 48.

[28] BOA/DH.ŞFR, no. 64/29, Coded telegram from the Interior Ministry's General Directorate of Security to the Province of Trebizond, dated 15 May 1916.

[29] BOA/DH.ŞFR, no. 54-A/116, Coded telegram from the Interior Ministry's General Directorate of Security to the Provinces of Hüdâvendigâr (Bursa), and Edirne, and to the Provincial Districts of İzmir and Çatalca, dated 27 July 1915.

settle elsewhere: "those Greeks from Antalya who were evicted from their areas of settlement because of the war and deported to the provinces of Bozkara, Elmalı, and Turgut are to be shown every courtesy and given the freedom to . . . return to their homes in Antalya; those who do not wish to return are free to go wherever they wish, apart from restricted military districts."[30] Similarly, a cable of 9 October 1915 orders officials in Bursa (Hüdâvendigâr) to "not allow those Greeks who have been removed from various regions on account of the war to receive documents [that would allow them] to come to Istanbul, but to all but those who appear untrustworthy or suspicious to go where they wish, outside of Istanbul and restricted military areas."[31] Another aspect of the removal of Greek villagers is that a separate decision was given for each area of settlement.[32] A cable to Edirne in August 1915 mentions that "the relocating to the interior of the population of the villages, for which a clear need for removal, is approved," thereby giving a green light for the operation to go ahead.[33]

The displaced Greeks of the Black Sea region were to be resettled in the area of Kastamonu and Sivas. The May 1916 cable to Trebizond mentioned above also acknowledges the approval of "the dispatch of those who are to be relocated to the interior to Kastamonu and those districts of the province of Sivas in which there are no Muslim refugees."[34] Other messages, such as the following examples sent to various provinces in late June 1916, report that "it has become clear that those Greeks . . . [who were previously] reported have been transported to Sivas for military reasons,"[35] or

[30] BOA/DH.ŞFR, no. 54-A/82, Coded telegram from the Interior Ministry's General Directorate of Security to the Provincial District of Antalya, dated 6 September 1915.

[31] BOA/DH.ŞFR, no. 56/332, Coded telegram from the Interior Ministry's General Directorate of Security to the Province of Hüdâvendigâr (Bursa) and the Provincial Districts of Karesi (Balıkesir) and İzmit, dated 9 October 1915.

[32] This situation is clearly understood in the Patriarchate's report. For instance, the population of some of the villages around Yalova were deported to the Bursa (Hüdâvendigâr) region on the pretext that they had been providing fuel for British submarines. See Greek Patriarchate, *Persecution of the Greeks*, 53.

[33] BOA/DH.ŞFR, no. 55/219, Coded telegram from the Interior Ministry's General Directorate of Security to the Province of Edirne, dated 24 August 1915.

[34] BOA/DH.ŞFR, no. 64/29, Coded telegram from the Interior Ministry's General Directorate of Security to the Province of Trebizond, dated 15 May 1916.

[35] BOA/DH.ŞFR, no. 65/126, Coded telegram from the interior minister Talat to the Province of Sivas, dated 29 June 1916.

that "in light of a military plan it has become vital that the Greeks be sent to the southern portions of the [Kastamonu] province."[36]

Various communiqués to certain regions make a point of stating that there was no need to take such measures in areas deemed militarily "secure." A coded telegram from the Security Directorate to the district of Karesi (Balıkesir) can be given as an example: "The measures that were adopted and implemented in regard to the relocation of the Greeks of the coastal regions to the interior were limited to those coastal villages in which [other] means of [maintaining security and] discipline [i.e., gendarmes in sufficient number] were absent, but in those places that possess these means in sufficient quantity, such as Bandırma and Erdek, the steps that have already been taken will have to suffice."[37]

As mentioned, a decision to evacuate for military reasons was occasionally reversed, as in the interesting case of Urla in Aydın Province. In February 1916, in response to a request by the army, the decision was handed down to "evacuate Urla and its environs."[38] Several days later, however, a Security Directorate cable stated that "in light of the absence of any military necessity, the evacuation of Urla is to be abandoned for the time being."[39] Nevertheless, the decision was reversed once more on 9 March 1916 in a message explaining that "the military aspect was recently discussed [again]. If it appears absolutely necessary to evacuate, it also seemed appropriate that the evacuation be done in a quiet and orderly manner and with all possible ease and facilitation." The evacuation must "appear as if it is [being done] for the protection of the population."[40]

In other areas, reports indicate that there was no need to remove the Greek population. A May 1916 cable from the AMMU to Antakya (An-

[36] BOA/DH.ŞFR, no. 65/136, Coded telegram from the interior minister Talat to the Province of Kastamonu, dated 1 July 1916.

[37] BOA/DH.ŞFR, no. 54/363, Coded telegram from the Interior Ministry's General Directorate of Security to the Provincial District of Karesi (Balıkesir), dated 8 July 1915.

[38] BOA/DH.ŞFR, no. 61/53, Coded telegram from the Interior Ministry's General Directorate of Security to the Province of Aydın, dated 19 February 1916.

[39] BOA/DH.ŞFR, no. 61/149, Coded telegram from the Interior Ministry's General Directorate of Security to the Province of Aydın, dated 26 February 1916. The report by the Patriarchate also gives several examples of districts that are initially slated to be evacuated for military reasons, but for which plans to do so are subsequently canceled. See, for instance, Greek Patriarchate, *Persecution of the Greeks in Turkey*, 49.

[40] BOA/DH.ŞFR, no. 61/231, Coded telegram from the Interior Ministry's Private Secretariat to the Province of Aydın, dated 9 March 1916.

tioch), for instance, states that the Greek inhabitants of the district of İskenderun "were not to be subject to relocation."[41] The reason for such a notification in the first place was that the Greek inhabitants of Ersöz County (in the district of İskenderun) had been deported without the knowledge or permission of the central government. The cable further demands that "the identities of those Greeks who were deported and the reason for their removal be reported."[42] A similar incident occurred in Biga in August 1916. An AMMU cable to the district speaks of there being "no need to remove the Greeks living in Biga."[43]

THE POLICY TOWARD THE GREEK POPULATION CHANGES AGAIN AT THE END OF 1916

In the fall of 1916, the Ottoman policy toward the Greeks began to take the shape of a more comprehensive evacuation. The principal factors in the government's decision to broaden the scope of its Greek policy were: (1) the Entente's occupation of the Aegean islands of Midilli (Mytilene, Lesbos), Sakız, and Sisam the previous spring; (2) the Russian advance into eastern Anatolia; and (3) the expectation of an imminent Greek entry into the war on the side of Russia and Britain. From a number of cipher messages from Talat Pasha to the provinces in September 1916, one can see that such a situation had been expected and that the local officials were being instructed to prepare for the deportation of the Greek inhabitants of their respective jurisdictions. An 11 September 1916 cable, for instance, orders that "in light of the present situation, the necessary steps and preparations are to have been already made so that, in the likely event that Greece joins the war against us, the [Ottoman] Greeks living in the border regions can, upon the initial order emanating from here, be immediately moved to the interior and settled in suitable places there; this state of affairs is to be

[41] BOA/DH.ŞFR, no. 64/62, Coded telegram from the Interior Ministry's General Directorate of Tribal and Immigrant Affairs to the Presidency of the Commission for the Liquidation (of Abandoned Property) in Antakya, dated 18 May 1916.

[42] BOA/DH.ŞFR, no. 64/72, Coded telegram from the Interior Ministry's General Directorate of Tribal and Immigrant Affairs to the Province of Aleppo, dated 18 May 1916.

[43] BOA/DH.ŞFR, no. 66/224, Coded telegram from the Interior Ministry's General Directorate of Tribal and Immigrant Affairs to the Provincial District of Kale-i Sultaniye (Çanakkale), dated 12 August 1916.

kept strictly secret and information [regarding the status of the operation] reported back here."[44]

And again, in another cable sent the same day to the provincial district of Çatalca, Talat informs the governor's office that "on the basis of the current situation in Greece, which greatly increases the possibility that it will enter the war on the side of our enemies," the Greek population will have to be removed, and that the ministry is to be informed of each and every town and village of the region from which the Greeks are to be expelled, as well as their destinations.[45]

So that there should be no confusion about the aim of such "necessary" preparations, it was spelled out in detail: "the purpose of the preparations is that the necessary means and measures are to be considered at length and completed so that, when the order is given from here, the areas and districts to which the Greek population that is to be moved to the interior is to be settled will already be determined, and that means will be in place for the deportations to proceed in a calm and orderly fashion."[46] Other regions were queried as to how many displaced Greeks they would be able to receive: "since it is planned that, in the event that Greece enters the war on the side of our enemies, the Greeks from the coastal areas will be moved inward and that the twelve to twenty thosand that will come from İzmir will be settled in Isparta, [we request that] the possibility of settling and provisioning this many persons in this area be studied and that we be informed [of your conclusions]."[47] From the increasing frequency of messages of this type to the provinces concerned, it can be inferred that these population transfers began to be implemented on a large scale in 1917.[48]

One of the recurrent themes of the telegram sent to the provinces during these months is the insistence that the local representatives of the gov-

[44] BOA/DH.ŞFR, no. 67/243, Coded telegram from interior minister Talat to the Provinces of Hüdâvendigâr (Bursa), Aydın, and Edirne, and to the Provincial Districts of İzmit, Balıkesir, Çanakkale (Kale-i Sultaniye), and Menteşe, dated 11 September 1916.

[45] BOA/DH.ŞFR, no. 67/241, Coded telegram from interior minister Talat to the Provincial District of Çatalca, dated 11 September 1916.

[46] BOA/DH.ŞFR, no. 68/80, Coded telegram from interior minister Talat to the Provincial District of İzmit, dated 21 September 1916.

[47] BOA/DH.ŞFR, no. 68/146, Coded telegram from interior minister Talat to the Province of Konya, dated 1 October 1916. A similar cable of inquiry was sent to the Provincial District of Karahisar-i Şarki (see BOA/DH.ŞFR, no. 68/163).

[48] For other cables in this vein sent to various provinces and provincial districts, see BOA/DH.ŞFR, nos. 68/30, 35, 48, 80.

ernment refrain from action until they receive orders from the military authorities. Talat wrote to a number of the eastern provinces, "As long as the Army [High] Command has not given any special permission to do so, for clear military needs, no township or town is permitted to be evacuated, nor is the population to be allowed to flee."[49] Again and again it would be repeated in the following months that the areas to be evacuated would be identified by the military authorities. A cable of April 1917 shows that the provincial district of Karesi (Balıkesir) was to be evacuated "for military reasons."[50]

The government was particularly fearful that Greeks in the central and eastern Black Sea area might collaborate with advancing Russian military units. Therefore, on 21 January 1917, most of the provinces of north-central Anatolia were alerted that "the Command of the Third Army has deemed it to be of urgent necessity that the Greek population around the Samsun basin be removed to points further inward and that it was vital that they be placed in villages in the provinces of Sivas, Kastamonu, and Ankara and the provincial district of Bolu."[51] A coded message from Talat to the provincial district of Samsun on 11 January 1917 contains the following: "I spoke with Enver Pasha. He says that the arrangements have been made by the Third Army. The goal is to take the Greeks along the coast some thirty to fifty kilometers inland. Nevertheless, it is of the utmost importance that no assaults be made on any persons or property during the course of the deportations."[52]

In fact, the execution of this order did not go as requested. In some villages, the inhabitants were deported on a few hours' notice; in others, the men were conscripted into labor battalions, the women and children were not allowed to bring anything with them, and the villages themselves were looted by their Muslim neighbors. What is more, the inhabitants of the raided and looted villages were often forced to sign affidavits that their

[49] BOA/DH.ŞFR, no. 68/161, Coded telegram from interior minister Talat to the Provinces of Erzurum, Sivas, Diyarbekır, and Mamuretülaziz, dated 2 October 1916.

[50] BOA/DH.ŞFR, no. 75/81, Coded telegram from the Interior Ministry's General Directorate of Tribal and Immigrant Affairs to the Provincial District of Karesi (Balıkesir), dated 19 April 1917.

[51] BOA/DH.ŞFR, no. 72/62, Coded telegram from the Interior Ministry's General Directorate of Security to the Provinces of Sivas, Kastamonu, and Ankara, and to the Provincial District of Bolu, dated 21 January 1917.

[52] BOA/DH.ŞFR, no. 71/234, Coded telegram from interior minister Talat to the Provincial District of Samsun, dated 11 January 1917.

attackers had been Armenians.[53] The messages arriving from Istanbul also reveal that the central government was well aware of what was going on. For instance, in one coded telegram to Samsun from early February 1917 one reads the following statement: "It has been reported that not only were no committees formed in order to store, protect, and administer the possessions and livestock of those Greeks who were evacuated, but the depots themselves were not sealed, and the houses were allowed to be vandalized and destroyed."[54]

A key figure in the evacuation of Greek villages—particularly in the Samsun region—was CUP Central Committee member Bahaeddin Şakir. Indeed, from his arrival in the region in December 1916, the process took on a far more systematic character; by the end of the month, at least eighteen villages were completely evacuated, and another fifteen partially emptied. During the first month of 1917, some eighty notables of Samsun were arrested and four thousand inhabitants were deported, first to Havza and later to Çorum. The Greek deportees were resettled in the former homes of deported Armenian villagers. Soon afterward followed the evacuation of the Giresun and Amasya regions; from the outset the Ottoman central government was well informed about the looting and destruction that accompanied the expulsion of the villagers there. In a cable to the provincial district of Canik on 26 February 1917, Talat Pasha demands that "an investigation be undertaken and the results reported regarding which villages were burnt and destroyed up to now in the course of bandit raids."[55]

In a series of letters to the Patriarchate in Istanbul, the Greek Orthodox patriarch of Samsun, Germanos Karavengelis, states that roughly thirty thousand people had been deported from his area to the province of Ankara. Villages evacuated in three or four separate waves of expulsion had been subsequently looted and razed; additionally, the convoys of deportees had been attacked and both women and children had been killed.[56]

---

[53] For those events that were witnessed in the Giresun region, see Greek Patriarchate, *Persecution of the Greeks*, 103–7.

[54] BOA/DH.ŞFR, no. 72/181, Coded telegram from the Interior Ministry's General Directorate of Tribal and Immigrant Affairs to the Provincial District of Samsun, dated 8 February 1917.

[55] BOA/DH.ŞFR, no. 73/79, Coded telegram from interior minister Talat to the Provincial District of Canik, dated 26 February 1917.

[56] For a detailed account of the events of this period, see Stefanos Yerasimos, *Milliyetler ve Sınırlar, Balkanlar, Kafkasya ve Orta-Doğu* (Istanbul: İletişim Yayınları 1994), 351–427.

In March 1917, the bishop of Amasya reported that two-thirds of those deported from Amasya to Ankara had been massacred.[57]

A list of instructions was prepared and sent out on 3 February 1917 for the evacuations of coastal Greek communities, particularly those in the Black Sea region. It was "absolutely demanded that the statutes be scrupulously and completely followed by officials of the civilian administration," declared the communiqué: "1. The army will determine and dictate which Greek townships and populations are to be evacuated and who is to be deported to the interior." Most significant, "the expulsion and deportation operations from the coastal sector" were broadened to include "individuals from the cities."[58] Yet despite the large-scale operation to evacuate the coastal Greeks, the populations in some areas were largely left in place.[59]

In sum, it may safely be confirmed that compared with the previous limited operations, these "evacuations," which began in the summer of 1916 and continued into 1918, were "carried out with great brutality."[60]

MUSLIM REFUGEES ARE SETTLED IN THE VILLAGES EVACUATED FOR MILITARY PURPOSES

The existing documentation reveals that although the coastal Greeks were being removed to the interior ostensibly for military reasons, the central government had no intention of allowing the deportees ever to return home, for Muslims were quickly and systematically settled in the emptied Greek villages. Certain provinces were explicitly instructed that "no allowance [was to] be made for the Greeks to come back and resettle on the coast."[61] Provincial officials were also instructed to keep records of the evacuations. As the IAMM requested on 5 July 1915, "the number of Greeks who have up to now been evacuated from the coastal regions for military reasons and sent to other areas and the areas to which they have

[57] Greek Patriarchate, *Persecution of the Greeks*, 120–22.

[58] BOA/DH.ŞFR, no. 72/148, Coded telegram from the Interior Ministry's General Directorate of Security to the Provincial District of Canik, dated 3 February 1917.

[59] BOA/DH.ŞFR, no. 78/154, Coded telegram from the Interior Ministry's General Directorate of Tribal and Immigrant Affairs to the Province of Trebizond, dated 30 July 1917.

[60] Toynbee, *The Western Question in Greece and Turkey*, 143.

[61] BOA/DH.ŞFR, no. 63/264, Coded telegram from the Interior Ministry's IAMM to the Provincial District of Karesi (Balıkesir), dated 10 May 1916.

been sent should be reported, along with subsequent step-by-step reports of those still to be removed."[62]

A September 1915 cable from the IAMM to the Marmara region shows that the Interior Ministry was interested in documenting the evacuations/ relocations in special registries: the district governor's office in Karesi (Balıkesir) was asked to "put together and send . . . the registries that were requested containing the names of the settlements from those parts of the province on the shores of the Marmara Sea that have been evacuated up to now, as well as the number of Greeks deported from there, and the areas to which they will be sent."[63] The government from time to time reminded provincial authorities to ensure that they were keeping proper documentation of events. In a cable dated 6 August 1916, for instance, the Security Directorate asks provincial heads that "a list be put together that states the number of Greeks living in the towns and villages within the province and [its] districts."[64]

The resettlement of Muslim refugees in the emptied Greek villages began in the first months of the war. In the Terkos region, whose February 1915 evacuation was previously mentioned, Muslim immigrants and refugees were being resettled within two months.[65] Additionally, a 12 January 1916 cable to provinces and provincial districts states the necessity of "sending the immigrants to the areas on the coast that have been emptied of Greeks and settling the aforementioned towns and villages, one after another, with Muslims," thereby indicating that the government had already made a decision to do so.[66]

Another cable, sent to the provinces of Edirne and Çanakkale in April 1916, shows that the Security Directorate wished to be informed "if there

[62] BOA/DH.ŞFR, no. 54/312, Coded telegram from the Interior Ministry's IAMM to the Provinces of Edirne and Hüdâvendigâr (Bursa), and to the Provincial Districts of Kale-i Sultaniye (Çanakkale) and Karesi (Balıkesir), dated 5 July 1915.

[63] BOA/DH.ŞFR, no. 56/73, Coded telegram from the Interior Ministry's IAMM to the Province of Hüdâvendigâr (Bursa), dated 18 September 1915.

[64] BOA/DH.ŞFR, no. 66/194, Coded telegram from the Interior Ministry's General Directorate of Security to the Provinces of Adana, Aydın, Hüdâvendigâr (Bursa), Sivas, Kastamonu, Ankara, Trebizond, Konya, and Mamuretülaziz, and to the Provincial Districts of Canik, Çatalca, Karesi (Balıkesir), Jerusalem, Kale-i Sultaniye (Çanakkale), Menteşe, Teke, Kayseri, İzmit, Marash, Niğde, Eskişehir, İçel, Kütahya, and Karahisâr-ı Sahib (Afyon Karahisar), dated 9 August 1916.

[65] Greek Patriarchate, Persecution of the Greeks in Turkey, 26.

[66] BOA/DH.ŞFR, no. 59/279, Coded telegram from the Interior Ministry's IAMM to the Province of Hüdâvendigâr (Bursa) and the Provincial District of Karesi (Balıkesir), dated 12 January 1916.

were Greek villages that had been evacuated on account of enemy submarines, and whether or not these villages had been settled with [Muslim]
refugees."[67] Throughout 1916 and 1917 the government would continue to
empty Greek villages and resettle them with Muslim refugees and immigrants. A steady stream of information was demanded from the provinces
about the Greek towns that had had been evacuated: a Security Directorate cable to Karesi (Balıkesir), sent on 18 April 1916, asks: "Which Greek
townships and settlements in the district were evacuated, both before and
after [the date of this telegram], and were they completely or only partially
emptied out? At this moment how many Greeks are left in these settlements and in which ones have [Muslim] immigrants been settled?"[68]

Such interrogatories were sent out repeatedly at set intervals, even to
the same regions.[69] "Have any of the inhabitants of the Greek villages
returned to their villages? If so, how many, and are there Muslim immi-
gants and Greek inhabitants? How many of each are there, and in which
villages? Please provide information by telegraph."[70]

From the fact that the central government felt that it could demand such
information by the very next day ("Please report by tomorrow evening
which Greek villages have been partially or wholly evacuated because of
the enemy submarines in the province/provincial district and whether or
not immigrants have been settled in them";[71] "Please provide by tomorrow
the information requested regarding the evacuated Greek villages"[72])—
and even within the same day ("[Please provide] the information requested on the Greek villages by this evening"[73])—it is reasonable to

[67] BOA/DH.ŞFR, no. 63/101, Coded telegram from the Interior Ministry's General Directorate of
Security to the Province of Edirne and the Provincial District of Çanakkale, dated 25 April 1916. See
also BOA/DH.ŞFR, no. 63/257.
[68] BOA/DH.ŞFR, no. 63/34, Coded telegram from the Interior Ministry's General Directorate of
Security to the Provincial District of Karesi (Balıkesir), dated 18 April 1916.
[69] For a cable concerning the county of Erdek, see BOA/DH.ŞFR, no. 63/80, Coded telegram
from the Interior Ministry to the Provincial District of Karesi (Balıkesir), dated 23 April 1916.
[70] BOA/DH.ŞFR, no. 63/88, Coded telegram from the Interior Ministry's General Directorate of
Security to the Province of Hüdâvendigâr (Bursa), dated 24 April 1916.
[71] BOA/DH.ŞFR, no. 63/101, Coded telegram from the Interior Ministry's General Directorate
of Security to the Province of Edirne and the Provincial District of Çanakkale, dated 25 April 1916.
[72] BOA/DH.ŞFR, no. 63/46, Coded telegram from the Interior Ministry's General Directorate of
Security to the Provincial District of Karesi (Balıkesir), dated 19 April 1916.
[73] BOA/DH.ŞFR, no. 63/73, Coded telegram from the Interior Ministry's General Directorate of
Security to the Provincial District of Karesi (Balıkesir), dated 18 April 1916.

assume that the whole process of evacuation and resettlement was carried out under the strictest supervision and control.

The resettlement of the empty Greek villages with Muslim immigrants and refugees continued into 1917. A cable from April of that year to Afyon, for example, demands that "since 1,000 immigrants have been sent in order to be placed in the Greek villages inside your provincial district, [please] determine and inform us of the way-stations until their arrival, and the neighborhoods and areas in which they are to be placed."[74] The evacuated coastal Greeks were largely relocated in Greek villages in the inner provinces,[75] and in some cases were resettled in the villages left behind by deported Armenians.[76]

PROPERTY LEFT BEHIND BY THE DEPORTED GREEKS

What was to become of the property of the Greek deportees to the interior? The available documentation indicates that there was no uniform policy on the matter at first, and that uniformity of practice spread, but slowly. The earliest documentary evidence on this subject is a cable of 10 June 1914 from Talat Pasha to the provincial district of Balıkesir. In it the interior minister requests that "the immovable property of those who have emigrated be protected well, and the transactions concerning the movable possessions be properly registered without any bureaucratic hitches or incumbrances."[77]

---

[74] BOA/DH.ŞFR, no. 75/113, Coded telegram from the Interior Ministry's Office and Tribal and Immigrant Settlement to the Provincial District of Karahisâr-ı Sahib (Afyon Karahisar), dated 25 April 1917.

[75] There are a great number of existing documents on this topic. For a few of the many examples, see BOA/DH.ŞFR, no. 75/114, Coded telegram from the Interior Ministry's General Directorate of Tribal and Immigrant Affairs to the Province of Konya, dated 14 April 1917; BOA/DH.ŞFR, no. 75/119, Coded telegram from the Interior Ministry's General Directorate of Tribal and Immigrant Affairs to the Provincial District of Küthya, dated 25 April 1917; BOA/DH.ŞFR, no. 75/120, Coded telegram from the Interior Ministry's General Directorate of Tribal and Immigrant Affairs to the Provincial District of Eskişehir, dated 6 May 1917.

[76] For instance, the Greek inhabitants who were evacuated in stages from the Uzunköprü region between September and October 1915 were resettled in the area around Malkara, in the houses left empty by the deported Armenians. See Greek Patriarchate, *Persecution of the Greeks in Turkey*, 33.

[77] BOA/DH.ŞFR, no. 41/208, Coded telegram from interior minister Talat to the Provincial District of Karesi (Balıkesir), dated 10 June 1914.

A subsequent telegram, which was sent to a great many provinces and districts on 6 July 1914, concerned the Greek deportees' abandoned property and possessions that were in danger of being stolen; consequently, the request is made that they not be disturbed but instead turned over to the regional Community Property Accounts (Mahalli Mal Sandıkları):

in view of the difficulties with preserving and protecting the houses, gardens, commercial goods, animals, livestock, and other articles and products left behind by the departing Greek inhabitants, and their increasing delapidation and deterioration over the course of time, as well as [the danger of] their theft, misuse, or abuse, an official decree should be given that the[se possessions] be placed in community property accounts, with the condition that they should be put into some sort of trust by secure means and the names of their owners registered so that they could be returned to their owners upon request; the matter should be conducted in said manner.[78]

Another cable, this one from the Interior Ministry's Office of Communication and dated 11 July 1914, deals with the disposition of abandoned Greek property:

In the Imperial Decree that has recently been handed down and approved by the Council of Ministers, it was ordered that those possessions which were left behind by the departing Greeks and which can be protected should be gathered up and placed in depots in the appropriate neighborhoods, while some of their livestock and other possessions are to be made secure by placing them in the care of reliable individuals. The required steps are to be taken to carry out this order accordingly.[79]

Over the following months, the provinces were reminded of the policy toward the Greeks and their property, which differed from the policy

[78] BOA/DH.ŞFR, no. 42/211, Coded telegram from the Interior Ministry's General Directorate of Security to the Provinces of Edirne, Aydın, and Hüdâvendigâr (Bursa), and to the Provincial Districts of İzmit, Çatalca, Karesi (Balıkesir), and Kale-i Sultaniye (Çanakkale), dated 6 July 1914.

[79] BOA/DH.ŞFR, no. 42/255, Coded telegram from the Fourth Department of the Interior Ministry's General Office of Communication to the Provinces of Edirne, Aydın, and Hüdâvendigâr (Bursa), and to the Provincial Districts of İzmit, Çatalca, Karesi (Balıkesir), and Kale-i Sultaniye (Çanakkale), dated 11 July 1914.

toward the Armenians. A January 1916 cable reminds the provincial district of Çanakkale that "in the present state a policy of tolerance and benevolence is to be followed in regard to the Greeks" and that "their moveable and immoveable properties in [the region of] Gallipoli are to be treated accordingly," whereas "separate instructions are to be given . . . in regard to property belonging to the Armenians."[80]

A cable to the Black Sea provinces of Trebizond and Samsun on 16 January 1917 states that "[Muslim] immigrants are being settled in the areas left empty [by the Greeks], and especially in those areas in the coastal regions. The moveable property is to be protected in churches and depots." Local officials are notified that "a separate set of instructions regarding the property of the Greeks is currently being sent by post."[81] One of these sets of instructions, sent to the provincial district of Canik on 24 February 1917, shows that they had been dispatched eleven days before and that "Greek properties are not subject to liquidation as Armenian properties are." Instead, "the moveable and immoveable properties belonging to them [i.e., the Greeks] are to be guarded and those things that are either breakable or prone to deterioration are to be given to the [new] immigrants and military in exchange for a receipt of acknowledgment."[82]

Yet despite the differential instructions in a number of cables to the provinces at this time regarding the disposition of Greek and Armenian abandoned property, the point was emphasized that the decrees concerning the property of Armenians were also valid for Greek properties. A July 1915 cable to the province of Hüdâvendigâr (Bursa), for example, informs the governor's office that "since there does not exist a separate set of instructions for the Greeks who are to be moved, the instructions that were previously sent concerning the protection and preservation of the abandoned property of the Armenians should be applied."[83] The commis-

---

[80] BOA/DH.ŞFR, no. 59/260, Coded telegram from the Interior Ministry's General Directorate of Security to the Provincial District of Çanakkale, dated 10 January 1916.

[81] BOA/DH.ŞFR, no. 72/28, Coded telegram from the Interior Ministry's General Directorate of Tribal and Immigrant Affairs to the Province of Trebizond and the Provincial District of Canik, dated 16 January 1917.

[82] BOA/DH.ŞFR, no. 73/69, Coded telegram from the Interior Ministry's General Directorate of Tribal and Immigrant Affairs to the Provincial District of Canik, dated 24 February 1916.

[83] BOA/DH.ŞFR, no. 54/296, Coded telegram from the Interior Ministry's IAMM to the Province of Hüdâvendigâr (Bursa), dated 6 July 1915.

sions that had been established according to these instructions in order to dispose of Armenian property were also to be responsible for that of the Greeks. A February 1917 telegram to Canik also mentions that the Liquidation Commission previously set up for Armenian property would be looking after abandoned Greek property.[84]

Nevertheless, even though the same decrees and commissions were engaged for Armenian as well as Greek properties, the latter were not in fact completely liquidated; instead, much of the Greek property was to be "preserved." Moreover, there was a noteworthy distinction in the disposal of the two different communities' properties, because the supervision and administration of the procedure had been assigned to two separate ministries. In the previously quoted cable from the IAMM to the provincial district of Canik (24 February 1917), the Settlement Office states that the "abandoned property of the Greeks belongs to the civil administration [mülkiye]," and not to the Finance Ministry, as is the case with the Armenian property; therefore, the Greek property "is not subject to liquidation. Moreover, there was no need to establish a new liquidation commission, as such commissions that already exist can oversee the matter with the assistance of the central government." This information is repeated in the letter cited above to the commission, and it is said that "unlike the Armenian property, the Greek property is not subject to liquidation, and those things belonging to the persons deported are to be left to family members and [business] partners." In other words, it was necessary "to protect and preserve the movable and non-movable property" of the Greeks, and only "those things that are perishable or liable to deteriorate should be given to [Muslim] immigrants and the military in exchange for a receipt of acknowledgement."[85]

[84] BOA/DH.ŞFR, no. 72/229, Coded telegram from the Interior Ministry's General Directorate of Tribal and Immigrant Affairs to the Provincial District of Canik, dated 13 February 1917. This matter was also reported to the presidency of the Liquidation Commission in Canik in a separate correspondence, in which it was written that "transactions concerning the [abandoned] Greek property shall be conducted by the Liquidation Commission in areas in which it is present, whereas in districts in which it is not they shall be conducted by a commission to be formed under the chairmanship of the highest ranking officials of the civil administration" (BOA/DH.ŞFR, no. 74/69, Coded telegram from the Interior Ministry's General Directorate of Tribal and Immigrant Settlement to the Presidency of the Canik Liquidation Commission, dated 20 March 1917).

[85] BOA/DH.ŞFR, no. 73/69, Coded telegram from the Interior Ministry's General Directorate of Tribal and Immigrant Affairs to the Provincial District of Canik, dated 24 February 1917.

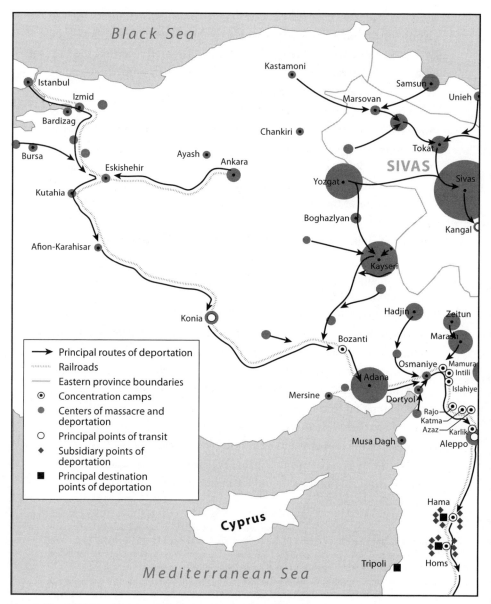

Map 3. The 1915 Armenian Genocide in the Turkish Empire. *Source*: Adapted from a map by the Armenian National Institute (ANI).

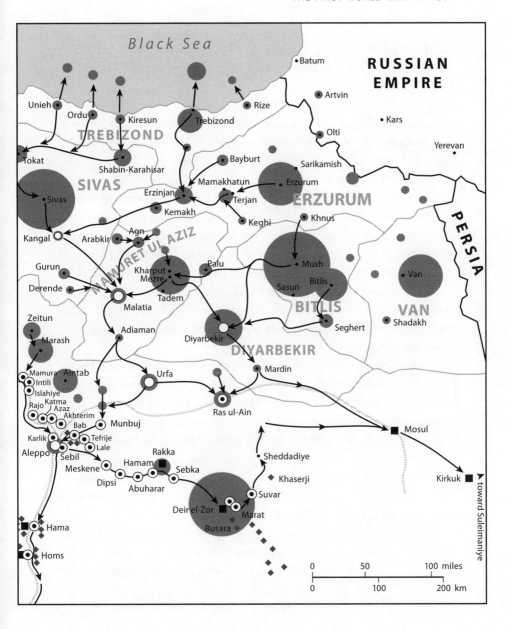

CONCLUSION: THE GREEKS AND ARMENIANS WERE SUBJECTED TO DIFFERENTIAL TREATMENT DURING THE WAR

A handful of foreign travelers in Anatolia directly witnessed the differential treatment of Greeks and Armenians during the war; they frequently recorded in their journals and reports that compared to the Armenians, the Greeks were not subjected to especially violent or brutal measures. In a lengthy report for the *Kölnische Zeitung*, a correspondent named Tyszka characterized the evacuation of Greek towns and villages from the Marmara region as "emptying out without the imposition of violence."[86] A teacher at the American college at Marsovan (Merzifon) observed: "While journeying to Constantinople, we passed some of the Greek exiles from European Turkey. They did not seem to be in such a pitiful condition as the Armenians, as they had considerable property with them. Because they traveled by boat and rail, they were obliged to suffer less danger and hardship on the way."[87]

A representative of the American Consulate in Edirne informed his superiors on 5 March 1916 that the government's Turkification policies in Thrace were continuing unabated: "The persecutions of these people, to which I have referred from time to time, and which are conducted by the authorities with a view to the Turkification of Thrace and the enriching of the Mussulmans at the expense of their more intelligent and thriftier compatriots, has never ceased but since the time of the general expulsion of Armenians, it has been conducted more quietly and in a less barbarous manner, said to be due to German guidance."[88]

Indeed, even during the most intense period of Armenian deportations and massacres, Greeks who had mistakenly been deported on the assumption that they were Armenians were often allowed to return to their

---

[86] DE/PA-AA/R 14087, "Secret" report from Tyszka to the German Foreign Ministry, dated 5 September 1915.

[87] NA/RG 59, 867.4016/106, Report from Ambassador Morgenthau, dated 26 July 1915, in *United States Official Records*, ed. Sarafian, 143.

[88] NA/RG 59, 867.00/786, Report by the American assistant consul in Edirne, Charles E. Allen, to the American Consulate in Istanbul, dated 5 March 1916, in *United States Official Records*, ed. Sarafian, 493.

homes. This can been seen in cables such as that sent to Karahisâr-ı Sâhib (Afyon Karahisar) in November 1915, confirming that "the petitioner Garigor oğlu, who is [now] understood to be Greek, is to be allowed to return to his village of Aristinyos."[89]

Additionally, many sources attest that Armenians were hidden by Greek neighbors and others during the deportations. An example can be given here of an American missionary who reported from Merzifon that the number of Armenians hidden among the Greek villages in their mountain villages ran into the "thousands" in her district alone.[90] This happened so frequently that in some regions, such as Tokat, the authorities razed Greek village houses in order to flush out Armenians thought to be hiding there.[91]

Despite the increasingly severe wartime policies, in particular for the period between late 1916 and the first months of 1917, the government's treatment of the Greeks—although comparable in some ways to the measures against the Armenians—differed in scope, intent, and motivation. The following chapters will examine Ottoman government policy concerning the Armenians in greater detail.

[89] BOA/DH.ŞFR, no. 58/36, Coded telegram from the Interior Ministry's General Directorate of Security to the Provincial District of Karahisâr-ı Sahib (Afyon Karahisar), dated 16 November 1915.

[90] NA/RG 59, 867.4016/252, Report dated 22 December 1915 by Miss Frances C. Gage, an American missionary working in Merzifon, to the State Department, via ambassador to the Porte, Henry Morgenthau. Reproduced in United States Official Records, ed. Sarafian, 407, 414. Additionally, on the subject of the situation of the Greeks of Anatolia during the annihilation of the Armenians, see Ioannis K. Hassiotis, "The Armenian Genocide and the Greeks: Response and Records (1915–23)," in History, Politics, Ethics, Hovannisian, 129–52.

[91] Greek Patriarchate, Persecution of the Greeks in Turkey, 98.

Extant Ottoman documents reveal that the
Unionist government made clear distinctions in its wartime policies between the Armenians and the empire's other Christian communities. The
Greeks, as has been seen, were deported and expelled with brutality, but
the Armenians were targeted for outright annihilation. In the decision to
exterminate them, the Unionists' overarching objective of homogenizing
the population of Anatolia undoubtedly played an important role; however, it would be incorrect to infer a direct line of causation between the
two. The available evidence does not indicate that the restructuring of the
general population resulted automatically in the annihilation of a particular
group. The central question, then, concerns the nature of the relationship
between demographic policy and genocide. Moreover, although the importance of World War I as the context for genocide cannot be discounted,
the deportation of the Ottoman Armenians was neither a military necessity nor a contingency of war, as has been so often claimed by the propo-
nents of the official Turkish version of history. The reason for the decision
of deportation encompassed much more than this, for the Unionists' major
problem, prior to the outbreak of hostilities, was the question of Armenian
reforms. As stated by no less a figure than interior minister Talat Pasha,
their primary intent, again unconnected with the war, was "eliminating [the
Armenian problem] in a manner that is comprehensive and absolute [*esaslı
bir suretde hal ve faslı ile külliyen izalesi*]."[1]

In the course of the war, following a series of military defeats, the Ottoman rulers came to believe that the issue of Armenian reforms had become
a lethal threat to the empire's national security and territorial integrity. The
policy decisions regarding the Armenians can thus be seen to have ema-
nated from the dual context of general ethnic cleansing in Anatolia and the

---

[1] *Ati*, 24 February 1920.

military defeats that transformed the long-standing question of Armenian reforms into an existential national security issue for the Ottoman state.[2]

In light of new documentary evidence from the Ottoman archives, this chapter will illustrate the evolution of Unionist policy toward the Armenians in this dual context, from early measures at the beginning of the war to the increasingly radical decisions that escalated into the annihilation of the Armenian people.

SOME OBSERVATIONS

The question of premeditation is central to debates on the chronology of the Armenian Genocide, from conception and planning to execution. On one hand, those scholars who emphasize the theme of continuity seek to explain the decision for annihilation in terms of culture, ideology, or mentality. In this approach, such concepts as a "subculture of massacre" and the "Ottoman-Turkish propensity to resolve acute conflicts . . . by resort[ing] to violence," as well as statements like "Islamic doctrines and traditions . . . embodied an inherent resistance to change," occupy an important place.[3] The Armenian Genocide is viewed as the outcome of a decision that was made at some point prior to World War I and implemented opportunistically in the favorable environment of military conflict.[4] The first steps taken against the Armenians in August 1914 are presented as "the first crippling initiative of the genocide," that is, as the enactment of a long-standing policy decision.[5] Vahakn N. Dadrian, one of

---

[2] For a more detailed discussion of the role of the military setbacks in the Unionist decision to annihilate the Armenians, see Akçam, *A Shameful Act*, 111–29.

[3] For these concepts, see V. N. Dadrian, *The History of the Armenian Genocide: Ethnic Conflict from the Balkans to Anatolia to the Caucasus* (Providence and Oxford: Berghahn Books, 1995), 4–6, 121.

[4] In his article, "The Armenian Genocide and the Pitfalls of a 'Balanced' Analysis," *Armenian Forum* 2 (Summer 1998): 73–131, V. N. Dadrian summarizes his views on this topic in detail and additionally proposes a second look at his earlier works: "Naim-Andonian Documents on the World War I Destruction of Ottoman Armenians: The Anathomy of a Genocide," *International Journal of Middle East Studies* 18 (1986): 311–60; "Genocide as a Problem of National and International Law: The World War I Armenian Case and Its Contemporary Legal Ramifications," *Yale Journal of International Law* 14, no. 2 (Summer 1989): 300–301; "The Armenian Genocide in Official Turkish Records," special issue containing the collected essays of V. N. Dadrian, *Journal of Political and Military Sociology* 22, no. 1 (Summer 1994): 29–96; *History of the Armenian Genocide*, 324–26.

[5] V. N. Dadrian, "The Armenian Genocide: An Interpretation," in *America and the Armenian Genocide of 1915*, ed. Jay Winter (New York and Cambridge: Cambridge University Press, 2003), 62.

the foremost defenders of this thesis, suggests two alternative occasions for this decision: the Committee of Union and Progress Congresses of 1910 or 1913.[6]

Another group of scholars, while not excluding facts that are explained by "continuity," sees the war not only as an opportune moment but also as a causal or determinative factor. Here the stress is more on the concept of contingency, as in the following statement: "The Genocide did not result primarily from Turkish racial or religious hatred of the Armenians . . . or from long-term planning by militant nationalists. The Genocide was, rather, a contingent event, initiated at a moment of imperial near-collapse, when the Young-Turks made a final, desperate effort to revive and expand the empire."[7]

These debates about continuity and contingency in the Armenian Genocide resemble those between "functionalists" and "intentionalists" concerning the Holocaust.[8] At one time, academics who took a side in this debate, or positioned themselves somewhere in the middle, made important contributions to the understanding of the Holocaust, but Holocaust scholarship has by now moved far beyond this distinction. In particular, the opening of archives in Eastern European countries and the increased availability of source material have resulted in much richer interpretations.[9] It is not difficult to conjecture that Armenian Genocide research will move in a similar direction.

Although a detailed discussion of these schools of thought is beyond the scope of this work, three further points must be stressed. The first pertains to the limited nature of available source materials on the Armenian Genocide, one of the most significant challenges in Armenian Genocide

[6] See V. N. Dadrian, "The Convergant Roles of the State and a Governmental Party in the Armenian Genocide," in *Studies in Comparative Genocide*, ed. Levon Chorbajian and George Shirinian (London: Macmillan; New York: St. Martin's Press, 1999), 92–125.

[7] Ronald Grigor Suny, "Empire and Nation: Armenians, Turks, and the End of the Ottoman Empire," in *Armenian Forum* 2 (Summer 1988): 17.

[8] For a broader summary of different points of view on this issue, see Richard Hovannisian, "The Armenian Genocide: Wartime Radicalization or Premeditated Continuum," in *The Armenian Genocide: Cultural and Ethical Legacies*, ed. Richard Hovannisian (New Brunswick and London: Transaction, 2007), 3–19.

[9] For more detailed information on this topic, see Ian Kershaw, *Hitler, the Germans, and the Final Solution* (New Haven and London: Yale University Press, 2008), 237–81; Richard Bessel, "Functionalists vs. Intentionalists: The Debate Twenty Years On *or* Whatever Happened to Functionalism and Intentionalism?," *German Studies Review* 26, no. 1 (Feb. 2003): 15–20.

research. Russian and Ottoman archival sources, along with a wide variety of Armenian primary sources, have yet to be sufficiently incorporated into our understanding of the Armenian Genocide, with the inescapable consequence that discussions of continuity, contingency, and the like may occasionally take on a speculative character. Rather than taking sides in a debate based on insufficient resources, this volume gives priority to presenting new evidence from Ottoman documents that help to illuminate various characteristics of the unfolding genocidal process.

Second, the debate on continuity and contingency in the Armenian Genocide hinges on the questionable presupposition that a single, final decision can be demonstrated. During the long years of debate on the Holocaust, the functionalists and structuralists eventually came to realize that the search for such a "final decision" for annihilation was not very meaningful. Instead, they were faced with a sequence of decisions, each one triggering the next. Understanding the process came to be seen as more important than focusing on a single decision and attempting to ascertain its date.[10] The writer of these lines, relying on the Ottoman documents that he has at hand, feels closer to the concept of process. The annihilation of the Armenians seems not to have resulted from a single decision on a given date; rather, the genocide appears to have been the cumulative outcome of a series of increasingly radical decisions, each triggering the next in a cascading sequence of events.

Third, the clear-cut separation and opposition of continuity and contingency cannot be very meaningful. To be sure, historical processes include both dimensions, and in this sense both sides of the debate make some correct points and have contributed significantly to our understanding of the genocidal process. More important, however, is the interaction of these themes during the process of annihilation. In light of the new evidence presented in this chapter, the issue of continuity versus contingency in the Armenian Genocide may be formulated as follows: Why did the demographic plan for homogenizing Anatolia, as decided by the Unionists in 1913, turn genocidal in the case of Armenians? This question cannot be answered with speculative hypotheses about intent or a "single deci-

---

[10] Christopher R. Browning, "The Decision-Making Process," in *The Historiography of the Holocaust*, ed. Dan Stone (New York: Palgrave Macmillan, 2004), 173–97.

sion," but through the analysis of a dynamic process as revealed by extant documents.

THE 1914 ARMENIAN REFORM PLAN AND TALAT'S REPORT

In the explanation of historical events, the identification of critical turning points is a long-standing tradition. The 1878 Treaty of Berlin, the 1894–96 pogroms during the reign of Abdülhamid, and the 1909 Adana massacres are often mentioned as turning points for the "Armenian Question."[11] If one accepts the 1912–13 Balkan Wars as a historical hinge of the demographic policies under construction for Anatolia, the Armenian Reform Agreement with Russia in February 1914 is another such point in the process that culminated in the annihilation of the Armenians.[12]

Encouraged by the success of the Balkan states, Armenians began to seek foreign aid for the solution to their own problems. This quest coincided with the Great powers holding discussions about how to share the territories remaining to the Ottomans. The French ambassador to Berlin, in charge of the talks between the Great powers, wrote on 25 September 1913 that the discussions taking place would settle "collectively and finally [the] future shares and present spheres of influence in Asia Minor."[13] The ultimate outcome was a series of bilateral agreements among France, Germany, Britain, and Italy, which divided Anatolia into zones of economic influence. However, as the same French ambassador noted on 16 March 1914, "the aim of this bargaining was not merely . . . to divide up Asia Minor in an economic sense, but also to partition it politically."[14] After signing the Baghdad Treaty with Great Britain in March 1914, Prince

---

[11] It is possible to find detailed information about the above-mentioned turning points in all works concerning the Armenian Genocide. For a short general summary, see Richard Hovannisian, "The Armenian Question in the Ottoman Empire," in *The Armenian People from Ancient to Modern Times*, vol. 2, *Foreign Dominion to Statehood: The Fifteenth Century to the Twentieth Century*, ed. Richard Hovannisian (New York: St. Martin's Press, 1997), 203–38.

[12] Unfortunately, there is no comprehensive work on the negotiations for the Armenian reforms, which began immediately after the Balkan Wars. The most detailed information on this topic can be found in Bayur, *Türk İnkılabı Tarihi*, vol. 2, part 3, 18–187. In addition, see Taner Akçam, *A Shameful Act*, 98–102.

[13] Ibid., 144.

[14] Ibid., 477.

Lichnowsky, the German ambassador to London, wrote to Berlin that "in reality the aim of this agreement is to divide Anatolia into zones of influence. But in order to appear respectful of the Sultan's rights, utmost care must be taken never to use this expression."[15] Russia's growing interest in Anatolia and the Middle East after 1905 was not unknown to any of the powers. Under these conditions, it was inescapable that the Armenians' search for foreign assistance would give birth to a competition between the Great powers.[16]

Negotations on the Armenian reforms began in spring 1913 with the participation of England, Germany, France, and Russia. These Great powers were in agreement on what the Ottomans regarded as, in essence, "the step toward partition."[17] "Asiatic Turkey cannot live for very long," said the French chargé d'affaires in St. Petersburg, who proposed "to establish small states based on nationalities, such as Armenian, Syrian and Arabian" in Anatolia.[18] The German ambassador in Istanbul, Hans von Wangenheim, declared on 30 June 1914 that "this matter means the beginning of the partition."[19] Russian representative André Mandelstam, who prepared Russia's first reform proposal, described the initiative as "the first step toward rescuing Armenia from Turkish oppression."[20] The Austrian ambassador to the Porte, Count Pallavicini, heard from the Russians that with the realization of the reforms, the division of Asiatic Turkey was as good as accomplished.[21]

The parties eventually reached an understanding known as the Yeniköy Accord, which the Ottomans were compelled to sign on 8 February 1914 despite their strong opposition. According to the agreement, the eastern provinces would be combined into two large provinces, and a foreign inspector invested with complete authority would be appointed for each

[15] Ibid., 475.

[16] For more information on Russian policy and the Armenian reforms, see Roderic Davison, "The Armenian Crisis, 1912–1914," in *American Historical Review* 53, no. 3 (April 1948): 481–505.

[17] Description of the reforms and negotiations by Marling, the British chargé d'affaires in Istanbul, in a report of the meetings that he sent to London (see Bayur, *Türk İnkılabı Tarihi*, vol. 2, part 3, 131).

[18] Ibid., 140.

[19] Ibid., 117.

[20] André Mandelstam, *Das Armenische Problem im Lichte des Volker und Menschenrechts* (Berlin: G. Stilke, 1931), 31.

[21] HHStA PA 12, 463, Yeniköy, 11 July 1913, no. 38/B, in *Österreich-Armenien, 1872–1936: Faximiliesammlung Diplomatischer Aktenstücke*, ed. Artem Ohandjanian, vol. 5 (Vienna: Self-published, 1995), 4069.

province. For the Unionist leaders this was a fateful, perhaps fatal step, for Serbia, Greece, Romania, and Bulgaria had been lost to the empire through just such a process. The Armenians, as the intended beneficiaries of these reforms, were thereafter viewed as a serious and permanent threat to the empire's continued existence.

The ominous words of the English military attaché in Istanbul turned out to be prophetic in 1915: "If the Great Powers, without consulting Turkey, attempt to force it to accept . . . Armenia's . . . autonomy, those today in power in Istanbul rather than submitting to this will set all the provinces on fire." And, he continued, "[i]f the Russian plan is accepted, it will open the way for massacres throughout the country."[22] What was finally accepted differed somewhat from the Russian proposal, but the result was the same.

The intolerable burden of the 1914 Armenian Reform Agreement lent urgency to the Ottomans' decision to enter the war. "Our sole goal was to be freed by means of this world war from all the foreign treaties that existed, each of which constituted a blow to our internal independence," recalled Unionist leader Cemal Pasha, adding that "the ripping up of the agreement concerning the reforms of eastern Anatolia was also desired."[23] Far from being compelled to enter the war, the Ittihadists welcomed it, as confirmed by Cemal Pasha in Damascus, 29 December 1914. "[I] guarantee you that Germany did not force us into the war, as some claim," declared Cemal, "no, we strive for an alliance with Germany because we know that our future will only be secured through the war."[24]

Armenian political leaders at the time of the reform negotiations later recalled that the Unionists had threatened them for appealing to the Great powers and thereby opening the way to the breakup of the Ottoman Empire. The Unionists had declared that this would end with the annihilation

[22] Bayur, *Türk İnkılabı Tarihi*, vol. 2, part 3, 83–84.

[23] Cemal Pasha, *Hatıralar ve Vesikalar* (Istanbul: Vakit, n.d.), 502. For the English translation, see *Memories of a Turkish Statesman, 1913–1919* (New York: George H. Doran, 1922), 276. To learn why the Unionists entered the war and what the other causes were, read Taner Akçam, *A Shameful Act*, 111–26.

[24] DE/PA-AA/R 19951/24-33/A4492/no. 50, enclosure 1, Ambassador Wangenheim to Chancellor Bethmann-Hollweg, dated 28 January 1915. Wangenheim reported that Cemal Pasha gave this talk on 29 December 1914 in the "Oriental Club in Damascus," and that, according to the report of the German consul, it left a good impression in Arab circles. I thank Wolfgang Gust for bringing this document to my attention.

of the entire Armenian people.[25] A "historic meeting" between Unionist and Tashnag leaders was held in the home of Bedros Halajian, himself a Unionist. "The Turkish statesmen were extremely angry at the Armenians ... in the encounters between Talat, Cemal[,] and Halil, and Agnuni, Shahrikian, Pastırmacıyan, Vartkes, and Zohrab, the Ottoman statesmen[,] asked the political figures in vain to stand up and take a position against Boghos Nubar Pasha ... That night the Turkish politicians left B. Halajian's house in an uneasy state and found that their only solution was the choice of massacre."[26] Additional sources mention "warnings" to the Armenians from Unionist leaders such as Enver, Cemal, Talat, and Halil Menteşe.[27] Thus, after officially entering the war in November 1914, the Unionists annulled the reform agreement,[28] but in the winter of 1915, there was a danger of its being revived. The Russian armies were advancing, and the occupation of the provinces, which was the subject of the reforms, could come at any moment and lead to the establishment of an independent Armenia. The Unionists saw just one way to halt this process: the cleansing of the Armenians.

The most important evidence of a connection between the 1915 extermination and the Armenian reforms is an official note from the Ottoman Interior Ministry dated 26 May 1915 to the grand vizierate. According to this document, the deportation of the Armenians had created the possibility of "eliminating [the Armenian problem] in a manner that is comprehensive and absolute."[29] The rationale behind the decisions about the Armenians is explained thus:

[25] On these memoirs and warnings, see V. N. Dadrian, "The Convergent Roles of the State and a Governmental Party," 120–24; *History of the Armenian Genocide*, 208, 211; and *Warrant for Genocide: Key Elements of Turko-Armenian Conflict* (New Brunswick and London: Transaction, 1999), 125–26.

[26] Dzerugin Hişadagneri, "Memoirs of 'Old Man,'" *Jagadamard*, 2 March 1919. (I thank Stephen Ohanian for the translation of the relevant passages.)

[27] On Halil Menteşe's "warnings," see *Osmanlı Mebusan Meclisi Reisi Halil Menteşe'nin Anıları* (Istanbul: Türkiye İş Bankası Yayınları, 1986), 175; on Talat Pasha, see Johannes Lepsius, *Der Todesgang des armenischen Volkes: Bericht über das Schicksal des Armenischen Volkes in der Türkei während des Weltkrieges* (Potsdam: Der Tempelverlag, 1919), 220–22; on Enver Pasha, see DE/PA-AA/ Bo.Kons./Band 170, "Notes of Marine Attaché Humann about a Conversation with Enver," dated 6 August 1915.

[28] The date of the annulment of the agreement was 16 December 1914 (Bayur, *Türk İnkılabı Tarihi*, vol. 3, part 3, 12).

[29] Although this document has been cited or mentioned in various publications dealing with the subject, it has never been completely translated into modern Turkish. For the citations in question, see Gürün, *Ermeni Dosyası*, 277–78; and Azmi Süslü, *Ermeniler ve 1915 Tehcir Olayı* (Van: Yüzüncü

[A]s the question of reform, which is a completely internal matter of the Ottoman State, has now become an international question as a result of the intervention of foreign countries, and with some of the Ottoman provinces now passing under foreign influence, it is demanded that certain concessions [be granted] and that a special administrative organization be created. Nevertheless, since it has been seen through bitter experience that reforms and organizations that are created under foreign influence and pressure have led to the dividing and partition of the Ottoman homeland, and *while delib-erations were under way as to how to prepare and implement the means for eliminating this trouble [gaile—*meaning the Armenian problem], *which represents an important section in the list of vital questions of the Ottoman state, in a manner that is both comprehensive and absolute,* finally a part of the Armenians living in areas near the war zones collaborated with the enemy to carry out armed attacks against [our] military forces and innocent civilians within the country . . . the Government began to activate the army, which was fighting on the [various] fronts, in consultation with local officials and military commanders as to what needed to be done . . . this action was neces-sary in order to restore order in a deliberate manner and on the basis of appropriate laws and principles [etc.].[30] (italics added)

Talat often expressed similar reasoning in his discussions with foreign diplomats. In a report to Chancellor Bethmann-Hollweg on 17 June 1915, German ambassador Wangenheim stated that "it was very clear that the Armenian deportations were not being carried out simply for military purposes," and relayed the substance of a meeting between the interior minister and German consul general Mordtmann. According to the am-bassador, Talat told Dr. Mordtmann that he wished "to use the world war as a pretext for cleansing the country of its internal enemies—namely, its Christian population—without having to face the diplomatic interven-tions of foreign countries," adding that this would also be "to the advantage

---

Yıl Üniversitesi Rektörlüğü Yayını, Yayın no. 5, 1990), 110. For a lengthy excerpt (but unfortunately not the entire text) of the document in modern Turkish, see Muammer Demirel, *Birinci Dünya Har-binde*, 53.

[30] *Ati*, 24 February 1920. The key passage of the Ottoman original is: "esâslı bir suretde hal ve faslı ile külliyen izâlesi esbâbının tehiyye ve ihzârı tasavvur ve mülâhaza edilmekde iken."

of Germany, which was Turkey's ally," because "in this manner Turkey will be strengthened."[31]

In the notes on his recollections of the period, American ambassador Henry Morgenthau mentions the following conversation with Talat, which took place on 9 July 1915: "Talat said that they had discussed the matter very thoroughly and arrived at a decision to which they would adhere. When I said they would be condemned by the world, he said they would know how to defend themselves; in other words, he does not give a damn."[32]

The important passage of this official memo from Talat, which is dated 26 May 1915, is the statement, "for eliminating this trouble [the Armenian problem] . . . in a manner that is both comprehensive and absolute." However one may interpret this phrase, it is clear that the final steps toward a decisive solution were not solely connected to the contingencies of war. The matter characterized as the Armenian Question, and which Talat described as a constant "trouble" or "worry" (*gaile*), was the ultimate outcome of administrative reforms in the six eastern provinces where much of the Armenian population was concentrated; in light of the areas affected, this question came to acquire dimensions that raised the prospect of a further partitioning of the Ottoman state. In blunter terms, behind this "troubled" (worrisome) problem that required resolution lay the possibility that the Armenians would eventually attempt to establish an independent state of their own. From the Unionists' standpoint, such a possibility would have to be eliminated.

In a later cable (29 August 1915) to most of the Ottoman provinces, Talat would make this concern quite explicit: "The objective that the government expects to achieve by the expelling of the Armenians from the areas in which they live and their transportation to other appointed areas is to ensure that this community will no longer be able to undertake initiatives and actions against the government, and that they will be brought to a state in which they will be unable to pursue their national

[31] DE/PA-AA/R 14086, Report from Ambassador Wangenheim to Chancellor Bethmann-Hollweg, dated 17 June 1915.

[32] Henry Morgenthau, *United States Diplomacy on the Bosphorus: The Diaries of Ambassador Morgenthau, 1913–1916*, comp., ed., and intro. Ara Sarafian (London: Taderon Press with Gomidas Institute, 2004), 273.

aspirations related to the advocating for a[n independent] government of Armenia."[33]

THE DECISION TO ANNIHILATE IS TAKEN AFTER LONG DELIBERATIONS

There is additional evidence that the decisions taken vis-à-vis the Armenians in the spring of 1915 were the result of prolonged and careful discussion by the CUP Central Committee. According to the 1919 indictment of the former Unionist leaders in Istanbul, "the killing and annihilation of the Armenians was the result of decisions taken by the Unionist Central Committee"; moreover, these decisions were made only after "wide-ranging and in-depth deliberations." The indictment also quotes Central Committee member Dr. Nâzım as having called the Armenian Question "a problem for which a decision was reached by the Central Committee after lengthy and in-depth deliberations," and stating that "this initiative would resolve the Eastern Question."[34]

Celal, governor-general of the province of Aleppo during the deportations, published his memoirs in the Ottoman daily *Vakit* in December 1918. There, he recalled that the same statement was conveyed to him via a parliamentary deputy from Konya. He wrote,

> Upon returning from Istanbul, one of these [parliamentary] deputies relayed the greetings of an individual who was a member of the Central Committee and said, "Since the decision in this matter was arrived at by the Central Committee only after long and in-depth discussions, it would be impossible to change [it], and the deportation of the Armenians was necessary for the sake of our national ideals," and thus I should put aside my own personal consideration on this matter; finally, he said "they would get rid of me were I to

[33] BOA/DH.ŞFR, no. 55/292, Coded telegram from the Interior Ministry's General Directorate of Security to the Provinces of Hüdâvendigâr (Bursa), Ankara, Konya, İzmit, Adana, Marash, Urfa, Aleppo, (Der) Zor, Sivas, Kütahya, Karesi (Balıkesir), Niğde, Mamuretülaziz, Diyarbekır, Karahisâr-ı Sahib (Afyon Karahisar), Erzurum, and Kayseri, dated 29 August 1915. This cable was basically written in order to persuade the Germans. Talat Pasha would actually hand-deliver a German translation of the document to the German Embassy on 31 August 1915. The translation can currently be found in the German archives.

[34] *TV*, no. 3540, 5 May 1919. The trial's first session was held on 27 April 1919.

oppose their point of view on this question, and Konya would no longer have me."[35]

Yet another account corroborates Talat's letter of 26 May 1915, the indictment of the Unionist leaders, and the testimony and memoirs of Aleppo governor Celal. That the deportation of the Armenians was an attempt to find a fundamental and permanent solution to the "Eastern Question," rather than planned and implemented as a result of temporary military need, was stated in a letter by Bahaeddin Şakir (as reported by Turkish journalist and writer Ahmet Emin Yalman).[36] Şakir, whom Yalman presents as a proponent of the policy of the "general annihilation" of the Armenians, wrote, "It was clearly understood that the presence of Armenians living in the area of the Russian border constituted a great danger for the continued viability of the country. National well-being demands that everything possible be done to remove this danger."[37] Yalman added that the goal of these policies was understood and implemented by "some politicians" as "the elimination of the Armenian minority for the purpose of creating racial homogeneity in Anatolia."[38]

ARRIVING AT THE DECISION TO ANNIHILATE

As Talat Pasha claimed in the previously mentioned lengthy letter of 26 May 1915, with the war's outbreak several temporary measures were taken against Armenians; however, it subsequently became necessary to modify them in an attempt to fundamentally resolve the problems of "reform," as it has been termed above, and "the Armenian national movement for an [independent] state." These anti-Armenian measures and the motivations behind them—as they are described in Talat's aforementioned cable—stand as the clearest possible refutation of the Turkish of-

---

[35] Celal Bey, "Ermeni Vakâyi-i ve Esbâb-ı ve Tesîrâtı," *Vakit*, 12 December 1918.

[36] Another significant point is the similarities between the letter by Bahaeddin Şakir mentioned here and reproduced by Yalman, and those published letters that Aram Andonian claims were written by Şakir. See Andonian, *Memoirs of Naim Bey*, 49–52.

[37] Ahmet Emin Yalman, *Turkey in the World War* (New Haven: Yale University Press, 1930), 220. Although the author quotes Şakir's very same letter in his far more extensive Turkish-language memoirs, *Yakın Tarihte Gördüklerim ve Geçirdiklerim (1888–1918)*, vol. 1 (Istanbul: Yenilik Basımevi, 1970), 332, he does not include the accusatory expressions that are found in the English version.

[38] Ibid., 220.

ficial version of the events of 1915, which insists that the policies toward the Armenians were the result of wartime exigencies. On the contrary, Unionist policy was aimed at resolving the issue of Armenian reforms in a definitive manner.

A reading of Ottoman archival materials suggests that these early measures, such as the disarming of Armenian recruits in the Ottoman Third Army and their transfer to labor battalions, the searching of Armenian villages for weapons, and the staging of raids against these villages to appropriate food and other necessities for the war effort, might have been temporary measures rather than the first steps of a predetermined plan.[39] However, the absence of any evidence on this topic makes it necessary to refrain from speculative discussions. Without a doubt, the Unionists considered the Armenian reforms as an existential issue, and they certainly wanted to cast off the February 1914 Armenian Reform Agreement. However, considering a matter as potentially lethal is not the same thing as adopting the annihilation of a group (the Armenians) as party policy. There remains the question of linkage between the two.

Too great a focus on questions of intent—for example, "When did the intent to annihilate take form in the minds of the Unionists?"—creates a serious obstacle to understanding genocide as a political process. The search for the formulation of intent may assume an inexorable progression of events from A to Z. "This is mostly a misinterpretation of political development reconstructed with hindsight (because the end of the event is known): the persecution of German Jews at the very beginning of Hitler's regime did not in any way imply that the Auschwitz scenario was already written."[40] For this reason, it is better to think in terms of a process than a "continuum." This avoids predetermining an outcome and implies a variable dynamics of destruction that is liable to change at any point. There is also an implicit *teleology* in the former approach, which takes the last point of destruction (Auschwitz, Der Zor) as a starting point and looks backward to violent expressions in the perpetrators' early speeches and writings, treating them as a "serious declaration of intent."

[39] The measures taken against the Armenians in August 1914 have been discussed in detail elsewhere. For a more detailed discussion of the matter, see Taner Akçam, *A Shameful Act*, 140–48.

[40] Jacques Semelin, *Purify and Destroy*, 325.

Moreover, an approach that "affixes the marks of intent" hinders the understanding of historical processes. Such a view perforce attempts to understand and explain all social and political processes as the evolution of a preexisting intent, and social clashes in essence are arranged in this mold. Such an approach, aside from being teleological, does not provide correct information about the historical process under way. As an example, throughout the 1908–13 period, until they seized power through the January 1913 military coup and established a dictatorial regime, the Unionists were unable to rule alone.[41] Plagued by frequent internal divisions, they were far from giving the impression of a party settled on a unified, definite program. At times they entered into the ranks of the opposition and risked being shut down.

Moreover, the political events of the era were not experienced as an ethnic conflict between Armenians and Turks. There was no political process with Turks and their political parties on one side and Armenians and their political parties on the other. The contemporary developments were much more complicated, much more complex, as in the 1912 elections, when the CUP and the Armenian Revolutionary Federation (ARF) formed a joint coalition.[42]

Meanwhile the Freedom and Unity Party (Hürriyet ve İtilaf Fırkası), which opposed the Unionists,[43] entered into an accord with another Armenian party, the Hunchaks,[44] and the two sides announced their alliance

[41] For a general summary of political developments in the post-1908 period, see Erik Zürcher, *Turkey: A Modern History* (London: Tauris & Co. Ltd., 2005), 93–133; Feroz Ahmad, *The Committee of Union and Progress in Turkish Politics, 1908–1914* (Oxford: Clarendon Press, 1969).

[42] The Armenian Revolutionary Federation (ARF) was the most important political party of the Armenians during the period under discussion. Founded in Tiflis (Tbilisi) in 1890, it assumed the leading role in the Armenian reforms movement at the turn of the century. The relations of the CUP and the Armenian Revolutionary Federation have not been sufficiently studied. The only serious and important study on this topic is Dikran Kaligian, *Armenian Organization and Ideology under Ottoman Rule: 1908–1914* (New Brunswick, NJ: Transaction, 2009).

[43] This is a party known for its liberal views, which was created in November 1911 through the union of the parties in opposition to the CUP. For more detailed information about the party, see Ali Birinci, *Hürriyet ve İtilaf Fırkası: II. Meşrutiyet Devrinde İttihat ve Terakki'ye Karşı Çıkanlar* (Istanbul: Dergah Yayınları, 1990).

[44] The Hunchakian Party is one of the oldest political parties in Armenian history, established in 1887 in Geneva, Switzerland. For some general information about the party, see Louise Nalbandian, *The Armenian Revolutionary Movement: The Development of Armenian Political Parties through the Nineteenth Century* (Berkeley: University of California Press, 1975, third printing), 104–32.

around an eight-point common platform.[45] However, Krikor Zohrab, one of the Armenian intellectuals murdered in the summer of 1915, acted in common with another group of parliamentary deputies known as the Group of Independents (Müstakiller Grubu), and attempted to remain equally distant from the other groupings.[46] Another important fact is that the CUP went through an extremely difficult period from the spring of 1912 until the January 1913 military coup. The party was divided by internal quarrels. It turned into an opposition party, its central offices were shut down temporarily by the government, several of its founders, including Talat, were arrested, and some of its officials either hid or fled abroad.[47]

In this tangled web of political relations, which I will not go into here, the argument that the CUP had decided on a policy of annihilation and was awaiting an opportune moment to put it into practice is speculative in nature.

THE GENERAL MOBILIZATION OF AUGUST 1914 AND ITS AFTERMATH

The records of the Interior Ministry's Cipher Office show that by the time of the general mobilization of the Ottoman Army in August 1914, the leaders of the CUP had placed the Armenian population—especially in eastern Anatolia—under close supervision and monitoring. Many of these documents mention the armed Armenian gangs that were organized by the Russians and sent to the Ottoman interior as brigands and raiders; there is also much information on the actions of these gangs in the border regions. These documents make it clear that the government in Istanbul was petrified by the prospects of an Armenian uprising.

A telegram from the Interior Ministry's General Directorate of Security to the eastern provinces on 28 August 1914 informs local officials that the government

> has received completely reliable reports to the effect that the Russians have, through the assistance of the Armenians in the Caucasus,

[45] Ali Birinci, *Hürriyet ve İtilaf Fırkası*, 139–40.
[46] Ibid., 53.
[47] Tunaya, *Türkiye'de Siyasal Partiler*, vol. 3, 215–27, 422–27.

incited the Armenians among us by promises that they will hand over to them the portions of the Ottoman lands that they conquer and will ensure their independence and they [i.e., the Russians] are presently attempting to form armed gangs by sending a great many individuals in village garb into the Armenian villages. Additionally, they have brought weapons and munitions with the intent of depositing them at certain places along the border so that, should war be declared, the Armenian individuals in [our] army should go over, with the weapons, to the Russian side; should our army [meet with success and] advance, [the Armenians] should remain quiet and compliant, but if our army should retreat [these Armenians] will then arm themselves and, forming themselves into armed gangs, go into action against us.[48]

And Istanbul is proposing various countermeasures to deal with this situation (more on this below).

The actions of voluntary Armenian units along the border were already being closely monitored. Regular reports were sent to the capital on their activities; in mid-August a cable to the eastern provinces contained the following information:

The Armenians in the Caucasus—especially the members of the armed gangs—have sent their families to Yerevan and all of the gang members themselves in Erzurum have also been carting off their entire families in the direction of Russia and Yerevan; and Armenians in Russia are harassing and humiliating [*tahkîr*] the Muslims there. They have said that they are going to take revenge for [the events of] 1894–1895 and are celebrating [their expected victory] and holding banquets for and giving gifts to the leading members of the General Government of the Caucasus.

The telegram then requests that the local officials report on whether such actions as these "are simply of a local or more overall character." Ad-

---

[48] BOA/DH.ŞFR, no. 45/115, Coded telegram from the Interior Ministry's General Directorate of Security to the Provinces of Van, Bitlis, Mamuretülaziz, Adana, Diyarbekır, and Sivas, dated 28 August 1914. Another coded cable, sent on 24 September 1914 by Third Army commander general Hasan İzzet Pasha to the Ottoman High Command makes it clear that these orders were also distributed to various units in the army. See *Askeri Tarih Belgeleri Dergisi* 32, no. 83 (March 1983): 7, Doc. no. 1894.

ditionally, it is requested that said officials "investigate and report back soon . . . on how many Armenian families have as of now left for the Caucasus and whether or not there is such a revolutionary movement or sensibility as this is present among the Armenians living there or if it is limited [to those mentioned]."[49] A telegram sent from the province of Erzurum on 17 August shows that detailed replies to these requests were sent from the relevant provinces. It reports that

> in light of the responses received from the various locales within the province, [it appears that] no Armenian families from [said] areas have recently gone to Russia; instead, from the beginning of June until 20 July only 101 men and women from 23 households have gone from the aforementioned country of the Erzurum [Province], and from 20 July until now some 15 persons from six households; additionally, in the past two months the members of two households from the county of Eleşkird have gone to Russia with passports, and only to visit, so at present there is no revolt or uprising or revolutionary ferment whatsoever and the friendly relations and coexistence with the Muslim [population] is continuing.[50]

Another coded telegram, sent on 8 October 1914 by Trebizond governor Cemal Azmi, reports the number of Armenian volunteers along the border who are being armed by the Russians and lists the areas in which they were in action.[51]

Some telegrams communicate the movements of some Armenian volunteers along the border and their resultant skirmishes with the Ottoman Army. A telegram of 3 September 1914 reveals that as the result of one such clash, one Armenian was killed and four were captured.[52] Other telegrams concern Armenians fleeing to Russia or joining voluntary

[49] BOA/DH.ŞFR, no. 44/43, Coded telegram from the Interior Ministry's General Directorate of Security to the Provinces of Van, Bitlis, Erzurum, Mamuretülaziz, Trebizond, Diyarbekır, Sivas, and Adana, dated August, 1914. (By looking at the dates of the previous and succeeding documents/ telegrams, it can safely be concluded that the date of the document must have been between 15–18 August 1915.)

[50] BOA/DH.EUM, 2. Şube, no. 1/39, Coded telegram from the acting governor of the Province of Erzurum, Cemal, to the Interior Ministry, dated 30 August 1914.

[51] *Askeri Tarih Belgeleri Dergisi* 31, no. 81 (December 1982): 35, Doc. no. 1809.

[52] BOA/DH.EUM.EMN, no. 30/12, Telegram from Erzurum Province to the Fourth Branch of the Department of General Correspondence of the Interior Ministry, received 3 September 1914.

Russian paramilitary units, particularly in villages along the border. A communication sent from the province of Erzurum to the headquarters of the Third Army on 31 October 1914 reports that in the district of Beyazıd and its environs there were "a great many Armenians; both those who were in the army as well as those who were in the villages have fled to Russia with the assistance of certain Kurdish guides with the intent of joining the armed gang in İkdir [Iğdır] formed by an individual named Surin."[53]

Bulgaria and Romania formed important bases for the creation of Armenian volunteer units, with the open support of Russia. The Ottoman embassies in Sofia and Bucharest, and consulates in the region, followed these activities closely and sent detailed information to Istanbul, including the number of people joining the volunteer units. For example, on 20 November 1914 the ambassador reported from Sofia that "during the last two weeks the greater part of over six hundred Armenians who are Ottoman subjects in Ruscuk and have reached the age of military service were gradually sent by the Russian consul in the aforementioned city to Russia, and they will enter the Ottoman lands as raiding bands [çete]."[54]

A cable sent out to a great many provinces and districts on 21 November 1914 indicates that in the very first weeks of the war the Ottoman government was already requesting lists of those of its subjects who had voluntarily gone to Russia, as well as the members of their families. In a telegram to the provinces in question, the Interior Ministry asked for "a report of the Armenians who have voluntarily gone to Russia, along with the identities of their family members who still remain in the areas [within the Ottoman Empire]."[55] Istanbul also took pains to stay aware of the numbers of Armenians crossing the border.[56] As a matter of fact, in reply to

---

[53] *Askeri Tarih Belgeleri Dergisi* 32, no. 83 (March 1983): 27, Doc. no. 1899.

[54] BOA/HR.SYS, no. 2871/1-13, Report from the ambassador at Sofia to grand vizier and minister of foreign affairs Said Halim Pasha, dated 20 November 1914. For a report from the Bucharest Embassy, which arrived on 21 December 1914, see Genelkurmay Başkanlığı [The Presidential Office of the General Staff], *Arşiv Belgeleriyle Ermeni Faaliyetleri, 1914–1918*, vol. 1 (Ankara: Genelkurmay Basım Evi, 2005), 49–50.

[55] BOA/DH.ŞFR, no. 47/107, Coded telegram from the Interior Ministry's General Directorate of Security to the Provinces of Sivas, Trebizond, Van, Bitlis, and Erzurum, dated 21 November 1915.

[56] BOA/HR.SYS, no. 2879/19, doc. no. 2, Telegram from the Foreign Ministry's General Directorate of Political Affairs to the Interior Ministry, dated 25 April 1915.

this letter, the embassy in Sofia reported that the consulate was preparing a detailed list of the identities of those Armenians who were Ottoman subjects.[57]

The attacks against the postal roads, the cutting of telegraph lines, attacks on police stations, and other hostile actions were duly and regularly reported to the capital. For instance, a "secret and urgent" cable sent by interior minister Talat to the province of Van on 20 December 1914 reveals that on the previous day, Cevded, the governor of Van, had forwarded information to the effect that "the telegraph lines between Reşâdiye and Vostan and between Vostan and Van had been cut by the Armenians and that the commander of the police station at Pelli had been murdered by these [same Armenians]; and serious clashes had begun to occur between the Armenians and the gendarmes in the retinue of the district official of Gevaş who were in the area."[58]

It should be added that in some instances the reports arriving in Istanbul about "postal [routes] being attacked by bandits . . . were without any foundation in truth,"[59] and that those attacking the Ottoman postal vehicles and officials were actually military deserters. These former soldiers would go around in mixed groups that might consist of Armenians, Greeks, and Muslims of all stripes. Moreover, in most cases the attacks had no political motivation whatever. For example, in a cipher telegram on 21/22 October 1914, Cemal Azmi, the governor of Trebizond, reported on the identities of the group responsible for attacking an Erzurum postal wagon near Gümüşhane: "of the brigands who attacked the Erzurum postal wagon and who are [approximately] 20 in number, the majority are understood to be Armenian and the minority belong to the Muslim and Greek communities; three of them are [former soldiers] belonging to regular units, and the remainder to the Baybur[t] labor battalion."[60] Some

[57] BOA/HR.SYS, no. 2871/1-13, Report from the embassy at Sofia to grand vizier and minister of foreign affairs Said Halim Pasha, 3 December 1914.

[58] BOA/DH.ŞFR, no. 48/85, Coded telegram from interior minister Talat to Cevded, governor of Van, dated 20 December 1914. For similar telegrams, see BOA/DH.ŞFR, nos. 48/7, 48/182, and 48/188.

[59] BOA/DH.EUM, 2. Şube, no. 2/40/2, Coded telegram from Van governor, Tahsin, to the Interior Ministry, dated 21 October 1914.

[60] BOA/DH.EUM, 2. Şube, no. 2/33/1-2-3, Coded telegram from Trebizond governor, Cemal Azmi, to the Interior Ministry, dated 21/22 October 1914.

of the culprits had been arrested and confessed their guilt.[61] Additional examples can be given of similar attacks, such as one carried out "against the Mosul [to Nusaybin] postal route . . . some five hours from Nusaybin . . . by as many as 20 Yezîdîs" wherein "the wagon driver was beaten and his mail pouches seized."[62]

As the Ottoman war effort turned progressively worse, the problem of armed gangs, which were formed by members of every ethnic and religious group in Anatolia—and in particular, by military deserters—gradually began to assume major proportions for the Ottoman government.[63] Military deserters favored mountainous regions so that they would not be easily caught or killed. Their concentrations in these areas reached such proportions that in order to preserve security, gendarmerie or army units could not depart from their locations, and this became a negative factor that affected the course of the war. For example, a message arriving from Dersim on 20 January 1915 stated that "it is understood from the communication taking place . . . [from] the Eleventh Elaziz Army Corps Command that the Dersim Mobile Gendarmerie Battalion, which was left for the preservation of peace of the provincial district, also will be sent to the site of war." It went on to report that as there were "numerous Muslim and non-Muslim military deserters" in the region, even the news of the military unit's departure from the region led to an increase in the attacks of the deserters on the populace, so that appropriate measures were immediately requested.[64] In some situations, the reports of such activities from the

[61] Report from the Third Army acting field inspector (*Üçüncü Ordu Menzil Müfettiş Vekili*) to the Third Army Command in Erzurum, dated 9/10 November 1914, in *Askeri Tarih Belgeleri Dergisi* 32, no. 83 (March 1983): 31, Doc. no. 1900. The colonel who conducted the investigation upon which the report is based also provides the individual names of the apprehended suspects.

[62] BOA/DH.ŞFR, no. 51/2, Coded telegram from interior minister Talat to the Province of Diyarbekır, dated 14 March 1915.

[63] Military deserters were a serious issue during World War I, and by the later phases of the war, their numbers attained a proportion of nearly one-half the regular army. A work relying on sources from the Turkish army's general staff gives a figure of five hundred thousand deserters, and this number alone is sufficient to indicate the seriousness of the matter (Edward Erickson, *Ordered to Die: A History of the Ottoman Army in the First World War* [Westport, CT: Greenwood Press, 2001], 243).

[64] BOA/DH.EUM, 2. Şube, no. 4/60/8, Cipher telegram from Dersim to the Cipher Office of the Interior Ministry, dated 20 January 1915. On the question of security created by military deserters during World War I, see Mehmet Beşikçi, "Birinci Dünya Savaşı'nda Devlet İktidarı ve İç Güvenlik: Asker Kaçakları Sorunu ve Jandarmanın Yeniden Yapılandırılması," in *Türkiye'de Ordu, Devlet ve Güvenlik Siyaseti*, comp. Evren Balta Paker and İsmet Akça (Istanbul: Bilgi Üniversitesi Yayınları, 2010), 147–74.

provinces forced Istanbul to send back queries asking, "Is the aforementioned armed gang a Muslim, Armenian or Greek gang? Investigate and report on the nationalities [of its members]."[65]

In a 30 December 1914 "secret and urgent" telegram to the province of Van, interior minister Talat takes the province's governor to task for having failed to enact harsh measures against the gangs of brigands in his region. "Although it would be possible to fundamentally root out and eliminate [such gangs] with [a series of] decisive and powerful strikes," says Talat, "the governor has not done so, instead contenting himself with ineffective measures such as [forming and] dispatching an investigatory and advisory delegation and sending out parliamentary deputies [to question the villagers], which is a very weak and ineffective measure." Such measures, the interior minister goes on, are the equivalent of allowing the escape of "murderers, of armed gangs who are known to have foreign Armenians within their ranks."[66]

It was not only Armenian volunteers who were active in the region. Ottoman forces also clashed with various Kurdish tribes that were collaborating with Russia, especially in the vicinity of Van. In a coded cable to the office of the provincial governor on 13 November 1914, the Security Directorate mentions the "reports from the province of Erzurum that assaults [carried out] by Abdürrezzak and his accomplices on the border [near] Van were successfully repulsed," and requests further details of the clashes and their outcome.[67]

In order to complete the picture it must be added as an aside that violence in the Caucasus and the province of Van was not the sole domain of Armenian armed volunteer groups. The Ottoman government, along with the Germans, was also very active in the region. After the general mobilization of 2 August 1914, the CUP reshaped the SO in a way "that would facilitate our army's actions on enemy soil, whether we entered the world war or not. On the outbreak of the war, the irregular groups, which were to be armed through the Special Organization, would carry out raids

[65] BOA/DH.ŞFR, no. 57/85, Coded telegram from the Interior Ministry's General Directorate of Security to the Provincial District of Canik, dated 23 October 1915.

[66] BOA/DH.ŞFR, no. 48/220, Coded telegram from interior minister Talat to Cevded, governor of the Province of Van, dated 30 December 1914.

[67] BOA/DH.ŞFR, no. 47/2, Coded telegram from the Interior Ministry's General Directorate of Security to the Province of Van, dated 14 November 1914.

against enemy territory."[68] These special units would be active primarily in the Caucasus and Lake Van areas, where they would operate with the intention of contributing to "Islamic unity and Turkish nationalism, which related to uniting Turks outside of Turkey."[69] The SO had a domestic task as well: "there are individuals inside the country to be eliminated. We are acting according to this point of view."[70] The "individuals" were the Armenians. As a result of these decisions the Ottoman government sent its special gangs across the border into the Caucasus and Iran.[71] The plan involved provoking revolts in the Caucasus, Iran, and India against the English and the Russians, and inciting them to enter the war.[72] It can readily be understood from the existing papers of the Interior Ministry's Cipher Office that the Ottoman leaders had been pursuing an aggressive policy toward Russia, especially in the Caucasus. The relations between the SO and the Ottoman Interior Ministry will be examined later, but for now let it suffice to provide a few examples concerning armed activities on the border near Van.

The first is a cable sent to the province of Van on 6 September 1914 instructing the governor's office that the problem "should be resolved personally." "Our political situation is now becoming more secure and [based] on surer foundations," it states. "We have reached understandings with the Bulgarians on all points. The armed gangs should have already completely organized themselves within Iran. The order to go into action will be given separately."[73] Likewise, these armed gangs would then go to Iran and begin their activities there. It should be noted that the Ottoman government was neutral and had not entered the war officially as of early September 1914.

A report from Cevded Bey, dated 17 October 1914, and sent by coded cable, contains detailed information about such cross-border incursions into Russia:

---

[68] A. Mil, "Umumi Harpte Teşkilat-ı Mahsusa," part 11, *Vakit*, 2 November 1933.

[69] Ibid.

[70] Mil, "Umumi Harpte," part 13, 15 November 1933.

[71] For detailed information on this subject, see Taner Akçam, *A Shameful Act*, 130–40.

[72] Wolf Dieter Bihl, *Die Kaukasus-Politik der Mittelmächte, Teil I: Ihre Basis in der Orient-Politik und ihre Aktionen, 1914–1917* (Vienna, Cologne, and Graz: Böhlau, 1974), 4.

[73] BOA/DH.ŞFR, no. 44/201, Coded telegram from the Interior Ministry's General Directorate of Security to the Province of Van, dated 6 September 1914.

[F]or one week now armed gangs, border units and individual volunteers from the [Kurdish] tribes have been clashing with enemy forces consisting of approximately 2,000 foot soldiers and an entire battery of horse-drawn artillery in and around Iran's Selmas region and between Cahari and Hanasorı. It has been learned that in the violent clashes that took place throughout the day yesterday and on into the evening enemy casualties have consisted of two officers and as many as 100 recruits. From our side there have been nine killed, one of whom was an officer, and twenty wounded.[74]

These gangs, in which Kurdish tribesmen and Ottoman soldiers operated together, attacked Christian villages and perpetrated massacres. In a cable sent to the provinces of Van and Mosul on 11 October 1914, the events of the previous month were recounted:

[T]he Ottoman reserves, led by a[n officer of the rank of] captain, carried out operations in the areas of Beykik Masforan and Seros Sartik, both in their disguises and in their military uniforms, and after crossing the border in the area around Rumiyye, the Ottoman Kurds returned to Ottoman territory with the spoils and booty that they had acquired; the cavalry units of Perestanı[?] Koçzâ and Rüstem Bey left Ottoman territory for Terceder after looting Barad, and again on 19 September the Kurds attacked and looted Kevhir, in which the Mavana Christians are settled, and, passing on to the most barbaric acts and deeds against the defenseless Christians, [they] tortured to death approximately ten people, both men and women, before being driven off.[75]

The cable makes clear that the report of these deeds came from the Russian Consulate and that the Ottoman central government was asking its own local authorities to authenticate the information received. The following day (18 October 1914), the Russian Embassy in Istanbul delivered an oral protest to the Ottoman government on account of the great number of cross-border attacks. In this protest, the Russian ambassador

[74] BOA/DH.EUM, 2. Şube, no. 2/72/2, Coded telegram from Cevded Bey, the governor of the Province of Van to the Interior Ministry, dated 17 October 1914.
[75] BOA/DH.ŞFR, no. 45/242, Coded telegram from the Interior Ministry's General Directorate of Security to the Provinces of Van and Mosul, dated 11 October 1914.

recounted seven separate attacks that had been made between 20 August and 11 September alone.[76]

As should be clear from all these documents, there was already an undeclared war in the Caucasus between the Ottoman Empire and Russia at least as early as September 1914. Both Istanbul and St. Petersburg were following policies based on exploiting the region's various ethnoreligious groups and using them to attack one another, even organizing their members into special units for the purpose of carrying out these assaults. As the Turkish historian of the period Yusuf Hikmet Bayur has stated, by the months of September and October, "a real war had already begun on the Ottoman border."[77]

INITIAL MEASURES BETWEEN AUGUST 1914 AND MARCH 1915

The available Cipher Office documents, including a number of cables sent in August 1914, make it clear that even before the world war was officially declared, local Ottoman officials had been informed of the activities of Russian Armenians in the border region between the two empires. Two noteworthy aspects of these events were the countermeasure of ordering that every non-Muslim who crossed the border be killed and the decision to form militia units from among the Muslims who did not serve in the regular Ottoman Army in order to counter the actions of voluntary Armenian gangs.

In the aforementioned telegram of 28 August 1914, the Ottoman Security Directorate calls for the following measures to be taken against the actions of Russian Armenians in the border areas: "[T]hose non-Muslim individuals who cross the border without a passport in hand [are to be] arrested and those found to be attempting to bring across weapons and ammunition are to be summarily executed." Additionally, "those Muslim populations [found in the Third Army's area of jurisdiction] who do not serve in the army are to remain in their villages and made into an orga-

[76] BOA/DH.EUM, 2. Şube, no. 2/34/8, Transcription of verbal note by the Russian Embassy (in Istanbul) delivered by the Interior Ministry of the Sublime Porte to the Imperial Foreign Ministry, dated 18 October 1914.

[77] Bayur, *Türk İnkilabı Tarihi*, vol. 3, part 1, 226.

nized body of militia in case of need."[78] The telegram indicates that these measures were originally sent by "the command of the Imperial Third Army to the Province of Erzurum." The ministry repeats that this information was very important and that the provinces must carry out investigations on these issues. It advises that the provinces "through consultations with the commander of the army corps act in the same fashion, and send information here about the steps which are being taken."[79]

Another measure that was taken against both those fleeing Ottoman soil for the Russian Empire and those entering from Russia to carry out paramilitary actions was violent reprisals against their families who stayed behind and against villagers found to be harboring such fugitives, as well as their deportation and the destruction of their villages. A document from 1 October 1914 makes it clear that a circular had been sent on 23–24 September as to the steps to be taken against fugitives. After stating that "it has been reported that the Russians have armed Russian and Ottoman Armenians and Greeks in the Caucasus and formed them into armed gangs, and then have sent them across the border in order to increase the numbers of these organizations in Ottoman territory . . . and this has increased the number of Armenians deserting from [Ottoman military] units," the communiqué directs, "I have presented you on 23/24 September 1914 with circular no. 347 on the measures that are to be taken in this regard. Additionally, harsh measures are to be taken regarding the families of deserters and traitors and villagers harboring [members of] armed gangs are to be severely punished; [the population of] any village in which an armed gang is encountered is to be dispersed and the reasons for this action to be [publicly] made known."[80]

Circular number 347, dated 23/24 September, which is mentioned in this document, repeats the information found in the government's telegram of 29 August 1914 cited above. However, it contains one important additional decision: the Armenian soldiers in the army, "to the extent possible being separated from the non-combattants, in the event of a movement against us will be immediately suppressed with violence,

---

[78] BOA/DH.ŞFR, no. 45/115, Coded telegram from the Interior Ministry's General Directorate of Security to the Provinces of Van, Bitlis, Mamuretülaziz, Adana, Diyarbekır, and Sivas, dated 28 August 1914.

[79] Ibid.

[80] *Askeri Tarih Belgeleri Dergisi* 31, no. 81 (December 1982): 39, Doc. no. 1810.

and the audacious ones will be killed."[81] The order is clear—in any case, the first ones to be killed will be the Armenians who were enrolled in the army.

The first of the decisions to be put into practice was the formation of Muslim militia, a process that began within the structure of the Third Army. In a cable sent to the office of the lieutenant governor of Erzincan and officials of the provincial districts of Bayburt, Tercan, and Kığı, for instance, it was stated that "at the suggestion of the Third Army commander, an Islamic militia unit was formed under the leadership of Dr. Bahaeddin Şakir Bey."[82] Such units were to carry out operations inside the Caucasus and Iran. Germans were also involved in the operation of these gangs. For example, the gangs active in the Kars-Artvin region were under the direction of the German colonel Stange.[83] An additional bit of information is that some governors opposed the idea of establishing militias directed against the Armenians, and shared their concerns on this topic with the government.[84]

Labor battalions of Armenian soldiers began to be organized. It is necessary to add that this procedure applied to all Christian soldiers but included only a certain portion of them as needed for road construction. The pertinent decision was made when military mobilization was

---

[81] For this circular, see *Askeri Tarih Belgeleri Dergisi* 32, no. 83 (March 1983): 7, Doc. no. 1894.

[82] Mil, "Umumi Harpte," part 13, 15 November 1933.

[83] There are two primary sources about Stange's involvement in the SO. His involvement is first attested to by Yusuf Riza, the commander of the SO units headquartered in Trebizond and a cohort of Stange, who testified at the Istanbul Courts-Martial, which were held between 1919 and 1921 in Istanbul. After stating that he worked closely with Stange, he declared that "we were handling our communications through the medium of Stange's cipher" (*TV*, 15 May 1919, no. 3549, 8 May 1919, fourth session). Second, Bahaeddin Şakir, the operational chief of the SO, in one of his cipher telegrams sent to the chiefs of SO units operating in the area of Trebizond, declared, "you, along with your troops, are subject to the authority of Stange" (Mil, "Umumi Harpte," part 94, 6 February 1934), thereby clearly confirming Stange's involvement in the SO operations.

[84] BOA/DH.EUM, 2. Şube, no. 2/32/1, Coded telegram from Azmi Bey, the governor of Konya, to the Interior Ministry, dated 21 October 1914: "I have learned that İzzet Pasha, the commander of the army corps in Erzurum, has communicated orders to the various army units that they should remain alert that members of the Armenian population within Ottoman lands might revolt because of the incitements of Armenian revolutionary committees, and should prevent attacks, if necessary, by protecting the Muslim population and so forth, and that these instructions have also also circulated widely all the way down the chain of command, by means of a general communiqué, to the heads of the various branches of the military recruiting offices. Even if these reports are indeed reliable, I see the amount of damage that their distribution in such a fashion, and the notice of Muslim people surrendering and so forth reaching the people, are going to cause, as inexplicable."

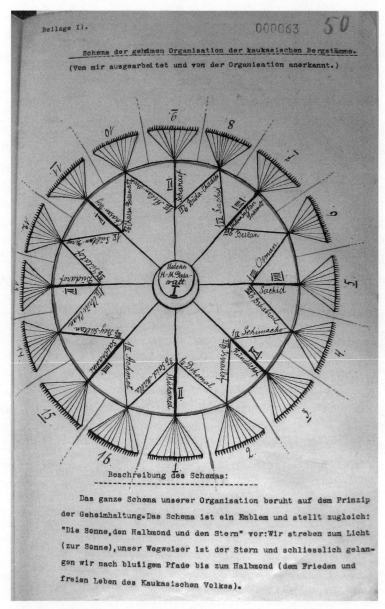

Figure 5.1. German Archive Document. See Chart of Secret Organization established by German and Ottoman military in Caucasus. *Source*: DE/PA-AA/R 21016, Der Weltkrieg 1914, Geheime Akten, Report from Usden H. M. Gasawatt to German Headquarters, 13 December 1915. My special thanks to Mehmet Uluışık for providing this document.

declared.[85] Meanwhile, Armenian and other Christian soldiers continued to serve in combat units. Lieutenant Commander Hans Humann reported on 16 October 1914 that the labor battalions comprised of Greeks and Armenians were formed in October 1914.[86]

Following the government's decision of 28 August 1914, it seems that a second decision was made at the beginning of September. On 6 September 1914 in a cable sent by interior minister Talat Pasha to a number of provinces and districts and marked "confidential and to be taken care of personally [bi'z-zat hal olunacakdır]," the officials addressed are requested to make preparations to arrest those who are known to have been among the leaders of Armenian political and subversive activities, as an order to that effect would be forthcoming: "[It is requested that the practice be implemented of] following and monitoring the behavior and movements of people there from among the leaders of Armenian political party and committee leaders who do not refrain from the dissemination of sedition and abominable deeds against Ottomanism and who for a long time have pursued political aspirations, and when necessary, action be in conformity to the communications that are occurring."[87]

On the same date, another telegram was sent to the provincial district government (mutasarrıflık) of Canik (today's Samsun), the contents of which are quite important: "The transportation of women and children to the interior, especially from the provinces on the Black Sea coast, cannot at this moment be a subject of discussion. So that there will be no cause for confusion in the future, the requisite measures must be prearranged and determined now, but while there is no clear need, it is necessary to take no action, and not allow opportunities for excitement to occur."[88] It is not clear

[85] BOA/DH.ŞFR, no. 43/214, Coded telegram from the Interior Ministry's Department of General Correspondence to the Provinces of Edirne, Erzurum, Adana, Ankara, Aydın, Bitlis, Basra, Baghdad, Beirut, Aleppo, Hüdâvendigâr (Bursa), Diyarbekir, Damascus, Sivas, Trebizond, Kastamonu, Konya, Mamuretülaziz, Mosul, and Van, and to the Provincial Districts of Urfa, İzmit, Bolu, Canik, Çatalca, Zor, Karesi (Balıkesir), Jerusalem, and Kale-i Sultaniye, dated 10 August 1914.

[86] Christopher Dinkel, "Der Einfluss hoher deutscher Offiziere im Osmanischen Reich auf die zum Völkermord und den Armeniern führenden Massnahmen: Ratgeber und/oder Vollzugsgehilfen," unpublished manuscript, 38.

[87] BOA/DH.ŞFR, no. 44/200, Coded telegram from interior minister Talat to the Provinces of Edirne, Erzurum, Adana, Bitlis, Van, Hüdâvendigâr (Bursa), Aleppo, Sivas, Mamuretülaziz, and Diyarbekır, and to the Provincial Districts of İzmit and Canik, dated 6 September 1914.

[88] BOA/DH.ŞFR, no. 45/206, Coded telegram from Interior Ministry's General Security Directorate to the Provincial District of Canik, dated 6 September 1914.

whether the telegram refers to Greeks or Armenians, but as the directive was composed together with another command issued the same day, the probability that Armenians are intended is extremely high. In any case, considering that the Ottomans have yet to enter the war as of early September, the deportation of women and children separately from men to the interior of the country is more than an idea: it already exists as a concrete political alternative, the implementation of which may be required.[89]

The first conclusion that can be drawn from the documents above is that the civil and military authorities appear to have made the first serious decisions concerning the Armenians as of the beginning of September. It was decided that the families of military deserters and those who hid "armed gang members" in their homes would be punished, and that labor battalions of Armenian soldiers and Muslim militia would be formed. The military authorities and the SO seem to have taken the responsibility for these matters. As for the civil authorities, they planned to keep Armenian notables under close surveillance and were prepared to arrest them, if necessary, upon an order that would be sent in the future.[90]

An Interior Ministry telegram to Erzurum of 10 October 1914 appears to pertain to the execution of these orders. It indicates that "raids and forced searches" had begun to be carried out against Armenians in the region. Local officials were "to content [themselves] for the time being with this and to forgo further pressure and investigations," while "nevertheless remaining vigilant and not tolerating further Armenian incitements or provocations."[91] Likewise, Lieutenant Commander Hans Humann reported that "extensive measures for the surveillance of the Armenian Patriarchate, Armenian leaders, and suspicious Armenian people" were under way from the beginning of November.[92]

In the same vein, at the outbreak of war additional plans were already in place to deport or exile the employees of foreign organizations that served

---

[89] It would not be correct to claim that the statements in the document applied to Muslim women and children. The Ottoman state had not entered the war, nor was the probability of an occupation of Samsun, the place to which the order had been sent, on the horizon. In addition, it would be strange to even think of Muslim families being separated from their males and deported.

[90] Erdal Aydoğan, İttihat ve Terakki'nin, 66.

[91] BOA/DH.ŞFR, no. 45/237, Coded telegram from the Interior Ministry's General Directorate of Security to the Province of Erzurum, dated 10 October 1914.

[92] Dinkel, "Der Einfluss," 38.

the Ottoman Armenians, especially in eastern Anatolia: "It is foreseen that in the event of a war, the functionaries of foreign institutions, who are quite numerous in the eastern provinces, and especially all those who engage in providing education and instruction to Armenians, would be detained and transported en masse to areas far away from the war zones where they would be forced to remain and reside." Local officials are asked for "their opinions in this regard" and to investigate and report "as to what, if any, foreign institutions are present in your [respective] province[s], what manner of and how many functionaries they have, and where it would be appropriate to [re]settle them."[93]

To judge from the wording of three cables, November was an important month for decisions about the Armenians. The first telegram, sent to Erzurum on 18 November, reveals that an overall decision on the Armenian situation was imminent. From Erzurum it was demanded that "you act in accordance with the exigencies of your area . . . with measures as befits a ruler, until definite instructions concerning the Armenians are given."[94] Another cable of similar content was sent to the province of Van on 29 November 1914: "Until firm and concise orders are given in regard to the Armenians, those things that local conditions make necessary are to be implemented and carried out in a dominating and controlling manner."[95] The third measure was to confiscate the devices used by Armenians to communicate with one another and with parties abroad. A cable from the Security Directorate to the provincial authorities in Van, for instance, inquires as to the results of a raid to seize a radio transmitter/ telegraph machine at the Armenian school in Van.[96]

What all of these documents clearly show is the following reality: by August 1914, the Unionist leaders were already in the process of deciding

[93] BOA/DH.ŞFR, no. 46/119, Coded telegram from the Interior Ministry's General Directorate of Security to the Provinces of Erzurum, Trebizond, Van, Bitlis, Mamuretülaziz, Diyarbekır, and Mosul, dated 31 October 1914.

[94] BOA/DH.ŞFR, no. 46/303. Coded telegram from the Interior Minister to the Province of Erzurum, dated 18 November 1914. The telegram ends in a strange way with the following words: "The performing of Muhiddin's hernia operation has been delayed somewhat. If you desire somebody else, I will send [him]."

[95] BOA/DH.ŞFR, no. 47/236, Coded telegram from the Interior Ministry's General Directorate of Security to the Province of Van, dated 29 November 1914.

[96] BOA/DH.ŞFR, no. 47/60, Coded telegram from the Interior Ministry's General Directorate of Security to the Province of Van, dated 17 November 1914.

current and future policy toward the Ottoman Armenians. The primary targets of this policy were political groups and circles thought to be connected with Russia, and in particular the probable aid they could give to Armenian volunteer units. Some of the decisions, such as the dismissal and deportation of government officials and others, were imminent, and to this end, local officials were already under orders to make the "necessary preparations" for an expected second round of instructions from the capital. By this time, also, the transfer of women and children from the shores of the Black Sea to the interior probably had been decided upon (or could be at any moment), but the execution of this measure was not yet desired. The government was girding itself to "give firm and concise orders" in regard to the Armenians.

From a secret order cabled by Talat Pasha to the provinces of Erzurum, Van, and Bitlis on 27 December 1914, one can infer that some decisions had been made earlier that month in Istanbul. Talat's call for the termination of all Armenian government officials in the provinces reflects an escalated stage of development:

> Since it was necessary to terminate the employment of the police commissioner and officials, who are members of the Armenian community and were likely, on account of their positions, [to be] instruments of evil and intrigue [it is requested that] the [official] documents [of appointment] of those in whom, having been earlier identified in this manner, no confidence remains, and for whom no [administrative] obstacle can be foreseen in the revoking of their documents, be revoked by the local administration. In the event that difficulties arise in the performing of such actions, the provinc[ial officials] should send [these people] to the far-off areas of the province, force them to resign, and revoke their [official] documents. If this proves unworkable or inconvenient, [local authorities] should send a list of these persons' names so that they can be sent off by [the officials] here to other provinces.[97]

Another source confirms that decisions were made in December 1914. Lieutenant Commander Hans Humann reported on 30 December that a

[97] BOA/DH.ŞFR, no. 48/166, Coded telegram from the Interior Ministry's General Directorate of Security to the Provinces of Erzurum, Van, and Bitlis, dated 27 December 1914.

decision had been made "when [if?] necessary to form a militia which at any time is capable of taking action against the Christian elements of the Triple Entente and also against the opposition in Turkish politics."[98]

As these initial decisions about the Armenians were being made, the course of the war was also changing, and not in the Ottomans' favor. They were defeated on two fronts: Sarıkamış (December–January 1915) at the hands of the Russians, and Egypt-Sinai (February 1915) by the British. The noose was tightening around Istanbul.

[98] Hans Humann, "Vertrauliche Mitteilung," 30 December 1914, in Yale University Library, Ernst Jäckh Papers, Group No. 467, Box 1, Folder 19.

SIX   FINAL STEPS IN THE DECISION-MAKING PROCESS

The battle of Sarıkamış (January 1915) was a complete disaster for the Ottoman Army, which lost, by its own count, more than sixty thousand soldiers, most of whom froze to death in the snows of the Caucasus Mountains. Along with this great loss, many soldiers deserted from the army and, in order to survive, turned to brigandage.[1] Another setback, though perhaps not of the same magnitude, was experienced in Egypt, when Cemal Pasha's Fourth Army was seriously defeated by the English in February 1915 in what became known as the First Canal Expedition. Meanwhile, the plan to get the Muslims who were living in Egypt and India to revolt against the English, which was seen as a condition for a successful expedition to Egypt by Cemal Pasha, achieved nothing.[2] The SO units, on which great hopes were placed, were unsuccessful in the areas of the Caucasus and Van, and they began to turn into a problem for the Ottoman Army.[3]

The fear that the English were going to land somewhere in the İskenderun region, and following this, the commencement of a great naval movement in order to seize Istanbul via Çanakkale, led the Unionists to believe that the end of the empire was certainly at hand. Almost everyone believed that the capture of Istanbul was imminent. At the main trial of Unionist leaders after the war, Cevat testified that "it wasn't known in what sort of condition Istanbul would be eight hours hence."[4] The 259-day battle of Gallipoli for Istanbul was an "inferno,"[5] a "ritual of fire and death."[6]

[1] Mareşal Fevzi Çakmak, *Birinci Dünya Savaşında Doğu Cephesi* (Ankara: Genelkurmay Basımevi, 2005), 73–74.

[2] On Cemal Pasha's Canal Expedition, see Nevzat Artuç, *Cemal Pasha: Askeri ve Siyasi Hayatı* (Ankara: Türk Tarih Kurumu, 2008), 219–30.

[3] Akçam, *A Shameful Act*, 137–42.

[4] Fifth session, *Takvim-i Vekayi (hereafter TV)*, no. 3554, 14 May 1919.

[5] Tarık Zafer Tunaya, *Türkiye'de Siyasal Partiler*, vol. 3, 514.

[6] Şevket Süreyya Aydemir, *Makedonya'dan Ortaasya'ya Enver Paşa*, vol. 3 (Istanbul: Remzi Kitabevi, 1972), 228.

Every one of those 259 days was a back-and-forth struggle between death and resurrection.

The first deportation decision was made under these circumstances. The evacuation of Armenians from certain regions due to military and political reasons presaged another important turning point. As will be seen in greater detail later, the fact that the European states were at war played an important role in these deportations, which were carried out first in Dörtyol and then in Zeytun, both in the region of Cilicia. While events in Zeytun were taking place at the beginning of March 1915, a telegram sent from Istanbul to the Fourth Army Command spoke of "the need, during a time like this when the European states are busy, to punish ... the Armenians." But the telegram concluded, "at this point it is evident that such a venture is not going to be suitable."[7] The Unionists believed that the war created favorable conditions for them, but the proper time had not yet arrived.

THE DEFEAT AT SARIKAMIŞ: A TURNING POINT

The disastrous Ottoman defeat at Sarıkamış, and the Entente's attempt—albeit unsuccessful—to force the Dardanelles in February (as a prelude to the Gallipoli landing two months later), played a major role in bringing about a transformation, as the Ottomans increasingly saw themselves as beset by dangers from all sides. On the Russian front in particular, where the Ottoman forces faced a series of defeats in rapid succession, increasing blame was heaped on Armenian militias, who were said to be acting as a fifth column for Russian forces inside Ottoman territory.

Thus, during February and March, the Unionist leaders began to concoct a more sinister explanation of the extent and purpose of Armenian activities in the war, and to broadcast this exaggerated account all over the country. The claim of "Armenian armed revolts" was a scapegoating device through which the Unionist leadership attempted to mask, or at least excuse, their defeats on the battlefield, especially at Sarıkamış. Eventually this new anti-Armenian propaganda would serve as one of the main ratio-

---

[7] BOA/DH, 2. Şube, no. 68/30/2, Cipher telegram from the Interior Ministry to the military headquarters of Damascus, Beirut, Aleppo, and their surroundings, n.d. (probably 9 March 1915).

nales for the eventual mass deportation and annihilation of the empire's Armenian population.[8]

Along these lines, in February one begins to see frequent mention of Armenian revolts or preparations for the same, both in cables sent by acting minister of war Enver Pasha to the affected locales and in telegrams to the capital from officials and army officers in the area under the jurisdiction of the Ottoman Third Army. A "secret" cable, sent by Enver Pasha on 25 February 1915, states that "certain Armenian bandits have appeared in Bitlis and other Armenian military deserters have also taken to banditry; there have been attacks by Armenians against military personnel and gendarmes in Aleppo and Dörtyol and a great store of bombs has been discovered in the houses of Armenians in the provincial district of Kayseri."[9]

As an initial step, ostensibly against such actions, all Armenian soldiers were forced to return their weapons and were removed from all positions in military headquarters. It was decreed that "without exception, Armenian recruits are to no longer be employed in any armed service, either in active and mobile army units, or in either mobile or stationary gendarmerie units, and are no longer allowed to serve in the retinues or offices of military staff or headquarters."[10]

Additionally, army units were given the authority to "exterminate [*imha etmek*]" all those who disobeyed government commands: "if any of the population is seen to act contrary to government orders in any way or to participate in armed assaults or rebellions, the army and corps commanders, corps and acting divisional commanders and station commanders are obliged to act immediately with military forces to suppress [such events] in the severest manner possible, and during violent uprisings they are authorized to liquidate [any and all offending people]." Military commanders could also "declare martial law immediately in any locale where they feel it necessary to do so."[11]

---

[8] This discussion will be limited to certain documents from the Interior Ministry's Cipher Office that reveal the steps of the process by which the general deportation decision was made. For further information on this subject, see Akçam, *A Shameful Act*, 111–49.

[9] *Askeri Tarih Belgeleri Dergisi* 34, no. 85 (October 1985): 23, Doc. no. 1999.

[10] Ibid.

[11] Ibid.

Over the next several months, the government was continually advised that the Armenians were in revolt and that such a situation posed a serious threat to the army. Among such communiqués, those from Third Army commander Mahmud Kamil Pasha are particularly noteworthy. For instance, in a cable of 22 April 1915, Kamil Pasha states that "[t]oday the Armenians are in a state of revolt and rebellion in parts of the province of Sivas and in the entire province of Van. It is to be assumed that the other provinces will follow suit and join [these provinces in revolt] in the appropriate time." He adds that "the attacks were planned in advance and organized by the Dashnaktsoutiun and other [Armenian revolutionary] committees."[12]

According to Kamil Pasha, the Armenians were "sowing discord in the army's rear. . . . Armenian individuals [who were under arms have entirely] deserted to the side of the enemy or to the latter's countries." The general, who perceived signs of revolt in the province of Sivas and the full-scale uprising in Van, felt that these events, which occurred "at a time when the Imperial Army was in a state of war . . . confirm and prove the Armenians' treason toward the [Ottoman] government and their collaboration with and aiding of the enemy." As a result of these events, he made the following decision (and so informed Istanbul):

> to preserve the life and existence of our nation it has become necessary—if distressing—to punish with full severity and deport those who have revolted, [and for this purpose] the provincial officials and acting army corps commanders have been notified by telegrams on the dates 7 and 8 April [1915] that all of those bearing weapons have been employed when necessary; and that individuals between the ages of 46 to 50 [in addition to those 18–46 years old] have been put under arms; and that, while taking care not to harm the population still loyal to the state or those [who are] defenseless, the decision has been made to mercilessly extirpate, down to the last man, all traitors who are conducting armed revolt against the government.[13]

---

[12] *Askeri Tarih Belgeleri Dergisi* 34, no. 85 (October 1985): 45–46, Doc. no. 2004. In this work, the date of the document was incorrectly transcribed as 9.12.[13]31 (i.e., 22 May 1915). The same document was published with the errors corrected in Genelkurmay Başkanlığı, *Arşiv Belgeleriyle Ermeni Faaliyetleri*, vol. 1, 123.

[13] Ibid. Here, at the cost of diverging from the topic, I wish to call attention to a parallel between the deportation orders published on 22 April and 27 May 1915, and the Barbarossa Decree. The Bar-

Similar telegrams reporting the Armenian population to be in revolt were sent to the capital by various Third Army departments or functionaries throughout its area of control. For example, an undated military report, bearing the signature "Şükrü" and sent from Van, individually lists the various instances of rebellion taking place in the region and states that "the Third Army has understood from the various preparations and measures mentioned above that a large-scale revolutionary action inside the country is being prepared."[14]

Cables of this sort would continue to be sent throughout the months of June and July. Mahmud Kamil Pasha stated on 19 June 1915 that "in the provinces of Erzurum, Van, and Bitlis, the Armenians, having deserted and fled to the side of the enemy, are acting as armed gangs and cutting the roads, murdering the population, raiding the [supply and arms] depots, and thereby showing their true faces," adding that "the Armenians are pursuing the same agenda in the provinces of Sivas, Diyarbekır, and Elazığ [Mamuretülaziz]." The general furthermore wrote that "from the point of view of the army's supply and security, the fact that the region that would feed the army and the places through which our present border passes are teeming with [members of] this community that harbors hostile aspirations is a great danger." As a result, he suggested that "from this point on, the Armenians in the aforementioned provinces should be deported to and resettled in the regions of Aleppo and Mosul" and requested that "assistance and advice be given so that the communications and instructions on this matter that the army send to the governors not be delayed."[15]

---

barossa Decree authorized collective reprisals against civilians in the event of resistance or sabotage against German forces. All partisans, real or suspected, were to be executed without trial by front-line combat units. Lieutenant General Eugen Müller of the Wehrmacht's legal branch defined partisans as "those civilians who resist, or promote resistance against the German armed forces (examples: rabble-rousers, those who disseminate propaganda leaflets or fail to obey German ordinances, arsonists, etc). In cases of uncertainty, suspicion alone should suffice" (Horst Boog, Jürgen Förster, and Joachim Hoffmann, *Das Deutsche Reich und der Zweite Weltkrieg. Bd.4: Der Angriff auf die Sowjetunion* [Stuttgart: DVA, 1983], 428–29). In the official deportation decision on 27 May 1915, Ottoman Army commanders were given the authority to "deport to other places and settle ... the inhabitants of villages and towns whose espionage and treachery are perceived" (*TV*, 1 June 1915). The parallelism is striking.

[14] Genelkurmay Başkanlığı, *Arşiv Belgeleriyle Ermeni Faaliyetleri*, vol. 1, 100. The entire document can be found on 97–108 and 389–418.

[15] Ibid., 187.

Whether or not there is a direct connection between this and similar reports sent by the Third Army to Istanbul and the deportation of Armenians from certain provinces is an important question that still awaits a full investigation but is not within the present purview. As is known, during the hearings held by the Ottoman Parliament's Fifth Department (the name of the commission that was formed by the Chamber of Deputies in November 1918 in order to investigate the wartime crimes of Ottoman government members), the members of the Unionist wartime cabinet claimed that in deciding to carry out the Armenian deportations, they had acted within their full authority as members of government, and they defended their decision as having been made entirely on the basis of military necessity.[16] I will here limit myself to examining certain aspects of these reports.

AN IMPORTANT NOTE REGARDING MILITARY DOCUMENTS

A closer look at the events characterized in the Third Army reports as "Armenian uprisings" reveals the striking character of the reports themselves. After the defeat at Sarıkamış, in particular, a change can be observed in the language used in the Third Army's communications. But, interestingly, there is no change whatsoever in the nature of events discussed.

First of all, despite the frequent use of the terms "uprising" and "revolt," a close reading of the reports makes it clear that the events under discussion actually consist of armed clashes with military deserters. For instance, a detailed account from the province of Bitlis on 29 October 1914, "via the Sasun road," is concerned with the killing of a group of gendarmes. The report explains that the assailants were a group of twenty-one military deserters and that "the houses of five of the deserters were razed." It also contains

---

[16] The minutes of the Commission of Investigation were subsequently published in book form (see footnote 19 in chapter 1 of this volume). The exact level and character of the Ottoman War Ministry and the army's involvement in the deportation and annihilation operations against the country's Armenians is a topic of serious debate, but one whose dimensions have yet to be fully brought to light. For a discussion of the issue, see V. N. Dadrian, "The Role of the Turkish Military in the Destruction of Ottoman Armenians," *Journal of Political and Military Sociology* 20, no. 2 (Winter 1992): 257–88; and "Party Allegiance as a Determinant in the Turkish Military's Involvement in the World War I Armenian Genocide," in *Hakirah: A Journal of Jewish and Ethnic Studies* 1, no. 1 (2003): 57–67.

the statement that "leading Armenians and [various] committee members claim that the events were not a planned action but personal [in nature]." The village inhabitants were given three days to hand over the guilty parties, and the latter were "surrendered to the government on the second day of the grace period, with the assistance and direction of the leading persons of the settlement of Geligüzan."[17]

A number of incidents in the Muş and Bitlis regions in February and March 1915 were of a similar nature. By and large these were clashes with military deserters, clashes usually won with ease by the government forces involved. According to a coded telegram from the province of Bitlis dated 21 February 1915, "weapons were used against our gendarmes in two different places on the Plain of Muş, and they were also used against our battalion that came to the settlement of Serveng which is attached to the capital county of Muş in order to arrest deserters. . . . The village was [surrounded and] put under blockade. As a result of the clashes, nine of the assailants were killed. The homes of the deserters were put to flames."[18]

Another coded cable from the Third Army Command, sent to the Office of the High Command in Istanbul (within the Ministry of War) on 27 February 1915, states that "the first Armenian incident began with [Ottoman forces being involved in] a clash with a 50-man-strong armed gang in the vicinity of Muş. . . . Although there were subsequent incidents in various places in the province of Bitlis, they were quickly suppressed."[19]

Two other noteworthy points that emerge from a close reading of such reports are, first, that the events in question do not in fact constitute an organized rebellion, and second, that there was no popular involvement. In the aforementioned, undated military report from Van, when the author (Şükrü), who speaks of a "large-scale revolutionary movement," recounts the events around Muş and Bitlis, he explains that "the Armenian leaders in both Muş and Bitlis, who are not [members of the revolutionary organization] Dashnaktsoutiun, have publicly condemned the events." This report also shows that the Armenian parliamentary deputy from Van,

[17] BOA/DH.EUM, 2. Şube, no. 2/48/2-3, Coded telegram from Bitlis governor Mustafa Bey to the Interior Ministry, dated 28–29 October 1914.

[18] Askeri Tarih Belgeleri Dergisi 31, no. 81 (December 1982): 61, Doc. no. 1815.

[19] Askeri Tarih Belgeleri Dergisi 34, no. 85 (October 1985): 33–34, Doc. no. 2001.

Vahan Papazian, was in the area at the time. According to author Şükrü, Papazian claimed that the Dashnaks (members of the Dashnaktsoutiun Party) had no connection with the incidents and wished, as Dashnaks, to "assist the state."

These same documents and others also indicate that the Armenian patriarch would subsequently submit a formal letter complaining of the extremely harsh measures to which the civilian population had been subjected on account of the military deserters, that the Third Army would conduct an investigation in response to the complaint, and that a delegation would be sent to the villages in which the incidents took place and file a report on the matter.[20] In the aforementioned telegram sent by Mahmud Kamil Pasha on 22 April 1915, the Third Army commander replies point by point to the complaints of the Armenian patriarch, stating that, "The [previous] cables that have been sent about the daily occurrences from the aforementioned provinces as well as by me have all shown that the Armenians have not been in a state of replying in kind or of lawful self-defense against the violence and oppressions of the gendarmes; rather, they are the ones in the role of the hostile assailant."[21]

A general communiqué sent by minister of war Enver Pasha on 20 April 1915 to the Third Army Command with instructions to forward the information to other units is quite explicit as to the nature of the events in question. In it, Enver states that "small bands comprised of Armenian and Greek individuals who have deserted—a small number from regular armed units and the majority after having served in the [unarmed] Labor Battalions—have deserted and are roaming here and there and using weapons against all of the gendarmes who were sent to arrest them."

Enver, who claims that the deserters consist of both Muslims and non-Muslims, also reports that the number of deserters is increasing by the day due to the insufficient number of gendarmes. Regarding the deserters, Enver suggests that "effort should be made to employ the local population in effecting their arrest. . . . Regardless of who they are, any of the local inhabitants who apprehends one of these individuals, be they Muslim or non-Muslim, and delivers them over to either the local officials or

---

[20] Genelkurmay Başkanlığı, *Arşiv Belgeleriyle Ermeni Faaliyetleri*, vol. 1, 107–8, 416–17.
[21] Ibid., 123–25, 419–21.

the military authorities [is to be given] a monetary award of not less than 1,000 liras."[22]

The second noteworthy point found in these reports is the exaggeration that was often encountered in the relating of these events, or, in other cases, the reporting of incidents that never occurred. A good example from the latter category is a report of 6 April 1915 to the Third Army Command from an officer in Sivas, the "commander of the Voluntary Special Organization Regiment." Among other things, the author states that the Armenian organization Dashnaktsoutiun

> has armed and trained each of the Armenian youths in the area of Sivas, and with the declaration of mass mobilization has fully outfitted with Mausers and Martini [rifles] some 30,000 persons from among the Armenian population of said province and sent some 15,000 of them to Russia, with the other 15,000 recruits remaining here. Upon receiving instructions to set out from Russia at some future time in the war, they will be instructed to continue their revolt for one month through [armed] uprising and revolution, with each recruit receiving a daily allowance of 1,000 cartidges.[23]

The same information is repeated in a coded cable from Sivas governor Muammer, dated 22–23 April 1915: "it has been confirmed from the mouths of captured suspects that the Armenians have trained and armed 30,000 persons from this province and that 15,000 of them have since joined the Russian Army, while [the other] 15[,000] persons have been entrusted with the task of occupying [areas] and threatening [Ottoman forces and villagers] from behind [military] lines in the event—God forbid!—that our army is unsuccessful."[24]

As can be clearly seen, the information in the two documents does not entirely square with reality. According to Ottoman figures, the total number of Armenians living within the province of Sivas at the time was 143,406.[25] If one reasonably assumes that close to half of these people

[22] *Askeri Tarih Belgeleri Dergisi* 32, no. 83 (March 1983): 91, Doc. no. 1907.
[23] Ibid., 85–86, Doc. no. 1906.
[24] Ibid., 111, Doc. no. 1911.
[25] Karpat, *Osmanlı Nüfusu*, 226.

were women, and that of the approximately 72,000 men close to half were
either children or elderly, then the able adult male population cannot have
been much more than 36,000. Moreover, it is well known that with the
declaration of general mobilization on 2 August 1914, these very same
people were taken into the military. Thus, taking the reports at face value,
one must conclude that nearly all of the Armenian men of draft age living in the Sivas Province fled the military and formed—or were formed
into—hostile, armed military units and then secretly hid themselves
within the region between August 1914 and March 1915!

It should be added that these very same documents have been used
by scholars and researchers, such as Justin McCarthy, who uphold the
official Turkish version of events, which is important support for the
argument that "the events of 1915 were in fact a civil war between
the Armenians and Turks."[26] By employing McCarthy's own method
of calculating population figures and classifying individuals by gender
and age, Vahakn N. Dadrian has shown the ridiculousness of this claim.
With full justification, he asks rhetorically, Where did these 30,000
people hide themselves between August 1914 and April 1915? Where
did the necessary supplies, weapons, and provisions for 30,000 people
come from, and where were they hidden? Who would have—and could
have—given them food, shelter, and military training? Moreover, how
is it that some 15,000 armed people, setting out from the Sivas Province in central Anatolia, traveled hundreds of miles through a region
entirely under the control of the Ottoman Third Army and arrived in
Russia without being seen by a single soul, without a single arrest or
armed clash?[27]

Another example can be given on the topic, this time in regard to the
claims of armed uprisings within the provincial district of Yozgat. A cable
sent to the First Army Corps Command on 23–24 July 1915 contains the

[26] McCarthy, *Muslim and Minorities*, 136, and Justin McCarthy and Carolyn McCarthy, *Turks and
Armenians: A Manual on the Armenian Question* (Washington, DC: Publication of Committee on Education, Assembly of Turkish American Associations, 1989), 48.

[27] As I explained in chapter 1 in the section "How Should the Documents Found in the Archives
Be Evaluated?," these are the type of documents that have led V. N. Dadrian to suspect the reliability
of the Ottoman documentation in general. For Dadrian's discussion and analysis of the subject, see
"Ottoman Archives and Denial," 291–94.

following account: "In the area around the county of Boğazlayan some 300 armed Armenian rebels from the area of Avanos arrived at the settlement of Boğazlayan [where they] carried out murders and razed buildings ... It is understood from the cable that was received that ... almost 250 recruits have been sent."[28] The information in this report was forwarded on the same day to the High Command in Istanbul by Fifth Army Corps acting commander in Ankara, Colonel Halil Recai, with the following addendum: "It was reported by the acting command of the 15th Division in Kayseri, on the basis of reports from local officials and heads of government offices, that a part of the Armenian population has been so bold as to attack the areas of Muslim habitation in Boğazlayan, killing, looting and pillaging."[29]

It is asserted that in addition to the environs around Boğazlayan, an "uprising" also began in the Akdağmadeni region, both areas falling within the provincial district of Yozgat. In a cable of 22 July 1915 to Colonel Halil Recai, the commander of the Fifteenth Division in Kayseri, Colonel Şahabettin, conveys the news "from a cable received from the acting department head in Akdağmadeni that some 250 aggressive Armenian bandits carried out raids on the settlements of Emirbey and Dere ... [illegible print]."[30] In a reply telegraphed the same day, Colonel Halil Recai demands that "the revolutionary and violent movements that have appeared in the villages and small towns of the counties of Boğazlayan and Akdağmadeni" be suppressed "forcefully and with dispatch, but without harming the loyal inhabitants."[31]

Documents within the archives of the Cipher Office deal with these incidents and their suppression. A coded telegram from Talat Pasha to the province of Ankara on 3 August 1915 relays a report from the province of Sivas that a (security) force was sent "in order to transfer Armenians who are found in large numbers in the settlements in the Akdağmadeni and Boğazlıyan counties that border the county of Tenos and who are likely

---

[28] *Askeri Tarih Belgeleri Dergisi* 32, no. 83 (March 1983): 145, Doc. nos. 1919 and 1920 (the quotation is from the first document).

[29] *Askeri Tarih Belgeleri Dergisi* 31, no. 81 (December 1982): 171, Doc. no. 1835.

[30] AAPJ, Box 17, File H, Doc. no. 593.

[31] Ibid., Doc. no. 595.

to engage in attacks in the future," and requests that contact be made with Sivas on the subject.[32] In another cable, sent to the province of Sivas on 15 September 1915, the Security Directorate in Istanbul requests that local officials "inform the Province of Ankara [so as to] combine their efforts and activities and quickly take the [necessary] measures in order to transport the Armenian bandits that have appeared in the environs of Boğazlıyan and Akdağ."[33]

The claims of an uprising alleged to have erupted within the provincial district of Yozgat have been repeated in a number of recently published works in Turkish, chief among them a reprinted propaganda piece originally issued by the Ottoman government in 1916, "The Aims and Revolutionary Actions of the Armenian [Revolutionary] Committees: Before and After the Declaration of the [Second] Constitutional Revolution." Even today, apologists for the official version of Turkish history continue to cite this "Yozgat rebellion" as a principal justification for the Armenian deportations.[34]

Unfortunately, the allegations of an Armenian revolt in the documents above have no basis in reality but were deliberately fabricated. In November 1918, the Commission for the Investigation of Crimes,[35] which was formed to investigate wartime crimes against the Armenians, obtained a number of cables, sent during the tenure of the Unionist government, that clearly showed the information in those documents to be incorrect. The cables were read into the record at sessions of the Yozgat trial beginning in February 1919. The subject was broached on 8 February at the trial's second session.

During the hearing the presiding judge asked county official Kemal about the Armenian uprisings in the Boğazlayan region. When Kemal insisted that there were indeed uprisings, the judge accused him of lying

---

[32] BOA/DH.ŞFR, no. 54-A/257, Coded telegram from interior minister Talat to the Province of Ankara, dated 3 August 1915.

[33] BOA/DH.ŞFR, no. 56/14, Coded telegram from the Interior Ministry's General Directorate of Security to the Province of Sivas, dated 15 September 1915.

[34] Erdoğan Cengiz, ed., *Ermeni Komitelerinin Âmâl ve Harekât-ı İhtilâliyesi: İlân-ı Meşrutiyetten Evvel ve Sonra* (Ankara: Başbakanlık Basımevi, Ankara, 1983), 253–55; Taha Niyazi Karaca, *Ermeni Sorununun Gelişim Sürecinde Yozgat'ta Türk Ermeni İlişkileri* (Ankara: Türk Tarih Kurumu 2005), 189–93.

[35] *Vakit*, 24 November 1918.

and read out a cable of 27 July 1915 from Colonel Şahabettin, acting commander of Kayseri, to Halil Recai, acting commander of the Fifth Army Corps in Ankara. Şahabettin reports "that there is not a shred of evidence regarding a revolt in the country of Boğazlayan." What is more, the remaining Armenians in the area were, according to Şahabettin, in a great panic, to the point that they dared not set foot outside their houses, because throughout the region "frightful looting and pillaging was being carried out by gendarmes, mounted Circassian cavalry and the Muslim population."[36]

The subject of uprisings and revolts within the provincial district of Yozgat continued to come up during succeeding sessions of the trial, with Colonel Şahabettin himself on the witness stand at the trial's eighth session (20 February 1919). Having initially testified that he sent more than two hundred troops in order to suppress the Boğazlayan uprising (which was mentioned in his related cable above), he admitted under cross-examination that the event in question amounted to no more than the pursuit of five or six military deserters.[37] At the trial's eleventh session on 5 March 1919, Yozgat district head Cemal gave a similar account, saying that there had been no indications of an uprising in the district, "only a few military deserters."[38]

So if there were no such uprisings in Yozgat, why send cables to the capital claiming the contrary? Perhaps the most striking trial testimony regarding these reports by the Third Army was given by retired general Pertev Pasha, who had served on the staff of the Third Army's Tenth Battalion in Sivas during the Armenian deportations. "[Third Army commander] Kamil was the person most responsible for the Armenian atrocities," declared the general. "When submitting his reports, he would exaggerate minor events and blame the Armenians for any defeats [that

[36] Newspaper accounts of the trial's sessions have been distilled from the February 1919 editions of the Armenian- and English-language papers *Nor geank, Zhamanag, Zhoghovourti tzayn, Renaissance,* and *Stanbul,* and presented by V. N. Dadrian in his unpublished research article, "Trials of Yozgat and Trabzon." A copy of the aforementioned cable can be found in AAPJ, Box 21, File M, Doc. no. 479.

[37] *Renaissance* and *Yeni Gazete,* 21 February 1919. Colonel Şahabettin, who was initially summoned to trial as a witness, would later be arrested and tried separately for the killing of Armenians in Yozgat and Kayseri.

[38] *Renaissance, Yeni Gazete,* 6 March 1919.

our forces suffered]. I am free of any of this responsibility [for the atrocities] because I possess the cables [that Kamil sent to us] ordering the massacres."[39]

The reality that emerges from all these documents is that the incidents in question were simply the work of armed bandit gangs of Muslim and non-Muslim military deserters that appeared—particularly in the eastern provinces—in the first months of the Ottoman entry into the war between fall 1914 and the first few months of 1915: it is simply not possible to speak of a planned, organized Armenian revolt. What is also seen, especially after the Ottoman defeat at Sarıkamış in the first months of 1915, is a change in how the Unionist Party and government viewed and interpreted these events.

FEAR OF A REVOLT

Cipher Office documents make it clear that after the start of the war Ottoman leaders were beset with constant fears of an Armenian uprising, fears that increased exponentially with the series of military setbacks at the hands of Russia and Great Britain in early 1915, and that grew, irrespective of the actual scope and potential threat posed by incidents involving Armenians.

But it should be mentioned that Istanbul was in mortal fear of provincial revolt even before the war began, and it was out of this concern that the demand arose for regular reports from the provinces. What can be understood from the Cipher Office papers is that toward the end of August 1914, the likelihood of a revolt in the provinces was investigated; for this purpose a list of questions were sent to provincial officials. Significantly, the responses of the various provincial governors are strikingly similar, each and every one of them informing Istanbul that there was no chance of an uprising or similar danger. For example, in the coded cable of 17 August 1914 seen above, the assistant governor of Erzurum informed his superiors in the capital that the Armenians in his province were not engaged in any sort of uprising whatever; rather, they lived close to and interspersed among the Muslims, with whom they got along quite well.[40]

[39] Quoted in V. N. Dadrian, "Party Allegiance," 57–67.
[40] *Askeri Tarih Belgeleri Dergisi* 31, no. 81 (December 1982): 35, Doc. no. 1809.

A similar picture emerges from a report sent by Tahsin Bey, the governor of Van (and later Erzurum), on 25 August 1914. In his report Tahsin Bey states that "neither before the general mobilization nor after has there been a single person from the Armenian population who has immigrated to Russia [or] Iran or fled [their home]. Among the local Armenians there are neither thoughts of revolt or even opposition to the government. . . . On the contrary," he adds, "among the Dashnaks one can see [an attitude of] vocal support for and assistance vis-à-vis the government in regard to the general mobilization and the war." In fact, the only observation that the governor considers worthwhile to report is that "in the private clubs in which the younger Armenian merchants and leaders meet," they are saying that "they do not want the Russians to be defeated by the Germans, and that the [push for] Armenian Reforms can [only] go forward if Russia were to become dominant in Europe." Tahsin concludes that "apart from these persistent wishes there are no efforts afoot toward any [political or military] action among the Armenians."[41]

The contents of a reply sent on the same day (25/26 August 1914) by the governor of Bitlis Province are similar to the information given by Tahsin Bey. After stating that "[n]o traces of revolutionary activity have been heard of or witnessed among the Armenians in the province," the governor adds that neither is there "anyone who is currently transporting Armenian families from the province to the Caucasus. While some Armenian merchants did travel to the Caucasus before the general mobilization for the purpose of raiding and looting, these were very few in number." In unequivocally stating that there were no serious problems of this nature in his province, the governor makes the following remarks on local Muslim-Christian relations, comments that, interestingly enough, closely parallel reports of the situation in Erzurum: "In the present war, all Muslims down to the most lowly villager are partisans of the Germans, while the Armenians without exception take the side of the Russians, and while there are indeed disputes among them due to [mutual] feelings of hostility, they remain on the verbal level. Apart from this present situation of oppositional feelings, there is no enmity between these two communities."

[41] BOA/DH.EUM, 2. Şube, no. 1/31/1, Coded telegram from Van governor, Tahsin Bey, to the Interior Ministry, dated 25 August 1915.

In fact, the governor's principal concern regarding Bitlis Province was not for Muslim-Christian strife per se, but rather for an outbreak of clashes between Kurds and Armenians; for this reason he found it incorrect for "all of the military units and gendarmerie forces [in the province] to be sent to the [provincial] borders and to leave [Bitlis itself] thoroughly empty." The Armenians, he stated, were hesitant to provoke the Kurds to attack them with the hope of getting the Russians to invade the area. Indeed, the Armenians did not dare do so, because, according to the governor, they knew that such a move "would be answered with tremendous violence." Regarding the situation of Armenian revolutionary organizations in his province, the governor had the following to say:

> in an honorable display of patriotism following the declaration of the general mobilization, the Dashnaks from among the Muş Armenians began to exhort and encourage the people [to participate] in order to facilitate the general mobilization, while the Hunchaks and the [Armenian] Church prevented them from fulfilling their national duty. Four or five days after clear directives were given to the Church, and the Hunchaks had understood that a firm decision had been given to face all difficulties for the sake of securing the national interest, they all began to comply fully with the government's directives.[42]

Another such report to the same effect was sent to the capital from the province of Mamuretülaziz (present-day Elazığ) on 5 October 1914. There were no signs that the Armenians were planning to organize an uprising, related the governor, so there was no need to form a Muslim militia. "As for talk of forming a militia, [the officials of] this province do not see a need for urgent action [to create such an] organization that would be solely reserved for the Muslim population," he stated, assuring his superiors that he would "discuss [this idea] further with the [local] acting army corps commander" and "would take the necessary measures and steps for [such an organization] to be formed if the need arose."[43]

---

[42] BOA/DH.EUM, 2. Şube, no. 68/17/1, Coded telegram from Mustafa Bey, governor of the Province of Bitlis, to the Interior Ministry, dated 25/26 August 1915.

[43] BOA/DH.EUM, 2. Şube, no. 2/10/1, Coded telegram from Sabit Bey, governor of the Province of Mamuretülaziz, to the Interior Ministry, dated 5 October 1914.

Through the Cipher Office papers one can trace the increasing concern in the capital, particularly over the months of February and March 1915. A cable of 28 February from the Security Directorate to various eastern provinces lists the recent events in Bitlis, Zeytun, and Dörtyol, calling them "evidence that a revolutionary effort is in preparation by our enemies within the country" and stating that, "As a precaution general and specific instructions [have been sent] from the Office of the Chiefs of Staff of the Imperial Army regarding Armenian individuals who are currently performing military service, as well as actions to be taken in the regions in which events like this have been reported."[44]

As seen above, the "instructions" refer to a 25 February 1915 general communiqué from the Ottoman chiefs of staff to the army's field commanders granting them the authority to take certain measures in the face of events that might arise in their areas of jurisdiction.[45] The Ottoman Interior Ministry instructed its civil officials in the provinces to establish a line of communication with the local military commanders in order to clarify what duties were to fall to them in the event of such an occurrence. "It is strongly suggested that extraordinary attention and effort be given to the thorough implementation—without delay and in direct consultation with the military—of those aspects [of the operation] that concern the civil administration."[46]

On 14 March 1915, a separate order was sent to the civilian governors of the empire's eastern provinces concerning the need to remain in communication with the Third Army Command in regard to the measures to be taken against the Armenians: "The Office of the High Command has informed [you] of the need to contact the Third Army command in

[44] BOA/DH.ŞFR, no. 50/127, Coded telegram from the Interior Ministry's General Directorate of Security to the Provinces of Erzurum, Adana, Ankara, Aydın, Bitlis, Aleppo, Hüdâvendigâr (Bursa), Diyarbekır, Sivas, Trebizond, Mamuretülaziz, and Van, and to the Provincial Districts of İzmit, Bolu, Canik, Karesi (Balıkesir), Kayseri, and Karahisâr-ı Sahib (Afyon Karahisar), dated 28 February 1915.

[45] Askeri Tarih Belgeleri Dergisi 34, no. 85 (October 1985): 23, Doc. no. 1999.

[46] BOA/DH.ŞFR, no. 50/127, Coded telegram from the Interior Ministry's General Directorate of Security to the Provinces of Erzurum, Adana, Ankara, Aydın, Bitlis, Aleppo, Hüdâvendigâr (Bursa), Diyarbekır, Sivas, Trebizond, Mamuretülaziz, and Van, and to the Provincial Districts of İzmit, Bolu, Canik, Karesi (Balıkesir), Kayseri, and Karahisâr-ı Sahib (Afyon Karahisar), dated 28 February 1915.

regard to Armenian actions and the necessary measures to be taken [in response]."[47]

The existing documentation shows that the Unionist leaders were particularly concerned that the Armenians might unite in a common cause with the Kurds. This fear is expressed openly by Talat Pasha in a "secret" message to the eastern provinces on 9 March 1915, when he requests a clarification as to whether or not an order has been issued in this regard: "[Please] report as to whether or not there exists the possibility in certain areas of the Armenians uniting with the Kurds, who have the propensity to deceive [müsta'idd-i iğfâl], and acting against the government, or whether there is the possibility of such activity or such a movement arising within [your] province."[48]

Another cable sent by Talat on 14 March 1915 to Cevded, the governor of Van Province, shows that a number of declarations had already been made to this effect by Armenian and Kurdish leaders. After claiming that "joint declarations by Bedirhânî Kâmil and Pastırmacıyan" had been understood as signifying an Armenian Kurdish partnership, the interior minister demands that, "should subsequent events confirm that certain leaders of these communities have been observed engaging in suspicious actions and initiatives, they are to be arrested and deported without delay."[49] Another example of this much-feared collaboration occurred in Malatya, where a number of Armenian military deserters formed a bandit gang with Alevi Kurds.

A coded telegram from Talat to the province of Mamuretülaziz says as much:

> the province of Sivas has reported that a number of [deserting] Armenian soldiers from the area who entered the district [nahiye] of Kürecik, which is in the county of Akçadağ in the provincial district of Malatya and borders on Darende, have come together with the Alevî Kurds who live there to form a bandit gang; that there have

---

[47] BOA/DH.ŞFR, no. 51/15, Coded telegram from the Interior Ministry's General Directorate of Security to to the Provinces of Erzurum, Van, Bitlis, and Diyarbekır, dated 14 March 1915.

[48] BOA/DH.ŞFR, no. 50/210, Coded telegram from interior minister Talat to the Provinces of Van, Bitlis, and Erzurum, dated 10 March 1915.

[49] BOA/DH.ŞFR, no. 51/14, Coded telegram from interior minister Talat to Cevded, governor of the Province of Van, dated 14 March 1915.

been attempts to pursue and arrest them by the Province of Sivas, and [in the process] it has emerged that the illegal oppressions by some officials from Malatya have caused some of the Kurds to have since taken to the mountains in revolt; but there are reports that have been deemed reliable by the bandits' leader Mehmed Ali and his companions that they are prepared to surrender and obey the government if the necessary just measures and treatment are meted out to them. [It is ordered that] an investigation be conducted and the necessary measures be fully and thoroughly implemented.[50]

The changes that took place in the early months of 1915 in regard to the "fears of a revolt" can be seen as a change in the policies pursued toward the Armenians. In these changes—and especially the major change in policy that occurred in April of that year—the role of the Unionist leader Dr. Bahaeddin Şakir must not be understated. Şakir, who experienced the negative developments in the Caucasus both before and after the defeat at Sarıkamış, including narrowly escaping death himself, was "of the opinion that it was as necessary to be afraid of the enemy within as with those outside the borders" because of "the oppositional stance that the Armenians had taken toward Turkey and the assistance that they were affording to the Russian army."[51] After obtaining a number of documents concerning the activity of Armenian armed gangs in the region, Şakir went to Istanbul at the end of February, where he worked to convince his Unionist colleagues of the need to eliminate this danger.[52]

DEPORTATIONS BETWEEN FEBRUARY AND APRIL 1915

In the months of February and March 1915, the Ottoman government began to deport certain groups because of political and military considerations. During the first deportation, the Armenians living in the area of Dörtyol

---

[50] BOA/DH.ŞFR, no. 51/130, Coded telegram from interior minister Talat to the Province of Mamuretülaziz, dated 25 March 1915.

[51] Mil, "Umumi Harpte," part 98, 10 February 1934.

[52] "Doctor Bahaeddin Şakir Bey, bringing them [the documents obtained] to the attention of the CUP central committee, was busy discussing the steps necessary to be taken to save the army from a great danger." Mil, "Umumi Harpte," part 100, 12 February 1934.

were relocated to the inner provinces of Anatolia. According to a coded telegram sent by the governor of Adana on 26 February 1915, it had been determined that the Armenians were establishing contact with the British warships off the coast, and the governor had therefore decided that "the Armenians in Dörtyol [are to be] deported in their entirety to Osmaniye, Ceyhan, and Adana, so that not a single Armenian would remain in the region."[53] In reply, the Interior Ministry confirmed the appropriateness of "deporting the Armenians of Dörtyol to the locations reported in your cable of 26 February." In addition, the ministry requested that "no place be allowed for any conditions to arise that might produce a revolt or rebellion" and that the local authorities "should act with the utmost force and despatch"; "it is necessary to thoroughly suppress any incident by harsh and decisive means, along with the immediate causes for the specific events."[54]

From German documents it is possible to extract more detailed information about these initial deportations from the Dörtyol environs. According to these sources, before the Armenian population was sent off to the aforementioned destinations, the entire population was forbidden from going in or out of the city, and a complete search of the area was conducted for the purposes of both discovering whether there had been any efforts on the part of the British to seek out potential allies in the area and to capture military deserters.[55] The men were subsequently removed from the region and put to work constructing roads to the Aleppo region.[56] Some people were arrested and sent off to Adana, where they were tried and executed.[57]

The deportation of the Armenians of Zeytun to the Anatolian interior in April 1915 would follow that of the Dörtyol Armenians, and came

[53] Genelkurmay Başkanlığı, *Arşiv Belgeleriyle Ermeni Faaliyetleri*, vol. 1, 55.

[54] BOA/DH.ŞFR, no. 50/141, Coded telegram from interior minister Talat to the Province of Adana, dated 2 March 1915.

[55] DE/PA-AA/Bo.Kons., vol. 168. Report by the German acting consul in İskenderun (Alexandretta), Hoffman, to the German ambassador in Istanbul, Wangenheim, dated 7 March 1915.

[56] DE/PA-AA/Bo.Kons., vol. 168. Report by the German consul in Adana, Büge, to the German ambassador in Istanbul, Wangenheim, dated 13 March 1915. At the time of this writing, Aram Arkun is completing a doctoral thesis on the developments in the Çukurova region entitled "The Fall of the Eagles' Nest: The Fate of Armenians of Hajin, Zeitun, Sis and Marash, 1914–1921."

[57] For the order concerning the capture and trial of suspects, see Genelkurmay Başkanlığı, *Arşiv Belgeleriyle Ermeni Faaliyetleri*, vol. 1, 56; for their death sentences and executions, see DE/PA-AA/R 14085, Report by German ambassador in Istanbul, Wangenheim, to Chancellor Bethmann-Hollweg, dated 15 April 1915. For more on Dörtyol, see Lepsius, *Der Todesgang*, 11, 43.

about in large part as a result of the events of the intervening month. Nevertheless, the events at Zeytun are still depicted in recent works advancing the official version of Turkish history as the first systematic attempt by the Armenians to stage a general uprising against the Ottoman authorities,[58] although events in Zeytun were entirely local in nature and fundamentally involved not political agents but military deserters.

There is a great deal of agreement among the Ottoman, German, and American documents dealing with the subject, and the documentation from all three archives gives largely similar information regarding the events in question. The initial incident was actually limited to a simple clash between a group of Armenian military deserters and a local gendarmerie unit, which subsequently found the former group locking themselves in an Armenian church and refusing to surrender. Marash provincial district governor Mümtaz, who sent the first reports on this incident on 9 and 13 March 1915, reported that there was nothing other than gendarmes on patrol being fired upon by "brigands [eşkıya]."[59] In his 30 March report, he wrote, "and today many people from the deserters and the remainder from suspect individuals were taken. The Investigation Committee continues its investigations." He concluded that the incidents essentially had ended.[60]

In a report to the Ottoman Fourth Army Command sent on 14 March 1915, the author states that he "does not entertain the possibility of a general Armenian uprising" and states that "in the face of the oppositional stance and rebellion displayed by certain Armenian military deserters in Zeytun, the state has attempted to take measures [to punish them]." He relates the local population's attitude toward the events as follows: "A large portion of our Armenian compatriots are sorely grieved by these actions of just a small, wicked remnant; their sense of connection to the homeland is beyond all doubt and suspicion." Additionally, the report provides

---

[58] For two examples, see Azmi Süslü, *Ermeniler ve 1915*, 71–72 and İhsan Sakarya, *Belgelerle Ermeni Sorunu* (Ankara: Genelkurmay Başkanlığı, 1984), 185–87. The information contained in these works is repeated almost verbatim in a great number of popular works. One example is Dr. Ali Güler and Dr. Suat Akgül, *Sorun Olan Ermeniler* (Ankara: Berikan, 2003), 201–2.

[59] BOA/DH.EUM, 2. Şube, nos. 68/30/1 and 68/31/1, Telegrams of Marash Provincial District governor Mümtaz, noted as "important and extremely urgent," to the Interior Ministry, dated 9 and 13 March 1915.

[60] BOA/DH.EUM, 2. Şube, no. 68/35/1, Cipher telegram of Marash Provincial District governor Mümtaz, marked "urgent," to the Interior Ministry, dated 30 March 1915.

the information that the military deserters "were not captured as the result of [their armed] clashes [with the gendarmes] but with the assistance of the leading [Armenian] inhabitants of Zeytun," who surrendered them of their own accord.[61]

This information is corroborated by several memoirs of the period. Hovsep Bıştikyan states that "Sahak Khabayan, who at that time was the Catholicos of Cilicia, sent in a written message [to the barricaded deserters] saying, 'For God's sake, have mercy; do not shoulder your weapons; Surrender!' He even went as far as Zeytun itself. We were all school kids at the time; they brought us out to meet him. He calmed the population down by vowing and persuading us that everything would turn out all right, and this was the reason that the inhabitants of Zeytun did not go out to fight."[62]

Reports that the deserters were ultimately convinced to surrender through the assistance of the Zeytun Armenians are also found in the American documents.[63] This information is corroborated in the memoirs of the Protestant pastor of Zeytun, who recounted that the Zeytun Armenians, who "sincerely disliked and dreaded" the deserters, were persuaded to report their activities to the Ottoman government "to ensure their own safety and the safety of the other Armenians in Cilicia."[64] A contemporary German journalist by the name of Tyszka provided a similar account of the local Armenians' stance. According to him, as events were transpiring, the Armenian patriarch himself paid a visit to Talat Pasha and was told by the interior minister "that he was extremely pleased with the behavior of the Zeytun Armenians [in this matter]."[65]

In late March 1915, Wangenheim, the German ambassador to the Porte, informed his superiors in Berlin that on the basis of the reports from his consulates in Adana and Aleppo, both of which had been following the events in the region closely, "it would not be possible to speak [of the

[61] Genelkurmay Başkanlığı, *Arşiv Belgeleriyle Ermeni Faaliyetleri*, vol. 1, 71–72, 355–61.

[62] For Hovsep Bıştikyan's memoirs see http://ermeni.hayem.org/turkce/vkayutyun.php?tp=ea&lng=tr&nmb=138.

[63] NA/RG 59, 867.00/761, Report of American consul in Aleppo, J. B. Jackson, to American ambassador in Istanbul, Morgenthau, dated 21 April 1915. Reproduced in *United States Official Records*, ed. Sarafian, 10.

[64] Bryce and Toynbee, *The Treatment of Armenians*, 489.

[65] DE/PA-AA/R 14088, Letter from German journalist in Istanbul Tyszka to the assistant Foreign Ministry advisor, Zimmermann, dated 1 October 1915.

events in question] as a pre-meditated and organized Armenian uprising, but rather as certain disturbances in reaction to military conscription."[66] The governor of Aleppo Province, Celal Bey, would give a similar depiction of events in his memoirs, which were published during the Armistice period in the Turkish daily *Vakit*. Referring to the deportation of the population of Zeytun to Konya and Sultaniye in the wake of the disturbances, Celal calls it "an unnecessary action."[67]

Two related factors appear to have played an important role in the wholesale removal and deportation of the Armenians of both Zeytun and Dörtyol. Reports began to be received that the British were making preparations for a landing and invasion force at İskenderun (Alexandretta). The already existing fears of a general uprising in the area were now exacerbated with the ominous possibility that any such revolt would be coordinated and made to coincide with the impending invasion. In a report dated 13 March 1915, Büge, the German consul in Adana, mentioned that British warships and landing craft were at present free to approach the coast for the purposes of conducting business. Thus, through service to the British, some local Armenians were able to establish communication with Armenians in other areas.[68] According to an Armenian captured during the events at Zeytun, "they [i.e., the Armenians] had been informed by the committee that the British already landed at İskenderun." What was being asked of them (i.e., the Armenians) was "to support the English by revolting and, by doing so, making things more difficult for the government and hindering their efforts at mobilization."[69]

Rössler, the German consul at Aleppo, would spend two weeks in the spring of 1915 investigating whether there was any connection or tie

[66] DE/PA-AA/R 14085, Report from German ambassador in Istanbul, Wangenheim, to Chancellor Bethmann-Hollweg, dated 26 March 1915. The most detailed foreign accounts of the developments in the region are contained in a report by the German consul in Aleppo, Rössler, to Chancellor Bethmann-Hollweg, dated 12 April 1915 (DE/PA-AA/R 14085). The report is based on the information personally collected by the consul, who toured the area between 28 March and 10 April 1915.

[67] Celal Bey, "Ermeni Vakâyi-i."

[68] DE/PA-AA/Bo.Kons./Band 168, Report from German consul in Adana, Büge, to Ambassador Wangenheim in Istanbul, dated 13 March 1915.

[69] İsmet Parmaksızoğlu, ed., *Ermeni Komitelerinin İhtilal Hareketleri ve Besledikleri Emeller* (Ankara: DSİ Basım ve Foto, 1981), 79–80.

between the Armenians at Dörtyol and those at Zeytun. At the conclusion of his investigation, he would inform his superiors that,

> according to the things that I have been told by an impartial indi-
> vidual who is in close contact with the Armenians and very well in-
> formed, some letters were written at first by those living in Dörtyol
> to Zeytun stating that now would be an opportune time for an up-
> rising. Communication had been established with British warships
> [in the eastern Mediterranean]. My source does not know whether
> or not the letters ultimately reached their destination. If my source's
> sources were good, this can be considered evidence [that these let-
> ters] are a call to revolt. It is not known what sort of reaction the
> persons addressed showed to this call.[70]

Various sources have claimed that Great Britain, at the insistent urging of Russia, was indeed considering a military landing and invasion in
the area.[71] As far as can be discerned from the British sources, there were
attempts not only to establish communication with the Armenians in the
Çukurova region, but a series of meetings was also held with Armenian
organizations abroad, during the course of which the representative of the
Armenian Revolutionary Committee claimed that his organization could
muster approximately twenty thousand volunteers to fight for the British
in the Çukurova and İskenderun regions. Similar proposals were made by
the Armenian National Defense Committee of America. A certain Varan-
dian, speaking on behalf of the organization, reported that half of these
volunteers were already in America and the Balkans and prepared to go,
and he proposed that British-controlled Cyprus be used as a base of operations.[72] Nevertheless, Great Britain did not take these proposals seriously
and soon abandoned the idea of a landing in or near İskenderun.

[70] DE/PA-AA/R 14086, Letter from German ambassador in Istanbul, Wangenheim, to Chancellor Bethmann-Hollweg, dated 27 May 1915. Rössler's aforementioned report also accompanied this letter.

[71] For additional information on the topic, see Donald Bloxham, *The Great Game of Genocide: Imperialism, Nationalism, and the Destruction of the Ottoman Armenians* (Oxford and New York: Oxford University Press, 2005), 78–83.

[72] For the relevant reports concerning these conversations, see Muammer Demirel, *Ermeniler Hakkında İngiliz Belgeleri (1896–1918) British Documents on Armenians* (Ankara: Yeni Türkiye, 2002), Doc. nos. 417, 418, 419, 420, 421, and 667–71. To the extent that it can be understood from the docu-

Cipher Office cables show that the Ottoman leaders had been afraid of some sort of joint Dörtyol-Zeytun revolt at least as far back as the spring of 1914. A coded telegram to the governors' offices in Adana and Aleppo, which was sent on 19 April 1914, expressed this concern openly, stating that "it has been learned from a [certain] source that the revolt upon which the Armenians in Zeytun resolved to embark will soon begin in Dörtyol, [which is] in the environs of İskenderun. It has since [been] rumored—through the admission of certain leaders of the [Armenian revolutionary] committee who are in Egypt—that a large-scale action will be undertaken with the assistance of all of the Armenian political parties and that attempts have been made to import all manner of weapons into the area."

For its part, the Ottoman Interior Ministry was not convinced of the reliability of these reports and requested further information regarding the activities of the Armenians within the province. In the cable it asks, "What is the current attitude of the Armenians in the province vis-à-vis the government and the other communities and what sort of endeavors and preparations are they engaged in?"[73]

It would be no exaggeration to claim that the fear of a "general revolt" on the part of many in the Ottoman leadership was central to their decision to take such harsh measures in response to—and far out of proportion with—the events at Zeytun. Along these lines, the German general Bronsart von Schellendorf would demand, in his aforementioned cable of 18 March 1915, that "the perpetrators be severely punished." Fourth Army commander Cemal Pasha would go even further, stating that "it is imperative that both those who would ask mercy [and turned themselves in] as well as those whose [continued] residency in Zeytun and Marash would be detrimental be sent off to Konya." The commander's sense of urgency stemmed from the fear that the British would once more build up their forces on the Egyptian front, and that a failure to deport such people "would necessitate a concentration of a very large force in these areas

---

ments published in this work, one can surmise that the Armenian Revolutionary Committee in the Balkans had made similar proposals to both the Russians and the French.

[73] BOA/DH.ŞFR, no. 40/45, Coded telegram from the Interior Ministry's General Directorate of Security to the Provinces of Adana and Aleppo, dated 19 April 1914.

[Zeytun and Marash] merely to maintain law and order."[74] In the end, on the following day (9 April) the deportations got under way for a portion of Zeytun's Armenians.[75] As also seen above, another measure considered by Cemal Pasha in mid-April was the settling of Muslim immigrants and refugees in the region.

What is important here is the fact that even as late as April 1915, Ottoman military and civilian leaders, as well as the German military and diplomatic functionaries who were stationed in or toured the region and were thus able to gather firsthand information, were reporting back to their superiors that there was, for all practical purposes, no uprising whatsoever being prepared by the Armenians. However, a primary eyewitness, Marash provincial district governor Mümtaz, seemed to be predicting deportation measures in his report of 30 March: "The Zeytun trouble is nothing new, it is old. If a fundamental step is not taken, there is no doubt that it will recur in the future." According to him, the main cause of such incidents in the past and in the future consisted of "the places being mountainous and the villages in the area all being inhabited by like-minded Armenians." Consequently, for such incidents to not recur, it was necessary for "some Armenian families previously confirmed as criminal to be deported to other places." Provincial district governor Mümtaz suggested that it was time to organize a relocation in the area. In his words, "At this juncture when I believe that conditions are favorable to decrease the Armenian population and increase the Muslim population, a summons and settlement of certain Armenian peasants of importance to be transferred to the plains while refugees who have yet to be settled be moved in their place is appropriate."[76] It appears that the Unionists wanted to use favorable conditions created by the war to solve an old problem. The deportation of the Zeytun Armenians to the interior of Konya in Anatolia must have resulted from such a thought.

---

[74] *Askeri Tarih Belgeleri Dergisi* 31, no. 81 (December 1982): 111, Doc. no. 1823.

[75] NA/RG 59, 867.00/761, Report from United States consul in Aleppo, J. B. Jackson, to Ambassador Morgenthau, dated 21 April 1915, in *United States Official Records*, ed. Sarafian, 10.

[76] BOA/DH.EUM, 2. Şube, no. 68/35/1, Cipher cable from Marash Provincial District governor, marked as "urgent," to the Interior Ministry, dated 30 March 1915.

THE FATEFUL DECISION AND ITS INITIAL
IMPLEMENTATION

There is a strong possibility that the final decisions to eliminate the Armenian population were made during discussions held in Istanbul at the end of March. As a result of these discussions, "it was decided in Istanbul that, while the Special Organization concerned itself with matters concerning [the country's] foreign enemies, Bahaeddin Şakir Bey would occupy himself with the country's internal enemies."[77] In other words, Bahaeddin Şakir was entrusted with the task of destroying the empire's Armenian population. Arif Cemil, who was also active in the SO with Şakir, states that "these conversations ultimately resulted in the publication of the Law of Deportation," and that "it was clear that Dr. Bahaeddin Şakir Bey returned shortly thereafter to the Caucasian front in an entirely new [capacity and] position."[78] Records exist in the Prime Ministerial Ottoman Archive that confirm the information that Arif Cemil gave regarding Bahaeddin Şakir Bey's trip to Istanbul and his later return to the region. Among these, the most important is delivered with the instructions "Personal Delivery, Extremely Urgent and Private" and dated 24 January 1915, in which Bahaeddin Şakir requests permission to travel to Istanbul to report on conditions in the region. Şakir, who stated, "the commanders don't know the situation here [at the Caucasian front] as well as we do," also said that if certain measures were not taken, "one can speak of the danger of an emotional ruination as well as a material one." According to Şakir, "the central focus points of this war aren't in Egypt or Basra or Rumeli [the Balkans]." His intentions were quite clear: "in order to meet to discuss this and other related issues . . . send consent for my arrival in Istanbul."[79] From another cipher cable on 5 April 1915 from the Interior Ministry, stating that "Bahaeddin Şakir Bey shall return soon and special [budgetary] appropriations will be sent for the [Muslim] immigrants," we

[77] Mil, "Umumi Harpte," part 98, 10 February 1934.
[78] Ibid., part 100, 12 February 1934.
[79] BOA/DH.ŞFR, no. 459/4, Coded telegram from Bahaeddin Şakir to Interior Ministry, dated 24 January 1915.

can surmise that the relevant decisions in this regard had been made at the end of March or the very beginning of April.[80]

There is additional evidence that March 1915 was a turning point for certain major decisions. The Grand National Assembly (Parliament) went into recess on 1 March months ahead of schedule, "due to extraordinary circumstances."[81] On 18 March, foreign minister Halil Menteşe traveled to Berlin for talks with the German government on the Armenian deportation. (Finance minister Cavit Bey, who opposed Ottoman entry into the war, was also in Berlin at this time but was not trusted in the Armenian matter.) Upon returning to Istanbul, Menteşe was welcomed at the train station by Talat, who greeted him thus: "Tell me, dear Halil, what did you discuss in Berlin regarding the deportation of Armenians?"[82]

Two separate decisions were most likely made at these meetings in Istanbul in late March. The decision to deport the Armenian population to present-day Syria and Iraq was sent to the provincial governors via the Interior Ministry's official channels. Subsequently, the decision to annihilate the Armenians was conveyed to the regions by CUP emissaries, in particular, the party's so-called responsible secretaries. One may confidently claim that a dual-track mechanism—similar to that which had been used against the Greek population in spring and summer 1914—was redeployed for the deportation and annihilation of the Armenians. When reports of the events in Van reached the capital, a series of comprehensive policies were put into effect almost immediately, giving the distinct impression that preparations for these actions must have been under way long before.

Initially, during the night of 23–24 April, a large-scale operation of mass arrests rounded up Armenian leaders and other "undesirables" in Istanbul.[83] A telegram to the province of Ankara on 24 April reports that "the Armenian arrestees will be sent to Ayaş" and demands that the Ayaş military depot be

[80] BOA/DH.ŞFR, no. 51/215, Coded telegram from interior minister Talat to the Province of Erzurum, dated 5 April 1915.

[81] MMZC, Period 3, Assembly Year 1, vol. 1, 1 March 1915, Session 33, 480–82.

[82] All this information was reported by Menteşe himself (Halil Menteşe, Osmanlı Mebusan Meclisi Reisi, 213–16).

[83] For a detailed account of the first wave of overnight arrests in Istanbul and the list of those deported to Ayaş and Çankırı, see Balakian, Armenian Golgotha: A Memoir of the Armenian Genocide, 1915–1918, trans. Peter Balakian and Aris Sevag (New York: Alfred A. Knopf, 2009), chapter 13, sections 6–10.

readied for this development.[84] In another cable, sent the following day, the Interior Ministry reports that upon arrival, the 180 arrestees from Istanbul were to be separated into two groups and resettled in Ayaş and Çankırı.[85] In fact, the final numbers were a little higher, as Ottoman documents show that 71 people were placed under supervision in Ayaş and 155 in Çankırı.[86] A subsequent cable to the provinces clarified that the latter group "had not been arrested" and that "since there was, in fact, no likelihood of them fleeing, they should be left to move freely within the town" and protected.[87]

A series of cipher cables were sent to all provincial and district governors on 24 April 1915. The first cable prohibited travel, ordering that "no travel documents or permissions to go abroad whatsoever be given to those Armenians who are known by the government to be suspicious, and especially not to the leaders and prominent members of planning and active committees."[88] The scope of the prohibition on travel would be broadened in the ensuing months, and the decision would include

[84] BOA/DH.ŞFR, no. 52/94, Coded telegram from interior minister Talat to the Province of Ankara, dated 24 April 1915.

[85] BOA/DH.ŞFR, no. 52/102, Coded telegram from interior minister Talat to the Province of Ankara, dated 25 April 1915. The cable says the same thing: "Some 180 Armenians, leaders of revolutionary committees and others whose [continued] residency here is seen as undesireable, will be placed, while being accompanied by a 75-person-strong escort composed of 15 police officers, two military officers, a commissioner, a civil servant and others, on the Number Eight train departing from Haydar Pasha [Station] this evening at 10:23 p.m.; they will then be sent off on the Number 124 train, which will arrive at Ankara the following day at 8:00 a.m. Of these some 60–70 individuals will remain under arrest at the Ayaş military depot as was written in yesterday's coded telegram, and the rouhly 100 remaining will be sent by the Ankara road to Kangırı [i.e., Çankırı] to be resettled. Those to be sent to Ayaş will be brought to the Sincanköy station and with security forces at the ready, they will be held at the aforementioned station until they are separated from one another and sent to Ayaş; alternately, all of them will first be sent to Ankara, where they will be divided into two separate groups and from there sent on to Ayaş and Kangırı; the [final] decision on [the questions of] protection and simplicity in this matter will be left to you."

[86] For more on those under observation in Çankırı, see BOA/DH.EUM, 2. Şube, no. 10/73; for the list of those that were held in Ayaş, see BOA/DH.EUM, 2. Şube, no. 67/31.

[87] BOA/DH.ŞFR, no. 52/184, Coded telegram from the Interior Ministry's General Directorate of Security to the Province of Kastamonu, dated 2 May 1915. Although these people were initially detained as those leading the preparations for a large-scale uprising, the fact that those who were exiled to Çankırı were not even considered to have been "arrestees"—to the point that they were not considered flight risks and allowed to wander the city freely—remains a strange paradox indeed.

[88] BOA/DH.ŞFR, no. 52/95, Coded telegram from interior minister Talat to the Provinces of Edirne, Erzurum, Adana, Ankara, Aydın, Bitlis, Aleppo, Hüdâvendigâr (Bursa), Diyarbekır, Sivas, Trebizond, Konya, Mamuretülaziz, and Van, and to the Provincial Districts of Urfa, İzmit, Kütahya, Karahisar-ı Sahip, Bolu, Canik, Karesi (Balıkesir), Kayseri, Marash, Niğde, and Eskişehir, dated 24 April 1915.

the orders "that no Armenians whatsoever, male or female, be allowed to enter Ottoman domains from abroad, and that Armenian males between the ages of 17 and 50 not be permitted to travel abroad at all without receiving special permission of the Exalted Office of the High Command."[89] Even more stringent measures would follow closely on the heels of this decision: on 21 August 1915, all provincial governors and district officials were instructed by circular that "no Armenian male or female of any age be allowed to leave the country without a command from the High Command."[90]

On 24 April 1915, several other critical government decisions were made and orders sent to the local authorities that, especially in light of the recent events in Zeytun, Bitlis, Sivas, and Van, Armenians were to be arrested and kept under supervision throughout the country.[91] By means of such orders, which were also sent in some fashion to the Ottoman High

[89] BOA/DH.ŞFR, no. 53/334, Coded telegram from the Interior Ministry's General Directorate of Security to the Provinces of Edirne, Erzurum, Adana, Ankara, Aydın, Bitlis, Basra, Baghdad, Beirut, Aleppo, Hüdâvendigâr (Bursa), Diyarbekır, Damascus, Sivas, Trebizond, Kastamonu, Konya, Mamuretülaziz, Mosul, and Van, and to the Provincial Districts of Urfa, İzmit, Niğde, İçel, Bolu, Canik, Çatalca, Zor, Karesi (Balıkesir), Jerusalem, Kale-i Sultaniye (Çanakkale), Menteşe, Teke, Kütahya, Marash, and Eskişehir, dated 13 June 1915.

[90] BOA/DH.ŞFR, no. 55/141, Coded telegram from the Interior Ministry's General Directorate of Security to the Provinces of Erzurum, Adana, Ankara, Bitlis, Aleppo, Hüdâvendigâr (Bursa), Diyarbekır, Damascus, Sivas, Trebizond, Konya, Mamuretülaziz, and Van, and to the Provincial Districts of Urfa, İzmit, Canik, Zor, Karesi (Balıkesir), Karahisâr-ı Sahib (Afyon Karahisar), Kayseri, Marash, Niğde, and Eskişehir, dated 21 August 1915.

[91] These cables, which are invaluable documents, also have the advantage of recounting the very same thing: "As a result of the revolutionary and political organizations of the Armenian [revolutionary] committees within the Ottoman state and the efforts that they have been expending for quite some time to obtain administrative control for themselves, the hostile actions of the Dashnak Committee and the Russian Armenians toward us following the declaration of war and the decision that the Armenians within the Ottoman state took to throw themselves entirely behind the effort to revolt after having seen the weakened state of the [Ottoman] Army, their gall to exploit every opportunity to engage in traitorous actions that would affect the life of the state and its future—and especially during this period, when the country is in the midst of a general war this has once more been confirmed by the recent rebellious events in Zeytun and Bitlis, Sivas and Van . . . and by the bombs that were discovered in Kayseri, Sivas and other districts, by the actions of the leaders of the Armenian [revolutionary] committees who, having formed voluntary units from the Russian army, have attacked the country in coordination with the Russians but who are originally members of the Ottoman [Armenian] community, the manner in which they threaten the Ottoman Army from the rear and the actions that they have taken and publications that have produced in very great number. Naturally, since the government cannot ever countenance or tolerate these plans and efforts that constitute in its eyes a vital question [for the country], nor view as lawful the continued existence of

Command,[92] all Dashnak and Hunchak committees and organizations were to be dissolved, their newspapers closed, and their leaders arrested and brought before military tribunals yet to be formed. Two days later, war minister Enver Pasha sent a special communiqué to all army commanders informing them of the government's decision to close Armenian organizations, confiscate their documents and papers, arrest their members, and search their premises for weapons; the commanders were ordered to "remain in communication with the civil officials in this regard" and "place importance on quickly providing all manner of assistance that might be requested by them."[93]

An "urgent and secret" circular of 2 May 1915, "to be handled personally" by all provincial officials, shows that a temporary law had been issued on 26 April in accordance with the 24 April decision to conduct a wide-ranging search for weapons. The circular explains that "the temporary law [of 26 April 1915] concerns the goal of ensuring that weapons and bombs in the hands of non-Muslim communities—and particularly, of the Armenians—be confiscated." Additionally, special attention was

---

[revolutionary] committees that are the source of disorder and sedition, it has felt the urgent need to eliminate [ilga] all [Armenian] political organizations. Therefore, it is being suggested with all urgency that the Hunchak, Dashnak and similar [Armenian revolutionary] committees['] branches within the province be shut down . . . and all of the papers and documents found in their [various] branch headquarters be immediately confiscated without giving them the opportunity to damage or destroy them; that the leaders and prominent members of the committees be immediately arrested along with those Armenians deemed by the government to be either important or injurious; that those whose continued residency in their present districts would seem ill-advised be concentrated in places that would appear suitable within the provincial district and that no possibility be given them to escape or flee; that searches for weapons should be commenced in coordination with the [military] commanders in the face of any situation that arises; that it has been the individuals, who will [be] arrested as a result of the examination of papers and documents that will be acquired and [whose contents shall be] fully revealed in the course of this operation, shall be delivered over to the courts-martial; that the necessary measures, having been decided through discussions with the Army High Command, are to be thoroughly and immediately implemented and continuous reports are to be sent regarding operations and the number of individuals arrested" (BOA/DH.ŞFR, no. 52/96-97-98, Coded telegram from interior minister Talat to the Provinces of Edirne, Erzurum, Adana, Ankara, Aydın, Bitlis, Aleppo, Hüdâvendigâr [Bursa], Diyarbekır, Sivas, Trebizond, Konya, Mamuretülaziz, and Van, and to the Provincial Districts of Urfa, İzmit, Karahisâr-ı Sahib [Afyon Karahisar], Bolu, Canik, Karesi [Balıkesir], Kayseri, Marash, Niğde, and Eskişehir, dated 24 April 1915).

[92] Genelkurmay Başkanlığı, Arşiv Belgeleriyle Ermeni Faaliyetleri, vol. 1, 127–29, 423–25.

[93] Genelkurmay Başkanlığı, Askeri Tarih Belgeleri Dergisi 31, no. 81 (December 1982): 137–38, Doc. no. 1829.

given in the circular to reminding its readers that this temporary law should not, in fact, be understood "to mean that weapons were to be collected from the Muslim population" and that the officials should act accordingly.[94]

The same distinction between Muslims and non-Muslims was made by the Ministry of War in an official response to the Ministry of the Interior in early July 1915, referencing an earlier note: "this is in response to state memorandum number 262 [of 3 July 1915]. The order concerning the collection of ammunition and explosive material is only to be implemented in regard to the non-Muslim communities and those members of the Muslim population who are are considered extraordinarily malicious or seditious; as it seems appropriate to leave other weapons in the hands of the remaining Muslims against a document signed by them, and a written communication has been sent to the army units in this regard. . . . In this regard, the decision is yours."[95]

Parallel to the widespread arrests, travel, and other prohibitions that began on 24 April 1915, the destination of the deportees from Zeytun and Marash, who were initially to be sent to Konya, was also changed. A cable to Cemal Pasha on 24 April requested that "apart from those already sent, no further Armenians be sent to the region, and in accordance with the wishes of the Pasha, who is the commander of the armed forces, the relevant persons are to be informed of the order to deport those whom it is seen as necessary to remove from regions such as İskenderun [Alexandretta], Dörtyol, Adana, Haçin, Zeytun and Sis, [and sent] to the regions of southeastern Aleppo, Der Zor, and Urfa."[96] The general direction of the deportations was to present-day Syria and Iraq.

A similar cipher cable was sent the following day (25 April) to the provinces of Adana and Aleppo and the provincial district of Marash,

---

[94] BOA/DH.ŞFR, no. 52/188, Coded telegram from interior minister Talat to the Provinces of Edirne, Erzurum, Adana, Ankara, Aydın, Bitlis, Aleppo, Hüdâvendigâr (Bursa), Diyarbekır, Sivas, Trebizond, Kastamonu, Konya, Mamuretülaziz, and Van, and to the Provincial Districts of Urfa, İzmit, Bolu, Canik, Karesi (Balıkesir), Marash, Niğde, and Eskişehir, dated 2 May 1915.

[95] BOA/DH.EUM, 2. Şube, no. 8/101/1, Telegram from the Imperial Ottoman War Ministry to the Interior Ministry (undated).

[96] BOA/DH.ŞFR, no. 52/93, Coded telegram from the Interior Ministry's General Directorate of Security to Fourth Army commander Cemal Pasha, dated 24 April 1915.

informing the officials there that the situation had also been reported to the Fourth Army Command.[97] Another cipher to the provincial district of Marash on 5 May 1915 demanded the "total deportation" of the Armenians of Zeytun.[98] The same order was repeated in a second cable sent four days later.[99]

As a result of the events in Van in late April, the earliest known telegram regarding the deportation of the Armenian population from Van and the surrounding provinces is from 2 May 1915. In it, a certain İsmet (later known as İsmet İnönü, Mustafa Kemal's amanuensis and successor as second president of Turkey) writes to the Interior Ministry on behalf of "the Office of the High Command of the Imperial Ottoman Army" and proposes that "the Armenians around Lake Van and especially in those places known to the provinc[ial government] of Van . . . should be removed from there and the hotbed of rebellion dispersed." The cable mentions that at the beginning of April the Russians deported the Muslim population within their own borders into the Ottoman Empire and states that in order to both suppress the revolt and to pay the Russians back in-kind for their actions, "it is necessary to either deport the aforementioned Armenians and their families to Russia or to disperse them into various places within the Anatolian interior." The High Command then requests that "the most suitable of these two paths be chosen and implemented."[100] It is understood that the Interior Ministry, in accordance with this proposal, ultimately opted for the second choice.

A second telegram in this regard was sent only to the provincial governors in Van and Bitlis on 6 May. Along with the directive to "see to th[e matter] personally," this communiqué informs the governors "that those Armenians around Lake Van and other places known and identified by the provincial governor's office in Van and which have been a constant

[97] BOA/DH.ŞFR, no. 52/112, Coded telegram marked "secret" from the Interior Ministry's General Directorate of Security to the Provinces of Adana and Aleppo and to the Provincial District of Marash, dated 25 April 1915.

[98] BOA/DH.ŞFR, no. 52/253, Coded telegram from the Interior Ministry's General Directorate of Security to the Provincial District of Marash, dated 6 May 1915.

[99] BOA/DH.ŞFR, no. 52/286, Coded telegram from the Interior Ministry's General Directorate of Security to the Provincial District of Marash, dated 9 May 1915.

[100] Askeri Tarih Belgeleri Dergisi 31, no. 81 (December 1982): 139–42, Doc. no. 1830.

breeding ground for revolt and rebellion are to be removed from [said] regions and locales and sent off into exile in the south." In addition, "it has been communicated by the Office of the High Command to the commanders of the Third and Fourth Armies that they are to afford any and all possible assistance to the governors for the speedy implementation of this decision." Notice of the evacuation operation would be given to "Van, the southern portion of Erzurum [Province] and the relevant counties [administratively] attached to the provincial center of Bitlis, and especially to Muş and the areas of Sason and Talori." Finally, it is requested that Tahsin Bey, the governor of Erzurum Province, also be informed of the situation and that the evacuation operation "be implemented speedily and in an orderly fashion."[101] Summoned to testify at the postwar trial in the Istanbul Court-Martial (Divan-i Örfi) of Unionists involved in the deportations and massacres around Harput (present-day Elazığ), Tahsin Bey told the court in its 2 August 1919 session that he had received the deportation order for Erzurum and its environs on 12 May 1915.[102]

However, as suggested by the testimony of some eyewitnesses and the reports of German consuls in the area, the evacuation of the villages surrounding Erzurum began sometime toward the end of April. For example, in the memoirs of Başkâtipzade Ragıp Bey, the author recalls that he arrived in Erzurum on 14 April 1915 and left twelve days later on 26 April. He writes of his time that "the disordered, impoverished, debased and dissolute state of the poor Armenian girls and women as a result of the Armenian deportations tore at our heartstrings."[103] In the aforementioned German consular accounts, it is reported that the emptying out of villages around Erzurum commenced at the beginning of May. "By 15 May," one of them states, "all of the villages had been evacuated."[104]

From the beginning of May, Talat Pasha began to concern himself personally with the questions of how many Armenians had actually been re-

[101] BOA/DH.ŞFR, no. 52/282, Coded telegram from the Interior Ministry's General Directorate of Security to the governor of Van, Cevded Bey, and the governor of Bitlis, Mustafa Abdülhâlik Bey, dated 6 May 1915. For another similar cable sent to the governor of Erzurum, Tahsin, see BOA/DH.ŞFR, no. 52/281.

[102] Yeni Gazete, 3 August 1919.

[103] Başkâtipzade Ragıp Bey, Tarih-i Hayatım (Ankara: Kebikeç Yayınları, 1996), 59–60.

[104] Lepsius, Der Todesgang, 43.

moved from the places slated for evacuation and where exactly they were to be resettled in the areas designated as such. In a 3 May 1915 cable to the provincial district of Marash, Talat asks, "[H]ow many Armenians are still in Zeytun? Up to now, how many have been removed and to where have they been sent?"[105] In another cable to the province of Adana, sent on 11 May, he requests reports on "[H]ow many Armenians have been removed from Haçin, Dörtyol and other locales up to the present . . . and to where have they been sent?"[106] In a cable to Aleppo on 5 May, he informs the governor that the arriving Armenians would have to be resettled in the eastern portions of the province,[107] and on 12 May, the Aleppo officials are asked to "disperse the Armenian [arrivals] in any manner [deemed] appropriate throughout the [area's various] villages or settle them in the new places."[108] It was also in this same period that Muslim refugees from the Balkans, Caucasus, and elsewhere began to be settled in the areas left empty of Armenians.

A cable to Fourth Army commander Cemal Pasha, sent on 20 April 1915, reports that "in accordance with the order given . . . the [Muslim] refugees in Ayıntab [present-day Gaziantep] have begun to be sent to Zeytun," where evacuations had actually begun between 8 and 10 April.[109] Although it would appear that the first stage of evacuation from Zeytun consisted of only a limited number of families and the "complete deportation" of the Zeytun Armenians was announced no earlier than 5 and 9 May,[110] the government's swift resettlement of Muslims there would seem to indicate that preparations for such a move had been made well in advance.

---

[105] BOA/DH.ŞFR, no. 52/203, Coded telegram from the Interior Ministry's General Directorate of Security to the Provincial District of Marash, dated 3 May 1915.

[106] BOA/DH.ŞFR, no. 52/338, Coded telegram from the Interior Ministry's General Directorate of Security to the Province of Adana, dated 11 May 1915.

[107] BOA/DH.ŞFR, no. 52/267, Coded telegram from the Interior Ministry's General Directorate of Security to the Province of Aleppo, dated 5 May 1915.

[108] BOA/DH.ŞFR, no. 52/335, Coded telegram from the Interior Ministry's General Directorate of Security to the Province of Aleppo, dated 12 May 1915.

[109] BOA/DH.ŞFR, no. 52/51, Coded telegram from the Interior Ministry's Office of Tribal and Immigrant Resettlement to Fourth Army commander Cemal Pasha, dated 20 April 1915.

[110] BOA/DH.ŞFR, no. 52/253 and 286, Coded telegrams from the Interior Ministry's General Directorate of Security to the Provincial District of Marash, dated 5 and 9 May 1915.

On 18 May interior minister Talat Pasha sent a "secret and urgent" reply to a request from Erzurum governor Tahsin Bey to send a group of local Armenians to Kastamonu and Sivas. Talat's communiqué reveals the new character that the deportation operation was taking on: "It is absolutely unacceptable to settle the Armenians removed from there in Kastamonu and Sivas. The highest officials have previously been instructed to send these persons to the south[ern provinces]. Therefore, the Armenians who have been reported to have been sent to Sivas by way of the Erzincan road are to be turned back immediately and sent to the southern parts of Urfa and Mosul and to the Provincial District of [Der] Zor." All further deportees are to be sent to these same locations, adds Talat.[111]

On 23 May 1915, the geographic scope of the Armenian deportations was broadened to include new regions, and for the first time the places from which they were to be deported are expressly listed. According to the list of instructions received by Cemal Pasha, which indicated that "the information has been given to the necessary provinces," the Armenian population was to be removed from: "(1) The provinces of Erzurum, Van, and Bitlis. (2) The provinces of Adana, Mersin, Kozan, and Cebel-i Bereket, apart from the population of [the cities of] Adana, Sis, and Mersin. (3) the provincial district of Marash, apart from the population of [the city of] Marash. (4) The towns and villages inside the counties of İskenderun, Bilan, Cisr-i Şugûr and Antalya, apart from the central county of the Aleppo province." As for the regions in which the Armenian deportees were to be resettled, the document continues,

> Those who have been deported from the provinces of Van, Erzurum, and Bitlis shall be resettled in the southern portion of the province of Mosul, but not the northern part [of the province], which shares a border with the province of Van; and in the provincial district of Urfa, but not the provincial district of [Der] Zor or its district center; those who are to be removed from the areas connected to Adana, Aleppo and Marash will be transported by the government

---

[111] BOA/DH.ŞFR, no. 53/48, Coded telegram from interior minister Talat to the Province of Erzurum, dated 18 May 1915.

to the places already designated in the eastern portion of the province of Damascus and the eastern and southeastern portions of the province of Aleppo, and resettled there.[112]

According to this new plan, the governors of the regions from which the Armenians were to be deported, and the local authorities in the regions where they would be resettled, were all informed separately by telegram.[113]

DEPORTATIONS AND MASSACRES: THE DUAL-TRACK MECHANISM

As has been explained above, in all likelihood the CUP Central Committee made two separate and parallel decisions sometime in late March or early April to deport and also annihilate the Armenian population of Anatolia. The most explicit acknowledgment of the dual manner in which these decisions were conveyed is in a speech by Reşid Akif Pasha, who served on the Council of Ministers in the Ahmed İzzet Pasha cabinet, the first cabinet formed in the Armistice period after Talat Pasha resigned and fled the country in October 1918. Addressing the Ottoman Chamber of Deputies on 21 November, Reşid Akif Pasha stated that the massacres began with the Interior Ministry's transmission of secret deportation orders to the provinces:

There are certain secrets that I learned in my most recent, brief service in the [İzzet Pasha] cabinet that didn't survive more than 25–30 days. Among these, I came across one peculiar thing. This deportation order was given openly and in official fashion by the Interior Ministry and communicated to the provinces. But after this official order [was given], the inauspicious order was circulated by the Central Committee to all parties so that the armed gangs [çete] could hastily complete their cursed task. With that, the

---

[112] BOA/DH.ŞFR, no. 53/94, Coded telegram from interior minister Talat to the commander of the Imperial Fourth Army, dated 23 May 1915.

[113] BOA/DH.ŞFR, no. 53/91, Coded telegram from interior minister Talat to the Province of Mosul and the Provincial Districts of Urfa and (Der) Zor, dated 23 May 1915; and BOA/DH.ŞFR, no. 53/92, Coded telegram to the Provinces of Adana and Aleppo and to the Provincial District of Marash, dated 23 May 1915.

armed gangs then took over and the barbaric massacres then began to take place.[114]

This speech, "in consideration of its particular importance," was subsequently published by a number of newspapers, which deemed it "worthy of the utmost notice."[115]

Similar information to that provided by Reşid Akif Pasha was also provided by Vehip Pasha. In his affidavit, which was based on the testimony of suspects that he himself had interrogated, Vehip Pasha affirmed that the official deportation orders were disseminated by means of the civilian provincial governors, whereas the annihilation order was in fact arranged by Bahaeddin Şakir. Vehip Pasha further stated that after being appointed to his position as Third Army commander, he began to investigate and had the gendarmes and their assistants, whom he saw as responsible for the massacre of the deportee convoys from Sivas, arrested, and he transcribed their testimony himself. These suspects told Vehip Pasha that "they had received their orders from Memduh Bey, who was serving as the district governor of Erzincan at that time for the purpose of acting in this manner, and those who were actively participating in the deplorable events received theirs from Dr. Bahaeddin Şakir Bey."[116]

The dual-track mechanism appears to have functioned more or less as follows: deportation orders were conveyed via official channels from the Interior Ministry to the provincial governors, who then circulated them to the security service units in the region; namely, the security organization connected to the Interior Ministry and the gendarmerie. As for the massacre of the deportee convoys, an operation overseen by Bahaeddin Şakir of the CUP Central Committee, coded killing orders were conveyed to the provinces primarily by the party's responsible secretaries.

Numerous sources confirm that the responsible secretaries did indeed transmit orders upon arrival in the regions where they were to be active. For example, in the postwar trial of the former Unionist leaders, the presiding judge frequently repeated that available documentation amply confirmed that the Unionist Party secretaries had brought the orders to the

---

[114] *Meclis-i Ayan Zabıt Ceridesi* [Minutes of the Ottoman Chamber of Notables; hereafter *MAZC*], 3rd Electoral Term, Year of Assembly 5, vol. 1 (Ankara: TBMM Basımevi 1990), 123.

[115] *İkdam*, 5 December 1918.

[116] Vehip Pasha's testimony.

provinces, and that the provincial governors who did not obey the orders orally transmitted by these secretaries were dismissed from office on the recommendations of the latter. Indeed, the judge separately questioned nearly every witness, each time along the lines of "the responsible pleni-potentiaries came to areas such as Ankara, Kastamonu, Erzincan, Yozgat, Trebizond, Sivas, and others; they delivered certain secret instructions to the [regions' respective] governors; [we]re you aware of this?"[117] Through-out the trial's sessions, the judge repeated that various governors, such as Mazhar Bey of Ankara, Reşid Pasha of Kastamonu, and Cemal Bey of Yozgat provincial district, had all been dismissed upon the urging of these secretaries.[118]

Corroborating testimony was given by these former governors, first before the Commission for the Investigation of Crimes (Tedkik-i Seyiyat Komisyonu), and later at various sessions of the Unionists' trials in the courts-martial. Former Ankara governor Mazhar Bey, for example, ex-plained his removal thus: "I acted as if I did not understand the orders concerning the deportation of Armenians that I received from the interior minister in Istanbul. As you know, other provinces had already completed their deportation operations that I had not yet begun. [Then] Atıf Bey ar-rived . . . He orally relayed to me the order regarding the killing and anni-hilation of the Armenians. I told him 'No, Atıf Bey, I am the governor, I'm not a bandit. I cannot do it. I will get up from th[e governor's] chair and you can come and do it.' "[119]

Kastamonu governor Reşid told a similar story. The verdict in the trial of the Unionist responsible secretaries states that Reşid was dismissed at the urging of responsible secretary Hasan Fehmi for having said, "I cannot have so much blood on my hands" (ben elimi kana boyamam).[120] Cemal, the governor of Yozgat provincial district, gave a similar account in his affidavit, which was delivered to the Commission for the Investigation of Misdeeds on 12 December 1918. Cemal attested that responsible secretary Necati Bey showed him an official order to annihilate the Armenians but refused to give it to him. The governor in turn refused to execute the order, telling Necati

---

[117] For example, see the account of the trial's fourth session in *TV*, no. 3549, 8 May 1919.

[118] *TV*, no. 3557, sixth session, 14 May 1919.

[119] AAPJ, Box 21, File M, Doc. no. 492.

[120] This information is found in the judges' decision in the trial of the responsible secretaries, deliv-ered on 8 January 1920, reproduced in *TV*, no. 3772, 10 February 1920.

Bey, "Since you do not have an official title, I will first have to ask for an official written request, and [until then] I cannot perform this action." Several days later, Cemal was dismissed from his post.[121] On 5 March 1919, at the eleventh session of the Yozgat trial, Cemal testified that Necati had told him that the order reflected the will of the CUP's Central Committee.[122]

In addition to the provincial and district officials who lost their positions, other local officials forfeited their lives. Hüseyin Nesimî, the senior administrator of Lice County, refused to carry out the order to massacre his Armenian residents. He first demanded to receive a written order to this effect. Soon thereafter he was removed from his position, summoned to Diyarbekır, and murdered en route.[123] His son, Abidin Nesimî, recalls that the order to dismiss state officials came from Diyarbekır governor Dr. Reşid Bey, and he names several other provincial and district heads who shared a similar fate: "Basra governor Ferit, Müntefak district governor Bedi Nuri . . . Sabit, the acting head official of Beşiri County, [and] the journalist İsmail Mestan" were among those killed. In order to carry out the annihilation of the Armenians, the younger Nesimî explains, "it was unavoidable that the administrative cadre that was likely to oppose [such a measure] would have to be removed. For this reason . . . it appeared necessary to eliminate the aforementioned persons."[124] The senior administrator of Midyat County was assassinated "upon the orders of the governor of Diyarbekır . . . for having resisted the order to kill the Christians in his county."[125] At the 11 May 1919 session of the Trebizond trial, Justice Ministry inspector Kenan Bey testified that during the period in question he had traveled to Samsun with the intention of conducting his own inquiry and that while there, "he observed the deportations take place . . . and the county head of Bafra was killed."[126]

The prominent Unionist journalist Hüseyin Cahit (Yalçın) writes in his memoirs that, in addition to the responsible secretaries, Bahaeddin Şakir himself "toured the eastern provinces and met with governors, district

[121] AAPJ, Box 21, File M, Doc. no. 494.

[122] *Renaissance*, 6, 7 March 1919.

[123] Lepsius, *Der Todesgang*, 76.

[124] Abidin Nesimi, *Yıllarım İçinden* (Istanbul: Gözlem Yayınları, 1977), 39–40.

[125] DE/PA-AA/Bo.Kons./Band 169, Cable from German consul in Mosul, Holstein, to Ambassador Wangenheim in Istanbul, dated 16 July 1915.

[126] *Alemdar*, 11 May 1919.

governors and others," and informed them of the Central Committee's decision.[127] During the main trial of the Unionist leaders, the presiding judge stated that Bahaeddin Şakir had suddenly been appointed overall commander of all the SO units.[128] Additionally, he stated that "both Nail Bey and Bahaeddin Şakir Bey toured certain provincial districts in the central regions of this province [of Trebizond], delivering secret orders," and he asked the witnesses whether or not they were aware of this.[129]

Additional evidence attests that the Central Committee's decision to annihilate the Armenians was delivered to the provinces by means of special couriers. At the time of the Armenian deportations, Ahmed Esat (later known as Esat Uras), was the head of the Second Department of the Interior Ministry–affiliated General Directorate of Security. During the Armistice period he approached the English occupation forces and attempted to sell them transcribed minutes from a meeting at which decisions were made regarding the Armenian massacres. Of the four documents he delivered to the English, the second one, which was written by Esat himself, reveals that the messages were sent to the various provincial governors by means of couriers, who were instructed to read them to the governors and then return with the original messages and destroy them.[130]

It was repeated in numerous indictments and verdicts of the court-martial trials in Istanbul that the order for annihilation was sent to the provinces via special couriers. For example, the verdict in the Bayburt trial mentions several times that the decision to annihilate the Armenians had been made by the Central Committee and transmitted to the provinces by special courier; the verdict made clear that special consideration had been given to the testimony of a certain Nusret, who was sentenced to death and executed. Nusret said during his interrogation that he received the order that "no Armenian be left," and if any were left, he was "threatened with execution." Consequently, the convoys were "sent ... with an official communiqué." Nusret was then asked why he did not get documents

---

[127] Hüseyin Cahit Yalçın, *Siyasi Anılar* (Istanbul: Türkiye İş Bankası Kültür Yayınları, 1976), 236.

[128] *TV*, no. 3549, 8 May 1335.

[129] Ibid.

[130] FO 371/4172/31307, Report dated 10 February 1919, 386. For the partial translation of this document and its analysis, see V. N. Dadrian, "The Secret Young-Turk Ittihadist Conference and the Decision for the World War I Genocide of the Armenians," *Journal of Political and Military Sociology* 22, no. 1 (Summer 1994): 173–77.

showing that he delivered the Armenians safe and sound. He replied, "at that time, the matter was finished."[131]

In addition, several corroborating testimonies state that these cables that ordered the massacres of the Armenians also contained the instructions to destroy the orders after reading. As seen above, in the main indictment in the trial of the Unionist leaders, it is recounted that Ali Suat, the governor of the provincial district of Der Zor, was given instructions to destroy the telegram he received after reading it.[132] Additionally, at the third session of the Yozgat trial (10 February 1919), the judge read out the testimony given by Kemal, the head official of Boğazlıyan County, before the Commission for the Investigation of Crimes. After reading it himself, Kemal stated that telegrams ordering the killings had been sent.[133] The same information was brought up at a later session of the trial (24 March 1919), with the public prosecutor stating that Kemal had written the testimony in question after "thinking about it for three or four hours."[134]

"DEPORTATION" MEANT ANNIHILATION

Beginning in April 1915, the deportation of the Armenian population meant their annihilation, and as the foregoing has shown, a great deal of documentation expresses this fact in some form or other. Many of the relevant records are cited in the main postwar indictment of the Unionist leadership. Of particular importance are the statements made by İhsan Bey, who served during the postwar period as director of the Interior Ministry's Private Secretariat. In his written testimony, İhsan Bey recalled that while he was serving as the head official of Kilis County, Abdullahad Nuri Bey came to him en route from Istanbul to Aleppo and revealed that the real purpose of the deportation was to annihilate the Armenians. "I was in contact with Talat Bey and received the annihilation order from him personally," explained Nuri Bey. "The safety of the country is tied to this."[135]

---

[131] *Tercüman-ı Hakikat*, 5 August 1920; *Vakit*, 6 August 1920.

[132] *TV*, no. 3540, 5 May 1919; the indictment was actually read at the trial's first session on 27 April 1919.

[133] *Renaissance* 11, 12 February 1919; *İkdam*, 11 February 1919.

[134] *Alemdar*, 25 March 1919.

[135] *TV*, no. 3540, 5 May 1919; this issue featured a report of the trial's first session, which was held on 27 April 1919.

Vehip Pasha, who was appointed commander of the Third Army in February 1916, declared in his aforementioned written statement to the investigatory commission that "the massacre and annihilation of the Armenians and their looting and pillaging by the killers were the result of a decision made by the [C]entral [C]ommittee of the [Committee of] Union and Progress." He also asserted that "these specific acts of violence, which [were] carried out in accordance with a comprehensive program and with a clear intent, were performed upon the instruction and urging, and with the supervision and follow-up of government functionaries, who were the tools of, first, the Central Committee of the CUP and its plenipotentiaries, and second, the wishes and aspirations of the CUP itself, which had discarded [all considerations of] law and conscience."[136] Despite having seen and heard of these crimes themselves, the general added, state functionaries took no steps to prevent them, even abetting them in many cases. This was one of the most important pieces of evidence testifying to the overall planned nature of the events that transpired.[137]

One of Vehip Pasha's most compelling and corroborating proofs of government administrators' direct responsibility for the tragedy was an account of the incidents in Trebizond witnessed by the Unionist deputy for this area, Hazıf Mehmed Emin Bey, wherein many local Armenian men, women, and children were loaded onto boats and then thrown into the Black Sea.

During debates on the subject in the Ottoman Chamber of Deputies, 11 December 1918, Mehmed Emin Bey, himself a loyal Unionist, stated that he "witnessed this incident . . . that is to say, the Armenian incident," adding that

[T]here was a county head in the military district. He loaded the Armenians onto a caïque on the pretext of sending them off to Samsun [by boat] and then dumped them into the sea. I heard that the

[136] From the written testimony of Vehip Pasha, delivered "to the President of the Commission for the Investigation of Crimes in the Office of the General [Directorate of] Security," dated 5 December 1918. I used the copy that is found in AAPJ, Box 7, File H, Doc. no. 171–82. Vehip Pasha's testimony played a critical role in the conviction of the defendants, not only in the main trial of Unionist leaders, but also of those tried for perpetrating the massacres in Trebizond and Harput. The entire testimony was actually read into the record in the second session of the Trebizond trial, held on 29 March 1919, and included in the judges' decision in the Harput trial.

[137] Ibid.

governor [of the province of Trebizond] Cemal Azmi performed this act personally . . . As soon as I arrived [in Istanbul], I told the interior minister those things that I had seen and heard. . . . But I was unable to persuade him to take any action whatsoever regarding the governor. I tried over a period of perhaps three years, but it was not to be. They would claim it [had happened in] the war zone, say things like this, and there was never any follow up or conclusion [on the matter].[138]

As seen from the series of cables from Talat Pasha in the indictment against the Unionist leaders in the main trial in Istanbul, what the interior minister requested from those local Unionist functionaries was not that they should prevent the killings from taking place nor even that they investigate such incidents; rather, they were ordered to clear the roads of all of the dead bodies that covered them. In his cables Talat warned the local officials that whoever failed to comply with the orders to remove the corpses would be severely punished. For instance, a coded telegram sent on 21 July 1915 to the provincial and district governors of Diyarbekır, Mamuretülaziz, Urfa, and Der Zor demands that "the dead who remain on the roads are to be removed and their corpses are to be thrown into the valleys, lakes, or rivers, and the possessions that they have abandoned on the roads are to be [taken and] burned." Moreover, in an order "which was sent in cipher by the governor of Mamuretülaziz to the provincial district governor of Malatya . . . [it is] reported that, despite the explicit orders [to the contrary], there are still many bodies present on the roads," and the governor informs his subordinate that "those officials who show laxity in this matter will face harsh punishments from the Imperial Interior Ministry."[139]

In addition to the foregoing evidence, there is also indirect proof that the decision to deport the Armenians was in fact made with the full intent of exterminating them. For example, here is a telegram sent by CUP Central Committee member Bahaeddin Şakir to the Unionist responsible secretary in Harput, Resneli Nazım, on 21 June 1915. In it Şakir asks, "[H]ave the Armenians who have been dispatched from there been liq-

[138] MMZC, Period 3, Assembly Year 5, vol. 1, 25 December 1918, Session 24, 300.

[139] TV, no. 3540, 5 May 1919; report of the trial's first session (27 April 1919).

uidated? (*tasfiye ol-*); have those detrimental and dangerous persons, whom you reported to have been exiled and sent off, been exterminated (*imhâ' edil*) or simply sent off into exile somewhere else? Please be explicit in your report, brother."[140] This cable would be used as a critical piece of evidence not only in the indictment in the main Unionist trial, but also in the trials of the local officials in Mamuretülaziz, the Unionist responsible secretaries, and several others.

Other telegrams with similar content were read into the record at the Yozgat trial, which began on 5 February 1919. Twelve such cables, which were submitted as evidence and read at the trial's ninth session (22 February 1919), contain descriptions of deportations that are clearly understood to be massacres and whole-scale killings. For example, in an exchange of communiqués on 5 August 1915, Boğazlıyan gendarmerie commander Mustafa reports to Fifth Army Corps acting commander Halil Recai that a group of Armenian "evildoers" who were rounded up the previous night from towns and villages in the area have been "sent to the predetermined places."[141] When Recai requests clarification of the phrase "sent to the predetermined places,"[142] Mustafa retorts that the Armenians were killed "because they were vermin."[143] A cable from Boğazlıyan gendarmerie commander Hulûsi, which was read at the trial's twelfth session, contains the same language and explains succinctly that the term "deportation means annihilation."[144]

In reports from the German Embassy and its consulates—and especially in field reports from German officers—one encounters numerous passages in which the Unionist leaders are said to have devised and put into place a plan that was thought to have simply entailed the order to deport the Armenian population, but actually aimed to annihilate them.[145] In a report dated 30 June 1915, German consul general Mordtmann recounts to his superiors a conversation with Ottoman interior minister

[140] Ibid.

[141] AAPJ, Box 17, File H, Doc. no. 616.

[142] AAPJ, Box 21, File M, Doc. no. 511.

[143] Ibid. For information dealing with the trial's ninth session, see the 23 February 1919 issues of *Renaissance*, *Yeni Gün*, and *İkdam*.

[144] AAPJ, Box 21, File M, Doc. no. 506; *Renaissance*, 7 March 1919.

[145] For two examples, see the German archives: Grosses Hauptquartier 194, Türkei 41/1, Cable from Wolff-Metternich to foreign minister Jagov, dated 1 July 1916; and DE/PA-AA/R 14094, Report by Scheubner Richter, dated 4 December 1916.

Talat Pasha, in which Talat very clearly explains the intended goal of the deportation. Regarding the deportation, Talat told him that "what we are talking about here . . . is the annihilation of the Armenians."[146] Separately, the report by the German officer Stange, sent on 23 August 1915 and marked "top secret," is of special importance. Stange, who served in 1914–15 with Bahaeddin Şakir in the SO, writes on the basis of his own personal observations that neither the Armenian deportations nor the massacres were carried out for military purposes or as the result of wartime conditions; rather, "what we are dealing with here is a long- and well-thought-out plan" that had been activated ostensibly in response to certain isolated events. "The decision to deport and annihilate [the Armenian population]," Stange states, "was taken by the Young Turk Committee in Istanbul" and coordinated by Bahaeddin Şakir in Erzurum.[147]

The key role played by the SO has been questioned by several historians. The chief claim is that no proof has been found about the direct participation of the SO or of its armed bands (çete) in the annihilation of the Armenians. This argument is important from the point of view of proving that the Armenian Genocide was not a centrally planned policy. If truly, as is claimed, it is not possible to demonstrate the direct role of the SO and its bands in the Armenian Genocide, the principal role of the central government in the murder of the Armenians can be easily denied. It can be proposed that the killings were the work of local structures that were out of control. In the following sections, this and similar arguments will be discussed, and an attempt will be made to show what information Interior Ministry documents contain on this topic.

[146] DE/PA-AA/Bo.Kons./Band 169, Report by Consul General Mordtmann, dated 30 June 1915.
[147] DE/PA-AA/Bo.Kons./Band 170, Report by Stange, dated 23 August 1915.

Despite all attempts to sanitize the archival re-
cord, as discussed at the beginning of this study, the surviving documents
in the Interior Ministry section of the Prime Ministerial Ottoman Archive
are sufficient to show the distinctive character of Ottoman wartime measures against the Armenians: having been uprooted and deported from
Anatolia, they were to be denied even rudimentary living conditions. As
shown in chapter 6, the orders to annihilate the Armenian population did
not reach the regional and district officials through the usual governmental channels but instead were hand-delivered by selected Unionist opera-
tives. Although, for this reason, the original orders are unlikely to be found
in official correspondence, the mobilization of several branches and agencies of government to implement the policy against the Armenians inevitably left a paper trail within the Ottoman state archive.

DOCUMENTS THAT SHOW THE GOAL OF THE
OPERATION TO HAVE BEEN ANNIHILATION

ANKARA

The clearest statement that the aim of the government's policies toward
the Armenians was annihilation is found in a cable of 29 August 1915 from
interior minister Talat Pasha to the province of Ankara. "The Armenian
question in the eastern provinces has been resolved," he asserted. "There's
no need to sully the nation and the government['s honor] with further
atrocities (*fuzuli mezâlım*)."[1] (See figure 7.1.) Talat's statement clearly
implied that up to the end of August 1915, such crimes had indeed been

[1] BOA/DH.ŞFR, no. 55/290, Coded telegram from Interior Minister Talat to the Province of Ankara, dated 29 August 1915.

committed. This document alone should put an end to many of the long-standing and unnecessary debates on this issue.

In the same cable Talat also mentioned—albeit briefly—the original reason for the complaint: "the centr[al government] has been greatly distressed, in particular, by the manner in which the Armenians were subjected to attacks in a locale near Ankara, by the general administrative incompetence of those entrusted with the deportations, and by the unleashing of the animal impulses of the [local] population and of the gendarmes assigned to this area to perpetrate rapes and thievery."

Talat was certainly referring to the annihilation of the Armenian Catholic population outside the city of Ankara—the news of which, unlike the massacres committed in more remote locations, was quickly relayed to Istanbul by Armenian railroad workers. According to one Armenian source, the German and Austro-Hungarian governments—and especially the Roman Catholic Church—protested to the Ottoman government over the affair.[2] Moreover, at this time Talat was engaged in fulfilling promises to Germany, which had been pressuring Turkey increasingly on this issue, that Catholics would not be deported.

After its earlier attempts at intervention failed to alleviate the harsh conditions of the deportations, Berlin delivered a note to the Ottoman government on 4 July 1915, so as not to be held responsible "for these harsh measures of the Turks" and "in order to be able to endure any future attacks by their enemies." The note further informed Istanbul that although the German government did approve "the deportation of the Armenians, which were carried out as the result of military exigency and with the purpose of preventing revolts, as [an] appropriate [measure]," the deportees "needed to be protected from looting and pillaging."[3]

The related note acknowledged receipt of news of the massacres, adding:

> It is unfortunate that, according to the information that has reached our embassy, local authorities have been unable to prevent events

[2] A firsthand account of the annihilation of the Catholic population of Ankara is recounted in Grigoris Balakian, *Armenian Golgotha: A Memoir of the Armenian Genocide, 1915–1918*, trans. Peter Balakian and Aris Sevag (New York: Alfred A. Knopf, 2009), chapter 13.

[3] DE/PA-AA/R 14086, Report to the Porte from German ambassador, Wangenheim, to Chancellor Bethmann-Hollweg, dated 7 July 1915.

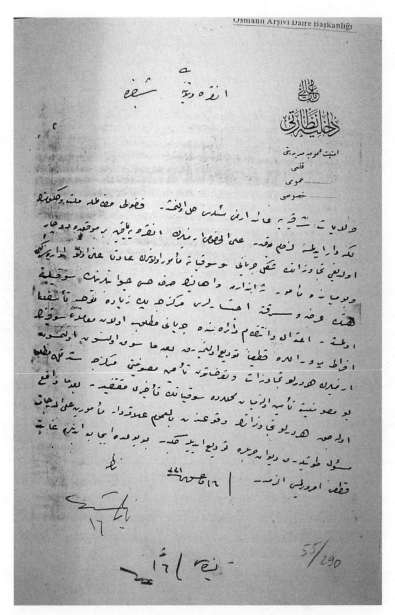

Figure 7.1. Ottoman Document 55/290. A cable from interior minister Talat Pasha on 29 August 1915 that reads, "The Armenian question in the Eastern Provinces has been resolved. There's no need to sully the nation and the government['s honor] with further atrocities [*fuzuli mezâlim*]."

such as these, which are disturbing in every sense. Enemy forces will exploit this situation in order to stir up indignation and outrage among the Armenians. . . . As a friend and power allied to Turkey, the German government sees itself as obligated to draw the Porte's attention to the potential negative consequences to our mutual interests, both during the current war and in the future. . . . Our embassy believes it necessary to give immediate and decisive orders in order to protect the lives and property of the Armenians who are forced to migrate, from the point that they are transported [until they are] in their new places of settlement.[4]

Soon after the reception of this note, the "Diyarbekır incident" (discussed below) erupted, and Germany began to engage in "more urgent" attempts to intervene with the Ottoman Porte.[5] Nevertheless, news of the continuing massacres compelled Berlin to submit a second, slightly sharper note on 9 August: "The systematic slaughter of the Armenian people who had been deported from their homes had taken on such an extent over the past few weeks that a renewed, forcible representation on our part against this coarse action, which the government not only tolerated but apparently supported, appeared to be imperative, particularly as in various places the Christians of other races and confessions were also no longer being spared."[6] Moreover, "The German Ambassador regrets having to determine that according to information he has received from impartial and undoubtedly reliable sources, incidents of this nature, instead of being prevented by the local authorities, regularly accompanied the expulsion of the Armenians in such a way that most of them perished before they reached their destination . . . [i]n certain places . . . all Christians, irrespective of their race or confession, have suffered the same fate."[7]

The note was hand-delivered to Talat, and during the ensuing conversation the Ottoman interior minister gave his word that he would prevent

---

[4] Ibid.

[5] DE/PA-AA/R 14093, Report prepared by the German Foreign Ministry for the German Reichstag, dated 27 September 1916.

[6] DE/PA-AA/R 14087, Report by German ambassador to the Porte, Hohenlohe-Langenburg, to Chancellor Bethmann-Hollweg, dated 12 August 1915. The note, dated 9 August (1915), appears as an appendix to the report.

[7] Ibid.

such incidents and that no Armenians would be deported from Istanbul. In fact, nothing changed. In response to the continuing situation, the German ambassador met separately with the grand vizier and the interior minister and pressed each of them for results. For their part, the Ottoman statesmen declared that the anti-Armenian measures had come to an end.[8]

On 31 August, as these discussions were taking place, Talat paid a visit to the German embassy, taking along the translations of several telegrams that he had sent to local officials in the provinces. In conversation with the German ambassador, Talat repeated the claim that the anti-Armenian measures had been stopped, uttering the now-famous statement: "The Armenian question no longer exists" (La question arménienne n'existe plus).[9] He had made the identical assertion in a cable to Ankara two days earlier (29 August).

One of the translated telegrams that Talat brought with him, which was quoted in chapter 5, appears to have been composed in order to convince the Germans. The goal of the Armenian deportations, the cable explained, was "to ensure that this community [the Armenians] would no longer be able to undertake initiatives and actions against the government, and that they would be brought to a state in which they will be unable to pursue their national aspirations related to the advocating for a[n independent] government of Armenia." The deportations were not aimed at "the annihilation of the aforementioned prominent individuals and personalities." Moreover, "Protestant and Catholic Armenians are not to be deported."[10] As will be shown in further examples below, Talat

[8] "In the wake of new unfortunate reports regarding the course of the resettlement, the ambassador, Prince Hohenlohe has, with the attached memorandum of 8 August, renewed his protest against the manner of dispatch. At the end of the month [August 1915] representations will again be made more urgently before the Grand Vizier. The Porte has declared that the measures against the Armenians will be abandoned . . ." (DE/PA-AA/R 14093, Report prepared by the German Foreign Ministry for the German Reichstag, dated 27 September 1916).

[9] DE/PA-AA/R 14087 and DE/PA-AA/Bo.Kons., vol. 170, Report by German ambassador to the Porte Hohenlohe-Langenburg to Chancellor Bethmann-Hollweg, dated 4 September 1915. Talat's words were also recorded by another German Embassy functionary, Göppert, during the 31 August conversations (DE/PA-AA/Bo.Kons., vol. 170).

[10] BOA/DH.ŞFR, no. 55/292, Coded telegram from the Interior Ministry's General Directorate of Security to the Provinces of Hüdâvendigâr (Bursa), Ankara, Konya, İzmit, Adana, Marash, Urfa, Aleppo, (Der) Zor, Sivas, Kütahya, Karesi (Balıkesir), Niğde, Mamuretülaziz, Diyarbekır, Karahisâr-ı Sahib (Afyon Karahisar), Erzurum, and Kayseri, dated 29 August 1915.

sent another cable to Ankara on 31 August (the day of his conversations at the German Embassy), demanding an investigation of the murder of Dr. Rupen Chilingirian, a prominent Istanbul Armenian intellectual, and his four companions.

DIYARBEKIR AND GOVERNOR REŞID

A second example can be given from a group of documents that show that the actual aim of the Armenian deportations was annihilation. It consists of a set of four telegrams from interior minister Talat to Dr. Reşid, governor of Diyarbekır Province. In the first of these, sent on 12 July 1915,[11] Talat informed the governor that he had received reports

> that in recent days massacres have been planned of the Armenians in the province, as well as of the other Christians without any difrerntiation according to sect or confession . . . [and] that in Mardin the Armenian bishop and some 700 persons from among the Armenian and other Christian population were taken outside the city and slaughtered like sheep by some persons who arrived from Diyarbekır; it is estimated that up to now some 2,000 persons have been killed in these massacres, and it is feared that, if no serious and decisive solution is found for this [phenomenon], the Muslim population of the surrounding provinces will rise up and massacre the entire Christian population.

In response, the interior minister commanded:

> Since the disciplinary and political measures adopted vis-à-vis the Armenians do not in any way apply to the other Christians, an immediate end should be put to such events, which will have an extremely negative effect on public opinion and which randomly threaten the

[11] This is the most well known, and has already been reproduced in several other works. This telegram first appeared in Devlet Arşivleri Genel Müdürlüğü, *Osmanlı Belgelerinde Ermeniler, 1915–1920*, Doc. no. 71, p. 69. The document, which is listed as Catalog no. 54/406, does not appear in the catalogs of the Prime Ministerial Ottoman Archive. The numeration in the relevant catalogs of Cipher Office documents jumps from 54/405 to 54/407. Had the General Directorate of the Turkish State Archives not published this document in the aforementioned book, no one would have known of its existence. An unanswered question remains as to whether the document was intentionally removed from the archival catalog.

lives of Christians in particular; please provide an accurate report of the present situation.[12]

The real impetus behind this telegram came not from Talat himself but from the German Embassy, which, having received regular reports of events from its various consulates throughout the empire, wished to exert pressure on the Ottoman regime to stop the widespread killings. According to consular reports from the region, Governor Reşid had been ordering the local gendarmerie units to massacre the Christians. If no preventive measures were taken, it was feared, the "lower classes" would also join in. One of the consulates' principal sources of information about these events was the district governor of Mardin, who was in Diyarbekır at the time. The German Embassy relayed these reports directly to Talat Pasha and demanded that he take preventive action. Indeed, in his cables the Ottoman interior minister used the same language as that found in the consular reports, such as the description of the Christians being "slaughtered like sheep," and repeated the casualty figures as well.

As an example of the similarity of expressions used by both German consuls and Talat, here is a passage from a German report:

> The governor of Diyarbekır, Reshid Bey, is raging among the Christians of his province like a good bloodhound; in Mardin he has also recently rounded up some 700 Christians (mostly Armenians) in one night—among them the Armenian bishop—by means of gendarmes specially dispatched from Diyarbekır and had them slaughtered like sheep. Reshid Bey is continuing his bloody labors among the innocent, whose numbers—the district governor assures me— have presently exceeded 2,000.[13]

In light of this report, Talat's reference to "public opinion" may be read as an allusion to the Germans' displeasure and the pressure being exerted upon him. The language of Talat's telegram is unambiguously clear. Those mentioned in the cable, some of whom were state employees, were being

[12] BOA/DH.ŞFR, no. 54/406, Coded telegram from interior minister Talat to the Province of Diyarbekır, dated 12 July 1915.

[13] DE/PA-AA/Bo.Kons., vol. 169, Reports by German consul in Mosul, Holstein, to Ambassador Wangenheim, dated 10, 15 July 1915; and note (in French), hand-delivered from the German ambassador to Talat, dated 12 July 1915.

killed at the behest of the provincial governor, but this was not the matter to which the interior minister took exception: Talat's complaint was that a policy formulated specifically for the Armenian population was being implemented indiscriminately for other Christians as well, and his demand was that the killing operations against the Armenians not be carried out in a manner that would involve other Christian populations.

The deportations and massacres in Diyarbekır nevertheless continued in a manner that included all Christians. In response, Talat sent a second telegram marked "secret; see to personally" to Governor Reşid ten days later (22 July 1915); in it he declared quite plainly that the policy of annihilation was to be limited to the Armenians and not to include other Christian groups. "Despite the firm and explicit instructions within the province," he wrote, "one hears that operations have been undertaken against the Armenians and all other Christian [groups] without exception, and that this situation, which was repeatedly a cause for complaint, is now spreading to the surrounding provinces. The continuation of this situation . . . which will leave the government in a difficult position in the future, is entirely unacceptable."[14]

This second cable produced no discernible results. The governor of Diyarbekır continued to persecute all the province's Christian inhabitants without differentiating between Armenians and others. As a result, on 2 August Talat sent a third cable, once again informing Governor Reşid that reportedly, "despite firm and explicit instructions, certain armed gangs within the province have continued persecuting and killing Christians" and that, "as it was previously announced, the continuation of this situation is absolutely unacceptable. . . . It must not be forgotten that as a responsible representative of the present government, you are obliged to carry out the orders and instructions that are handed down from here, unconditionally and in accordance with our interpretation [of their meaning]." Talat concluded with a clear warning that his governor would be held responsible "for every action and incident in which bandits or armed gangs are involved."[15]

---

[14] BOA/DH.ŞFR, no. 54-A/73, Coded telegram from interior minister Talat to the Province of Diyarbekır, dated 22 July 1915.

[15] BOA/DH.ŞFR, no. 54-A/248, Coded telegram from interior minister Talat to the Province of Diyarbekır, dated 2 August 1915.

The important point is this: no criminal investigation was ever conducted against Reşid, who was openly accused of acting against the government's orders by carrying out deportation and murder operations against all Christians instead of simply the Armenians, and who ordered more than two thousand people "slaughtered like sheep"; nor was any legal sanction whatsoever imposed upon him. Even more significant, perhaps, is that Hilmi, the district governor of Mardin, who had reported the events to the German Consulate in the first place and opposed Reşid's crimes, *did* suffer government sanction, eventually being removed from his post.[16]

Moreover, Reşid's subordinate officials were rewarded for their success in carrying out the government's policies against the Armenians in Diyarbekır and its environs. On 28 July 1915, "some members of the police and commissioners who were instrumental in the capture of the leaders and other members of Armenian revolutionary committees in the province of Diyarbekır . . . were praised, given monetary rewards and citations of merit."[17]

As for Reşid, the only accounting demanded by the government concerned the fate of the jewelry and other possessions confiscated from the murdered Armenians that he had promised to send to Istanbul. For these, the governor was sent an official request "to see to the matter personally." In a cable—the fourth of those mentioned—of 6 October 1915, Talat informed Reşid that "it has been reported by parliamentary deputies that the money, jewels, and other possessions belonging to the Armenians who were deported and robbed along the way have not been lost but rather secured and sent to the capital due to the measures that you have taken. Please report back on the quantity [of valuables] and the manner in which they were recorded."[18] Talat's concern was not for the fate of the Armenians who were massacred, but rather for their valuables. No sense of injustice, nor any need to return the goods to their rightful owners, was expressed or even suggested anywhere in his telegram.

Following an investigation for embezzlement at Diyarbekır, Reşid was transferred to Ankara Province and bought a mansion on the Bosporus,

[16] Gaunt, *Massacres, Resistance, Protectors,* 170.

[17] BOA/DH.EUM.MEM, no. 2042/67/31/1333.N.15, 28 July 1915.

[18] BOA/DH.ŞFR, no. 56/315, Coded telegram from the Interior Ministry to the Province of Diyarbekır, dated 6 October 1915.

only to be removed from the governorship when Talat found out about the real-estate purchase. As journalist Süleyman Nazif expressed most succinctly, "Even more distressing than this is the fact that, although he thought of and referred to him as a 'killer,' Talat Pasha dismissed Reşid for having been a 'thief.' "[19]

In a postscript to this narrative, decades later additional information came to light concerning the fate of the jewelry and precious stones that were the subject of Talat's concern in the cables. According to a member of the Raman tribe, which inhabited the provinces of Diyarbekır, Siirt, and Mardin, Reşid summoned the leaders of the tribe and told them:

> I will give you convoy after convoy of Armenians . . . However much gold, money, jewelry, and valuable items they have with them, we will take it together. You will bring them with *kelek* [floatation devices made of inflated animal skins] across the Tigris. When you arrive at a place where no one can see or hear, you will kill them all and throw the[ir bodies] in the Tigris. You will cut open their stomachs and fill them with rocks so that they won't float to the surface. All of the possessions you find are for your people. Of the gold, money, and jewels, half of it is yours, the other half you will bring to me to give to the Red Crescent. But no one can hear or know about this secret. If this secret is ever revealed both you and I will be destroyed.[20]

BOĞAZLIYAN AND KEMAL, ITS GOVERNING OFFICIAL

In the Yozgat trial, which was heard in the Istanbul Court-Martial beginning in February 1919, a number of telegrams were submitted in various sessions as evidence against Kemal, the district official in charge of Boğazlıyan and its environs. Kemal was subsequently convicted of organizing the massacre of Armenians in his county and executed in Istanbul's Beyazid Square on 10 April 1919. These cables represent further support for my assertions.

[19] *Hadisat*, 8 February 1919.

[20] The identity of the person whose recollection this is and who wishes to remain anonymous is known to the author. A draft of the events here was penned in 1983 with the title "Haver Delal" (unpublished manuscript), 70–71.

Among the Cipher Office documents is a cable sent by Talat Pasha to Ankara on 9 August 1915. In it, the interior minister stated that "up to now, of the Armenians found in the towns and villages of Boğazlıyan, some 3,160 have been killed by the Boğazlıyan county official."[21] According to the telegram, this information came from the head of the military branch in Boğazlıyan, where it was passed on to the command of the Fifteenth Division, and thence to the Army Corps Command and the Army High Command. Talat demanded a thorough investigation and regular reports on its results.

The cable from Boğazlıyan local commander Mustafa Bey had indeed reached Istanbul through military channels. Mustafa Bey reported the situation by cipher telegram to Şahabettin, the acting commander of the Fifteenth Division in Kayseri, who forwarded the information to Halil Recai, the acting commander of the Fifth Army Corps in Ankara. Halil Recai then relayed the report to the Ottoman High Command. There are other cables that also attest to crimes organized by Kemal.[22]

During the investigations and interrogations preceding the Istanbul trials, these telegrams were read back to him, and he was asked for further information in the matter. According to the minutes of the interrogation, the commission chairman Mazhar Bey asked the following questions:

> Question: On the basis of the testimony, the Divisional Command was informed by Boğazlıyan branch commander Mustafa Bey that more than 1,500 Armenians had been killed in the towns and villages of Boğazlıyan. The Kayseri divisional commander then informed the Army Corps [commander].
>
> Read [into the record] the translation of the cipher [telegrams] of the branch commander of Boğazlıyan, number 18, dated 14 July 1915 and of Şehabettin Bey, number 17, dated 14 July 1915 . . . Read also the cipher translation of the cable of the divisional

---

[21] BOA/DH.ŞFR, no. 54-A/326, Coded telegram from interior minister Talat to the Province of Ankara, dated 9 August 1915.

[22] Examples of such telegrams can be found in the AAPJ. All of these documents were given, along with their codification numbers from the aforementioned archive, in a work written in Armenian about the events at Yozgat. See Krigér, *Yozghadi hayasbanut'ean vaveragan badmut'iunê* (New York: n.p., 1980). In particular, see pages 324–29 for the documents in question.

commander to the Army Corps [commander], number 169,
dated July 1915 ...

Question: It is written in the translations of cipher number 207,
dated July 23, 1915, sent by Division Commander Şehabettin Bey
to the Army Corps [commander] that until [that date] he [i.e.,
Kemal] had had 3,660 Armenians killed in the villages and towns
of Boğazlıyan. This very amount is the number of Armenians who
were killed by 23 July.[23]

In another telegram read out during the Yozgat trial itself—and especially during the hearing of 22 February 1919—the local commander in
Boğazlıyan reported that Kemal had organized the killing of 1,500 Armenians. Afterward, the judge read one of the telegrams from the chain
of military command, which Talat mentions in his 9 August 1915 cables.
The following day's newspapers cited this telegram in which the killing of
3,160 Armenians was reported.[24]

One reason that I have chosen to dwell on this matter at such length and
in such detail has certainly been to show the consistency of the documentation in the Prime Ministerial Ottoman Archive in Istanbul, the Archive
of the Armenian Patriarchate in Jerusalem, and contemporary newspaper
accounts. But beyond this reason there is another. No investigation whatsoever was opened into the actions of this county head about whom such
incriminating evidence is now—and was then—available; on the contrary, he was to receive a promotion for the "successes" he had achieved in
carrying out his duties. "In the testimony he gave on 19 December 1918,
before the president of the investigatory committee in Istanbul and in his
subsequent testimony [at the Yozgat trial], Şakir Bey, the deputy for Yozgat, claimed that Kemal Bey . . . had boasted that he had been promoted
to acting district governor of Yozgat [for] having slaughtered Armenians."
Kemal allegedly told him, "I slaughtered the Armenians in Boğazlıyan, I
became acting district governor; I'm killing [them] here, too. I'll be made
the governor of a provincial district, or maybe even of a province."[25] Indeed, while still serving as head official of Boğazlıyan County, he was pro-

[23] For further information, see ibid., 328–30.
[24] *Alemdar, Yeni Gazete,* and *Renaissance,* 23 February 1919.
[25] AAPJ, File M, no. 494.

moted to the governorship of the provincial district of Yozgat between 19 August and 8 October 1915, and on 23 April 1916, he was again promoted to a higher position.[26]

More significant than this, perhaps, is the fact that although no investigation was ever opened against Kemal for the murders he had ordered to be committed, he would subsequently be investigated and tried for the property and possessions that came into his possession during the Armenian deportations. At the first session (6 February 1919) of the Yozgat trial, the defense argued that Kemal had already been tried and acquitted in Yozgat for the Armenian deportations and therefore could not be tried again for the same offense. In response, the judge read a report (found among the interrogation documents) that was written by an inspector who had investigated the related charge against Kemal. According to the report, Kemal had actually been judged for "abuses" (*suistimal*) during the course of the deportations.[27]

Upon the insistance of the attorneys, the court had a telegram sent to Yozgat in order to learn of the situation there. At the trial's second session on 8 February, the reply was read. Afterward, "it was reported that since Kemal Bey had abused his governmental position by purchasing abandoned Armenian property at prices far below actual value, on the basis of the official report prepared by the civil administration, it was decided by the court [to sentence him] to five months' imprisonment and to remove him from his position for five months. On a subsequent appeal it was decided to acquit and release him. No evidence could be found that he had already been tried for the murders."[28]

In fact, by administrative decisions of the Administrative Council of the Province of Ankara (8 January 1917) and of the Council of Ministers (12 April 1917), during his tenure as head official of Boğazlıyan County, Kemal had already been convicted of involvement in improprieties and abuse of his position in relation to his acquisition of abandoned Armenian properties. As a result, he was removed from his position on 13 June 1917. On 7 October 1917, he was at first sentenced to three months'

[26] Nejdet Bilgi, *Ermeni Tehciri ve Boğazlıyan Kaymakamı Mehmed Kemal Bey'in Yargılanması* (Ankara: Köksav Yayınları, 1999), 85.

[27] *Alemdar, Yeni Gazete, İkdam,* and *Memleket,* 6 February 1919.

[28] *İkdam,* 9 February 1919.

imprisonment for "having purchased items in his official capacity," but he was subsequently acquitted in a superior court on 25 July 1918.[29] The similarity of circumstances and outcomes in the cases of both Kemal and Reşid is significant evidence of the policies of the central government in regard to the Armenian deportation.

SPECIAL EFFORTS TO RESCUE THE KILLERS: THE MURDER OF DR. RUPEN CHILINGIRIAN

In light of the previous examples of Reşid and Boğazlıyan county head Kemal, the telegram sent to Ankara clearly shows that Istanbul was well aware of the murders and other crimes in the provinces. But, as will be seen in the case of Dr. Rupen Chilingirian, the Unionist government in Istanbul was not only aware of these crimes but in the case of several well-intentioned local administrators who made extraordinary personal efforts to identify and bring the murderers to justice, the state took pains to ensure that the perpetrators would go free.[30]

To gain some insight into this phenomenon, let us examine the events surrounding the murder of Dr. Rupen Chilingirian, one of the Armenian intellectuals taken into custody during the mass arrests, which began on 24 April 1915 and continued over the following months. He was arrested on June 1915 and deported to Çankırı. According to a report prepared by the District Governor's Office in Çankırı (dated 24 August 1915), Dr. Chilingirian and four friends had been pardoned by an Interior Ministry decision of 4 August 1915 and allowed to leave Çankırı.[31] But on 26 August—two days after the report was sent—Rupen Chilingirian and his four friends were taken to the outskirts of Ankara and murdered.[32]

[29] This information is found in Bilgi, *Ermeni Tehciri ve Boğazlayan*, 86.

[30] For more detailed information on the Dr. Chilingirian case, see Taner Akçam, "The Chilingirian Murder: A Case Study from the 1915 Roundup of Armenian Intellectuals," *Holocaust and Genocide Studies* 25, no. 1 (Spring 2011): 128–45.

[31] BOA/DH.EUM, 2. Şube, 10/73 20 L 1333, Cipher cable from the provincial governor of Kastamonu to the Interior Ministry, dated 31 August 1915.

[32] There is an important detail worth mentioning in regard to the Ottoman document under discussion here. Çankırı is a district within the province of Kastamonu, and the report prepared by the district governor of Çankırı was first sent to the provincial center on 24 August. It was only passed on to Istanbul on 31 August, or seven days later. Dr. Chilingirian and his colleagues had already been found murdered four days before it was sent.

As shown by the records of the postwar military tribunals in Istanbul, the real events were as follows: Dr. Chilingirian and his four friends were ambushed by a Kurdish gang run by Kurd Alo and his friends and killed in the vicinity of the Tüney gendarmerie post, near Ankara.[33] The ambush and murder was organized by Cemal Oğuz, the Unionist responsible secretary for Çankırı, and a group of several other officials. However, İzzet Bey, the acting district governor of Çankırı, had promised Dr. Chilingirian, as a matter of honor, that he and his friends would be transported to Ayaş safe and sound. İzzet Bey was joined by the commander of the military police of Kastamonu Province and a number of investigative judges and police officials, and together they toured the scene of the crime. Their investigation led to the Kurds' arrest for murder.[34]

Istanbul was fully informed of the crimes. By cable, Talat demanded a report on "which province it was where the attacks took place against Rupen Chilingirian and his four colleagues, who are understood to have been killed by Hacı Ali Oğlu [Kurd Alo] and 11 companions while being deported from Çankırı," adding that "the perpetrators are to be pursued and captured [immediately]."[35] Apprehended through the initiative of local officials and convicted by a court-martial established in Ankara, the defendants, including Kurd Alo, were sentenced to eight years in prison. Even so, the real outcome of the trial remains clouded in uncertainty.

The trial and punishment of Kurd Alo and his codefendants in Ankara was first mentioned in the indictment in the main trial against the Union and Progress leaders, which opened in April 1919. Document 18 of the

---

[33] In the Ottoman documents the person in question is referred to alternately as Kurd Alo, Kurd Ali, or Haci Ali. I will hereafter use Kurd Alo, since it is the name most commonly used. In Talat Pasha's cables the name "Ali" is written *'ayn-lam-ya* (علی). In the indictment printed in the Ottoman gazetteer *TV* (issue no. 3540) and the 29 April 1919 edition of *Alemdar*, the word is written *ayn-lam-vav* (علو), or "Alo." In their account of the judges' ruling in the Cemal Oğuz trial on 9 February 1920, *Alemdar* spelled the name of Kürd Ali *'ayn-lam-ya* (علی), whereas *Ati* and *Peyam-ı Sabah* wrote of "Kürd Alo" *'ayn-lam-vav* (علو). In its 2 May 1920 edition, *Peyam-ı Sabah* again wrote the name as "Kürd Alo" in a reprint of the Istanbul Court-Martial decision rejecting that of the Military Court of Appeal. In the Armenian sources the gang in question is always referred to as the "Kürt Alo Gang." See Dadrian and Akçam, *"Tehcir ve Taktil,"* preface.

[34] For a detailed account of the murders, see Grigoris Balakian, *Armenian Golgotha*, chapter 14.

[35] Talat Pasha was directly contending with a great amount of pressure from his German allies during those days, and the investigation that was ordered may well have been a direct result of this pressure (BOA/DH.ŞFR, no. 55/338, Coded telegram from interior minister Talat to the Province of Kastamonu, dated 31 August 1915).

indictment includes the pretrial testimony of a certain Cemal Asaf, who recounted the events of Dr. Chilingirian's murder.[36] Unionist responsible secretary Cemal Oğuz was formally accused of the crime and arrested on 3 April 1919, but for some unknown reason he was subsequently released.[37] Nevertheless, Oğuz would be rearrested and his case integrated into the trial of the responsible secretaries at the 27 October 1919 session (most likely the fifth one) of this trial. The most significant charge against Oğuz was that he had arranged for the killing of Dr. Chilingirian and his four friends. For this reason, the matter came up in numerous sessions of the trial, and a number of eyewitnesses testified about the events.[38]

At the trial's 29 November 1919 session, the case against Cemal Oğuz was separated from that of the other reponsible secretaries due to health reasons.[39] Nevertheless, the review of Cemal Oğuz's case continued on 27 January 1920 as a separate case.[40] The question of the murders was raised in this trial at the 5 February 1920 session, during which Mîhâil Ohannes Effendi gave the following eyewitness testimony:

> Five of [my] friends were dispatched to Ayaş. The wagons that carried them departed on Thursday and arrived on Friday. It is widely known that the guards later handed these five friends over to bandits. In response, the acting district governor, İzzet Bey[,] went to

[36] "The recorded testimony of Cemal Asaf Bey regarding the manner in which some of those deported earlier were killed by the Kürd Alo gang, which was formed by Kangırı [i.e., Çankırı] Responsible Secretary . . . Cemâl Oğuz Bey, is but one part of the actions and activities of the committee representatives that must be connected to the Committee's central organization [doc. no. 18]," *TV*, no. 3540, 5 May 1919; Report of the trial's opening session, ibid., 27 April 1919, 7 (left-hand column).

[37] For a more detailed discussion of Cemal Oğuz and his activities, see Dadrian and Akçam, *"Tehcir ve Taktil."* The information on Oğuz is found in the preface (by Dadrian) and the chapters on his trial.

[38] For example, at the session at 27 October 1919, the written testimony of Rahib (Priest) Karabityan Effendi was read into the record; in his account the witness claimed that Cemal Oğuz had killed five people who had been deported to Ayaş (*Ati*, 28 October 1919). At the 12 November 1919 session, the testimony of pharmacist Krikor Effendi was heard. In his testimony, he stated that "in that period the acting governor of the provincial district was İzzet Bey," and recounted that this İzzet Bey had mentioned to an Armenian friend that he was greatly upset by the murders of Chilingirian and others and that he had "sobbed uncontrollably" (*Ati*, 13 November 1919). At the trial's 22 November 1919 session, the architect (*mimar*) Simon Effendi recounted, "I was in Kangırı [i.e., Çankırı] at the time that five Armenians were killed near the Tüney police station. The government conducted an investigation of this matter. According to what I heard, they arrested somebody," and held Cemal Oğuz accountable for the incident (*Ati*, 23 November 1919).

[39] *Ati, Alemdar*, 30 December 1919.

[40] *Ati*, 28 January 1920.

the site of the incident and conducted an investigation. It was also widely known that Cemâl Oğuz Bey and Nûreddin Bey were quite satisfied with these incidents. Following this question[ing,] two brigands were arrested and thrown in prison.[41]

At the 8 February 1920 session, Cemal Oğuz was sentenced to imprisonment for having ordered the murder of Chilingirian. In their ruling, the judges wrote that Oğuz was guilty of murder in the second degree,

> for having known and for aiding and abetting the actual assailants involved in the events; for having sent the deserter Captain Nûreddin Bey and Kürd Ali [to Çankırı] and given them the necessary instructions and planning for the murder of Dr. Chilingirian and his four known companions, who were all killed in the area around Çankırı's Tüney police station; for having shown them the way; for organizing the murder of other individuals and for ensuring that the perpetrators would be neither opposed nor hindered [in their crimes]; for facilitating the aforementioned crimes at the outset and for ensuring their subsequent completion.[42]

On the basis of this conviction Cemal Oğuz was sentenced to five years, four months in prison, while the aforementioned Captain Nûreddin received a six-year, eight-month sentence in absentia.[43]

Cemal Oğuz's case was subsequently transferred to the Military Court of Cassation and on 23 March 1920, the court overturned his conviction for the murders of Chilingirian and his companions. The court's reasoning was as follows: a court-martial was set up in Ankara in 1915 and Cemal Oğuz was included among those defendants charged and sentenced for the aforementioned crimes. Therefore, efforts to retry this same case in Istanbul were illegal since (1) the case was not within the Istanbul court's jurisdiction, and (2) the same case could not be heard twice.

Nevertheless, the case of Cemal Oğuz was reexamined in the Istanbul Court-Martial on 29 April 1920. This court rejected the earlier ruling of the Military Court of Appeal and insisted on rendering its own ruling,

[41] *Alemdar*, 6 February 1920.
[42] Ibid., 9 February 1920.
[43] Ibid.

based on the following line of reasoning: "In truth, although the real perpetrators of the aforementioned crimes were tried and sentenced by the
Ankara Court-Martial in 1915, the aforementioned defendant [Cemal
Oğuz] was not previously mentioned [in the court] and the ruling of said
court [on this matter] has to this day never been finalized; no trial was
subsequently held in the [relevant] area for Cemal Oğuz Bey."[44]

I have dwelled at length on the events surrounding the murder of Dr.
Chilingirian and his colleagues and on the subsequent trials in order to
better understand the extensive efforts of Talat Pasha and the rest of the
Unionist government in Istanbul on behalf of Kurd Alo and the other assailants who were captured and tried as a result of the initiative taken by
local authorities and not the central government. As will be seen below,
Talat Pasha would later have Kurd Alo and his colleagues released, their
indictment for murder notwithstanding. The court-martial's assertion that
the Ankara court's decision had "never been finalized" was correct, and the
reason was that Talat Pasha had taken pains to ensure this outcome.

One of the most important documents to highlight Talat Pasha's attitude toward these murders and their perpetrators is a "secret" telegram
he sent to Ankara on 13 May 1916. In it, Talat Pasha stated that "individuals who have been convicted or arrested as a result of crimes they have
committed may, in accordance with the special statute, be released into
the army, to provide service to the army, if they so wish, through either judicial pardon or postponement [of prosecution]," wrote the interior minister, adding that "it is considered appropriate that the aforementioned
who have been detained by the military tribunal be released to the army,
singly or in pairs through the processing office reporting to the Ministry of
Justice."[45] With these words, Talat ordered the provincial office in Ankara
to cooperate with the Ministry of Justice and free the detainees.

Reading this telegram in the context of the other documents, one can
also understand that the individuals for whom Talat requested a pardon
were none other than the members of the Kurd Alo gang. Talat was most
likely making tacit reference to the fall 1914 temporary law releasing con-

[44] *Peyam-ı Sabah, Vakit*, 2 May 1920.
[45] BOA/DH.ŞFR, no. 63/301, Coded telegram from interior minister Talat to the Province of Ankara, dated 13 May 1916.

victs from prison. The purpose of the special statute was to provide manpower to paramilitary units associated with the army.

Some eighteen months after the country's jails and prisons were first emptied as the result of a law passed in the autumn of 1914,[46] Talat again invoked the same law in order to secure the release of convicted murderers who were serving time in the Ankara prisons. The following cables show quite clearly how Talat Pasha and others invested great effort in order to save a number of murderers who had been arrested and brought to justice. In the first of these directives, which was sent on 5 June 1916, Talat demanded "that those actions deemed necessary, according to the official written communication nos. 788 and 832 sent on 26 and 30 April 1916 respectively, regarding the [illegible text] and the views expressed in the copy of the cable sent on 18 May 1916 to the CUP Central Committee and signed by Nallıhanlı Mehmed Ali from the Ankara Prison, be accelerated and that their results be reported."[47] The last document makes clear that despite Talat Pasha's "secret" cable of 13 May 1916, the aforementioned Ali had yet to be released, most likely because the correspondence with the Ministry of Justice had not yet arrived. In response, Ali sent a telegram to the CUP Central Committee on 31 May; Talat replied on 5 June, asking that the orders included in his 13 May communication concerning Ali be implemented.

A second cable, sent on 7 or 8 June 1915 and marked "secret," significantly clarifies the obstacles that emerged when the wheels of government and bureaucracy began to turn. According to this cable, the defendants would have to be convicted and sentenced before they could be pardoned; however, the trial had not yet reached that stage. On the other hand, Talat was concerned that an unconditional pardon would incur Berlin's displeasure.

[46] A general order marked "secret" was sent to all the provinces on 4 November 1914 by the Interior Ministry and the General Administration of Prisons and informed them that an amnesty was to be issued and the prisons and jails emptied. See BOA/DH.ŞFR, no. 46/186, Coded telegram from the Interior Ministry to the Provinces of Edirne, Adana, Ankara, Aydın, Basra, Beirut, Hicaz, Aleppo, Trebizond, Kastamonu, Konya, Mamuretülaziz, Van, and Yemen; the Provincial Districts of Bolu, Canik, Asîr, Karesi (Balıkesir), Jerusalem, Kale-i Sultaniye (Çanakkale), Menteşe, Teke, and Kayseri; and to the Guardianship (Muhâfızlık) of Medina, dated 4 November 1914.

[47] BOA/DH.ŞFR, no. 64/214, Coded telegram from interior minister Talat to the Province of Ankara, dated 5 June 1916.

"As long as no decision is rendered by the courts-martial in regard to the aforementioned detainees, just as it is not possible to issue a pardon, neither would it be appropriate to issue such a pardon without any terms or conditions on this matter, which carries with it political implications," wrote the interior minister. "So much so, in fact, that, although it is not desirable that the persons such as these continue their confinement, it is preferable that the problem be solved by . . . first producing a decision to suspend the consequences [of their legal prosecution]."[48] The solution, in other words, was to halt the legal process so that no pardon would be necessary.

According to a July 1918 Interior Ministry cipher telegram, Kurd Alo's gang continued to ask for assistance from the Ottoman government, which viewed their request favorably. The "extremely urgent" cable to the province of Ankara reads: "The request by the brigand Kurd Alo and the Karasu gang for protection in exchange for their being placed into service, on the Syrian Front for instance, is acceptable."[49] No further information has come to light on the ultimate fate of the killers.

These documents show very clearly that those suspects who were subjected to the judicial process were eventually released from custody and protected by the direct efforts of the government, often over the following several years. These documents not only reveal the government's attitude toward the killers and toward the court's rulings in regard to those guilty of committing crimes against Armenians, but also show that there were some local authorities who did not hesitate to prosecute the criminals.

LANGUAGE THAT BETRAYS AN AWARENESS OF THE CRIMES

The meaning and construction of the language of Ottoman official documents deserve separate, serious, and thoroughgoing research. What follows must be understood as an attempt to highlight a feature of Ottoman correspondence that has been observed throughout this study.

[48] BOA/DH.ŞFR, no. 64/257, Coded telegram from interior minister Talat to the Province of Ankara, dated 7/8 June 1916.

[49] The cable was sent in reply to one sent by the provincial governor of Ankara on 27 June 1918; a note in the margin states, "Resent on 11 July 1918." BOA/DH.ŞFR, no. 89/39, Coded telegram from Interior Ministry to Province of Ankara, dated 8 June 1918.

Among the Cipher Office papers are numerous documents, some composed by Talat himself, that reveal his knowledge of, and indifference to, the crimes being committed. For example, in a widely circulated cable of 26 July 1915, including instructions to "see to the matter personally," Talat ordered local officials to "determine to the most accurate extent possible, the number [of] Armenians who have perished in the province from the beginning of the war till now as the result of disease, rebellion and military actions, and report back quickly."[50]

One indication of Talat's indifference to the Armenian deaths was his consistent choice of neutral words (e.g., "perish," *telef ol-*) in describing such situations, particularly in regard to the Armenians.[51] Such rhetoric within the context of other documents may be seen to reflect a certain mind-set. Consider, for example, Talat's cabled response to reports of large-scale massacres in June 1915. After stating that "reports have arrived from the Province of Erzurum that a convoy of 500 Armenians who were deported from Erzurum has been murdered by Kurds between Erzincan and Erzurum," Talat commented,

> naturally, to the extent that it is possible, efforts are being made to protect the lives of the deported Armenians [during the time that they are] on the[ir] journey, and of disciplining those attempting to escape during the course of the deportation and those who are liable to attack those entrusted with defending [the convoys]. However, the [local] population should never become involved in this [operation], and absolutely no place or possibility must be given for such

[50] BOA/DH.ŞFR, no. 54-A/112, Coded telegram from interior minister Talat to the Provinces of Trebizond, Erzurum, Sivas, Diyarbekır, Mamuretülaziz, Adana, and Bitlis, and to the Provincial Districts of Marash and Canik, dated 26 July 1915.

[51] In similar fashion, a cable sent in April 1915 during the events in Van and containing the note "urgent and secret; to be seen to personally" contains the passage "how many soldiers and Muslim civilians have perished and been wounded up to now in the areas that the Armenians attacked [?]" (BOA/DH.ŞFR, no. 52/200, Coded telegram from interior minister Talat to the Province of Van, dated 3 May 1915). But there are also other documents in which very careful and precise language is used in regard to the Muslim population. On the subject of the Armenians, however, it is possible to detect a certain consistency in language. See, for instance, the cable sent in the wake of the September 1915 incidents in Urfa: "Report back on the number of soldiers and civilians who have been martyred, wounded and captured from the beginning of the incident until now and how many [?] to those of the insurgents who have perished . . . or have been apprehended (*derdest edil*)" (BOA/DH.ŞFR, no. 57/178, Coded telegram from the Interior Ministry to the Provincial District of Urfa, dated 28 September 1915).

incidents to arise that would produce clashes between the various communities and would simultaneously look very bad to the outside world.[52]

The main subject of the document was the massacre of five hundred people. Talat confirmed that those Armenians who attempted to flee or attack the convoy escort were to be punished without exception. Within this context, he stated that in order to protect the Armenian deportees, efforts were being expended "to the extent possible." In fact, the preservation of Armenian lives does not appear to have been Talat's main concern. Rather, he wished to prevent civilian participation in the massacres or, alternatively, the development of a situation that would create a negative impression on public or world opinion.[53]

The government was well aware of, but quite unconcerned about, the annihilation of the Armenians, additional telegrams show. A cable from the Security Directorate to Ankara on 10 February 1916 demanded a report "whether or not those identified Armenians who have been deported and exiled are still alive and[, if so,] their location at present."[54] In essence, what the government wished to know was simply the location of the Armenian survivors—assuming there were any.

The Ottoman Interior Ministry Papers likewise reflect this awareness of, but indifference to, the murder of Armenians. Throughout the entire period of the Armenian deportations, Talat kept himself closely informed of the fate of the convoys. In cables to the provinces he often requested

[52] BOA/DH.ŞFR, no. 54/9, Coded telegram from interior minister Talat to the Provinces of Diyarbekır, Mamuretülaziz, and Bitlis, dated 14 June 1915.

[53] Ibid. At the end of this cable, Talat says, "it is therefore necessary that all measures and means be thoroughly employed to prevent those [Kurdish] tribes and villagers who are found along the route from attacking Armenians who will travel these roads, and to forcefully punish those who would dare to kill or rob them or their defenders." This demand, however, would appear to have been no more than a fleeting afterthought—and a temporary one at best, as there is not a single shred of evidence that any investigation, criminal or otherwise, was ever opened against such perpetrators. There is more than enough evidence, however, to suggest that Talat wrote this cable as a result of pressure exerted on him by the German Embassy to take some measures toward protecting the Armenian deportees. See Hilmar Kaiser, "'A Scene from the Inferno': The Armenians of Erzurum and the Genocide, " in *Der Völkermord an den Armeniern und die Shoah*, ed. Hans-Lukas Kieser and Dominik J. Schaller (Zürich: Chronos Verlag, 2002), 129–87.

[54] BOA/DH.ŞFR, no. 60/288, Coded telegram from the Interior Ministry's General Directorate of Security to the Province of Ankara, dated 10 February 1916.

information on the status of individual deportees. For example, a "secret" cable to Trebizond on 11 September 1915 reads:

> Tahtacıyan, Fadkyan [and] Mısıryan, about whom the communication of earlier investigations and the ascertaining of their whereabouts is reported, are among the relatives of Aram Effendi of the Senate [Ottoman Chamber of Notables]. It is necessary to find them if they are [still] alive and, in any case, for the truth to be learned in a confidential manner. You are to categorically report the information that you have regarding these persons.[55]

The question was unambiguous: Talat, well aware that these people were likely to have been killed already, demanded to be secretly informed as to whether those in question had indeed been put to death.

Similarly, a 17 January 1916 telegram to the province of Sivas requested that the recipient "report after investigating the time of deportation and destination of Meryem, the paternal aunt of the [parliamentary] deputy Tomayan and the widow of Onnig's son, and whether or not she is still alive today."[56] According to the reply received, Talat would continue to follow the fate of the aforementioned individual. On 3 February 1916, he wrote to the province of Mamuretülaziz: "as has been understood from the report from the Province of Sivas that Meryem Kadın [Madame Meryem], the sister of Sivas deputy Barsamyan Effendi and the widow of the late Özmekyan Agob, was deported to Malatya in August; please investigate as to her present location and whether or not she is still alive."[57] The central government knew perfectly well that Armenians were being slaughtered throughout Anatolia. For this very reason, inquiries about whether or not certain people were still alive could be—and repeatedly were—made with such complete nonchalance.

A meaningful document in this context is a telegram sent by Talat Pasha on 20 July 1916 to all of the provinces announcing that the deportations

[55] BOA/DH.ŞFR, no. 55-A/208, Coded telegram from interior minister Talat to the Province of Trebizond, dated 11 September 1915.

[56] BOA/DH.ŞFR, no. 60/40, Coded telegram from interior minister Talat to the Province of Sivas, dated 17 January 1916.

[57] BOA/DH.ŞFR, no. 60/218, Coded telegram from interior minister Talat to the Province of Mamuretülaziz, dated 3 February 1916.

from Anatolia were in large measure complete. "As a result of wartime conditions and other reasons, in many locales the lives, liberty and property of certain members of the population are being either directly or indirectly violated by means of a number of orders that were arbitrarily given by certain state officials without any regard for law and order," the cable began. Local officials were reminded that the responsibility for this situation was theirs and theirs alone, and that they would have to take preventive steps: "Even if the war necessitated certain conditions and exceptional measures, these conditions and aforementioned measures were restricted and fixed upon special laws [that were passed] since the start of the war."[58] The telegram ended with the directive that those illegal actions were going to be punished.

This statement is significant in three ways. First, it openly acknowledges that the "life, liberty and property of the people" were violated. Second, it admits that during the war certain "conditions and exceptional measures" were developed to deal with wartime circumstances, and then further reveals that these measures were restricted by "special laws." Talat's clear purpose was to signal that the central administration (chiefly himself) would not be held accountable for the crimes. Third, regarding the possibility of an investigation or indeed any government effort to bring the criminals to justice, the telegram is silent. This should be taken as yet another confession of guilt.

[58] BOA/DH.ŞFR, no. 66/44, Coded telegram from interior minister Talat to the Provinces of Edirne, Erzurum, Adana, Ankara, Aydın, Bitlis, Baghdad, Beirut, Aleppo, Hüdâvendigâr (Bursa), Diyarbekır, Damascus, Sivas, Trebizond, Kastamonu, Konya, Mamuretülaziz, and Mosul, and to the Provincial Districts of Urfa, İzmit, İçel, Marash, Kütahya, Bolu, Canik, Çatalca, (Der) Zor, Karesi (Balıkesir), Jerusalem, Kale-i Sultaniye (Çanakkale), Menteşe, Teke, Kayseri, Niğde, Eskişehir, and Karahisâr-ı Sahib (Afyon Karahisar), dated 20 July 1916.

EIGHT   DEMOGRAPHIC POLICY AND THE ANNIHILATION OF THE ARMENIANS

If the annihilation of the Armenians was the outcome of a sequence of decisions, each one triggering the next, questions arise as to the possible relationship between demographic policy and genocidal practice. Were they distinct responses to different needs? Or was genocide the ultimate fulfillment of a demographic vision? I will argue that there was such a causal relationship. Demographic anxieties shaped the Armenian deportations: the population ratios where Armenians were deported and where they remained were decisive, and the deportations were carried accordingly.

The course of the war and accompanying security fears powerfully shaped decisions about the annihilation of the Armenians. Had the Ottomans not been defeated at Sarıkamış, and if, in March 1915, the loss of Istanbul had not been looming in a mere matter of days, the final, fatal blow against the Armenians might have been stayed. Talat Pasha's memorandum of 26 May indicates, however, that removal of the threat known as the "Armenian reform issue" was widely considered a necessity among the Unionists even before the war, and that efforts were made to eliminate this perceived threat.

Demographic policy was first formulated against another perceived threat to national security, the Greeks in western Anatolia, and enacted between 1913 and 1914. Three factors appear to have prevented the ethnic cleansing of the Ottoman Greeks from escalating into genocide: the Great War had not yet begun, there was a country to which the Greeks could be expelled, and the Armenian-inhabited regions to the east were potentially subject to Russian occupation and eventual Armenian statehood. During the 1915 events in Zeytun, a telegram from Istanbul to the Fourth Army Command spoke of "the need to punish . . . the Armenians" while "the European states were preoccupied."[1] The Unionists were clearly aware that

[1] BOA/DH, 2. Şube, no. 68/30/1, Cipher telegram from the Interior Ministry to the General Command of Damascus, Beirut, Aleppo, and their surroundings, n.d. (probably 9 March 1915).

the war had created favorable conditions, and they intended to make full use of the opportunity.

Whether a demographic policy toward the Armenians might have existed prior to the war remains an open question. Likewise, it is unclear that the Unionists ever seriously considered expelling the Armenians to Russia. Apart from the decision of 24 April 1915, at what point in time were they destined for the deserts of Syria and Iraq? The answers are as yet unknown, and there is no need for excessive speculation. In the case of the Armenians, demographic engineering took the form of genocide. Most important, the 5 to 10 percent criterion was decisive in their annihilation.

This section will highlight demographic policy as a backdrop for the deportation of the Armenians and consider the role of the 5 to 10 percent principle in this policy. In this fashion, I hope to clarify the relationship between demographic policy and the Armenian Genocide. The following discussion will also address such unfounded appraisals as, "the events of 1915 were in fact a civil war between the Armenians and Turks."[2] Not a single top secret document at the highest levels of the state makes the slightest allusion to a civil war or "intercommunal warfare."[3] On the contrary, Ottoman documents show that Armenian areas were evacuated under tight government control.

THE ARMENIAN DEPORTATIONS AS ONE PART OF A COMPREHENSIVE POPULATION POLICY

Faced with the logistical impossibility of deporting the entire Armenian community at once, the government ordered Armenians to be sent out in convoys over an extended period of time. Provincial authorities were instructed not to allow the "arrangement of Armenians in caravans" to "cause . . . crowding and the interruption of military transport."[4]

---

[2] McCarthy, *Muslim and Minorities*, 136, and McCarthy and McCarthy, *Turks and Armenians*, 48.

[3] The description belongs to Justin McCarthy. For one of his works in which he has systematically examined the thesis claiming that the events of 1912–23 constituted an "Ottoman civil war," see Justin McCarthy, *Death and Exile: The Ethnic Cleansing of Ottoman Muslims, 1821–1922* (Princeton, NJ: Darwin Press, 1995), 181–203.

[4] BOA/DH.ŞFR, no. 54-A/392, Coded telegram to the Commissions for the Liquidation (of Abandoned Property) of the Provinces of Erzurum, Adana, Ankara, Bitlis, Aleppo, Hüdâvendigâr (Bursa), Diyarbekır, Sivas, Trebizond, Mamuretülaziz, Mosul, and Van, and to the Provincial Districts

The Ottoman gendarmerie was assigned the responsibility for constituting, guarding, and transporting the convoys as far as the provincial border, where the deportees were transferred to a new set of escorts. Interior Ministry records sometimes specify the province from which gendarmes should come to take over a convoy and the crossing point at which this should be done. Authorities in Mosul, for example, were notified that the provincial government of Diyarbekır wanted a convoy from Erzurum to be taken over by gendarmes from Mosul Province at the Diyarbekır border.[5]

The transfers of Armenian convoys were regularly reported to Istanbul. On 20 July 1915, for instance, Talat Pasha instructed authorities in Mamuretülaziz that "afterward, the convoys that are to arrive should be handed over at the border of the province."[6] In another cable sent to the province of Marash on 28 July 1915, Talat discerned that a problem had arisen during the handover and demanded that such a situation not be repeated.[7]

The importance of official documents on the transport and transfer of convoys under the control of provincial gendarmes also emerged in the 1919–21 Istanbul Military Tribunals. During both the preliminary investigations and the trials, judges continually asked the accused whether they had received such documents.[8] In addition to reporting handovers, provincial and subprovincial administrators continually informed their superiors about the number of Armenians sent off or remaining behind, and these figures were reviewed by Istanbul in the form of regular reports. Each province and provincial district recorded the actions and movements within its borders.

Here are a few limited examples of the telegrams received on a single date, 17 September 1915, from various provincial locations. This detailed report was sent by the governor of Ankara Province:

---

of Urfa, İzmit, Canik, (Der) Zor, Karesi (Balıkesir), Kayseri, Karahisâr-ı Sahib (Afyon Karahisar), Marash, Eskişehir, and Niğde, dated 13 August 1915.

[5] BOA/DH.ŞFR, no. 56/387, Coded telegram from interior minister Talat to the Province of Mosul, dated 13 October 1915.

[6] BOA/DH.ŞFR, no. 54-A/59, Coded telegram from interior minister Talat to the Province of Mamuretülaziz, dated 20 July 1915.

[7] BOA/DH.ŞFR, no. 54-A/157, Coded telegram from interior minister Talat to the Provincial District of Marash, dated 28 July 1915.

[8] Transcription of the verdict of the Bayburt trial (see *Tercüman-ı Hakikat*, 5 August 1920).

The number of Armenians deported up until the present from the center and surrounding areas of the province is 21,237. There are in the provincial district of Yozgat, 1,916; in the center of Kırşehir, 747; 60 in Haymana; 479 in Nallıhan; [and] 576 Armenians in Sungurlu; these are composed of families and children in the interior of Yozgat whose deportation in part to specified zones, and others whose distribution to Muslim villages determined according to need, is necessary. There are at present 550 people at the Ankara station in the process of deportation. The direction of their journeys is toward the areas of Aleppo and [Der] Zor. With the center of the province being deported, the number of the population remaining at present and the set of those staying in Keskin Kalacık and being distributed to Muslim villages will be shown separately.[9]

In a telegram from İzmit, "It is submitted that the approximately 58,000 Armenians found in the center and surroundings being completely deported, today in the [train] stations of the provincial district there are no concentrations of Armenians."[10] From Eskişehir, it was written that "the Armenians found in the vicinity" had been "completely deported."[11]

As the deportations began in late April and early May 1915, cables went out from Istanbul to each and every province; the central government demanded reports on the number of Armenians being sent off, the destinations of the deportees, the route they were to take, and the number and situation of the Armenians remaining. "[H]ow many Armenians have been removed from Haçin, Dörtyol, and other places up to now, and where have they been sent?" the province of Adana was asked in early May; additional details on these figures were requested.[12] "[A]s soon as the Armenian villages have been emptied out," the provinces were later

---

[9] BOA/DH.EUM, 2. Şube, no. 68/66, Coded telegram from the Province of Ankara to the Interior Ministry, dated 17 September 1915. In this and the following original telegrams, the population figures were spelled out as words, but for ease of reading I have translated them as numerals.

[10] BOA/DH.EUM, 2. Şube, no. 68/67, Coded telegram from the Provincial District of İzmit to the Interior Ministry, dated 17 September 1915.

[11] BOA/DH.EUM, 2. Şube, no. 68/15, Coded telegram from the Provincial District of Eskişehir to the Interior Ministry, dated 17 September 1915.

[12] BOA/DH.ŞFR, no. 52/338, Coded telegram from interior minister Talat to the Province of Adana, dated 12 May 1915.

instructed, "the providing of regular reports should be arranged containing the number of [deportees], the names of the villages and places of deportation."[13]

Communications to the provinces from the very first days of the Armenian deportations show that these actions were part of the Ottoman government's overall population policy. The requested information was not limited to the numbers of Armenians sent off or remaining behind. According to a general communiqué of 14 June 1915, the provinces were to report without delay on

> the names of the Armenian villages that had been emptied out, their geographic location, the nature and condition of their lands, and their potential for cultivation; the number of persons from the population who have been deported and the quantities and character of the abandoned properties and lands, and the best estimates and opinions about where it would be most beneficial to settle [Muslim] immigrants, as well as what type [of the latter] and from where.[14]

Diyarbekır Province, which had been tardy in replying, was sternly reminded that "since the central government sees it as extremely necessary that the desired economic, [and] environmental information regarding the Armenian villages be taken into consideration in the [execution of the] general deportations and resettlement, comprehensive information [in this regard] is to be assembled by the state bureaucrats."[15]

In addition to reports on the conditions in the provinces, Istanbul required detailed registries of the Armenians deported or left in their villages, and a very close supervisory apparatus was set up for the preparation and submission of such ledgers. These recorded "the number of deported Armenians," along with the names of the townships and villages from which they had been deported. Tardy submissions resulted in warnings

[13] BOA/DH.ŞFR, no. 53/113, Coded telegram from the Interior Ministry's IAMM to the Provinces of Adana, Aleppo, Erzurum, Van, and Bitlis, dated 25 May 1915.

[14] BOA/DH.ŞFR, no. 54/15, Coded telegram from the Interior Ministry's IAMM to the Provinces of Adana, Aleppo, Erzurum, Bitlis, Van, and Diyarbekır, and to the Provincial District of Marash, dated 14 June 1915.

[15] BOA/DH.ŞFR, no. 54/39, Coded telegram from the Interior Ministry's IAMM to the Province of Diyarbekır, dated 17 June, 1915.

to provincial officials along the lines of: "the previously requested registry has not yet arrived; send immediately."[16] Deadlines and submission instructions were frequently included. In a cable of 25 July 1915 to a number
of eastern provinces, the Security Directorate instructed that "it should be
reported regularly and in highly accurate fashion as to how many Armenians within the province/provincial district have been deported to this
day, as well as the number who are in the process of being deported and
how many still remain."[17]

On 13 August 1915, nearly all Ottoman provinces were given a five-day
deadline to submit their reports:

> Since it is seen as necessary to know the number of Armenians pre-
> viously residing within [your respective] province[s]; the number
> of such persons and households deported up to now as a result of
> the deportations up to this point; the number of persons remaining
> [in their respective homes] today, as well as what manner of order
> or permission was given for them to do so; please put together and
> send at your first means possible and within five days at the latest
> individual notebooks containing this information.[18]

A questionnaire was included in these cables to ensure that the answers
would be given fully, separately, and with plenty of detail. In mid-August
1915, local officials in more than a dozen provinces and districts were
asked:

> (1) Of those Armenians to be deported how many still remain
> within the province/district; (2) How many Armenians are cur-
> rently there who are scheduled to be deported to the designated
> locations? And where are these persons? How many Armenians cur-

[16] BOA/DH.ŞFR, no. 54-A/97, Coded telegram from the Interior Ministry's General Security Directorate to the Province of Trebizond and the Provincial District of Canik, dated 24 July 1915.

[17] BOA/DH.ŞFR, no. 54-A/100, Coded telegram from the Interior Ministry's General Security Directorate to the Provinces of Erzurum, Adana, Bitlis, Aleppo, Diyarbekır, Sivas, Trebizond,
Mamuretülaziz, and Van, and to the Provincial Districts of Urfa and Marash, dated 25 July 1915.

[18] BOA/DH.ŞFR, no. 56/57, Coded telegram from the Interior Ministry's General Security Di-
rectorate to the Provinces of Edirne, Erzurum, Adana, Ankara, Bitlis, Aleppo, Hüdâvendigâr (Bursa),
Diyarbekır, Damascus, Sivas, Trebizond, Konya, Mamuretülaziz, and Van, and to the Provincial
Districts of Urfa, İzmit, Karahisâr-ı Sahib (Afyon Karahisar), Kütahya, Canik, (Der) Zor, Karesi
(Balıkesir), Kayseri, Marash, Eskişehir, and Niğde, dated 18 August 1915.

rently being deported are there on the roads, at [railroad] stations and in the villages? (3) How many Catholic and Protestant Armenians are there within [your] province/ provincial district? How many of these have already been sent off and how many still remain at this time? What are the respective percentages of [Armenian] Protestants and Catholics relative to the Muslim population?

The answers were expected "within three days."[19]

A Security Directorate cable of September 1916 near the end of the deportations gives an idea of the scope and detail expected of Armenian "registries."Armenians were to be enumerated by religion and social status in the following categories:

(1) local Armenians; (2) foreign Armenians; (3) those who were not deported because they were Catholic or Protestant; (4) those who were exempted [from the deportation] because they were the family of a soldier; (5) those who converted [to Islam] and were [therefore] not deported; (6) those who were not deported due to some special order.[20]

From the very beginning, as we have seen, provincial officials were expected to report in detail not only on the general population of Armenians, but also on specific subcategories such as the Armenians already sent, those subject to deportation but not yet sent (and the location of those still in transit), and those remaining behind. Similarly, in April 1916, "clear and explicit reports" were requested "within two days at the most regarding the number of local Armenians not deported and left where they were, those coming from other regions who have been temporarily

[19] BOA/DH.ŞFR, no. 55/208, Coded telegram from the Interior Ministry's General Security Directorate to the Provinces of Erzurum, Adana, Ankara, Bitlis, Aleppo, Hüdâvendigâr (Bursa), Diyarbekır, Sivas, Trebizond, Konya, and Mamuretülaziz, and to the Provincial Districts of İzmit, Canik, Karesi (Balıkesir), Karahisâr-ı Sahib (Afyon Karahisar), Kayseri, Marash, Niğde, and Kütahya, dated 25 August 1915.

[20] BOA/DH.ŞFR, no. 68/112, Coded telegram from the Interior Ministry's General Security Directorate to the Provinces of Edirne, Adana, Ankara, Aydın, Bitlis, Baghdad, Beirut, Aleppo, Hüdâvendigâr (Bursa), Diyarbekır, Damascus, Sivas, Trebizond, Kastamonu, Konya, Mamuretülaziz, and Mosul, and to the Provincial Districts of Urfa, İzmit, Bolu, Canik, Çatalca, (Der) Zor, Karesi (Balıkesir), Jerusalem, Kale-i Sultaniye (Çanakkale), Menteşe, Teke, Kayseri, Karahisâr-ı Sahib (Afyon Karahisar), İçel, Kütahya, Marash, Niğde, and Eskişehir, dated 25 September 1916.

left [in your province/district], and how many are currently in transit to other areas."[21]

The following month (May 1916), a similar questionnaire was cabled to the provinces.[22] Some of these directives explained the rationale for such detail and clarity:

> As was reported in the cable of 22 April 1916, the purpose in demanding [to know] the number of Armenians in the province is to understand how many of the local Armenians there are who have been spared deportation and left in place and how many have come from other regions and been temporarily left [in your province], as well as how many are currently on the roads, traveling to other areas. [Please] respond quickly with separate answers to each of these questions.[23]

The demand for such detailed information—in particular, the exact population ratios of the various ethnoreligious communities—reflected the determining factors in the government's population policies of deportation and resettlement. Indeed, the fact is clearly stated in some of the documents. On 5 December 1915, the provincial government of Konya was asked to report "in which areas within the province those Armenians are to be [re]settled in accordance with the [correct] population ratios."[24] When replies from the provinces failed to specify the ethnic origins of the populations in question, follow-up queries were sent: "It is to be stressed that there is no information to be found regarding the place of origin of some of the individuals whose names are listed in the registries submitted."[25]

[21] BOA/DH.ŞFR, no. 63/72, Coded telegram from the Interior Ministry's General Security Directorate to the Provinces of Adana, Ankara, Edirne, Aleppo, Hüdâvendigâr (Bursa), Diyarbekır, Damascus, Sivas, Kastamonu, Konya, Mamuretülaziz, and Mosul, and to the Provincial Districts of İzmit, Bolu, Canik, (Der) Zor, Karesi (Balıkesir), Kayseri, Urfa, İçel, Kütahya, Niğde, and Eskişehir, dated 22 April 1916.

[22] BOA/DH.ŞFR, no. 64/49 and 51, Coded telegram from the Interior Ministry's General Security Directorate to the Provincial District of Karahisâr-ı Sahib (Afyon Karahisar) and the Province of Hüdâvendigâr (Bursa), dated 17 May 1916.

[23] BOA/DH.ŞFR, no. 63/259, Coded telegram from the Interior Ministry's General Security Directorate to the Provinces of Aleppo and Adana, dated 9 May 1916.

[24] BOA/DH.ŞFR, no. 58/202, Coded telegram from the Interior Ministry's General Security Directorate to the Province of Konya, dated 5 December 1915.

[25] BOA/DH.ŞFR, no. 57/368, Coded telegram from interior minister Talat to the Province of Edirne, dated 10 November 1915.

Such exhaustive demographic reports were deemed necessary for deporting the Armenians in an orderly fashion. Provincial leaders were therefore cautioned to send any missing information without delay:

> Either because certain parties have still failed to respond to the original or follow-up requests for information regarding the number of Armenians removed, the names of the deportees and the places from where they were deported, or since [the reports that they have sent] have not contained the essential information in order to determine [re]settlement policy or [be able to implement the] orders to resettle [new] immigrants and refugees, it is necessary to again [request that these parties] report on . . . the number of Armenians deported, the dates on which they were deported and the places to which they were sent, [as well as] the names of the villages and settlements that are either partially or entirely included [in the deportations], the [names of the] places, and whether or not it is necessary to send the immigrants there and in what number. [Please] send the [requested] necessary information and assessment.[26]

Throughout the course of the deportations, the central government kept up its demand for detailed statistical information at all points along the route. The Armenians' places of origin, destinations, and every stopping place in between was closely monitored so that the regime could maintain accurate demographic figures from beginning to end. "How many Armenians are there currently waiting to be sent to the designated areas[?]" the regions were asked in August 1915. "Where are these [people] at present[?] [T]o what location are they being sent and by which route[?] How many Armenian [deportees] have arrived up to now[?] How many souls are there awaiting deportation [?] Report [back with this information] by three days from now at the latest."[27]

In December 1915, the provincial authorities were to "report back clearly and fully, and within three days at the latest, as to the number of

---

[26] BOA/DH.ŞFR, no. 54/412, Coded telegram from the Interior Ministry's IAMM to the Provinces and Provincial Districts of Adana, Erzurum, Bitlis, Aleppo, Diyarbekır, Sivas, Trebizond, Mamuretülaziz, Marash, İzmit, Canik, and Kayseri, dated 12 July 1915.

[27] BOA/DH.ŞFR, no. 55/211, Coded telegram from the Interior Ministry's General Security Directorate to the Provinces of Damascus, Adana, Konya, Ankara, and Aleppo, and to the Provincial Districts of Edirne, (Der) Zor, Marash, dated 25 August 1915.

local Armenians who have been spared deportation and left in place; of those who have arrived [in your district or province] from somewhere else and who are temporarily remaining there in accordance with the afore-mentioned laws and regulations; as well the number of Armenians who are currently in transit to other areas."[28] Talat Pasha interrogated the province of Konya in April 1916 as follows:

(1) How many Armenians are there within the province at this moment? How many of these are local and how many from outside the province? (2) How many Armenians were sent into the province to be settled, and to where were they sent? What is their percentage of the population relative to the Muslim population, and where are these Armenians from? (3) Of those [Armenians] sent off for deportation and left there [in the province], how many are they in number and what population[s] are they from?[29]

As mentioned above, way stations along the deportation route were closely monitored. A Security Directorate cable sent to several provinces in late August 1915 asked, "How many Armenians have been assembled at the stations for deportation and not yet deported, and where have they been assembled? It is expected and very important that [this information] be reported back by this evening at the latest."[30] On 23 October 1915, Talat asked Cemal Pasha to report "separately on how many Armenian [deportees] there are in transit and where they are."[31]

The deportation routes were sometimes changed because of crowding, as seen in a telegram of 26 September 1915 to Mamuretülaziz Province. "In order to lessen the crowding created due to the excess of the caravans

[28] BOA/DH.ŞFR, no. 59/76, Coded telegram from the Interior Ministry's IAMM to the Provinces of Adana, Ankara, Aleppo, Hüdâvendigâr (Bursa), Diyarbekır, Damascus, Sivas, Konya, Mamuretülaziz, Bitlis, and Mosul, and to the Provincial Districts of Urfa, Eskişehir, Niğde, Karahisâr-ı Sahib (Afyon Karahisar), Kütahya, İzmit, Karesi (Balıkesir), Kayseri, (Der) Zor, dated 21 December 1915.

[29] BOA/DH.ŞFR, no. 63/119, Coded telegram from interior minister Talat to the Province of Konya, dated 26 April 1916.

[30] BOA/DH.ŞFR, no. 55/279, Coded telegram from the Interior Ministry's General Security Directorate to the Province of Konya and the Provincial Districts of İzmit, Kütahya, Eskişehir, and Karahisâr-ı Sahib (Afyon Karahisar), dated 28 August 1915.

[31] BOA/DH.ŞFR, no. 57/80, Coded telegram from interior minister Talat to Fourth Army commander Cemal Pasha, dated 23 October 1915.

going by the aforementioned route . . . the sending of the caravans hence-forth via Diyarbekir to Mosul" is requested.[32] Diyarbekır was notified the same day. "The Armenian caravans coming to the province in order to be deported to Mosul not being sent to Urfa, [but] being sent via Mardin, and in this way removing the crowding produced in Urfa" was requested.[33] Kastamonu was informed on 16 March 1916 that because Sivas Province "was extremely busy" and "the possibility did not exist" of sending Arme-nians onward from there, the deportation should not be conducted along that route.[34]

The Armenian convoys' final destinations received similar oversight. Telegrams were regularly sent to the designated provinces and subprovin-cial districts that requested the number of arrivals and the percentage of the local population they now comprised. On 1 July 1915, the Office of Tribal and Immigrant Settlement (IAMM) asked administrators in Mosul and Urfa, "[H]ow many Armenians have arrived [in your area] up to now in order to be settled there, and where are they from? What are the places to which it was decided to deport and resettle them? [Please] report back quickly and provide information regularly as they arrive."[35]

Cables of this type, asking for "quick reports regarding the number of Armenians who have arrived thus far and their places of origin and reset-tlement," were sent to the provinces at regular intervals.[36] "[Please] report back quickly and in as exact figures as possible the number of Armenian families and individuals [who] are being settled in [your] district until now, how many Armenian families have arrived and from the population of which province have they come, and where they have been sent."[37] It

[32] BOA/DH.ŞFR, no. 56/168, Coded telegram from the Interior Ministry's General Security Di-rectorate to the Province of Mamuretülaziz, dated 26 September 1915.

[33] BOA/DH.ŞFR, no. 56/180, Coded telegram from the Interior Ministry's General Security Di-rectorate to the Province of Diyarbekır, dated 26 September 1915.

[34] BOA/DH.ŞFR, no. 62/50, Coded telegram from interior minister Talat to the Province of Kastamonu, dated 16 March 1916.

[35] BOA/DH.ŞFR, no. 54/271, Coded telegram from the Interior Ministry's IAMM to the Province of Mosul and the Provincial District of Urfa, dated 1 July 1915.

[36] BOA/DH.ŞFR, no. 54-A/58, Coded telegram from the Interior Ministry's IAMM to the Provin-cial Districts of Mosul and (Der) Zor, dated 20 July 1915.

[37] BOA/DH.ŞFR, no. 54-A/106, Coded telegram from the Interior Ministry's General Security Directorate to the Provinces of Aleppo and Damascus, and to the Provincial Districts of Urfa and (Der) Zor, dated 25 July 1915.

was expected that such reports would be submitted in an orderly and regular fashion.

On 21 August 1915, provincial and district administrators in the southeast received orders that "regular reports be put together regarding the number of Armenians arriving from other provinces up to this point, and that the number of persons and their general condition be reported as soon as they arrive."[38] At times it was even demanded that the information be reported back within twenty-four hours. "[R]eport back by tomorrow evening on the number of Armenians who have been deported up to now from the capital and surrounding areas, as well as the number awaiting deportation, those who are currently under way and at assembly points, and on their present condition," the Security Directorate ordered local officials in September 1915.[39] In like manner, an "urgent" order of May 1916 demanded "an answer ... by tomorrow evening to the cable sent on 9 April 1916 asking for a report on the number of Armenians."[40]

At certain intervals throughout the period of the deportations, a specific day was selected for a "general inventory" of operations: for example, "Report back on the number of Armenians living within your province or district on 6 November 1915, as well as how many there are being deported or who have come from other areas in order to be sent on further."[41] Also subject to regular monitoring were the prospective final destinations for Armenian deportees—the district of Der Zor in particular—as well as the number of Armenians who had already arrived there. As will be seen below, telegrams were regularly sent to these places.

[38] BOA/DH.ŞFR, no. 55/140, Coded telegram from the Interior Ministry's IAMM to the Provinces of Aleppo, Damascus, and Mosul; to the Provincial Districts of Urfa and (Der) Zor; and to the president of the Commission on Abandoned Property of Aleppo, dated 21 August 1915.

[39] BOA/DH.ŞFR, no. 56/45, Coded telegram from the Interior Ministry's General Security Directorate to the Provinces of Hüdâvendigâr (Bursa), Sivas, Mamuretülaziz, and Diyarbekır, and to the Provincial Districts of Kayseri, Niğde, and Urfa, dated 16 September 1915.

[40] BOA/DH.ŞFR, no. 63/253, Coded telegram from interior minister Talat to the Provinces of Ankara, Damascus, Sivas, Kastamonu, and Mosul, and to the Provincial District of Karahisâr-ı Sahib (Afyon Karahisar), dated 9 May 1916.

[41] BOA/DH.ŞFR, no. 57/282, Coded telegram from the Interior Ministry's General Security Directorate to the Provinces of Adana, Ankara, Bitlis, Aleppo, Hüdâvendigâr (Bursa), Diyarbekır, Damascus, Sivas, Konya, Mamuretülaziz, and Mosul, and to the Provincial Districts of Urfa, İzmit, Karasi, Kale-i Sultaniye (Çanakkale), Kayseri, Niğde, Eskişehir, Kütahya, Marash, and Urfa, dated 5 November 1915.

THE BLACK BOOK OF TALAT PASHA, OR A RÉSUMÉ OF DEPORTATIONS AND KILLINGS

In 2008 Turkish journalist Murat Bardakçı published some documents that he identified as "the daily journal of Talat Pasha." The titles of these undated documents are important: (1) "The Numbers of Armenians Deported"; (2) "A General Accounting of the Armenian Population after Deportation"; (3) "Armenian Orphans (Numbers Distributed to Muslims and Existing Today)"; (4) "Quantity of Abandoned Empty Houses from Armenians"; (5) "Table Showing Farm Estates Abandoned by Armenians"; and (6) "Mining Concessions in the Charge of Armenians." In particular, the document called "A General Accounting of the Armenian Population after Deportation" provides detailed figures for cities in every province and provincial district on the numbers of "local Armenians," "outsider Armenians and where they came from," and how many of the Armenians of that city were to be found in other cities.[42]

No date is given on the documents, but it is quite probable that they were prepared in early 1918 and contain a general accounting of the deportations. Work on them began at the end of 1916. In the last months of 1916, a final inventory was attempted in order to determine how many Armenians had survived the deportations and killing operations. For this purpose Talat Pasha sent a general communiqué to all provinces and districts on 24 September 1916, asking each local administrator to prepare a list containing the number of remaining Armenians within their respective jurisdictions. The request was repeated on 29 and 30 October with follow-up cables to local administrators who were reminded to "send the first draft of the list concerning the number of Armenians in your province/provincial district as requested on 24 September 1916."[43]

[42] Bardakçı, *Talat Paşa'nın Evrak-ı Metrukesi*, 76, 89–94, 101–3, and 108–45. Bardakçı claims that these documents cannot possibly date from 1915–16.

[43] BOA/DH.ŞFR, no. 69/120, Coded telegram from interior minister Talat to the Provinces of Edirne, Adana, Ankara, Bitlis, Baghdad, Beirut, Aleppo, Hüdâvendigâr (Bursa), Diyarbekır, Damascus, Sivas, Trebizond, Kastamonu, Konya, Mamuretülaziz, and Mosul, and to the Provincial Districts of Urfa, Bolu, Canik, (Der) Zor, Karesi (Balıkesir), Jerusalem, Menteşe, Teke, Kayseri, Kütahya, Marash, and Karahisâr-ı Sahib (Afyon Karahisar), dated 29 October 1916.

These lists were expected to answer a number of questions that had originally been sent to all regions. The Interior Ministry closely monitored which provinces submitted their reports in a timely fashion. Those that failed to do so received follow-up requests—accompanied by veiled warnings—to submit the required information. A 5 December 1916 cable to Adana demanded "the speedy compilation and dispatch of a list concerning the number of Armenians."[44] On the same day, the provincial district of Urfa was asked to "quickly send back the list concerning the number of Armenians [in your area] without leaving out a single locale."[45] The 25 December 1916 telegrams to the provinces of Diyarbekır, Damascus, and Mamuretülaziz, and to the provincial district of Der Zor serve as further examples: "Resend with the first post the list, requested on 24 September 1916, containing the figures for the number of Armenians in [your] province/provincial district."[46]

Some communications included an explicit rationale for demanding the lists. A cable to Kütahya on 14 February 1917, having criticized the previous report for "not clarifying the places of origin of the Armenians inside the provincial district," explained that "the purpose in asking the numbers of these [people] is to understand their place of origin, the condition in which they have arrived and remained there. It is necessary that these aspects be clearly and fully explained."[47] According to another cable, which was sent three days later to a number of districts and provinces,

> the purpose in asking about the number of Armenians within the provincial district/province is to understand their place of origin and the province and provincial district from which they arrived there. ... Therefore, [please conduct] a thorough examination of [all the places in] the province and report by telegram the total number of these persons, how many are local and how many [not, as well as]

[44] BOA/DH.ŞFR, no. 70/183, Coded telegram from the Interior Ministry's General Security Directorate to the Province of Adana, dated 5 December 1916.

[45] BOA/DH.ŞFR, no. 70/186, Coded telegram from the Interior Ministry's General Security Directorate to the Provincial District of Urfa, dated 25 December 1916.

[46] BOA/DH.ŞFR, no. 70/190, Coded telegram from the Interior Ministry's General Security Directorate to the Provinces of Diyarbekır, Damascus, and Mamuretülaziz, and to the Provincial District of (Der) Zor, dated 25 December 1916.

[47] BOA/DH.ŞFR, no. 73/5, Coded telegram from interior minister Talat to the Provincial District of Kütahya, dated 14 February 1917.

the province, provincial district and county from which the [others] came, and then record the number of persons in place of origin, including their clan and county on the lists to be prepared along these lines and send them along with the first post.[48]

A "very urgent" cable of 26 March 1917 to a number of provinces asked for the number of Armenians remaining in each jurisdiction; administrators were reminded that separate cables to the same effect had previously been sent out on 11 and 18 February. On occasion, when figures on the remaining Armenian populations were delayed, Talat Pasha himself would send out communications to the governors, demand the reason for such delays, and order that reports be sent within three days. In such orders, "the need to report the names of the county heads who caused [this] delay ... is urgently communicated."[49]

A telegram of 29 July 1917 reveals that in addition to the number of surviving Armenians, questions were asked about the quantity of Armenian-owned goods, their value, and the amount that had already been distributed to Muslims:

(1) What is the total number of Armenians deported from within your province or provincial district to some other location, as well as the value of the abandoned property belonging to them? (2) How many Armenians are there presently [residing in your province or provincial district] and how many of them are residing within their own homes? (3) How many of the abandoned houses belonging to the deported Armenians were given to [Muslim] immigrants, and how many were put up for auction by the Finance Ministry? Please report back speedily and in cipher on the existence of information concerning the aforementioned matters.[50]

[48] BOA/DH.ŞFR, no. 73/29, Coded telegram from interior minister Talat to the Provinces of Adana, Ankara, Aydın, Beirut, Aleppo, Damascus, Sivas, Kastamonu, Konya, and Mosul, and to the Provincial Districts of Urfa, İzmit, İçel, Eskişehir, Bolu, (Der) Zor, Karesi (Balıkesir), Jerusalem, Karahisâr-ı Sahib (Afyon Karahisar), Marash, and Niğde, dated 17 February 1917.

[49] BOA/DH.ŞFR, no. 74/115, Coded telegram from interior minister Talat to the Provinces of Adana, Aydın, and Damascus, and to the Provincial Districts of Urfa, (Der) Zor, and Karesi (Balıkesir), dated 13 March 1917. Another cable with an identical message was sent to the provinces of Kastamonu and Konya later in the day (BOA/DH.ŞFR, no. 74/118).

[50] BOA/DH.ŞFR, no. 78/225, Coded telegram from the Interior Ministry's General Directorate of Tribal and Immigrant Affairs to the Provinces of Edirne, Adana, Ankara, Beirut, Aleppo,

Another cable, sent to the provinces on 21 August, demanded that "separate investigations be conducted regarding the number of Armenians currently remaining in the province, as well as the breakdown of locals [versus those from somewhere else] and the province or provincial districts from which they came, and it should be sent by telegram; this information should then be entered into lists that are to be prepared in this regard and sent off with the first post."[51]

All this material clarifies that the Talat Pasha documents published by Bardakçı were the product of exacting effort over a long period of time. They show that the entire deportation operation was carried out under close government supervision in accordance with a demographic policy. Now let us examine more closely the 5 to 10 percent rule as a defining factor in that policy.

THE 5 TO 10 PERCENT REGULATION AND THE DESTRUCTION OF THE ARMENIANS

If the Unionists applied the 5 to 10 percent criterion both to the settlement of Armenians and to that of other ethnoreligious groups, was there any connection between this ratio and the annihilation of the Armenians? The thesis being proposed here is that the Armenian Genocide was not implemented solely as demographic engineering, but also as destruction and annihilation, and that the 5 to 10 percent principle was decisive in achieving this goal. Care was taken so that the number of Armenians deported to Syria, and those who remained behind, would not exceed 5 to 10 percent of the population of the places in which they were found. Such a result could be achieved only through annihilation.

The story of Dikran Kelegian illustrates the extreme importance of statistics during the course of the Armenian Genocide. An Armenian intel-

Hüdâvendigâr (Bursa), Diyarbekır, Damascus, Sivas, Trebizond, Kastamonu, Konya, Mamuretülaziz, and Mosul, and to the Provincial Districts of Eskişehir, Urfa, İçel, Bolu, Teke, Canik, Çatalca, (Der) Zor, Jerusalem, Karahisâr-ı Sahib (Afyon Karahisar), Kale-i Sultaniye (Çanakkale), Karasi, Kayseri, Kütahya, Marash, Niğde, and Cebel-i Lübnan, dated 29 July 1917.

[51] BOA/DH.ŞFR, no. 72/210, Coded telegram from interior minister Talat to the Provinces of Adana, Ankara, Aydın, Beirut, Aleppo, Damascus, Kastamonu, Konya, and Mosul, and to the Provincial Districts of Urfa, İzmit, Eskişehir, İçel, Bolu, (Der) Zor, Karesi (Balıkesir), Jerusalem, Karahisâr-ı Sahib (Afyon Karahisar), Kütahya, Marash, and Niğde, dated 8 August 1917.

lectual who helped reorganize the Committee of Union and Progress in 1905–6, Kelegian was especially close to CUP Central Committee member Bahaeddin Şakir. "It is a sacred duty for me to help in any way I can an enterprise that a brother like you has begun with sincerity and purity," wrote Kelegian to Şakir, adding that, "as my personal connection to you is eternal, under whatever circumstances or wherever I may be found . . . have no doubt that whatever assistance I can give will be a good fortune for me."[52] The attempt to organize an assassination of Sultan Abdülhamid took place in 1905 during this period of assistance.[53] Unfortunately for Kelegian, Şakir became an architect of the genocide, and his "brother" was among the Armenian intellectuals arrested on 24 April 1915. Afterward, Kelegian said of the CUP, "They were going to implement the Armenian massacres with mathematical accuracy."[54]

Whether or not Kelegian had the 5 to 10 percent principle in mind, it was certainly no coincidence that the Department of Statistics was among the most important units of the Interior Ministry's IAMM, which was charged with all deportation matters.[55] Here, one is confronted with genocide as a calculated attempt to impose a demographic formula over a wide territory.[56] The documentary record shows that this ideal ratio was strictly implemented in the western Ottoman provinces and the southern destinations to which the Armenians were deported (corresponding mainly with today's Syria and Iraq). The implementation in the eastern provinces was slightly different.

[52] Kelegian went so far as to prepare a false passport for Şakir so that he could travel. Erdal Aydoğan and İsmail Eyyüpoğlu, *Bahaeddin Şakir Bey'in Bıraktığı Vesikalara Göre İttihat ve Terakki* (Istanbul: Alternatif Yayınları, 2004), 317, 339, and 347.

[53] Ibid., 326–28 and 340–45.

[54] Andonian, *Exile, Trauma and Death*, 160.

[55] Nedim İpek, *İmparatorluktan Ulus Devlete Göçler* (Istanbul: Serander, 2006), 142–67.

[56] Fuat Dündar was the first to call attention to the great importance of statistics in the Armenian deportations. In his work connected with this topic, he wrote that his fundamental thesis was "to bring out the basic role that statistics and mathematics played in ethnic matters," and that "the Unionist operation was a mathematical operation" (Fuat Dündar, *Modern Türkiye'nin Şifresi*, 21 and 32). See also his *Crime of Numbers: The Role of Statistics in the Armenian Question*, 1 and 105–6. Both the English and the Turkish editions uncritically accept some denialist arguments of the Turkish state. For a criticism of some of Dündar's views, see Taner Akçam, " 'Ermeni Meselesi Hallolunmuştur' Kitabına Yönelen Eleştiriler ya da Tarihçinin Belgeyle İlişkisi Üzerine," in Akçam, *1915 Yazıları* (Istanbul: İletişim Yayınları, 2010), 39–111; for a comprehensive critique of his book, see Ayhan Aktar and Abdulhamit Kırmızı, " 'Bon Pour L'Orient': Fuat Dündar'ın kitabını deşifre ederken. . . . " *Tarih ve Toplum* no. 8 (Spring 2009): 157–86.

The Armenians were also deported en masse from western Anatolia. However, in some western provinces where the Armenian population was not as concentrated, the policy was either to leave them where they were or to subject them to an "internal dispersion" within their home province, according to the 5 percent rule. An August 1915 coded telegram from the Security Directorate to the provincial district of Antalya, for instance, informed local officials that "in light of their small numbers, there is at present no need to deport the Armenians from there."[57] The directorate advised the district of Çanakkale in early June that "if a suitable destination for deportation and resettlement within the district can be found [send them there], but if such a place cannot be found, send them to Karesi (Balıkesir)."[58] The Armenians dispatched from Bursa (Hüdâvendigâr) were to be resettled in the evacuated Armenian villages of Bilecik, according to a cable from the Tribal Office (IAMM) to the respective provinces. A follow-up report on the results of this action was also requested.[59]

A security directive advised the district governor's office in Kayseri that "the Armenians of the village of Küçük İncesu be deported to some area within the province of Konya where there are currently none, such as Aksaray."[60] İzmit was another provincial district to which such directives were sent. In early August 1915, the Security Directorate requested that some of the Armenians be "exempted from deportation."[61] The provincial district governor was to "ensure that the Armenian laborers and officials working in the [illegible text] company be settled along with their families in Muslim villages on the condition that they do not exceed 5 percent [of the total population] and in a manner that will ensure their continued service until they are [able to be] replaced."[62] According to a

[57] BOA/DH.ŞFR, no. 55/59, Coded telegram from the Interior Ministry's General Directorate of Security to the Provincial District of Antalya, dated 17 August 1915.

[58] BOA/DH.ŞFR, no. 53/289, Coded telegram from the Interior Ministry's General Directorate of Security to the Provincial District of Kale-i Sultaniye, dated 8 June 1915.

[59] BOA/DH.ŞFR, no. 54/335 and 336, Coded telegram from the Interior Ministry's IAMM to the Province of Hüdâvendigâr (Bursa) and the Provincial District of Karesi (Balıkesir), dated 7 July 1915.

[60] BOA/DH.ŞFR, no. 53/246, Coded telegram from the Interior Ministry's General Directorate of Security to the Provincial District of Kayseri, dated 5 June 1915.

[61] BOA/DH.ŞFR, no. 54-A/263, Coded telegram from the Interior Ministry's General Directorate of Security to the Provincial District of İzmit, dated 4 August 1915.

[62] BOA/DH.ŞFR, no. 54-A/293, Coded telegram from the Interior Ministry's General Directorate of Security to the Provincial District of İzmit, dated 7 August 1915.

follow-up cable the same day, "it has been reported to the High Command that the Armenian workers whose continued service at the felt factory in İzmit is currently necessary should, in light of their deportation, be settled in Muslim villages [so as to constitute no more than] 5 percent [of the total population] and in a manner that will not prevent their continued employment."[63]

In some areas, such as Aleppo and Kayseri, only Protestant and Catholic Armenians were to be dispersed among the local Muslims. On 28 August 1915, the Aleppo authorities were ordered to

> report separately on the population figures for both Protestant and Catholic Armenians who have until now not been deported and are currently there; and if the numbers of those who have not yet been deported are not large in relation to the Muslim population in the areas in which they live, have them dispersed and distributed to the [surrounding] Muslim villages according to the guidelines contained in the relevant circulars or in special communications.[64]

The governor of the Kayseri provincial district reported on 18 September 1915:

> It is submitted that in the center and environs there are 46,463 Armenians [of the Armenian Church], 1,517 Catholics [Armenians], and 1,957 Protestants [Armenians], so that in all the Armenian population is registered as 49,947, of whom 44,271 have been deported to the provinces of Aleppo, Damascus, and Mosul, and 765 people while having also earlier set out, in view of their fleeing, returning and hiding, were again seized and were in the course of deportation; and the 4,911 [members] of soldier's families remaining in the

[63] BOA/DH.ŞFR, no. 54-A/294, Coded telegram from the Interior Ministry's General Directorate of Security to the Provincial District of İzmit, dated 7 August 1915. It is highly probable that this cable and the one in the previous note relate to the same events. The subject under discussion is the temporary delay in deporting the Armenian workers. From the wording of both communications ("until they are replaced"), there is nothing to preclude the possibility that these Armenians were in fact subjected to deportation at a later date.

[64] BOA/DH.ŞFR, no. 55/265, Coded telegram from the Interior Ministry's General Directorate of Security to the Province of Aleppo, dated 28 August 1915. It is perhaps telling that this and the previously cited cable were sent precisely at the period when interior minister Talat was assuring German officials that Protestants and Catholics (as opposed to members of the Armenian Apostolic Church) would be excluded from the deportations.

provincial district, with the insignificant number of Protestant and Catholic remnants, were distributed to the villages in a 5 percent proportion.[65]

The most detailed explication of the 5 percent dispersion rule for western Anatolia—both in principle and in practice—was issued on 16 August 1915. This document is a copy of an order sent to all army commands and the Ministry of Internal Affairs:

> Those Armenians who are going to be made to move whose guardians are either soldiers or officials will remain in the places where they were before. If these [Armenians] are more than five houses in the town or village in which they are staying, the excess, first from families of soldiers, will be distributed to the Muslim villages that they desire in the counties and provincial districts to which they are subject, on condition that the same density is not surpassed and the 5 percent relationship up to only one hundred is respected. In this way, in a Muslim village of twenty houses only one house of Armenians may be found, and in villages and towns of more than one hundred houses, not more than five houses may be found. The Interior Ministry too informed the provinces of this way through a circular. Lists of military families must be quickly prepared and distributed to local civil service officials.[66]

In some places, calculations based on the number of houses failed to yield an exact total of the Armenians to be dispersed. For example, on 6 January 1916 the provincial district of Kütahya was requested to report within two days "how many Armenians were to be found in 67 houses."[67]

Some evidence suggests that Armenians themselves were aware of the 5 percent practice. Witness a petition from the Armenians of Karahisar, Konya Province, who were to be expelled through an order of 5 August

[65] BOA/DH.EUM, 2. Şube, 68/75, Coded telegram from the Cipher Office of the district governor of Kayseri to the Interior Ministry, dated 18 September 1915.

[66] BOA/DH.EUM.VRK, no. 15/49, Copy of an order from the Supreme Military Command, to the First, Third, and Fifth Army Corps Commands, dated 16 August 1915.

[67] BOA/DH.ŞFR, no. 59/232, Coded telegram from Interior Ministry's Generel Security Directorate to the Provincial District of Kütahya, dated 6 January 1916.

1915:[68] "as it . . . is evident to your exalted government that the Armenian people forming approximately 2 percent of the population living in our provincial district since the formation of the eternal Ottoman state under no circumstances permitted its reputation of loyalty to be stained, we ask that the imperial mercy that your just government abundantly commanded for the Armenian people of Burdur and Isparta also be deservingly ordered for the innocent people of our land."[69]

There is conflicting information about the 5 percent rule for the eastern provinces. Some official documents suggest that the rule was not implemented in this region. All of the Armenians were deported, without separation or internal dispersion. In May 1915, during the initial phase of the deportations, the interior minister declared to Erzurum that "since the province is on the border with Russia, according to the principle that we follow, not a single Armenian is to be allowed to remain there."[70] The eastern provinces were directed on 20 June 1915 that "all Armenians living in the towns and villages in the province are to be deported along with their families, [and] without exception, and sent to the Province of Mosul and in the directions of Urfa and [Der] Zor."[71]

Nonetheless, other sources indicate that the 5 percent regulation was indeed implemented in these provinces. The memoirs of Ali Fuat Elden, who was in the retinue of Cemal Pasha (the governor of Syria and commander of the Fourth Army during World War I) and who held various high-level positions, such as chief of staff, include a telegram from Bahaeddin Şakir to Cemal Pasha. "We are sending 95 percent of the immigrants from Trebizond, Erzurum, Sivas, Mamuretülaziz, [and] Diyarbekır to the

---

[68] BOA/DH.ŞFR, no. 54-A/276, Coded telegram from Interior Ministry's General Directorate of Security to the Provinces of Ankara and Hüdâvendigâr (Bursa), and to the Provincial Districts of Kayseri, Karahisâr-ı Sahib (Afyon Karahisar), Niğde, Eskişehir, and Karesi (Balıkesir), dated 5 August 1915.

[69] BOA/DH.EUM, 2. Şube, no. 12/11/1, Telegram from Nikogos oğlu Ohannes, Mızrakyan Artin, Papaz oğlu İstepan, and Nersis oğlu Markada in the name of the people of Karahisâr-ı Sahib (Afyon Karahisar) of Konya to the Exhalted Prime Ministerial Office, dated 5 October 1915. It is understood from the letter that the first request took place on 1 September 1915.

[70] BOA/DH.ŞFR, no. 53/129, Coded telegram from the Interior Ministry's General Directorate of Security to the Province of Erzurum, dated 27 May 1915.

[71] BOA/DH.ŞFR, no. 54/87, Coded telegram from the Interior Ministry's General Directorate of Security to the Provinces of Trebizond, Mamuretülaziz, Sivas, and Diyarbekır, and the Provincial District of Canik, dated 20 June 1915.

south of Mosul," wrote Şakir.[72] Other documents also indicate that some Armenians were not deported from this area. Evidently, there were some exceptions being made. For example, the governor of Malatya provincial district reported to the province of Bitlis that "of the 3,341 males and 3,594 females in the 1,582 houses registered in Malatya, 3,246 males and 3,492 females in 1,550 houses were deported, and in the remaining 32 houses, 95 males and 102 females were left as artisans." In addition, 315 Catholics, 130 Protestants, and 30 Latins (Orthodox) remained together with those who had come from other places.[73] Bitlis governor Sabit Bey, in a telegram in response to this information, states, "there is no harm in artisan women being left, on the necessary condition that they are to the greatest degree chosen from Catholics and Protestants, and do not exceed ten or fifteen [in number]."[74] It must be added that although all the Armenians of this province were to be removed, male and female children were being assembled for assimilation into Muslim families.

THE 10 PERCENT RULE IN THE PLACES TO WHICH ARMENIANS WERE SENT

The earliest correspondence about the areas designated for Armenian settlement and their proportion to the local population dates from the end of April 1915. An Interior Ministry telegram of 24 April 1915 defined the resettlement areas as "the southeastern portion of [the province of] Aleppo, and the vicinities of [Der] Zor and Urfa."[75] A more detailed description is found in a cable of 23 May to Fourth Army commander Cemal Pasha and the governors of Erzurum, Van, and Bitlis. The Armenians were to be resettled "in the southern portion of the province of Mosul, apart from the the northern section, which borders the province of Van, the provincial

---

[72] Ali Fuad Elden, *Birinci Dünya Harbinde Suriye Hatıraları* (Istanbul: Türkiye İş Bankası Kültür Yayınları, 2005), 150. When Ali Fuad Elden wrote immigrant (*göçmen*), he meant Armenians. This cable is included in the section of his book concerned with the Armenian deportations, and after the telegram, he continues to relate his memories about the deportations.

[73] AAPJ, Carton 7, File H, Doc. no. 109, Telegram from the governor of the Provincial District of Malatya to the Province of Bitlis, dated 13 November 1915.

[74] AAPJ, Carton 7, File H, Doc. no. 645, Cipher telegram from Bitlis governor, Sabit, to the Malatya Provincial District government, dated 25 November 1915.

[75] BOA/DH.ŞFR, no. 52/93, Coded telegram from the Interior Ministry's General Directorate of Security to Fourth Army commander Cemal Pasha, dated 24 April 1915.

districts of [Der] Zor and Urfa (apart from the central part), the eastern part of the province of Damascus and the eastern and southeastern parts of the province of Aleppo."[76]

The Interior Ministry informed the grand vizierate on 26 May 1915 that the Armenian deportations had begun. The Armenians were to be relocated "to Mosul province, excluding the northern part which borders Van province, and Zor provincial district, to the southern part of Urfa provincial district excluding Urfa's center; to the eastern and southeastern part of Aleppo province, and the eastern part of Damascus province."[77]

On 31 May, the Council of Ministers prepared a fifteen-article circular designating these areas for Armenian resettlement.[78] A note dated 26 May from the Ottoman Ministry of War to the Interior Ministry stated that "the Armenian population must not exceed 10 percent of the number of [nomadic] tribal and Muslim inhabitants of the place to which they are sent."[79]

Over the next few months the resettlement areas were expanded. A ciphered cable distributed to a great number of provincial and local administrative officials on 5 July 1915 redefined the borders as:

(1) the existing towns and villages eighty kilometers from the border of Iran in the district of Kerkük, areas south and west of the province of Mosul;

(2) the southern and western areas in the district of Der Zor, within twenty-five kilometers from the border of Diyarbekır and including all inhabited locations in the valley of the Habur and Euphrates rivers;

(3) excluding the northern portion of the province of Aleppo, all of the villages and towns east and south and southwest, and including the districts of Havran and Kerek in the province of Damascus, all villages and towns within twenty-five kilometers from the railway route.

[76] BOA/DH.ŞFR, no. 53/94, Coded telegram from interior minister Talat to the Command of the Fourth Imperial Army, dated 23 May 1915. Another coded telegram with the same information was sent on the same day to the Provinces of Erzurum, Van, and Bitlis; see BOA/DH.ŞFR, no. 53/93.

[77] For the relevant correspondence, see Bayur, *Türk İnkilap Tarihi*, vol. 3, part 3, 37–42.

[78] Genelkurmay Başkanlığı, *Arşiv Belgeleriyle Ermeni Faaliyetleri*, vol. 1, 131.

[79] İhsan Sakarya, *Belgelerle Ermeni Sorunu*, 224; Kamuran Gürün, *Ermeni Dosyası* (Ankara: Bilgi Yayınevi, 1988), 277.

Map 4. Historic map of Der Zor Province.

The document ended with the reminder that the Armenians "should be distributed and settled among the Muslim population according to a 10 percent ratio."[80] The situation was explained on the same day with the same telegram to the provincial district government of Der Zor, and it was requested that those arriving be settled in conformance with this ratio.[81]

Two days later, the provincial district of Der Zor reported that "the [number of] Armenians who have already arrived and who are on their way has in fact exceeded the figure of 10 percent of the district's total registered population."[82] The cable also noted that the tribes in Der Zor were nomadic, and it mentioned difficulties in matters of census and settlement. In response, the IAMM sent off a cable to numerous regions on 12 July 1915 and reminded the local officials that the "Armenians were to be settled in the southern part of the province of Aleppo, the eastern part of the province of Damascus and the provincial district of Kerkük," and, therefore, "those who were to be deported and sent to the provincial district of [Der] Zor, which has already exceeded its 10 percent [limit]" should no longer be sent there, but instead to the new destinations mentioned above.[83] On one occasion, a population ratio of just 2 percent was allowed for the dispersion of Armenians within the borders of Damascus Province. A cipher telegram of 18 October 1915 states,

> Regarding the distribution of the 30,000 [Armenians] who are found in Aleppo . . . the settlement exceptionally of some of them, who are

[80] BOA/DH.ŞFR, no. 54/315, Coded telegram from the Interior Ministry's IAMM to the Provinces of Adana, Erzurum, Bitlis, Aleppo, Diyarbekır, Damascus, Sivas, Trebizond, Mamuretülaziz, and Mosul; to the president of the Commission on Abandoned Property in Adana and Aleppo; and to the Provincial Districts of (Der) Zor, Marash, Canik, Kayseri, and İzmit, dated 5 July 1915.

[81] BOA/DH.ŞFR, no. 54/308, Coded telegram from Interior Ministry's IAMM to the Provincial District of Der Zor, dated 5 July 1915.

[82] BOA/DH, 2. Şube, 3/60/1, Coded telegram from Kamil on behalf of the Provincial District of Der Zor to the Interior Ministry, dated 7 July 1915.

[83] BOA/DH.ŞFR, no. 54/413, Coded telegram from the Interior Ministry's Office of Tribal and Immigrant Settlement to the Provinces of Adana, Erzurum, Bitlis, Aleppo, Diyarbekır, Sivas, Mamuretülaziz, and Urfa, and to the Provincial Districts of Kayseri, Canik, and İzmit, 12 July 1915. A different telegram sent on the same day to the same places informed that the Armenians sent to Der Zor exceeded 10 percent of the population there. See BOA/DH.ŞFR, no. 54/308. These two documents are helpful in explaining another phenomenon. As will be seen below, at the start of 1916 Armenians again began to be sent to Der Zor in an intensive fashion, though the 10 percent limit had been exceeded there. This shows that the Unionists starting at this time had abandoned their settlement policy. Armenians were being sent to Der Zor to be exterminated.

officials or in the service of the state and those who provide good service to the state and who have not supported a seditious idea, with the purpose of bettering their conditions to a degree, has been decided with the consent of the command of the Fourth Army on condition that it does not exceed 2 percent of the people present in the cities and towns, with the exception of the places which are found on the route of the railroad and the towns of Damascus, Hama, and Homs; and their dispatch by means of special documents given by the Aleppo police director included in special instructions has begun.[84]

As is understood from the telegram, a handful of Armenian professionals from a group of thirty thousand were exempted on the basis of merit and permitted to resettle in nonstrategic areas, where they would be outnumbered 50:1 (this dispersion will be discussed at greater length below on the section concerning assimilation).[85] From a telegram sent by the IAMM director Şükrü Kaya, it is possible to understand that the 10 percent rule was followed during these months in the distribution within Damascus Province. In a telegram dated 26 October 1915, Şükrü Kaya reports that "as a result of the information obtained on the refugees who are to be settled in the localities connected with the Syrian Province, from consultation by way of the Fourth Army Command" in a predetermined area within the province, on condition of not being east of a set line, the Armenians in the province "are to be settled so as to not exceed 10 percent of the population of the city and towns."[86] As is shown, with the exception of one single incident, the 5 to 10 percent rule is consistent throughout all documents. Throughout the deportation and resettlement process, special attention would continue to be focused on the question of population ratios. Wherever the concentration of Armenians threatened to exceed the

---

[84] BOA/DH.EUM, 2. Şube, no. 68/80, Cipher telegram from the Cipher Office of the Interior Ministry to the Provinces of Damascus and Aleppo, dated 18 October 1915. This decision was communicated in another telegram of Şükrü Bey, then director in Aleppo of the Interior Ministry's Office of Tribal and Immigrant Settlement (IAMM), dated 25 October 1915 (see BOA/DH.ŞFR, no. 57/125).

[85] Yervant Odian was one of these relatively fortunate Armenians who settled in Hama with a document he succeeded in obtaining (Yervant Odian, *Accursed Years: My Exile and Return from Der Zor, 1914–1919* [London: Gomidas Institute, 2009], 96–97).

[86] BOA/DH.ŞFR, no. 494/109, Coded telegram from the director of Immigrant Affairs, Şükrü Kaya, to the Interior Ministry, dated 26 October 1915.

prescribed figures, the government intervened immediately to send Armenians to other regions.

In a cable to the province of Aleppo on 8 September 1915, the Security Directorate advised that "the wholesale receiving of [all] the Armenians sent there from various locales and their resettlement in the [provincial] center and periphery is not acceptable since it will subsequently result in them forming a relative majority in this area," and therefore, "they should be constantly monitored from this consideration and all of those [Armenian deportees] apart from those who have arrived already should not be sent to the interior of the province and instead be sent to the area around Urfa."[87]

A similar telegram dated 11 January 1916, and again sent to the province of Aleppo, asked about the causes of unwanted accumulations of Armenians in Islahiye:

> It is informed by Adana Province that Armenians constantly are coming from Aleppo to Islahiye by land and train without the province being informed as to whether or not they possess documents, and the assembly despite this much self-sacrifice of fifteen, twenty thousand Armenians in Islahiye and its surroundings cannot be suitable. The communication of the clarification through investigation of where and at what date the order and permission for their being sent to that area was issued [is requested].[88]

Population ratio of the Armenians for the targeted settlement areas was crucial throughout the deportation process. With the exception of this single incident, the 5 to 10 percent rule is consistent throughout all documents.

IS THERE A CONNECTION BETWEEN THE 5 TO 10 PERCENT POLICY AND GENOCIDE?

The 5 to 10 percent rule is found in ciphered and top secret correspondence at the highest level of the state, and its significance is not in doubt. If the dispersion of the Armenians in a fashion not to exceed 10 percent of

[87] BOA/DH.ŞFR, no. 55-A/145, Coded telegram from the Interior Ministry's General Directorate of Security to the Province of Aleppo, dated 8 September 1915.

[88] BOA/DH.ŞFR, no. 59/277, Coded telegram from the Interior Ministry's General Directorate of Security to the Province of Aleppo, dated 11 January 1916.

the local Muslim population for the targeted settlement areas was planned in advance, this can be considered as a concrete indication that the policy toward Armenians was indeed genocidal. The 10 percent ratio seems to have been the operational goal in implementing that policy throughout the entire process of genocide, notably during the second wave of massacres in the summer of 1916.[89]

The Interior Ministry laid out the general framework of the deportation policy in a November 1915 communiqué to Aleppo: "The purpose of sending away certain people is to safeguard the welfare of our fatherland for the future, for wherever they may live they will never abandon their seditious ideas, so we must try to reduce their numbers as much as possible."[90] Abdullahad Nuri, who headed the Aleppo resettlement office, clearly understood the relationship between the 5 to 10 percent regulation and the effort to reduce the numbers of "certain people" as much as possible. "Enquiries having been made[;] it is understood that hardly 10 percent of the Armenians subjected to the general deportations have reached the places destined for them; the rest have died from natural causes, such as hunger and sickness," reported Nuri on 10 January 1916. "We inform you that we are working to bring about the same result with regard to those who are still alive, by using severe measures."[91]

The language of numbers is very clear. According to the 1914 Ottoman census, the population of the empire, including the Arab provinces, was approximately 18.5 million. Excluding the latter provinces, the estimated population of Anatolia was between 15 and 17.5 million.[92] The prewar Ar-

---

[89] The Armenian survivors who arrived at the settlement areas mentioned above were the targets of a second wave of massacres that intensified in the summer months of 1916 and continued to the end of that year. For a detailed report on these massacres, see Raymond Kévorkian, ed., "L'extermination des déportés arméniens ottomans dans les camps de concentration de Syrie-Mésopotamie (1915–1916)," Special Issue, *Revue d'histoire arménienne contemporaine* 2 (1998). For further information, see http://www.imprescriptible.fr/rhac/tome2/.

[90] Aram Andonian, *Memoirs of Naim Bey*, 4. The contents of this telegram are nearly identical to those of Talat Pasha's directive of 29 August 1915 to all provinces (BOA/DH.ŞFR, no. 55/292; see chapter 5, footnote 33 in this volume). The similarities of the telegrams published by Aram Andonian to this and other extant Ottoman documents make a reexamination of the validity of the Andonian telegrams necessary.

[91] Aram Andonian, *Memoirs of Naim Bey*, 57–58.

[92] Kemal Karpat estimates the Anatolian population at about 15 million (*Ottoman Population*, 188). On the basis of several upward corrections of these numbers, Justin McCarthy puts the figure for Anatolia alone at 17.5 million (*Muslims and Minorities*, 110).

menian population of Anatolia, according to the Ottoman census, was 1.3 million (according to Justin McCarthy, about 1.5 million), while according to the Armenian Gregorian Church, the figure was 2.1 million.[93] As we have seen, the Ottoman administration aimed to deport the Armenians to several Ottoman provinces in what is now Syria and Iraq without exceeding 10 percent of the local population, which was overwhelmingly Muslim. How was this going to take place?

Relying on the 1914 Ottoman state statistics at hand, let us examine more closely the number of Muslims in these regions.[94] While estimating this population, I would like to stress one point. Government communiqués from May and June 1915, while stating that the Armenians were going to be settled within the borders of provinces like Aleppo, Damascus, and Mosul, also noted some restrictions: for example, "excluding the northern portion of the province of Aleppo," or "in the southern portion of the province of Mosul, apart from the the northern section," and later again for Mosul, "the southern and western portions of the province." I wish to look at the population of this region without paying excessive attention to these restrictions.

For Mosul there are no accurate numbers. However, based on Ottoman statistics of previous years, Justin McCarthy estimates a population of 828,000 for the year 1909.[95] According to a census conducted by the British after they occupied the region in 1919, the total population of the province was 703,378, of which 601,893 were Muslims.[96] Based on

[93] The purpose here is not to debate the question of Armenian population figures and their losses. Rather, it is simply to shed some light on the connection between the 5 to 10 percent policy and genocide. In regard to the subject of Armenian population figures within the Ottoman Empire, in addition to the aforementioned works by Kemal Karpat and Justin McCarthy, a good general distillation of the available sources can be found in Hikmet Özdemir et al., *Ermeniler: Sürgün ve Göç* (Ankara: Türk Tarih Kurumu, 2004), 5–53. For Armenian sources, see Kevork Pamukciyan, "Zamanlar, Mekânlar, İnsanlar," in *Ermeni Kaynaklarından Tarihe Katkılar*, vol. 3 (Istanbul: Aras Yayıncılık, 2003), 289–92; and Levon Marashlian, *Politics and Demography: Armenians, Turks and Kurds in the Ottoman Empire* (Toronto: Zoryan Institute, 1991).

[94] For the 1914 Ottoman statistics, see Karpat, *Ottoman Population*, 188–90. To what degree these figures are accurate is the topic of a different discussion; for one example, see Levon Marashlian, *Politics and Demography*. However, this discussion is not important for the present topic.

[95] Justin McCarthy, *Population History of the Middle East and the Balkans* (Istanbul: ISIS Press, 2002), 205n4.

[96] İhsan Şerif Kaymaz, *Mosul Sorunu* (Istanbul: Otopsi Yayınları, 2003), 27.

McCarthy's figure, the Muslim population of Mosul may be liberally estimated as 750,000.[97]

The total population of the province of Damascus for 1914, according to the official Ottoman figures, was 918,409 souls, of whom 791,582 were Muslim.[98] According to these same figures, the provincial district of Der Zor contained 66,294 inhabitants, of whom 65,770 were Muslim.[99]

In the 1914 census, the population of Aleppo Province was 667,790, of whom 576,320 were Muslim. It should also be added that the counties of Aleppo, such as Antep, İskenderun, Antakya, and Kilis, were not chosen as settlement destinations for deported Armenians; on the contrary, the Armenians living there were themselves deported. As for the city of Aleppo, the provincial capital was initially chosen as a destination for the deportees, but later the Armenians who arrived there were expelled in the direction of Mosul and Der Zor.[100] The general population figures of these places are as follows, with the numbers of Muslims in parentheses: the city of Aleppo 126,676 (93,976); İskenderun 18,875 (14,140); Antakya 91,573 (78,054); Antep 110,810 (89,769); and Kilis 84,814 (78,905).

According to these numbers, the total Muslim population of places that were not proclaimed to be part of the Armenian region of the settlement of

---

[97] In *Population History*, Justin McCarthy estimates that the population increased from 1909 to 1914 by a factor of 0.011. There is nothing recorded as to how much of this increase refers to Muslims or to non-Muslims. If the difference of 100,000 with the 1919 English census is taken as a basis, the figure of 750,000 that I use here is a very generous one.

[98] Karpat, *Ottoman Population*, 188–200. Justin McCarthy gives the figure of 1,017,322 total inhabitants of the province for the years 1911–12, of which some 876,835 were Muslim (McCarthy, *Population History*, 185).

[99] Karpat, *Ottoman Population*, 190. Based on McCarthy's figures for 1911–12, which give the total population of the Der Zor district as 83,120, Karpat adds a corrective 25 percent to bring the figure to 103,900 (McCarthy, *Population History*, 198).

[100] On Aleppo being selected as the arrival point for the deportations, see BOA/DH.ŞFR, no. 54-A/389, Coded telegram from the Interior Ministry's IAMM to the Province of Aleppo and to the president of the Commission (of Abandoned Properties), dated 31 July 1915. There exists a considerable amount of information on the deportations from Aleppo. Here, it is sufficient for me to simply provide some of the relevant document classification numbers: BOA/DH.ŞFR, nos. 57/53; 62/135; 63/306; 63/307; 64/175; 65/32-1; and 65/51. Despite the war, the German and American governments collaborated in great efforts to attempt to prevent the deportations from Aleppo, and there is abundant information on this subject in both of these countries' archives. For one example, see NA/RG 59, 867.4016/296, Report from Hoffman Philip to the secretatry of state, dated 1 September 1916, cited in *United States Official Records*, ed. Sarafian, 534–40.

Aleppo Province, and where deportations were conducted, was 354,844. That means that the Muslim population of the remaining parts of Aleppo Province, which were considered for Armenian settlement, was 221,476.[101] If the Muslim population of Mosul is considered to be 750,000 and the entire Muslim population of Aleppo is included, the number of Muslims in the region, which was foreseen for the settlement of Armenians, is in the neighborhood of 2,183,672. Excluding those places that were listed above within the province of Aleppo as destinations for settlement, the figure could reach as high as 1,850,000 Muslims.

It is useful to add one more bit of information to the picture. In essence, although Mosul was proclaimed to be a place of deportation, the dispatch of Armenians there was halted because of the war, and only later was a very limited number of Armenians sent there: "The adherence of the Armenians being deported to the interior of Mosul province to the Russian forces found in the south of Van is probable, and from the point of view of easily managing their conduct, their deportation in the directions of Urfa and Zor is seen as suitable," stated a security directive from the Interior Ministry, adding that "[c]onformity of action accordingly [is desired]."[102]

A detailed circular was prepared in October 1915 about the new settlement areas arranged for the Armenians and the administrative statutes for the existing camps, but these regulations did not indicate Mosul as a place of settlement.[103] Although a limited number of convoys were sent to Mosul after autumn 1915, this was halted by early June 1916 because Mosul had been declared a war zone.[104] The local German consul reported in September 1916 that "it has been 3½ months therefore that no new caravan has arrived in Mosul."[105] If we exclude Mosul as a region of Armenian settlement,

[101] Karpat, *Ottoman Population*, 176–72.

[102] BOA/DH.ŞFR, no. 54-A/198, Coded telegram from the Interior Ministry's General Security Directorate to the Provinces of Diyarbekır and Mamuretülaziz, dated 31 July 1915.

[103] BOA/DH.EUM.VRK.15/71-1-6, Communication from the director of the IAMM of the Interior Ministry, Kaya, to the Interior Ministry, dated 8 October 1915.

[104] BOA/DH.ŞFR, no. 64/239 and BOA/DH.ŞFR, no. 64/248, Coded telegrams from the Interior Ministry's General Security Directorate to the Province of Aleppo and Provincial District of Zor, dated 7 June 1916.

[105] DE/PA-AA/R 14093, Report of Mosul consul, Hoffmann, to German Embassy, Istanbul, dated 5 September 1916.

the general population comes to 1.85 million; including Mosul, it is 2.18 million. In round numbers, the Ottoman government's 10 percent ceiling must have allowed for an influx of no more than 185,000 to 218,000 Armenian settlers. In that case, the calculation is simple. According to official Ottoman statistics, it was necessary to reduce the prewar population of 1.3 million Armenians to approximately 200,000.

Several figures approach an accurate count of the Armenians deported from their homes and those who arrived in the deportation regions. Two of the documents belonging to Talat Pasha that were published by Murat Bardakçı contain such detailed information. The first document bears the title "Number of Armenians Deported," and gives a total number of 924,158. It is necessary to make some additions to this figure because the list of provinces and provincial districts omits a great many places from which there is decisive proof that Armenians were deported.[106] Many of these "missing" locations—Istanbul, Edirne, Aydın, Bolu, Kastamonu, Van, Teke (Antalya), Kale-i Sultaniye (Çanakkale), Biga, Eskişehir, İçel (Silifke), Kütahya, Menteşe (Muğla), Çatalca, and Urfa—were far from inconsequential areas of Armenian settlement.[107]

The second document enumerates the Armenians who survived the deportation and compares these figures with the 1914 population. The Ottoman officials who prepared the document appended an important gloss: "It is appropriate to increase this number by 30 percent."[108] Thus, based on both documents, one can confidently say that the number of deported Armenians was around 1.2 million. Consequently, Toynbee's estimate of 1.2 million or the German pastor Lepsius's estimate of 1.3 million Armenians deported are perhaps close to the truth.[109]

---

[106] The document contains the names of only eighteen provinces and provincial districts. See Bardakçı, *Talat Paşa'nın Evrak-ı Metrukesi*, 77.

[107] For a complete list of the provinces and provincial districts of the period, see Dahiliye Nezâreti İdare-i Umumiye-i Dahiliye Müdüriyeti, *Teşkilât-ı Hâzıra-i Mülkiyeyi ve Vilâyet, Livâ, Kazâ ve Nâhiyelerin Hurûf-i Hecâ Sırasıyla Esâmîsini Hâvî Cedveldir* (Istanbul: Matbaa-i Âmire, [1331] 1915).

[108] Bardakçı, *Talat Paşa'nın Evrak-ı Metrukesi*, 109.

[109] Bryce and Toynbee, *The Treatment of Armenians*, 646; Johannes Lepsius, *Deutschland und Armenien, 1914–1918: Sammlung diplomatischer Aktenstücke* (Potsdam: Der Tempel Verlag, 1919), lxv. Similar numbers were published in several contemporary Arab-language newspapers. In the 30 May 1916 edition of the daily *El-Mokattam*, the figure 1.2 million is given for the number of Armenians deported (cited in Faiz El-Ghusein, *Martyred Armenia* [New York, Montreal, and London: Tankian, 1975], 58).

Table 1. Number of Deported Armenians

Names of Provinces and Provincial Subdivisions	Population Transferred
Province of Ankara	47,224
Province of Erzurum	128,657
Province of Adana	46,031
Province of Bitlis	109,521
Province of Aleppo	34,451
Province of Bursa[a]	66,413
Province of Diyarbekır	61,002
Province of Sivas	141,592
Province of Trabzon	34,500
Province of Elazığ[b]	74,206
Provincial Subdivision of İzmit	54,370
Provincial Subdivision of Samsun[c]	26,374
Provincial Subdivision of Balıkesird	8,290
Provincial Subdivision of Karahisar	7,327
Provincial Subdivision of Kayseri	47,617
Provincial Subdivision of Maraş	27,101
Provincial Subdivision of Niğde	5,101
Province of Konya	4,381
Total Sum	924,158

Source: Murat Bardakçı, *Talat Paşa'nın Evrak-ı Metrukesi: Sadrazam Talat Paşa'nın özel arşivinde bulunan Ermeni tehciri konusundaki belgeler ve hususi yazışmalar* [The Abandoned Documents of Talat Pasha: The Records and Private Correspondence on the Armenian Deportation Found in the Private Archive of Vizier Talat Pasha] (Istanbul: Everest Publications, 2008), 77.

[a] Bursa was formerly known as Hüdavendigâr.
[b] Elazığ was formerly known as Mamuretülaziz.
[c] Samsun was formerly known as Canik.
[d] Balıkesir was formerly known as Karesi.

The question that remains is how many Armenian survivors arrived at these new settlement areas. These figures are also consistent. The American consul in Aleppo, Jesse B. Jackson, reported that according to reliable sources, since 3 February 1916 some 486,000 Armenians had been living in the environs of Aleppo and Damascus and along the Euphrates River as far as Der Zor.[110] Rössler, the German consul in Aleppo, reported to

[110] NA/RG 59, 867.48/271, Report from Aleppo consul, Jesse B. Jackson, to Ambassador Henry Morgenthau, dated 8 February 1916, reproduced in *United States Official Records*, ed. Sarafian, 489–90.

Table 2. General Calculation of the Post-Deportation Armenian Population
(possibly 1915–16)[a]

	Current local population	Foreign population	Locals now in other locations	According to the population records of 1912 [1330]
Ankara	12,766	410	4,560	44,661
Mosul	253	7,033	0	0
Niğde	193	850	547	4,939
İzmit	3,880	142	9,464	56,115
Kütahya	3,932	680	0	4,023
Eskişehir	1,258	1,096	1,104	8,620
Bolu	1,539	551	56	3,002
Afyonkarahisar	2,234	1,778	1,484	7,498
İçel	252	116	0	350
Balıkesir	1,852	124	1,696	8,663
Kayseri	6,650	111	6,778	47,974
Adana	12,263	4,257	19,664	51,723
Maraş	6,115	198	2,010	27,306
Sivas	8,097	948	3,993	141,000
Beirut	50	1,849	0	1,224
Kastamonu	3,437	185	211	9,052
Konya	3,730	14,210	3,639	13,078
Aydın	11,901	5,729	0	19,710
Syria	0	39,409	0	0
Zor	201	6,778	0	63
Bursa	2,821	178	10,251	59,038
Aleppo	13,679	13,591	19,091	37,031
Erzurum	0	0	3,364	125,657
Bitlis	0	0	1,061	114,704
Van	0	0	160	67,792
Diyarbekır	0	0	1,849	56,166
Trabzon	0	0	562	37,549

Chancellor Bethmann-Hollweg on 20 December 1915 that "at the most 500,000 [Armenians] came to Syria and Mesopotamia."[111]

Beginning in May 1915 and continuing through the summer and fall, as convoy after convoy of deported Armenians arrived in Syria, thousands

[111] DE/PA-AA/R 14089, Report from German consul in Aleppo, Rössler, to Chancellor Bethmann-Hollweg, dated 20 December 1915. In a different report sent on 4 October 1916 from the embassy in Istanbul, the number of survivors was said to be 425,000 (DE/PA-AA/R 14093, Report from the German Embassy in Istanbul to Chancellor Bethmann-Hollweg, dated 4 October 1916).

Table 2. (*Cont.*)

	Current local population	Foreign population	Locals now in other locations	According to the population records of 1912 [1330]
Elazığ	0	0	2,201	70,060
	97,247	106,910	94,206[b]	1,032,614
Istanbul	80,000	0	0	80,000
	177,247	106,910	94,206	1,112,614
	106,910			
	284,157			

Source: Murat Bardakçı, *Talat Paşa'nın Evrak-i Metrukesi: Sadrazam Talat Paşa'nın özel arşivinde bulunan Ermeni tehciri konusundaki belgeler ve hususi yazışmalar* [The Abandoned Documents of Talat Pasha: The Records and Private Correspondence about the Armenian Deportation Found in the Private Archive of Vizier Talat Pasha] (Istanbul: Everest Publications, 2008), 109. *Note*: In the summary figures from 1912 [1330], the general population of Gregorian Armenians had been listed as 1,187,818, the Catholic Armenians as 63,967, and in aggregate 1,256,403 for both. Since the entire population was not accurately reflected in the written records, not only could the number be actually closer to 1,500,000, as a precaution, an estimate of approximately 30 percent should be added to the combined figure of 284,157 for current local and foreign populations shown above, in which case, the actual current figures would be closer to 350,000–400,000.

[a] The years 1915–16 given by Murat Bardakçı are not correct. The date should be 1918.

[b] This figure is actually inclusive of the figure for foreign population. The number according to the population of 1912 is 68,433.

died of starvation, disease, and other causes. Even so, the number of survivors must have been much greater than 10 percent of the local Muslim population. By February 1916 there was an excess of approximately 275,000 Armenians whose annihilation was deemed necessary. And this was realized through a second wave of massacres that began in March 1916 with the emptying of the Armenian camps and reached its zenith that summer. Afterward, many sources agree, only about 200,000 deported Armenians remained alive.[112] The Ottoman government had successfully applied the 10 percent policy.

[112] Lepsius, *Deutschland und Armenien*, lxv. Raymond Kévorkian, who has written a detailed work on the second stage of the genocide, gives the figure of the Armenians who reached Syria as 870,000, based on Armenian sources, and states that roughly 240,000 of these survived. Of the remaining 630,000 people, 130,000 died from hunger and sickness in the camps by February 1916. Of the remaining 500,000 people still living, perhaps 200,000 were annihilated during the summer of 1916 in the Der Zor area. See Kévorkian, "L'extermination des déportés arméniens," 16, 61.

Table 3. Summary of Ottoman Population, 1914

Administrative Area	Muslims	Rums[a]	Armenians	Jews	Catholics	Armenian Catholics	Protestants	Orthodox	Assyrian Christians	Old Assyrians
Edirne	360,417	224,459	19,725	22,515	221	48	115	1		
Erzurum	673,297	4,859	125,657	10	5	8,720	2,241		88	
Istanbul	560,434	205,375	72,962	52,126	387	9,918	1,213	2,905	562	
Adana	341,903	8,537	50,139	66	437	2,511	5,036	174	467	
Ankara	877,285	20,226	44,507	1,026	14	7,069	2,381			
Aydin	1,249,067	299,096	19,395	35,041	1	892	479	1,793	2	
Bitlis	309,999		114,704			2,788	1,640		3,992	
Beirut	648,314	87,244	1,188	15,052	24,210	277	3,823	3,367	491	
Aleppo	576,320	13,772	35,104	12,193	8,182	5,739	8,643	1,776	2,956	
Bursa	474,114	74,927	58,921	4,126		1,278	992			
Diyarbekir	492,101	1,822	55,890	2,085	113	9,960	7,376		37,976	4,133
Syria	791,582	60,978	413	10,140	27,662	247	1,873	2,991	3,079	
Sivas	939,735	75,324	143,406	344		3,693	4,575		3	
Trabzon	921,128	161,574	37,549	8		1,350	1,338			
Kastamonu	737,302	20,958	8,959	8						
Konya	750,712	25,071	12,971	4	79		254	1		
Elazığ	446,379	971	76,070			3,751	8,043	715	2,234	
Van	179,380	1	67,792	1,383						
Eskişehir	140,578	2,613	8,276	728		316	215			
Antalya	235,762	12,385	630	250						
Urfa	149,384	2	15,161	865		1,557	1,652	39	2,328	

İçel	102,034	2,500	341	10	7	449	1,937	10	3
İzmit	226,859	40,048	55,403	428	5	9	2	1	1
Bolu	399,281	5,146	2,961	20					
Samsun	265,950	98,739	27,058	27		261	1,257		
Çatalca	20,048	36,797	842	1,480					
Zor	65,770	18	67	2	27	215	1	1	141
Jerusalem	266,044	26,035	1,310	21,259	1,086		1,733	9,880	427
Afyon[b]	277,659	632	7,437	7		2	9		
Balıkesir	359,804	97,497	8,544	362		109	51	2	
Çanakkale[c]	149,903	8,541	2,474	3,642	9		67		
Kayseri	184,292	26,590	48,659			1,515	2,018		
Kütahya	303,348	8,755	3,910			638			
Maraş	152,645	11	27,842	251	23	4,480	6,111	1,189	
Menteşe	188,916	19,923	12	1,615			769		
Niğde	227,100	58,312	4,890						
Total	15,044,846	1,729,738	1,161,169	187,073	62,468	67,838	65,844	24,845	54,750	4,133

Source: Kemal Karpat, *Osmanlı Nüfusu (1830–1914): Demografik ve Sosyal Özellikleri* (Ottoman Population [1830-1914]: Demographic and Social Characteristics) (Istanbul: Tarih Vakfı Publications), 226.

a The term "Rum" refers to those citizens of the Ottoman Empire who were ethnic Greeks.

b Afyon was formerly known as Karahisâr-ı Sahib.

c Çanakkale was formerly known as Kale-i Sultaniye.

THE EXISTENCE OF A LIMITED SETTLEMENT POLICY

I believe that the Ottoman government anticipated that the number of Armenians reaching Syria would be in the neighborhood of two hundred thousand and wanted to implement a limited settlement policy accordingly. Although the Ottoman, Armenian, and foreign diplomatic sources are full of references to the early settlement policies, this aspect of the Armenian Genocide has received scant attention. This relative neglect is likely based on an overly narrow concept of genocide, as well as a tendency on the part of scholars to counter the denial policy of the Turkish state by focusing on those aspects of the Armenian Genocide that most closely resemble the Holocaust.

From the Ottoman documents at hand, one can discern two important aspects of the early settlement policy. First, the Armenians were to be removed either to existing villages and counties or alternatively to new areas reserved for them alone. A careful distinction was made between old and new places of settlement in all telegrams to the region. Second, local communities would be permitted to offer humanitarian assistance.

The earliest policy directive, a "confidential" cable dated 12 May 1915, was sent even before the first major wave of deportations had begun. "[T]he Armenians who have been deported there should be distributed amongst the villages and settled according to whichever of the villages is determined appropriate depending on location, and since their sustenance cannot be provided by the government over the long term, it should be obtained directly from them from this time forward," ordered interior minister Talat. "Report back on the amount needed to cover the anticipated expenses, which shall be paid out of the budget for unexpected expenses."[113] As will be seen below, the Armenian community in Syria (especially Aleppo) was indeed allowed to assist the arriving deportees.

In a second telegram sent to Mosul and Der Zor on 23 May 1915 and recirculated the next day to other provinces, as well as the Fourth Army Command, the settlement of Armenians in their new areas was outlined more clearly: "The Armenians to be sent will be transported to places de-

[113] BOA/DH.ŞFR, no. 52/335, Coded telegram from the Interior Ministry's General Security Directorate to the Province of Aleppo, dated 12 May 1915.

termined by the government, and settled there," read the directive. "The Armenians arriving in places of settlement will be placed in houses that will be built in existing villages and towns in accordance with the requirement of the situation or place or in a dispersed fashion; or in villages to be newly established in places to be decided upon by the government." The only restriction was that "the lines of contiguity of the borders of the villages and towns of Armenian settlement as well as the Armenian villages to be newly founded with the Baghdad railway" be at least twenty-five kilometers distant.[114]

The most detailed definition of this topic is to be found in a 31 May 1915 decision of the Council of Ministers. Attached to the ruling was a set of fifteen guidelines. The fourth guideline stated: "Depending on the condition and location of the Armenians who reach the established settlement locations, they [the Armenians] will be settled either by constructing homes in existing villages and towns, or by establishing villages in assigned locations to be set up by local authorities." The fifth guideline added, "In the event that land which is adequate, vacant, abandoned or state-owned is not available in established villages in the settlement areas, the allotment of farms or villages that are state property for settlement is appropriate."[115]

A document dated 7 October 1915 specified the existing camps created up to that date and their administrative statutes.[116] This information is consistent with the Armenian sources used by Raymond Kévorkian. Rakka, Havran, and Der Zor were identified as settlement areas; Aleppo, Katma, Müslimiye, Suruç, and Ras ul Ayn as "areas of centralized gathering and detention"; and Deyrü'l-hafr, Meskene, Ebû Hüreyre, Hamâm, Sıhhiye, Maden Şerîası, and Tibni as "rest stops along the route." The Armenians were to be concentrated at temporary central locations, such as Aleppo or

---

[114] BOA/DH.ŞFR, no. 53/91, Coded telegram from interior minister Talat to the Province of Mosul and the Provincial District of (Der) Zor, dated 23 May 1915. Similar telegrams were sent the same day to the provincial offices in Erzurum, Van, and Bitlis (BOA/DH.ŞFR, no. 53/93), and to the Office of the Imperial Commander of the Fourth Army (BOA/DH.ŞFR, no. 53/94).

[115] The title of the set of fifteen articles mentioned here is "Guideline for the Settlement and Provisionings of Armenians Transferred to Other Locations due to the Exigencies of War and Extraordinary Political Necessity." See Genelkurmay Başkanlığı, *Arşiv Belgeleriyle Ermeni*, 131–33, 427–31.

[116] BOA/DH.EUM.VRK.15/71-1-6, Communication from the director of the IAMM of the Interior Ministry, Şükrü Kaya, to the Interior Ministry, dated 8 October 1915.

Katma, and eventually sent on to preassigned settlement areas. The document also outlines the organization of new "deportation offices" and their operation under the authority of established offices in "Aleppo, Meskene, [Der] Zor [and] Rakka."

Armenian sources and the reports of foreign diplomats indicate that limited settlement work was conducted in the early months. A German official returning from the region on 11 November 1915 reported: "Sabcha [Sebka/Rakka] . . . the first settlement location. Previously there existed a population of several hundred, now 7,000 people (the words of the township administrator) . . . the new settlement site is being expanded on the ridge of the mountain . . . long rows of rubble lie there . . . 100 houses stand out . . . In a short time 250 more houses will be ready . . . many are still living in rented houses." A German doctor made similar observations at Der Zor: "The officials daily clean all corners and streets carefully, build new living quarters as in Sabcha, distribute money to the people, as well as bread and flour, but with the exception of [those] preferring death to life [i.e., those Armenians who refuse this food from the government]."[117] The picture that Consul Wilhelm Litten drew of Der Zor was more rosy: "Der Zor is a friendly small town with straight streets and sidewalks. The Armenians enjoy absolute freedom; they can do whatever they want . . . also in connection with their food, which they themselves must purchase. Whoever has no money gets nothing."[118]

Similar information is found in Armenian sources. As the first deportees were arriving in Aleppo in May 1915, a refugee committee was formed there within the structure of the Armenian Church with official permission from the provincial government. The minutes of the meetings of that committee, which continued its activities until 1917, contain important information about the "settlement policies" that were being implemented in the summer and fall of 1915 in Syria.[119] The first noteworthy matter is the

[117] DE/PA-AA/R 14089, Medical captain Dr. Schacht's report, dated 11 November 1915, appended to the report of Aleppo consul, Rössler, to Chancellor Bethmann-Hollweg, dated 16 November 1915.

[118] DE/PA-AA/R 14090, Report by Consul Litten, dated 6 February 1916, attached to the report of Aleppo consul, Rössler, to Chancellor Bethmann-Hollweg, 9 February 1916.

[119] This information has been taken from the unpublished manuscript of Vahram L. Shemmassian, which is entitled "Humanitarian Intervention by the Armenian Prelacy of Aleppo during the First Months of the Genocide." I thank Vahram for sharing this extremely important work with me and giving permission for its use. The page numbers referred to here are from the manuscript version I possess.

coordinated effort of the committee and the government for the distribution of aid. For example, the two sides determined their respective fields of aid so that assistance could reach larger sectors. The committee's records state that the government's refugee commission gave five meteliks (equivalent to less than half a loaf of bread; one metelik is equal to a U.S. penny) daily to each adult, and three meteliks to each underage refugee, and the church committee's members were also present during the distribution of these funds.[120] Another important point is the participation of state officials in the meetings of the church committee. At one such meeting on 17 June 1915, a state official demanded a list of Armenian orphans in Aleppo, and the committee complied. In October, the committee established its own orphanage, which continued in operation until early 1917.[121]

The first refugees to arrive in Aleppo were from the region of Cilicia, and some of them were immediately dispersed to the surrounding towns and villages. German documents recorded their arrival and the order for their dispersal in the Aleppine villages.[122] Committee members went to these settlement locations and attempted to distribute aid there. The committee members who went to the areas of Munbuj and Bab, for example, judged that although the government's aid was not sufficient, its officials "deserve praise for their caring." The refugees in Munbuj expressed their "satisfaction with the local Circassian population," as well as the district governor.[123] A letter of gratitude was written to the local official Nevruz Pasha at the settlement of Maara for his "care and protection" of the deportees.[124] In the Idlib district, committee reports revealed that the government settled deportees in "suitable homes."[125] However, the government's distribution of relief was also riddled with persistent irregularities in all these places.[126]

[120] Ibid., 12. Metelik was the colloquial name of the 10-para coin, four of which were equal to one kuruş (or kurush)—the main currency. The following consumer prices for 1-kg. quantities were current in Istanbul as of July 1914: "sugar: 3 kuruş; rice: 3 kuruş; pasta: 3 kuruş; white beans: 4 kuruş; cheese: 12 kuruş; lamb meat: 7 kuruş." Tevfik Çavdar, *Milli Mücadele Başlarken Sayılarla Vaziyet ve Manzara-i Umumiye* (Istanbul: Milliyet yay, 1971), 116.

[121] Ibid., 10.

[122] DE/PA-AA/Bo.Kons., vol. 169, Report from Aleppo consul, Rössler, to the German Embassy, Istanbul, dated 3 June 1915.

[123] Shemmassian, "Humanitarian Intervention," 17.

[124] Ibid., 20.

[125] Ibid., 18–19.

[126] Ibid., 18.

Deportation official Naim Bey also mentioned the existence of these settlement policies: "At the start of the deportations, villages in the area of Aleppo were chosen for the Armenian refugees . . . Many Armenians were settled in those villages, and many of these began to work."[127] Aram Andonian, who reported this information and confirmed that Armenians were settled in "Aleppo and the cities of Ayaz, Kilis, Bab, Maara, and Muncup in the [same] province," stated that he did not know "whether there really was a decision of the government on this topic."[128] Raymond Kévorkian, relying extensively on Armenian archival materials, provides similar information on Rakka and Der Zor (and Ras ul Ayn, which was administratively attached to Der Zor) as settlement regions. Kévorkian writes that in Rakka, where the Armenian Patriarchate and American and Swiss organizations distributed aid, the county head received government assistance for the settlement of several thousand deportees: "a minority [of deportees] succeeded within a few months in opening shops for crafts or commerce. . . . Up to the month of June 1916, this population found in some way normal living conditions, and without a doubt had the feeling that it would be able to live there continuously."[129]

Some fifteen thousand Armenians were settled in the city of Der Zor, and "as in Rakka . . . did not delay in revitalizing local commerce and crafts, encouraged by the provincial governor Ali Suad Bey."[130] The new district governor Salih Zeki, who was sent to Der Zor in order to organize the second stage of the genocide in the summer of 1916, visited "the market, where he was particularly irritated to see the flourishing state of the Armenians," an eyewitness recalled. "The latter had created a veritable Armenia from it—as in Damascus, Hama, and Homs—and the market was largely in their hands."[131]

Ras ul Ayn, connected administratively to Der Zor, numbered twenty to thirty Chechen households that settled there after the Russo-Turkish War of 1878. The Ottoman state population figures for 1914 give the population of Ras ul Ayn as 2,667. This very small town was turned into a camp

---

[127] Aram Andonian, *Medz Vojire* (Boston: Bahag,1921), 89. I thank Armand Mirijanian for his translation of these sections of the original Armenian text.

[128] Ibid., 22

[129] Kévorkian, "L'extermination des déportés arméniens," 36.

[130] Ibid., 38.

[131] Ibid.

that sheltered around fifty thousand people. "Yusuf Ziya Bey, the local county head who remained in his post until February 1916 . . . authorized the deportees who had the means to live in the city; he also authorized local small commerce. . . . During four months, from November 1915 to the end of February 1916, this camp functioned, compared to other institutions of the same type in the region, under conditions which for this type of structure were nearly normal."[132]

It is necessary here to prevent a misunderstanding. The existence of a "settlement policy" does not mean that the situation of the refugees arriving in Syria was good or that deaths did not occur. Quite the contrary. Consul Litten, whose rosy picture of Der Zor was noted above, characterized the area between Der Zor and Sabha (Sebka?) as a "place of corpses." Rössler, who forwarded the consul's report, said he was informed that 1,029 Armenians had died in another concentration camp at Bab in January 1916.[133] According to the German doctor quoted above, an Ottoman state physician working at Der Zor told him that approximately 150 to 200 people were dying there each day.[134]

Armenian sources provide detailed information about the situation of the transitory camps for halting and dispersion. Scarcity of food, epidemics, and lack of shelter were among the basic causes of mass death. Let us survey the camps from west to east. At Mamoura, half an hour distant from Osmaniye, where during the months of August, September, and October 1915 approximately eighty thousand Armenians on average were sheltered under makeshift tents, "every day, six to seven hundred people died. . . . The bodies of the dead without burial gathered in heaps. The field was covered with them."[135]

The situation at Islahiye was not much different: "There were days when, under tens of thousands of tents, people died not by the tens but by the hundreds. Healthy men could no longer be found to collect the bodies and bury them. . . . The first victims were poor little children . . . One would

---

[132] Ibid., 30–31.

[133] DE/PA-AA/R 14090, Report from Aleppo consul, Rössler, to Chancellor Bethmann-Hollweg, 9 February 1916, with a report attached by Consul Litten, 6 February 1916.

[134] DE/PA-AA/R 14089, Report of medical captain Dr. Schacht, dated 11 November 1915, appended to the report of Aleppo consul, Rössler, to Chancellor Bethmann-Hollweg, dated 16 November 1915.

[135] Kévorkian, "L'extermination des déportés arméniens," 19.

have said that we were crossing a field of battle: the entire plain in front of Islahiye was embossed with hillocks of varying sizes. These were the tombs of Armenians buried fifty or one hundred at a time. . . . Alas, some were as high as hills."[136]

At Radjo, Katma, and Azaz, "corpses piled up in groups under tents made from old pieces of fabrics. . . . There were corpses everywhere." Andonian stated that sixty thousand had died from typhus and famine in these camps in the autumn of 1915.[137] Later these camps were closed down for military reasons.[138] At Bab, the situation was the same. Fr. Dajad Arslanian, who arrived at the end of November 1915, was horrified to see that "a multitude of dead and dying were stretched out along the sides of the tents whom the Armenian deportee gravediggers chosen by the authorities were barely able to evacuate. . . . [I]n the field that was serving as a cemetery there were dead without burial who remained thus for entire days, many semi-naked or completely undressed. My God, what a sight."[139] Fr. Arslanian, who in this camp assumed the obligation of burying the dead with as much respect as possible and according to traditions, reported that from the end of November 1915 to the end of February 1916, roughly fifty to sixty thousand Armenians lost their lives. At the Ras ul Ayn camp described above, where conditions were said to be good, some fourteen thousand people perished between November 1915 and February 1916. Raymond Kévorkian, who has carried out the most detailed research on the Syrian camps, says that by February 1916, "more than three hundred thousand deportees out of a total of over eight hundred fifty thousand had died in autumn 1915 and winter 1915–1916 on the routes of Syria and Mesopotamia or in the concentration camps."[140]

Ottoman government documents also confirm that hunger and disease opened the way for a great number of deaths among the Armenians who reached Syria. A telegram sent on 17 October 1915 to Damascus Province

[136] Ibid., 20.

[137] Ibid., 22.

[138] DE/PA-AA/R 14090, Report from Aleppo consul, Rössler, to Chancellor Bethmann-Hollweg, dated 9 February 1916.

[139] Kévorkian, "L'extermination des déportés arméniens," 87.

[140] Raymond Kévorkian, *The Armenian Genocide: A Complete History* (London: I. B. Tauris, 2011); the quote is in Chapter 9, "The Decision to Liquidate the Last Deportees." I thank Raymond for making the chapter available to me.

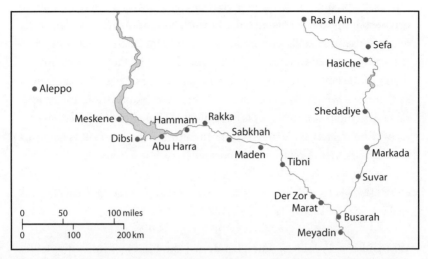

Map 5. Map of Syria showing the resettlement areas and camps. *Source*: Adapted from a map by George Aghjayan, provided by courtesy of the *Armenian Weekly*.

reported that each day, at least seventy to eighty refugees in the region were dying of sicknesses like fever, typhus, and dysentery; IAMM director Kaya in Aleppo was to be contacted so that the necessary measures could be taken.[141] Similarly, a telegram sent 26 October 1915 to Aleppo acknowledged that "deaths were occurring every day from hunger in the Armenian caravans" and reported that money "from the Fourth Army Command . . . for the procuring of their food supplies" had been allocated.[142]

These widespread deaths must be understood as part of the limited settlement policy under discussion. The existence of a limited settlement policy at the beginning, as is frequently claimed in the official Turkish accounts, does not prove that the aim of the policy toward the Armenians was anything less than the destruction of this community; nor, on the other hand, is it correct to speak of this genocide solely in terms of physical annihilation, and for this reason not mention the settlement policies.

[141] BOA/DH.ŞFR, no. 57/71, Coded telegram from the Interior Ministry's General Security Directorate to the Province of Damascus, dated 17 October 1915.

[142] BOA/DH.ŞFR, no. 57/110, Coded telegram from the Interior Ministry's General Security Directorate to the Province of Aleppo, dated 26 October 1915

The predominant conception of genocide as physical annihilation alone is reflected up to the present time in works on the Armenian Genocide, where settlement policies are either not mentioned or are attributed to the actions of well-intentioned local officials. While there is certainly no doubt of the good intentions of some local officials, I believe that limited settlement—which was abondoned later—and assimilation are inseparable structural components of the Armenian Genocide. Assimilation policy will be treated separately below. The immediate question is why this limited settlement policy was abandoned.

POPULATION CENSUSES AND THE ABANDONMENT OF THE SETTLEMENT POLICY

Why did the Unionists, who abandoned the policy of limited resettlement, decide to remove most of the Armenian survivors east to Der Zor for their final destruction? The evident reason for this drastic change in policy was that the number of deportees who arrived in Syria exceeded the planned resettlement ratio of 10 percent, beyond which threshold any living Armenian would be considered a threat to national security. Consequently, a second wave of massacres was launched, in Talat's words, "to reduce the [Armenian] number as much as possible,"[143] and a central topic of discussion among the CUP functionaries was "how they were going to decrease the numbers of the Armenians."[144] The extent to which military necessity, a justification found in some German reports and Ottoman telegrams, may have influenced the second wave of deportations has not been substantiated. I will discuss the second phase of the annihilation process below.

On 10 July 1916 the German ambassador reported that the "persecution of the Armenians in the eastern provinces has reached its final stage."[145] Raymond Kévorkian, relying on the testimony of Armenian journalist Aram Andonian, writes that the settlement policies were abandoned beginning in December 1915 to January 1916. The deportation official Naim

---

[143] Aram Andonian, *Memoirs of Naim Bey*, 4.

[144] Ibid., 4–6.

[145] DE/PA-AA/R 14092, Report of German ambassador Wolff-Metternich to Chancellor Bethmann-Hollweg, dated 10 July 1916.

Bey recorded that orders to change the Armenian settlement areas arrived in November 1915: "When the decision of the government specifying Maara, Bab, and other areas of Aleppo as the [re]settlement area for local Armenians was altered to [indicate] the region around the Habur River Deir-el-Zor, I understood that the situation was not a simple tragedy, but that more frightful things were going to happen."[146] The telegram informing local officials of the change in the settlement regions followed Talat Pasha's telegram that was quoted above with the passage, "to reduce the [Armenian] number as much as possible." Recalling Abdullahad Nuri's telegram of January 1916, which was quoted earlier ("we inform you that we are working to bring about the same result with regard to those who are still alive, by using severe measures"[147]), one can infer that the shift in policy took place between December 1915 and January 1916.

With the necessary preparations completed, the camps in Syria were emptied, and the second stage of the Armenian Genocide began, culminating in the summer of 1916 with the annihilation of close to two hundred thousand people in Der Zor. Under the leadership of provincial district governor Zeki, during the five-month period from the end of July to the end of December, approximately two hundred thousand Armenians were massacred in this region.[148] In January 1919, when the British expeditionary forces entered Der Zor, they found only 980 Armenians there.[149]

The Cipher Office of the Ottoman Interior Ministry kept track of these developments. Some conjectures can be made about why the limited settlement policies were abandoned and the second wave of massacres was organized. In particular, the connection between the start of the uprooting and removal of Armenians from the places in which they settled and the population figures of the area is quite striking. As discussed in detail earlier, the Interior Ministry kept the deportation process under very strict supervision and control, and at every stage of deportation immediately demanded continual reports about changing population compositions

---

[146] Andonian, *Medz Vojire*, 22

[147] Aram Andonian, *The Memoirs of Naim Bey*, 57–58.

[148] Kévorkian, "L'extermination des déportés arméniens," 24, 33, 44. Raymond Kévorkian's study deals with the emptying of the camps and the annihilation of the Armenians. Relying on Ottoman documents here, I will focus on the part of this topic connected with population numbers.

[149] T. H. Greenshielde, "The Settlement of Armenian Refugees in Syria and Lebanon, 1915–1939," PhD dissertation, University of Durham, 1978, 56.

from every relevant region. This supervision and control was operative for Aleppo and its environs in particular.

A telegram sent to Aleppo on 29 July stated that "because the Armenians are being deported via various routes and means of transportation, it is not possible for the deportation to be administered from the center and the places of settlement be determined here [by the central government]." Instead the dispersions would be conducted on a regional basis.[150] Aleppo was designated as the administrative center for organizing the arrival and distribution of the Armenians.[151] To establish the new branch office, IAMM director Şükrü Kaya departed for Aleppo at the end of August, and Nuri was appointed as his assistant.[152] All relevant provincial and provincial district governments were informed of this situation.[153] Regional administrators were to contact Kaya about deportation matters and follow his directives.[154] In addition, some provincial district governors were invited to a meeting in Aleppo at the beginning of October for direct discussions.[155]

The first decision for the region was to regulate the goals of the camps and their administrative relations. Accordingly, instructions were prepared and submitted for government approval. A 20 September 1915 telegram from Istanbul to Kaya in Aleppo stated that as "instructions about the organization and legislation of the deportation are seen as suitable by the general committee [meaning either the Ottoman cabinet or the Central Committee of the CUP], the need for its application in provinces and provincial districts which require [it] has been communicated."[156] The prob-

---

[150] BOA/DH.ŞFR, no. 54-A/167, Coded telegram from the Interior Ministry's IAMM to the Province of Aleppo, dated 29 July 1915.

[151] BOA/DH.ŞFR, no. 54-A/389, Coded telegram from Interior Ministry's IAMM, dated 13 August 1915.

[152] BOA/DH.ŞFR, no. 56/385, Coded telegram from the Secretariat of the General Security Directorate of the Interior Ministry to IAMM director Kaya, Aleppo, dated 12 September 1915.

[153] BOA/DH.ŞFR, no. 55-A/16, Coded telegram from the Interior Ministry's General Security Directorate to the Provinces of Konya, Ankara, Hüdavendigâr, Adana, and Aleppo, and to the Provincial Districts of İzmit, Eskişehir, Kütahya, Karahisar-ı Sahip, and Marash, dated 31 August 1915.

[154] BOA/DH.ŞFR, no. 56/69, Coded telegram from the Interior Ministry's General Security Directorate to the Provinces of Mosul and Damascus, and to the Provincial Districts of Urfa, Zor, and Ayıntab, dated 18 September 1915.

[155] BOA/DH.ŞFR, no. 56/173, Coded telegram from the Interior Ministry's General Security Directorate to the Provincial Districts of Urfa and Zor, dated 26 September 1915.

[156] BOA/DH.ŞFR, no. 56/85, Coded telegram from interior minister Talat to the director of the Office of Settlement of Tribes and Refugees of the Interior Ministry, Kaya, then in Aleppo, dated 20 September 1920.

able reference was to the above-mentioned instructions that were sent to the regions on 7 October 1915.[157] With the first deportation caravans arriving in Aleppo in the middle of May, no serious preparation was made for the settlement of the Armenians.

Two further important decisions were made. The first was "the deportation without exception towards Rakka, Zor, and Kerek" of the Armenian deportees who had come to Aleppo. Istanbul approved Kaya's desire,[158] and in a separate cable to Aleppo Province, the Interior Ministry asked that appropriate steps be initiated.[159] The second decision was to organize an extensive regional census of population. A telegram of 8 December 1915 to the provinces of Aleppo and Damascus, as well as to the provincial district of Urfa, listed the places where a census would be conducted: the majority were areas where camps existed, such as Harran, Maara, İdlib, Bab, Mencib, and Rakka. In particular, an attempt was to be made to register the nomadic tribes of the area.[160]

The funds necessary to conduct a census were sent to Aleppo and Damascus Provinces. Each was to "take measures for the carrying out of the registration [census] order in an orderly and speedy fashion, and according to local needs; and communciate with the command of the Fourth Army in this respect if it was seen necessary."[161] The Der Zor provincial district government informed the capital on 11 December 1915 that "the registers of the current population along with the map of the provincial district that had been ordered" were sent to Istanbul.[162]

[157] BOA/DH.EUM.VRK.15/71-1-6, note from the director of the IAMM of the Interior Ministry, Kaya, to the Interior Ministry, dated 8 October 1915.

[158] BOA/DH.ŞFR, no. 57/53, Coded telegram from the Interior Ministry's General Security Directorate to the Province of Aleppo, dated 17 October 1915.

[159] BOA/DH.ŞFR, no. 57/5, Coded telegram from the Interior Ministry's General Security Directorate to the Province of Aleppo, dated 17 October 1915.

[160] Interior Ministry's Cipher Office to the Province of Aleppo (BOA/DH.ŞFR, no. 58/231); the Provincial District of Urfa (BOA/DH.ŞFR, no. 58/230), dated 8 December 1915; and the Province of Damascus, dated 25 December 1915 (BOA/DH.ŞFR, no. 59/91).

[161] Coded telegrams from the Interior Ministry's Cipher Office to the Province of Aleppo (BOA/DH.ŞFR, no. 69/239) and to the Province of Damascus (BOA/DH.ŞFR, no. 69/241), dated 12 November 1915.

[162] BOA/DH.EUM.KLU, no. 10/36, Telegram from the Provincial District of Zor to the Interior Ministry, dated 11 December 1915. While the map of Der Zor and a notebook registering its population should have been in the relevant dossier of the archive, this registry is missing, and there is information only about the population of the town of Göksun and Medina in the file. The notebook had not been placed in this dossier.

In addition to the population census that regional officials were planning to conduct directly, the Interior Ministry, as noted above, continued
to receive almost weekly reports from the regions about the changing population ratios as the Armenian convoys moved to different locations. Two
telegrams of 13 January 1916 requested the population figures from Beirut
and Zor within twenty-four hours, as well as information from Damascus
Province on "the number of foreign Armenians that are reported as arriving from outside, together with local Armenians found in Damascus, and
where they are being deported."[163]

Now came the time for the evacuations, as camps were emptied in the
direction of Der Zor. From late January 1916, the Interior Ministry maintained systematic records on the convoys, which were surging wave after
wave into Der Zor. On 31 January 1916, "One thousand five hundred Armenians more came by way of Aleppo."[164] On 7 March 1916, "Two thousand five hundred Armenians of Ayıntâb and İzmit yesterday arrived at
[Der] Zor."[165] On 8 March 1916, "one thousand four hundred forty people
from the Armenians of Ayıntâb, Tekfurdağı, Karahisâr, [and] Akşehir yesterday arrived at [Der] Zor."[166] On 11 March 1916, "four hundred Armenians of İzmit and Samsun arrived."[167] On 12 March 1916 it was reported
that "Yesterday, two hundred eighty more Armenians of Marash, Bursa,
and Adapazar arrived."[168] Here let me remind readers that in the preceding months, the number of Armenians in Der Zor had already exceeded
10 percent of the number of the existing population, and orders had been
given that no more Armenians be sent there.

Similar developments can be traced in German and Armenian sources.
Aleppo consul Walter Rössler reported that the emptying of the camps

---

[163] Coded telegrams from the Interior Ministry's General Security Directorate to the Province of
Beirut, the Provincial District of Zor (BOA/DH.ŞFR, no. 60/32), and the Province of Damascus
(BOA/DH.ŞFR, no. 60/35), dated 16 January 1916.

[164] BOA/DH.EUM, 2. Şube, no. 69/5, Coded telegram from provincial district governor Ali Suad
to the Interior Ministry, dated 31 January 1916.

[165] BOA/DH.EUM, 2. Şube, no. 69/6, Coded telegram from provincial district governor Ali Suad
to the Interior Ministry, dated 7 March 1916.

[166] BOA/DH.EUM, 2. Şube, no. 69/7, Coded telegram from provincial district governor Ali Suad
to the Interior Ministry, dated 8 March 1916.

[167] BOA/DH.EUM, 2. Şube, no. 69/8, Coded telegram from provincial district governor Ali Suad
to the Interior Ministry, dated 11 March 1916.

[168] BOA/DH.EUM, 2. Şube, no. 69/9, Coded telegram from provincial district governor Ali Suad
to the Interior Ministry, dated 12 March 1916.

between Adana and Aleppo began in early December, and the deportees had been sent toward Bab and Der Zor.[169] Raymond Kévorkian, relying on Andonian's records, likewise states, "After the Constantinople authorities had decided to cleanse northern Syria of its Armenian deportees, between December 1915 and January 1916 . . . the camps of Mamura, Islahiye, Raco, Katma, Azaz, Bab, Akhterim, Munbuc, and Mârra, all situated somewhere in the periphery of Aleppo, were then closed down one by one and the survivors of these camps were sent along the line of the Euphrates or to Ras ul-Ayn."[170]

In March 1916, this time Ras ul Ayn and other places to the east of Aleppo began to be emptied, and their temporary residents were sent to Der Zor. At the beginning of April, there was great crowding at Ras ul Ayn. The Der Zor provincial district government was told that "news was received that until now only very few of the Armenian caravans assembling at Ras ul Ayn in order to be deported to [Der] Zor had been deported, and the great part of them is still held there." The Interior Ministry ordered "their . . . deportation as a whole, preferably with speed and effort, within a short period to the places determined."[171]

The next step in organizing a second wave of annihilation was to declare the region off-limits. Foreigners and non-Muslim merchants were forbidden to wander through the region for any purpose. A security directive requested that "as the coming and going in the places where the Armenians are being deported and settled of some foreigners, and, for instance, merchants possessing American nationality, or even the wandering of some Ottoman non-Muslim merchants in that area for the goal of commerce is not seen as suitable, those who do not have the confidence of the government not be permitted to travel and voyage in such sectors."[172] Likewise, the distribution of aid to the deportees was absolutely prohibited. Humanitarian workers and the government

[169] DE/PA-AA/R 14090, Report from German consul of Aleppo, Rössler, to Chancellor Bethmann-Hollweg, dated 9 February 1916.

[170] Kévorkian, "L'extermination des déportés arméniens," 24, 32–33.

[171] BOA/DH.ŞFR, no. 62/199, Coded telegram from Interior Ministry's General Security Directorate to the Provincial District of Zor, dated 1 April 1916.

[172] BOA/DH.ŞFR, no. 61/32, Coded telegram from Interior Ministry's General Security Directorate to the Provinces of Aleppo, Adana, Mosul, and Diyarbekır, and to the Provincial Districts of Urfa and (Der) Zor, dated 13 February 1916.

officials who closed their eyes to these distributions were to be "severely punished."[173]

The December 1915 map and census figures for Der Zor proving insufficient, an official correspondence began in March 1916 to organize a new census. Again, it should be underscored that while Istanbul was deciding on a new regional population count, officials unceasingly continued to solicit information about the changing locations of the Armenians and the new population balances that resulted. For example, a general communiqué of 11 May 1916 requested "the rapid communication of the information demanded . . . about the number of the people and the place of deportation and settlements."[174] On 31 May 1916, the Der Zor provincial district government was asked to "quickly communicate the number of Armenians having come from other places that are being left inside the provincial district, and those on the road to be deported to other places."[175]

"[T]he registration of the population of Armenians has begun," reported the Der Zor provincial district government in early April 1916. Further information about this regional population census can also be found in Armenian sources. Krikor Ankout, who was in Rakka in May 1916, wrote in his memoirs, "Under the administration of Fahri [county head of Rakka], the census of the deportations began, and this continued under his successor."[176] Minas Tilbéian said that during these months a census took place in the Ayran and Intili camps: "During the course of May 1916, the commander of the gendarmerie, the county head of Osmaniye, and his [the latter's] assistant in Baghche came to Ayran and Intili in the name of the Province of Adana in order to count the Armenians: they found their numbers to be large."[177]

The census required significant funding at the regional level. The Der Zor provincial district requested an "order for payment of sixteen thousand five hundred kurush, the expenditure of which is necessary for the two months'

[173] Communication from interior minister Talat to the Command of the Ottoman Army, dated 25 March 1916, cited in Genelkurmay Başkanlığı, *Arşiv Belgeleriyle Ermeni Faaliyetleri*, vol. 2, 5.

[174] BOA/DH.ŞFR, no. 63/289, Coded telegram from the Office of Statistics and officials of the Interior Ministry's General Directorate of Tribal and Immigrant Settlement to the Provinces of Konya, Adana, Aleppo, Damascus, and Mosul, and to the Provincial District of Zor, dated 11 May 1916.

[175] BOA/DH.ŞFR, 64/165, Coded telegram from the Interior Ministry's General Security Directorate to the Provincial District of Zor, dated 31 May 1916.

[176] Kévorkian, "L'extermination des déportés arméniens," 165.

[177] Ibid., 67

salary of the registration [census] committee and travel allowances for setting out to the places subject [to the provincial district], and miscellaneous
expenditures."[178] The Interior Ministry's Population Administration Directorate, observing that "the dispatch of an order for payment of sixteen
thousand five hundred kurush has been repeated[ly] communicated by the
local provincial district government for the registration [census] of the Armenians who are arriving in [Der] Zor provincial district and there are no
appropriations alloted for the registration of population in the current year's
budget," asked that the payment be made from discretionary funds.[179] The
payment was indeed made at the end of June from secret funds, and the Der
Zor provincial district government was informed of this.[180]

The government appealed to Parliament to appropriate the necessary
funds. On 8 March 1916, a bill was proposed "concerning adding 680,000
kurush for the registration of population . . . of the provinces of Aleppo and
Damascus, and the provincial district of Urfa to the 1916 Interior Ministry
budget." However, the assembly rejected the proposal.[181] For this reason,
the payment was made from secret appropriations.

To save themselves from deportation and death, many Armenians
managed to bribe the census takers in Der Zor to register them under the
names of deceased individuals. Governor Zeki, who had been appointed
in order to organize massacres in the district, wanted "these registrations
which had no official value whatsoever to be considered as if they never
occured," and wrote that "if God wills, within the span of one or two
months, after the conclusion of the desired settlement, what it required
would be carried out and presented in accordance with the situation that
is produced." In other words, Zeki wanted the population figures that were
going to be reported after the massacres to be taken as the true state of
affairs.[182] Finally, the Armenians who remained in the interior districts

[178] BOA/DH.SN.THR, no. 69/46, Communication written to the Interior Ministry's General Security Directorate, marked as "secret," dated 6 April 1916.
[179] BOA/DH.SN.THR, no. 69/46, Note from the Secretariat of the Registration of Population of
the Interior Ministry, dated 20 June 1916.
[180] BOA/DH.ŞFR, no. 65/105, Coded telegram from Interior Ministry's Cipher Office to the Provincial District of (Der) Zor, dated 28 June 1916.
[181] MMZC, Period 3, Assembly Year 2, vol. 2, 24 February 1331 (8 March 1916), Session 41, 392,
397.
[182] BOA/DH.SN.THR, no. 69/46, Telegram of Der Zor provincial district governor, Salih Zeki, to
the Interior Ministry, dated 20 July 1916.

were expelled to Der Zor. The deportation orders were cabled on 10 July 1916 to Konya and on 18 July 1916 to Diyarbekır.[183]

No further obstacle was left. Talat Pasha's telegram of 19 July 1916 was like a signal to begin the massacres: "Forbidding harmful Armenian people from congregating along military routes and the immediate deportation of the latter to the interior are appropriate." Talat also informed the Office of the (Army) High Command of the situation.[184] On 29 July 1916, he wrote openly that the Army Command had informed the Sixth Army of the "steps that are required for the distribution and settlement to suitable places of the Armenians whose congregation in the river basin of the Euphrates and at the military route is going to be dangerous for military transport."[185]

The Armenians no longer had anywhere to go. The massacres would last throughout the summer and fall. Anticipating that extra manpower would be needed for the killing operation, Zeki asked Istanbul to send additional gendarmes from the Fourth Army to Der Zor.[186] Two weeks later, he requested three hundred more soldiers from the Sixth Army.[187]

From this point on, in the government's view, the Armenians amounted to no more than a set of figures. The mathematical reduction of their numbers by systematic massacre was monitored through a constant stream of official requests for the latest population statistics. In a special cable sent in August 1916 to the district governor's office in Der Zor, Talat requested an update of the situation there:

(1) How many Armenians are there presently within the provincial district of [Der] Zor? (2) In which sectors [of the district] are these persons currently located, and what is their ratio [to the total population]? (3) How many Armenians have arrived [in the district] since the beginning of the deportations and where have they been

[183] Coded telegrams from Interior Ministry's General Security Directorate to the Province of Konya, dated 10 July 1916 (BOA/DH.ŞFR, no. 65/176) and to the Province of Diyarbekır, dated 18 July 1916 (BOA/DH.ŞFR, no. 66/21).

[184] BOA/DH.ŞFR, no. 66/19, Coded telegram from interior minister Talat to the Provincial District of Zor, dated 19 July 1916.

[185] BOA/DH.ŞFR, no. 66/94, Coded telegram from interior minister Talat to the Provincial District of Zor, dated 29 July 1916.

[186] BOA/DH.ŞFR, no. 66/118, Coded telegram from interior minister Talat to the Fourth Army Command, dated 30 July 1916.

[187] BOA/DH.ŞFR, no. 67/7, Coded telegram from interior minister Talat to the Sixth Army Command, dated 14 August 1916.

sent? (4) How many have come from Aleppo and other districts in this time? What is the overall Armenian population, including these [Armenians]?[188]

In an "urgent" telegram of 5 December 1916, he asked for "telegraphic information [about the situation] and the dispatch by the first post, without making further communication necessary, of the requested tabulated list . . . about the number of Armenians in the provincial district/province."[189]

Did military considerations play a role in the annihilation of the Armenians who were arriving at their places of exile? Information exists in this regard in German consular reports. In December and January, according to Rössler, Armenians in the region stretching from Adana to Aleppo "had to be removed" toward Ras ul Ayn and Der Zor "for military reasons, to make the lines of communication [the railway] free and prevent the transmission of communicable diseases to the army."[190]

Ottoman documents likewise state that military considerations were a factor in certain relocations of the Armenians in Syria. In a telegram of 18 June 1915 to the government of the province of Aleppo, Talat Pasha said that as "the dispatch of the foreign Armenians, whose transportation and expulsion to another direction was decided by the army, to the provinces of Damscus and Mosul was found dangerous because of the present conditions of the war, their deportation to [Der] Zor is necessary."[191] In his telegrams to Der Zor in July and August 1916, Talat repeated the rationale that the accumulation of Armenians along military routes was undesirable and could obstruct military transport. It is important to note that one year earlier, he had ordered Armenians deported to Der Zor for military reasons; one year later, he ordered Armenians deported *away from* Der Zor, again for military reasons.

[188] BOA/DH.ŞFR. no. 66/170, Coded telegram from interior minister Talat to the Provincial District of (Der) Zor, dated 8 August 1916.

[189] BOA/DH.ŞFR, no. 70/190, Coded telegram from interior minister Talat to the Provinces of Diyarbekır, Damascus, and Mamuretülaziz, and to the Provincial District of (Der) Zor, dated 5 December 1916.

[190] DE/PA-AA/R 14090, Report from Aleppo consul, Rössler, to Chancellor Bethmann-Hollweg, dated 9 February 1916.

[191] BOA/DH.ŞFR, no. 65/32-1, Coded telegram from the Interior Ministry's IAMM to the Province of Aleppo, dated 18 June 1916.

As additional gendarmes were being requested from the Fourth and Sixth Army Commands, Talat invoked military necessity once more: "for the protection of public order and the securing of discipline, in consequence of the Armenians deported to Zor today being present in a concentrated and compact state."[192] Obviously, Talat was concealing his orders to the head of Der Zor provincial district to "drive out the Armenians from Der Zor," and the fact that Der Zor was being emptied, from the army commanders. At the same time, he was using the concentration of Armenians in Der Zor to justify his request for gendarmes. This apparent contradiction can only be explained as Talat's use of military necessity as a rationale for his operation. Nevertheless, the notion of "military necessity" needs further research. A dwindling group of miserable deportees, sick, hungry, and exhausted, was in no position to challenge the Ottoman Army. Why were they seen as a threat? And why were such orders not issued from within the military command hierarchy?

Survivor memoirs, as well as Ottoman documents, show that the issue of annihilation in Der Zor provoked serious disagreement between the army and civil authorities.[193] The Ottoman Sixth Army, which was preparing to confront the English forces in Mesopotamia (Iraq), needed manpower for the construction of roads as well as other work. The military authorities in Der Zor tried to set up a labor battalion (*amele taburu*) attached to the Sixth Army and separated about five hundred Armenians who were soldiers, laborers, and artisans for the army's needs. To counter this attempt, Governor Zeki had some of the Armenians arrested, deported, and even murdered.[194] The traces of this clash remain in the documents of the Interior Ministry.

[192] Coded telegrams from interior minister Talat to the Fourth Army Command, dated 30 July 1916 (BOA/DH.ŞFR, no. 66/118) and to the Sixth Army Command, dated 14 August 1916 (BOA/DH.ŞFR, no. 67/7).

[193] Actually, disagreement and discord between military and civil authorities in the region was a serious problem throughout the deportation process. For example, in a report on the region written to the Ministry of the Interior by the director of the provincial district Mount Lebanon, Ali Münif, he tells the state that "in this region [today's Syria] there is often mutually distinct positions and opposition between the ministry and the army command on the subject of the deportation and banishment of Armenians" and reports that this leads to hesitation among state personnel. BOA/DH.ŞFR, no. 488/80, Coded telegram from Aleppo Province to the Interior Ministry, dated 10 September 1915.

[194] Details on the incident are found in the memoirs of Aram Zirekyan and Aram Andonian (Kévorkian, "L'extermination des déportés arméniens," 175–82).

Zeki was made uncomfortable by the initiative of the Sixth Army and on 26 July 1916 complained to Istanbul. After meeting with the military authorities, Talat responded as follows: "It is communicated in response from the Office of the High Command that the Sixth Army Command was ordered that the station commander [of Der Zor] does not have the authority to choose of his own accord artisans from among the Armenians, and of the necessity of assuring the unity of action of the civil administration and the military recruitment [office]."[195] Although a later directive to Zeki stressed the importance of coordinating with the Sixth Army on this issue,[196] the obstacle of the local military authority in Der Zor, which was working to prevent the massacres because of its own needs, appears to have been overcome. The ultimate resolution of this conflict is not important here. What is important is that an argument in the sense that the massacres were carried out for military reasons is not very illuminating.

Perhaps the important question is not the military situation in the east and west of Syria but rather Anatolia. The passing of Erzurum into Russian hands in February 1916 may have played a greater role than military needs in Syria. Whether this Russian advance and occupation retriggered the Unionists' fear of the February 1914 Armenian Reform Agreement remains unclear. Perhaps also, the "surplus" Armenian population in Syria was considered a security risk for this reason, in addition to the Unionists' demographic anxieties. If the war were lost, the returning Armenians could form the basis of an Armenian administration in the region.

THE 10 PERCENT RULE IN THE REPORTS OF GERMAN AND AMERICAN CONSULATES

The resettlement of Armenians in accordance with the 10 percent criterion, and the significance of this figure in their annihilation, are also discussed in German and American documents. American consul Leslie Davis reported from Harput on 30 December 1915, "Of nearly a hundred thousand Armenians who were in this Vilayet a year ago, there are

[195] BOA/DH.ŞFR, no. 66/159, Coded telegram from the Interior Ministry's General Security Directorate to the Provincial District of Zor, dated 6 August 1916.
[196] BOA/DH.ŞFR, no. 67/220, Coded special telegram from interior minister Talat to the Provincial District of Zor, dated 10 September 1916.

probably not more than four thousand left. It has been reported recently that not more than five per cent of the Armenians were to be left. It is doubtful if that many remain now."[197]

German consul Rössler in Aleppo reported likewise on 27 April 1916. "[A]ccording to what I have learned from a Turkish officer who arrived from Der Zor on 20 April 1916, the district governor of the Der Zor Provincial District received an order to leave [only enough] Armenians so that they would make up [no more than] 10 percent of the [total] local population while the rest should be sent further on to Mosul," Rössler recorded. "The population of Der Zor can be estimated at about 20,000 souls. It is said that at least 15,000 of these are Armenians who were sent there, meaning that at least 13,000 of them will have to be deported [to somewhere else]."[198]

On 29 July 1916 Rössler informed the German Embassy that on the seventeenth of the month the Armenians in the Der Zor district had been ordered from the region: "Yet this near idyll through the misery of the Armenians quickly changed into a spot in hell after it was ordered that only 10 percent of the residents are allowed to be Armenians, and above all, the humane governor Suad Bey was transferred to Baghdad and had been replaced by the brutal Circassian Zeki Bey." The consul added that "it would be necessary to annihilate those who were left over." In line with this goal, Der Zor district governor Suad was removed from his post and transferred to Baghdad; in his place the district "received a merciless successor."[199]

American consul J. B. Jackson summarized an entire period when he wrote, "the most horrible butcheries imaginable occurred, the facts of which were related to me by a few survivors who miraculously escaped and who were given shelter by friendly Arabs and later returned to Aleppo after suffering great hardships."[200] An arrest warrant for Governor Zeki,

---

[197] NA/RG 59, 867.4016/269, Report by Harput consul, Leslie Davis, to Ambassador Henry Morgenthau in Constantinople, dated 30 December 1915, in *United States Official Records*, ed. Sarafian, 473.

[198] DE/PA-AA/R 14091, Report from Aleppo consul, Rössler, to German chancellor Bethmann-Hollweg, dated 27 April 1916.

[199] DE/PA-AA/R 14093, Report from Aleppo consul, Rössler, to German chancellor Bethmann-Hollweg, dated 29 July 1916.

[200] NA/RG 59, 867.4016/373, Report from American consul, J. B. Jackson, formerly at Aleppo, Syria, now in Washington, dated 4 March 1918.

the chief architect of the crimes of Der Zor, was issued in 1918,[201] and on 28 April 1920, he was sentenced to death in absentia.[202] Salih Zeki later became one of the founders of Turkey's Communist Party, and as the representative of this party, he came to Erzurum to negotiate an alliance with the Kemalist Nationalists.[203]

[201] BOA/DH.ŞFR, no. 94/6, Coded telegram from the General Directorate of the Interior Ministry's Investigation Committee to the Provincial District of Mardin, dated 1 December 1918.

[202] Dadrian and Akçam, *"Tehcir ve Taktil,"* 170 and 715–17.

[203] Mete Tunçay and Erden Akbulut, *Türkiye Halk İştirakiyun Fırkası (1920–1923)* (Istanbul: Sosyal Tarih Yayınları, 2007), 391n333.

NINE ASSIMILATION: THE CONVERSION AND FORCED MARRIAGE OF CHRISTIAN CHILDREN

In his autobiography, *Totally Unofficial Man*, Raphael Lemkin, who coined the term "genocide," recalled his struggle to persuade the United Nations to recognize "cultural genocide." This concept, wrote Lemkin, "meant the destruction of the cultural pattern of a group, such as the language, the traditions, the monuments, archives, libraries, churches. In brief: the shrines of the soul of a nation."[1]

The original third article of what would become the UN Convention on the Prevention and Punishment of the Crime of Genocide (1948) defined cultural genocide as any of the following: (a) the forcible transfer of children to another human group; (b) the forced and systematic exile of individuals representing the culture of a group; (c) the prohibition of the use of the national language even in private intercourse; (d) the systematic destruction of books printed in the national language or of religious works or prohibition of new publications; or (e) the systematic destruction of historical or religious monuments or their diversion to alien uses, destruction or dispersion of documents and objects of historical, artistic, or religious value and of objects used in religious worship.[2] In the discussions, however, Article 3 was deleted from the definition of genocide.[3] "I defended it successfully through two drafts," wrote Lemkin, but "there was not enough support for this idea in the Committee.... So with a heavy

[1] John Docker, "Are Settler-Colonies Inherently Genocidal? Rereading Lemkin," in *Empire, Colony Genocide: Conquest, Occupation and Subaltern Resistance in World History*, ed. Dirk Moses (New York and Oxford: Berghahn Books, 2008), 82.

[2] The first draft of the convention, including Article 3, was prepared by the UN secretariat in May 1947. See http://www.preventgenocide.org/law/convention/drafts/.

[3] For more detailed information about the debates on the concept of cultural genocide, see Matthew Lippman, "The 1948 Convention on the Prevention and Punishment of the Crime of Genocide: Forty-Five Years Later, " in *Temple International and Comparative Law Journal* 8, no. 1 (1948); or "The Drafting of the 1948 Convention on the Prevention and Punishment of the Crime of Genocide," *Boston University of International Law Journal* 3, no. 1 (1985): 1–66.

heart I decided not to press for it."[4] Although an element of cultural geno-cide—the crime of "forcibly transferring children of the group to another group"—was incorporated into the final text of the 1948 Convention, Lemkin had to abandon an idea that "was very dear to me."

In addition to cultural genocide, Lemkin's original concept differed from the UN definition in another, less recognized respect. Whereas the 1948 Convention gave legal form to a concept of genocide as a unitary event, Lemkin also understood it as a series of connected acts, a process that unfolded over time. "Generally speaking," Lemkin wrote in *Axis Rule in Occupied Europe,* the work that introduced the term, "genocide does not necessarily mean the immediate destruction of a nation."[5] Lemkin's al-ternative vision of a prolonged process was narrowed to the immediate destruction of a "national, ethnical, racial or religious group."

The UN Convention, while allowing some leeway for interpretation, also tends to characterize genocide primarily as an act of physical destruc-tion. For the inventor of the word, however, physical destruction was only one aspect of the genocidal process. As a social reality, Lemkin understood, genocide constructs as much as it destroys. "Genocide has two phases," he wrote, "one, destruction of the national pattern of the oppressed group; the other, the imposition of the national pattern of the oppressor."[6]

While the second stage of genocide can take many different forms, in the end the targeted group is compelled to adopt the lifestyle, culture, and institutions of the dominant group. Without doubt, assimilation is among the most effective ways to achieve this result. Scholarly debates on geno-cide have neglected the constructive phase of genocide for far too long.

There are two further reasons why the concept of assimilation was detached from the study of genocide. First, Armenian Genocide studies have suffered from the general weaknesses of the emerging field. Occu-pying the central place in these debates as a sine qua non, the Holocaust became the yardstick against which an event might or might not measure up as a genocide. Consequently, researchers spent enormous amounts of

---

[4] John Docker, "Are Settler-Colonies Inherently Genocidal? Rereading Lemkin," in *Empire, Colony Genocide: Conquest, Occupation and Subaltern Resistance in World History,* ed. Dirk Moses (New York and Oxford: Berghahn Books, 2008), 82.

[5] See Raphael Lemkin, *Axis Rule in Occupied Europe* (New York: Carnegie Endowment for Inter-national Peace, 1944), 79.

[6] Ibid.

energy trying to prove that other incidents of mass violence were in some way comparable to the Holocaust.[7] Exacerbating this general problem was the Turkish Republic's long-standing denial of the Armenian Genocide. Whether or not to apply the 1948 definition, or other definitions, to the physical extermination of the Armenians became the touchstone for all debate. As with other instances of mass violence, the fear that the events of 1915, collectively, would not be considered genocide if they did not resemble the Holocaust precluded serious analysis along the lines of dynamic social processes. Meanwhile, a concerted effort was made to ignore all the differences—such as forced assimilation—that might arise between any two discrete episodes of mass violence.

Second, our understanding of assimilation as a process of the Armenian Genocide has been hampered by the character of available sources, mainly German and American consular reports, as well as missionary and survivor accounts. These narratives tended to generalize, and to telescope, long periods of time: while vividly conveying the terror and chaos on the ground, they failed to illuminate the coolly systematic policy framework behind the scenes. Without direct knowledge of government decision making, the consuls, missionaries, and survivors could not capture, with chronological precision, evidence of the administrative changes then in progress. For these observers, as well as later readers, lack of access to Ottoman records partially obscured what was taking place.

The conceptual, rhetorical, and observational limitations outlined above have in turn clouded our understanding of religious conversion and forced assimilation during the events of 1915. Conversion has been seen as a practice that varied from one region to another at the discretion of local administrators and that was primarily motivated by Muslim fanaticism. It has also been assumed that Armenians were unable to save themselves through religious conversion, because converts were also annihilated. "Certainly, the possibility of conversion was, since the beginning of the genocidal policy, a sort of myth maintained by the deportees to allow them to believe that they still had a gate of exit," writes scholar Raymond Kévorkian, adding, "the forced conversion of Armenians never was at

---

[7] The relationship between the Holocaust and other genocides is a much-debated topic. For an overview of the literature, see Dirk Moses, "The Holocaust and Genocide," in *The Historiography of the Holocaust*, ed. Dan Stone (New York: Palgrave Macmillan, 2004), 533–55.

any moment a serious option envisioned by the Unionist Committee."[8] As a result, scholarly analysis has largely ignored a topic that merits closer study. In light of new documentary evidence from the Ottoman archives, I will argue below that religious conversion and the assimilation of Armenian children into Muslim households were two of the most significant structural components of the Armenian Genocide.

Armenians were assimilated in several ways: religious conversion, a temporary policy of dispersed settlement, the reassignment of children from Christianity to Islam, and the forced marriage or concubinage of young Christian women and adolescent girls with Muslim men. As is shown below, throughout the entire process of deportation and destruction, the concepts of *temsil* and *temessül* in Ottoman, which mean "assimilation," openly referred to the settlement of Armenian survivors in Syria, and, when suitable, were also used in connection with Armenian boys and girls. *Bakım ve terbiye*, which means "care and upbringing," was anoher phrase used especially for the assimilation of children. What is remarkable is the manifestation of clear distinctions in the course of the assimilation policy and the changes the latter underwent. It is possible to follow these distinctions and changes through Ottoman documents. [9]

If assimilation was integral to the Armenian deportations and annihilation, what was the relationship between assimilation and physical destruction? In light of the 5 to 10 percent principle discussed in chapter 8, and other documents to be presented below, I argue that the Ittihadists consistently took *governability* as their central principle. Wherever Armenians could be dissolved within the Muslim majority, religious conversion was allowed. But wherever assimilation constituted a danger, the Ittihadists abandoned the policy and turned instead to physical annihilation. Even at that

[8] Kévorkian, "L'extermination des déportés arméniens ottomans," 55. Ara Sarafian's evaluations on this topic form an exception. Without having seen the relevant Ottoman documents, he correctly determined that both religious conversions and the dispersion of children within Muslim families were part of a systematic governmental policy, and consequently must be considered a structural element of genocide (Ara Sarafian, "The Absorption of Armenian Women and Children into Muslim Households as a Structural Component of the Armenian Genocide," in *In God's Name: Genocide and Religion in the Twentieth Century*, ed. Omer Bartov and Phyllis Mack [New York: Berghahn Books, 2001], 209–21).

[9] The information that I present below should be read in a distinctly cautious manner. While I will be quoting from commands of the central government and discussing the relevant government policies, the extent and manner in which these orders were carried out in the provinces is the topic of a separate work.

stage, however, Armenians were again allowed to assimilate (for example, through conversion), as long as they were deemed "governable."

The balance between assimilation and physical annihilation was of key importance throughout a deportation, but the principle of governability was what weighted the scales. From this point of view, population statistics again prove to be significant, and it is possible to say that the constant enumeration of Armenians significantly influenced Unionist policy on religious conversion. Regardless of the method they chose, the Unionists intended to maintain the Armenian remnants at a manageable level. Survivors were to be prevented from acting collectively or preserving their nationality and culture.

RELIGIOUS CONVERSION DURING DEPORTATION

At the commencement of the deportations, religious conversion was permitted, and Armenian converts were dispersed to various towns and villages in their home province. But on 1 July 1915, religious conversion was prohibited, and it was only allowed again four months later, although with certain restrictions. In Syria, at the convoys' destination, a similar process took place. Settlement and the assimilation policy connected to it were pursued at first, but not with the aim of religious conversion. In Syria, too, religious conversion was permitted at the end of 1915. The next spring, however, the Syrian region saw a distinct shift in policy.The so-called Cemal Pasha's Armenians, survivors who had earlier been settled in the areas of Hama, Homs, and Damascus, were made to choose between conversion and the certain death of deportation to Der Zor. Forcible Islamization operated in parallel with annihilation.[10]

In this initial stage, mass conversion to Islam was not only allowed but even encouraged. The earliest known document on conversion is a "confidential" cipher telegram of 22 June 1915 to the seven provinces (Erzurum, Van, Mamuretülaziz, Diyarbekır, Sivas, Bitlis, and Trebizond), which had

[10] I would like to caution that this summary should be read with undivided attention. First, the picture has as its basis official Ottoman documents—it would be valuable to look more closely at how the procedures were carried out in the provinces; second, there's a dearth of information concerning the fate of Armenians who had chosen conversion to Islam prior to July 1. Although consular reports indicate that these people remained alive, further research on this topic is still necessary, particularly in Armenian survivor accounts.

been promised reforms in the February 1914 agreement with the Russians. Local officials were instructed that "the Armenians who have been deported from your province to the south [and] who converted to Islam individually or collectively be detained, and those who are found assembled together be dispersed in the province." The final directives to "inform those who will be executing [the orders] of our communication; take the copy of this cable from the telegraph office and destroy it" are very interesting.[11] This is one of only three known Ottoman archival documents that command the reader to destroy the telegram—and all three documents are telegrams on the topic of assimilation.

German and American documents show that religious conversions began prior to this order and were carried out intensively. As early as 2 June 1915, German consul Scheubner-Richter reported from Erzurum that "the Armenians who are converting are not being removed from their places."[12] It is also understood from American consul William Peter's report of 10 June 1915 that religious conversions were well under way: "until now about 150 families have been converted to Islamism and the rest have been sent to the Interior. " The consul added, "a great part of the persons who have gone are now willing to follow the example of the 150 families converted." On 25 June 1915, the German consul at Samsun reported that "the government sent fanatical, strictly religious Muslim men and women into all Armenian homes to spread propaganda for conversion to Islam, of course with the threat of serious consequences for those who remain true to their beliefs. As far as I know, many families have already converted up to the present, and the number is increasing daily." According to the consul, "[a]ll the Armenian villages in and around Samsun had been Islamicized."[13]

[11] BOA/DH.ŞFR, no. 54/100, Cipher telegram from interior minister Talat to Cevded Bey (governor of the Province of Van), to Cemal Azmi Bey (governor of the Province of Trebizond), Tahsin Bey (governor of the Province of Erzurum), Mustafa Bey (governor of the Province of Bitlis), Sâbit Bey (governor of the Province of Mamuretülaziz), Reşid Bey (governor of the Province of Diyarbekır), and Muammer Bey (governor of the Province of Sivas), dated 22 June 1915.

[12] DE/PA-AA/Bo.Kons., vol. 168, Report by Erzurum consul, Scheubner-Richter, dated 2 June 1915.

[13] DE/PA-AA/R 14086, Report of Samsun consul, Kuckhoff, to Ambassador Wangenheim, dated 4 July 1915 (in the report Kuckhoff included the telegram dated 25 June), appended to the report by Ambassador Wangenheim, dated 16 July 1915.

An Armenian woman who was deported from Samsun stated in her memoirs that after the announcement of the deportation, a *hoca* (meaning in this case an imam or Muslim religious leader, often affiliated with a mosque) visited their house two or three times a week to press them to convert to Islam.[14] In Merzifon (a city and district in Sivas Province), "it was publicly announced that people could save themselves if they would become Mohammedans. Large numbers, it is said 1,000 families, put in petitions to the Government."[15] American missionary Dr. J. K. Marden, who was then in the same city, wrote, "In the town of Marsovan, from 13,000 Armenians, over 11,500 were deported and about 1,500 accepted Mohammedanism as an alternative to sure death."[16] An American teacher at the College of Marsovan stated, "During this reign of terror, notice was given that anyone who accepted Islam would be allowed to remain safely at home. The offices of the lawyers who recorded applications were crowded with people petitioning to become Mohammedans. Many did it for the sake of their women and children, feeling that it would be a matter of only a few weeks before relief would come."[17]

The German consul mentioned "mass religious conversions" in his report from Trebizond on 26 June.[18] In the first week of July, Ambassador von Wangenheim wrote to his superiors that "Armenians in Trebizond have converted to Islam in droves in order to avoid deportation and save their lives and property."[19] For his part, the American ambassador to the Porte, Henry Morgenthau, sent a "top secret" cable to the State Department on 10 July in which he relayed reports of mass deportations and

[14] Pailadzo Captanian, *1915 Der Völkermord an den Armenien: Eine Zeugin berichtet* (Leipzig: Gustav Kiepenheuer 1993), 20.

[15] Statement by Miss Gage, a foreign (American) traveler in Turkey, communicated by the American Committee for Armenian and Syrian Relief, in Bryce and Toynbee, *The Treatment of Armenians*, 371.

[16] NA/RG 59, 867.4016/292, Report from Maurice Francis Egan, American Embassy, Copenhagen, to secretary of state, dated 3 July 1916, including statement from Dr. J. K. Marden (undated), in *United States Official Records*, ed. Sarafian, 525.

[17] NA/RG 59, 867.4016/106, Report from Ambassador Morgenthau to the State Department, dated 26 July 1915, in *United States Official Record*, ed. Sarafian, 143.

[18] DE/PA-AA/R 14086, Report from Ambassador Wangenheim to Chancellor Bethmann-Hollweg, dated 7 July 1915.

[19] DE/PA-AA/R 14086, Report from Ambassador Wangenheim to Chancellor Bethmann-Hollweg, dated 7 July 1915.

murders of Armenians and stated, "Many Armenians are becoming Moslems to avoid persecution."[20]

Religious converts, even if not deported, were not allowed to remain at home. According to the provincial district governor of Samsun, the converts were to be dispersed to the neighboring province and districts, and this matter was included in the telegraphic order of 22 June.[21] The Balkan section of the Dashnaktsoutiun Committee quoted some figures in an August 1915 report to Morgenthau: "at Ordou [present-day Ordu] 160 families out of 250 have embraced Islamism; at Kirassunde [present-day Giresun] 200 families out of 400."[22] American missionary Dr. Clark, who was stationed in Sivas, reported that of the 25,000 Armenians in that city, 1,000 chose Islam in the summer of 1915.[23]

Other consuls reported that the Armenian converts were not being deported.[24] On 15 October 1915, appealing for a halt to the massacres of Armenians, prominent German ministers stated that "Many hundreds of Christian families who decided to accept Islam were exempt from deportation."[25] A missionary in Kayseri wrote, "Women who were taken from our compound were deported because they did not become Moslems. . . . Those who accepted Islam were allowed to stay, but were sent out to villages."[26] On 12 December 1915, Mordtmann, the German consul general at Istanbul, relayed reports on conversions in Trebizond, Adana, and Konya.[27]

[20] NA/RG 59, 867.4016/74, Cable from Ambassador Morgenthau to the State Department, dated 10 July 1915, in *United States Official Records*, ed. Sarafian, 52.

[21] William Peter, Samsun, to Henry Morgenthau, dated 10 July 1915, in *United States Official Records*, ed. Sarafian, 62 (LC/HM[Sr.]/Reel 7/619).

[22] NA/RG 59, 867.4016/122, Report of Dashnaktsoutiun (spelled here Daschnaktzoutioun) Committee, Balkan Section, Sofia, "No. 5: The Extermination of the Armenian People," dated 2 August/20 [sic] July 1915, appended to letter of Ambassador Morgenthau to the secretary of state, dated 10 August 1915, in *United States Official Records*, ed. Sarafian, 163.

[23] NA/RG 59, 867.4016/288, Report of Dr. Clark, dated 31 May 1916, appended to Hoffman Philip, Istanbul American Embassy, to secretary of state, 12 June 1916.

[24] For example, it is learned from a report sent on 28 June 1916 by Werht, the secretary of the German Consulate in Sivas, that those who converted in Sivas were allowed to remain in their places of residence (DE/PA-AA/Bo.Kons./Band 172).

[25] DE/PA-AA/Bo.Kons./Band 171, German chancellor Bethmann-Hollweg to the chargé d'affaires of the embassy (Neurath), 15 November 1915.

[26] Report of Stella Loughridge, in *"Turkish Atrocities": Statements of American Missionaries on the Destruction of Christian Communities in Ottoman Turkey, 1915–1917*, comp. James L. Barton (Ann Arbor, MI: Gomidas Institute, 1998), 117.

[27] DE/PA-AA/Bo.Kons./Band 172, Consul General Mordtmann's personal notes, dated 21 December 1915.

Mass conversions to Islam took place, especially in the Black Sea region. In telegrams from Ordu, Samsun, and Fatsa, local officials, religious leaders such as imams or *müftüs*, or groups of Armenians petitioned the government to accept the new converts as Muslims and not deport them. The Armenian converts in Ordu declared themselves not at all "in any relations in any fashion with the Armenians who all along were filthy [*mülevves*] and traitors to the homeland Armenians," adding that, "as we were innocent, if by dispersing three to five families each to three hundred Muslim villages the possibility of our staying in our homeland would not be suitable, we request our deportation to a suitable and nearby place in the interior, while leaving our families and children behind, with [the dispersion] of only the family leaders to be deemed sufficient."[28]

A telegram sent from the provincial district government of Canik on 9 July 1915 reveals that the deportations of Armenians from the area were completed and that Armenian converts were settled in places in the region in a scattered fashion:

It is submitted that the final caravan of Armenians being expelled from Samsun departed four days ago with [their] religious leaders and the last caravan of those [being removed] to Alaçam earlier because they were troublemakers also today was deported by way of Kavak Havza; and in this way the expulsion process concluded, and those remaining for the purpose of carrying out the procedures in view of their demonstration of conversion on the condition of immediately being transferred to town and villages were distributed one or two each to Muslim and village neighborhoods, and in their places refugees and emigrants and Muslim people are being settled.[29]

By July 1915, it was clear that too many Armenians were willing to convert in order to escape death, and the policy of conversion was therefore abandoned. "It is understood that some of the Armenians being expelled pledged to convert in mass or individually, and in this fashion worked to

[28] BOA/DH.EUM, 2. Şube, no. 8/61-a/2, Telegram from Ölmezoğlu Ali Kemal and Muhtar Bünyadoğlu Ahmed Niyazi in Ordu to the Interior Ministry, dated 30 June 1915. For examples of other telegrams, see BOA/DH.EUM, 2. Şube, no. 8/61-a/1, a/3, and 8/70/1.

[29] BOA/DH.EUM, 2. Şube, no. 10/78/1, Cipher telegram of Canik provincial district governor Necmi Bey, dated 9 July 1915.

secure the way for them to remain in their native lands," observed Talat in a cable to provincial administrators. Noting that the Armenians chose this way because "they saw themselves . . . in danger," the interior minister directed that "the applications of this sort of people categorically should not be given a favorable importance." He added that "Deportation still to the designated neighborhoods, even if they convert," of such people must continue.[30] As reported by Trebizond German consul Bergfeld on 9 July, the governor-general of Trebizond told Armenians desirous of conversion that "an Armenian converted to Islam would then be deported as a Mohammedan Armenian."[31]

The general circular prohibiting religious conversion was reinforced by separate orders in response to questions from the provinces. Kayseri was informed on 13 July 1915 that "the conversion [to Islam] of Armenians shall not delay their deportation, since their conversions are only undergone for the purpose of securing personal advantage."[32] In many areas, it appears that conversions to Islam nevertheless continued, with the encouragement of local officials. American missionaries reported that despite the prohibition, some wealthy people were willing to look the other way.[33]

For this reason, a new order marked "secret, to be taken care of personally," was sent immediately to all regions. No permission whatsoever was to be given for religious conversion, and the converts were to be immediately deported. Pointing out that "some of the Armenians being expelled were left in their places on the occasion of their conversion . . . and . . . it is understood that some officials in the civil service assisted them," the directive continued,

> as was informed in a cipher telegram dated 1 July 1915, in consideration of the basis of these types of conversion which take place

[30] BOA/DH.ŞFR, no. 54/254, Coded telegram from the Interior Ministry's General Security Directorate to the Provinces and Provincial Districts of Erzurum, Adana, Bitlis, Aleppo, Diyarbekır, Trebizond, Mamuretülaziz, Mosul, Van, Urfa, Kütahya, Marash, İçel, and Eskişehir, dated 1 July 1915.

[31] NA/RG 59, 867.4016/118, Translation of the report of German consul, Heinrich Bergfeld, in Trebizond, dated 9 July 1915, in *United States Official Records*, ed. Sarafian, 154.

[32] BOA/DH.ŞFR, no. 54/427, Coded telegram from interior minister Talat to the Provincial District of Kayseri, dated 13 July 1915.

[33] Myrtle O. Shane's report in *"Turkish Atrocities,"* Barton, 9.

only compelled by [self-]interest, they have no official value, and so making an exception in treatment for the converts is absolutely not permissible. Consequently, with the absolute preservation of the decrees of the previous communication, the need to not give any favorable importance to such insincere and temporary conversions is announced through a circular.[34]

Even in spite of this repeated general order, religious conversions must have continued in various areas, much to the irritation of the central government. Testy telegrams flew out from Istanbul all summer long, querulously reminding the provinces that the message "conversion not being possible to accept" had been "communicated numerous times."[35] In a cable to the provincial governor of Ankara, sent 3 August 1915 with the note "to be taken care of personally," Talat Pasha reiterated that "since these potential conversions have only taken place for the sake of securing personal advantage, they are not officially recognized," adding that "no exceptional treatment whatsoever is to be afforded to those converts who have attempted, in this manner, to remain in place [and avoid deportation] and . . . no opportunity shall be given for malfeasance in this regard."[36] In a stream of directives "concerning not paying attention to such conversions," the regions were ordered to "conform to the previous communications."[37]

In addition to the bribes and other inducements taken from those with wealth, provincial officials may have been moved by the grievous state of the Armenian deportees. "Save us! We will become Muslims!" cried the

[34] BOA/DH.ŞFR, no. 54-A/49, Coded telegram from the Interior Ministry's General Directorate of Security to the Provinces of Erzurum, Adana, Bitlis, Aleppo, Diyarbekır, Sivas, Trebizond, Mamuretülaziz, Mosul, and Van, and to the Provincial Districts of Urfa, Canik, Zor, Niğde, Kütahya, Marash, İçil, Eskişehir, dated 20 July 1915.

[35] BOA/DH.ŞFR, no. 55-A/85, Coded telegram from the Interior Ministry's General Directorate of Security to the Province of Sivas, dated 5 September 1915.

[36] BOA/DH.ŞFR, no. 54-A/232, Coded telegram from interior minister Talat to the Province of Ankara, dated 5 August 1915.

[37] BOA/DH.ŞFR, no. 56/88, Coded telegram from the Interior Ministry's General Directorate of Security to the Provincial District Eskişehir, dated 22 September 1915. Two more distinct examples connected to this topic: BOA/DH.ŞFR, no. 54-A/277, Coded telegram from interior minister Talat to the Province of Kastamonu, dated 5 August 1915; BOA/DH.ŞFR, no. 55/93, Coded telegram from the Interior Ministry's General Directorate of Security to the Province of Konya, dated 18 August 1915.

women of a convoy an hour away from Erzincan. "We will become Germans! We will become anything you want, just save us! They are taking us to the Kemah Pass to cut our throats!"[38]

Despite this clear, empire-wide policy, local officials continued to appeal to the capital, requesting special permission in regard to converts. In each case, the decision to either grant or deny such permission was given by Talat Pasha personally. In an 18 August 1915 cable to the provincial district of Niğde, Talat stated that "those Armenian girls who have converted to Islam may be married off to Muslims on the condition that absolutely no abuse [of the conversion policy] is allowed."[39] In a cable to Konya the same day, however, the interior minister declared that "the conversion of Armenians is not acceptable."[40] Also denied were petitions from the provincial districts of Kayseri and Urfa, including, in the latter case, a request to "convert a church into a mosque."[41]

Talat also decided where to settle Armenian converts and prospective converts, whether individually or as a group. "There is no need for the reported 156 Protestants to convert to Islam," he cabled to Sivas on 30 August 1915. "Let them remain as they are."[42] Six days later, noting that, "although it has been communicated numerous times already that [their] conversions are unacceptable, Manusacıyan and Dağılyan have converted," Talat demanded an immediate report on "the manner in which [these people] converted and whether or not official action was taken in their regard."[43] He also complained to the provincial governor of Adana that "Bogos Kaltakcıyan, who is understood to be in Tarsus and who has changed his name to Yusuf Bedri on account of having converted to Islam, has been allowed to return to İzmir."[44]

---

[38] DE/PA-AA/Bo.Kons./Band 170, Report by Wedel-Jarlsberg, in which he recounts his observations, dated 28 July 1915.

[39] BOA/DH.ŞFR, no. 55/92, Coded telegram from interior minister Talat to the Provincial District of Niğde, dated 18 August 1915.

[40] BOA/DH.ŞFR, no. 55/93, Coded telegram from interior minister Talat to the Province of Konya, dated 18 August 1915.

[41] BOA/DH.ŞFR, no. 55/94 and 55/100.

[42] BOA/DH.ŞFR, no. 55/336, Coded telegram from interior minister Talat to the Province of Sivas, dated 31 August 1915.

[43] BOA/DH.ŞFR, no. 55-A/83, Coded telegram from interior minister Talat to the Province of Sivas, dated 5 September 1915.

[44] BOA/DH.ŞFR, no. 62/35, Coded telegram from interior minister Talat to the Province of Adana, dated 16 March 1916.

PERMISSION IS AGAIN GIVEN FOR RELIGIOUS CONVERSION

At the end of October 1915, the prohibition on religious conversion was lifted. The provincial district of Bolu was notified on 25 October that "the practice of the procedure of conversion of Armenians in due form is suitable."[45] On the following day, Adana was instructed that "the necessity of carrying out the procedure of conversion [to Islam] in due form at the end of October of Çolak oğlu Kazarosyan of Yozgat with his family, who was mentioned in the telegram . . . which was sent by Kemaleddin Effendi, the kadı [the judge of Islamic law] of Islâhiye, on 14 October 1915 to the Directorate of Public Security [police] be communicated to those requiring it."[46]

All the provinces and provincial districts, including settlement areas in present-day Syria and Iraq, were notified of this change through a "secret" order on 4 November. "The points below concerning the conversion of Armenians must be taken into consideration," the message began. "(1) The conversion [to Islam] of those who remained in the neighborhoods where they resided from of old and were not deported is accepted. (2) The conversions are acceptable of those who, while being deported during the general proceedings, are detained and diverted from the deportations as a result of a special order communicated from the center, and either returned to their original places of residence or remain at a location."[47]

Religious conversion was arranged and accepted according to certain principles that did not include everybody. Deportees who for various reasons were delayed en route did not qualify. Only those whose deportation had been postponed by ministerial order were able to take advantage of this right. In response to questions from the provinces, the Interior

[45] BOA/DH.ŞFR, no. 57/115, Coded telegram from the Interior Ministry's General Directorate of Security to the Provincial District of Bolu, dated 25 October 1915.

[46] BOA/DH.ŞFR, 57/124, Coded telegram from interior minister Talat to the Province of Adana, dated 26 October 1915.

[47] BOA/DH.ŞFR, no. 57/281, Coded telegram from interior minister Talat to the Provinces of Erzurum, Aydın, Hüdâvendigâr, Trebizond, Van, Adana, Bitlis, Diyarbekır, Konya, Ankara, Aleppo, Mamuretülaziz, Sivas, and Mosul, and to the Provincial Districts of Urfa, Zor, Kayseri, Marash, İzmit, Karahisâr ı Sahib, Karesi Eskişehir, Canik, Kal'a i Sultâniye, Niğde, and Kütahya, dated 4 November 1915.

Ministry clarified the conditions under which religious conversions would (or would not) be accepted. "As the permission in the first and second articles of the instructions concerning conversion is with regard to the limited number of people exempted from deportation through a special order of the ministry and whose names are communicated," read a March 1916 cable to Konya Province, "the support of the conversions of the Armenians who remained in Ereğli simply because of the delay of their deportation and who will be subject to the deportations as soon as the roads open, naturally cannot be suitable for [this] policy."[48]

Just as he did while religious conversion was prohibited, interior minister Talat continued to decide individual cases. In November 1915 he informed the provincial district of Menteşe that "there is no obstacle to recognizing the conversions of Armenians who have petitioned to do so,"[49] while declaring to the provincial district of Afyon that "it is impermissible to recognize the conversion of those Armenian women whose husbands are still alive and serving in the military."[50] Other than a change of mood, what might have prompted such contradictory judgments? A general appraisal of this topic will be made below.

German diplomats also noted the renewal of permission to convert. "[T]he order to send the Armenians in Kayseri away to Sivas was issued," wrote Aleppo consul Rössler in January 1916, adding, "this expulsion means death. Perhaps the Mutesarrıf [provincial district governor] announced that those converting to Islam would be exempt with the intention of saving them [the Armenians]. Many people converted."[51]

At the same time, Armenian soldiers in the Ottoman Army were being forced to convert to Islam. "[S]everal days earlier the War Ministry gave the order that all Armenians being employed in the service of the army must become Muslim," noted Consul General Mordtmann of the Ger-

---

[48] BOA/DH.ŞFR, no. 61/252, Coded telegram from interior minister Talat to the Province of Konya, dated 7 March 1916.

[49] BOA/DH.ŞFR, no. 57/344, Coded telegram from interior minister Talat to the Provincial District of Menteşe, dated 7 November 1915.

[50] BOA/DH.ŞFR, no. 58/146, Coded telegram from interior minister Talat to the Provincial District of Karahisâr-ı Sâhib, dated 29 November 1915.

[51] DE/PA-AA/R 14090, Report by Aleppo consul, Rössler, to German chancellor Bethmann-Hollweg, dated 31 January 1916.

man Embassy on 16 November 1915; "they [the Armenians] must now simply take on Muslim names, with the true formalities (circumcision) of religious conversion in consideration of the conditions of war to be left for later." According to Mordtmann, Istanbul Armenian families were also being forced to abandon Christianity.[52] Already in September and October, reported the Bucharest committee of the Dashnaktsoutiun, "The Armenian soldiers working in the railway [province of Konya] have been forced, under threat of death, to embrace Islamism. More than 1,500 soldiers have been already converted by force."[53]

ASSIMILATION AND RELIGIOUS CONVERSION AT THE ENDPOINTS OF THE DEPORTATIONS

The Armenian survivors in Syria were expected to assimilate, but religious conversion was not at first required as part of the process. A telegram to Mosul and Der Zor in the summer of 1915 sheds light on the initial plans for those who reached Syria alive.

What is important about this telegram is that it was sent before the great part of the deportation caravans had even entered the deserts of Syria, and in this sense, it must be considered the expression of a previously planned policy. The 23 June cable, which was "to be taken care of personally," contains the following order:

> The Armenian population from the same counties and districts [of a province] is to be broken up and settled in different regions, and no space or permission is to be given for the opening of Armenian schools in their areas of settlement; thereby, their children are to be forced to continue their studies at the government schools and care and attention is to be given that the villages in which they are to be settled be at least five hours distant from one another and that they

[52] DE/PA-AA/Bo.Kons./Band. 172, Notes of the consul general in the Constantinople Embassy (Mordtmann), 16 December 1915.

[53] NA/RG 59, 867.4016/226, Report of Dashnaktsoutiun Committee, Balkan Section, Bucharest, "The Extermination of the Armenian People in Turkey," dated 28/15 October 1915, appended to Ambassador Morgenthau to the secretary of state, 9 November 1915, in *United States Official Records*, ed. Sarafian, 342.

be in no place or condition that would allow for self-rule or defense. . . . [This telegram] is to be destroyed after its contents have been communicated to the necessary parties.[54]

Sent just one day after the 22 June directive that permitted religious conversions, this is the second of the three Ottoman documents related to assimilation that was to be destroyed.

Additional "decisions about the Armenians" arrived the following week in a detailed communiqué from the Supreme Military Command:

(1) the language of domestic and foreign communication and correspondence is to be Turkish for those Armenians who have been or are to be removed and dispersed there from the Eastern Anatolia[n provinces] adjacent to the Russian border, Zeytun, Damascus, Adana, and the coastal areas; (2) Absolutely no permission shall be given for the establishment of Armenian schools in the areas in which the Armenians are to be resettled and all Armenian youth are to be educated in government schools; (3) At present permission is given to publish Armenian-language newspapers only in Istanbul; Armenian newspapers in other provinces are to be prohibited.[55]

The Armenians approaching Syria in the summer of 1915 were to be assimilated through dispersion, language, and education, but not religious conversion. However, this policy was abandoned through the order of 4 November. A directive of 21 December, intended specifically for the settlement areas, confirmed the new approach: "to accept in accordance with the plan the conversions of the Armenians who desire [this] from [those] who arrived for the purpose of settlement from other places, after the date of their arrival in the new areas."[56]

As late as the fall of 1915, permission for religious conversion did not yet mean forcible Islamization. According to the memoirs of some Armenian deportees, at this stage there was no compulsion at all. Yervant Odian, an

---

[54] BOA/DH.ŞFR, no. 54/122, Coded telegram from the Interior Ministry's IAMM to the Province of Mosul and the Provincial District of (Der) Zor, dated 23 June 1915.

[55] BOA/DH.ŞFR, no. 54/261, Coded telegram from interior minister Talat to the Provinces of Damascus, Aleppo, and Mosul, and to the Provincial Districts of Urfa and (Der) Zor, dated 1 July 1915.

[56] BOA/DH.ŞFR, no. 59/83, Coded telegram from the Interior Ministry's General Security Directorate to the Provinces of Aleppo, Damascus, and Mosul, and to the Provincial Districts of Urfa and (Der) Zor, dated 21 December 1916.

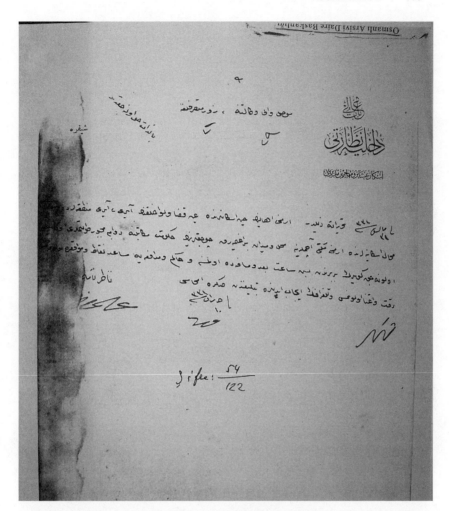

Figure 9.1. Ottoman Document 54/122. A cable from the Ministry of the Interior on 23 June 1915 that reads, "No space or permission is to be given for the opening of Armenian schools in their areas of settlement . . . [this telegram] is to be destroyed after its contents have been communicated to the necessary parties."

editor of the Istanbul Armenian-language newspaper *Zhamanag*, recalled one group of Armenians, in particular craftsmen, who were assembled for settlement near Damascus and Hama by order of Cemal Pasha, governor of Syria and commander of the Ottoman Fourth Army. "As artisans we're going there to work in government factories," Odian was told. "They are especially looking for tailors, shoemakers, metalworkers, carpenters and weavers."[57]

THE FINAL CHOICE: ISLAM OR DEPORTATION

The spring of 1916 saw an important change in the policies of religious conversion. Both the Armenians remaining in Anatolia and those who had been allowed to settle in Syria as Christians were made to choose between Islam and deportation to Der Zor. Those who understood that deportation meant death were compelled to accept forcible religious conversion.

That enforced Islamization took place at the same time as another change in policy was a meaningful coincidence. It was in spring 1916 that the emptying of all the Armenian settlement sites and camps in Aleppo and its environs began, and throughout that summer a second large massacre was organized. A direct connection can be discerned between the decision for massacre and the new assimilation policy of forcible Islamization.

Evidence of this policy change can be traced in the reports of the German and American Consulates during spring 1916. Three to four hundred Armenian families in the city of Antep had not been sent away in the first deportation. On 8 February, American consul J. B. Jackson reported that "these remaining families in Aintab have been notified that if they become Muslims they may remain."[58] The sole requirement for staying was to abandon Christianity. Similar reports arrived from Sivas. German consular secretary Werth wrote on 28 June, "yesterday morning the Armenians who are still remaining here who belong to road building, construction, and engineer regiments, as well as all who are in the trade school, and also all Greeks were locked up in the Armenian church here. The Greeks and the Armenians who accepted Islam were released after a fierce bastinado. Other Armenians were advised by the authorities to convert to Islam; if they do not accept they will be deported and sent to an unknown place. The Armenians fear a fourth slaughter."[59] As of 23 July, "Armenian doc-

---

[57] Odian, *Accursed Years*, 97.

[58] NA/RG 59, 867.4016/275, Report of Aleppo consul, J. B. Jackson, to American Embassy, dated 8 February 1916, in *United States Official Documents on the Armenian Genocide*, vol. 1, *The Lower Euphrates*, ed. Ara Sarafian (Boston, MA: *Armenian Review*, 1993), Doc. no. 61, 117.

[59] DE/PA-AA/R 14092, Telegraphic report of Sivas consular secretary Werth to the Istanbul German Embassy, dated 28 June 1916.

tors of all ranks are being threatened and forced to become Muslim. All of them are forced to convert [religions]. An Armenian health employee was temporarily imprisoned."[60]

In Syria there were similar developments. Ali Kemal Bey, CUP responsible secretary in Damascus, personally took on the task of forcible Islamization and traveled through the region to speed up the process. "The operation was very simple. Ittihad [CUP] had prepared thousands of applications on which only old and new names had to be entered and signed, in place of which a piece of paper, with the new Islamic name and a number on it, was given to them . . . Thus, 5,000 Armenian deportees became Muslims in Hama in this way in four or five days."[61]

When Çerkes Hasan Amca (Circassian Uncle Hasan), who was assigned the task of sending the Armenians in the Harran plain to Damascus and Jerusalem, began the job at the end of August 1916, his first instructions concerned "the order of conversion of all the refugees being carried out."[62] Special teachers of religion were appointed. The Armenians who refused to abandon Christianity were left to starve.[63] During this period, approximately 150,000 Armenians, identified by Raymond Kévorkian as "Cemal's Armenians," dispersed essentially between Hama and Damascus, were forcibly Islamized.[64] The extent to which these Armenians, having assimilated, were allowed to remain alive as a result of Cemal Pasha's personal interventions is the topic of another discussion.[65]

The wave of forced conversions that began in Syria in spring 1916 also left its traces in consular reports. "At the end of February and the beginning of March, nearly all of the Armenians in the labor battalion of Aleppo, urged upon partly with success, were converted to Islam," wrote Consul Rössler. "During the month of March, lists of Armenians in Aleppo were drawn up by the police as preparation for deportation, and the news was spread through the police that the only path to salvation from deportation

---

[60] DE/PA-AA/Bo.Kons./Band 172, Telegraphic report of Sivas consular secretary Werth to the Istanbul German Embassy, dated 23 July 1916

[61] Odian, *Accursed Years*, 114–15.

[62] "Çerkes Hasan Bey'in Hâtırâtı: Tehcîrin İç Yüzü," *Alemdar*, 28 June 1919.

[63] *Alemdar*, 20 June 1919.

[64] Kévorkian, "L'extermination des déportés arméniens ottomans," 51.

[65] DE/PA-AA/R 14093, Report of German ambassador Wolff-Metternich to Chancellor Bethmann-Hollweg, dated 18 September 1916.

was conversion to Islam. Then when a succession of families applied for conversion, they were treated as if the granting of the request was a special favor."[66] In May, Ambassador Wolff-Metternich related that word of a new campaign to forcibly convert Armenians to Islam had reached the Germans. Wolff-Metternich discussed this with Unionist leaders Halil Menteşe and Talat Pasha, but they decisively denied such a thing.[67] However, on 30 June 1916 the German consul in Damascus reported that in this region "all the Armenians were more or less forcibly turned into Muslims."[68] A similar report came from Aleppo: "According to mutually corroborating news from Hama, Homs, Damascus, and other places, in the last weeks those sent away en masse [the Armenians] were pressed to convert to Islam through the threat of further deportations. This [conversion process] took place in a purely bureaucratic fashion: Applying, and then changing of name."[69] American consul J. B. Jackson of Aleppo confirmed that "at Hama, Homs, Marash[,] etc. thousands have been forced to become Mohammedans."[70]

Dispatches from Jerusalem told the same story. Consul Brode reported that, according to the Armenian patriarch, "The Armenians settled in the East Jordanian region were forcibly converted to Islam." It was also reported that as "[Hüseyin] Kazım Bey, the official entrusted with the settlement of the Armenians, was found to be too mild, he was removed from his post, while the man brought in his place, Kemal, applied cruel methods, and as a result of such pressure, 3,500 people converted."[71]

This consular information confirms the testimony of Yervant Odian and Circassian Uncle Hasan quoted earlier. Annihilation and forcible Is-

[66] DE/PA-AA/R 14091, Report of Aleppo consul, Rössler, to Chancellor Bethmann-Hollweg, dated 27 April 1916.

[67] DE/PA-AA/R 14091, Report of German ambassador Wolff-Metternich to Chancellor Bethmann-Hollweg, dated 11 May 1916.

[68] DE/PA-AA/Bo.Kons./Band 173, Telegram of Damascus consul Loytved Hardegg to the German Embassy, dated 30 June 1916.

[69] DE/PA-AA/R 14093, Report of Aleppo consul Hoffmann to the German Embassy, dated 29 June 1916.

[70] NA/RG 59, 867.4016/298, Letter from Mrs. Jesse Jackson, wife of Aleppo consul J. B. Jackson, to the State Department, dated 13 October 1916. Mrs. Jackson copied information from her husband's letter and sent it on because he had difficulties in sending out mail. Reproduced in *United States Official Documents*, ed. Sarafian, Doc. no. 61, 119.

[71] DE/PA-AA/R 14092, Report by Jerusalem consul (Dr.) Brode, dated 26 June, 1916.

lamization coincided with the last stage of the Armenian Genocide. Together, these parallel operations aimed to complete the destruction of the Armenians.

FACTORS DETERMINING THE RELIGIOUS CONVERSION POLICY

The question that requires an answer is whether a rationale can be discerned behind the changing policies of religious conversion and cultural assimilation. Why did Ottoman officials at first permit religious conversion, then forbid it, then again insist forcibly that outside of death, Islam was the only choice remaining?

As all these fluctuations have shown, the policies of religious conversion cannot be attributed solely to Muslim fanaticism. Quite the contrary: however incomplete when first put into practice, this policy was based on a cold-blooded calculation. Wolff-Metternich's observations on this topic are important. On 10 July 1916, the German ambassador reported that "despite all the official disavowals, Islamization played a great role in this last phase of Armenian persecutions." Wolff-Metternich, who said, "At the same time, no measure prompted by religious fanaticism must be seen in the forcible Islamization of the Armenians," concluded that "such sentiments must be foreign to the Young Turk rulers." Based on his meetings with government authorities, Wolff-Metternich said, "the decisive motivation in the forcible conversion of the Armenians' religions is not religious fanaticism but the blending of the Armenians with the Muslim people of the Empire."[72] Consul General Mordtmann, who believed that "forcible Islamization of the Armenians is not a goal in and of itself, but only serves to Turkify the converts," likewise stressed that the goal was assimilation.[73]

After 1 July 1915, it is easy to understand from the expressions "assure the means to stay in their native lands [*memleketlerinde kalmak çâresini*

[72] DE/PA-AA/R 14092, Report of Ambassador Wolff-Metternich to Chancellor Bethmann-Hollweg, dated 10 July 1916. In a report dated 18 September, Wolff-Metternich repeats the same information. See DE/PA-AA/R 14093, Report of German ambassdor Wolff-Metternich to Chancellor Bethmann-Hollweg, dated 18 September 1916.

[73] DE/PA-AA/Bo.Kons./Band 101, Mordtmann's notes in the margin of the report of Aleppo consul, Rössler, to the German Embassy, dated 20 April 1917.

temin]," "compulsion of interest [ilcâ' i menfa'at]," and "false and temporary [ca'lî ve muvakkat]," which were used in the documents forbidding
religious conversion, that the Unionists worried that the Armenians had
no sincere intention of abandoning their religion but rather aimed to preserve their identity.

In his report mentioned above, Wolff-Metternich also stressed this
point. After relating that the Armenians converted of their own volition
in order to be saved from deportation and death, and to prevent their
goods from being seized, he stated that the "officials did not favor this
movement and nevertheless deported the converts." He explained the
change in this policy as follows: "apparently it is feared that through
further mass conversions the true goal of the Armenian deportations—the complete neutralization of the Armenian people—might be
thwarted."[74]

The German ambassador explained that the change in attitude toward
charitable institutions, such as the orphanages, hospitals, and schools run
by the German and American missionaries, was due to the fear that the Armenians could preserve their national identity. Recalling that nothing had
initially been said about the work of these institutions, Wolff-Metternich
made an important observation about the reason for this, while communicating that in the last stage of the annihilation of the Armenians, these
institutions also became targets: "The Turkish government has rightly understood that the schools and orphanages run by foreigners have a great
influence on the awakening and development of Armenian national feeling. It is also logical from its standpoint to take them under strict control,
or completely have them close."[75]

For this reason, numbers were important. In correspondence with
the provinces, the number of Armenian converts, especially compared
with that of the remaining Armenians and the Muslim population, were
requested in a systematic fashion. Several examples can be provided. On
28 October 1915, "the communication of the number of Armenians who
have not yet completed the process of conversion" was requested in a tele-

[74] DE/PA-AA/R 14092, Report of Ambassador Wolff-Metternich to Chancellor Bethmann-
Hollweg, dated 10 July 1916.
[75] Ibid.

gram sent to the provincial district government of Canik.[76] In a telegram
sent again from Canik on 13 February 1916, "the communication of how
many Armenians have been announced as requesting conversion from
those who came out of places of escape and hiding" was demanded.[77]

An order sent to all provinces and districts in July 1916 asked that a
tabulated list be prepared on this issue and sent back: "The need is communicated via circular for the rapid preparation and dispatch of a tabulated list by district [kaza] containing the quantities within the province/
district of (1) local Armenians, (2) foreign Armenians, (3) those left as
Catholics and Protestants, (4) those kept in their places as families of soldiers, (5) those remaining by converting, [and] (6) Armenians remaining
due to special orders."[78]

The documents reveal that alongside the general concern over population, security was another factor in the issue of religious conversion. According to a telegram of 31 January 1916 to the provincial government of
Niğde, during the period when religious conversions were again being
permitted, special permission was required from the War Ministry for the
acceptance of religious conversions. This telegram stated, "It has been informed in response by the Supreme Military Command's deputy that the
accepting of the requests of the Armenians through the desires of their
consciences for religious conversion is suitable."[79]

Occasionally, requests for religious conversion were rejected for security reasons. A cipher telegram of 20 February 1916 to Kale-i Sultaniye
(present-day Çanakkale) states, "Basically, religious conversion is not an
obstacle to deportation. If the presence of non-Muslims there is a forbidden danger, this restriction cannot be removed. Considering that the

[76] BOA/DH.ŞFR, no. 59/119, Coded telegram from interior minister Talat to the Provincial District of Canik, dated 28 December 1915.

[77] BOA/DH.ŞFR, no. 59/267, Coded telegram from interior minister Talat to the Provincial District of Canik, dated 13 February 1916.

[78] BOA/DH.ŞFR, no. 68/112, Coded telegram from the Interior Ministry's General Security Directorate to the Provinces of Edirne, Adana, Ankara, Aydın, Bitlis, Baghdad, Beirut, Aleppo, Hüdâvendigâr (Bursa), Diyarbekır, Damascus, Sivas, Trebizond, Kastamonu, Konya, Mamuretülaziz, and
Mosul, and to the Provincial Districts of Urfa, İzmit, Bolu, Canik, Çatalca, (Der) Zor, Karesi, Jerusalem, Kale-i Sultaniye (Çanakkale), Menteşe, Teke, Kayseri, Karahisâr-ı Sâhib, İçel, Kütahya, Marash,
Niğde, and Eskişehir, dated 24 September 1916.

[79] BOA/DH.ŞFR, no. 60/183, Coded telegram from the Interior Ministry's General Directorate of
Security to the Provincial District of Niğde, dated 31 January 1916.

deportation of such [people] has been shown necessary from a military standpoint, the requests to be left on condition of religious conversion cannot be seen as worthy of acceptance."[80]

The Interior Ministry ordered a thorough police investigation of every prospective convert and based its decision on the results. On 24 April 1916, the Interior Ministry's General Directorate of Security informed the Departments of the Judiciary and Sects of the Ministry of Justice that because "Tatyos son of Sahak, of Kayseri origin, who wants to convert" is in relations with Armenian revolutionaries, and "it is understood from an investigation of the facts that his conversion was caused by fear," the refusal of this request was desired.[81] Talat Pasha is again the name found in the midst of all these investigations.[82]

Although religious conversions in general had begun to be allowed, permission for the group conversion of all the Edirne Armenians was refused. In this matter, the pressures of foreign ambassadors, in addition to concerns about security and numbers, may have played a role. A telegram to Edirne on 6 March 1916 stated that "in the Edirne region the Armenians' mass conversions were very ugly and would not be possible to reconcile with the present policy of the state," and immediately therefore, "its [the aforementioned religious conversions] correction in a definitive fashion is necessary."[83] Three days later, the government expressed its concern much more clearly: because "the mass conversion in a place like Edirne which is called Europe's gate is incompatible with the direction of the policies of the state," officials were requested to consider "that the religious conversion operation never existed."[84]

[80] BOA/DH.ŞFR, no. 61/61, Coded telegram from the Interior Ministry's General Directorate to the Provincial District of Kale-i Sultaniye (Çanakkale), dated 20 February 1916.

[81] BOA/DH.EUM, 2. Şube, no. 20/42, Note from the Directorate of Public Security of the Interior Ministry to the Ministry of Justice and Sects, marked "confidential" and dated 24 April 1916. For another similar investigation and rejection of a religous conversion, see BOA/DH.EUM, 2. Şube, no. 21/14.

[82] BOA/DH.EUM, 2. Şube, no. 30/49, "On İranos oğlu Dacat Who Wishes to Convert," note of Assistant Permanent Undersecretary (Müsteşar Muavini) Osman Bey in the name of interior minister Talat Bey to Director General of the Police Ahmed Bey, dated 17 August 1916.

[83] BOA/DH.ŞFR, no. 61/211, Coded telegram from the Interior Ministry's General Directorate of Security to the Province of Edirne, dated 6 March 1916.

[84] BOA/DH.ŞFR, no. 61/257, Coded telegram from the Interior Ministry's General Directorate of Security to the Province of Edirne, dated 9 March 1916.

As a matter of fact, in March 1916 the American consul in Edirne corroborated the forcible return of the Armenians to Christianity: "these people [converted Armenians] have during the past few days been summoned to the konak and have been accorded the privilege of resuming their Christian names and religion. Inasmuch as it is uncertain what will be the ultimate fate of the Armenians, some of them have declined to take advantage of this privilege and have insisted upon remaining Mussulman."[85] This changed attitude was said to have been adopted under Austrian pressure.

Armenian converts were being investigated and their movements kept under control as late as 1918. In April of that year, all provinces and districts were required to prepare "a detailed tabulated list—about the names of those who converted of the Armenians at present living in the province/district, the date and manner of conversion, the names of the members of their families, the degree of relationship to the head of the family, with what business after their conversions they have been busy, how they became known by the local officers with their circumstances and movements before and after conversion." The circular "carefully" advised the dispatch of this information "in an orderly manner and with [all] possible speed."[86]

ASSIMILATION OF CHILDREN AND OLDER GIRLS

That a policy of assimilation was a structural element of the Armenian Genocide is especially clear from the treatment of Armenian children. Ottoman documents clearly show that the government of the Committee of Union and Progress systematically and more or less successfully aimed to dissolve Armenian youth within the Muslim majority. Girls and young boys were forcibly Islamized, then placed in Muslim orphanages or distributed to Muslim families. The older girls were married off by force to

[85] NA/RG 59, 867.00/786, Report of American consul general, G. Bie Ravndal, Constantinople, dated 18 March 1916, in *United States Official Records*, ed. Sarafian, 495.

[86] BOA/DH.ŞFR, no. 86/45, Coded telegram from the Interior Ministry to the Provinces of Edirne, Adana, Ankara, Aydın, Bitlis, Beirut, Aleppo, Hüdâvendigâr, Diyarbekır, Damascus, Sivas, Trebizond, Kastamonu, Konya, Mamuretülaziz (Elazığ), and Mosul, and to the Provincial Districts of Urfa, İzmit, Bolu, Canik, Çatalca, Zor, Karesi, Kale-i Sultaniye, Menteşe, Teke, Kayseri, Karahisâr-ı Sâhib, Eskişehir, İçel, Kütahya, Marash, Niğde, and Cebel-i Lübnan, dated 3 April 1918.

Muslim men. The important point is that assimilation was planned before the start of the deportations.

This is not to say that there was no policy of annihilation directed at Armenian children. Throughout the entire deportation, young girls and boys were killed outright or abandoned to die of hunger and disease.[87] In some places, along with their mothers, they were drowned in the Black Sea. At the fourth session of the Trebizond postwar trial, on 3 April 1919, "one woman's confirmed testimony" revealed that "Cemal Azmi Bey ordered the gendarmes to collect Armenian men and take them by boat to Kumkale. On the way they were all killed—some shot, others thrown into the sea."[88] "Around Değirmendere," said the same indictment, "the women and children were loaded onto boats, taken to the sea and thrown off to drown."[89]

In a similar fashion, rape, sexual abuse, and prostitution of Armenian women were extremely widespread. "Do to them whatever you wish," declared the military commanders who escorted the convoys, giving their soldiers "the full right of usage of [Armenian] women."[90] In Der Zor, members of the German Army directly encouraged and led the opening of a brothel.[91] Unlimited license turned the whole deportation process, from beginning to end, into a "laboratory in total domination."[92]

[87] On the topic of the physical destruction directed against women and children in particular, the following sources may be examined: Wolfgang Gust, *Der Völkermord an den Armeniern 1915/16: Dokumente aus dem Politischen Archiv des deutschen Auswärtigen Amts* (Springe, Germany: Verlag zu Klampen, 2005), 22–25; V. N. Dadrian, "Children as Victims of Genocide: The Armenian Case," *Journal of Genocide Research* 5, no. 3 (September 2003): 421–27; Matthias Bjørnlund, "'A Fate Worse than Dying': Sexual Violence during the Armenian Genocide," in *Brutality and Desire: War and Sexuality in Europe's Twentieth Century*, ed. Dagmar Herzog (New York: Palgrave Macmillan, 2009), 16–58; Donald E. Miller and Lorna Touryan Miller, *Survivors: An Oral History of the Armenian Genocide* (Berkeley: University of California Press, 1993), 94–117; Sarafian, "Absorption of Armenian Women and Children," 209–21; Katharine Derderian, "Common Fate, Different Experience: Gender-Specific Aspects of the Armenian Genocide, 1915–1917," *Holocaust and Genocide Studies* 19, no. 1 (2005): 1–25; Donald E. Miller and Lorna Touryan Miller, "Women and Children of the Armenian Genocide," in Hovannisian, *The Armenian Genocide: History, Politics, Ethics*, 152–72.

[88] *Alemdar*, 4 April 1919. Similar statements were given at the seventh session of the trial; see *Alemdar*, 9 April 1919. Of the trials held after World War I during the years 1919–21 in Istanbul, the Trebizond trial was one of the most important.

[89] *Alemdar*, 16 April 1919.

[90] DE/PA-AA/R 14086, German missionary Blank's testimony, appendix 3 in a report from Ambassador Wangenheim to Chancellor Bethmann-Hollweg, dated 27 May 1915. For similar accounts in German reports, see Gust, *Völkermord an den Armeniern*, 36–39.

[91] Odian, *Accursed Years*, 196–97, 209–11.

[92] Hannah Arendt, *Essays in Understanding, 1930–1954* (New York: Houghton Mifflin Harcourt, 1994), 304, quoted in Matthias Bjørnlund, "'A Fate Worse than Dying,'" 24.

Sexualized violence was everywhere. "[T]he rape of women and girls are ordinary and daily facts," stated an eyewitness.[93] In Cilicia, "The rapes of children of both sexes could not even approximately be counted or described."[94] Girls eight and ten years of age were violated and then murdered.[95] The creation of a harem by nearly every senior official involved in the deportations and annihilations, the organization of sex parties,[96] the trafficking of young girls as "presents,"[97] and still more abuses of young girls and women could be endlessly elaborated. Speaking of the mass rapes and other assaults, Bergfeld, the German consul at Trebizond, was justified in saying, "The Turkish government at the least was not sorry to see the attacks against the Armenians which led to their nearly complete destruction in Eastern Anatolia, and today too still sees things in the same way."[98]

The systematic organization of the rapes came out during the Istanbul trials of 1919–22, and, for example, was underscored in the reading of the verdict of the Trebizond trial, dated 22 May 1919.[99] Rape was also a reason for the death sentence and was meted out to Nusret, the county

[93] Bryce and Toynbee, *The Treatment of Armenians*, Doc. no. 138, 551.

[94] NA/RG 59, 867.4016/190, Report of the Dashnaktsoutiun Committee, Balkan Section, Bucharest, "The Extermination of the Armenian People in Turkey," dated 22/5 September 1915, appended to letter of Ambassador Morgenthau to the secretary of state, dated 17 September 1915, in *United States Official Records*, ed. Sarafian, 259.

[95] Ibid., Doc. no. 24, 128. For other examples, see Miller and Miller, *Survivors*, 102–3.

[96] For example, the Red Crescent Hospital in Trebizond had been reduced to a "pleasure dome" where the province's governor-general, Cemal Azmi, and other officials were using young girls as sexual slaves. The topic was on the agenda of the 26 March session of the Trebizond court-martial trial, and the judge had recourse to the testimony of the accused and eyewitnesses. See *Yeni Gazete*, 27 March 1919; for other examples, see Matthias Bjørnlund, "'A Fate Worse than Dying,'" 23, and footnote 53.

[97] "The best looking of the older girls . . . are kept in houses for the pleasure of members of the gang which seems to rule affairs here . . . a member of the Committee of Union and Progress here has ten of the handsomest girls in a house in the central part of the city for the use of himself and friends," wrote the American consul inTrebizond (NA/RG 59, 867.4016/128, Report of Oscar S. Heizer to Ambassador Henry Morgenthau, dated 28 July 1915, in *United States Official Records*, ed. Sarafian, 180). It was also reported that the *kaymakam* (county chief) of Tel Ebiad offered three German officials of the Baghdad Railway one Armenian girl each for the night (DE/PA-AA/R 14087, Letter from the director of the Deutsche Hülfsbund für christliches Liebeswerk im Orient [German Aid Union for Christian Charity Work in the Orient], Friedrich Schuchardt, to the German Foreign Ministry, dated 20 August 1915). For other examples, see Dadrian, "The Armenian Genocide," 83–84.

[98] DE/PA-AA/R 14104, Report of Trebizond consul, Bergfeld, to Chancellor Hertling, dated 1 September 1918.

[99] Akçam and Dadrian, "*Tehcir ve Taktil*," 706.

head (*kaymakam*) of Bayburd, in August 1920.[100] Salih Zeki, the county
head of Everek, was indicted for torture, bribery, and rape.[101] To sum
up, the social and political construction of all this sexualized violence
and the question of whether it was centrally organized as a structural
component of the Armenian Genocide are important topics for further
study.

Here, without dwelling upon this dimension of physical destruction,
which is the topic of many survivor accounts and studies, I will attempt
to show, by relying on Ottoman archival documents, that throughout the
period of the deportations, assimilation was as much a structural element
of genocide as physical destruction. Mass violence or its extreme form,
genocide, is an extremely complex, many-layered process that cannot be
reduced solely to one dimension. Assimilation and other forms of destruction should therefore be approached together.

The collection of children and older girls, and their dispersion in Turkish homes, was carried out by official and unofficial means. Children
were "voluntarily" surrendered to Muslim families or "purchased" on
the road, kidnapped while officials closed their eyes, or seized and sold
into slavery.[102] Trafficking in Armenian girls and women was one of the
most important sources of income for the gendarmes who accompanied
the convoys. In many memoirs, local Muslims are said to have come to
the stopping places, with the gendarmes' permission. "*Gavurlar satılık
çocuklarınız var mı?* Infidels, have you any children to sell?" they called
out. "We want to buy them."[103] In Cilicia, "Armenian girls and women
were sold for sixty piasters each."[104] "Deportees were sold at auction as sex
slaves, marketed in Damascus naked so that bidders might better judge

---

[100] Ibid., 667–68.

[101] For the results of the investigation into the deportation crimes of Kayseri, see Çalıka, *Rifat
Çalıka'nın Anıları*, 33–35. Salih Zeki was later sent to Der Zor as *kaymakam* and organized massacres
there. The Istanbul Court-Martial sentenced him to death in absentia as a result of this crime. For the
decision from the trial, see Akçam and Dadrian, *"Tehcir ve Taktil,"* 715–16.

[102] On this topic, for some examples, see Miller and Miller, *Survivors*, 100–103; Richard G. Hovannisian, "Intervention and Shades of Altruism during the Armenian Genocide," in his *The Armenian
Genocide: History, Politics, Ethics*, 173–208.

[103] Abraham H. Hartunian, *Neither to Laugh nor to Weep: An Odyssey of Faith; A Memoir of the Armenian Genocide*, 3rd ed. (Belmont, MA: NAASR, 1999), 102.

[104] NA/RG 59, 867.4016/190, Dashnaktsoutiun Committee, "The Extermination of the Armenian
People," 22/5 September 1915.

their worth ... naked Armenian girls and women ... were put up for auction and the whole lot disposed of, some for two, three, and four francs. Only Mohammedans were allowed to buy."[105]

Among the Arab tribes, "Armenian women were sold like pieces of old furniture, at low prices, varying from one to ten liras, or from one to five sheep."[106] The German consul at Mosul, Holstein, visited regions where the maximum price of a woman was 5 piastres (95 pfennig).[107] The American consul at Harput, Leslie A. Davis, observed an encampment of deportees passing through Harput (Mamuretülaziz) Province: "As one walks through the camp mothers offer their children and beg one to take them. In fact, the Turks have been taking their choice of these children and girls for slaves, or worse. In fact, they have even had their doctors there to examine the more likely girls and thus secure the best ones."[108]

Sometimes the selection and dispersion of children took place directly in front of government buildings. On the testimony of eyewitnesses, the Armenian patriarch of Constantinople, Zaven Der Yeghiayan, recounted on 15 August 1915 that

> when the deportees ... arrived ... [the] caravan was stopped in front of the government building, all boys and girls were taken from their mothers and led into rooms; the caravan was forced to continue on its way. Announcements were made in the surrounding villages for everyone to come and choose from these children ... In this way, as soon as caravans of women and children arrived in a town or burg, they were exhibited in front of the government building so that local Muslims could make their selection.[109]

In addition to the procedure described above, little Armenian children were assembled by government officials, collected in certain centers, and

---

[105] Katharine Derderian, "Common Fate, Different Experience," 11–12.

[106] Faiz el-Ghusein, *Martyred Armenia*, 33–34.

[107] DE/PA-AA/R 14090, Letter of Holstein, dated 15 November 1915, 2nd supplement to report of Aleppo consul, Rössler, to Ambassador Wolff-Metternich, dated 3 January 1916.

[108] NA/RG 59, 867.4016/127, Report of Mamouret-ul-Aziz (Harput) consul, Leslie A. Davis, to American ambassador Henry Morgenthau, dated 11 July 1915, in *United States Official Records*, ed. Sarafian, 172.

[109] Zaven Der Yeghiayan, *My Patriarchal Memoirs* (Barrington, RI: Mayreni, 2002), 88.

there, after being forcibly Islamized, were either placed in orphanages or with Muslim families.

THE ASSIMILATION OF CHILDREN AND ADOLESCENT GIRLS IN OTTOMAN DOCUMENTS

The Prime Ministerial Archive in Istanbul is replete with documents showing that forced assimilation was a centrally planned government policy. The sources in this archive confirm that young Christian boys and girls were taken from their families and raised according to Muslim customs and traditions. They were dispersed to Muslim villages in which there were no Armenians, forced to marry Muslims, or placed in orphanages.

Policy directives on the treatment of Armenian children and older girls were cabled to the regions in June and early July 1915, just as the large-scale deportations began in earnest. Forced assimilation, in other words, was no accidental by-product or unintentional result; on the contrary, it preceded the deportations both in concept and design. In the Ottoman archival documents, assimilation policies are clearly described as having been previously "considered" or "thought over" (*düşünülmüş*).

The first such cable was sent to the provinces in late June (26 June 1915, to be precise). Significantly, it was sent by the Ministry of Education rather than the Interior Ministry, which is normally in charge of deportation. This shows that the issue of children and older girls had been discussed in the cabinet, a decision had been made, and the Ministry of Education was to implement the measures. The telegrams sent directly by the education minister, with the notations "secret" and "[to be deciphered] according to the Interior [Ministry's] Cipher [Office Code]," contain the following instructions:

> Since consideration has been given to [the idea of] the education and upbringing of the children under the age of ten of those Armenians who have been relocated or in some fashion deported, either through the establishment of an orphanage or the gathering of them into an already existing orphanage, [it is requested that] it be reported back with all haste how many [such orphaned] children

there are within the province, and whether or not there is a suitable building in existence for the establishment of an orphanage.[110]

Almost two weeks afterward, another telegram was sent, this time from the Interior Ministry's IAMM to numerous provinces and provincial districts:

> For the purpose of the care and upbringing [bakım ve terbiye] of children who probably will be left without a guardian [i.e., become orphans] during the course of the Armenians' transportation and deportation, their [the children's] distribution to notables and men of repute in villages and kazas [counties] where Armenians and foreigners are not found, and the payment of thirty guruş [kurush] monthly from the special appropriations for immigrants for the children who will be left over after the distribution and will be given to those who do not have the means of subsistence, are seen as suitable. It is notified by circular that this be communicated to those for whom it is necessary and it be carried out as required in that way, and after this cipher telegram is shown to those necessary it be destroyed.[111]

This is the third telegram directly related to assimilation that was to be destroyed. Just why this was desired is difficult to understand and still open to interpretation.

The phrase "the children who are likely to become orphans" is extremely important. Clearly, such an outcome to the deportations was known in advance and taken into account: in other words, it was preplanned. Perhaps the destruction of the telegram was to conceal this official policy to shatter Armenian families. Regardless of how the "care and upbringing" of children was going to be realized, Istanbul was intent on assimilation.

[110] BOA/DH.ŞFR, no. 54/150, Coded telegram from the Private Secretariat of the Ministry of Education to the Provinces of Diyarbekır, Adana, Aleppo, Trebizond, Erzurum, Sivas, Bitlis, Mamuretül-aziz, and Van, and to the Provincial District of Marash, dated 26 June 1915.

[111] BOA/DH.ŞFR, no. 54/411, Coded telegram from the Interior Ministry's IAMM to the Provinces of Adana, Aleppo, Diyarbekır, Erzurum, Bitlis, Van, Trebizond, Sivas, Hüdâvendigâr (Bursa), Edirne, and Mosul, and to the Provincial Districts of İzmit, Canik, Kayseri, Marash, (Der) Zor, and Urfa, dated 12 July 1915.

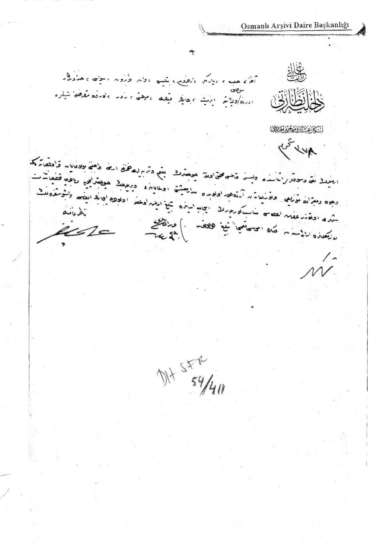

Figure 9.2. Ottoman Document 54/411. A cable from the Ministry of the Interior on 12 July 1915 that ordered that Armenian children should be distributed among Muslim families, "for the purpose of the care and upbringing [*bakim ve terbiye*]," and that "after this cipher telegram is shown to those necessary, it be destroyed."

Moreover, painstaking efforts were made to induce Muslim families to adopt Armenian children and accept Armenian brides. The incentive of this "program to encourage assimilation" was economic: the families that took in Armenian youth were to be recognized as their heirs. A telegram sent on 1 August 1915 to all the chairmanships of the Abandoned Property Commissions explained: "The personal property of the children who are to be left with people worthy of trust for the purpose of education and upbringing, together with that of those converting or marrying, will be preserved, and if their testators have died, their hereditary shares will be given."[112]

The importance of this order will be better understood in context. According to American missionary Henry Riggs, the governor-general (*vali*) of Harput (Mamuretülaziz) Province "was not ashamed to say ... '[e]very person sent into exile is considered by the government as dead.' "[113] It was the starter's pistol in a race to plunder Armenian property. Though officials of the Abandoned Property Commissions took an early lead, local administrators and notables sought to advance by adopting the children of prominent Armenian families or by forcibly marrying older girls and women whose husbands had been deported. The inclusion of a girl from Harput in the harem of a Turkish notable eager to seize her inheritance, or the forcible marriage of wealthy Armenian women in the Erzurum convoy, are only a few of the examples that can be given of this plunder.[114]

First on the agenda of the "care and upbringing" of Armenian children was their education in state schools. Three days before and five days after the education minister's message of 26 June 1915, the Interior Ministry sent, as we have seen, a policy directive on the resettlement of Armenian survivors. It was ordered that "[Armenian] children be required to

[112] BOA/DH.ŞFR, no. 54-A/382, Cipher telegram from the Interior Ministry IAMM Statistics Department to the Provinces of Adana, Ankara, Erzurum, Bitlis, Aleppo, Hüdâvendigâr, Diyarbekir, Damascus, Sivas, Mamuretülaziz, Mosul, Trebizond, and Van; to the Provincial Districts of İzmit, Urfa, Eskişehir, Zor, Canik, Kayseri, Marash, Karesi, Kale-i Sultaniye, Niğde, and Karahisâr-ı Sâhib; and to the Abandoned Property Commission Chairmanships of Adana, Aleppo, Marash, Mamuretülaziz, Diyarbekir, Trebizond, Sivas, Canik, and İzmit, dated 11 August 1915.

[113] Henry H. Riggs, *Days of Tragedy in Armenia: Personal Experiences in Harpoot, 1915–1917* (Ann Arbor, MI: Gomidas Institute, 1997), 93.

[114] Cited in Hans-Lukas Kieser, *Der Verpasste Friede: Mission, Ethnie und Staat in den Ostprovinzen der Turkey, 1939–1938* (Zurich: Chronos Verlag, 2000), 426–27.

continue in government schools,"[115] and "absolutely no permission shall be given for the establishment of Armenian schools in the areas in which the Armenians are to be resettled and all Armenian youth are to be educated in government schools."[116]

Subsequent directives further clarified what was meant by "care and upbringing." Armenian youth were to be raised according to the Muslim religion, usage, and customs; to that end, forcible Islamification and forcible marriage are defined as "necessity." In a 30 December 1915 telegram to the provincial district of Niğde, Talat Pasha stated, "it is necessary that assistance be provided to those without guardians or [living] relatives, that the children be placed in orphanages and Muslim villages in which there are no Armenians or foreigners, and that the young women and girls be married off to Muslims, so that they will be raised according to Islamic principles."[117]

Officials were aware that these measures amounted to forcible assimilation. The words *temsil* and *temessül*, which signified assimilation, were openly used. Thus on 20 April 1916, the Interior Ministry instructed Kastamonu Province that "those Armenian families from which the males have been sent off must be forced to assimilate [*temessül*] in the areas in which they are found as a result of their dispersion and resettlement among villages and towns in which there are no Armenians or foreigners."[118] This telegram explicitly announces that only males will be deported, and shows that the destruction of family ties was a government policy.

Certain regions were chosen for the assimilation of children. A 15 February 1916 cable to Sivas Province stated that Armenian orphans and children without any living relatives had been selected. "It is not appropriate for those Armenian orphans currently in Aleppo to be left there; rather, they are to be sent back and gathered together here [in your province]," officials were instructed. "Sivas is the most suitable environment for their

---

[115] BOA/DH.ŞFR, no. 54/122, Coded telegram from the Interior Ministry's IAMM to the Province of Mosul and the Provincial District of (Der) Zor, dated 23 June 1915.

[116] BOA/DH.ŞFR, no. 54/261, Coded telegram from interior minister Talat to the Provinces of Damascus, Aleppo, and Mosul, and to the Provincial Districts of Urfa and (Der) Zor, dated 1 July 1915.

[117] BOA/DH.ŞFR, no. 59/150, Coded telegram from Talat Pasha to the Provincial District of Niğde, dated 30 December 1915.

[118] BOA/DH.ŞFR, no. 63/60, Coded telegram from the Interior Ministry's IAMM to the Province of Kastamonu, dated 20 April 1916.

upbringing and assimilation [*terbiye ve temsîllerine*]. You are ordered to communicate with [the officials in] Aleppo so that these [orphans] can be assembled there and placed in orphanages."[119] Another cable to Sivas the following week (February 22) stated that "there are almost 500 orphans in Aleppo," and ordered that "the necessary expenditure be made from the allocations [designated] for immigrants" based on "the existing numbers there and for their education and assimilation."[120] Konya was another such destination. At the beginning of 1916, Consul Hoffman of Mosul learned from a state official who was charged with the settlement of the Armenians in the city that the dispatch of orphan children to an orphanage that was being established in Konya was imminent.[121]

According to an exchange of communications with Der Zor, only certain areas were chosen for the assimilation of children, and local officials were not allowed to dispatch them anywhere at will. The Interior Ministry, asking the provincial district government of Der Zor on 27 October 1915 what had been done for the Armenian orphans, was told: "As the deportation still has not been brought to an end and aspects of settlement and feeding have not been fully assured, it was not possible to do anything up until now with the aim of education and upbringing for the Armenian children who remain without guardians."[122] In response, "since the deportation to the north of motherless and fatherless children would be injurious to their upbringing and assimilation [*terbiye ve temsîlleri*]," on 3 November, the Interior Ministry requested "their not being included in the general deportation, [and] the rapid communication of their numbers along with their feeding and maintenance from the appropriations for protection and refugees."[123] Two days later the request was again made for "the communication of the estimated number of Armenian children remaining without guardians."[124]

[119] BOA/DH.ŞFR, no. 61/20, Coded telegram from the Interior Ministry's IAMM to the Province of Sivas, dated 15 February 1916.

[120] BOA/DH.ŞFR, no. 61/79, Coded telegram from the Interior Ministry's IAMM to the Province of Sivas, dated 22 February 1916.

[121] DE/PA-AA/R 14093, Report from Mosul consul, Hoffmann, to the German Embassy in Istanbul, dated 5 September 1916.

[122] BOA/DH.ŞFR, no. 503/50, Coded telegram from the Provincial District of Der Zor to Interior Ministry, dated 31 October 1915.

[123] BOA/DH.ŞFR, no. 60/230, Coded telegram from the Interior Ministry's IAMM to the Provincial District of Der Zor, dated 3 November 1915.

[124] BOA/DH.ŞFR, no. 59/214, Coded telegram from the Interior Ministry's IAMM to the Provincial District of Der Zor, dated 5 November 1915.

The distribution of children to the newly opened orphanages was organized either directly by, or in coordination with, Istanbul. A telegram of November 1915 to Damascus and Aleppo Provinces demanded that "in the province . . . if there are orphan children without anybody, their sending to Istanbul for education and upbringing" be carried out.[125] At the beginning of 1917, the Third Army Command was asked whether the children of the Armenians deported from Samsun had been distributed to existing orphanages and whether measures were being taken for their upbringing.[126]

In addition, it was important to understand whether children were placed in orphanages by age-groups. Accordingly, the distribution of very young children to Muslim families and the placement of the others in dormitories was requested. A cable sent to Sivas on 25 August 1915 stated that, "as was communicated earlier with special emphasis, the distribution of young lone Armenian children to Muslim villages is necessary. Their placement in orphan dormitories later necessitates many inconveniences."[127] Another telegram of the same period (30 August 1915) sent to Ankara said, "it is not right for Armenian children to be found in official institutions," and directed that "the remainder be distributed to Muslim villages."[128] Moreover, the provinces were frequently asked for "the rapid communication of what up until now was done for the purpose of education and upbringing of Armenian children remaining without guardians, and the numbers of those distributed to leading notables and those present today."[129]

The most comprehensive and detailed document on the deliberate breakup of Armenian families was a telegram of 30 April 1916 from the Interior Ministry's IAMM to almost all provinces:

[125] BOA/ DH.ŞFR, no. 58/34, Coded telegram from the Interior Ministry's General Directorate of Security to the Provinces of Damascus and Aleppo, and the Guardianship of Medina, dated 16 November 1915.

[126] BOA/DH.ŞFR, no. 77/5, Coded telegram from the Interior Ministry's IAMM to the commander of the Third Army, dated 2 June 1917.

[127] BOA/DH.ŞFR, no. 55/206, Coded telegram from the Interior Ministry's General Directorate of Security to the Province of Sivas, dated 25 August 1915.

[128] BOA/DH.ŞFR, no. 55/323, Coded telegram from the Interior Ministry's General Directorate of Security to the Province of Ankara, dated 30 August 1915.

[129] BOA/DH.ŞFR, no. 55/206, Coded telegram from the Interior Ministry's General Directorate of Security to the Province of Sivas, dated 25 August 1915.

(1) The distribution in a dispersed fashion of families without guardians whose men are deported or in the army to villages and towns where there are no Armenians and foreigners and, assuring their maintenance from the immigrant appropriations, their becoming familiar with local customs; (2) the giving in marriage of young and widowed women; (3) the distribution of children up to twelve years old to local orphanages and dormitories; (4) if the number of the orphanages is not sufficient, their [children] being given to Muslims for their upbringing and assimilation [terbiye ve temsîllerine] in accordance with local customs, [and] (5) if Muslims to receive and bring them up are not found, their distribution to villages on condition that thirty kuruş from the immigrant appropriations be given for the expense of maintenance.

Included in the plan were "step-by-step" reports "based on numbers and quantities of the actions and efforts that are going to take place in the preceding manner."[130]

The surviving women and children were not to be placed in urban areas, as this might hinder their assimilation. Aleppo governor Bekir Sami was warned on 9 August 1915 that "it is unacceptable that those Armenian women and families now bereft of male members be placed in the large cities" and reminded that "those boys and girls who are still young and bereft of relatives can be placed in small numbers and in dispersed fashion in Muslim villages."[131]

From the following telegrams, it can be seen that absolute consistency on this topic was maintained: on 16 February 1916 the provincial district of Der Zor was told, "it is absolutely unacceptable that those orphaned Armenian girls whom certain officials have taken in, in order to raise them, [be allowed to] travel to Istanbul";[132] and on 13 May 1916, Niğde was instructed that "it is not right that the children be detained in the center

[130] BOA/DH.ŞFR, no. 63/142, Coded telegram from the Interior Ministry's IAMM to the Provinces of Adana, Erzurum, Edirne, Aleppo, Hüdâvendigâr (Bursa), Sivas, Diyarbekır, Mamuretülaziz (Elazığ), Konya, Kastamonu, and Trebizond, and to the Provincial Districts of İzmit, Canik, Eskişehir, Karahisâr-ı Sâhib, Marash, Urfa, Kayseri, and Niğde, dated 30 April 1916.

[131] BOA/DH.ŞFR, no. 54-A/325, Coded telegram from the Interior Ministry's General Directorate of Security to Aleppo provincial governor Bekir Sami Bey, dated 9 August 1915.

[132] BOA/DH.ŞFR, no. 61/23, Coded telegram from the Interior Ministry's General Directorate of Security to the Provincial District of (Der) Zor, dated 16 February 1916.

[city]. Distribution to other places is more appropriate. The carrying out of the distribution accordingly [is requested]."[133]

Some officials asked whether they could bring the children they had taken to Istanbul. A telegram from Der Zor states that "some officials were asking for permission concerning wanting to bring up Armenian girls without family or friends, taking them either to the places they were going or to Istanbul," and information was requested as to what should be done.[134] Such requests were generally denied: "The bringing to Istanbul of the children in question is not suitable. The distribution of the afore-mentioned infants to orphanages in the provincial district and nearby provinces [is] to be endeavored."[135] Although "the sending of Armenian girls without family or friends taken by some officials for upbringing to Istanbul is absolutely impermissible," read another dispatch, "There is no objection to their being taken to other provinces."[136]

The arrival in Istanbul of Armenian women who married soldiers after becoming Muslim was also not desired. Such a woman was permitted to travel to other cities only if she possessed a document that proved her husband was an officer: "It was communicated in response by the War Minis-try that when Armenian women who married officers after conversion to Islam have in hand a certified document given by army corps command-erships about having officer husbands there should be no obstruction to their departures to places other than Istanbul."[137]

Bringing unauthorized people to Istanbul was grounds for an investiga-tion. Just how seriously this matter was taken can be understood from the investigation launched on 22 October 1916 against Major Hayri Bey, who had brought several Armenian girls to Istanbul from Aleppo. In "extremely confidential and urgent" correspondence with Enver, Talat called for the

---

[133] BOA/DH.ŞFR, no. 64/8, Coded telegram from Interior Ministry's IAMM to the Provincial District of Niğde, dated 13 May 1916.

[134] BOA/DH.ŞFR, no. 509/48, Coded telegram from the Provincial District of Der Zor to the In-terior Ministry, dated 13 December 1915.

[135] BOA/DH.ŞFR, no. 64/82, Coded telegram from the Interior Ministry's IAMM to the Provin-cial District of Kayseri, dated 20 May 1916.

[136] BOA/DH.ŞFR, no. 61/23, Coded telegram from interior minister Talat to the Provincial Dis-trict of Der Zor, dated 16 February 1916.

[137] BOA/DH/ŞFR, no. 81/151, Coded telegram from Interior Ministry's General Directorate of Security to the Province of Konya, dated 14 November 1917; a similar telegram was sent on 12 Decem-ber 1917 to the Province of Mamuretülaziz (BOA/DH/ŞFR, no. 82/87).

officer to be severely punished.[138] The reason was that bringing Armenians to Istanbul was a way of helping them escape, and ultimately saving them from genocide. The real goal of prohibiting their coming to Istanbul was to block that possibility.

The government's policy of assimilation of children can be followed in German and American consular documents. Reports from the regions show that Armenian families were allowed to leave their children in places chosen by the government. These sources were also in accord on the age-groups of children who were going to receive instruction and upbringing in orphanages. Early in July 1915, the American consul wrote from Trebizond, "The children, when the parents so desired, were left behind and placed in large houses in different parts of the city. There are approximately three thousand such children retained in these houses called by the Turks 'Orphanages.' Girls up to 15 years of age inclusive, and boys to 10 years of age inclusive are accepted; those over these ages are compelled to go with their parents."[139] American missionary Mary L. Graffam, who was allowed to accompany an Armenian convoy from Sivas, wrote from Malatya on 7 August 1915, "Boys under ten and girls under fourteen are accepted here as orphans."[140]

These reports supplement the Ottoman documents with additional necessary information about the treatment of children in various age-groups. On 29 August 1916, the German consul of Aleppo summed up the fate of as many as eight hundred motherless children from disbanded Swiss, American, and German orphanages:

> The local government appointed a special commissioner for these orphanages who will carry out their transfer to Turkish management. According to secretly conducted inquiries, the following principles will be applied: boys over thirteen years old will be sent away, young girls over thirteen will be married (naturally with Muslims). Children between ten and thirteen years old, because they

---

[138] BOA/DH.EUM, 2. Şube, no. 8/61, Note from interior minister Talat Bey to Acting Commander in Chief Enver Pasha, dated 22 October 1916, with the notation "extremely confidential and urgent."

[139] NA/RG 59, 867.4016/103, Report of Trebizond consul Oscar S. Heizer to Ambassador Henry Morgenthau, dated 7 July 1915, in *United States Official Records*, ed. Sarafian, 126.

[140] NA/RG 59, 867.4016/187, Appendix to Morgenthau's report to the State Department, dated 13 September 1915, ibid., 244.

still are under the effects of what they lived through, are going to be separated from younger ones and will be placed in pure Turkish orphanages in order to learn a trade. Children under ten years old will be brought up in special orphanages. This means in other words: boys over thirteen years old will be deported and probably killed, young girls of this age will be put into harems . . . the younger children will be Islamified, as far as they survive the Turkish orphanage administration.[141]

The memoirs of surviving children show that the consul was not exaggerating.[142] Hampartzoum Mardiros Chitjian of Peri County, Harput (Mamuretülaziz) Province, was left with his three brothers at the school they called the "dreadful building" when his family was deported.[143] The group soon grew to more than two hundred as Armenian boys from four to sixteen years old were brought in from all the nearby villages.[144] According to plan, the children were pressured to assimilate. "We were to become Turkified," recalled Hampartzoum. "The very first thing they did was to change our Armenian names into Turkish names. My name was changed to Rooshdee [Rüştü]. Next they demanded we no longer speak Armenian. They insisted we speak only in Turkish." Hampartzoum was not surprised at how quickly they picked up the language: "What surprised me more was how quickly and unconsciously we completely forgot how to speak Armenian."[145] Later the Islamization stage began: "One day a *mullah* (religious figure) would come and the next day a *hoja* (teacher)." Then,

---

[141] DE/PA-AA/R 14093, Report of Aleppo consular agent Hoffmann to German Consulate in Istanbul, dated 29 August 1916.

[142] Many memoirs have been written about growing up in orphanages according to Muslim principles and then returning to prior identities. The most extensive work on Armenian orphans, in three volumes, is Libarid Azadian, *Hay orbere Mets Egherni* [*The Orphans of the Armenian Genocide*] (Los Angeles, CA: Tparan April [Abril Publishers], 1995). For further work on this topic, see Aram Arkun, "A Preliminary Overview of Armenian-Language Primary Sources Published on the Armenian Genocide," paper presented at the workshop "The State of the Art of Armenian Genocide Research: Historiography, Sources, and Future Directions," Clark University, April 2010.

[143] Today it is called Akpazar. It is a town in Mazgirt County, Tunceli Province, that is also referred to as Çarsancak.

[144] Hampartzoum Mardiros Chitjian, *A Hair's Breadth from Death* (London and Reading: Taderon Press, 2003), 98–99.

[145] Ibid., 100.

"[f]or more than two weeks early in the morning and again in the evening, we were forced to recite their Moslem prayers. At the end of each week, we were tested."[146]

Another step was the separation of the children by age-group: "Three weeks later without warning, about ten o'clock in the morning, three gendarmes entered . . . without a word they promptly started to separate boys according to physical size and age." Hampartzoum learned why this division was carried out: "[a]s it turned out, the older boys were separated from the group because they were designated to be killed on that day. The Turks knew the older boys were not going to convert and become Turk and therefore would continue to be a threat . . . we knew we were destined to be killed." Hampartzoum managed to escape, but "to this day," he recalled wistfully at the age of 102, "I have not heard about the fate of the other boys. For eighty-eight years I have searched for them [to] no avail."[147] The other children who remained in the orphanage were later distributed to Muslim families to serve as *yanaşma*, a type of house servant or serf, with the exception of those too young to be useful for any kind of work. These little children, including Hampartzoum's youngest brother, were killed like the older ones.[148] The story of Hampartzoum Chitjian illustrates the general pattern in the progression of events, a pattern that can be observed in Ottoman, consular, and survivor accounts. All these sources supplement and corroborate one another.

What of Armenian children who were hidden in Muslim homes for safekeeping instead of assimilation? The government was convinced that such children would preserve their Armenian identity, and in the future become the source of problems. Addressing this serious issue, Third Army commander Mahmud Kamil Pasha put the provinces on notice: "The executions of those who hide Armenians who are being deported to the interior is communicated. The punishment [for this] . . . does not apply to . . . those who are keeping women and children . . . officially entrusted by the existing government. However, those hiding Armenians of any sex and religion in their homes without the knowledge of the government, and in

[146] Ibid., 101.
[147] Ibid., 103–5.
[148] Ibid., 156–57.

whose homes girls or women are found, without official marriage, shall be punished in the aforementioned manner."[149]

All these policies of assimilation were directed only at Armenian children, not those of other Christian denominations or ethnic groups. A telegram to Mosul at the end of July bears this out: "The assumption of the upbringing and maintenance of Assyrian and Chaldean women and children coming from Başkal'a and Siird who are not Armenian by their own communities is suitable."[150]

CHANGES IN ATTITUDE TOWARD MISSIONARY SCHOOLS

Schools opened by foreign missionaries in the Ottoman Empire were an obstacle in the successful application of assimilation policies because they continued to protect the ethnocultural identities of their Armenian students. It was necessary therefore to close these schools, and indeed this was done—the schools were shut down and their buildings confiscated. Although the Ottoman administration had felt extremely uncomfortable about missionary activities, it was too weak to counter them prior to the war.[151] The declaration of war in November 1914 offered an opportunity to expel foreign nationals of enemy states, and this was done without delay.[152] In time, the activities of American and German missionaries were also prohibited.

Enver Pasha, writing in the newspaper *Atî* in 1918, expressed the general opinion of the Ottoman rulers about missionary activities. In his view, missionaries did not want "to leave any Muslim government on the face of the earth"; foreign governments likewise intended "to remove us [the Ottomans or Muslims] from the surface of the earth." According to the pasha, who said "no foreign government has or can have the right to

---

[149] AAPJ, Carton 17, File H, Doc. no. 309, Cipher telegram from the Third Army Command to Sivas Province, dated 1 August 1915.

[150] BOA/DH.ŞFR, 54-A/154, Cipher telegram from the Interior Ministry EUM to Mosul Province, dated 28 July 1915.

[151] The missionary schools and their fate is the topic of a separate work unto itself and will not be treated here. For more detailed information on this topic, see Kieser, *Der Verpasste Friede*, 327–59; and Şamil Mutlu, *Osmanlı Devletinde Misyoner Okulları* (Istanbul: Gökkubbe, 2005), 333–71.

[152] Kieser, ibid., 345.

send missionaries and open schools on this continent," Anatolia had to be saved from "foreign influence and intervention."[153] And this is what was done.

At first, American and German missionary schools were allowed to operate unmolested. On 17 August 1915, Sivas was informed that "there is no harm in the female teachers and children in the orphanage remaining there for now,"[154] and on the same date Adana was told of "the Armenian children in the orphanage not being objected to."[155] In October 1915, Kayseri was sent a similar directive about "Armenian children who are reported to be in the presence of American missionaries not being interfered with and for now remaining."[156]

The first blow against the mission schools was the deportation of native faculty, staff, and students. Nor were the schools allowed to function as orphanages. "The important American religious and educational institutions are losing their professors, teachers, helpers and students, and even the orphanages are to be emptied of the hundreds of children therein, and which ruins the fruits of 50 years of untiring effort in this field."[157]

"It is perceived that the American and German schools, which are understood not to have been able to find students after the Armenian emigration, after being converted into orphanages are again being filled with Armenian children," warned the minister of education in a secret message to the provinces. "Moreover, the conversion of schools into orphanages is contingent on obtaining permission with an exalted [i.e., imperial] decree, so it is necessary to prohibit those schools which dare to [do] this behavior without obtaining permission."[158] Proclaiming the government's real purpose of freeing itself from missionary activities, the minister continued, "I request with the greatest urgency not to allow losing the means

[153] For the full article, see ibid., 561–64.

[154] BOA/DH.ŞFR, no. 55/42, Coded telegram from the Interior Ministry's General Directorate of Security to the Province of Sivas, dated 17 August 1915.

[155] BOA/DH.ŞFR, no. 55/43, Coded telegram from the Interior Ministry's General Directorate of Security to the Province of Adana, dated 17 August 1915.

[156] BOA/DH.ŞFR, no. 57/270, Coded telegram from the Interior Ministry's General Directorate of Security to the Provincial District of Kayseri, dated 1 January 1916.

[157] NA/RG 59, 867.4016/126, Report from Aleppo consul J. B. Jackson to American ambassador Henry Morgenthau, dated 3 August 1915, cited in *United States Official Records*, ed. Sarafian, 170.

[158] BOA/DH.ŞFR, no. 55-A/155, Coded telegram from the education minister to the Provinces of Mamuretülaziz, Sivas, and Diyarbekır, dated 9 September 1915.

and opportunity of saving the country from the institutions which are the source of the misrepresentations [as good] of foreigners."[159]

Later in the process, the mission schools and other establishments were closed, one by one, and their buildings appropriated for government use under the pretext of necessities of war. The American schools in Mersin, Tarsus, and Adana were the first to be seized in this way.[160] The orphanage seized in Kayseri was turned into a hospital.[161] Later, American institutions in Bitlis were also taken.[162] The remaining institutions carried out their work under very difficult conditions, and when America entered the war in spring 1917, they were left to German and Swiss organizations.[163] It was no longer possible for these institutions to obstruct assimilation policies. During this process, certain provinces were again warned that "the orphaned children [should] be placed at as great a distance as possible from the sight of the American missionaries."[164] In spring 1917, an orphanage under German control in Aleppo was also closed, and the children were initially distributed to an orphanage that was newly opening in Beirut, as well as to various places in Anatolia.[165] Henceforth, no obstacle remained in the way of the Islamization of Armenian children.

"Women who were taken from our compound were deported because they did not become Moslems. Their children and little babies were taken from them. Those who accepted Islam were allowed to stay, but were sent out to villages, their children taken away from them, and in those cases I

[159] Ibid.

[160] For the protest of the American government, see BOA/HR.HMŞ.İŞO, 71/1-4, and Şamil Mutlu, ibid., 333.

[161] BOA/DH.ŞFR, no. 63/265, Coded telegram from Education Ministry to the Provincial District of Niğde, dated 10 May 1916. The first efforts at closings began in November 1915, according to a letter dated 16 November 1915 from American missionary Henry K. Wingate in Kayseri to American ambassador Morgenthau (see LC/HM[Sr.]/Reel 7/770, in United States Official Records, ed. Sarafian, 349).

[162] BOA/DH.ŞFR, no. 68/148, Coded telegram from the Interior Ministry's General Directorate of Security to the Province of Bitlis, dated 1 October 1916.

[163] Kieser, Der Verpasste Friede, 432.

[164] BOA/DH.ŞFR, no. 63/276, Coded telegram from the Interior Ministry's IAMM to the Provincial District of Kayseri, dated 11 May 1916.

[165] There is much correspondence in the archives of the German Foreign Office on the topic of the closing of the orphanage in Aleppo. See DE/PA-AA/R 14095, Aleppo consul, Rössler, to Chancellor Bethmann-Hollweg, dated 14 February 1917; DE/PA-AA/R 14095, Undersecretary of the Foreign Office Stumm, Berlin, to the embassy in Constantinople, dated 1 March 1917; DE/PA-AA/R 14095, Ambassador Kühlmann to the Foreign Office, dated 7 March 1917.

know of, were forced to marry Turks."[166] These words of American missionary Stella Loughridge are in effect a summary of the main lines of the assimilation policy.

ABOUT THE NUMBERS

No one knows how many children were distributed to Muslim homes. In many works, it is estimated that between 5 and 10 percent of Ottoman Armenians were converted and absorbed into Muslim households in the course of 1915. This translates to a figure of one hundred thousand to two hundred thousand people.[167]

How many of these children remained in orphanages or were distributed to families is likewise unknown. The figures at hand are very disparate. According to a document that does not bear an official date, in a notebook belonging to Talat Pasha, the number of Armenian children distributed to Muslim people was 6,768, and the number of children in orphanages was 3,501. However, this figure can easily be shown to be extremely low.[168] During discussions held in the Ottoman Senate in 1917 about proposed laws on orphanages, the national education minister declared that as of March 1917, there were sixty-nine orphanages in all, and the number of children in them was twenty thousand. Of these, five thousand were girls and the remainder boys.[169] General Harbord, who was sent to Anatolia and the Caucasus in 1919 by President Wilson to prepare a report on the possibility of an American mandate over Armenia, reported that in the

---

[166] Stella Loughridge's report, in *"Turkish Atrocities,"* Barton, 117.

[167] Sarafian, "Absorption of Armenian Women and Children," 211; Lepsius, *Deutschland und Armenien*, lv; Özdemir et al., *Sürgün ve Göç*, 5–53.

[168] Bardakçı, *Talat Paşa'nın Evrak-ı Metrukesi*, 89. The numbers in this document, which was prepared in 1918, are incomplete at best. There were a total of 46 Ottoman provinces and independent provincial districts (25 provinces and 21 independent provincial districts), and while roughly 35 of these were directly affected by the deportations and distributions, Talat Pasha's list includes a total of 16 places of settlement (10 provinces and 6 provincial districts), and does not give any information about other ones. The lack of such provinces of central importance as Damascus, Ankara, Mamuretülaziz, Kastamonu, Konya, and Beirut in the list is just one example that can be given about this situation. The figures given for the settlement areas in the list are also deficient. For example, according to the list, no children are shown as distributed to the Muslim population in places like Kayseri, Der Zor, Urfa, İzmit, Mosul, and Aleppo, and it is clear that this is not true.

[169] *MAZC*, Period 3, Assembly Year 3, session of 27 March 1917, 397. The minister stated that it was not known how many of these children were from families of fallen soldiers and how many were the remainder, so he estimated that it could be "half and half."

places he passed through, "fully 50,000 orphans are to-day receiving Government or other organized care."[170] Harbord probably obtained this figure from Kazım Karabekir, commander of the Turkish Army, with whom he met in Erzurum.[171] A report prepared in 1921 by the Armenian Patriarchate of Istanbul stated that "there are still Armenian orphans and young girls in Moslem houses, who have not yet been liberated," and estimated their number as 63,000.[172]

Without entering into disputes over numbers based on all the estimates, one can safely assert that after World War I, when Istanbul was occupied by the Allied forces, the recovery of children and girls distributed to Muslim households was a very serious issue.[173] Through at least three separate channels, the Allied forces, the Ottoman government, and the Armenian Patriarchate attempted to organize the collection of women and children from Muslim homes; various joint commissions were also founded to work on solving problems. For example, an Armenian-Greek Section was formed within the structure of the English High Commission and worked with other officials of the commission to assemble Armenian children dispersed in Muslim homes.[174]

Harsh articles criticizing the policies of the Unionists in connection with children held in Muslim homes appeared in the contemporary press. With statements like the following, they demanded that the new government take relevant steps: "Oppressing the poor Armenian nation, the Union and Progress Celâlîs [sixteen- to seventeenth-century Ottoman rebels] who committed improprieties in this connection, not being satisfied with the blood they spilled and the immense wealth they stole, stretched their hands as far as the innocent girls without any family or friends who remained here and there." The government, feeling the need

---

[170] Maj. Gen. James G. Harbord, *Report of the American Military Mission to Armenia* (Washington, DC: Government Printing Office, 1920), 8.

[171] Kazım Karabekir also gives the same figure in his memoirs (quoted by İbrahim Ethem Atnur, *Türkiye'de Ermeni Kadınlar ve Çocuklar Meselesi [1915–1923]* [Ankara: Babil Yayıncılık, 2005], 129).

[172] NA/RG 59, 867.4016/398, cited in Özdemir et al., *Sürgün ve Göç*, 120–26.

[173] The question of Armenians who converted and who were distributed among Muslim families is outside of the scope of this work and for this reason will not be discussed here. For more information, see Akçam, *A Shameful Act*, 272–80; Atnur, *Kadınlar ve Çocuklar*, 129–94.

[174] On the activities of the commission and the minutes of its sessions, see Vartkes Yeghiayan, *British Reports on Ethnic Cleansing in Anatolia, 1919–1922: The Greek-Armenian Section* (Glendale, CA: Center for Armenian Remembrance, 2007).

to take action due to this pressure, cleared all obstacles in the way of the return of the Armenians, and gave official permission for their return;[175] it also sent orders to all regions for the collection of children kept by Muslim families, demanding "the immediate surrender to guardians or [their] communities of Armenian orphans, girls, and women who are found in Muslim families, and official and private institutions."[176] It was announced that legal investigations would be conducted regarding those who would not surrender children that they had with them.[177]

Such attempts were not very successful. As a 1921 report of the Armenian Patriarchate declared, "many Armenians had adopted Islam to get rid of the unspeakable crime and the persecution organized by the İttihad and many others . . . lived in different districts in disguise . . . many Armenians still hide themselves . . . and do not dare to come out for fear being subject to persecution even now."[178]

THE UNIONISTS AND ASSIMILATION: A GENERAL ASSESSMENT

As a general observation, we can say that "transfer of children from the victims' group to the perpetrators' community is common in genocide, but why it takes place is less well understood."[179] It might be too easy to explain this phenomena with "legitimate war booty" or a "triumphalist" attitude toward the "internal enemy."[180] There ought to be deeper reasons

[175] Actually, the return of the Armenians to their homes began to be permitted in a limited manner beginning in August 1918. It was necessary to undergo a police investigation in order to return. The first order on this topic that I have been able to find is dated 19 August 1918 (DH.ŞFR, no. 90/176). On 18/20 October 1918, a general order announced that it had been decided "by the Council of Ministers that returning to the places from which they were expelled be allowed for all the people who were deported to other places, being removed from a place by military decision as a result of war conditions" (DH.ŞFR, 92/187).

[176] BOA/DH.ŞFR, no. 92/196. The second document is cited in Atnur, *Kadınlar ve Çocukları*, 143–45 (BOA/DH.EUM.ECB, no. 21/63).

[177] Confidential letter from Interior Minister Mustafa Arif to the Foreign Office, dated 1 November 1918. Cited in Devlet Arşivleri Genel Müdürlüğü [General Directorate of State Archives], *Osmanlı Belgelerinde Ermeniler (1915–1920)*, document number 210 (BOA/HR.MÜ, no. 43/34).

[178] NA/RG 59, 867.4016/398, cited in Özdemir et al., *Sürgün ve Göç*, 126.

[179] Keith David Watenpaugh, "The League of Nations' Rescue of Armenian Genocide Survivors and the Making of Modern Humanitarianism, 1920–1927," *American Historical Review* 115, no. 5 (December 2010): 1315–39.

[180] Ibid.

that would explain these practices, and I would like to assert some general observations here and put forth some theses on the subject. The questions requiring an answer here are why did the Unionists permit religious conversion at all and why did their assimilation policy disperse Armenian youth among Muslim families by forcibly Islamizing children and forcibly marrying off older girls? Before answering these questions, it will be helpful to clarify a point. Forcible assimilation, the type being discussed here, was used as a means to destroy an ethnoreligious group. Moreover, forcible assimilation and physical destruction existed on a continuum of genocidal practice. These alternatives, and the transitions between them, were imposed, regulated, and enforced by the Unionists as a matter of government policy. Further, some methods of forcible assimilation, in and of themselves, amounted to annihilation. For example, what was done to a young girl who was forcibly Islamized and either married against her will, trafficked, prostituted, or otherwise sexually abused can be defined as a type of destruction, and in this sense, assimilation may be considered as a kind of "structural violence."

That the Unionists used forcible assimilation and physical annihilation in an intermeshing fashion while distributing Armenian children to Muslim families sheds light on their motives for genocide. Moreover, the existence of a systematic policy of assimilation lends support to a long-held scholarly consensus that racism, as currently understood, was not the basis of Unionist policy, nor did it motivate the annihilation of the Armenians.

This point has not been an especially weighty issue in the debates about 1915. Even for writers who argue that the decision for genocide was made much earlier than the war, even in the period of Abdülhamid, the issue is very clear: "In the final analysis, there was little racism in the ideology that authorized and legitimized the genocide of the Armenians."[181] In the usage of the period, the term "race" (ırk) was often understood in a broader sense than a biological one: depending on the context, it could also signify "ancestry" or "ethnicity."[182]

[181] V. N. Dadrian, "The Role of Turkish Physicians in the World War I Genocide of Ottoman Armenians," *Holocaust and Genocide Studies* 1, no. 2 (1986): 184.

[182] For a discussion on this topic, see Suavi Aydın, "Nazan Maksudyan'ın kitabı 'Türklüğü Ölçmek' üzerine," *Tarih ve Toplum* 2 (Fall 2005): 155–84; and Nazan Maksudyan, "The Turkish Review of Anthropology and the Racist Face of Turkish Nationalism," *Cultural Dynamics* 17 (2005): 291–322.

Although the race concept isn't being used here in its narrow biological meaning, the connection between racism and Unionist thought
requires a more detailed and careful debate, and we need to accept that
the relationship between racism and assimilation—and racism and nationalism—is more complex than is depicted here. The subject is in fact
directly related to what must be understood from the actual context of
racism. It is possible to derive definitions of comprehensive racism that
encompass the possibility of assimilation of other ethnic and religious
groups while nevertheless being based on a concept of "pure blood" that
yet differs from "exclusionary" racism. One could give Étienne Balibar's
"colonial racism" concept as an example of this.[183] Like this, pan-Turkism,
which could be defined as a form of racist thought, is also not "exclusionary." Some researchers have proposed the idea that it is a form of "inclusive" racism.[184]

Keeping this general theoretical reservation before us and continuing
along these lines, I contend that although some within Unionist ranks were
indeed inclined toward racism or social Darwinism,[185] the mainstream of
Unionist thought was nourished from other sources. The Unionists in
general saw the Christians as second-class citizens, and the roots of this
disdain were centuries old. Having grown up in an atmosphere that accepted the cultural, political, and legal superiority of Muslims, they lacked
the ability to change Ottoman society and institutions at such a profound
level. In contrast, the religious concept of a "ruling nation" (*millet-i ha-
kime*) based on Ottoman Islam was readily redefined as a nationalist concept based on modern Turkishness. The traditional subordination of the
Armenians as Christians allowed the Unionists to target them all the more
easily, not just as enemies of the state, but also as aliens to the nation.

The hatred and resentment that drive a mass crime such as genocide
were fueled, in this case, by the cultural background of Ottoman Islam, not
modern racist thought. Moreover, the existence of non-Turkish Muslim

---

[183] Étienne Balibar and Immanuel Maurice Wallerstein, *Race, Nation, Class: Ambiguous Identities*
(New York: Verso, 1991), 37–69.

[184] Nizam Önen, *İki Turan, Macaristan ve Türkiye'de Turancılık* (Istanbul: İletişim Yayıncılık, 2005),
27.

[185] For a work on the influence of ideologies like social Darwinism and racism on Ottoman intellectuals, see Atilla Doğan, *Osmanlı Aydınları ve Sosyal Darwinizm* (Istanbul: Bilgi Üniversitesi Yayınları,
2006).

groups in the empire, and the difficulty of defining ethnic "Turkishness" according to clear and evident objective criteria, drove the Unionists toward cultural nationalism. The inherited tradition of constructing and excluding social "otherness" on religious, not racist, grounds was what enabled this philosophical shift. As a result, the Unionists were able to recognize the right to life of the "other," but only when the "other" gave up its "otherness." Such was the ideological foundation of CUP assimilation policy during the Armenian Genocide.

Union and Progress political thought was not only synthetic but pragmatic in nature. Having taken possession of an empire, with its more than six centuries of state tradition, the Unionists were confronted with the central question of how to protect it. Saving the state was their alpha and omega, and all other principles were means to that defining end. Consequently, the Unionists took an instrumental, not dogmatic, view of such ideologies as Ottomanism, Turkism (and Turanism), Islamism, and Westernization. They had little problem in passing from one to another as justified by the needs of the state.[186]

Of course, they were nationalists, but as has been said, their political philosophy may be described as a cultural nationalism that had not cut all its ties with religion, rather than as an ethnic nationalism based on clear, let alone "objective," criteria.[187] Their nationalism was defined not by the doctrines they chose, but rather by "state interests," making the Unionists a type of "state nationalist." The difference between a state-centered na-

---

[186] The connection of the Union and Progress Party with various ideologies is a topic that has been widely discussed. For more detailed information and a bibliography on this subject, see Taner Akçam, *A Shameful Act*, 82–109.

[187] Many works have been published on the widely discussed topics of the birth of Turkish nationalism, the various stages it passed through, Unionist and Kemalist nationalism, and the relationship of Turkish nationalism to racism. See Masami Arai, *Jön Türk Dönemi Milliyetçiliği* (Istanbul: İletişim Yayınları, 1994); Masami Arai, "The Genç Kalemler and the Young Turks: A Study in Nationalism," *METU Studies in Developments* 12, nos. 3–4 (1985): 194–244; Tanıl Bora, *Türk Milliyetçiliğinin Üç Hali* (Istanbul: Birikim, 2009), 13–52; Tanıl Bora, "Nationalist Discourses in Turkey," in *Symbiotic Antagonisms: Competing Nationalisms in Turkey*, ed. Ayse Kadioglu and Fuat Keyman (Salt Lake City: University of Utah Press, 2011); Ahmet Yıldız, *"Ne Mutlu Türküm Diyebilene": Türk Ulusal Kimliğinin Etno-Seküler Sınırları (1919–1938)* (Istanbul: İletişim Yayınları, 2001), 47–87; Dündar, *Modern Türkiye'nin Şifresi*, 41–85; Ayhan Aktar, *Varlık Vergisi ve Türkleştirme Politikaları* (Istanbul: İletişim, 2000), 71–101; Ayhan Aktar, *Türk Milliyetçiliği, Gayrimüslimler ve Ekonomik Dönüşüm* (Istanbul: İletişim 2006); Etienne Copeaux, *Tarih Ders Kitaplarında (1931–1993) Türk Tarih Tezinden Türk-İslam Sentezine* (Istanbul: Tarih Vakfı Yurt Yayınları, 1998); Büşra Ersanlı Behar, *İktidar ve Tarih: Türkiye'de "Resim Tarih" Tezinin Oluşumu (1929–1937)* (Istanbul: Afa Yayınları, 1992).

tionalism and nationalism as a political and intellectual movement is important for understanding the Unionists' political decisions.[188]

The Unionists' embrace of cultural and state nationalism helps to explain what impelled them to annihilate the Armenians. State-centered thinking, guided by the premise of "protecting the state," led them to believe that such a decision was necessary. From the moment the Unionists took power, they saw their first duty as saving the empire from extinction. During World War I, they came to view the Armenians as an existential threat. Extinguishing this threat was therefore a priority.

Faith in science—especially the natural sciences—held a central place in the modernist philosophy of the Young Turks. They envisioned themselves on a historical mission that was entrusted to them by a force outside their own society, that is, by "science." Just as physicians cured their patients by means of medicine, the Unionists would cure society's ills through the proper application of science.

This scientific bent led them to act as "social engineers," and their policy in this regard can be called "social engineering."[189] Perhaps they invented the 5 to 10 percent formula for this reason. With the Armenians reduced in numbers to the point where they could no longer pose a threat to the empire, the Unionists were content to dissolve the remnants within Ottoman society. Their aim was to establish complete control over a "problem" group, the Armenians, through forcible assimilation and physical annihilation. Moreover, the conversion to Islam and the Turkification of a particular group of Armenians, or Armenian children's absorption into Muslim

---

[188] In fact, these various forms of nationalism always existed in Turkish political life, and they were explained through different concepts. For example, in one work, the concepts of *Türk ulusçuluğu* (Turkish nationalism) and *Türkçülük* (Turkism) are used as two different categories to distinguish Kemalism and its state-centered nationalism in the republican period from (the popular) nationalist movements defending the ideology of Turkism. See Günay Göksu Özdoğan, *"Turan"dan "Bozkurt"a: Tek Parti Döneminde Türkçülük* (Istanbul: İletişim Yayınları, 2006).

[189] There is a wide range of literature on the topic of social engineering. See, for example, Milica Zarkovic Bookman, *The Demographic Struggle for Power: The Political Economy of Demographic Engineering in the Modern World* (Portland, OR: Frank Cass, 1997); John McGarry, " 'Demographic Engineering': The State-Directed Movement of Ethnic Groups as a Technique of Conflict Regulation," *Ethnic and Racial Studies* 21, no. 4 (July 1998): 613–38. For Ottoman Turkish cases, see Nesim Şeker, "Demographic Engineering in the Late Ottoman Empire and the Armenians," *Middle Eastern Studies* 43, no. 3 (2007): 461–74; Uğur Ümit Üngör, "Geographies of Nationalism and Violence: Rethinking Young Turk 'Social Engineering,'" in *European Journal of Turkish Studies* no. 7 (2008). See online at http://ejts.revues.org/index2583.html.

families, presented the Unionists with military, economic, and political advantages.

From the Unionists' point of view, the existence of Christian majorities in strategic regions of Anatolia constituted a major security risk that was exacerbated by the ongoing war and the Russian threat. Moreover, the February 1914 Reform Agreement, which was one of the most important reasons for the deportation of the Armenians, had foreseen the formation of autonomous Armenian provinces. It was therefore extremely important to replace the Christians with a Muslim Turkish majority. The Unionists knew, however, that removing the Armenians from these areas would drastically reduce local populations. To make matters worse, Muslim men of fighting age (twenty to forty-five) had been taken into the army, and it was not clear when they would return. From this perspective, the Islamization of Armenian children offered a long-term strategic solution.

Added to the security risk was a very serious shortage of able-bodied workers in the region. Men were often conscripted into the army before the harvest, and the Armenians were deported in this same season. Economically, therefore, the Islamized Armenian children represented a windfall opportunity with long-term dividends. Even in normal times, eastern Anatolia's agrarian society was chronically short of cheap labor. The writer, having grown up in this environment, vividly recalls the child labor customs that served to fill this gap, including the socially defined roles of the *morbed*, *nöker*, and *yanaşma*. A *morbed* is a kind of seasonal worker, hired for a short time in exchange for a specific payment. A *nöker* is a relatively poor child, such as an orphan or half orphan, who has been "adopted" to work for a rich family, although in many cases, the child of a well-known family or a relative may be fostered as a *nöker*. Lowest in social status, like a serf in feudal society, is a *yanaşma*. While a *nöker* might enjoy a quasi-familial standing in the household, this is not even considered with a *yanaşma*. In exchange for being looked after, the *yanaşma* must do every sort of task. Yet the *yanaşma* also signifies a degree of social solidarity, because children who would otherwise have died are thus protected. Islamized Armenians, according to the attitude of the family, would have been assigned a social status between *nöker* and *yanaşma*.

Finally, Islamized Armenian children were distributed not only as an economic commodity, but also as a political incentive. Because the Unionists did not enjoy broad-based public support, their anti-Armenian policy might have proved unpopular among villagers who were themselves struggling for subsistence. The Muslim masses, seeing the Armenians religiously and culturally as the "other," might be won over with sufficient material incentives. The "gift" of Armenian children was a way to buy loyalty—in other words, a type of bribe. Later events would prove the Unionists' calculations correct.[190]

The last point that can be added to this picture concerns young girls in particular and pertains to the existence of an Ottoman institution with deep historical roots. It was a widespread practice to place young girls as foster children in the homes of families who were well off. This practice was called *besleme* (foster daughter/servant). The importance and impact of this institution on the distribution of girls among Muslim families during genocide is a topic for further research.[191]

[190] There are various explanations about the motivations of the Unionists in allowing Armenian children to be distributed to Muslim families. "Unlike the racist Nazis, for example, the Ottoman Turks were quite appreciative of the value of the gene pool that Armenian children embodied" (Dadrian, "Children as Victims of Genocide," 423; or, "According to some contemporary Western observers, one of the reasons that the CUP in some instances preferred conversion to murder was that some of the perceived 'racial' traits of Armenians were deemed desirable if somehow disassociated from any actual 'Armenianness'" (Matthias Bjørnlund, "'A Fate Worse than Dying,'" 38). Such types of explanation are not only unsatisfying but also risk encouraging racist thinking, which of course is neither acceptable nor correct.

[191] For an extensive study of this institution, see Nazan Maksudyan, "Foster-Daughter or Servant, Charity or Abuse in the late Ottoman Empire," *Journal of Historical Sociology* 21, no. 4 (December 2008): 488–512; Ferhunde Özbay et al., "Adoption and Fostering: Turkey," in *Encyclopedia of Women and Islamic Cultures*, vol. 2, *Family, Law, and Politics*, gen. ed. Suad Joseph (Leiden, 2005).

The deportations left an enormous amount of abandoned Armenian property and possessions in their wake. This posed the question of what policy the government and local officials should take in regard to its preservation or liquidation. The ultimate answer of the Unionist government is highly instructive regarding the ultimate aims of their Armenian policy. On the basis of existing Interior Ministry Papers from the period, it can confidently be asserted that the goal of the CUP was not the resettlement of Anatolia's Armenian population and their just compensation for the property and possessions that they were forced to leave behind. Rather, the confiscation and subsequent use of Armenian property clearly demonstrated that Unionist government policy was intended to completely deprive the Armenians of all possibility of continued existence.

THE FIRST LEGAL STEPS

A series of laws and statutes were passed with the aim of regulating the question of assistance that would be given to the deported Armenians in their new place of settlement and regarding the use and sale of the property and possessions the Armenians left behind. This legislation would be upheld by the Ottoman government as one of the central proofs that it harbored no aim of annihilating its Armenian population. It was claimed that while there may have been instances of abuse and looting—and these, the government argued, were not within its power to fully prevent—the state had taken measures to protect and preserve Armenian property and possessions, and these losses were compensated in various ways in the areas where the Armenians were settled. The improprieties and illegalities that appeared, they argued, were not the result of conscious government policy, but occurred despite its stated policies, since the government had actually expended all possible effort to prevent them.

In truth, a large number of regulations were passed on this matter, mostly in the form of temporary laws or decrees. The first of these was a decision of the Ottoman Council of Ministers on 31 May 1915 that decreed that possessions and lands would be distributed to the Armenians in their new places of residence in accordance with their previous financial and economic status.[1] Additionally, the state would have dwellings constructed for the homeless, seed would be distributed to farmers, and tools and materials given to artisans; after the value of this abandoned property had been determined, it would be distributed to the Muslim immigrants settled there. A registry of other immovable properties would be kept, wherein the type, value, and quantity of such items would be recorded, after which it, too, would be distributed among Muslim immigrants. The income of those revenue-producing properties, such as lands, shops, factories, bazaars, and warehouses, which were produced through sale by public auction or rent, were to be placed in a trust and given to their Armenian owners. A statute would be prepared for the purpose of carrying out all of these forseeable actions, and commissions were even established in which officials from the Interior and Finance Ministries were to be entrusted with carrying out these statutes in the regions affected.

Among the decisions made by the Council of Ministers on 31 May was the ratification of a fifteen-article statute that would be sent as a separate document to the Interior, Finance, and War Ministries on the following day.[2] In fact, the various sections of this statute were largely a reiteration of the aforementioned legislative decree. Special mention was made in it of the guidelines and principles according to which the Armenians were to be resettled in their new locations, although there were no instructions whatsoever as to what was to be done with the property and possessions left behind, how its value was to be determined, or how the

---

[1] For the full text of the decision, see Genelkurmay Başkanlığı, *Arşiv Belgeleriyle Ermeni Faaliyetleri*, vol. 1, 131–33, 427–31; and Azmi Süslü, *Ermeniler ve 1915*, 111–13. In order to make it more easily understood, my explanation was based on the modernized "Turkish" version of the text found in the publication of the chiefs of staff (*genelkurmay*).

[2] For the full version of the text sent to the other ministries, see Azmi Süslü, *Ermeniler ve 1915*, 115–16. Azmi Süslü says that the decree under discussion was published separately by the Interior Ministry's IAMM (113).

income or revenue from the sale of such property was to be transferred to its original owners should it be sold or given to the new inhabitants of the area.

The first detailed regulation concerning this matter, prepared on 10 June 1915, was composed of a lengthy introduction and thirty-four separate articles.[3] An examination of this legislation produces the following picture: the first ten paragraphs deal with what was to be done with the abandoned Armenian properties. They included the following instructions: a listing of the properties as well as the type, amount, and estimated value of each was to be recorded in registries; it was to be collected and stored in places such as bazaars, churches, and warehouses, and the identity of its owners preserved in a clear fashion; the income accruing from products that would be necessary to sell would be credited to the accounts of its original owners, and all of these would be overseen and administered by the Commission for the Administration of Abandoned Property.

Among all these paragraphs, the tenth one stands out: "In regard to the use of immovable properties belonging to the population that has been deported, no further action shall be taken in regard to the proxy agreements that were written up after the[se properties] were [legally] separated from their owners." In other words, Armenians were forbidden from taking any legal actions to reclaim the properties in the places they had left behind; nor could they concern themselves with properties and possessions for which a trustee had been appointed. They were also not allowed to use, buy, or sell their properties. As will be shown below, any deeds of trust or other transactions performed by the Armenians in regard to the disposal or administration of their property and possessions were in practice considered invalid, whether they occurred before or after their deportation. Those who today tend to characterize the deportation operations as having consisted of nothing more than a relocation of the empire's Armenian inhabitants are hard-pressed to give a reasonable explanation for this situation. What sort of "relocation" is it in which the people subjected

[3] For the full text, titled "Instructions Regarding the Administrative Status of Property, Possessions and Real Estate belonging to the Armenians Transported to Other Regions on Account of Wartime Conditions and Extraordinary Political Exigencies" [Ahval-i Harbiye ve Zaruret-i Fevkalade-i Siyasiye dolayısıyla Mahall-i Ahire Nakilleri İcra Edilen Ermenilere Ait Emval ve Emlak ve Arazinin Keyfiyet-i İdaresi Hakkında Talimatname], see Genelkurmay Başkanlığı, Arşiv Belgeleriyle Ermeni Faaliyetleri, vol. 1, 139–42, 433–38; and Süslü, Ermeniler ve 1915, 117–21.

thereto lose all right of possession and disposal over their own property, even being forcibly prevented by law from reclaiming it?

Paragraphs eleven through twenty-one deal with the issue of resettling Muslim refugees and immigrants in the places vacated by the Armenians. These largely consist of regulations on matters such as the guidelines by which certain people and groups would be settled and where and how land and existing buildings would be distributed to them. They also deal with how lands, possessions, and breakable items that could not be distributed were to be administered, and what to do with cases of natural increase in the value of items and rental fees.

From the twenty-fourth paragraph on, the regulations deal with the authority, jurisdiction, and working conditions, salaries, and other aspects of the Commissions for the Administration of Abandoned Property that were to be set up in the affected regions. One noteworthy paragraph is the twenty-seventh, which entrusts these commissions with delivering a "summary report" of their decisions and actions to a ministerial official of the central government or a provincial governor's office every fifteen days.

There was not a single point in the entire detailed communiqué concerning the manner or mechanism that would be used to deliver monetary or other recompensation for the value of their abandoned possessions and property to the original Armenian owners, or what the regulations and guidelines would be for such transactions. There is only the following statement in paragraph twenty-two: "The amounts obtained from the price of sales and rents will be placed in a secure trust in the names of the owners and subsequently delivered to the owners according to the statutes and regulations that will be announced." However, there is no information about any such instructions ever being created in the following months, nor any regulations whatsoever being enacted in this regard. All such ordinances that were created concerned only the disposal, use, sale, and such of the abandoned properties. The Unionist government never fully took up the question—and certainly did not have a coherent or complete plan for such matters as the relocation of the Armenian population and the problems that arose from this operation.

As will be seen in great detail below, although the Interior Ministry Papers contain literally hundreds of documents concerning questions such as the proper use and disposal of abandoned properties, and describe the problems that might (and did) emerge from the use of such practices and their proper resolution, there are almost no such documents or correspondence concerning the problems involved in the resettlement of Armenians or their compensation for the value of their abandoned property. In a sense, such a question simply did not exist for the Ottoman bureaucracy.

Equally important, no documents or information attest that the detailed operations described and decided upon in the regulations were actually carried out. For instance, although there are instructions to maintain registries containing the type, amount, value, and original owners of possessions and property that the Armenians were forced to leave behind, and that stipulate that the originals of these registries were to be delivered in an approved manner to the government and to the commissions for abandoned property, there is no evidence as to the fate or present location of these records. Moreover, although it was decided that all of the aforementioned commissions were to inform the central or provincial government of their decisions and actions every fifteen days, no information whatsoever is available on whether or not such reports were actually ever created, their eventual fate, or even of correspondence on these matters between the commissions and the government. The fact that nearly a century has passed since this time and not a single shred of evidence of their actual existence and functioning has emerged leaves much room for speculation.

NEW REGULATIONS

On the subject of the administration of abandoned Armenian possessions and property, the correspondence between the center and the periphery was quite frequent. Messages were often exchanged for the purpose of clarifying points on which the local officials were unclear, or solving problems that had emerged during the implementation of these regulations. For example, in a cable sent on 5 July 1915 to a number of provincial destinations on the subject of fields that had already been sown, the Settlement Office stated that "it has been understood that in the areas that have been evacuated by the Armenians, it has not been possible in certain areas to implement certain sections listed in the manual of instructions regarding the disposal and acquisition of sown fields that have been abandoned," and that it would therefore be appropriate "for these to be given from the [lands] allocated to the [Muslim] immigrants, reaped and harvested by the government, under the supervision of the Commissions of Abandoned Property." With this goal in mind, the Settlement Office requested that a report be given "within two days time, along with regular examinations and assessments as to how much labor and what types of machines, tools and supplies are needed, either from the army or from the local population in order to dispense with the aforementioned products."[4]

Another telegram sent on the same day (5 July) to Trebizond Province shows that a special eight-point list of instructions had been prepared "on the administration and preservation of the abandoned properties." These instructions explain individually how abandoned property is to be registered, how the registry books are to be kept, where the movable property is to be stored, to whom the property and perishable possessions are to be given, how immovable properties are to be sold, where the income from such transactions is to be placed, and how it is to be recorded when property and possessions are given to the resettled immigrants.[5]

All of the provinces were notified on 13 July that after the commissions on abandoned property were formed, "these commissions were to be entrusted not only with the functions of monitoring and supervision of the abandoned Armenian properties, but also with taking care of the various details surrounding the settlement of the immigrants and [Kurdish] tribes in the evacuated villages and towns." If necessary, these commissions were to also form subcommissions that would be "responsible for reporting back [on their activities] to a ministerial office every 15 days."[6]

Among the other regulations and ordinances, of particular importance was a telegram sent to Trebizond on 11 July 1915; other cables containing similar content were subsequently sent to other regions.[7] The gist of the

---

[4] BOA/DH.ŞFR, no. 54/301, Coded telegram from the Interior Ministry's IAMM to the Provinces of Sivas, Diyarbekır, and Mamuretülaziz, dated 5 July, 1915.

[5] BOA/DH.ŞFR, no. 54/310, Coded telegram from the Interior Ministry's IAMM to the Province of Trebizond, dated 5 July 1915.

[6] BOA/DH.ŞFR, no. 54/442, Coded telegram from the Interior Ministry's IAMM to the Provinces of Adana, Aleppo, Erzurum, Bitlis, Diyarbekır, Mamuretülaziz, Trebizond, Sivas, Hüdâvendigâr (Bursa), and Edirne; to the Provincial Districts of Marash, Canik, İzmit, Kayseri, Marash, (Der) Zor, and Urfa; and to the Commissions on Abandoned Property in Adana and Aleppo, dated 13 July 1915.

[7] BOA/DH.ŞFR, no. 54/393, Coded telegram from the Interior Ministry's IAMM to the Province of Trebizond, dated 11 July 1915. The original telegram, which was written as a reply to a question from

Trebizond cable is this: All of the deeds and statements of ownership concerning the promissory notes in the hands of the Armenians are to be collected and recorded in registries, and the Armenians are not to be allowed to transfer them via some fictitious arrangement to others. Likewise, no sales of property will be permitted that would allow such properties to pass into the hands of foreigners or others. The cable also adds that all possessions apart from animals and "those likely to be spoiled over time" are to be placed under guard. Here the state is seen openly issuing decrees denying its citizens their right to freely dispense with their property and forcibly appropriating the property belonging to the Armenians.

There are also existing documents that indicate that these regulations and ordinances that were put into effect were not limited to Trebizond. For example, a telegram sent on 28 August 1915 to nearly all provinces and districts requested that "it be hastily reported back within three days whether or not there was property or land sold to foreigners by the Armenians in the province who were deported, from the time that the aforementioned persons' deportation was announced [*mübaşeret*] until eight days ago, or the time of their [actual] deportation. If there was, please report the quantity and location [of such property]."[8]

The government's interest in obtaining this information was evident in another cable sent ten days later on 8 September to Adana Province:

> There was no doubt that, from the date in which the deportation order was announced until their actual deportation took place, those Armenians whom it was decided to deport would engage in all manner

---

the office of the governor of Trebizond on 8 June, reads as follows: "The dates and type of transfer deeds [*senet*] that are to be received in connection with the properties claimed to belong to Armenians sent to the interior are to be already recorded in the registries, as was done during the liquidation of the properties. No pre-arranged [fictitious] exchanges [*danışıklı döğüş*] as a result of these deeds are to be allowed, nor are the properties in the possession of Armenians to be allowed to pass into the hands of foreigners, nor are transactions that are likely to be fictitious exchanges to be approved. Those items among the moveable properties, apart from animals and things that are likely to lose their value or fall into ruin over time, are to be preserved. The claims of banks and commercial institutions are to be preserved and to be exercised after they are confirmed by the courts."

[8] BOA/DH.ŞFR, no. 55/280, Coded telegram from the Interior Ministry's IAMM to the Provinces of Erzurum, Adana, Ankara, Bitlis, Aleppo, Hüdâvendigâr (Bursa), Diyarbekır, Sivas, Trebizond, Mamuretülaziz, Van, and Konya; to the Provincial Districts of Urfa, İzmit, Canik, Karesi (Balıkesir), Kayseri, Karahisâr-ı Sahib (Afyon Karahisar), Marash, Eskişehir, and Niğde; and to the presidents of the Commissions on Abandoned Property in Aleppo, Adana, Sivas, and Trebizond, dated 28 August 1915.

of deception and subterfuge in order to convert the moveable and immoveable properties in their possession to currency. Since such agreements and transactions, the disastrous effects of which are obvious, cannot, of course, be officially recognized, it is necessary not to legally accept those contracts and acquisitions undertaken from the date that the deportation order was first announced until the beginning of the deportation and subsequently.[9]

These documents are of the utmost importance for showing that the Ottoman government did not permit those soon-to-be (deported) Armenians from collecting on promissory notes, selling their possessions, or leaving them in the hands of a third party. Moreover, the categorization of some possessions as "likely to lose value or deteriorate over time" opened the door to a great deal of looting and illicit self-enrichment by local inhabitants and officials. Last, the invalidation of all sales and transfers of Armenian movable and immovable properties undertaken from the initial announcement of the deportation order to its actual execution is an action of central importance. This ordinance, passed on 26 September 1915, would be reiterated when it was subseqeuntly included as one of the most fateful sections of the law on the use of Armenian property.

This action on the part of the state, which effectively prevented its Armenian citizens from disposing of their property and possessions before being deported, reveals much about the actual goals of that deportation. In the end, the government itself would appropriate the lion's share of abandoned Armenian property. Along these lines, when reports began to arrive that the abandoned properties and possessions were being disposed of at very low prices, a general communiqué was sent to the provinces demanding that all such transactions be invalidated and ordering that "no foreigners or suspicious or unknown persons are to be permitted to enter or travel around in the areas [from which the Armenians] are to be evicted, and those who do enter are to be removed immediately."[10]

---

[9] BOA/DH.ŞFR, no. 55-A/171, Coded telegram from the Interior Ministry's IAMM to the Province of Adana, dated 8 September 1915.

[10] BOA/DH.ŞFR, no. 54-A/388, Coded telegram from the Interior Ministry's IAMM to the Provinces of Erzurum, Adana, Ankara, Aydın, Bitlis, Aleppo, Hüdâvendigâr (Bursa), Diyarbekır, Damascus, Sivas, Trebizond, Mamuretülaziz, Mosul, and Van; to the Provincial Districts of Urfa, İzmit,

A clear explanation of the goal of the deportations—namely, the con-fiscation of Armenian property on behalf of the state—can be found in a telegram sent to Sivas on 24 August 1915: "The state has decided to ex-propriate the immovable property and possessions of the deported Arme-nians, and to pay off their [outstanding] debts. Therefore, it is necessary to preserve the rights devolving upon to government and to reconcile [these actions] with the laws on the transfer of property."[11]

Additionally, throughout this period the Ottoman regime felt com-pelled to enact a number of regulations aimed especially at preventing abuses by its own officials. For instance, a message sent on 24 July 1915 to Sivas Province states that "the sale of abandoned property and possessions to [government] officials has been deemed inappropriate, since it will open the door to malicious rumors and abuses."[12] On 3 August a similar cable, stating that the government had received reports of state officials openly participating in public auctions and transferring the auctioned property to their own possession by various means, was sent to all districts and provinces. As a result, state officials would heretofore be forbidden from purchasing abandoned Armenian properties.[13] Special orders were sent to some regions concerning individual government branches and of-fices. For instance, a cable was sent to the president of the Commission on Abandoned Property in Aleppo stating that "the profession[al code] of Justice Ministry officials prevents them from involving themselves in matters concerning abandoned properties."[14] To other regions, however,

---

Canik, Zor, Karesi (Balıkesir), Kayseri, Karahisâr-ı Sahib (Afyon Karahisar), Marash, Eskişehir, and Niğde; and to the presidents of the Commissions on Abandoned Property in Adana, Aleppo, Marash, Diyarbekır, Sivas, Trebizond, Mamuretülaziz, Erzurum, and İzmit, dated 11 August 1915.

[11] BOA/DH.ŞFR, no. 55/196, Coded telegram from the Interior Ministry's IAMM to the Province of Sivas, dated 24 August 1915.

[12] BOA/DH.ŞFR, no. 54/382, Coded telegram from the Interior Ministry's IAMM to the Province of Sivas, dated 24 August 1915.

[13] BOA/DH.ŞFR, no. 55-A/259, Coded telegram from the Interior Ministry's IAMM to the Prov-inces of Adana, Edirne, Erzurum, Bitlis, Diyarbekır, Aleppo, Hüdâvendigâr (Bursa), Sivas, Trebi-zond, Mamuretülaziz, and Van; to the Provincial Districts of İzmit, Canik, Çatalca, Kayseri, Karesi (Balıkesir), Marash, Kale-i Sultaniye (Çanakkale), and (Der) Zor; and to the presidents of the Com-missions on Abandoned Property in Adana, Erzurum, Aleppo, Marash, Trebizond, Canik, Sivas, Mamuretülaziz, and Diyarbekır, dated 3 August 1915.

[14] BOA/DH.ŞFR, no. 54/160, Coded telegram from the Interior Ministry's IAMM to the Presi-dency of the Commission on Abandoned Property, dated 26 June 1915.

permission was given "for government officials to purchase Armenian residences on the condition that payment was made up front."[15]

Apart from the difficulties experienced at the local level, such as looting and appropriation of property, another major problem was the fact that the list of state regulations did not explain how foreign firms—Germany foremost among them—were to collect on claims from their Armenian clients. Germany's various consuls were preoccupied with producing lists that contained their own firms' claims in the provinces in which they were stationed.[16] What they were looking for was a way in which to collect on these claims. Since the very beginning of the deportations, Germany had made several entreaties to the Ottoman government in this regard. On 8 August 1915, for instance, it officially informed the Porte that "it would hold the Ottoman regime responsible for losses it incurred." When these efforts failed to produce the desired results, Berlin filed an official letter of protest on 13 September.[17]

Finally, on 26 September, two days before the opening of the Ottoman Parliament, the Council of Ministers issued a temporary eleven-point law regulating the use of abandoned Armenian property.[18] The entire law dealt with the question of how abandoned property was to be used, without a single direction—or even mention—of how the income from the sale of the deportees' property and possessions should be transferred to the deportees. Perhaps the most important section of the law was (as explained above) the paragraph negating the Armenian deportees' right to dispose of their own property. According to the law, "where a court of

[15] BOA/DH.ŞFR, no. 55/107, Coded telegram from the Interior Ministry's IAMM to the Province of Hüdâvendigâr (Bursa), dated 11 August 1915.

[16] DE/PA-AA/R 14086, Report by German consul in Samsun, Kuckhoff, dated 4 July, appended to a report, dated 16 July 1915, from German ambassador to the Porte, Wangenheim, to Chancellor Bethmann-Hollweg: "According to the governor's account, a commission will be entrusted with ordering commercial matters. I am producing a list of German firms and their claims [from individuals] that have come from the banks and commissionaires. I have received lists from the Ottoman Bank, the Salonica Bank and the Hochstrasser Bank that show the debtors and the amounts of their debts. I spoke with the district governor regarding the measures that are to be taken on this matter."

[17] Hilmar Kaiser, "1915–1916 Ermeni Soykırımı Sırasında Ermeni Mülkleri, Osmanlı Hukuku ve Milliyet Politikaları," in İmparatorluktan Cumhuriyete Türkiye'de Etnik Çatışma, ed. Erik Jan Zürcher (Istanbul: İletişim Yayınları, 2005), 137–38.

[18] The law was published in the 27 September 1915 edition of the Ottoman gazette TV (no. 2303) as "The Temporary Law on the Abandoned Possessions and Properties and Outstanding Debts of Persons Transported to Other Districts" [Âhir Mahallere Nakledilen Eşhâsın Emvâl ve Düyûn ve Matlûbât-ı Metrukesi Hakkında Kanun-ı Muvakkat].

law has confirmed the presence of a fictitious transaction or duplicitous deal in deals involving the surrendering of property within the fifteen-day period preceding the aforementioned persons' deportation, these understandings and agreements are considered void and invalid."

When the Ottoman Parliament opened the following year, the president of the Senate, Ahmed Rıza, leveled harsh criticism at the temporary law and the spirit behind it, calling it "an oppression. Seize me by my arm, throw me out of my village, and then sell my property and possessions: such a thing is never allowable or proper. Neither the law, nor the conscience of the Ottomans can accept this."[19] Nevertheless, all of the senator's efforts to have the law repealed and its implementation halted came to naught. Furthermore, despite the fact that the temporary law was sent to the parliamentary commission for review, it would never be debated in Parliament itself.

In a report to Washington, Ambassador Morgenthau provides an interesting detail regarding the debates and discussions in the Ottoman Parliament. According to the ambassador, Talat Pasha placed enormous pressure on Ahmed Rıza to abandon his efforts, and when the senator continued to maintain a position sympathetic to the Armenians, the interior minister threatened to take even harsher measures against them. Morgenthau reports on this issue in the following manner: "From other sources it is stated that the Cabinet promised to modify their attitude towards the Armenians if Ahmed Rıza and his friends would agree not to interpellate the Government. This Ahmed Rıza and his friends did."[20]

One further decree that must be mentioned here was issued on 8 November 1915 in connection with the law of 26 September. This decree explains in a very detailed fashion how the points raised in the law were going to be realized. What is important is that the law of 26 September and the 8 November decree created the legal basis for the government later, in the republican period, to control and distribute Armenian properties, and they remained in effect for many years.[21]

[19] For the Ottoman Parliament's discussion and debates on this matter, see Bayur, *Türk İnkılabı Tarihi*, vol. 3, part 3 (Ankara: Türk Tarih Kurumu, 1983), 48.

[20] NA/RG 59, 867.00/797.5, Report marked "Private and Strictly Confidential," from Ambassador to the Porte Morgenthau to Secretary of State Lansing, dated 4 November 1915, in *United States Official Records*, ed. Sarafian, 317. For more on the subject, see Dadrian, "Genocide as a Problem," 267–69.

[21] *TV*, 8 November 1915, no. 2343.

WERE THE ARMENIANS RECOMPENSED FOR THEIR PROPERTY AND POSSESSIONS?

The laws and regulations passed on 30 May, 10 June, and 26 September 1915 that are summarized above are often presented as the strongest evidence for the argument that the Ottoman government had no intention of destroying the Armenians.[22] But as the correspondence between the Ottoman government and the periphery and the orders sent out by the former clearly attest, the government's principal aim was to confiscate the property and possessions left behind by the Armenian deportees and thus cause the material destruction of the Armenian community. Upon the adoption of the temporary law of 26 September, Anatolian Railroad Company director Arthur Gwinner, who was in Berlin at the time, submitted a French translation of the law to the German Foreign Ministry. Apparently unaware of the Ottoman government's 24 August cable to Sivas (mentioned earlier in footnote 11), Gwinner, with more than a hint of derision, summed up the new law thus: "[The law] can be described simply and clearly in two paragraphs. Paragraph 1—Armenian property is to be appropriated; Paragraph 2—The [Ottoman] Government is to possess the property of those who have been deported and will or will not pay [their] debts."[23] Basing themselves on the reports and opinions of businessmen in Istanbul, the legal experts at the German Embassy (which conducted a legal analysis of the aforementioned law) described the legislation as "a legalization of pillaging," a description that was not far from the truth.[24]

The foreign diplomats who witnessed the manner in which this looting was carried out in the provinces sent their respective capitals a virtual torrent of reports that contained eyewitness testimonies and factual information on the events taking place.[25] The connecting thread of many of these reports is well expressed by J. B. Jackson, the American consul

[22] Halaçoğlu, *Ermeni Tehciri ve Gerçekler*, 68–69; Süslü, *Ermeniler ve 1915*, 109–22.

[23] DE/PA-AA/R 14088, Letter from Anatolian Railways Company director Arthur Gwinner to the German Foreign Ministry, dated 7 October 1915.

[24] Hilmar Kaiser, "1915–1916 Ermeni Soykırımı Sırasında Ermeni Mülkleri," 141.

[25] For a detailed discussion of this subject, see Gust, *Völkermord an den Armeniern*, 44–50; Taner Akçam, *A Shameful Act*, 272–74; Hilmar Kaiser, ibid., 141.

in Aleppo, who witnessed the events in the region. He summarized the events as "a gigantic plundering scheme as well as a final blow to extinguish the race."[26]

But what I will attempt to answer here is not how the various measures were enacted or carried out, or even how the abandoned Armenian properties were looted, but these more central questions: What does the existing Ottoman documentation say concerning the measures enacted in regard to the Armenians in their areas of resettlment? What manner of correspondence—mentioned in the 31 May 1915 regulations—is there on the question of giving away or transferring compensatory lands, houses, and other possessions to resettled Armenians? What documents and papers are available concerning the financial or material reimbursements of the Armenian deportees for the property and possessions they left behind and for the problems that inevitably arose when conducting such transactions?

In researching these very questions in the Ottoman archives, up until now no researcher has been able to find a single document of substance regarding the questions of resettlement, the distribution of land or habitations to Armenians at their new areas of resettlement, or the delivering of compensation to said Armenians for the property they were forced to leave behind. But as will be shown below regarding the various governmental actions taken in order to facilitate the resettling of Muslim immigrants, there are numerous documents in existence concerning the dispatch of inspectors to the relevant provinces, how they were to deal with the problems of resettlement, and the measures that were taken by the Ottoman regime on the basis of the inspectors' reports. On this subject a special communiqué containing sixteen separate points in all provided ample instructions as to how the health, food, clothing, rehabilitation, and other immigrants' needs were to be provided for, and listed the conditions that must be met in order to do so.[27]

For the Muslim immigrants in Bafra (Samsun Province) alone, there are at least four or five documents dealing with the various problems

[26] NA/RG 59, 867.4016/148, Report from Aleppo consul, Jesse B. Jackson, to Ambassador Henry Morgenthau, dated 19 August 1915, in *United States Official Records*, ed. Sarafian, 207.

[27] BOA/DH.ŞFR, no. 62/100–101, Coded telegram from the Statistics Branch of the Interior Ministry's IAMM to the Province of Mosul, dated 23 March 1917.

encountered during their resettlement. For example, a cable sent to the district governor of Canik (Samsun) on 25 December 1916 stated that "several abuses in the distribution of daily stipends and supplies to the immigrants in the province were reported by Hilmi Bey, the official responsible for export shipping who is located in Terme, during the course of his overseeing of events." It demanded that "the necessary investigations be immediately [undertaken] in regard to this important matter," and that the problem be resolved.[28]

Another cable to Canik, sent on 30 January 1917, informed the district officials that it had been learned from the inspectors dispatched to the region that "the [Muslim] immigrants and refugees in Bafra were not only settled in a poor manner by not being properly given homes, lands and seeds, but in addition, immigrants who were already resettled were removed from their homes." The Directorate of Tribal and Immigrant Affairs demanded that "the affairs of the immigrants and refugees in Bafra be ordered and corrected, and an end be put to the endless [stream of] complaints from Bafra."[29]

However, one would search in vain for similar cables on the issue of settling the deported Armenians. Again, there does not appear to have been any serious consideration in the minds of the Unionist leaders in regard to the resettlement policies for the Armenians, the transfer of compensation for their abandoned property, or the problems that would arise as a result of this process. And this is the main reason that it is not possible to find a single document dealing with this subject. This reality alone is sufficient to show the real goal of the deportation policies.

In one work penned with the aim of defending the official version of Turkish history, Yusuf Halaçoğlu claims that "the money obtained from the sale of [abandoned] properties was sent to the [respective property] owners by the Commissions on Abandoned Property. Similarly, the [Armenian] deportees who arrived at the areas of resettlement established businesses with the money transferred to them and thereby were able to adapt to their new environment."[30] This thesis stands in direct opposition

---

[28] BOA/DH.ŞFR, no. 71/70, Coded telegram from the Interior Ministry's General Directorate of Tribal and Immigrant Affairs to the Provincial District of Canik, dated 25 December 1915.

[29] BOA/DH.ŞFR, no. 72/124, Coded telegram from the Interior Ministry's General Directorate of Tribal and Immigrant Affairs to the Provincial District of Canik, dated 30 January 1917.

[30] Yusuf Halaçoğlu, *Ermeni Tehciri ve Gerçekler*, 69.

to the argument being forwarded here, and should thus be examined at greater length.

As proof of his claims, Halaçoğlu cites three separate documents, all telegrams. What is interesting here is that he neither quotes them nor even explains the contents of any of these cables, even briefly. If he had done so, the following information would have emerged: All three documents concern one specific event, and all three were sent on the same day to three separate destinations. Above all, none of the cables have anything to do with the question of returning any compensation for the sale of property and possessions left behind to Armenians.

According to its archival numeration, the first cable, identified as number 50/348, was sent by the IAMM to the director of the same office, Kaya, who was in Aleppo at the time. In the cable, the IAMM informed him that "six hundred thousand kurush from the amount of the proceeds from [the sale of] abandoned properties in Aleppo along with another two hundred thousand kurush from the proceeds will be sent from Eskişehir and can be expended on the provisioning and deportation of the Armenians."[31] The second telegram, numbered 50/349, was sent to the acting governor of Aleppo and informs him that the money will arrive from Eskişehir and that he is "authorized to spend [this money] on the provisioning and deportation of the Armenians."[32] The third cable was sent to the district governor of Eskişehir and requests that the aforementioned funds be sent to the Registrar's Office in Aleppo.[33]

As can be seen, all three messages refer to the same event: the provincial governor of Eskişehir is being asked to send certain amounts resulting from the sale of abandoned Armenian property to Aleppo Province to cover the expenses incurred during the course of the Armenian deportations. From another cable sent on the same day to Aleppo—and one that Yusuf Halaçoğlu does not mention—it is also clear that all this money was to be used to cover the government's expenses: "the province has been notified that it is appropriate that 600,000 of the 645,000 kurush reported

[31] BOA/ŞFR.DH, no. 57/348, Coded telegram from the Interior Ministry's IAMM to the director of Immigrant Affairs (Muhacirin Müdürü) in Aleppo, Kaya, dated 8 November 1915.

[32] BOA/ŞFR.DH, no. 57/349, Coded telegram from the Interior Ministry's IAMM to the acting governor of Aleppo, dated 8 November 1915.

[33] BOA/ŞFR.DH, no. 57/350, Coded telegram from the Interior Ministry's IAMM to the Provincial District of Eskişehir, dated 8 November 1915.

in your cable [to have been gained] from the sale of the animals from the abandoned [Armenian] propety be expended for the costs of the deportation and provisioning of the Armenians."[34]

It is telling in the extreme that a person who serves as director general of the Ottoman archives, who has the opportunity to access every single document and paper contained therein, cannot locate a single document actually showing a specific case of Armenians being recompensed in their places of resettlement for the property and possessions left behind, and that the only sources he uses to justify his argument are several documents without any connection to the subject at hand.

In conclusion, what is promised in the various Ottoman laws and regulations from the period—namely, the supplying of land, houses, seeds, supplies, and other means of subsistence to deported Armenians—finds no confirmation in the Ottoman documentation of ever having been fulfilled.

HOW WERE THE REVENUES FROM THE SALE OF ARMENIAN PROPERTY ULTIMATELY USED?

Although no documentation has been found in the Ottoman archives that deals with actual cases of deported Armenians being recompensed for their abandoned property, a great number of documents deal with the disposal of the property itself, including the people to whom it should be given, how it is to be liquidated, and how the proceeds are to be used. The reality on display in these documents is this: in regard to the use of abandoned Armenian property, the Ottoman leadership of the time pursued a preplanned and thoroughly systematic policy—regardless of how successful this policy ultimately was in the face of widespread local corruption. The Unionist regime exploited these properties and funds so thoroughly that, in the end, nothing remained that could be given to the Armenians. These possessions and the revenues from their sale were used for six primary purposes: (1) the needs of Muslim immigrants; (2) the creation of a Muslim bourgeoisie; (3) the needs of the army; (4) the government's expenses for the deportations; (5) various government needs; and (6) the needs of militia

---

[34] BOA/DH.ŞFR, no. 57/342, Coded telegram from the Interior Ministry's IAMM to the presidency of the Commission for the Administration of Abandoned Property in Aleppo, dated 8 November 1915.

organizations. If we look more closely at these points, we can understand why what was happening was an organized state plunder of Armenian properties, and why there was nothing left to give to the Armenians.

THE NEEDS OF MUSLIM IMMIGRANTS

As was mentioned earlier on the origins of the government's deportation and resettlement policies, the removal of the Armenian population and re-settlement of Muslims in their place had been decided on long before these policies were put into effect. According to several documents, the decision on where to settle which Muslim immigrants and refugees had been de-cided even before the Armenians were cleared out. As a result, once the Armenian deportations took place, the actual resettlement of Muslims was able to begin almost immediately, and it was only natural for the aban-doned lands, property, and possessions of the Armenians to be given to the new arrivals. The manner in which this redistribution was to take place was organized in ordinances issued on 30 May and 15 June 1915.

Among the surviving papers of the Interior Minister's Cipher Office are literally hundreds of cables that were sent to the provinces regarding the resettlement of Muslim immigrants and refugees in abandoned Armenian homes and the division of the latter's possessions among the newcomers. For example, a telegram sent to Aleppo, Urfa, and Marash on 26 February 1916, marked "to be kept secret," contained this passage:

> One portion of the refugees who have fled from the war zones to Diyarbekır shall be sent off to Ayıntab [Antep], Marash and Urfa and settled there. Just as the abandoned [Armenian] houses will be used by the refugees in this manner, after the value has been esti-mated of abandoned property necessary for the provisioning and clothing of the refugees, the immigrants' share of the allocation is also to be calculated and can be delivered over to them as well. The Commissions on the Liquidation [of Abandoned Property] have been sent a written account of this state of affairs.[35]

---

[35] BOA/DH.ŞFR, no. 61/117, Coded telegram from the Interior Ministry's General Directorate of Tribal and Immigrant Affairs to the Province of Aleppo, and to the Provincial Districts of Urfa and Marash, dated 26 February 1916.

On the same day an identical order was sent by cable to Trebizond, again with the notice "to be kept secret"; the only difference was that the name "Diyarbekır" was replaced by "Sivas, Canik, and Çorum," whence the Muslim immigrants "were to be sent to the neighboring provinces and provincial districts and settled there."[36]

In similar fashion, the provincial governor of Bitlis is specially informed that he must exploit "the existing supplies, clothing and other items found among the abandoned property" for the clothing and other needs of the new Muslim arrivals.[37] For this purpose special cables were also sent to the Liquidation Commissions of Abandoned Properties. A cable sent to various provinces on 4 March 1916 demanded "the distribution of both processed and non-processed materials in the depots and warehouses of abandoned property to those in need in order to cloth the refugees in the province."[38] In another cable sent to several provinces and districts, the Office of Tribal and Immigrant Resettlement requested that "those helpless persons who are without anyone [to help them] and who have fled the war zones . . . as well as those who are in need" be settled "in those houses from among the abandoned properties" and that, in addition to "the procuring of possessions and provisions [for them] from among the [aforementioned] abandoned property . . . an attempt is to be made by the regional governments and municipalities to find work for these persons and to ensure that every avenue is exploited for their advantage . . . so that they may be able to provide [for them] a daily wage."[39]

The Muslim immigrants had the first right to refuse the acquisition and use of the abandoned Armenian property. Wherever these rules and practices were either not followed or consciously abandoned, the local authorities received a warning from the central government. For instance, a June

[36] BOA/DH.ŞFR, no. 61/122, Coded telegram from the Interior Ministry's IAMM to the Province of Trebizond, dated 26 February 1916.

[37] BOA/DH.ŞFR, no. 61/120, Coded telegram from the Interior Ministry's IAMM to the Province of Bitlis, dated 26 February 1916.

[38] BOA/DH.ŞFR, no. 61/247, Coded telegram from the Interior Ministry's IAMM to the Trebizond Liquidation Commission, dated 4 March 1916.

[39] BOA/DH.ŞFR, no. 63/261, Coded telegram from the Interior Ministry's IAMM to the Provinces of Ankara, Adana, Aleppo, Hüdâvendigâr (Bursa), Diyarbekır, Kastamonu, Mamuretülaziz, Sivas, and Trebizond, and to the Provincial Districts of İzmit, Eskişehir, Urfa, Canik, Karesi (Balıkesir), Kayseri, and Niğde, dated 10 May 1916.

1916 cable to almost all regions of the empire demands the "preferential allocation of those empty houses that are found among the abandoned properties to the refugees who fled the war zones."[40]

Orders were sent out instructing local officials that in certain cases, wherein abandoned Armenian properties had been purchased or rented at low prices by local notables or government officials, these houses were to be immediately repossessed and given to the immigrants:

> It has been learned from the content of reports arriving from certain provinces that abandoned residences have been occupied by the locals—and in particular by [local] notables and certain government officials—with the aim of purchasing and[/or] renting them cheaply. Since it is absolutely unacceptable for residences like these to be given to the influential persons and notables [within these communities] when there are so many refugees and immigrants that are in need and worthy of such protection and assistance, it is to be announced that all possible residences are to be immediately evacuated and allocated to immigrants and refugees, and in complete disregard of any resistance or opposition [that might be encountered from these people].[41]

In the face of continued house acquisitions by locals, a more harshly worded reiteration of the earlier order was sent to the provinces in October 1916, informing local officials that "those abandoned residences that have been occupied by government officials and the local population are to be immediately evacuated and turned over to immigrants and refugees and without regard to any obstacles or requests [posed by the locals],"

[40] BOA/ŞFR, no. 65/36, Coded telegram from the Interior Ministry's IAMM to the Provinces of Erzurum, Aydın, Bitlis, Beirut, Damascus, Konya, Mosul, and Van, and to the Provincial Districts of İçel, Bolu, Teke, Cebel-i Lübnan, (Der) Zor, Kale-i Sultaniye (Çanakkale), Karahisâr-ı Sahib (Afyon Karahisar), Kütahya, Menteşe, Marash, dated 16 June 1916. A similar cable was also sent on the same day to the Provinces of Ankara, Adana, Aleppo, Hüdâvendigâr (Bursa), Diyarbekır, Kastamonu, Mamuretülaziz, Sivas, and Trebizond, and to the Provincial Districts of İzmit, Eskişehir, Urfa, Canik, Karesi (Balıkesir), Niğde, and Kayseri, dated 19 June 1916. See BOA/DH.ŞFR, no. 65/37.

[41] BOA/DH.ŞFR, no. 68/155, Coded telegram from the Interior Ministry's General Directorate of Tribal and Immigrant Affairs to the Provinces of Ankara, Adana, Aleppo, Hüdâvendigâr (Bursa), Diyarbekır, Sivas, Trebizond, Kastamonu, Mamuretülaziz, Erzurum, Aydın, Bitlis, Beirut, Damascus, Konya, Mosul, and Van, and to the Provincial Districts of Urfa, İzmit, Eskişehir, Canik, Karesi (Balıkesir), Kayseri, Niğde, İçel, Bolu, Teke, Cebel-i Lübnan, (Der) Zor, Kale-i Sultaniye (Çanakkale), Karahisâr-ı Sahib (Afyon Karahisar), Kütahya, Menteşe, and Marash, dated 3 October 1916.

adding that "the instructions on this matter are not to be repeated; please report the results [of these efforts]."[42]

In certain regions, the abandoned houses were rented out to the new-comers, but when it was learned that some of those refugees or immigrants who could not or would not pay rent had been evicted, another general order was sent to all the provinces ordering an immediate end to such evictions. A cable from 1 September 1917, for instance, announced that

> it has been learned . . . [that rent has been demanded] from the refugees and immigrants who have settled in the abandoned prop-erties [and] that it has been ordered that those not paying were to be tossed out and the houses evacuated. . . . [it is ordered that] the abandoned properties that have been given to refugees and immi-grants are not to be evacuated . . . immovable properties must be allocated to immigrants and refugees and, to the extent possible, not sold, and immigrants and refugees must not be evicted from their houses.[43]

As mentioned above, some Muslim groups were removed for what were essentially political reasons, especially from certain regions controlled by Cemal Pasha as commander of the Fourth Army. From some documents it can be understood that special directives had been issued in regard to the resettlement and housing of these groups. A message marked "urgent," and sent to the relevant provinces on 13 April 1916, demanded that "great care is to be taken that those families sent off by the Fourth Army Command should have no reason for complaint or discomfort whatsoever," and that "they are to be immediately housed in those houses from among the aban-doned properties that are suitable and in accordance with their former economic and social standing, and that they be well cared for through the

[42] BOA/DH.ŞFR, no. 69/148, Coded telegram from the Interior Ministry's General Directorate of Tribal and Immigrant Affairs to the Provinces of Ankara, Sivas, Diyarbekır, Mamuretülaziz, Adana, Konya, and Aleppo, and to the Provincial Districts of Niğde, Kayseri, Urfa, Marash, and Eskişehir, dated 14 October 1916.

[43] BOA/DH.ŞFR, no. 79/172, Coded telegram from the Interior Ministry's General Directorate of Tribal and Immigrant Affairs to the Provinces of Adana, Ankara, Aydın, Bitlis, Aleppo, Hüdâvendigâr (Bursa), Diyarbekır, Konya, Mosul, and Kastamonu, and to the Provincial Districts of Urfa, İzmit, Bolu, Canik, (Der) Zor, Karasi, Menteşe, Kayseri, Teke, Karahisâr-ı Sahib (Afyon Karahisar), İçel, Kütahya, Eskişehir, Marash, and Niğde, dated 1 September 1917.

acquisition and supply of [various] various necessities."[44] Cemal Pasha was also informed of the situation and of recent events that had transpired by means of a detailed report that was delivered to him that day and marked "private."[45] Soon thereafter (26 April), the Directorate of Tribal and Immigrant Affairs prepared and sent a special fourteen-point list of instructions "concerning the manner in which those families removed from the Fourth Army's area of jurisdiction are to be settled and provisioned" to the affected provinces.[46]

THE CREATION OF A MUSLIM BOURGEOISIE

The property and possessions left by the Armenians were distributed to Muslim individuals or institutions—sometimes for free, others for very low prices or at low payment installments—all with the goal of creating a "Muslim bourgeoisie." Accordingly, as seen in the relevant sections above, detailed lists were compiled of businesses and/or commercial enterprises that belonged to Istanbul Armenians or foreigners or that were run by Armenians who had been deported or had Armenians on their boards of directors.[47]

The Ottoman Interior Ministry sent numerous telegraphic messages to provinces concerning the process of transferring abandoned Armenian lands, property, and businesses to Muslim firms. The purpose of many of these communications was either to clarify the general lines along which

[44] BOA/DH.ŞFR, no. 62/307, Coded telegram from the Interior Ministry's General Directorate of Tribal and Immigrant Affairs to the Provinces and Provincial Districts of Kütahya, Yozgat, Ankara, Çorum, Sivas, Amasya, Tokat, Konya, Isparta, Bolu, Kastamonu, and Hüdâvendigâr (Bursa), dated 13 April 1916.

[45] BOA/DH.ŞFR, no. 62/308, Coded telegram from the Interior Ministry's IAMM to Minister of the Navy and Fourth Army commander Cemal Pasha, dated 13 April 1916.

[46] BOA/DH.ŞFR, no. 63/123, Coded telegram from the Interior Ministry's General Directorate of Tribal and Immigrant Affairs to the Provinces and Provincial Districts of Kütahya, Yozgat, Ankara, Çorum, Sivas, Amasya, Tokat, Konya, Ertuğrul, Isparta, Bolu, Kastamonu, and Hüdâvendigâr (Bursa), dated 26 April 1916.

[47] BOA/DH.ŞFR, no. 57/24, Coded telegram from the Interior Ministry's IAMM to the Provinces of Adana, Erzurum, Bitlis, Aleppo, Marash, Hüdâvendigâr (Bursa), Diyarbekır, Sivas, Trebizond, Canik, Mamuretülaziz, and Konya, and to the chairmen of the Commissions on Abandoned Property of the Provincial Districts of İzmit, Eskişehir, Niğde, Kayseri, and Karahisâr-ı Sahib (Afyon Karahisar), dated 1 November 1915.

this practice was to be carried out or to resolve the various problems that arose during the course of the individual transfers.

An extremely important document in this regard is the cable sent personally by Talat Pasha to all the provincial commissions on abandoned property on 6 January 1916, which showed the general lines and guiding principles of the government's policy on this matter. In it, the interior minister openly declared that one of the aims in utilizing the abandoned Armenian property was "to multiply the number of Muslim enterprises in our country," and in accordance with this objective "companies [are to be] formed that are composed of Muslims." He directed that the abandoned Armenian "moveable properties are to be handed over to them [Muslims] with the appropriate stipulations and conditions." Specifically, Talat mentioned that "for the sake of the future [of those companies that will be formed] care be taken that the founders, boards of directors and representatives be selected from among the well-respected and powerful members [of their respective communities]." Special attention was to be given "to ensure that capital didn't pass into foreigner hands so in order to pave the way for greater acquisition of the new companies by Muslim notables, shares were issued in small par value sums." Furthermore, local authorities were requested to show "attention to the development of commercial life among the Muslim population," that "effort [be displayed] in this regard, and that information [be given] consistently to the ministry about the results of these actions and transactions."[48]

The ultimate objective, however, was not simply the transfer of Armenian property to existing Muslim companies; rather, the matter was approached as a vast social project aimed at fostering and expanding commercial activity and participation among the empire's Muslim population. A cable sent for this purpose to nearly all Ottoman provinces on 16 February 1916 emphasized this point, while again reiterating that the goal of

[48] BOA/DH.ŞFR, no. 59/239, Coded telegram from the Interior Ministry's IAMM to the Provinces of Erzurum, Adana, Ankara, Bitlis, Aleppo, Hüdâvendigâr (Bursa), Diyarbekır, Sivas, Trebizond, Mamuretülaziz, Konya, and Edirne; to the Provincial Districts of Urfa, İzmit, Canik, Karesi (Balıkesir), Kayseri, Karahisâr-ı Sahib (Afyon Karahisar), Eskişehir, Niğde, Kütahya, and Marash; and to the chairmen of the Commissions on the Liquidation of (Abandoned Property) in Tekfurdağı, Adana, Cebel-i Bereket, Kozan, Yozgat, Ankara, Erzurum, Bitlis, Aleppo, Marash, Antakya, Hüdâvendigâr (Bursa), Gemlik, Bilecik, Diyarbekır, Sivas, Merzifon, Tokat, Samsun, Ordu, Trebizond, Konya, Mamuretülaziz, İzmit, Adapazarı, Eskişehir, Sivrihisâr, Kayseri, Develü, Niğde, Karahisâr-ı Sahib (Afyon Karahisar), and Urfa, 6 January 1916.

the operation was "the accustoming of Muslims to commercial life and the increasing of the number of Muslim commercial enterprises." Despite this goal, the cable stated that in many regions, reports had been received of Armenian properties simply being turned over wholesale to existing Muslim firms without any attempt to encourage the rest of the Muslim population to participate in the public auctions and thereby expand its holdings. The cable stressed that such actions were wrong. In addition, information had been received that "the items purchased by a majority of these firms had been then sold to others at several times their [original purchase] price, and that [the owners of these companies] had thereby quickly grown rich." As a result of such reports, the cable reiterated the demand that such practices be halted and the Muslim population be encouraged to establish commercial enterprises themselves, and that, in line with this aim, they be afforded full assistance and protection.[49]

These instructions were repeated in another cable that was sent to nearly all Ottoman provinces on 16 May 1916:

It was previously communicated that, in order that those [commercial] establishments left by the Armenians, such as factories, shops and mills, not be left empty and unused, they [the establishments] were to be turned over, under the appropriate conditions, to Muslim companies, and all manner of facilitation and assistance be afforded for this purpose. It is suggested that they be rented or sold to Muslim applicants at low prices and that they be shown the necessary assistance [for this to happen].[50]

Since the aim of all this was "the wholesale transfer of productive and commercial establishments to Muslims," it was ordered that "shops and warehouses not be sold off in an arbitrary and desultory manner, that a down payment of an acceptable portion of their value be given [for their

[49] BOA/DH.ŞFR, no. 61/31, Coded telegram from the Interior Ministry's IAMM to the Provinces of Aleppo, Adana, Mosul, and Diyarbekır, and to the Provincial Districts of Urfa and (Der) Zor, dated 16 February 1915.

[50] BOA/DH.ŞFR, no. 64/39, Coded telegram from the Interior Ministry's IAMM to the Provinces of Edirne, Adana, Ankara, Erzurum, Bitlis, Aleppo, Hüdâvendigâr (Bursa), Diyarbekır, Sivas, Trebizond, Mamuretülaziz and Konya; to the Provincial Districts of İzmit, Eskişehir, Niğde, Karahisâr-ı Sahib (Afyon Karahisar), Kayseri, Urfa, Marash, Karesi (Balıkesir), and Canik; and to the chairmen of the Commissions on Liquidation (of Abandoned Property), dated 16 May 1916.

purchase] and that they be put in the hands of honorable youth who are enthusiastic about commerce, when the latter are able to come up with a reliable security [for these properties]."[51] Another method that was followed in some instances was the renting out of such economic enterprises to Muslim companies at very low prices.[52]

Economic transfer operations such as these were actually first begun during the operations to expel the Greek population from the empire's Aegean coastal areas. Only later, during the deportation operations, was the policy applied to the Armenians and their property. A cable sent to the Aegean province of Aydın on 19 November 1914, which proposed that abandoned Greek properties be handed over to the Anatolia Cotton Company, can be given as an example of the earlier use of this policy.[53] Interestingly, a message sent to Adana during the period of the Armenian deportations (16 September 1915) proposes the handing over of certain lands and properties left by the Armenians to the same firm.[54]

THE NEEDS OF THE ARMY

One of the most significant beneficiaries of the abandoned Armenian property was the military, which used it where necessary to meet its own material needs—needs that increased exponentially as the war dragged on. The two main avenues of exploitation were the appropriation of abandoned edifices and structures for military use and the army's receipt of revenues from the sale of the produce of fields, vineyards, and gardens.

[51] BOA/DH.ŞRF, no. 60/129, Coded telegram from the Interior Ministry's IAMM to the chairman of the Commission on Liquidation (of Abandoned Property) in Trebizond, dated 26 December 1915. Another cable containing similar content would be subsequently sent to many other regions. See the cable sent to the Ordu Liquidation Commission Chair, BOA/DH.ŞRF, no. 60/277.

[52] BOA/DH.ŞFR, no. 64/39, Coded telegram from the Interior Ministry's IAMM to the Provinces of Edirne, Adana, Ankara, Erzurum, Bitlis, Aleppo, Hüdâvendigâr (Bursa), Diyarbekır, Sivas, Trebizond, Mamuretülaziz, and Konya; to the Provincial Districts of İzmit, Eskişehir, Niğde, Karahisâr-ı Sahib (Afyon Karahisar), Kayseri, Urfa, Marash, Karesi (Balıkesir), and Canik; and to the presidents of the Liquidation Commissions (for Abandoned Property), dated 16 May 1916.

[53] BOA/DH.ŞFR, no. 47/87, Coded telegram from the Private Secretariat of the Interior Ministry to the Province of Aydın, dated 19 November 1915.

[54] BOA/DH.ŞFR, no. 56/50, Coded telegram from interior minister Talat to the Province of Adana, dated 16 September 1915. In the Ottoman statistics for industry for the years 1913–15, no documentary reference to "Anatolia Cotton Company" has been found. There exists the possibility that it was actually a Unionist "shell company" of sorts.

Military need was the main impetus for issuing the prohibition on the sale of certain items of abandoned Armenian property. A general directive sent to many of the provinces on 13 August 1915 made this clear, even listing the various items needed by the military that were not to be sold:

> [U]pon receiving reports that various items that are of particular military necessity and that the Armenians were not able to take with them, such as shoes, scarves, shoe leather, rawhide sandals, roan and the like, are being sold for next to nothing, it is ordered that after these and similar items, which are the most urgently needed by the military units, have been thoroughly compiled in special lists or tables with their corresponding values or purchase prices and receipts issued, they are to be sent to Istanbul for the purpose of general supplies and provisions.[55]

This general directive was also sent separately to the provinces and districts within the military jurisdiction of the Third and Fourth Armies, and the local authorities were instructed to pass on the notebooks they compiled of the aforementioned items to their respective army commanders.[56]

Similar telegrams were dispatched by the Interior Ministry to a great many provinces and ordered the compiling of lists of items readily available from among the abandoned Armenian possessions and property, such as dry goods, pulses, and grains that could be used for the military's needs, and for these things to be delivered to those local officials in charge of army commissaries and silos. A list or bill of such goods would have to be compiled and submitted to the army should it so demand.[57] Due to the important nature of the matter, the Ministry of War directly informed the local officials and advisories on proper procedure for the Liquidation

---

[55] BOA/DH.ŞFR, no. 54-A/390, Coded telegram from the Interior Ministry's IAMM to the Provinces of Adana and Ankara, and to the Provincial Districts of İzmit, Eskişehir, Karesi (Balıkesir), and Karahisâr-ı Sahib (Afyon Karahisar), dated 13 August 1915. It is unclear from the wording of the telegram whether it is the lists or the actual items listed—or both—that are to be sent to Istanbul.

[56] BOA/DH.ŞFR, no. 54-A/390-1, Coded telegram from the Interior Ministry's IAMM to the Provinces of Erzurum, Bitlis, Trebizond, Sivas, Aleppo, Diyarbekır, and Mamuretülaziz, and to the Provincial Districts of Marash and Urfa, dated 13 August 1915.

[57] BOA/DH.ŞFR, no. 55/210, Coded telegram from the Interior Ministry's IAMM to Erzurum, Adana, Ankara, Bitlis, Aleppo, Hüdâvendigâr (Bursa), Diyarbekır, Sivas, Trebizond, Mamuretülaziz, and Van, and to the Provincial Districts of Urfa, İzmit, Canik, Karesi (Balıkesir), Kayseri, Karahisâr-ı Sahib (Afyon Karahisar), Marash, Eskişehir, and Niğde, dated 25 August 1915.

Commissions that were formed. For example, a cable sent by Enver Pasha on 9 September 1915 contained the following statement:

> It is reiterated here that, in order to prevent these items from passing into [private] hands and to cover any remaining needs of the army, those provisions and such that are among those items and possessions left by the relocating Armenians and that are needed by the army, after their prices have been estimated by the the Commissions on Military Levies, are to be purchased in accordance with the special law and that the type and amount of provisions purchased are step by step [gradually] to be reported as the transactions are made.[58]

The fourth paragraph of the 6 January 1916 regulation (mentioned earlier in the paragraphs concerning the creation of a Muslim bourgeoisie) was devoted to this subject. The relevant passage requests that "among the perishable items and animals that are among the abandoned possessions and property, those things that are of military necessity" are to be given "in exchange for a special receipt."[59]

Apart from the reiteration of general principles, correspondence was also conducted with many individual regions, and instructions were given on how such material could be and should be transferred to the military's jurisdiction. One of the subjects frequently discussed in these communications was the question of how the abandoned Armenian fields were to be harvested. One such message instructed that the government was to carry out the harvest and then deliver the proceeds to the military:

[58] BOA/DH.ŞFR, no. 55/A-143, Coded telegram from Enver Pasha, via the Cipher Office of the War Ministry's Secretariat, to the Provincial District of Kütahya, dated 9 September 1915.

[59] BOA/DH.ŞFR, no. 59/239, Coded telegram from the Interior Ministry's IAMM to the Provinces of Erzurum, Adana, Ankara, Bitlis, Aleppo, Hüdâvendigâr (Bursa), Diyarbekır, Sivas, Trebizond, Mamuretülaziz, Konya, and Edirne; to the Provincial Districts of Urfa, İzmit, Canik, Karesi (Balıkesir), Kayseri, Karahisâr-ı Sahib (Afyon Karahisar), Eskişehir, Niğde, Kütahya, and Marash; and to the chairmen of the Commissions on the Liquidation of (Abandoned Property) in Tekfurdağı, Adana, Cebel-i Bereket, Kozan, Yozgat, Ankara, Erzurum, Bitlis, Aleppo, Marash, Antakya, Hüdâvendigâr (Bursa), Gemlik, Bilecik, Diyarbekır, Sivas, Merzifon, Tokat, Samsun, Ordu, Trebizond, Konya, Mamuretülaziz, İzmit, Adapazarı, Eskişehir, Sivrihisâr, Kayseri, Develü, Niğde, Karahisâr-ı Sahib (Afyon Karahisar), and Urfa, 6 January 1916.

In those areas left empty by the Armenians a portion of those, the abandoned cultivated lands . . . allocated to the needs of [new Muslim] immigrants [and refugees and] which are under the supervision of the Commissions on Abandoned Property, are to be assessed and divvied out, and then harvested by the government; it is appropriate that the remainder of the produce received [from these holdings] is to be delivered over to the army according to the price that is to be assessed. After the military has ensured active assistance through the labor battalions, a quick examination and assessment is to be given, and within two days, the amount of labor, the types of machines and tools and [other] equipment that are needed from the military or from the local population in order to remove and transfer said produce are to be reported.[60]

Similar operations were indicated for vineyards and gardens. Numerous examples can be given of telegrams sent to Çanakkale ("concerning the assessment of the value of grapes in the abandoned vineyards, and [after] a valuation report is made, they are to be surrendered to the military"),[61] other provinces ("concerning the donation of the grapes and figs found on the abandoned Greek properties to the military"), and the various Liquidation Commissions.[62]

THE GOVERNMENT'S EXPENSES FOR THE DEPORTATIONS

The revenues obtained from the sale of abandoned Armenian properties were also used to cover the expenses incurred by the government during the deportation of the Armenians. The telegrams cited above in regard to

[60] BOA/DH.ŞFR, no. 54/301, Coded telegram from the Interior Ministry's IAMM to the Provinces of Sivas, Diyarbekır, and Mamüretülaziz, dated 5 July 1915. Similar cables were sent to other provinces. For one sent to Urfa on 12 July 1915, see BOA/DH.ŞFR, no. 54/382.

[61] BOA/DH.ŞFR, no. 67/106, Coded telegram from the Interior Ministry's General Directorate of Tribal and Immigrant Affairs to the Provincial District of Kale-i Sultaniye (Çanakkale), dated 27 August 1916.

[62] BOA/DH.ŞFR, no. 68/178, Coded telegram from the Interior Ministry's General Directorate of Tribal and Immigrant Affairs to the Provinces of Aydın and Hüdâvendigâr (Bursa); to the Provincial District of Karesi (Balıkesir); and to the chairmen of the Liquidation Commissions in Bursa (Hüdâvendigâr) and Karesi (Balıkesir), dated 4 October 1916.

the Yusuf Halaçoğlu case can be given here as an example. These cables, which were sent to Aleppo and Eskişehir, inform local officials of the need to deliver the revenues earned from the sale of Armenian property to the revenue authorities to cover government expenses.[63]

The documents openly stated that in certain situations the Armenian deportees were expected to cover the expenses for their relocation, while the government would only pay its own expenses. The first instance that I have found of the application of this policy is in relation to the Armenians deported from Zeytun to Konya in April 1915: "Since it [is] neither possible nor appropriate that the Armenians deported from Zeytun be supplied by the government [from now on], it is necessary for them to secure and acquire their own means of support and subsistence; please report the amounts expended for their resettlement and their support up to this time so that it may be sent."[64]

A similar implementation can be seen in May 1915 in Aleppo and the surrounding region; a Security Directorate cable to the provincial governor ordered him "to first resettle the deported Armenians in separate townships in the villages or mountains, whichever is suitable based on local conditions . . . and since it will not be possible for the government to cover their provisions, they will subsequently have to secure these by themselves."[65] In a November 1915 cable to the director for immigrant affairs, Şükrü Kaya, who was in Aleppo at the time, the following suggestion was made regarding a similar operation: "Your plan is acceptable in regard to making those Armenians who wish to [go to] the villages of Hama, Homs and Damascus pay the travel expenses themselves."[66] It is of great significance that a state that has confiscated property left by the Armenians it deported then refused to cover the latter's expenses.

[63] BOA/ŞFR.DH, no. 57/342, 348–49, and 350, Coded telegram from the Interior Ministry's IAMM to Kaya, the director of Immigrant Affairs in Aleppo; to the acting governor of Aleppo; and to the Provincial District of Eskişehir, dated 8 November 1915.

[64] BOA/DH.ŞFR, no. 52/292, Coded telegram from the Interior Ministry's General Directorate of Security to the Province of Konya, dated 9 May 1915.

[65] BOA/DH.ŞFR, no. 52/335, Coded telegram from the Interior Ministry's General Directorate of Security to the Province of Aleppo, dated 12 May 1915.

[66] BOA/DH.ŞFR, no. 57/54, Coded telegram from interior minister Talat to Kaya, the director of Immigrant Affairs in Aleppo, dated 18 October 1915.

VARIOUS GOVERNMENT NEEDS

In some cases, abandoned Armenian buildings that were deemed suitable were appropriated by the government for a variety of purposes. When not left for the military's use, such buildings were employed as anything from schools and jails to police stations and medical clinics. A few examples include:

Jails: In May 1916, the Interior Ministry asked the provincial officials to "report back quickly on whether, in areas in which there is a need for prisons, the abandoned Armenian buildings can be used as jails, and if so, what condition they are in and what manner of repairs they might need."[67]

Schools: In a cable that went out to local officials in nearly every region in the first months of the deportations, the Tribal and Immigrant Settlement Office said that "it is necessary the schools in towns and villages evacuated by the Armenians be allocated as schools for the Muslim immigrants who are to be settled there, while amount of educational tools and equipment and value that comprise [a part of] the buildings are to be recorded, along with the present value of the buildings, in registries and put separately in the general ledgers."[68] From some regions it was demanded that a portion of the money collected and held in the Commission for Abandoned Properties be devoted to the construction of schools or to covering the expenses of existing ones.[69]

[67] BOA/DH.ŞFR, no. 64/18, Coded telegram from the Interior Ministry's Office of Administrative Buildings and Prisons to the Provinces and Provincial Districts of Edirne Adana, Ankara, Diyarbekır, Sivas, Konya, Mamuretülaziz, Urfa, İzmit, Bolu, Canik, Karesi (Balıkesir), Kale-i Sultaniye (Çanakkale), Kayseri, Marash, İçel, Kütahya, Eskişehir, Niğde, and Karahisar, dated 14 May 1916.

[68] BOA/DH.ŞFR, no. 54/101, Coded telegram from the Interior Ministry's IAMM to the presidents of the Commissions on Abandoned Properties of Adana, Aleppo, and Marash; to the Provinces of Adana, Erzurum, Bitlis, Diyarbekır, Aleppo, and Hüdâvendigâr (Bursa); and to the Provincial Districts of Marash, Kayseri, and Karesi (Balıkesir), dated 22 June 1915.

[69] For a cable on the subject of "the allocation of a portion of the [revenues from the Commission on] Abandoned Properties for a Medical School," see BOA/DH.ŞFR, no. 57/59, Coded telegram from the Interior Ministry's IAMM to the Province of Mamuretülaziz, dated 18 October 1915.

Hospitals and Clinics: A Health Directorate cable of 1 August 1915 asked local officials that "the conditions be put fully in place for the maintenance and administration of the buildings and health and medical institutions left by the departing non-Muslims so that they may [continue to] improve and alleviate local medical needs."[70]

Police Stations: In a late July 1917 cable to Ankara, the Interior Ministry demanded "from the Ankara Police Ministry the money order for the rent on the two buildings belonging to the deportees and [currently] being used as a police station."[71]

THE NEEDS OF MILITIA ORGANIZATIONS

A cable sent to Mamuretülaziz Province in August 1915 clarifies that the expenses incurred by militia organizations that were formed in Dersim and its environs had been covered from resources acquired through the sale of abandoned Armenian property:

[Your] valuable ideas regarding the militia organizations in Dersim are both appropriate and accurate. It is necessary to select the leaders upon whom military ranks will be conferred from among those individuals whose [sense of] connection to the government and loyalty can be depended upon, and whose power and influence over the various [Kurdish] tribes can truly be exploited by the state, and from this point to fully prepare and complete the conditions so that such persons will be unable to subsequently abuse their positions and influence. It is appropriate for the allocation that is to be given to them to be taken from the abandoned [Armenian] properties.[72]

[70] BOA/DH.ŞFR, no. 54-A/218, Coded telegram [?] from the Interior Ministry's General Directorate of Health to the Provinces and Health Directorates of Erzurum, Bitlis, Mamuretülaziz, Sivas, Mosul, and Trebizond, and to the Health Centers and Provincial Districts of (Der) Zor and Samsun, dated August 1915.

[71] BOA/DH.EUM.MH, 148/17, Coded telegram from the Interior Ministry's Office of Accounting to the Province of Ankara, dated 23 July 1917.

[72] BOA/DH.ŞFR, no. 54-A/354, Coded telegram from the Interior Ministry's General Directorate of Security to Mamuretülaziz provincial governor Sabit Bey Effendi in Dersim, dated 10 August 1915.

The cable goes on to demand that information be supplied regarding the activities of the militia organizations and the effect that they would have.

Taken together, these documents reveal that the Unionists strove in a highly systematic fashion to exploit abandoned Armenian properties in the pursuit of clear ends, and in this effort used its power and influence to prevent looting by private individuals. Thus the picture that emerges explains in large part why the Armenians who survived the deportations were never recompensed for the property and possessions they were forced to leave behind. Ottoman government records indeed corroborate the quote given earlier by American consul J. B. Jackson, that the appropriation of abandoned Armenian property and possessions was "a gigantic plundering scheme as well as a final blow to extinguish the race."[73]

[73] NA/RG 59, 867.4016/148, Report from Aleppo consul, Jesse B. Jackson, to Ambassador Henry Morgenthau, dated 19 August 1915, in *United States Official Records*, ed. Sarafian, 207.

ELEVEN

SOME OFFICIAL DENIALIST
ARGUMENTS OF THE
TURKISH STATE AND
DOCUMENTS FROM THE
OTTOMAN INTERIOR
MINISTRY

There are certain theses in the discussions about the Armenian Genocide that people have not gotten sick of repeating to such a degree that they practically become memorized. These include the now-classic arguments that Armenian Catholics and Protestants, and the Armenians of Istanbul and İzmir, were not deported. Families of soldiers were not touched, and despite it being wartime, the government opened investigations against state officials who acted badly toward the Armenians during the deportations. It tried 1,397 people, issued long prison sentences, and even had some people executed. All possible aid was given to the Armenians on the roads and at their destinations, including the acceptance of aid from foreign countries. Another important argument added in recent years is that the organization known as the Special Organization, which in fact enjoyed an official status through its association with the War Ministry, had no connection whatsoever with the annihilation of the Armenians. It is claimed that no document can be shown to demonstrate such a connection. In this chapter, I will closely examine some of these arguments and share information from the Prime Ministerial Ottoman Archive on this topic. As I will demonstrate one by one, the Interior Ministry documents very clearly show that all these claims are baseless.

TALAT PASHA'S TELEGRAMS AND THE CATHOLIC AND PROTESTANT ARMENIANS

A central piece of evidence used to support the Turkish regime's "official history" of this period is the group of telegrams sent directly by Talat Pasha to the provinces in order to ensure that the deportations proceeded in an orderly fashion; the existence of these telegrams is said to show that the deportations were never conducted with the intent of annihilating Armenians, and that Talat also ordered the exemption of Armenian Catholics and Protestants.

First of all, official channels were not employed for correspondence concerning killings. This is a situation often encountered in other historical instances of genocidal operations. Those responsible often expend great effort to "cover their tracks." Moreover, the Unionist regime was forced to hide its operations even from its own allies.

The Ottoman archival materials clearly show that Talat Pasha did indeed send such orders to the provinces. Nevertheless, as will be seen below, his main goal in doing so was to avoid German and Austrian pressure. As the reports of massacres came in from Anatolia at increasing rates, the German and Austrian ambassadors to the Porte made ever more frequent entreaties before the Ottoman government that such actions be stopped. The German government pressured the Porte to exclude, at the very least, Armenians of the Protestant and Catholic faith from deportation. Seeing that these requests were not fulfilled and that reports of the killings continued to arrive apace, Berlin felt compelled to send the Ottoman regime two separate notes of protest on 4 July and 9 August 1915.[1] As if to accede to German and Austrian wishes, Talat ordered the provinces to conduct the deportations fairly, but the same recipients soon received his second cable, voiding the preceding instructions.

This practice can be demonstrated in the deportation of Catholic and Protestant Armenians. As already mentioned, those who deny any genocidal intent in the 1915 deportations typically argue that these groups were not subjected to deportation. For example, Yusuf Halaçoğlu, who served as the director of the Prime Ministerial (i.e., Ottoman) Archive between 1989 and 1992 and who was the chairman of the Turkish Historical Society between 1993 and 2008, writes, "Just as the infirm and blind were not deported, those [Armenians] belonging to the Catholic and Protestant denominations, families with men serving in the army, government functionaries, merchants, and some laborers and craftsmen were also ex-

---

[1] On the question of German efforts to this effect beginning at the end of June 1916, see Gust, *Der Völkermord an den Armeniern*, 76–97; Lepsius, *Deutschland und Armenien*, xxvi–xxxiii.

empted from the deportations."[2] In recent years a number of other scholars have likewise begun to claim that the Ottoman government, under pressure from the German government and public opinion, did indeed exempt Catholic and Protestant Armenians from the deportations. Guenter Lewy, for example, claims repeatedly throughout his work that the deportations of Catholic and Protestant Armenians were blocked, chiefly as a result of German governmental pressure.[3] Fuat Dündar writes, "permission was given for families of three groups to remain in Anatolia: families of craftsmen, soldiers, and Protestants and Catholics."[4] The truth is that these groups were also deported. Orders to the provinces that they not be touched were produced for German consumption and quickly rescinded by follow-up cables.

Here I am primarily interested in the situation concerning Protestant and Catholic Armenians, and will not discuss the other two groups. Suffice it to say that in certain areas, in a very limited manner, the army kept essential artisans from being deported. However, other artisans were indeed exiled. Yervant Odian's memoirs (mentioned in chapter 9) show how the Fourth Army assembled artisans who had been deported to Syria and settled them in the regions of Hama and Homs. The situation of soldiers' families was no different. A great majority of them were deported, particularly after the Armenians in the army were killed. Those few who were allowed to remain in their homes were mainly found in the provinces of western Anatolia where the 5 percent rule was enforced. Meanwhile, the Second Department of the Interior Ministry's General Directorate of Security was flooded with petitions from Armenian soldiers who somehow continued to serve and who were asking for the whereabouts of their deported families.[5] The Interior Ministry also instructed all regions that the deported families of soldiers could not return without special permission.[6]

[2] Yusuf Halaçoğlu, *Ermeni Tehciri* (Istanbul: Babıali Kültür Yayıncılığı, 2004), 82.

[3] Guenter Lewy, *The Armenian Massacres in Ottoman Turkey: A Disputed Genocide* (Salt Lake City: University of Utah Press, 2005), 176, 184–86, and 206–8.

[4] Fuat Dündar, *Modern Türkiye'nin Şifresi*, 298.

[5] It is only necessary to give a few examples here: BOA/DH, 2. Şube, nos. 20/48, 20/57, 21/35, and 22/31.

[6] BOA/DH.ŞFR, no. 58/89, Coded telegram from the Interior Ministry's General Security Directorate to the Provinces of Edirne, Erzurum, Adana, Ankara, Bitlis, Aleppo, Hüdâvendigâr (Bursa), Diyarbekır, Damascus, Sivas, Trebizond, Konya, Mamuretülaziz, Mosul, and Van, and to the Provincial

As for Protestant and Catholic Armenians, orders to the provinces in the first months of the deportations openly and clearly stated that all Armenians, regardless of their religion, were to be deported. I have already presented ample documentation to show that it was seen as necessary for "all of the Armenians found in the towns and villages in the province, without exception, to be deported, along with their families."[7] I also learned from the Ottoman documents that at least from the beginning of deportations in May until the beginning of August, the Ottoman government expelled all Armenians without exception, in spite of German diplomatic efforts on behalf of the Catholics and Protestants.[8]

Nevertheless, under increasing pressure, Talat appeared to accede to his allies' demands. On 4 August 1915, the interior minister ordered that "those Armenian Catholics that *still remain* should be exempted from deportation" (italics added).[9] A similar directive eleven days later stated that "those Armenians *not yet deported* who are of the Protestant denomination are to be exempted from deportation" (italics added).[10] It is worth noting that both directives exempted these groups "if any are still left"; in addition, nothing in these cables suggests that those Catholic and Protestant Armenians already deported would be allowed to return to their homes: on the contrary, this was explicitly forbidden.

Having thus, at least temporarily, appeased his allies in Berlin, Talat Pasha lost no time in rescinding his previous orders. In a directive of

---

Districts of Urfa, İzmit, Canik, Çatalca, Zor, Karesi (Balıkesir), Kale-i Sultaniye (Çanakkale), Kayseri, Marash, İçel, Karahisâr-ı Sahib (Afyon Karahisar), Eskişehir, Niğde, and Kütahya, dated 22 November 1915.

[7] BOA/DH.ŞFR, no. 54/87, Coded telegram from the Interior Ministry's General Directorate of Security to the Provinces of Trebizond, Mamuretülaziz, Sivas, and Diyarbekır, and to the Provincial District of Canik, dated 20 June 1915.

[8] The only exception that I was able to find on this topic is a cable sent to Erzurum on 17 June 1915. In it permission is given for "Armenian Catholic missionaries" in the city to remain there for the time being with registration papers (BOA/DH.ŞFR, no. 54/55, Coded telegram from the Interior Ministry's General Directorate of Security to the Province of Erzurum, dated 17 June 1915).

[9] BOA/DH.ŞFR, no. 54-A/252, Coded telegram from interior minister Talat to the Provinces of Erzurum, Adana, Ankara, Bitlis, Aleppo, Diyarbekır, Sivas, Trebizond, Mamüretülaziz, and Van, and to the Provincial Districts of Urfa, Canik, and Marash, dated 3 August 1915.

[10] BOA/DH.ŞFR, no. 54/20, Coded telegram from interior minister Talat to the Provinces of Erzurum, Adana, Ankara, Bitlis, Aleppo, Hüdâvendigâr (Bursa), Diyarbekır, Sivas, Trebizond, Konya, Mamuratülaziz, and Van; and to the Provincial Districts of Urfa, İzmit, Canik, Karesi (Balıkesir), and Karahisâr-ı Sahib (Afyon Karahisar), and to the Provincial Districts of Marash, Niğde, and Eskişehir, dated 15 August 1915.

4 August to the provinces that reported the deportation of Armenian Catholics, he demanded that "the Armenians from Adana, Sis and Mersin whose deportation was previously announced as delayed are to be completely removed, together with other Armenians left within the province, and deported to those places appointed."[11] Simultaneously, a similar telegram was sent to Marash, the other main city of the region.[12] The supposed exemption of the Armenian Catholics had lasted less than a day.

Not content to inform one city at a time, Talat sent a follow-up "circular" cable on 11 August to all the provinces in question, reminding local officials to "deport the Armenian Catholics along with the others" and demanding that "the action be carried out in that manner."[13] The same day, he ordered that "the Catholic population in the province of Ankara be sent off and exiled like the other Armenians."[14]

Responding to questions from provincial administrators, Talat clarified that the order to halt the deportations did not include the Catholics and Protestants who had already been sent off. His 14 August cable to the provincial district of İzmit said that the Protestants and Catholics en route to Eskişehir would not be allowed to return.[15] Next, on 30 August, Eskişehir received word that "[t]here is no need for those Armenian Catholics and Protestants who were sent [to your district] from İzmit and other areas to be returned [to their homes]. The order [not to deport Armenian Catholics and Protestants] does not include those who have [already] gone." Such messages leave no doubt that the

[11] BOA/DH.ŞFR, no. 54-A/271, Coded telegram from interior minister Talat to Adana provincial governor İsmail Hakkı Bey, dated 4 August 1915.

[12] BOA/DH.ŞFR, no. 54-A/272, Coded telegram from interior minister Talat to the Provincial District of Marash, dated 4 August 1915.

[13] BOA/DH.ŞFR, no. 54-A/384, Coded telegram from interior minister Talat to the Provinces of Adana and Aleppo, and to the presidents of the Commissions (on Abandoned Property) in Adana, Aleppo, and Marash, dated 11 August 1915.

[14] BOA/DH.ŞFR, no. 55-A/373, Coded telegram from the Interior Ministry's IAMM to the Province of Ankara, dated 11 August 1915. On the other hand, another cable sent to Ankara on 4 June 1916 shows that some Armenian Catholics still remained in Ankara. Talat Pasha asks that "it be reported back quickly the manner in which Catholics are being treated at present and whether or not all of the Catholics in Ankara have been allowed to conduct religious ceremonies by the German priest who is temporarily there [in Ankara]" (BOA/DH.ŞFR, no. 64/210).

[15] BOA/DH.ŞFR, no. 55-A/55, Coded telegram from the Interior Ministry's General Directorate of Security to the Provincial District of İzmit, dated 14 August 1915.

deported members of these two Christian communities would not be sent back home.[16]

Naturally, Talat's attempts to deceive the Western powers did not succeed for long, as Berlin was soon enough aware of the true situation and exerted pressure anew on the Porte. As a result, Talat Pasha would send a second "general communiqué" to the provinces on 29 August that demanded a halt to the deportation of Catholics and Protestants; this time he paid a visit to the German Embassy and showed the ambassador the telegram. The German authorities, who believed the Ottoman interior minister, duly informed their functionaries in the provinces that the deportations had been stopped.[17] In fact, Talat's order used elliptical and unclear expressions in demanding that these Armenian communities not be deported. Perhaps more important, the new order was emphatically not retroactive but solely applied to "the Armenians who were not [already] uprooted and deported."[18]

The vagueness in the wording of this telegram was not all, however. A subsequent order from Talat made it clear how the local authorities were to understand the 29 August cable. In no uncertain terms, Talat informed his provincial officials to disregard the message he had sent and subsequently shown to the Germans as proof that Catholics and Protestants were no longer being deported. In an order sent to the governor of Adana on 2 September with the accompanying notation "resolve the matter yourself," the interior minister explained how the general communiqué of four days earlier was to be understood. Aware that the province had been emptied of Armenian Catholics and Protestants, Talat directed that if any somehow remained, local authorities should pretend that "the order to delay the deportation 'arrived' only after they have [already] been deported"; furthermore, these Catholics and Protestants were to be

[16] BOA/DH.ŞFR, no. 55/321, Coded telegram from the Interior Ministry's General Directorate of Security to the Provincial District of Eskişehir, dated 30 August 1915.

[17] DE/PA-AA/Bo.Kons./170, Note by legal advisor of the German Embassy in Istanbul, Göppert, dated 31 August 1915.

[18] BOA/DH.ŞFR, no. 55/292, Coded telegram from the Interior Ministry's General Directorate of Security to (the Provinces of) Hüdâvendigâr (Bursa), Ankara, Konya, İzmit, Adana, Marash, and Aleppo, (and to the Provincial Districts of Der) Zor, Sivas, Kütahya, Karesi (Balıkesir), Niğde, Mamuretülaziz, Diyarbekır, Karahisâr-ı Sahib (Afyon Karahisar), Erzurum, and Kayseri, dated 29 August 1915.

"deported along with their families."[19] The message to the provinces was essentially this: the deportation of Armenian Catholics and Protestants would continue, but if the Germans pressed the government and local authorities too hard, the latter should act as if the new order had come too late, and thus there was nothing more they could do.

Another cable, sent to Marash on 24 October, would seem to indicate that Talat had instructed the provinces throughout the summer on how to proceed on the issue of deporting Catholics and Protestants. In it, the interior minister mentioned that he had sent cipher telegrams to the provinces on 5 August and 2 September (nos. 4917 and 5945, respectively) regarding the need for all Armenians to be deported without exception, Protestants and Catholics included. In recalling this, Talat said that "the reasons have not been understood for the fact that, although notice has already been given as to the need to deport the Armenians of Marash and send them to the appointed areas . . . there are more than 2,500 Armenians and more than 3,000 Protestant Christians remaining in Marash itself," and demanded an explanation for this situation.[20]

But Talat did not limit himself to telegraphic communications; he also sent "inspectors" to various provinces. Among these targeted regions, Adana was an area of great importance due to the particular interest that the German Consulate there took in the issue. At one point Consul Eugen Büge reported to his superiors that Talat had sent Ali Münif (Çetinkaya) Bey to the province as an inspector and that the latter had arrived with the message for local officials that the previous cables on halting the deportations were null and void. As a result, Büge wrote that "the explanation given to the Chancellor's Embassy by the Porte on 31 August was simply

[19] BOA/DH.ŞFR, no. 55-A/22, Coded telegram from interior minister Talat to the Province of Adana, dated 2 September 1915.

[20] BOA/DH.ŞFR, no. 57/96, Coded telegram from the Interior Ministry's General Directorate of Security to the Provincial District of Marash, dated 24 October 1915. It can be understood from another cable sent to the same provincial district months later (22 April 1916) that some Catholics were still residing within the city of Marash. "I have communicated with the Fourth Army Command," wrote Talat. "The Catholics are all to remain." But in light of the fact that the order to deport the remaining Catholics was sent in October 1915, it is likely that those that remained in Marash at that time had earlier been deported there from other regions (BOA/DH.ŞFR, no. 63/76, Coded telegram from interior minister Talat to the Provincial District of Marash, dated 22 April 1916).

a great deception," [21] for "state functionaries" acted in accordance with the inspectors and follow-up decrees sent by Talat, and "the deportations continue regardless of what may be believed."[22] Indeed, in his memoirs Ali Münif admits that he himself had prepared the list of those Armenians to be deported from Adana.[23] Nevertheless, already in September officials from various provinces were reporting that no more Armenians remained in their territories.[24]

In response to the reports arriving from Adana, the German ambassador to the Porte, Prince Ernst Wilhelm Hohenlohe-Langenburg, wrote to Berlin on 25 September 1915,

> Further reports by the Imperial Consuls in Adana and Aleppo confirm that the well-known telegraphic instructions by the Porte for the improvement of the fate of the deported Armenians have on the whole not fulfilled their purpose due to the various exceptions to the privileges granted, which the Porte itself made at the beginning and later, and also due to the despotism of the provincial authorities. In Adana, as Dr. Buege [Büge] reported on 13th instant, widows, orphans, soldiers' families, even the sick and blind were to be deported.[25]

For this reason the ambassador's report referred to Talat as a "liar."

Numerous other dispatches found among the papers of the Ottoman Cipher Office show that the practice of sending a second telegram to rescind a previous order was a frequent modus operandi of Talat Pasha. As

[21] Talat told the German Embassy on 31 August 1915 that he had come straight to the embassy with the relevant telegrams in hand in order to show them to the ambassador and to explain the situation as it then stood; this example is important in that it shows that a relevant communiqué sent to the provinces on 29 August was subsequently ordered invalid not just by means of telegraphic messages but also by the inspectors sent to the region.

[22] DE/PA-AA/Bo.Kons./Band 170, Telegram from German consul in Adana, Büge, dated 10 September 1915.

[23] Taha Toros, ed., "Eski Nafıa Nazırı Ali Münif Yegane'nin Hatıraları: İstibdattan Cumhuriyet'e," *Akşam*, 26 October–21 December 1955, part 47.

[24] Such telegrams were sent from the Province of Diyarbekır on 5 September 1915, from the Provincial District of İzmit and Eskişehir on 17 September 1915, and from Niğde on 18 September 1915. All can be found in the publication of Devlet Arşivleri Genel Müdürlüğü [*General Directorate of State Archives*], *Osmanlı Belgelerinde Ermeniler (1915–1920)*, 94–97.

[25] DE/PA-AA/R 14088, Report from Ambassador Hohenlohe(-Langenburg), dated 25 September 1915.

another example of this, the telegram from Talat to the provincial district of Tekfurdağı (Tekirdağ) sent on 16 April 1914 can be given:

> The content of the written recommendations given yesterday to the 4–5 person delegation, sent by the Patriarchate upon the request of the Metropolitan [bishop] of Vize for the purpose of advising him, are to be ignored; on the other hand, those refugees in Ereğli are to be placed on a steamship at the first possible moment and their departure from Ereğli accelerated; the aforementioned delegation is to be put under observation and great efforts are to be taken [to ensure] that [this delegation's] efforts come to naught and that this is done without them catching word of this.[26]

Here we see Talat directing Ottoman regional officials to disregard his previous orders, as well as the list of proposals he had given to the Greek Patriarchate's delegation to the region; at the same time, he orders that the delegation be closely monitored and prevented from achieving their aims. This significant telegram reveals the strategy behind the Ottoman interior minister's behavior toward both foreign delegations and the country's own minorities throughout this period.

An Ottoman document that I found in the German archives will surely settle all disputes about Adana. This directive "from the office of the province" explains in detail how the deportations from Adana were to be conducted:

(1) Because it is decided that local and foreign Armenians in the center of Adana fully be deported by the 24th day of August, each person's tie and connection to Adana will be cut from now on, effective immediately.

(2) The application of those who are demanding extension of stay with the argument that their tie and connection has not been cut is absolutely not valid.

(3) Starting from this hour, all Armenians will be registered by applying to the police, and are going to obtain deportation documents.

[26] BOA/DH.ŞFR, no. 40/17, Coded telegram from interior minister Talat to the Provincial District of Tekfurdağı, dated 16 April 1914.

(4) Those who do not go on the appointed day will be arrested, placed under observation, and without stop be deported under guard.

(5) It is announced that because the police department is occupied with registration each night until morning, registration is also taking place by application at night too at the aforementioned department.[27]

All Armenians without exception were to be expelled from Adana. This document is so clear that discussion is unnecessary.

In light of all this information it becomes easier to understand why Talat was often called "deceitful" or a "liar," even in Turkish sources. Historian İsmail Hami Danişmend wrote that Talat had "broadened his notoriety as a liar, in particular."[28] The editor of the Turkish daily *Sabah* reports that Talat "told lies" in an almost mechanical fashion.[29] After Talat's escape from Istanbul, his contemporary, journalist Süleyman Nazıf, described him as someone "possessing no qualities apart from deceitfulness."[30] Mustafa Kemal (Atatürk) was said to have received his share of Talat's lies.[31]

Even Talat's close political associates identified him as a liar. His closest friend Hüseyin Cahit (Yalçın) admits that Talat "lied in governmental and political matters."[32] Falih Rıfkı Atay, Talat's personal secretary, referred to him as a person "who found no immorality in either lies or cruelties." Atay also recalled that his former boss would often dictate an open, official telegram and then follow it up with a cipher cable invalidating the previous message.[33] American ambassador Henry Morgenthau and Unionist deputy Halil Menteşe recalled that Talat, who had in his earlier years worked as a telegraphic agent in Edirne, had a private tele-

[27] DE/PA-AA/Bo.Kons./Band 170, Report from Adana consul, Büge, to the Embassy in Istanbul, dated 6 September 1915.

[28] İsmail Hami Danişmend, *İzahlı Osmanlı Tarihi Kronolojisi* (Istanbul: Türkiye Yayınevi 1961), 448. This and the two subsequent examples were taken from Dadrian, "Pitfalls of a 'Balanced' Analysis," 125.

[29] *Sabah*, 15 May 1915.

[30] *Hadisat*, 5 November 1918.

[31] Falih Rıfkı Atay, *Atatürk'ün Bana Anlattıkları* (Istanbul: Sel Yayınları, 1955), 9–10.

[32] Yalçın, *Siyasi Anılar*, 148.

[33] Falih Rıfkı Atay, *Zeytindağı* (Istanbul: Bateş A.Ş., 1981), 24–25.

graph line set up in his own house from which he would often send and receive communications.[34]

In an interview with Turkish journalist Murat Bardakçı in October 1982, the interior minister's widow, Hayriye Talat, confirmed this information. To the reporter's question, "Was there a telegraph machine in the Pasha's house—that is, in your house—during the time of the Armenian incidents?" she replied, "Yes, there was." Bardakçı then asked, "Would he use the machine himself?" to which she answered, "Both he would use it and . . . Ah, I can't remember his name . . . he later went blind . . . he only recently died. . . . Well, whatever it was, he would use it too, of course. He gave orders to all the provincial governors."[35]

Sending out orders and then immediately rescinding them was in fact a common practice among Ottoman leaders. The German officer Hans von Seeckt, chief of staff at Ottoman Army Headquarters during the war, recounted that as a rule, "official orders" were rescinded by secondary orders that reflected the secret decisions of the Ottoman regime.[36] Captain Selahattin recalled that the cables sent out by the war minister via official channels in order to appease the Germans would afterward be invalidated by follow-up messages from the "telegraph office" in Enver Pasha's own home.[37]

THE QUESTION OF INVESTIGATIONS DURING THE DEPORTATION

A widely disseminated major argument holds that the Ottoman government investigated those state functionaries who had abused or exploited the Armenian deportees, attacked convoys, or perpetrated murders and other grievous crimes. According to this argument, some officials were indeed guilty of abuses during the deportations, but "[individuals] who did not comply with [government] instructions, and those who were guilty, were arrested and sent for trial. A special investigative council was formed

---

[34] Menteşe, *Osmanlı Mebusan Meclisi Reisi*, 216; Morgenthau, *Ambassador Morgenthau's Story*, 143–44.

[35] Bardakçı, *Talat Paşa'nın Evrak-ı Metrukesi*, 211.

[36] Cited by V. N. Dadrian, "Documentation of the Armenian Genocide in German and Austrian Sources," in Charney, *Bibliographic Review*, 109–10.

[37] İlhan Selçuk, *Yüzbaşı Selahattin'in Romanı*, vol. 1 (Istanbul: Remzi Kitabevi 1993), 292.

at the Ministry of War to examine such irregularities . . . Those who were found guilty were sent to the martial law courts. The number of these individuals was . . . 1,397. They were given various sentences including execution."[38]

In the Prime Ministerial Ottoman Archive—and, most important, among the papers of the Interior Ministry's Cipher Office, where the majority of documents dealing with this subject are to be found—a researcher will look in vain for documents attesting to investigations being initiated against state officials accused of committing murders and other serious crimes against Armenian deportees. Indeed, as will be shown below, the Committee for Union and Progress, through various pretexts and rationalizations, eventually eliminated members of its own notorious Special Organization whom they feared might create problems for the committee in the future. Nevertheless, they at no time pursued any systematic investigation of improprieties by state or government functionaries.

These same documents reveal, moreover, that the Unionist government showed a particular concern and sensitivity toward "abandoned" Armenian property that was in no way extended to its deported owners. The Ottoman regime, which planned to exploit Armenian property and profit from its sale, worked hard to prevent looting and private embezzlement. Those officials who were indeed investigated or tried for alleged improprieties had not been accused of abusing Armenians, but rather of diverting Armenian property for personal gain.

The reason that those who claim a lack of genocidal intent behind the deportations have yet to publish documents corroborating their assertion is, simply, that no known documents attest to legal investigations against officials suspected of abusing Armenians. Kamuran Gürün, who put forth the figure of 1,397 prosecutions of state functionaries, has produced no documentation on the matter. Instead, after listing the figures for individual Ottoman provinces, he apparently deemed it sufficient to cite a single Ottoman document—without quoting from it. A similar situation can be witnessed in the case of Yusuf Halaçoğlu, who, relying on Gürün's work, repeats the same figures. After claiming that convicted government

---

[38] Kamuran Gürün, *Armenian File: The Myth of Innocence Exposed* (London: K. Rustem and Weidenfeld & Nicolson, 1985; New York: St. Martin's Press, 1986). http://www.eraren.org/index.php?Lisan=en&Page=YayinIcerik&IcerikNo=217/.

officials were "tried in the courts-martial and given severe sentences,"[39] Halaçoğlu cites twelve separate documents as proof, but provides no information whatsoever on their scope or content.

A closer look at these twelve documents readily reveals that not a single one had anything to do with abuses of Armenian people. Instead, they concerned crimes such as looting, thievery, bribery, and confiscation in regard to abandoned Armenian properties, and the majority do not mention prosecution.

Some of these documents were solely concerned with inquiring into reports regarding the confiscation of property, such as "a cable sent by the General Directorate of Security to the governor of the provincial district of Eskişehir about county head of Mihalıççık Yovanaki Effendi, who was understood to have forced Armenians to deliver over their possessions";[40] or investigations being undertaken over simple instances of robbery, confiscation, and bribery, such as "a telegram from the General Directorate of Security to the provincial district governor of Niğde dealing with a cable sent from Pozantı by Director of Immigrant Affairs Şükrü Bey, who was entrusted with the deportation of Armenians, in which he requests that an investigation be conducted over an event that had transpired in Ulukışla."[41] Others discussed the granting of permission to try cases of misappropriation and embezzlement, such as "a response sent by wire from the General Directorate of Security to the Province of Mamuretül-aziz concerning the delivering of county head of Besni, Edhem Kadri Bey to the Court-Martial, who as the result of investigations had been found to have turned a blind eye to the exploitation of Armenian property and possessions by government officials and had himself received a number of items without payment."[42]

Halaçoğlu also cites these documents as examples of "trials [taking place] in the court-martial" and of "the imposition of severe punishments," but not content with the misrepresentations above, he even sub-

[39] Yusuf Halaçoğlu, *Ermeniler Tehciri ve Gerçekler* (Ankara: Türk Tarih Kurumu, 2005), 62.

[40] BOA/DH.ŞFR, no. 59/196, Coded telegram from the Interior Ministry's General Directorate of Security to the Provincial District of Eskişehir, dated 4 January 1916.

[41] BOA/DH.ŞFR, no. 55-A/156, Coded telegram from the Interior Ministry's General Directorate of Security to the Provincial District of Niğde, dated 8 September 1915.

[42] BOA/DH.ŞFR, no. 61/165, Coded telegram from the Interior Ministry's General Directorate of Security to the Province of Mamuretülaziz, dated 1 March 1916.

mits documents in which praise was heaped upon state officials for their actions against the Armenians as support for his claims. One such document concerned a county official who, having been removed from his position by naval minister and Fourth Army commander Cemal Pasha, was later praised by interior minister Talat Pasha and restored to his post. In a cable of 28 November 1915, Talat reminded Cemal Pasha that an another official had been previously removed from his position by his (Cemal's) own request, and that Cemal did not possess the authority to remove another county official on his own.

After informing the naval minister that "state officials such as county heads (*kaymakam*) [and] provincial district governors (*mutasarrıf*) are not to be summarily removed from their positions, even in the event that it is reported or ordered by provincial governors; rather, their removal from office and replacement is only to be undertaken after an initial investigation is undertaken and their responsibility [in a given impropriety] has been determined,"[43] Talat admonished him that it was therefore improper for the county head in question "to be removed from his official position" merely in response to an army officer's report, and stated that he had reversed the separation process and restored the official to his position.[44] Cemal was not to intervene in such affairs, warned Talat, because efforts and activities concerning the deportation of Armenians were the responsibility of the Interior Ministry and the provincial government of Aleppo.

In a later cable to Adana Province, Talat demanded that "the [Interior] Ministry must first be asked in the event that it becomes necessary to return the county head of İslahiye, who was taken and sent to the capital due to his improprieties during the Armenian deportations, to his position on account of his [distinguished] efforts, or whether other county heads in similar positions were removed from their positions and then returned [to them later on]."[45] To cite this document as an example of how state officials who were guilty of crimes against Armenians were "punished with various

---

[43] BOA/DH.ŞFR, no. 58/141, Coded telegram from interior minister Talat Pasha to Fourth Army commander Cemal Pasha, dated 28 November 1915.

[44] Ibid.

[45] BOA/DH.ŞFR, no. 58/196, Coded telegram from interior minister Talat to the Province of Adana, dated 4 December 1915.

prison sentences and even death" is nothing less than scandalous—and undeserving of the description of scholarly research.

INVESTIGATORY COMMISSIONS ARE DISPATCHED TO THE PROVINCES

If there is one thing that all of these documents clearly show, it is the fact that the Ottoman government, intent on systematically exploiting the property and goods of deported Armenians and any revenue that could be gained from their sale, took great pains to prevent their acquisition—legal or otherwise—and use by private individuals. As will be explained in chapter 12, this is why the Commissions for the Administration of Abandoned Property were established, closely monitored, and obliged to submit reports of their activities to the capital every fifteen days.[46]

In order to prevent local Ottoman officials from laying hands on the property, laws and regulations were issued forbidding this. Moreover, the regime ordered the provinces to investigate such reported improprieties. On 26 August 1915, the governor of Mamuretülaziz was informed that "telegraphic reports have arrived from the administrative center of Kangal, signed by Edhem, the investigative judge for the county of Akçadağ, [stating that] officials and gendarmes in Malatya and Akçadağ have looted some five million lira worth of abandoned property. An investigation [is to be] immediately undertaken and the various points of the regulatory statute [are to be] strenuously implemented and [the results] reported."[47] Unfortunately, even according to Interior Ministry documents, the looting and pilfering soon reached such dimensions that in some cases one or two officials managed to appropriate for themselves all of the abandoned Armenian gardens, orchards, and buildings in the village.[48]

[46] BOA/DH.ŞFR, no. 54/442, Coded telegram from the Interior Ministry's IAMM to the Provinces of Adana, Aleppo, Erzurum, Bitlis, Diyarbekır, Mamuretülaziz, Trebizond, Sivas, Hüdâvendigâr (Bursa), and Edirne; to the Provincial Districts of Marash, Canik, İzmit, Kayseri, Marash, (Der) Zor, and Urfa; and to the presidents of the Commissions on Abandoned Property in Adana and Aleppo, dated 13 July 1915.

[47] BOA/DH.ŞFR, no. 55/255, Coded telegram from the Interior Ministry's IAMM to the Province of Mamuretülaziz and to the president of the Mamuretülaziz Commission on Abandoned Property, dated 26 August 1915.

[48] The "acquistion and purchase by certain administrative officials of Armenian properties at very low prices during the deportation of Armenians [from] the township of Karabük, in the subdistrict of

When it became clear that the central government's attempts to monitor the situation in the provinces by telegraphic communication alone had met with no success and were unlikely to in the future, Istanbul dispatched commissions to investigate improprieties such as looting, theft, and abuses by provincial officials. A 30 September 1915 communication from the Grand Vizier's Office to the Ministry of War indicates that three such commissions were formed.[49]

Four days earlier the Interior Ministry had relayed information to the other government ministries about the state of these commissions. Mazhar Bey, the former governor of Bitlis Province, was appointed to head a commission formed "in order to bring before the courts-martial those officials and gendarmes whose illegal actions and abuses were witnessed during the deportation of Armenians in the provinces of Sivas, Trebizond, Erzurum, Mamuretülaziz, Diyarbekır, and Bitlis and the provincial district of Cânik, and whose crimes have been confirmed through the necessary investigation,"[50] and the first president of the Investigative Court, Asım Bey, was appointed to chair the commission that was set up to "investigate illegalities in the provinces of Adana, Aleppo, and Damascus, and the provincial districts of Urfa, [Der] Zor, and Marash."[51] As for the third commission, Hulusi Bey, president of the Court of Appeals, was sent to the provinces of "Bursa [Hüdâvendigâr] and Ankara and the provincial districts of İzmit, Balıkesir, Eskişehir, Afyon, Kayseri and Niğde" in order to lead the commission for this area.

These commissions lacked the authority to investigate all crimes, however; rather, they were able to concern themselves only with economic irregularities. The clearest evidence in this regard emerged during the trial of Boğazlıyan county head Kemal. At the trial's 6 March 1919 session, the court made reference to both the testimony of witness Aziz Nedim, the

---

Akkaya [which is administratively] attached to Kastamonu" can be given as an example of this phenomenon. In this case, two officials acquired "all of the abandoned [properties]" and took them under their own protection. Regarding the investigation into this accusation, see BOA/DH.ŞFR, no. 94/20, 3 December 1918.

[49] Genelkurmay Başkanlığı, *Arşiv Belgeleriyle Ermeni Faaliyetleri*, vol. 1, 233.

[50] BOA/DH.ŞFR, no. 56/179, Coded telegram from interior minister Talat to Mazhar Bey, former governor of the Province of Bitlis, now in Sivas (via the Office of the Governor of Sivas Province), dated 26 September 1915.

[51] BOA/DH.ŞFR, no. 56/186, Coded telegram from interior minister Talat to Ankara Province civil service inspector Muhtâr Bey, dated 26 September 1915.

commission functionary who was assigned to conduct an investigation at Boğazlıyan in order to understand the results of a wartime investigation and trial concerning Kemal's activities, and to the written testimony of Mazhar Bey, who had chaired the regional investigation and had previously submitted to the commission, which was established in November 1918 to collect information about crimes during the war years.[52]

Nedim testified that according to the official order he had received during the period in question, he possessed the authority to investigate only economic irregularities, and "that he did not have any authority whatsoever in regard to investigating massacres." Later in this same session, prosecuting attorney Sami Bey assessed Nedim's testimony thus: "What we have understood from [his] testimony is that Aziz Nedim wished to clarify the questions of what exactly were the limits of the inspection that he was to undertake and of his own authority in the matter, and he was informed that the masssacres were outside of the scope of [his] investigation."[53]

In the 20 December 1918 edition of the Turkish daily İleri, one functionary who served in these commissions offered some enlightening explanations as to their activities. The official (whom the paper did not name) stated that the scope of investigative commissions was extremely limited and did not include the authority either to conduct investigations of high-ranking officials or send the latter to the courts-martial for further investigation or trial. What is more, he complained, no one paid attention to their reports. As for the authority they *did* possess, "The commissions had been sent in the role of officials entrusted with preliminary investigations, and were only able to send minor officials to the courts-martial for misdemeanors demanding further investigation, because they did not possess the authority [to do more]. As for the others [commissions], it could [also] be said that the reports that they submitted had almost no effect at all."[54]

It must be added that, before submitting complaints to the courts-martial for illegalities and abuses, even for county heads (*kaymakam*), the commissions were required to obtain permission from the relevant

[52] *Memleket*, 7 March 1919.
[53] V. N. Dadrian, "Pitfalls of a 'Balanced' Analysis," 73–130 and 121–12.
[54] *İleri*, 20 December 1918.

ministry in Istanbul. An October 1915 telegram on the subject from Talat Pasha to Mazhar Bey, who had just been appointed head of one of the investigative commissions, clearly explained that "the results of the investigations of governors, provincial district governors and country heads will be first submitted to the ministerial office and subsequent actions . . . will be taken in accordance with the orders and reports that will be sent [from the ministerial office]."[55]

Among the surviving papers of the Ottoman Interior Ministry are a number of documents dealing with the permissions given for these investigations. To give one example:

> It has been learned from the current investigations that Besni county head Edhem Kadri Bey allowed officials within his retinue to abuse their positions in matters concerning the Armenians and that he himself received certain items without payment; it being seen as appropriate that he be turned over to the responsible court-martial for this reason, the necessary instructions have been communicated to the head of the Investigative Committee, Mazhar Bey.[56]

Economic improprieties would nevertheless continue throughout the period that the commissions were active, and the central government sent numerous cables to the provinces in an attempt to stem the rampant illegal activity.

Plenty of similar documents can be found within the archives of the Interior Ministry's Cipher Office, such as one stating that "it is being reported . . . that abandoned Armenian property in the county of Karacabey has passed into the hands of a variety of parties. Please report back quickly [after] investigating."[57] Another stated that "abuses have occurred . . . regarding the abandoned property in Silivri and [those responsible] for

[55] BOA/DH.ŞFR, no. 56/267, Coded telegram from interior minister Talat to the former governor of Bitlis, in Sivas (via the Office of the Governor of Sivas Province), 3 October 1915.

[56] BOA/DH.ŞFR, no. 61/165, Coded telegram from interior minister Talat to the Province of Mamuretülaziz, dated 1 March 1916. For another document dealing with permission being given for the removal from his position of Tenos county head Cemil Bey for improprieties, and his delivery to the court-martial, see BOA/DH.ŞFR, no. 57/105, Coded telegram from interior minister Talat to the Province of Sivas, dated 24 November 1915. Mazhar Bey would be informed of this situation by a separate cable.

[57] BOA/DH.ŞFR, no. 57/208, Coded telegram from the Interior Ministry's IAMM to the president of the Bursa (Hüdâvendigâr) Commission on Abandoned Property, dated 31 December 1915.

these [abuses] are primarily gendarmes and their unit commanders" and the need for those committing these abuses to be investigated.[58]

In his testimony before the postwar parliamentary commission of inquiry known as the Fifth Department (5. Şube), former grand vizier Said Halim Pasha acknowledged that the activities of the investigative commissions had, in the final analysis, produced little or no result. In his words, "investigative commissions were put together following the Armenian massacres (Ermeni kıtâli). These performed their functions and returned. However, the Interior Ministry did not wish to announce the results of the investigations. Despite all manner of entreaty and insistent demands, [the ministry] insisted on concealing the truth . . . for the entire period that Talat Pasha was at the Interior Ministry, he determined that no consequences would or could result from the investigations."[59]

Examples of some of the reports sent to the capital by the investigative commissions can be found in the Archive of the Armenian Patriarchate of Jerusalem. Some of the accounts found in the reports of the Ankara commission are instructive in the extreme. In one case, a witness was asked to tell all he knew about the illegalities that had occurred. "Sir, I have seen far more horrible things than this," he replied. "I saw the armed gangs and gendarmes kill the Armenians in the convoy with axes and pickaxes."

"I didn't ask you about that! Just answer my question!" warned the head of the parliamentary commission.

"Sir, I will answer it as well," the witness insisted, "but please lend your ear to these things I am compelled to say in the name of justice: I saw people just like us in a wagon who had been killed with axes and pickaxes." At this, he was ejected from the room.[60]

Many documents among the Cipher Office papers also dealt with instances wherein inquiries were made simply into the looting of Armenian property, abuses by officials, and other irregularities. To give one example, at one point during their activities, investigative commission chairman Mazhar Bey, who conducted investigations in the Malatya region, requested permission to investigate a county head for suspected

[58] BOA/DH.ŞFR, no. 61/276, Coded telegram from the Interior Ministry's IAMM to the Provincial District of Eskişehir, dated 13 March 1916.

[59] Kocahanoğlu, İttihat ve Terakki'nin Sorgulanması ve Yargılanması, 84.

[60] Dadrian, "Pitfalls of a 'Balanced' Analysis," 124.

malfeasance. Upon learning of this, Talat Pasha wrote a message to the Mamuretülaziz Province that is worth repeating at length:

> When Hakkı Bey, the county head of Kahta, left his official posi-
> tion and unlawfully crossed the border and entered the county in
> order to receive the Armenian convoy from Erzurum and from
> Malatya, he did so not upon the command or with the authority of
> the county head of Hısnımansur, who had been entrusted with the
> deportation [operation]; as a result of this, tension erupted between
> the two. Because this situation obliged the convoy to remain at the
> foot of the mountain for three days, and their property and posses-
> sions were looted, the convoy was forced into a state of of disarray.
> As a result of his own declaration, which was supported by reports
> and unambiguous evidence, it is understood that, even though a
> huge amount of money and possessions were taken by means of the
> official and individual channels that Hakkı Bey employed, only in
> the amount of around 10,000 kurush were surrendered to the trea-
> sury; as a result, Investigative Commission Chairman Mazhar Bey
> has announced the necessity of having the aforementioned Hakkı
> Bey brought before the Court-Martial. Please submit your opinions
> on this matter.[61]

As can be understood from the cable, Talat was not at all concerned with the fate of the Armenians in the convoys; rather, his sole interest was in the fate of the money and possessions taken by Hakkı Bey beyond 10,000 kurush. Similarly, among the dozens of other similar documents that could be cited here, one finds no information about investigations being opened into murders or other crimes against individuals that took place during the Armenian deportations.

As a comparison, consider the following: In the investigations that took place after November 1918, one finds numerous expressions such as, "it is understood that [given individuals] were involved in the crimes car-ried out during the course of the deportations,"[62] or "attempts have been

---

[61] BOA/DH.ŞFR, no. 59/146, Coded telegram from interior minister Talat to the Province of Mamuretülaziz, dated 29 December 1916.

[62] BOA/DH.ŞFR, no. 96/270, Coded telegram from the Interior Ministry's General Directorate of Security to the Provincial District of İzmit, dated 8 March 1919.

made to capture Akyazılı Abaza Kâzım and Kuru İbrahim, who, during the course of the deportations from Adapazarı, were involved in the oppression and torture of individual deportees and were responsible for their deaths."[63] On the other hand, among the documents found among Interior Ministry Papers and relating to the wartime investigations, one would be hard-pressed to find any such expression of concern—to say nothing of prosecution—for crimes committed against Armenian deportees.

It is worth providing a number of examples here from archival sources of the conditions under which permission was actually given to investigate local officials:

The head official of Tenos County Cemil Bey is to be removed from his position and distanced from all tasks now because of his inappropriate actions during the Armenian deportations. Investigative Commission chair Mazhar Bey has been informed in writing that the documents concerning the aforementioned [suspects] have been submitted at the court-martial.[64]

[Azîziye Kâ'im-i makâmı Hâmid] is to be removed from his position and distanced from all tasks immediately because of his inappropriate actions and events during the [Armenian] deportations. Investigative Commission Chair Mazhar Bey has been informed that the documents concerning the aforementioned [suspects] have been submitted at the court-martial.[65]

The reply has been given to the Investigative Commission chair of the need to hand over the head official of Görün County, Şuayib Effendi, to the court-martial, due to his inappropriate policies and actions during the Armenian [deportation]. The aforementioned is also to be removed from his position by the provincial government.[66]

---

[63] BOA/DH.EUM.AYŞ, no. 21/95, Written communication from the assistant chief prosecutor of the Istanbul Court-Martial [Dersaadet'ten Divan-ı Harbi Örfi Müdde-i Umumi Muavini] to the Interior Ministry, dated 27 September 1919.

[64] BOA/DH.ŞFR, no. 57/105, Coded telegram from interior minister Talat to the Province of Sivas, dated 14 October 1915.

[65] BOA/DH.ŞFR, no. 57/116, Coded telegram from interior minister Talat to the Province of Sivas, dated 25 October 1915.

[66] BOA/DH.ŞFR, no. 57/413, Coded telegram from the Interior Ministry's General Directorate of Security to the Province of Sivas, dated 13 October 1915. It is understood that these removals from

Please report the results of the investigation in a clear manner regarding regimental commander Captain Sâlih Effendi, who was reported to have received a 5,000-lira bribe from the Armenians arriving from [Der] Zor, so that they might serve as a basis for actions needing to be taken.[67]

Another reality that emerges from the Cipher Office papers is that investigations were indeed opened against state officials who were suspected of assisting Armenians for the purpose of rescuing them from deportation. The following examples from archival sources of such investigations can be given:

[Please] report the results of the investigation and pursuit of [train] station dispatch official Lieutenant Tahsin Effendi, who is known to have smuggled certain Armenians to Istanbul after issuing them false papers.[68]

It has been reported by the Office of the Provincial District Governor of [Der] Zor that they had learned that [only] two of the seven Armenians exiled from Istanbul to [Der] Zor and three of the seventy-two Armenians dispatched from Aleppo to [Der] Zor have arrived in [that location] while the others have been released in exchange for money by the gendarmes entrusted to protect them. Please complete any and all preparations so that the necessary investigation of the protecting gendarmes is quickly completed and that their dossiers are submitted to the court-martial and report on what is being done to prevent similar incidents from occurring.[69]

It has been learned that there are still 3,845 males and a little less than 5,000 women in Marash who have not been deported, and that of these, there are as many as 3,500 Gregorian Christians, while the

---

office mentioned in the previous two documents were carried out with the approval and desire of Mazhar Bey, who wished to be appointed to and serve in Sivas.

[67] BOA/DH.ŞFR, no. 66/55, Coded telegram from interior minister Talat to the Provincial District of (Der) Zor, dated 22 July 1916.

[68] BOA/DH.ŞFR, no. 66/167, Coded telegram from interior minister Talat to the Province of Konya, dated 8 August 1916.

[69] BOA/DH.ŞFR, no. 66/43, Coded telegram from interior minister Talat to the Province of Aleppo, dated 20 July 1916.

rest are Catholic and Protestant. It is thought that the Gregorian Christians are still there due to the recent communications regarding their exclusion from the deportation. In light of this situation, it is difficult to understand whether or not the provincial district governor supported or protected the Armenians [in question]. Nevertheless, civil administration inspector Haydar Bey has been sent to Marash to investigate.[70]

THOSE RECEIVING THE DEATH SENTENCE

There is indeed some evidence that during the course of the deportations a number of criminal investigations were opened against individuals—including members of the SO—who were afterward executed. As will be seen in the cables from Talat Pasha cited below, in "removing" these individuals (and in particular these SO functionaries), one of the chief motivations was the concern that they might cause problems for the government in the future. To give a few examples:

Çerkez Ahmed: He played a role in the massacre of Armenians in the regions of Van, Urfa, Diyarbekır, and Damascus, as well as in the killing of two Armenian members of the Ottoman Chamber of Deputies, Krikor Zohrab and Vartkes Serengülyan, on the orders of Cemal Pasha. A 21 August 1915 cable from Talat Pasha to Diyarbekır Province showed that Çerkez Ahmed's gang of brigands had already begun to pose a serious problem for the area. Talat Pasha wished to respond to this problem by having Çerkez Ahmed sent back to Istanbul; in it he mentions that "since it has been learned that the inappropriate actions of Provincial Governor's Aide Halil Bey and Sirozlu Çerkez Ahmed, who were sent to Urfa along with their gangs, have come to constitute a threat to the general peace and order of the provincial district, please communicate that they are to be immediately recalled."[71] On his journey back to the capital, Çerkez Ahmed was arrested on Talat Pasha's order as he reached Eskişehir and sent from there to Cemal Pasha in Aleppo. In a cable to Konya, sent on 27 August

[70] BOA/DH.ŞFR, no. 63/110, Coded telegram from interior minister Talat to Fourth Army commander Cemal Pasha, dated 26 April 1916.

[71] BOA/DH.ŞFR, no. 55/132, Coded telegram from interior minister Talat to the Province of Diyarbekır, dated 21 August 1915.

1915, Talat explained the situation: "Sirozî Ahmed and his companion Halil, who murdered Armenians and looted their goods, have been sent to Konya today so that they may be tried in the Fourth Army's court-martial. There should be absolutely no opportunity given for them to escape and they are to be held in confinement in Konya until the orders and instructions arrive from Cemal Pasha."[72]

Çerkez Ahmed would be subsequently tried in the court-martial in Aleppo, sentenced to death, and executed on 17 September 1915. Interior minister Talat Pasha approved the court's sentence, sending Cemal Pasha a telegram advising him that "his elimination is necessary in every sense. Otherwise, he might prove damaging in the future."[73] In his memoirs, Cemal Pasha's chief of staff, General Ali Fuat Erden, writes that "the debt of gratitude [owed] to killers and murderers is heavy. . . . The means that are employed in dirty business become necessary in times of need and [must be] used; but after they are employed, they must not be tolerated, but rather discarded (like toilet paper)."[74]

Yakup Cemil: As part of an SO unit formed of convicts released from prison as part of a special pardon, he played a central role in the massacre of Armenians in eastern Anatolia during the war.[75] Among papers of the Interior Ministry's Cipher Office are a number of documents of correspondence dealing with Yakup Cemil's activities in the Trebizond region and his subsequent transfer from Bitlis to Iraq.[76] After the war, a commission, named the Investigation of Misdeeds (Tedkik-i Seyyiyat),[77] was formed in order to investigate the Armenian deportation and massacres.

[72] BOA/DH.ŞFR, no. 55-A/177, Coded telegram from interior minister Talat to the Province of Konya, dated 9 September 1915.

[73] Ziya Şakir, *Yakın Tarihte Üç Büyük Adam* (Istanbul: Ahmet Sait, 1946), 58.

[74] Ali Fuad Erden, *Birinci Dünya Harbinde Suriye Hatıraları*, vol. 1 (Istanbul: Halk, 1954), 216. For a detailed account of Çerkez Ahmet's role in the Armenian Genocide, see Dadrian, "Documentation in Turkish Sources," 118–20.

[75] Aziz Samih, *Büyük Harpte Kafkas Cephesi Hatıraları* (Ankara: Genelkurmay Yayınları, 1934), 68. Aziz Samih, who served during the war in the Reserve Cavalry Corps, characterized Yakup Cemil's "crazy, immoral [çılgın, ahlaksız]" regiment as a bunch of "bloody, murderous convicts."

[76] BOA/DH.ŞFR, no. 55-A/95, Coded telegram from Major Cevad from the office of the SO (Teşkîlât-ı Mahsûsa'ya Memur), to Major Yakub Cemil Bey, via Trebizond governor Cemal Azmi Bey, dated 5 September 1915; BOA/DH.ŞFR, no. 58/58, Coded telegram from interior minister Talat to Yakub Cemil Bey to the Office of the Governor of Bitlis, dated 13 December 1915. In this cable Talat informs Cemil that "the order was given by Enver Pasha to the relevant parties for you to join Halil Bey in Iraq."

[77] *Vakit*, 24 November 1918.

This commission asked the War Ministry questions about the massacres in which Yakup Cemil participated. Yakup Cemil, having been found guilty of organizing a coup against the Unionist leaders, was executed on 11 September 1916 for "treason against the homeland."[78]

Kurdish armed band chief Şaftanlı Amero: He was entrusted by Diyarbekır provincial governor Dr. Reşid and acting governor Feyzi to murder 636 of the province's Armenian leaders. After transporting them across the Tigris River with flotation devices made of inflated animal skins, the Armenians were brought to the Bezuan Valley where they were stripped naked and given over to members of his tribe to be killed. Less than two weeks had passed before Amero was called to Diyarbekır, where he was to be given a medallion and reward for his heroism by Dr. Reşid and Feyzi Bey. Upon his arrival he was murdered by ten Circassians who had been entrusted with the task.[79]

"Kurdish" Murza Bey: He organized the killing of Armenians from Erzincan and Erzurum as they were in the area of the Kemah Pass. Later on, the Unionists had him arrested on the charge of having struck a gendarme, but the real reason was "because they felt that he might become dangerous." Once in custody, "he was secretly murdered."[80]

German Consular Reports: Dr. Rössler, the German consul in Damascus, stated in one of his reports that Fourth Army commander Cemal Pasha had a number of Kurds hanged for having organized an attack on a camp set up in the İslahiye region, in which, before the eyes of the German engineers, they pillaged, looted, and killed the Armenians there.[81] In a December 1915 report, Germany's ambassador to the Porte, Wolff-Metternich, wrote, "I spoke today about the condition of the Armenians with Talat Bey, who had returned from Anatolia. He has taken comprehensive

[78] AAPJ, Box 21, File M, Doc. no. 555.

[79] Thomas Mugurditchian, *Dikranagerdi nahankin chartere* (Kahire: Djihanian, 1919), 57–61, cited in Dadrian and Akçam, *"Tehcir ve Taktil."* Similar accounts of these events are recounted in the unpublished work "Haver Delal" (mentioned in chapter 7, note 20, in this volume), which was written by a member of the Kurdish Raman tribe. The account of these events is found on pages 70–71.

[80] FO 371/2781/264888, Report based on the testimony of Sait Ahmet Muhtar, an Indian Muslim serving in the British army, dated 27 December 1916, no. 2, 7. Additionally, see *Current History* 5 (February 1917), cited (with reference to the *Times [London]*) in Dadrian and Akçam, *"Tehcir ve Taktil,"* 210.

[81] DE/PA-AA/R 14090, Report by German consul in Damascus, Dr. Walter Rössler, dated 3 January 1916.

measures concerning the provisioning of Armenians who have been deported. Evil actions against the persons or possessions of Armenians have
been severely punished. Recently more than twenty persons convicted of
such untoward acts were sentenced to death."[82]

Kör (Blind) Nuri: He served with the rank of captain as the gendarmerie
commander for Şarkışla during the deportations. He was subsequently arrested for the murder of almost two thousand Armenian soldiers (who
had served in the labor battalions) and then sent by Third Army commander Vehip Pasha to the military court; upon his conviction, he was
sentenced to death. In the written testimony he subsquently gave to the
investigative commission in Istanbul, Vehip Pasha would provide detailed
information on this affair.[83]

Gendarmerie sergeant Tahsin: He took part in the killings of Armenians
in and around Mosul Province. Later on he was turned over to the court-
martial but was sentenced to death even before the end of his trial. The
presiding judge was actually forced to sign the death sentence after the execution had taken place. Information on this matter came to light during
two separate trials on wartime crimes that were held in Istanbul between
the years 1919 and 1921. In his testimony at the 19 April 1919 session of
the trial of Mosul central commander Nevzat Bey, former director of the
Interior Ministry's Private Secretariat Fuâd Bey gave the following information: "a soldier committed a murder while drunk. We tried him in the
court-martial. He was executed before a death sentence was handed down
and it was only communicated to us and ratified after the fact. If we had
complained [about it], each one of us would have gotten the same 'ration
of lead' [as that soldier]."[84]

Between 1919 and 1921, another Mosul-related trial was held against
Captain Ferit Bey. The former president of the Mosul Court for Serious

---

[82] DE/PA-AA/R 14089, Report from German ambassador to the Porte, Wolff-Metternich, to Chancellor Bethmann-Hollweg, dated 18 December 1915. The information given here by Talat deserves
special attention. J. B. Jackson, the American consul in Aleppo, reported that a number of Ottoman
citizens who had given assistance to Armenians had been executed on various pretexts (NA/RG 59,
867.4016/301, Report marked "Very Confidential," by ambassador to the Porte, Morgenthau, to the
State Department, dated 15 September 1916, in *United States Official Records*, ed. Sarafian, 550–51).

[83] AAPJ, Box 7, File H, Doc. no. 171–82, Written testimony of Vehip Pasha given to the Presidency
of the Commission of Criminal Investigation in the Office of the General Directorate of Security,
dated 5 December 1918.

[84] *Yeni Gazete*, 20 April 1919.

Crimes, Hasan Bey, testified in this trial against Ferit Bey, who was accused of having taken part in the crimes of central commander Nevzat Bey and in the "atrocities that had occurred in Mosul." Among other things, Hasan Bey claimed that the crime of Sergeant Tahsin, who was sentenced to death, had been "banditry."[85] According to another newspaper report of the trial, Hasan Bey stated at one point "as for Tâhir, who was executed, he was a person who had committed many murders."[86] Even if one cannot be sure at this point of the crime for which Sergeant Tahsin was executed, it appears likely that he played a role in murder and other crimes against Armenians.

To sum up, in 1915–17 there was no government policy to investigate and punish individuals (whether state employees or private citizens) who participated in the killings; in contrast, the misappropriation of Armenian property was indeed investigated. In some cases, infamous murderers were also "eliminated" as a potential danger to CUP operations.

THE QUESTION OF DEPORTATIONS FROM ISTANBUL AND İZMIR

One of the central arguments used by those claiming that there was no conscious attempt to annihilate the Armenian population is that had the Ottoman authorities actually intended to destroy the entire population, they would have also deported the Armenians of Istanbul and İzmir— which, it is claimed, did not happen. However, the documentation available among the Cipher Office papers shows that there were indeed Armenian deportations from these provinces.

ISTANBUL AND DEPORTATIONS

What is meant here by "deportations" from Istanbul is not merely the arrest of a limited number of intellectuals on 24 April 1915 and their exile to Ayaş and Çankırı but also small-scale deportations of Armenians from the imperial capital afterward and throughout the rest of the war. In fact, there were plans to eventually deport all of Istanbul's Armenian population, but

[85] *Alemdar*, 3 June 1919.
[86] *Yeni Gazete*, 3 June 1919.

it is understood that these plans were never implemented due primarily to early German pressure and, secondarily, to the later course of the Ottoman war effort. In an August 1915 report, for instance, the German ambassador to the Porte, Hohenlohe-Langenburg, told his superiors that he had hand-delivered a note to Talat Pasha, dated 9 August, protesting the ongoing crimes against Armenians and demanding that the Porte take measures to prevent further incidents. "Istanbul has given its guarantee that the Armenians of Istanbul shall not be deported," he claimed.[87]

In his memoirs, Archbishop Zaven Der Yeghiayan, who served as Armenian patriarch of Constantinople between 1913 and 1922, says that in the end, the deportation of Istanbul's Armenian population was prevented only as the result of German pressure. In fact, a German parliamentary delegation came to the Ottoman capital in January and February 1916 and, according to Der Yeghiayan, made the German government's concerns well known. Both its presence and its message were strongly enough felt that an understanding was reached between the two countries that the Armenians of Istanbul would not be deported.[88]

German, British, and American sources all testify that lesser piecemeal deportations from Istanbul were conducted throughout the war. Corroborating information about similar deportation orders can be found in the archives of the Ottoman Interior Ministry's Cipher Office. Significantly, the documents from these disparate archives do not contradict but rather largely confirm and corroborate each other.

The first document to be examined in this regard is found in the "Blue Book" published by James Bryce and Arnold Toynbee in 1916. In a letter of 15 August 1915, the Armenian patriarch of Constantinople reported on the question of deportations from the capital:

> So now it is Constantinople's turn. In any case, the population has fallen into a panic, and is waiting from one moment to another for the execution of its doom. The arrests are innumerable, and those arrested are immediately removed from the capital. The majority will assuredly perish. It is the retail merchants of provincial birth,

---

[87] DE/PA-AA/R 14087, Report from German ambassador to the Porte, Hohenlohe-Langenburg, to Chancellor Bethmann-Hollweg, dated 12 August 1915.

[88] Der Yeghiayan, *My Patriarchal Memoirs*, 105–6.

but resident in Constantinople, who are so far being deported.
. . . We are making great efforts to save at any rate the Armenians
of Constantinople from this horrible extermination of the race, in
order that, hereafter, we may have at least one rallying point for the
Armenian cause in Turkey.[89]

Another letter, written on 28 October 1915 by the Balkan branch of the
Dashnaktsoutiun (Armenian Revolutionary Federation) has the following to say about the deportations:

> Thousands of poor Armenians expelled from Constantinople are
> made to march on foot from İsmid to Konia and still further, after
> they have delivered up everything they possess to the gendarmes,
> including their shoes. Those who can afford to travel by rail are also
> fleeced by the gendarmes, who not only demand the price of the
> ticket from Constantinople to their destinations, but extract the
> whole of their money by selling them food at exorbitant prices. They
> demand payment even for unlocking the door of the water-closet.[90]

American missionary William S. Dodd, who was then stationed in
Konya, confirmed the above accounts of deportations:

> The other method of transportation, on foot, was carried out largely
> in the case of men from Constantinople who were there at work,
> without their families, their families living in the interior towns and
> villages. While the Turkish Government constantly maintained that
> they made no deportation of the Armenian population of Constan-
> tinople, they arrested and sent away those thousands of men who
> were earning their living for the support of their families. There were
> women also among these.[91]

The German archives likewise contain reports of large-scale deportations from Istanbul. On 5 December 1915, German foreign ministry

[89] Bryce and Toynbee, *The Treatment of Armenians*, Doc. no. 7, 53, Letter from the Armenian patriarch in Istanbul, dated 15 August [1915].

[90] Ibid., Doc. no. 11, 65. The Dashnak letter is a report that was sent by the State Department to the
American Relief Committee after being received.

[91] William S. Dodd, "Report of Conditions Witnessed in the Armenian Deportations in Konia,
Turkey," in *"Turkish Atrocities,"* Barton, 147.

secretary Jagov forwarded a report to Ambassador Wolff-Metternich that he had received from the Dashnak Committee's branch in Sofia. According to the report, "The Turkish government, in contradiction to the promises that it had previously given, has begun to deport Armenians from Istanbul as well. As of this moment, as many as 10,000 persons are said to have been deported and a large portion of these have been killed in the mountains of İzmit. A list has been prepared that contains [the names of] 70,000 persons [to be deported]." Jagov then gives Wolff-Metternich the following directive: "If these reports prove correct, please protest [the Ottoman government's behavior] energetically."[92]

In his reply on 7 December, the German ambassador confirmed the reports of the continued deportations, claiming that on the basis of information received from the director of security for Istanbul, some 30,000 Armenians had already been expelled from the capital: "I have learned from a very trustworthy source that according to information provided by the local chief of police, which I beg to keep secret, lately about 4,000 Armenians also from Constantinople have been deported to Anatolia, and that the remaining 80,000 Armenians still living in Constantinople are to be gradually cleared away, 30,000 having already been deported during the summer and a further 30,000 having fled. Should a stop be put to this, then more severe means are necessary."[93]

What can be understood from all these documents is that the deportation of Armenians from Istanbul was carried out in a piecemeal fashion and over a long period of time. It is possible to find information relating to the subject of small-scale deportations carried out from Istanbul both during the various court-martial trials held in Istanbul between 1919 and 1921 and in the contemporary press. Here are a few examples: On 18 December 1919, during the seventh session of the postwar trial held at the Istanbul Court-Martial and known as the County Directors Trial (Nahiye Müdürleri Davası), an Armenian who had been deported from Istanbul testified that he had been one of a two-hundred-person convoy deported between July and August 1915.[94] Celal Bey, who served as provincial governor of

[92] DE/PA-AA/Bo.Kons./Band 171, Telegram from German foreign ministry secretary Jagov to German ambassador to the Porte, Wolff-Metternich, dated 5 December 1915.

[93] DE/PA-AA/R 14089, Telegram from German ambassador to the Porte, Wolff-Metternich, to Chancellor Bethmann-Hollweg, date 7 December 1915.

[94] *Alemdar, Ati,* 19 September 1919.

Konya during the deportation operations, recalled that deportations from Istanbul were indeed carried out and puts the number of those deported "in the thousands": "The trains that left from Haydar Pasha carried thousands of Armenians every day. They tended to pile up in Konya. The command would arrive continually from Istanbul for them to be sent further. And when no rail cars were provided I would apologize, telling them that no further deportations would be possible."[95]

Interior Ministry documents confirm all the information above that Armenians from Istanbul were deported throughout 1915 and much of 1916. For example, a June 1916 cable to the provinces demands that "the Armenians who are to be deported from Istanbul and other locales and sent to [Der] Zor are to be sent there by way of the Kars-Marash-Pazarcık Road over Konya, Karaman, and Tarsus."[96] As can be understood from the cable, deportations from Istanbul continued at least into the summer of 1916.

The Interior Ministry documents further reveal that there were clear criteria for deportation, and that the deportees were largely sent to the provincial district of Der Zor. Essentially, the documents show that there were four main criteria according to which people were deported: (1) born outside of Istanbul, (2) unmarried, (3) unemployed, and (4) belonging to various organizations. It is useful to give some examples. An August 1915 cable from the Interior Ministry's Security Directorate to the provincial district of İzmit informed the local officials that the Armenians from İzmit who live in Istanbul are to be considered residents of İzmit and deported. It added that the police chief had also been informed that "those Armenians who are from İzmit and its surrounding areas but are currently in Istanbul and who wished to go to the aforementioned areas" must leave "[Istanbul] and not be returned here; they are to be expelled along with the others, since they are the population of those locales." Finally, the telegram asked that "the operation be carried out according to [this rule]."[97]

[95] Celal Bey, "Ermeni Vakâyi-i."

[96] BOA/DH.ŞFR, no. 65/95, Coded telegram from interior minister Talat to the Provinces of Edirne, Adana, Ankara, Aydın, Hüdâvendigâr (Bursa), and Konya, and to the Provincial Districts of İzmit, Bolu, Karesi (Balıkesir), Kayseri, Karahisâr-ı Sahib (Afyon Karahisar), Kütahya, Eskişehir, Niğde, Marash, and İçel, dated 26 June 1916.

[97] BOA/DH.ŞFR, no. 54-A/343, Coded telegram from the Interior Ministry's General Directorate of Security to the Provincial District of İzmit, dated 9 August 1915.

Another cable, this one sent directly from interior minister Talat Pasha to Konya Province in December 1915, shows that special documents were issued by the chief of police for the expulsion from the capital of Armenians from İzmit: "The provincial district of İzmit has been informed of the need to deport those Armenians from İzmit who could not be deported because they were in Istanbul at the time of the deportations and who were subsequently sent to İzmit on documents from the Police Directorate." The reason that the dispatch was sent to Konya was because of the request to the governor that this new group of Armenians would be "placed in the province somewhere other than the [province's administrative] center."[98]

A cable sent to Mosul in November of 1916 concerning "Simpat Kirkoyan, a manufacturing merchant from Bitlis who is from the provinces [taşralı] and unmarried and who was apprehended attempting to flee to Bulgaria on a forged passport and sent to the interior of the country on 20 July 1915" can be given as an example of the deportation of unmarried Armenian men and non-Istanbul natives.[99]

One of the cases appearing before the Istanbul Court-Martial during the Armistice period concerned individuals who were accused, among other things, of deporting unmarried Armenian men from Istanbul. The prosecution called for the defendant, a police official by the name of Hidayet Effendi, to be convicted and sentenced for the crime of "finding pretexts to deport unmarried Armenian men from the environs of Üsküdar and then entering their houses and confiscating the property and possessions of some of them."[100]

Another Interior Ministry cable to Kastamonu Province, sent in July 1915, shows that similar actions had been taken against those Armenians deported from Istanbul to Çankırı and Ayaş on 25 April 1915. According to the message, a registry of Istanbul Armenians had been created in which it was recorded whether they were originally from the provinces. Again, similar action was requested here in regard to the nonnatives: "Among those Armenians previously sent [to Çankırı and Ayaş] and who

---

[98] BOA/DH.ŞFR, no. 60/308, Coded telegram from interior minister Talat to the Province of Konya, dated 13 December 1915.

[99] BOA/DH.ŞFR, no. 70/119, Coded telegram from interior minister Talat to the Province of Mosul, dated 28 November 1916.

[100] For more information of the trial of Hidayet Effendi, see Alemdar, 17, 19 June and 9 July 1919; Yeni Gazete, 24 June and 16 July 1919.

are identified as persons whom it appears appropriate to release, if there are some by whose names there are notes in the registries identifying their place of origin as the provinces [taşralı] and who therefore are to be sent back to their residences, permission should given for them to forego being returned to their homes and to be sent to Istanbul instead."[101] The occasion for the telegram is clear: among those Armenians who were exempt from the deportation, those who were not from Istanbul but rather from the provinces were generally to be sent back to their region of origin; nevertheless, in this cable a special exception for these people was made.

Other documents show that there were also special "combined" categories for potential deportees, such as "unmarried, from the provinces" and "unemployed, from the provinces." Some examples from these documents: "Kirkor Karagözyan, the son of Karabet, who is originally from Bursa [Hüdâvendigâr], has been taken from Kumkapı, where he resides and sent to Konya, has been deported under the categories of 'unemployed' and 'from the provinces'";[102] "Nazarat, the son of Asador, has been deported from Istanbul to Konya for the reasons of his being single and from the provinces."[103] Likewise, there are examples of those deported for their membership in certain political organizations, such as "Serki, son of Kirkor, [who was] deported from Istanbul to Konya when it was learned that he was a member of the Dashnaktsoutiun Armenian Committee."[104]

In the Armenian sources it is possible to find a great deal of information on the exact criteria upon which the deportations were conducted. For example, one might mention the memoirs of Aleksan Tarpinyan, who was arrested along with six friends while they were staying "in Istanbul's Arnavutköy at 6:00 p.m. on the evening of 15 August 1915," and who was deported to Syria. In regard to the period after his arrest, Tarpiyan states that "they subjected us to interrogations, and especially wanted to know whether or not we were unmarried. All six of us were." Upon learning this, the decision to deport them was made.[105]

---

[101] BOA/DH.ŞFR, no. 54-A/150, Coded telegram from the Interior Ministry to the Province of Kastamonu, dated 29 July 1915.

[102] BOA/DH.EUM, 2. Şube, no. 16/16.

[103] Ibid., no. 15/16.

[104] Ibid., no. 15/4.

[105] Kévorkian, "L'extermination des déportés arméniens." For Alexan Tarpinyan's testimony, see http://www.imprescriptible.fr/rhac/tome2/p2t01/.

Foreigners who witnessed these deportations made mention of the fact that the deportations of Armenians from Istanbul were determined and carried out on the basis of certain specific criteria. A reporter for the German daily *Kölnische Zeitung*, von Tyszka, wrote in top secret reports of 5 and 6 September 1915 that he witnessed Armenians being sent away from Istanbul in a systematic fashion. "First of all, unmarried males (who were thought to have been from Sivas and the eastern Anatolian provinces); after that, all males, married or single, who were born in the Armenian provinces. . . . Up to the present 200 males and 50 families have been deported." Von Nahmer then reported that the deportations had been carried out in this manner because of the presence of the embassies of the various powers in Istanbul, and that he had heard from Germans who were close to the Ottoman government that once the deportations of those Armenians in Anatolia were complete, it would be the turn of those in Istanbul.[106]

İZMIR AND DEPORTATIONS

The claim that Armenians were not deported from İzmir is simply untrue. Various sources, among them documents found in the Prime Ministerial Archive in Istanbul, show that Armenians began to be deported from İzmir already in the summer of 1915—albeit in small groups. These deportations were halted in November 1916 as the result of intervention by German general Liman von Sanders. A letter from İzmir provincial governor Rahmi Bey to Talat Pasha on 26 May 1915 stated that "the order has arrived from the Ministry of War . . . regarding the wholesale deportation to the interior of those communities who are hostile [to the government]." The governor added that those whose deportation is desired "are those who were born here [i.e., İzmir], grew up and became rich here, and who have contributed to the economic development of country; [they] have supported aid to those who need help and are dignified and honorable persons; we may even say that they are more conscious of a sense of Turkishness than certain Turks." In Rahmi's opinion, "It is wrong to separate these persons from their wives and children and send them off to uninhab-

[106] DE/PA-AA/R 14087, Reports by *Kölnischen Zeitung* reporter von Tyszka to the German Foreign Ministry, dated 5–6 September 1915.

itable climes, those who thought that the administration of the government is in honorable hands and that no persecution or oppression would come to them from this regime and [therefore] do not feel the need to leave the country." Relying on his long friendship with the interior minister, Rahmi asked that the deportations be halted: "Therefore, in the name of our friendship I ask of both you and Enver that you speak with him and inform him that the execution of such measures in the province [of İzmir] should be abandoned."[107]

From the governor's letter alone it is not possible to know how many people altogether were slated for deportation, which of the aforementioned groups they were from, nor their ultimate fate. Nevertheless, on occasion one can learn from various telegrams about certain limited deportations of Armenians, and from others about specific permissions being granted for them to return. For instance, a 1 September 1915 cable asked for reports on "the return to İzmir of the Armenian Aşçıyan and Bulutyan families, who are [currently] in Ereğli";[108] another cable from Talat Pasha on 30 September spoke of the appropriateness of "allowing Captain Dikran Effendi's wife and father Kasbar to return to İzmir";[109] or others on the same date permitting the relatives of Onnig Effendi, parliamentary deputy for İzmir, to return to İzmir or to settle in Eskişehir. To these can be added telegrams from 3, 5, 10, and 25 October and 14 November 1915, which have largely the same content.[110]

Existing documents show that the first mass arrest and deportation of Armenians in İzmir was conducted in November 1915. A cable sent by the Security Directorate to Aydın Province on 2 December 1915 informs them that "it has been learned from the Office of the Governor of the Provincial District of [Afyon] Karahisar that 60 Armenians have come from İzmir to [Afyon] Karahisar under the guard of special officers in order to be sent to the place of their final destination. [Please] report

---

[107] BOA/DH.EUM, S. Şube, 20/62, Message from İzmir provincial governor Rahmi Bey, with the salutation "To Talat Bey Effendi," dated 26 May 1915.

[108] BOA/DH.ŞFR, no. 55/345, Coded telegram from interior minister Talat to the Province of Konya, dated 1 September 1915.

[109] BOA/DH.ŞFR, no. 56/271, Coded telegram from interior minister Talat to the Provincial District of Karahisâr-ı Sahib (Afyon Karahisar), dated 30 September 1915.

[110] BOA/DH.ŞFR, no. 56/270, Coded telegram from interior minister Talat to the Provincial District of Karahisâr-ı Sahib (Afyon Karahisar), dated 30 September 1915. For other documents, see BOA/DH.ŞFR, nos. 56/291, 56/301, 56/345, 57/29, 57/121, and 58/6.

the reasons for their removal and exile."[111] A cable sent to Afyon six days later reports that "61 Armenians sent away from İzmir have been sent to Mosul via the Diyarbekır road."[112] Another wave of arrests followed that of the aforementioned 61 people, and this time a group of 95 people from İzmir were deported to Mosul: "[Please] send off under guard the 61 persons who, on account of their being dangerous individuals, were sent from İzmir to [Afyon] Karahisar and from there on to Konya where they are being guarded, along with the further 95 Armenians who are yet to be dispatched, to Mosul by way of Diyarbekır."[113]

An October 1916 cable to Konya indicates that a group of Armenians deported from İzmir to Konya had been taken from Konya and sent to Pozantı to be settled there on 25 December 1915.[114] It is impossible to understand from the message whether this was one of the previously mentioned groups or a different one. Another cable sent to Afyon on 9 February 1916 states that "the Manisa textile factory owner Sarıyan, who was deported from İzmir on account of his being a member of the Dashnaktsoutiun Committee and who, according to the written reply I received from the province of Aydın, is presently in [Afyon], is to be sent on to Mosul by way of Diyarbekır like those before him. [Please] report [when this is done]."[115] From this, and from the German involvement in the deportation from İzmir in autumn 1916, it may be concluded that the arrests and deportations from İzmir continued into 1916.

The first information concerning the İzmir deportations and German involvement therein is mentioned in a November 1916 report from Germany's consul in İzmir, Prince von Spee. In his report, von Spee related that he was told by İzmir governor Rahmi Bey that CUP members in İzmir had made complaints to the central government about him due to his "soft" policy toward the Armenians in his province. In response, the

---

[111] BOA/DH.ŞFR, no. 58/191, Coded telegram from the Interior Ministry's General Directorate of Security to the Province of Aydın, dated 2 December 1915.

[112] BOA/DH.ŞFR, no. 58/247, Coded telegram from the Interior Ministry's General Directorate of Security to the Provincial District of Karahisâr-ı Sahib (Afyon Karahisar), dated 8 December 1915.

[113] BOA/DH.ŞFR, no. 59/20, Coded telegram from interior minister Talat to the Province of Konya, dated 16 January 1916.

[114] BOA/DH.ŞFR, no. 69/58, Coded telegram from interior minister Talat to the Province of Konya, dated 21 October 1916.

[115] BOA/DH.ŞFR, no. 60/282, Coded telegram from interior minister Talat to the Provincial District of Karahisâr-ı Sahib (Afyon Karahisar), dated 9 February 1916.

Unionist leaders in Istanbul began to exert pressure on him to deport the Armenian population of İzmir. As a result of this pressure, Rahmi eventually gave the İzmir police commissioner full authority to arrest all Armenians considered suspicious. On 8 November 1916 the first round of arrests was made, netting three hundred Armenians who, along with their families, were placed on trains and sent to the interior.[116] The German consul also reports that General Liman von Sanders, the commander of the army in İzmir, informed Rahmi Bey that he would not allow any further deportations because it would put the country's military situation at greater risk.

General Liman von Sanders, who informed Istanbul of the situation himself on 12 November, states in his report of the same date that the İzmir governor had told him that he had received the order to deport his province's Armenians from Talat himself, adding, "I warned the governor that I would not allow [any more such actions] after this and warned him that it was necessary to desist from arrests and deportations on this scale [in the future]. I then informed the governor that in the event that were such an event to be repeated I would prevent it by force of arms."[117]

Regardless of how much von Sanders might claim that the reason for his decision was clearly military, there were numerous rumors afoot that the decision to deport Armenians from İzmir had actually been made by the German government, and this likely played a greater role in influencing von Sanders's actions than any military considerations per se. Germany's ambassador to the Porte at the time, Dr. Richard von Kühlman, apprised Berlin of the situation and asked that it be announced that Liman von Sanders's decision had received support from the German government. In its reply, sent on 14 December 1916, the German Foreign Ministry announced that it stood behind its general.[118] As for von Kühlman, he sent off a note several weeks earlier (25 November) stating that "the deportation

---

[116] DE/PA-AA/Bo.Kons./Band 174, Report from German consul in İzmir (Prince von) Spee, dated 10 November 1916.

[117] DE/PA-AA/Bo.Kons./Band 174, Report from Liman von Sanders to the German Embassy in Istanbul, dated 12 November 1916.

[118] For the ambassador's message requesting support, see DE/PA-AA/R 14094, Report from German Embassy representative Radowitz, dated 13 November 1916. The German Foreign Ministry's statement of support for von Sanders's position is DE/PA-AA/R 14094, Note from German Foreign Ministry secretary Zimmerman, dated 14 November 1916.

of Armenians [from] İzmir has been postponed. It should thus be understood that the matter has been closed."[119]

From the Ottoman Interior Ministry archives, it is possible to follow the course of the deportations conducted in İzmir in November 1916. According to documents found there, the number of Armenians taken into custody in the first round of arrests—reported in the German sources as around 300— was actually 256, and they were deported almost immediately after their arrest. Five days after the arrests, a cable was sent to the provincial district of Karahisar that said, "a message was sent to the Office of the High Command, requesting that 256 Armenian [revolutionary] committee members who were sent off from İzmir [toward Karahisar] be sent to Marash by way of Adana, and should be put on trains [for this purpose]."[120] Other cables, such as one sent to Adana requesting that "the 256 Armenian committee members deported from İzmir who will be arriving in Adana in order to be sent on to [Der] Zor are to be sent [there] under guard, and by way of Marash,"[121] and one to Marash ordering that "the 256 Armenian committee members deported from İzmir who will be arriving there [in Marash] in order to be sent on to [Der] Zor are to be sent to [Der] Zor under guard,"[122] allow us to track the deportees step-by-step and to understand that, from the outset, their final destination was Der Zor.

THE ROLE OF THE SPECIAL ORGANIZATION (TEŞKILAT-I MAHSUSA) IN THE CRIMES

In his 2005 work *The Armenian Massacres in Ottoman Turkey: A Disputed Genocide*, Guenter Lewy has claimed that there is no connection between the Special Organization and the deportation and killing operations against the Armenians. This thesis has no basis whatsoever.[123]

[119] DE/PA-AA/R 14094, Report from German ambassador to the Porte, von Kühlmann, dated 25 November 1916.

[120] BOA/DH.ŞFR, no. 69/260, Coded telegram from the Interior Ministry's General Directorate of Security to the Provincial District of Karahisâr-ı Sahib (Afyon Karahisar), dated 13 November 1916.

[121] BOA/DH.ŞFR, no. 69/262, Coded telegram from the Interior Ministry's General Directorate of Security to the Province of Adana, dated 13 November 1916.

[122] BOA/DH.ŞFR, no. 69/261, Coded telegram from the Interior Ministry's General Directorate of Security to the Provincial District of Marash, dated 13 November 1916.

[123] Lewy, *Armenian Massacres*. A detailed critique by this author of Lewy's book appeared in serialized form in the Turkish Armenian newspaper *Agos* in July–August 2006, nos. 84–85. For the English-

According to the author, not a single document corroborating such a connection appeared in Istanbul between 1919 and 1921, including the indictment against the former Unionist leaders' trial, apart from descriptions coming from a few personal testimonies and claims.[124] Lewy also claims that during the trial sessions, "the defendants denied any connection between the SO [Special Organization] and the Central Committee of the CUP, however, as well as any role of the SO in the Armenian deportations and massacres."[125] Lewy's arguments, and in particular the reception of his book, are extremely important. This is a perfect example of how the denial industry operates, so it is worth examining closely.

Lewy's book and similar arguments elsewhere have been well received by Turkish state authorities. The author himself has been seen as worthy of various awards and accolades. The Avrasya Strategic Research Center (ASAM),[126] the Turkish government's central propaganda arm for disseminating and supporting the official line on the Armenian question, awarded Lewy its highest prize for research on "Crimes Against Humanity"; the chairman of Turkey's Grand National Assembly (TBMM), Bülent Arınç, presented him with the TBMM Medallion.[127] The Turkish Foreign Ministry has subsidized the free international distribution of Lewy's book, calling it their "official view," and in the Turkish press, there have been a number of articles about Lewy that have been gushing in their praise.[128]

---

language version of the article, see "Guenter Lewy's 'The Armenian Massacres in Ottoman Turkey,'" in *Genocide Studies and Prevention* 3, no. 1 (April 2008): 111–45.

[124] In Lewy's own words, "[Y]et there is no credible evidence, other than the assertion of the indictment of the main trial, for the allegation that the SO [Special Organization], with large numbers of convicts enrolled in its ranks, took the lead role in the massacres . . . there is no evidence anywhere that . . . any . . . SO detachment was diverted to duty involving the Armenian deportations," ibid., 84–85.

[125] Ibid., 86.

[126] ASAM was established in 1999. The Armenian Research Institute, which was also established within the framework of ASAM in 2001, now serves as the center for research and propaganda in support of Turkey's official version of history in regard to the Armenians. After undergoing a name change in 2005, it is now known as the Institute for the Research of Crimes Against Humanity (İnsanlığa Karşı İşlenen Suçlar Araştırma Enstitüsü). During a conference held at Gazi University in Ankara on 24–26 November 2005, Guenter Lewy was awarded ASAM's "Highest Award [in the field of] Crimes Against Humanity" (Gündüz Aktan, "Rövanş [1]," *Radikal*, 29 November 2005).

[127] http://www.meclishaber.gov.tr/develop/owa/haber_portal.haber_detay?p1=30684.

[128] To give two examples: "In both the book *Armenian Massacres in Ottoman Turkey* by the great genocide scholar Guenter Lewy and in Colonel Edward J. Erickson's *Enemies Within* there are detailed proofs that the Special Organization did not involve itself in the [Armenian] deportations as a state organization," Gündüz Aktan, "Bir Şey Söyle de," *Radikal*, 22 March 2007. See also Şahin Alpay, "'Soykırım' tezinin zaafları," *Zaman*, 3 September 2005.

It is worthwhile dwelling a bit on these claims of the author regarding the relationship between the SO and the crimes against the Armenians and examining what official Ottoman documents say about this issue.

As has been mentioned, the SO was reestablished in August 1914. The organization had two goals: externally, to incite a Muslim revolt against Russia and Great Britain, and internally, to take measures against the Armenians. It was decided to form militia forces for this purpose, and this was immediately begun. The ranks of these armed units were filled by recruiting from three separate sources: Kurdish tribes, Muslim refugees from the Balkans and the Caucasus, and convicts. During the main postwar trial of Unionist leaders, almost twenty separate documents that dealt with the formation of these units were read out during the fourth through seventh sessions alone.[129]

The SO militia units served in the Caucasus and Iran beginning in September. After their initial military setbacks at the beginning of the war, control of the SO units was taken away from the army and the Ministry of War, under which they had operated until that time, and were placed under the direct control of the CUP. Additionally, the units were reorganized and assigned to carry out the annihilation of the Armenian convoys.[130]

For his part, Lewy does not dispute the existence of these SO units, nor the fact that they were dispatched to the Caucasus region and Iran for the purpose of fomenting revolts. Rather, he disputes the claim that the units were used in the elimination of Armenians. He believes that the real perpetrators of these crimes were largely Kurdish tribesmen, gendarmes and militias, bandit gangs, and volunteers and irregulars, none of whom he completely identifies nor wishes to place in too close a connection with the CUP Central Committee: "[T]he common element is that *chettes* were irregulars who (no matter how recruited, directed, or composed) participated in the robbing and killing of Armenian deportees."[131]

According to Lewy, although these elements (whose nature and identity is never made entirely clear) may very well have carried out these

---

[129] For the minutes of the session, see Dadrian and Akçam, *"Tehcir ve Taktil,"* 471–599.

[130] For a more detailed discussion of the SO's units, see Taner Akçam, *A Shameful Act,* 130–40 and 149–59.

[131] Lewy, *Armenian Massacres,* 228.

crimes, the crimes themselves were made possible not through any action or intent of the Unionist center in Istanbul but rather by the actions of individual local officials, whom he identifies as the guilty parties: "[T]hese militia units were usually organized by local authorities, often under the influence of militants in the CUP clubs."[132]

Lewy's overall goal is to show that the killings of the Armenians were not the result of a central decision and operation, so that there is no cause to speak of genocide. The killings were rather local events, and the central government had no direct connection with them. Consequently, it will be of benefit here to briefly review some information that came to light during the Istanbul trials in particular and to show that they contain the same information and content as the documents from the Interior Ministry's Cipher Office and show the direct involvement of the military and Interior Ministry in the operations.

CONSTANT COMMUNICATION BETWEEN DIFFERENT INSTITUTIONS

The documents of the Interior Ministry and some evidence originating from the main trial of the Istanbul Court-Martial clearly attest that there was a constant and broad-ranging communication between the Command Center of the SO and the Ottoman Ministry of War, the Interior Ministry, and the CUP Central Committee. It is true that until the fifth and sixth sessions of the main trial of the Unionist leaders, the defendants denied any connection between the SO and the other aforementioned institutions. But during the fifth and sixth sessions, a number of documents were read into the record that showed the defendants that the SO had indeed been in communication with the CUP Central Committee, the Ministry of War, local party organizations, and voluntary armed units, and at this point the defendants began to admit that the documents had actually been written by their own hands and ceased denying these connections.

The fullest explanation of the coordination that went on between the various institutions was that given by Küçük Talat:

[132] Ibid., 223.

It is possible that the [Committee of] Union and Progress was in communication with the Special Organization, just as it was in communication . . . with every institution. . . . It is possible that the Special Organization made an appeal to the CUP Central Committee. Your own party said that it assisted us by means of your organization. It is natural that the Central Committee, which could not have remained indifferent to . . . an appeal made in this manner, whether from the Minister of War or from the Special Organization in the name of the ministry itself, would have possibly suggested . . . to some of the members of the organization that they should act in accordance with the demands of the Ministry of War, of the Special Organization or of the Interior Ministry.[133]

DEPOSITIONS OF WITNESSES AND SUSPECTS

During different trials in the court-martial in Istanbul, dozens of defendants and eyewitnesses testified that units of the SO were involved in the deportation and massacre of Armenians and that they were thus responsible for these crimes. During the fifth session of the main trial, for instance, the presiding judge directed a question to Yusuf Rıza, saying that "it is clear from your testimony that among the contingents involved in the matter of deportations and massacres, there also were [these] companies, which is to say Special Organization troops." In reply, Yusuf Rıza stated that there did indeed exist this type of local SO units, which were under the supervision of local administrators (governors, in this case) and the CUP's so-called responsible secretaries, and that these units were directly involved in the deportation operations.[134] In the seventh session of the same trial, when Yusuf Rıza was read some incriminating testimony and documents regarding the involvement of SO units in crimes, he responded that "it is a shame that conditions have now, today come to such a state [so as to show] that the Special Organization became a means for carrying out all

[133] *TV*, 25 May 1919, no. 3557, Report on the trial's sixth session (14 May 1919).
[134] *TV*, 21 May 1919, no. 3554, Report on the trial's fifth session (14 May 1919). Yusuf Rıza's claim that there were two different SOs was most likely an attempt to clear himself of any blame. During his testimony he stated that the units of the SO that were under the direction of the local officials (provincial governors) and Unionist secretaries were separate from those SO units connected to the Ministry of War, in which he served.

of these crimes under orders from the [CUP] Central Committee. Your servant cannot find words to reply to this [state of affairs], Your Honor." In short, under the weight of such compelling documentation, Yusuf Rıza was forced to admit that both the CUP's Central Committee and the SO had played an important role in the various wartime crimes against the Armenians and others.[135]

During various sessions of the different trials, many others—from Ottoman bureaucrats to army officers—would give testimony confirming the fact that units of the SO were directly involved in crimes against Armenians. These testimonies were then reported in the dailies of the period and often reiterated in the respective courts' rulings. For example, at the 2 August 1919 session of the Mamuretülaziz trial, Tahsin, the former governor of the province of Erzurum, stated that units of the SO (which was under the supervision and control of Bahaeddin Şakir) had been responsible for the annihilation of the Armenians:

> I was in Erzurum during the deportation of the Armenians . . . the convoys that were subjected to massacre were carried out by those who had been assembled on behalf of the Special Organization. There were two parts to the Special Organization. At the time that I left Erzurum the Special Organization [there] was a rather significant force. And these [units] would participate in the war. The army was aware of this. Afterward, there was a different Special Organization that was subject to the orders of Bahaeddin Şakir Bey, which is to say that he would send off telegrams here and there that he would sign "Head of the Special Organization" . . . Bahaeddin Şakir Bey also had a cipher machine. He was in communication with both the Porte and the Ministry of War. During the period of the deportations they were in communication with the army, as well . . . Bahaeddin Şakir Bey [had] two cipher machines, so that he could communicate with both the Porte and the Ministry of War.[136]

In the final verdict in this case, much space was given both to numerous documents and the testimony of Muslim Turkish eyewitnesses who

[135] *TV*, 29 May 1919, no. 3561, Report on the seventh session of the trial, 17 May 1919.
[136] *Alemdar*, 3 August 1919.

claimed that the crimes against the Armenians had been carried out by the SO.[137]

Another bit of evidence of the connection between the SO and the Armenian deportations is found in the written deposition of Kastamonu governor Reşid Pasha, which was read at the fifth session (27 October 1919) of the trial of the Unionist responsible secretaries. In his statement, the governor recounted that he had at one point received a memo from Bahaeddin Şakir (signed "Head of the Special Organization") announcing that the Armenians of Kastamonu were to be deported and informing him that he was being removed from his position for noncompliance with this order.[138]

In the verdict given in the Bayburt trial, a great number of quotations were taken from the testimonies of Muslim witnesses in regard to the killings and other crimes perpetrated by the SO. The Erzurum regimental commander Adil Bey, for instance, stated that the Armenians "were killed . . . by members of the Special Organization" and that he had learned this from the investigations that were carried out and from the written reply that he had received from the commander of the Bayburt gendarmerie.[139]

The trial that began on 13 July 1919 was referred to in the press as the "Trial of the Cretan Café Owner Necati Effendi," whose café was depicted as "one of the most important bases of operation for the Union and Progress gangs." It directly concerned the SO unit that operated in the environs of Diyarbekır and Urfa and their crimes. The defendants were members of an armed gang in Diyarbekır known as the Eşref Bey Gang. One of the defendants gave the following account: "I d[idn't] know that our regiment was called an armed gang. Our clothing, our headgear, everything we had was like the military; we were soldiers, Your Honor." Over the course of the trial, various coded cables sent from the region were read, along with the testimony of eyewitnesses, concerning the murders committed and the looting that took place.[140] One could literally go on for pages with the list of evidence.

---

[137] *TV*, 9 February 1920, no. 3771; the verdict in the Harput trial was delivered on 13 January 1920.

[138] *Atı, Alemdar*, 28 October 1919. Portions of these testimonies, which appeared in the daily papers at the time, would consistently be used in subsequent cases, such as in the verdict in the trial of the Unionist secretaries and in various sessions of the main trial of the Unionist leaders.

[139] *Tercüman-ı Hakikat*, 5 August 1920; *Vakit*, 6 August 1920.

[140] *Atı, Alemdar*, 27 October 1919.

DIFFERENT NAMES USED TO DEFINE THE SPECIAL
ORGANIZATION UNITS

Over the course of the trials, it came to light that different names were given to the SO units, which were the core of many of the armed gangs and voluntary militias. Moreover, this information did not just appear during the trials themselves; the archives of the Interior Ministry's Cipher Office are replete with similar information. To give a few brief examples: On 8 May 1919, at the fourth session of the main trial against the Unionist leaders, the presiding judge asked the defendants, "What was your purpose in using the term 'armed gang'? Is it proper to give the term 'armed gang' to a [military] detachment, to a battalion, to a detachment attached to the Ministry of War or the Army?" One of the defendants, Cevad, replied that different names like these were given to these units "on the orders that came from the Ministry of War," and that "they were sometimes called voluntary detachments, at other times, armed gangs."[141]

Likewise, in the cables and letters belonging to the Ministry of War, the SO, the CUP Central Committee, and the local organizations that were read into the record throughout the trial, the term "armed gang" is frequently used for SO units. At the trial's fifth session, for instance, an official correspondence from the CUP Secretariat in Samsun to the CUP Central Committee was read, informing the committee that a "55 person armed gang under the command of *Artvinli* [Artvin native] Tufan Ağa— the fifth such gang—has been sent off by motorized vehicle."[142]

At the same session, dozens of documents were read that referred to the SO units as "voluntary," and a number of witnesses gave testimony to the same effect. For instance, during the trial's fifth session, the defendant Cevad called these units "voluntary detachments" and "voluntary organizations," even reading out several telegrams to show that these terms were also used in official correspondence.[143] For his part, Ziya Gökalp stated that "after the general mobilization was announced the Ministry of War created the Special Organization and began to form voluntary detachments."

[141] *TV*, 15 May 1919, no. 3549, Report on the trial's fourth session, 8 May 1919.
[142] Ibid.
[143] *TV*, 21 May 1919, no. 3554, Report on the trial's fifth session, 14 May 1919.

RELATIONS BETWEEN THE INTERIOR MINISTRY AND
THE SPECIAL ORGANIZATION

The papers of the Interior Ministry's Cipher Office clearly show us that the Ottoman Interior Ministry had a direct hand in the formation of SO units. The terms "armed gang," "volunteer," and "individuals from the Special Organization" are all used in a manner that makes them practically interchangeable; furthermore, the purpose in forming these units is made quite clear. In a cable sent to Van on 6 September 1914 (mentioned in chapter 4), the Security Directorate openly writes that the armed gangs were organized for the purpose of carrying out attacks inside Iran: "Our current political situation is becoming more secure and [is established] on sound foundations. We have reached understandings with the Bulgarians on all points. The armed gangs should have already completely organized themselves within Iran. The order to act will be given separately."[144]

In a cable sent by the Interior Ministry's Security Directorate to a number of regions on 12 September 1914, it is openly stated that the aim of creating the armed gangs is "to attack enemy territories," and for this purpose, it orders the jails to be emptied and a list of those freed inmates to be sent to Istanbul:

> Those tribe members and other persons of influence who for past crimes are today confined in jails and prisons, or who have been sentenced but escaped, and about whom it is hoped that they might be exploited for military actions, are to all receive a general pardon; armed gangs are to be then formed under their leadership that, when necessary, will attack [across] enemy territory; this will be convenient in the future for the purpose of saving the country from the burden of these bandits and it will be appropriate that such persons who could perform such a task be appointed in cooperation with the [military] commanders. Since, in light of it having been announced by the High Command of the Imperial Army, the impor-

---

[144] BOA/DH.ŞFR, no. 44/201, Coded telegram from the Interior Ministry's General Directorate of Security to the Province of Van, dated 6 September 1914.

tance of this effort has been taken into account and a [final] decision will be subsequently taken here; if there are currently any individuals who could be employed by means of the amnesty decree[,] their names should be recorded and sent in.[145]

It can be understood from the existing documents that "voluntary regiments" had already begun to be formed from the first days of August, which was when the general mobilization order was given, and that this matter was largely left to the Ottoman Third Army. In fact, this is stated quite clearly in the official documents: "The need to form voluntary regiments was left by the War Ministry to [local] needs."[146] The same information would be repeated in another cable, sent to Mamuretülaziz Province nearly six months later, on 13 February 1915: "it has been reported by the War Ministry that the permission to form voluntary regiments from among the individual tribal members who have [thus far] avoided military service shall be left to the discretion and approval of the Third Army Command, and the situation as it stands is to be communicated to said command."[147]

Another telegram sent to Van Province on 15 August 1914 reveals that it was not only the recently formed voluntary units that as of August were put under command of the Third Army, but also the "tribal regiments," which were the Unionist successors to the notorious "Hamidiye regiments" of the Hamidian period: "The tribal cavalry units in Eastern Anatolia are to be placed under the command of the Third Army in Erzurum and, since their manner and place of service is to be determined by the aforementioned army commander[,] it is ordered that you act in a manner that will be established in communication [with the Third Army Command]."[148]

---

[145] BOA/DH.ŞFR, no. 44/224, Coded telegram from the Interior Ministry's General Directorate of Security to the Provinces of Van, Bitlis, Mosul, Erzurum, and Diyarbekır, dated 12 September 1914. An identical telegram was sent the following day to the Province of Trebizond. See BOA/DH.ŞFR, no. 44; and BOA/DH.ŞFR, no. 44/232.

[146] BOA/DH.ŞFR, no. 44/41, Coded telegram from the Interior Ministry's General Directorate of Security to the Provincial District of Karesi (Balıkesir), dated 18 August 1914.

[147] BOA/DH.ŞFR, no. 49/263, Coded telegram from interior minister Talat to the Province of Mamuretülaziz, dated 13 February 1915.

[148] BOA/DH.ŞFR, no. 44/24, Coded telegram from the First Branch of the Interior Ministry's General Office of Communication to the Province of Van, dated 15 August 1914.

During the period in which these armed gangs were being formed, in his role as interior minister, Talat Pasha assumed the task of coordinating actions between the CUP Central Committee, local officials, and army commanders. For example, in a 29 November 1914 cable to the provincial district of İzmit, after stating that "it would seem appropriate that those detainees in İzmit who have either been already sentenced or who are awaiting trial and who might be employed as armed gangs and brigands should have the charges against them lifted and their sentences removed through the procuring of a decree of amnesty in their regard [in exchange for] service and activities [on behalf of the Ottoman war effort] that they subsequently display," Talat orders that such people be therefore released from custody and sent to Istanbul.[149]

In addition, Talat also closely monitored various aspects of this operation, such as the questions of whether or not the necessary provisions were being secured for the gangs that were formed and whether or not they reached their intended destinations. One can cite numerous examples of this, such as the cable he wrote to Trebizond on 24 December 1914 demanding that the five-hundred-person militia under the command of gendarmerie captain Ahmed Bey have its needs provided for and that when they are dispatched from Samsun to the Caucasus, a steamship be secured for their passage to Trebizond.[150] In another telegram to Trebizond, this one sent two days later, he asked whether or not the two hundred volunteers under the leadership of the Sivas convict Çarşambalı (Çarşamba native) Hacı Bey have been assembled yet.[151] In these cables, the term "Special Organization unit" is used in place of the term "armed gang."

---

[149] BOA/DH.ŞFR, no. 47/245, Coded telegram from the Interior Ministry's General Directorate of Security to the Provincial District of İzmit, dated 29 November 1914.

[150] BOA/DH.ŞFR, no. 48/150, Coded telegram from interior minister Talat to the Province of Trebizond, dated 24 December 1914. "It has been understood from communications with the office of the provincial district governor of Canik that a 500-man force under the direction of gendarmerie captain Ahmed Bey has been put together and fully outfitted in order to take part in armed actions [çete müsâdemâtı] in the Caucasus, and we are informing you in response that the aforementioned force must be sent immediately to Trebizond. The direct shipment to the province of a quantity of weapons and supplies for said force is now pending."

[151] BOA/DH.ŞFR, no. 48/155, Coded telegram from interior minister Talat to the Province of Trebizond, dated 26 December 1914.

Additional documents attest to the correspondence between the Interior Ministry and the SO heads in the provinces. For example, there is ample existing correspondence between Talat Pasha and a certain Rıza,[152] the person responsible for SO activity in the Trebizond region, and it can be understood from this correspondence that the members of the SO also employed the Interior Ministry codes in their correspondence. On 18 November 1915, for instance, Talat Pasha ordered the provincial governor of Trebizond that the cable sent "by Rıza Bey, the head of the Special Organization delegation by the cipher of the county administrative center of Arhavi" be sent "immediately using the cipher of the province [of Trebizond]."[153] Yet another example that can be given in the matter is Talat Pasha's direct correspondence with Süleyman Askerî, who was the original head of the SO before going to the Mesopotamian front.[154]

Another noteworthy aspect of this correspondence that bears mention is the fact that the CUP's Central Committee employed the channels of communication of the Interior Ministry's Cipher Office in it. A cable sent to Trebizond Province on 20 November 1914 bears the heading "From the [CUP] Central Committee" and states that it was [written] for Rıza Bey," the aforementioned head of the SO activities in the region. The message also includes the following passage,

We request of you [that you find us] a few persons who know the coastal area between Poti and Sohum and who have engaged in smuggling activities there, as well as some capable individuals who are familiar with the regions of Kütayis[?], Tiflis, Dağıstan, Takata [?] and Rigodar[?]. Additionally, we will need two or three persons from among the Christian Georgians. Please report if you can find up to 100 persons who know the Caucasus Mountains and who are able to engage in brigandage and [armed] gang activities and whether or not you can assemble them in Trebizond within one

[152] This would be the same Rıza previously referred to in the text as "Yusuf Rıza." He would subsequently be arrested and appear as one of the defendants in the main trial of Unionist leaders after the war.

[153] BOA/DH.ŞFR, no. 47/73, Coded telegram from interior minister Talat to the Province of Trebizond, dated 18 November 1914.

[154] BOA/DH.ŞFR, no. 48/250, Coded telegram from interior minister Talat to Süleyman Askerî Bey, the provincial governor of Basra and commander of Iraq and its environs, dated 3 January 1915.

week at the latest; according to this we can get a good idea of what forces there are [available to us] here.[155]

As can be seen in all of these examples and many others, the terms "armed gang," "volunteer," and others were all used overtly and interchangeably for the various units of the SO. For example, in a telegram sent to Erzurum on 13 January 1915, the term "volunteers" is used for the armed gangs when ordering the emptying out of the prisons, and mention is made of these volunteers having been highly successful in combat: "It has been understood that those individuals who, after having been held in provincial jails and prisons were released and [formed] into armed gangs and sent to the theater of war, have secured great benefit [for our efforts]." For this reason, the telegram goes on, the order is given that "new 'volunteers' be rounded up and, after communicating on this matter with Third Army commander Hafız Hakkı Pasha, they are then to be sent off [toward the front]."[156] Likewise, in a 16 December 1914 cable to nearly all of the provincial governors, Talat wrote that the effort "to gather men for service in armed gangs" was continuing with great success.[157]

Among the existing Cipher Office papers are a number of official documents that openly use the term "Special Organization" and that state that these units were specifically employed against the Armenians. A cable sent by army headquarters in Istanbul (in the cipher of the Interior Ministry) to Mamuretülaziz Province on 2 June 1915 can be given as an example of this phenomenon. In this telegram the sender, Lieutenant Colonel Cevded, who is the SO member responsible for the region (later one of the defendants in the main postwar Unionist trial), asks the opinion of the governor about the Kurds and Armenians in the area, for the purpose of sending SO units:

[155] BOA/DH.ŞFR, no. DH.ŞFR, no. 47/96 and 47/96-1, Coded telegram from the Interior Ministry to the Province of Trebizond, dated 20 November 1914.

[156] BOA/DH.ŞFR, no. 48/344, Coded telegram from interior minister Talat to the Province of Erzurum, dated 13 January 1915.

[157] BOA/DH.ŞFR, no. 48/28, Coded telegram from the Interior Ministry's General Directorate of Security to the Provinces of Edirne, Ankara, Aydın, Hüdâvendigâr (Bursa), Sivas, Kastamonu, and Konya, and to the Provincial Districts of İzmit, Bolu, Çatalca, Karesi (Balıkesir), Kale-i Sultaniye, Menteşe, Teke, and Karahisâr-ı Sahib (Afyon Karahisar), dated 16 December 1914.

[R]elying on the known conditions among the Dersim Kurds, the Armenians have both evaded the pursuit detachments and with a specific revolutionary purpose in mind have entered Dersim with the purpose of stirring up confusion, quickly exploiting the Kurds' penchant for rapine, plunder and the rebellious tendencies for which they have long been known . . . and the situations such as hiding and provisioning Armenians by the thousands are well-known, with these two groups even displaying relations bordering on fondness for one another; matters have gone so far that infor-mal—even overly free-and-easy—behavior [by both sides] is being witnessed publicly. In light of this, I would like you to report your views and opinions on the situation, so as to know that the steps foreseen by the Special Organization might be taken when the time demands it.[158]

All the documents above, as well as additional examples too numer-ous to cite here, clearly show that the terms "gangs" and "volunteers" were indeed used in reference to the SO units, whose involvement in the Ar-menian Genocide is sufficiently clear. Moreover, the records of the Istan-bul Military Tribunals corroborates those of the Interior Ministry as pre-served in the Prime Ministerial Archive in Istanbul.

ANY TYPE OF ASSISTANCE TO THE CONVOYS IS DENIED

Those who argue that Armenian losses during the deportations were not the product of a central policy attempt to link the deaths to such general causes as epidemic diseases and hunger. According to such claims, epi-demics and famine were general problems that Muslims also had to con-front. The Ottoman government, despite the difficult conditions—so the argument goes—took advantage of all the possibilities at its disposal and attempted to aid the Armenian caravans. It even accepted the proposals of foreign countries to distribute aid and worked to lessen the suffering

[158] BOA/DH.ŞFR, no. 53/222, Coded telegram from Lieutenant Colonel Cevded of Army Head-quarters (Istanbul) to the Province of Mamuretülaziz, dated 2 June 1915.

of the Armenians. Let us examine the Interior Ministry documents that I have collected in order to see what they reveal about this subject.

It is true that during the years of World War I epidemics caused a great number of deaths.[159] And indeed, it is also certainly true that not only the Armenians but also large numbers of Ottoman soldiers and the population at large perished during this period as the result of hunger and disease. Nevertheless, Armenians were treated differently regarding health and the distribution of aid during the war years. The Ottoman government consciously and deliberately decided not to organize relief efforts for the Armenian deportees and refused the offers of assistance from foreign countries, even subsequently threatening legal proceedings against people and institutions accused of wishing to assist them. In this regard, the papers of the Interior Ministry archives contain documents and information of the utmost importance. These documents confirm the claims that the Ottoman government refused all offers of assistance from abroad and instead fully intended to annihilate the convoys of deportees—claims frequently repeated in German and American sources.[160]

In this sense, it would not be incorrect to speak of a high degree of internal consistency among these three different groups of sources. Additionally, the memoirs of a number of Turkish government officials who served in the region during that period give accounts similar to those found in both the Ottoman Interior Ministry and foreign archives (namely, German and American sources).

Celal Bey, the provincial governor of Aleppo, would write in his memoirs (serialized in the pages of the daily newspaper *Vakit*),

I admit, I did not believe that these orders, these actions revolved around the annihilation of the Armenians. I never imagined that any

---

[159] For a work on the epidemics that broke out during the war and the deaths they caused, see Hikmet Özdemir, *Salgın Hastalıklardan Ölümler, 1914–1918* (Ankara: Türk Tarih Kurumu, 2005).

[160] There are a number of works in existence on the subject of offers of foreign aid and their refusal by the Ottoman authorities. For a few examples of these, see Suzanne Elizabeth Moranian, *The American Missionaries and the Armenian Question: 1915–1927* (doctoral dissertation,University of Wisconsin-Madison, 1994); Barton, *"Turkish Atrocities"*; Rouben Paul Adalian, "American Diplomatic Correspondence," and Suzanne Elizabeth Moranian, "The Armenian Genocide and the American Missionary Relief Effort," in *America and the Armenian Genocide of 1915*, ed. Jay Winter (Cambridge: Cambridge University Press, 2003), 146–214; Hilmar Kaiser, in collaboration with Luther and Nancy Eskijian, *At the Crossroads of Der Zor: Death, Survival, and Humanitarian Resistance in Aleppo, 1915–1917* (Princeton and London: Gomidas Institute, 2002).

government could take upon itself to annihilate its own citizens in this manner, in effect destroying its human capital, which must be seen as the country's greatest treasure. I presumed that the actions being carried out were measures deriving from a desire to temporarily remove the Armenians from the theater of war and taken as the result of wartime exigencies.[161]

He later acknowledged that he had been mistaken. He claimed that no regard was given to the telegrams that he "wrote to the Interior Ministry" in which he requested "allocations in order to build shelters for the Armenians who were to be deported." Rather than assistance, however, the regime sent "an official who claimed to be entrusted with the resettlement of refugees, but who had actually been entrusted with the task of deporting the Armenians, along with their wives and children." According to Celal, what had occurred was "to attempt to annihilate" the Armenians.[162]

Hüseyin Kâzım, whom Cemal Pasha appointed as coordinator of assistance for Armenians arriving in Syria and Lebanon, told the German Consulate in Damascus at one point that "the government had not the slightest desire to assist the Armenian deportees and everyone was afraid that what had been planned was their systematic annihilation; this barbaric policy of obliteration was a cause of shame for Turkey."[163] In the memoirs he later penned, Hüseyin Kâzım, who eventually resigned from his post, recounted that in "Lebanon alone the number of persons who fell victim to the government's plot was 200,000."[164]

Çerkes Hasan Bey (aka Circassian Uncle Hasan), who would be brought in as Hüseyin Kâzım's replacement, had similar things to say about the government's attitude. In his memoirs he stated that when he first began his duties, the local civilian bosses told him, "see to it that you finish up the matter with these refugees in accordance with what the circumstances demand," and explained that they wanted "the matter resolved through the 'cleansing' [of the Armenians]."[165] After organizing the Arme-

---

[161] Celal Bey, "Ermeni Vakâyi-i," *Vakit*.

[162] Ibid.

[163] DE/PA-AA/R 14092, Report from Ambassador Wolff-Metternich, dated 19 June 1916, with appended report of Loytved Hardegg, dated 30 May 1916.

[164] Hüseyin Kâzım Kadri, *Türkiye'nin Çöküşü* (Istanbul: Hikmet Neşriyat, 1992), 255.

[165] "Tehcirin İç Yüzü," 26 June 1919.

nian deportations in an orderly fashion, in line with the special order he received from Cemal Pasha, Çerkes Hasan Bey learned that "these just and humane . . . actions" that he had performed for "the wretched masses . . . whom it was desired to rescue from death" were seen as "betrayal of the homeland." After being "accused of being a traitor," he was ultimately forced to resign his post.[166]

There is ample evidence in the German and American archives showing that no systematic and organized assistance was afforded by the government to the deportees, and that offers of assistance from outside were consistently refused. Already in the first days of the deportations, the German Embassy in Istanbul began to send reports back to Berlin that claimed that the Ottoman government did not provide "support for the deportation [columns], either in the way of money, of food, or of any other type."[167] German functionaries would often pass on reports from the regions to the effect that "the government has not lifted one little finger to provide even a smidgen of assistance to the deportees, and the police who adopt this stance of their commanders have, if anything, done everything in their power to increase the torment and cruelty that the Armenians have already experienced."[168]

German missionaries also reported that "the Turkish Government . . . has not taken the necessary measures to prevent the deportees from starving to death" and that it rejected "efforts to bring assistance to women and children, even those in difficult situations."[169] Wolff-Metternich, the German ambassador to the Porte, wrote in his report of 27 December 1915 that the Ottoman government had placed enormous obstacles in the way of all offers of assistance.[170]

---

[166] *Alemdar*, 27 June 1919.

[167] DE/PA-AA/R 14086, Report from Ambassador Wangenheim to Chancellor Bethmann-Hollweg, dated 17 June 1915.

[168] DE/PA-AA/Bo.Kons., vol. 170, Report from Lieutenant Colonel Stange (in Istanbul) to the German Military Mission, dated 23 August 1915.

[169] DE/PA-AA/Bo.Kons., vol. 171, Letter from Chancellor Bethmann-Hollweg to the German Embassy in Istanbul, dated 10 November 1915. In the letter the prime minister tells the German ambassador, "I would advise you to use your influence at the Porte on behalf of the Armenians, and in particular that you pay close attention that the Porte's standards [of behavior] not be extended to encompass the remaining Christian population in Turkey."

[170] DE/PA-AA/R 14089, Report by Ambassador Wolff-Metternich to Chancellor Bethmann-Hollweg, dated 27 December 1915.

A comparably large amount of information on this phenomenon also exists in the United States archives. American missionaries and others stationed in the region began reporting back to their superiors about the intransigence of Ottoman officials in regard to assisting the destitute Armenians that had arrived in their areas. For example, Dr. William S. Dodd, who served in Konya during this period, wrote to Ambassador Morgenthau on 6 May 1915:

> I went to the Police Mudir [commissioner] and asked permission to see them and was refused. The second time I went permission was granted, a police officer being present, so that I could get very little information. I went again and asked permission to give aid to them in the name of the Red Cross. . . . The Mudir refused permission, telling me to wait until the Vali [provincial governor] should come. The Vali came last night, and I called on him today. He told me that they were not in any need, and that I would not be allowed to give aid. I asked to see them and he refused.[171]

On the basis of these reports, Ambassador Morgenthau wrote to his superiors in Washington that the American missionaries were prevented from rendering any adequate assistance to the Armenians.[172]

Nor, it should be added, was this a covert policy on the part of the Ottoman government. Its officials openly and often stated that they would not accept any assistance. In his report of 20 August 1915, Ambassador Morgenthau wrote that the government had prevented the distribution of relief supplies that had been sent to Urfa, and that interior minister Talat Pasha had actually demanded of him that those regional consuls who attempted to have aid delivered to the region should be recalled.[173] Greg Young, who served in the American Consulate in Damascus during the war, related that he told Cemal Pasha during a conversation that "if the [Ottoman] Government permitted . . . I could secure funds from the American Red Cross to aid these people who undoubtedly would be

---

[171] Report by William S. Dodd (from Konya), dated 6 May 1915, in *United States Official Records*, ed. Sarafian, 37 (LC/HM[Sr.]/Reel 7/555).

[172] For an example, see NA/RG 59, 867.4016/90, Report from Ambassador Morgenthau to the State Department, dated 11 August 1915, in ibid., 77.

[173] NA/RG 59, 867.401.6/100, Report from Ambassador Morgenthau to the State Department, dated 20 August 1915, in ibid., 122.

very needy." Cemal Pasha replied that "the Government would not permit [any] of this and that the Government was doing everything possible, furnishing food, tents et cetera."[174]

Young traveled to the district near Damascus that was being used as a way station for Armenian deportees and gathered firsthand information, an approach that did nothing to endear him to the Unionist leadership. After Cemal Pasha reported to the Ottoman Ministry of War that the American consul was "preoccupied with the Armenian question," the Ottoman deputy foreign minister contacted Ambassador Morgenthau and delivered a demand by the Porte that the ambassador issue instructions to all American Consulates in the empire not to meddle in Ottoman internal affairs. Morgenthau, who reported on this situation to his superiors, wrote on 29 November 1915 that the "Minister of War and Minister of Foreign Affairs have repeatedly told me that they object to Americans distributing relief to Armenians because assistance by foreigners encourages such idealists as the Armenians to further resistance against the Government, although the Government has admitted at other times that Armenians are not in a position to effectively oppose the Government." Ottoman officials, he added, were demanding that any American aid be given directly to the Ottoman regime.[175]

One of the countless meetings that Ambassador Morgenthau reported holding with Ottoman officials and politicians was with Halil Menteşe, the speaker of the Ottoman Chamber of Deputies, on 12 November 1915. He recounted that Halil Menteşe, when reiterating the government's position on the matter, referred to the words of the minister of war: "Enver Pasha's opinion is that no foreigners should help the Armenians; whether his reasons are right or wrong, I give them to you as they are. Enver Pasha states that the Armenians are idealists and the minute they see foreigners approach them and help them, they will be encouraged in their national ideals. He therefore wishes to cut and sever for ever all relations between Armenians and foreigners."[176]

[174] NA/RG 59, 867.4016/212, Report from United States consular official in Damascus Greg Young to Ambassador Morgenthau (in Istanbul), dated 20 September 1915, in ibid., 296.

[175] NA/RG 59, 867.48/199, Report from Ambassador Morgenthau to the State Department, dated 29 November 1915, in ibid., 388.

[176] Interview of Ambassador Morgenthau with Halil Bey, minister for Foreign Affairs, at the American Embassy, 12 November 1915, in ibid., 346 (LC/HM[Sr.]/Reel 22/560–61).

Appeals to Cemal Pasha in Syria for assistance were categorically refused with the excuse that strict orders against this had been received from the capital. This explanation was given, among others, to Loytved, the German consul in Damascus, who suggested that humanitarian aid be provided for the deportees: "Under the direction of Hanauer, the German missionary who settled in Damascus three weeks ago, I wanted to establish a mess hall, a bath and an orphanage for the Armenians in Damascaus and its environs. I informed Cemal Pasha of this. He told me . . . that he had received clear instructions from Istanbul to prevent any German or American participation in assistance activities."[177] When asked why such offers of assistance were being rejected, Cemal Pasha explained that "the Armenians are resisting the Turkish government, and if they can be shown that they cannot expect any more assistance from foreign governments their morale can be broken."[178]

Not only individual appeals but also official offers to provide assistance from the German and American governments fell on deaf ears. In a report written on 28 April 1916, the German ambassador Wolff-Metternich informed his superiors in Berlin that his offer to assist the deportation convoys had been refused by the Ottoman government, which had explained that "[the government] cannot in any way allow foreign aid efforts for the Armenians since it will only inflate their hopes of receiving assistance from abroad"; the ambassador then added that "this response is word-for-word identical to the reply given by Cemal Pasha to Consul Loytved in Damascus."[179]

When it offered to provide assistance for the Armenian deportees, the American government would also find its offers rejected. Ambassador Morgenthau, who sent a lengthy report on the matter back to Washington on 26 July 1916, recounted in detail the explanation he had received from the Ottoman government for refusing his offer of aid. What is of crucial importance in the ambassador's account is that a high-ranking member of the Unionist regime rejects the claims that the Armenians who are perishing during the deportations are doing so because of hunger. Instead, the minister accuses the Entente forces of intentionally exaggerating the reports

[177] DE/PA-AA/R 14090, Report by Ambassador Wolff-Metternich to Chancellor Bethmann-Hollweg, dated 29 March 1916.

[178] Ibid.

[179] DE/PA-AA/R 14091, Report by Ambassador Wolff-Metternich to Chancellor Bethmann-Hollweg, dated 28 April 1916.

of death and hardship suffered by the Armenians in order to advance two separate purposes. The first of these was to create a rift in relations between the United States and the Ottoman Empire by creating propaganda that the latter had refused offers of assistance, while the second aim was to cause the Entente powers to appear more humanitarian and charitable in the eyes of the Syrian and Lebanese populations. All of the uproar about famines and deaths and the like was all being done in order to provoke an uprising in Syria of the type that had broken out in Mecca.[180]

In addition, in giving this explanation, the Ottoman minister denied that there actually was a famine. The government had opposed the distribution of aid by neutral parties because these people (who would receive the assistance) would be subjected to foreign propaganda and that would result in the interference of foreigners in the internal affairs of the empire.[181] Another American Embassy report from Istanbul, dated 12 August 1916, shows that the Ottoman foreign minister reiterated that the Ottoman government would never allow a neutral commission to distribute aid in Syria and Lebanon.[182]

The same words attributed to the Ottoman foreign minister in American reports were also expressed as government policy by Talat Pasha in a cable to Fourth Army commander Cemal Pasha. On 12 July 1916 he relates, "that Syrians [in the United States], distressed by the reports that they have seen in the American press of thousands of Syrians perishing from hunger, have appealed to the American government to assist their fellow countrymen," asking for both money and material aid. Elsewhere, the interior minister reports that "no one has died from hunger in Syria and the [Ottoman] foreign minister has been verbally appraised of the economic conditions in Syria," and says that the necessary information has been given to the Americans.[183] In the end, the foreign minister appears to have relayed Talat's words to Ambassador Morgenthau.

---

[180] NA/RG 59, 867.48/362, Report by American minister in Copenhagen Hoffman Philip (from Constantinople via Copenhagen) to the State Department, dated 26 July 1916, in *United States Official Records*, ed. Sarafian, 529.

[181] Ibid.

[182] NA/RG 59, 867.48/390, Report by Hoffman Philip (from Constantinople via Copenhagen) to the State Department, dated 12 August 1916, in *United States Official Records*, ed. Sarafian, 531.

[183] BOA/DH.ŞFR, no. 65/180, Coded telegram from interior minister Talat to Fourth Army commander Cemal Pasha, dated 12 July 1916.

INVESTIGATIONS ARE OPENED AGAINST THOSE PROVIDING ASSISTANCE

It is possible to follow all of these developments from the documents found in the Interior Ministry archives. The government's attitude toward providing aid itself or allowing assistance to be provided by others was clearly stated by Talat Pasha in an 8 April 1916 cable to Cemal Pasha marked "urgent, secret and private":

> I spoke with Enver Pasha. We do not want to allow aid to be delivered to the Armenians by means of a third party and do not wish to give them the sense that they will receive aid and protection from foreigners. For this reason it is appropriate that they be given receipts of payment in exchange for the money that they wish to distribute while the money itself [will be distributed] by means of either the local administration or state officials and in the manner that they deem appropriate.[184]

What in essence can be gleaned from the correspondence between Talat and Enver is that the Ottoman regime did not merely reject offers of assistance but worked to ensure that foreigners would be prevented from freely circulating in Anatolia and the deserts of Syria and Iraq in order to prevent them from actually seeing and coming into contact with the convoys of Armenian deportees. Many messages were telegraphed to the provinces and gave precise information on the movements of certain foreigners and Ottoman citizens, including the days of their departure and expected arrival, the routes taken, and the demand that local officials take the necessary measures to ensure that such people not encounter processions of Armenian deportees during the course of their travels.

To give one example, a cable from Talat Pasha to the district governor of Urfa, sent on 20 December 1915, stated that "a portion of those citizens of hostile states currently in Urfa are to be sent to Kayseri and Niğde. The aforementioned persons are not to encounter Armenian

---

[184] BOA/DH.ŞFR, no. 62/276, Coded telegram from interior minister Talat to Fourth Army commander Cemal Pasha, dated 8 April 1916.

convoys on the roads during the course of their travels."[185] Another cable with similar contents was sent out to all provincial, district, and county officials.[186]

Alongside the steps taken to ensure that foreigners traveling in Anatolia and the Levant would not encounter convoys of Armenian deportees, measures were also taken to reduce the chance of them coming across dead deportees along the roads, as special attention was taken to remove their corpses from routes traveled by these foreigners. Apart from the documents quoted in chapter 1 concerning the removal of corpses from the roadside, the reports of missionaries stationed in eastern Anatolia in particular are full of eyewitness accounts of the extraordinary efforts taken in this direction. For instance, in his memoirs, Henry Riggs, an American missionary serving in Harput (Mamuretülaziz) at the time, wrote of encountering corpses on the roads when traveling to Harput; he also explained that he passed by many places that had clearly been "cleaned up" recently, as evidenced by the newly dug graves or, as often as not, by the many shallow graves and hastily (and poorly) buried bodies. Additionally, Riggs recounted that the inhabitants of the villages through which he passed told him that government functionaries had come by and forced them to gather the corpses together and burn them, saying that "some [foreign] consuls were to come by that way."[187]

Among the existing Interior Ministry documents, there are some related to investigations conducted against foreigners who wished to lend aid to the Armenian convoys. In an 11 December 1915 cable from Talat Pasha to the provincial governor of Aleppo, for instance, the interior minister wrote that "Şükrü Bey, the director of refugee affairs, has reported that a number of German engineers are currently to be found in the environs of [Der] Zor and prepared to set out in order to ensure that the four-to-five hundred Armenians deported over the past months are returned to their homes, along with their families." Talat continued, saying that, "according to the reply from the Ministry of War, the identity of these persons and their purpose for engaging in this manner of action remains

[185] BOA/DH.ŞFR, no. 59/40, Coded telegram from interior minister Talat to the Provincial District of Urfa, dated 20 December 1915.

[186] BOA/DH.ŞFR, no. 59/46, 47, 49.

[187] Leslie A. Davis, *The Slaughterhouse Province: An American Diplomat's Report on the Armenian Genocide, 1915–1917*, ed. Susan K. Blair (New Rochelle, NY: Aristide D. Caratzas, 1989), 25.

unknown." He then requested that the governor investigate the matter further and forward the resulting information to him.[188]

When reports were received that the American Embassy was attempting to organize relief efforts for the deportees, the Ottoman Ministry of War wrote a note to the Interior Ministry on 21 January 1916 informing them that it had learned that money and material aid was being distributed to the Armenians "by secret means," and requested "that a thorough investigation of the matter be conducted and the results reported back [to the Ministry of War]."[189] In response, Talat Pasha sent a cable to all provinces and districts on 30 January ordering that a secret investigation be conducted into this situation:

> It has been reported that vast sums of money have earlier as well as recently been sent by Armenians living in America in order to meet the needs of Armenians within the Ottoman domains, and that these funds have been distributed by secret means. [After] conducting an extremely secret and thorough investigation into this matter report back as to whether or not money has been sent there by these means and who have been the parties distributing the arriving funds to the Armenians.[190]

Following this demand for an investigation, another order was sent out on 6 February 1916 that demanded that the funds being distributed to Armenians by the American Consulate or missionaries be confiscated so that it could be distributed by the government instead.[191]

Particular notice was paid to foreigners who approached the locations of Armenian convoys, and when reports of such incidents reached the capital, messages were sent out to local officials demanding immediate

[188] BOA/DH.ŞFR, no. 58/258, Coded telegram from interior minister Talat Pasha to the Province of Aleppo, dated 11 December 1915.

[189] Document, signed "Ali Seydi," sent to the Interior Ministry, dated 21 January 1916, in *Askeri Tarih Belgeleri Dergisi* 32, no. 83 (March 1983): 161, Doc. no. 1923.

[190] BOA/DH.ŞFR, no. 60/178, Coded telegram from interior minister Talat to the Provinces of Edirne, Adana, Ankara, Bitlis, Aleppo, Hüdâvendigâr (Bursa), Diyarbekır, Damascus, Sivas, Trebizond, Konya, and Mamuretülaziz, and to the Provincial Districts of Urfa İzmit, Karahisâr-ı Sahib (Afyon Karahisar), İçel, Niğde, Canik, (Der) Zor, Karesi (Balıkesir), Kütahya, Eskişehir, and Marash, dated 30 January 1916.

[191] BOA/DH.ŞFR, no. 60/281, Coded telegram from the Interior Ministry's General Security Directorate to the Provinces of Aleppo and Mamuretülaziz, and to the Provincial District of Kayseri, dated 6 February 1916.

steps to prevent the foreigners from coming into contact with deportees. One such cable from Talat Pasha to the provinces and districts in question informed the officials that

> since it is unacceptable that certain foreigners and merchants possessing American citizenship should come and go to the areas to which the Armenians have been deported and resettled or even that certain Ottoman non-Muslim merchants should circulate in those areas for the purpose of commerce, the government shall give no permission for travel and free movement for persons deemed unreliable such as these.[192]

These adopted measures were reported by Talat Pasha himself to the Ottoman High Command with an official note dated 26 March 1916. Talat stated that "the reports regarding the methods and persons involved in the distribution of funds sent [from abroad] to meet the needs of [local] Armenians have been investigated and communicated both to the concerned provinces and to districts which are not connected to any province," and added that "instructions and the final decision [on what to do] in this matter are the perogative of the Office of the High Command."[193]

In reply, Enver Pasha, commander of the Ottoman forces, demanded that they "severely punish state functionaries or officials who have either allowed or are aware of the secret distribution of funds to the Armenians."[194] That this correspondence and the decisions took place in March 1916 is very important. As seen earlier, this coincides with the prohibition of foreigners traveling around the deportation regions. It is clear that these steps were taken in order to organize the second stage of the genocide.

Secret investigations were occasionally ordered against individuals considered suspect. A February 1916 cipher cable to Ankara Province, for instance, demanded that "an investigation [be initiated] in a highly

---

[192] BOA/DH.ŞFR, no. 61/32, Coded telegram from interior minister Talat to the Provinces of Aleppo, Adana, Mosul, and Diyarbekır, and to the Provincial Districts of Urfa and (Der) Zor, dated 13 February 1916.

[193] Genelkurmay Başkanlığı, *Arşiv Belgeleriyle Ermeni Faaliyetleri*, vol. 2, 5. The date of the document is reproduced incorrectly as 25 March 1916; 26 March is the correct date, see 299.

[194] Genelkurmay Başkanlığı, *Arşiv Belgeleriyle Ermeni Faaliyetleri*, vol. 2, 5. A clerical error appears to have been committed during the copying of this document, as the document, whose actual date is 28 March 1916, is reproduced as 28 January 1917 (ibid., 300).

secretive manner against an American individual by the name of Drap-erdankl [?] who sent a letter to the American ambassador from Çorum, including [ascertaining] his identity, what his purpose is in traveling in those areas, and whether he is distributing provisions to Armenians."[195] Yet despite the government's various preventive measures, money and material assistance continued to reach the Armenian deportees through German and American aid agencies.

In response to continuing reports to this effect, another order was sent to numerous provinces and districts on 23 March that reiterated the government's demand that such activity be stopped: "It has been learned that in certain areas money [continues to be] distributed to the Armenians by American and German institutions. Since it is necessary that all money that is to be distributed to the Armenians should be distributed by government officials under the supervision of administrative functionaries, it is not permitted that distributions be made by any other means."[196] A similar order was sent three days later in response to the activities of the American consuls in the region after reports had been received that the Americans wanted to send a number of people to areas in which they had no consulates in order to distribute money; instead, it was stressed that any monetary or material assistance would have to be distributed by local government officials.[197]

Cables that demanded the investigation of the sources of assistance arriving in the region, and the people and institutions suspected of distributing it, were sent to the provinces with great frequency. A general communiqué sent by Talat Pasha on 30 March 1916, for instance, demanded that an investigation commence of the behavior and activities of a certain company (and its employees) that was being employed for the distribution of aid to Armenian refugees:

---

[195] BOA/DH.ŞFR, no. 61/48, Coded telegram from the Interior Ministry's General Security Directorate to the Province of Ankara, dated 19 February 1916.

[196] BOA/DH.ŞFR, no. 62/90, Coded telegram from the Interior Ministry's General Security Directorate to the Provinces of Edirne, Adana, Ankara, Bitlis, Aleppo, Hüdâvendigâr (Bursa), Diyarbekır, Damascus, Sivas, Trebizond, Kastamonu, Konya, Mamuretülaziz, and Mosul, and to the Provincial Districts of Urfa, İzmit, İçel, Kütahya, Eskişehir, Bolu, Canik, (Der) Zor, Karesi (Balıkesir), Kayseri, Marash, Karahisâr-ı Sahib (Afyon Karahisar), and Niğde, dated 23 March 1916.

[197] BOA/DH.ŞFR, no. 62/129, Coded telegram from interior minister Talat to the Provinces of Edirne, Ankara, Kastamonu, and Konya, and to the Provincial Districts of İzmit, Bolu, Çatalca, Karesi (Balıkesir), Menteşe, Kütahya, İçel, Eskişehir, and Niğde, dated 26 March 1916.

Please conduct a thorough investigation and report on whether the Abronasyan Trading House has branches within your province/provincial district, whether they have acted as intermediaries for the sending and distribution of funds sent to the Armenians by Armenians of foreign citizenship or by American consulates, and the status and actions of [government] officials who assisted them [in their efforts].[198]

Another telegram sent three months later ordered local officials to follow the trail of funds sent for the Armenians: "It has been learned that 50,000 lira have been sent by the American Embassy, via the Ottoman Bank, to be distributed among the Armenians deported to the environs of Syria, and that this money has reached Jerusalem. Please conduct a quick investigation, and report on the identity of those persons to whom the funds were distributed, and their means of distribution."[199]

One important challenge facing the government was the existence of local officials who either continued to assist the Armenian refugees or turned a blind eye to the efforts of others to do the same. On 3 April 1916 interior minister Talat Pasha sent a general order to the provinces and demanded that any official caught facilitating or allowing the distribution of aid to the deportees be severely punished:

It has been stated in a general communiqué by the Office of the High Command that both government officials who have permitted the secret and direct distribution of money to the Armenians by American or German institutions without the intercession or mediation of government officials, and those who have either been informed or aware of this [and have done nothing to prevent it] must be severely punished.[200]

[198] BOA/DH.ŞFR, no. 62/181, Coded telegram from interior minister Talat to the Provinces of Edirne, Erzurum, Adana, Ankara, Aydın, Bitlis, Aleppo, Hüdâvendigâr (Bursa), Diyarbekır, Sivas, Trebizond, Kastamonu, Konya, and Mamuretülaziz, and to the Provincial Districts of Urfa, İzmit, Bolu, Canik, (Der) Zor, Karesi (Balıkesir), Kayseri, Marash, Niğde, Kütahya, Eskişehir, and İçel, dated 30 March 1916.

[199] BOA/DH.ŞFR, no. 65/25, Coded telegram from the Interior Ministry's General Security Directorate to the Province of Damascus and the Provincial District of Jerusalem, dated 18 June 1916.

[200] BOA/DH.ŞFR, no. 62/210, Coded telegram from the Interior Ministry's General Security Directorate to the Provinces of Edirne, Adana, Ankara, Bitlis, Aleppo, Hüdâvendigâr (Bursa), Diyarbekır, Damascus, Sivas, Trebizond, Kastamonu, Konya, Mamuretülaziz, and Mosul, and to the Provincial

In the summer of 1916, when the presence of two Armenians who were secretly distributing money to deportees in the Der Zor region was reported, the Security Directorate sent a cable to the provincial governor of Aleppo on 22 July and demanded more information:

> It has been learned that two Armenians by the names of Papaz Sahak [Sahak the priest] and Eczâcı Sergis [Sergis the pharmacist] have traveled to [Der] Zor and secretly distributed money to the Armenians [there]; please submit a speedy and thorough report as to what need there was to allow these persons to come to [Der] Zor.[201]

Another cable that followed two days later demanded that the two people in question be arrested and sent back to Aleppo, and that confirmation of their arrival be given as well.[202]

Due to the government's attempts to monitor and prevent the delivery of outside assistance to the Armenian refugees—however mixed in their results—those wishing to provide such assistance were forced to maintain a certain level of secrecy in their distribution efforts. Some Muslim state officials were also a part of these efforts. Those attempting to organize aid efforts in Aleppo were often followed and closely monitored by government functionaries; their houses were frequently raided and they themselves were occasionally arrested.[203] Armenians who were determined to have received assistance from the local American Consulate would frequently be arrested, as can be seen in a November 1916 Security Directorate cable to Aleppo Province: "A telegraphic message has been received, addressed to a 'Dövik' in Aleppo and signed by 'İshak Tebon' who resides in the house of Dikranyan, stating that 1,000 lira have been received from the American Embassy and that 10,000 dollars have been received. [He] has been detained since the purpose [of the funds] could not be discerned."[204]

Districts of Urfa, İzmit, Karahisâr-ı Sahib (Afyon Karahisar), Marash, Niğde, Bolu, Canik, (Der) Zor, Karesi (Balıkesir), Kayseri, İçel, Kütahya, and Eskişehir, dated 3 April 1916.

[201] BOA/DH.ŞFR, no. 54-A/71, Coded telegram from the Interior Ministry's General Security Directorate to the Province of Aleppo, dated 22 July 1916.

[202] BOA/DH.ŞFR, no. 54-A/91, Coded telegram from the Interior Ministry's General Security Directorate to the Provincial District of (Der) Zor, dated 24 July 1916.

[203] For more detailed information on the subject, see Hilmar Kaiser, *At the Crossroads of Der Zor*, 37–52.

[204] BOA/DH.ŞFR, no. 69/210, Coded telegram from the Interior Ministry's General Security Directorate to the Province of Aleppo, dated 7 November 1916.

The archives of the Cipher Office of the Ottoman Interior Ministry contain many documents dealing with instances of "banditry" in Aleppo Province in the spring of 1916. A Security Directorate cable from 3 May 1916, for instance, stated that "it has been reported from the province of Aleppo that armed gangs have begun to be formed by the foreign Armenians in [the province]," and ordered that "these gangs not be allowed to operate; report on the results [of the measures you take against them]."[205] Ten days later another cable, this one from Talat to Aleppo Province, informed the governor that "apart from Catholics and Protestants, Armenians of foreign nationality in Aleppo" are considered by the Fourth Army Command as eligible for deportation, and demanded that "those individuals from among said Armenians who are understood to have been involved in these bandit organizations or those to whom we need resort for their knowledge of banditry are to be left there in custody" and investigated.[206]

No further information has come to light that would clarify what is meant in these documents by "armed gang activity"; furthermore, the question of whether or not these activities are somehow connected to the aid distribution activities being organized in the region cannot be answered, and awaits scholarly investigation.[207]

The army and the government were not making idle threats. If necessary, they did not even hesitate to threaten foreign diplomats. In a letter sent indirectly through German channels, the American consul in Aleppo, J. B. Jackson, relates incidents he experienced: "I am trying to keep those in the outside towns alive, also, but it is a terrible task, as many persons have been beaten to death, and some hung or shot for having distributed relief funds. . . . I sent Bernau there a few days ago. . . . Djemal Pasha threatened to bring him before the Court Martial if he paid money to Armenians."[208]

[205] BOA/DH.ŞFR, no. 63/175, Coded telegram from the Interior Ministry's General Security Directorate to the Province of Adana and to the Provincial Districts of Marash, Urfa, and (Der) Zor, date 3 May 1916.

[206] BOA/DH.ŞFR, no. 63/306, Coded telegram from interior minister Talat to the Province of Aleppo, dated 13 May 1916. The same message was also cabled to Cemal Pasha (see BOA/DH.ŞFR, no. 63/307).

[207] For some of the other cables reporting on bandit activity in Aleppo, see BOA/DH.ŞFR, no. 63/241, 248, 263, 282, and 307. Esat Uras, who was conversant in Armenian, was sent to Aleppo for the purpose of conducting an investigation into the matter.

[208] NA/RG 59, 867.4016/298, Letter from Aleppo consul J. B. Jackson's wife, Mrs. Jesse Jackson, to the State Department, dated 13 October 1916, containing letter from J. B. Jackson to Mrs. Jackson, in Sarafian, ed., United States Official Documents, Doc. no. 61, 119.

He also reports that a number of Ottoman citizens in the Der Zor region had been beaten—even killed in some cases—for distributing aid, and that some were even sentenced to death and executed on other pretexts. "There have been a number of persons (Ottomans) arrested at [Der] Zor for having distributed relief, some beaten to death and some hung really for that reason but said to be for others."[209] All this was not simply the acts of a government that was attempting to relocate its citizens.

A TENTATIVE NOTE ON THE ISSUES OF AID DISTRIBUTION AND EPIDEMIC DISEASES

On the basis of the few existing Cipher Office documents on the questions of aid distribution and the struggle against contagions during the deportations and in the refugee camps, one can assert with confidence that very different treatment was meted out to Muslim refugees than to the Armenian deportees. It can be claimed on the basis of the number, content, and language of the telegraphic communications sent that particular care and attention was shown toward the former group.

In addition to the special concern shown by the government to the difficulties that arose during the resettlement of Muslim refugees, the newcomers were provided with free housing, fields, food and clothing, and a monthly stipend for each individual. Government officials coming from occupied areas to the interior provinces would be appointed with the specific task of helping resolve the various problems associated with refugee resettlement.[210] Messages inquiring if all of the preparations were complete for assisting the newcomers and whether or not there remained other things to do in this regard were sent off to the provinces in question:

> It has been learned that, despite such efforts, it has unfortunately not been possible to fully meet the needs of the refugees arriving from the occupied provinces. As a result, please report back quickly and in

[209] NA/RG 59, 867.4016/301, Very confidential report from the American Embassy, Istanbul, to the secretary of state, dated 15 September 1916, with letter attached sent by German channels from Jesse Jackson, dated 3 September 1916, in *United States Official Documents*, ed. Sarafian, 124.

[210] BOA/DH.ŞFR, no. 66/150, Coded telegram from interior minister Talat to the Provinces of Ankara, Konya, Mosul, Sivas, Diyarbekır, Erzurum, Trebizond, and Kastamonu, and to the Provincial Districts of Urfa, Canik, and Kayseri, dated 5 August 1916.

detail as to what further type[s] of assistance for them and means of providing it must be secured, as well as the manner of transport and provision and what you think you will need [for this purpose].[211]

In addition to Kaya, the head of the General Directorate for Tribal and Immigrant Affairs, interior minister Talat Pasha also conducted regular inspections of the provinces and concerned himself firsthand with the problem of resettling Muslim refugees. While the former was touring the provinces, the latter would send individual cables containing similar messages, either to the army commanders or to the local administrators of the provinces and districts that Kaya would visit,[212] and instruct them to "assist and facilitate [the efforts] of the Director-General of Immigrants Şükrü Bey, as he will be arriving there in order to prepare the groundwork for the resettlement and provisioning of refugees and immigrants."[213]

Talat followed these efforts with his own inspections. In telegrams sent from Istanbul, the interior minister wrote to local administrators that he "was in Anatolia for the purpose of conducting inspection tours," and ordered them to prepare for him "the necessary documents and means to provide the required information on the condition of the refugees and the manner in which they are sent and resettled."[214] That cables such as these were sent separately to almost every administrative district, from provinces down to individual counties, is significant because it highlights the level of interest and engagement that the Ottoman government displayed in regard to the situation of its incoming Muslim refugee population.[215]

---

[211] BOA/DH.ŞFR, no. 66/154, Coded telegram from the Interior Ministry's General Directorate of Tribal and Immigrant Affairs to the Provinces of Erzurum, Trebizond, Sivas, Konya, Ankara, Adana, Aleppo, Diyarbekır, Mamuretülaziz, and Mosul, and to the Provincial Districts of Urfa, Kayseri, and Canik, dated 6 August 1916.

[212] BOA/DH.ŞFR, no. 66/180, Coded telegram from interior minister Talat to the Offices of the Second, Third, and Fourth Army commanders, dated 8 August 1916.

[213] BOA/DH.ŞFR, no. 66/181, Coded telegram from interior minister Talat to the Provinces of Aleppo, Diyarbekır, Mamuretülaziz, Sivas, and Trebizond, and to the Provincial Districts of Urfa and Canik, dated 8 August 1916.

[214] BOA/DH.ŞFR, no. 69/266, Coded telegram from the Interior Ministry's General Directorate of Tribal and Immigrant Affairs to the Provinces of Mamuretülaziz and Diyarbekır, and to the Provincial District of Urfa, dated 13 November 1916.

[215] To give some idea of just how much attention was given to the matter, it is sufficient here to simply give some of the archival numbers of documents dealing with the subject: BOA/DH.ŞFR, nos. 69/163, 166, 167, 169, 171, 173, 177, 179, 181, 185, and 186.

Additionally, funds were regularly and consistently sent to the provinces with the clear instructions that they were to be used solely for the needs of the newcomers. Among the Interior Ministry Papers, simply for the month of August 1916, there are literally dozens of telegraphic messages sent to the provinces along the lines of this cable to the district of Canik:

> ten thousand lira were sent by post today from the general [re]settlement expenses. The majority was in five-kurush notes. Daily allotments of up to three kurush per person for the provisioning of refugees may be given out according to the economic situation and current needs. Care should be taken to ensure [that the refugees receive] provisions until the money arrives. Absolutely no money should be allocated and spent for the area beyond that for the expenses of refugees and immigrants.[216]

A similar situation can also be seen in regard to the struggle against contagious diseases. During the course of the years-long effort to resettle Muslim immigrants, an enormous number of communications were conducted with the provinces in regard to dealing with the outbreaks of various contagions. There are numerous cables along the lines of this one from 12 November 1916, demanding that "the necessary measures be taken in order to improve and reorder the sanitary conditions of the refugees who now find themselves in difficult conditions in Çorum." Contagious diseases had broken out among the newcomers, living as they were in substandard conditions, and a health inspector had been immediately dispatched to the region as a result. The message concluded with the order that the "measures that are proposed [by the inspector] be quickly implemented and carried out."[217] Another cable would also be sent to Ankara demanding that sanitary measures be implemented the very same day.[218]

---

[216] BOA/DH.ŞFR, no. 66/197, Coded telegram from the Interior Ministry's IAMM to the Provincial District of Canik, dated 10 August 1916. For similar cables, see BOA/DH.ŞFR, nos. 66/26, 199, 204, 205, 209, 210, 212, 214, 216, 217, and 240.

[217] BOA/DH.ŞFR, no. 69/233, Coded telegram from the Interior Ministry's General Directorate of Tribal and Immigrant Affairs to the Provincial District of Çorum, dated 12 November 1916.

[218] BOA/DH.ŞFR, no. 69/234, Coded telegram from the Interior Ministry's General Directorate of Tribal and Immigrant Affairs to the Province of Ankara, dated 12 November 1916.

Another example that can be given is the correspondence regarding the outbreaks of cholera and typhus that appeared in their initial stages among the Muslim refugee populations settled in Harran, and the measures that the government advised to take against them. One cable began, "It has been reported in a telegram only now received from the Inspectorate for Immigrants [and Refugees] in Diyarbekır, where there have been two deaths from cholera and three [other undetermined but] suspicious deaths among the refugees in Harran," and then listed at length the necessary measures to take to counter the threat. It also reported that other provinces in the area, as well as the commands of the Second and Fourth Armies, had been informed of the problem.[219] And in truth, cables informing them of the necessary measures to take were indeed sent to the surrounding provinces on the same day.[220]

There are also many archived telegrams to the provinces dealing with other questions of the health and sanitary conditions of the refugees and their other needs. Among these is one "to the Provincial District of Yozgat . . . concerning the increase in the amount of daily allotment for the refugees in Yozgat and the securing of their clothing needs, due to their naked and very impoverished condition";[221] another to Ankara Province concerning the refugees in Çorum, "who are in a very impoverished condition, lacking clothing and firewood and other burnable materials," and the steps that are needed to be taken to alleviate their hardships;[222] and, finally, another "to the Province of Diyarbekır . . . concerning the improving of the situation . . . of the refugees in Silvan and Siverek, who are in an extraordinarily impoverished and bereft condition."[223]

In many cases inspectors, sanitation officials, and medicines were sent to regions in order to contend with contagious diseases and similar prob-

[219] BOA/DH.ŞFR, no. 69/257, Coded telegram from the Interior Ministry's General Directorate of Tribal and Immigrant Affairs to interior minister Talat (in Malatya), dated 13 November 1916.

[220] For the cable sent to Sivas, see BOA/DH.ŞFR, no. 69/256; for the one sent to the Second and Fourth Army Commands, see BOA/DH.ŞFR, no. 69/257; for the one sent to Urfa, see BOA/DH.ŞFR, no. 70/17.

[221] BOA/DH.ŞFR, no. 70/18, Coded telegram from the Interior Ministry's General Directorate of Tribal and Immigrant Affairs to the Provincial District of Yozgat, dated 15 November 1916.

[222] BOA/DH.ŞFR, no. 70/57, Coded telegram from the Interior Ministry's General Directorate of Tribal and Immigrant Affairs to the Province of Ankara, dated 21 November 1916.

[223] BOA/DH.ŞFR, no. 71/53, Coded telegram from the Interior Ministry's General Directorate of Tribal and Immigrant Affairs to the Province of Diyarbekır, dated 21 December 1916.

lems. In a November 1916 cable to Samsun, the Directorate of Tribal and Immigrant Affairs wrote that "[i]t has been reported that a health inspector will be arriving there shortly in order to study and implement the measures necessary for the improvement of the sanitary and health conditions of the refugees in the provincial district, and that as many minor sanitation officials as necessary will soon be sent, along with the quinine requested."[224]

Another telegram from the Directorate, this one sent on 23 March 1917 to Mosul Province, stated that in addition to other such cables sent to individual provinces, a "general communiqué" had been prepared to "ensure the feeding and provisioning of the population who have fled the theater of war, and to reorder and regulate the manner in which they are delivered to the areas in which they are concentrated," and that these instructions "have been communicated to the necessary [parties]." This sixteen-point communiqué contained both general information on sanitation, food, clothing, and housing; how these were to be provided; and a list of the individual actions that were to be carried out. Among these are, in order:

(2) Sheltered resting areas are to be set up at the halting places that coincide with the concentration points for refugees from the war zones, and care is to be given for their provisioning to the extent that circumstances allow; (3) By having sanitation officials present at these sheltered resting areas, no opportunity is to be allowed for an outbreak of contagious diseases among the refugees ... and those who come down with contagious diseases are to be immediately isolated...; (5) An explanatory list containing the number of persons comprising each convoy and their points of concentration and assembly is to be delivered into the hands of the officials in charge of the dispatch of convoys [on their journeys]...; (7) When the convoys are sent from one area to another, the officials in charge of the convoys shall be responsible for providing these persons with two days' worth of provisions and supplies, and with the protection of said provisions and supplies...; (10) Means of transport shall be allocated for those lacking the strength to go on foot, such as women

[224] BOA/DH.ŞFR, no. 70/20, Coded telegram from the Interior Ministry's General Directorate of Tribal and Immigrant Affairs to the Provincial District of Canik, dated 5 November 1916.

and children; (11) An official responsible for provisions and assistance shall be placed in the sheltered resting areas by area officials;
(12) Temporary hospitals are to be established in appropriate areas
of the halting places and local doctors are to be stationed there, while
the [ailing] refugees are to be placed under their supervision. . . ;
(14) The value of the provisions, clothing and other items among
the moveable property is to be assessed and deducted from the allocations for immigrants [and refugees], and delivered to the refugees;
(15) The provincial governors, district governors and county heads
are directly responsible for the sending and resettlement of the refugees. The civil service inspectors who are to be stationed in specific
locations and shall assist and supervise the proper implementation
of these measures as well as keep the provincial and government
ministry officials informed of the current situation. Regarding this
issue, the resources from the immigration funds can be allocated for
the deployment of the civil servants.[225]

In contrast to the enomous amount of energy, concern, and resources
that went into the care and resettlement of Muslim refugees and immigrants, one will search the archives in vain for *any* such messages
throughout the entire period of the deportations that reflect anything
close to this level of concern for the care and protection of the Armenian deportees, much less for detailed lists of instructions and resource
allocations. The paucity of correspondence between the center and the
periphery—a paucity that borders on total absence—concerning measures to deal with outbreaks of contagious diseases among the surviving Armenian deportees, despite their heavy toll in lives, highlights once
again the profound difference in the Ottoman government's treatment of
the deported Armenians vis-à-vis Muslim refugees. This difference can
also be seen more concretely in correspondence between interior minister Talat Pasha and Kaya, the director general of Tribal and Immigrant
Affairs who had gone to Aleppo in order to perform on-site supervision
of deportation activities. Kaya informed the interior minister that Armenian deportees in Hama were dying from a variety of diseases and there-

[225] BOA/DH.ŞFR, no. 62/100–101, Coded telegram from the Interior Ministry's IAMM to the
Province of Mosul, dated 23 March 1917.

fore needed to be sent elsewhere. In his reply, Talat stated that "reports have been received that the diseases of fever, typhus and dysentery that have appeared among the almost 20,000 deportees in Hama are causing some 70–80 deaths per day." Continuing, he said that it is appropriate for the deportees to be "sent, in communication with the Province of Damascus, to special areas at the soonest possible convenience for the sake of the preservation of public health," and he asks to be informed of the results of these actions.[226] For the government, what was important was not the deaths of Armenians from various diseases but the threat that these diseases posed for the remaining inhabitants of the province. This prompted the demand that the diseased people be physically distanced from the province as soon as possible.

Similar tone and content can be found in the messages that traveled in the other direction. Provincial officials did not demand that measures be taken for the treatment of Armenians suffering from contagious diseases; rather, they simply demanded that the Armenians be sent somewhere else so that the contagion would not spread to the army or the rest of the civilian population. On 22 September 1915, for instance, the district governor of Karahisar sent the following cable:

> [Y]esterday evening 44 wagons full of Armenians arrived, bringing their total number, including those [already] here, to 10,170 persons assembled at the station. Due to the dysentery prevailing among these persons and the possibility of the spread of one or other diseases to the military personnel who are being sent, the need is being strongly emphasized by the military branch for these [deportees] to be quickly sent and transported to other areas.

Additionally, the district governor requested that "permission be given for the Armenians to forcibly be marched by foot or to be transported by wagons, which will be paid for from the special funds allocated for the immigrants [*Muhacirin Tahsisatı*]," since it would not be possible to send them by train.[227]

---

[226] BOA/DH.ŞFR, no. 57/51, Coded telegram from interior minister Talat to the director of the Office for (Tribal and) Immigrant (Settlement), Kaya, then in Aleppo, dated 17 October 1915.

[227] BOA/DH.EUM, 2. Şube, no. 68/81, Coded telegram from Şevket, the district governor of Karahisar, to the Interior Ministry, dated 22 September 1915.

Another solution that was considered in light of the contagious disease and death prevalent within the Armenian convoys was to change
the routes that they would take. On 3 February 1916, Talat Pasha sent the
provincial governor of Der Zor a cable informing him that "since the Armenian deportees arriving in Ras ul Ayn on their way to Mosul are beset
by typhus and other contagious diseases," the Sixth Army Command has
requested (from Talat) that "the route to Mosul via Ras ul Ayn should not
be used in order to prevent the diseases from infecting military personnel."
Therefore, he requested that "another [route be used] so that the Armenian deportees will not subsequently pass through the resting spot of Ras
ul Ayn on the way to Mosul."[228] Again, no effort or consideration was given
to treating the Armenians who were suffering from contagious diseases;
the concern as such was that such people might infect military personnel.

A message sent to the Third Army Command regarding the Muslim
immigrants and refugees further reflected the different approach taken by
Ottoman authorities to displaced Muslims:

> A message has been written to the Ministry of War [requesting that]
> the military units that are found in the areas through which the refu-
> gees pass before reaching their place of [re]settlement are to provide
> assistance to [the refugees] and especially in regard to [their] sick
> and diseased [members]. It has also been communicated to the rel-
> evant provinces of the need for them to take pains to improve the
> refugees' general situation.

Finally, the message added that "it is necessary that assistance be provided
[to these people] in whatever manner [they may require]. It will be possible to ensure an improvement of their condition and the supplying of
them with [the necessary] provisions," and concludes with the encouragement that every possible step should be taken to meet the needs that
might arise.[229]

The website of the Prime Ministerial Archive devotes a special section to the "Armenian Issue according to the Archival Documents." Select

---

[228] BOA/DH.ŞFR, no. 60/219, Coded telegram from interior minister Talat to the Provincial District of (Der) Zor, dated 3 February 1916.

[229] BOA/DH.ŞFR, no. 71/171, Coded telegram from the Interior Ministry's General Directorate of
Tribal and Immigrant Affairs to the aide to the Third Army chief of staff, dated 4 January 1917.

documents related to the Armenian deportations are presented there in order to bolster the official Turkish state version of events. As a result of this sharply different treatment of displaced Muslim and Armenian populations, as mentioned above, it would be very difficult to present documents on the health, sanitation, and contagious diseases of Armenian deportees and the government measures taken in this regard. On this site, which contains approximately fifteen hundred documents at present, only six have been placed in the group labeled "The Protection of Armenians Subjected to Deportation and the Treatment of Their Health Problems," and not a single one of these has to do with measures taken or needing to be taken against contagious diseases. Only three documents are relevant: the first concerns the granting of permission for doctors from the municipality to be sent "in order to treat those among the Armenians arriving [in Ras ul Ayn] who are ill";[230] the second is a Security Directorate cable telling the officials in Konya not to leave those Armenians in Ereğli (in the province of Konya) who would appear to be suffering from dysentery or malaria "lying on the ground." Instead they "are to be quarantined in abandoned Armenian houses."[231] The third document is about what actions are to be taken regarding the health and sanitation reports about the Armenians that have been received.[232] From this lack of correspondence alone, a person not knowing otherwise might conclude that there simply was no real problem with contagious diseases among the Armenian deportees. In fact, it shows with great clarity the real policy of the Unionist regime toward the Armenians.

[230] BOA/DH.ŞFR, no. 54-A/153, Coded telegram from interior minister Talat to the Province of Aleppo, dated 28 July 1915.

[231] BOA/DH.ŞFR, no. 57/337, Coded telegram from the Interior Ministry's General Security Directorate to the Province of Konya, dated 7 November 1915.

[232] BOA/DH.ŞFR, no. 65/92, Coded telegram from the Interior Ministry's General Security Directorate to the Provinces of Edirne, Adana, Ankara, Aydın, Hüdâvendigâr (Bursa), Damascus, Sivas, Kastamonu, and Konya, and to the Provincial Districts of İzmit, Bolu, Canik, Karesi (Balıkesir), Kale-i Sultaniye (Çanakkale), Kayseri, Karahisâr-ı Sahib (Afyon Karahisar), Marash, Kütahya, Niğde, and Eskişehir, dated 26 June 1916.

The Armenian Genocide—the first large-scale mass murder of the twentieth century—must be placed in a new context and understood within that context: the commencement of the partitioning of the Ottoman Empire into nation-states. Far from an isolated campaign against a single ethnoreligious group, the annihilation of the Armenians was part of an extremely comprehensive operation that was accomplished in order to save the empire. For this reason, it is not correct to interpret the Armenian Genocide along the lines of a clash between the empire's Muslim groups (ethnic Turks, Kurds, Circassians, and others), more generally expressed by the concept of "Turk," and its Christian elements (Armenians, Greeks, and Syriacs). The Armenian Genocide must be understood and interpreted as a matter between the Ottoman state and its subjects that arose as a result of specific policies pursued by the regime. The rulers of the empire saw one group of Ottoman citizens, due to their religious and ethnic makeup, as the source of problems, indeed, as a threat. Thus they intended to expel this group from Anatolia, and failing that, to kill them.

Even if prior to the 1912–13 Balkan Wars it may have existed as an idea, the ethnoreligious homogenization of Anatolia arose as a concrete party and state policy from the ashes of military defeat. I have called it a demographic policy, and its goal, which was gradually systematized and put into practice after 1913, was to create a Turkish Muslim majority in Anatolia. The operational objectives of this enormous social engineering project were to assimilate (*temsil* or *temessül*) the Muslims of non-Turkish origin and reduce the Christians to no more than 5 to 10 percent of the Muslim population.

The first to be targeted were the Greeks of Thrace and the Aegean coast, who were expelled to Greece through force, threats, and massacres. The Armenians were treated differently from the other Christian groups, partly because of the nature of the conflict the regime perceived with them and especially because of the proximity of their homeland to the Russian border. The threat of Russian occupation and the existence of an international reform agreement cast Armenians as an existential danger. It was felt necessary to prevent them from uniting under an autonomous administration that might one day emerge as an independent Armenia; consequently, Unionist policy toward the Armenians was genocidal.

To document this thesis primarily through Ottoman sources has been a primary aim of this book. I have sought to demonstrate that there is no real contradiction between the material in Ottoman and various Western archives, despite frequent and ongoing claims to the contrary. All documentary sources, from their varied perspectives, attest to the same historical facts. In addition, the Ottoman documents demonstrate that the genocide was implemented as a demographic policy. The principle that the Armenian remnant not exceed 5 percent of the Muslim population in some western Anatolian provinces, while those deported were not to exceed 10 percent of the Muslims at their destinations, amounts to an order for their near-total annihilation.

Finally, I wish to emphasize one aspect of this history that is profoundly misunderstood in Turkey and possibly elsewhere. In the various debates concerning the events of 1915, it is often assumed that the principal question to be answered is whether the deportations and related measures constitute genocide. Political demands—particularly in the international arena—that Turkey recognize these events as a genocide have undoubtedly played no small part in producing this widely held conviction.

From the viewpoint of jurisprudence, how these events are to be characterized, and according to which article of international criminal law they would be most appropriately described, are certainly important points. I can comfortably assert that in light of the available documents, these events cannot be defined in any fashion other than that of genocide. Nevertheless, I believe that the fundamental issue is not legal but moral. And the moral responsibility—to acknowledge the injustice of what was done to the Armenians, and to undo, through indemnification, as much as possible of the damage it created—has no direct connection with the legal term to be used for the 1915 events. Irrespective of which term you might think is appropriate, this great injustice inflicted upon the Armenian people must be rectified. Although the legal aspect of the appropriate term may and must be debated, the current framing of this debate, especially in Turkey, reveals that the fundamental moral issue has yet to be fully addressed.

In order to be able to sensibly discuss the characterization of 1915 according to existing categories of international criminal law, it is first of all necessary to acknowledge that a *crime* was committed. Absent such acknowledgment, there is little point in debating such terms as "genocide," "crimes against humanity," or "war crimes." The question is whether or not the events of 1915 are considered as a transgression that would fall within the purview of criminal law.

What must be understood is that the thesis known in Turkey as the "official version" (and elsewhere as the "contra-genocide" view) of the events surrounding the last years of the Ottoman Empire and the transition to the Turkish Republic takes as its starting point the assumption that the events of 1915 were derived from governmental actions that were, in essence, within the bounds of what are considered normal and legal actions for a state entity and cannot therefore be explained through a recourse to criminality or criminal law. According to this assumption, under certain conditions a government or a state can resort to actions such as "forcible deportation," even if they result in the deaths of its own citizens, and there are no moral or legal grounds upon which such actions can be faulted.

I believe that regardless of how one describes it, a moral admission must be made: a recognition of the truth that a wrongful act took place, one so large and serious as to be deserving of moral opprobrium. Unless grounded on the assumption that the events of 1915 were due to morally and ethically indefensible actions on the part of the Ottoman government, no serious and productive discussion of the events in question can take place.

"Genocide" is not a term whose discussion belongs solely to the field of criminal law; it is also used very broadly in the social sciences. In this sense, it is entirely justified as a description of the mass murder that took place in 1915. Social scientists generally approach mass slaughters such as the Armenian Genocide with the intention of understanding or explaining them. One of their central motivations is the desire to shed light on the conditions under which such atrocities arise, and thus how they can be avoided in the future.

Regardless of the term used, it is necessary to fully confront the immense human tragedy whose repetition must absolutely be prevented. The palpable anger—even vehemence—of the Turkish government's refusal to face its recent past, and the difficulties of Turkish society in coming to terms with its own history, are very thought-provoking and very troubling. The reaction of state and society suggests that they might again resort to similar actions, and this is truly a frightening prospect.

Until a language is developed for understanding and discussing the bitter events of the past, and for condemning all crimes that target religious or ethnic differences, progress toward resolving the issue will not be possible. First and foremost, we must admit that these historical events were the intended result of deliberate government policies that were morally unacceptable. I believe that the powerful, recent surge of democratization in Turkey has paved the way for such recognition, and in this sense, the future looks a little more optimistic.

SELECTED BIBLIOGRAPHY

While a complete bibliography of genocide and ethnic cleansing in the late Ottoman period is beyond the scope of this work, the sources I have found most useful are listed below. Additional sources are cited in the footnotes.

ARCHIVAL COLLECTIONS

Following the name of each major collection is the abbreviation used in this book.

AUSTRIA

Haus- Hof- und Staatsarchiv, Politisches Archiv [Archives of the House, Court, and State]: HHStA Politisches Archiv: HHStA PA

GERMANY

Politisches Archiv des Auswärtiges Amt [Political Archive of the Foreign Office]: DE/PA-AA
  Botschaft Konstantinopel: DE/PA-AA/Bo.Kons.
    Reich: DE/PA-AA/R

ISRAEL

Archive of the Armenian Patriarchate of Jerusalem: AAPJ
  Boxes 7, 17, and 21

TURKEY

Prime Ministerial Ottoman Archive [Başbakanlık Osmanlı Arşivi]: BOA
Ministry of Foreign Affairs [Hariciye Nezareti]
  Harciye Hukuk Müşavirliği Odası [Foreign Affairs, Office of Legal Counsel]: HR.HMŞ.İŞO

Hariciye Nezareti Siyasî Kısım [Ministry of Foreign Affairs,
Political Division]: HR.SYS
Ministry of the Interior [Dahiliye Nezareti]
Dahiliye Nezareti Dahiliye Kalem-i Mahsus Evrakı [Ministry of the
Interior, Record Office of the Private Secretariat]: DH.KMS
Dahiliye Nezareti Emniyet-i Umumiye Asayiş Kalemi [Ministry
of the Interior, General Security, Secretariat of Public Order]:
DH.EUM.AYŞ
Dahiliye Nezareti Emniyet-i Umumiye Beşinci Şube [Ministry of
the Interior, Fifth Department of General Security]: DH.EUM,
5. Şube
Dahiliye Nezareti Emniyet-i Umumiye Birinci Şube [Ministry of
the Interior, First Department of General Security]: DH.EUM,
1. Şube
Dahiliye Nezareti Emniyet-i Umumiye Emniyet Şubesi Evrakı
[Record Office of the Security Branch of General Security of
the Interior Ministry]: DH.EUM.EMN
Dahiliye Nezareti Emniyet-i Umumiye Evrak Odası Kalemi Evrakı
[Record Chamber of the Documents Office of General
Security of the Interior Ministry]: DH.EUM.VRK
Dahiliye Nezareti Emniyet-i Umumiye İkinci Şube [Ministry of the
Interior, Second Department of General Security]: DH.EUM,
2. Şube
Dahiliye Nezareti Emniyet-i Umumiye Kalemi Umumi [Ministry
of the Interior, General Secretariat of General Security]:
DH.EUM.KLU
Dahiliye Nezareti Emniyet-i Umumiye Memurin Kalemi Evrakı
[Ministry of the Interior, Record Office of the General Security
Officials]: DH.EUM.MEM
Dahiliye Nezareti Emniyet-i Umumiye Muhasebe Kalemi Evrakı
[Office of Accounting of General Security of the Interior
Ministry]: DH.EUM.MH
Dahiliye Nezareti Emniyet-i Umumiye Üçüncü Şube [Ministry
of the Interior, Third Department of General Security]:
DH.EUM, 3. Şube
Dahiliye Nezareti Sicill-i Nüfus Tahrirat Kalemi [Ministry of the
Interior, Secretariat of Population Registry]: DH.SN.THR

Dahiliye Nezareti Şifre Kalemi [Ministry of the Interior, Cipher
Office]: DH.ŞFR

UNITED KINGDOM

Foreign Office Archives: FO
Class 371. *Political: General Correspondence, 1919–1920.*
Geographic Classification: 44. *Turkey and the Ottoman Empire.*
Files 2480, 2781, 4172, and 4174.

UNITED STATES ARCHIVES

National Archives and Records Administration (Washington, D.C.),
Record Group: NA/RG
Record Group 59. General Records of the Department of State.
Series 867. Internal Affairs of Turkey, 1910–1929. File
867.4016. Race Problems.

Private Papers
Ernst Jäckh Papers. Yale University Library.

OFFICIAL PUBLICATIONS

GERMANY

Foreign Office [Auswärtiges Amt]. *Die grosse politik der europäischen kabinette,*
1871–1914. Sammlung der diplomatischen akten des Auswärtigen amtes, im
auftrage des Auswärtigen amtes. Edited by Johannes Lepsius, Albrecht Men-
delssohn-Bartholdy, and Friedrich Thimme. Berlin: Deutsche veragsgesell-
schaft für politik und geschichte, 1922–27.

OTTOMAN EMPIRE AND TURKISH REPUBLIC

General Staff. Directorate of Military History and Strategic Studies [Genelkur-
may Başkanlığı. Askeri Tarih ve Stratejik Etüt ve Denetleme Başkanlığı]. *Arşiv*
Belgeleriyle Ermeni Faaliyetleri, 1914–1918 [Armenian Activities in the Archive
Documents, 1914–1918]. 8 vols. Ankara: Genelkurmay Basımevi, 2005–2007.
———. *Askeri Tarih Belgeleri Dergisi* [Documents on Military History]. 1982–
1999.
Grand National Assembly of Turkey. *TBMM Gizli Celse Zabitlari* [Minutes of
Closed Sessions]. Ankara: Türkiye İş Bankası Yayınları, 1985.

Grand National Assembly of Turkey *TBMM Zabıt Cerideleri* [Minutes of the Turkish Grand National Assembly]. Ankara: TBMM Matbaası, 1958.

Ministry of the Interior. Office of General Public Administration [Dahiliye Nezareti İdare-i Umumiye-i Dahiliye Müdüriyeti]. *Teşkilat-ı Hazıra-i Mülkiyeyi ve Vilayet, Liva, Kaza ve Nahiyelerin Huruf-i Heca Sırasıyla Esamisini Havi Cedveldir* [Alphabetical Register of Names of Provinces, Provincial Districts, Counties and Townships]. Istanbul: Matbaa-i Âmire, [1331] 1915.

Ottoman Parliament. Chamber of Deputies. *Meclis-i Mebusan Zabıt Ceridesi* [Minutes of the Chamber of Deputies]. Ankara: TBMM Basımevi, 1992.

———. Chamber of Notables. *Meclis-i Ayan Zabıt Ceridesi* [Minutes of the Chamber of Notables]. Ankara: TBMM Basımevi, 1990.

Prime Ministry. General Directorate of Legislation Development and Publication [Başbakanlık Mevzuatı Geliştirme ve Yayın Genel Müdürlüğü]. *Resmi Gazete* [Official Gazette]. 1934–1935.

———. General Directorate of State Archives [Başbakanlık Devlet Arşivleri Genel Müdürlüğü]. *Osmanlı Belgelerinde Ermeniler, 1915–1920* [Armenians in Ottoman Documents, 1915–1920]. Ankara: Başbakanlık Devlet Arşivleri Genel Müdürlüğü, 1994.

———. General Directorate of State Archives [Başbakanlık Devlet Arşivleri Genel Müdürlüğü]. *Arşiv Belgelerine Göre Kafkaslar'da ve Anadolu'da Ermeni Mezalimi* [Armenian Violence and Massacre in the Caucasus and Anatolia, Based on Archives]. 4 vols. Ankara: Başbakanlık Basımevi, 1995–1998.

———. General Directorate of State Archives [Başbakanlık Devlet Arşivleri Genel Müdürlüğü]. *Ermeniler Tarafından Yapılan Katliam Belgeleri* [Documents on Massacre Perpetrated by Armenians]. 2 vols. Ankara: Başbakanlık Basımevi, 2001.

———. General Directorate of State Archives [Başbakanlık Devlet Arşivleri Genel Müdürlüğü]. *Osmanlı Belgelerinde Ermenilerin Sevk ve İskanı* [The Deportation and Settlement of the Armenians (according to) Ottoman Documents]. Ankara: Başbakanlık Basımevi, 2007.

Takvim-i Vekayi [Chronicle of Events]. Official gazette of the Ottoman government. 1915, 1918–1922.

PUBLISHED DOCUMENTS

AUSTRIA

Ohandjanian, Artem. *Österreich-Armenien, 1872–1936: Faximiliesammlung Diplomatischer Aktenstücke.* Vienna: Ohandjanianverlag, 1995. 12 vols.

GERMANY

Gust, Wolfgang, ed. *Der Völkermord an den Armeniern 1915/16: Dokumente aus dem Politishcen Archiv des deutschen Auswärtigen Amts.* Springe: Zu Klampen Verlag, 2005.

Lepsius, Johannes. *Deutschand und Armenien, 1914–1918: Sammlung diplomatischer Aktenstücke*, Potsdam-Berlin: Tempel Verlag, 1919.

UNITED KINGDOM

Bryce, James, and Arnold Toynbee. *The Treatment of the Armenians in the Ottoman Empire, 1915–1916: Documents Presented to Viscount Grey of Fallodon by Viscount Bryce.* Princeton, NJ: Gomidas Institute, 2000.
Yeghiayan, Vartkes, ed. *British Reports on Ethnic Cleansing in Anatolia, 1919–1922: The Armenian-Greek Section.* Glendale, CA: Center for Armenian Remembrance, 2007.

UNITED STATES

Adalian, Rouben, ed. *The Armenian Genocide in the U.S. Archives, 1915–1918* (microform). Alexandria, VA: Chadwyck-Healey, 1991.
———. *Guide to the Armenian Genocide in the U.S. Archives, 1915–1918.* Alexandria, VA: Chadwyck-Healey, 1994.
Sarafian, Ara, ed. *United States Official Documents on the Armenian Genocide.* 3 vols. Boston, MA: Armenian Review, 1993–95.
———. *United States Official Records on the Armenian Genocide, 1915–1917.* Princeton and London: Gomidas Institute, 2004.

NEWSPAPERS

Akşam
Alemdar
Atî
Hadisat
İkdam
İleri
Memleket
Peyam-i Sabah
Renaissance
Sabah
Tercüman-ı Hakikat
Vakit
Yeni Gazete

MEMOIRS AND STUDIES

Books, journal and newspaper articles, and unpublished manuscripts are arranged by language and author.

ARMENIAN

Andonian, Aram. *Medz Vojire.* Boston: Bahag Printing House, 1921.

Azadian, Libarid. *Hay Orbere Mets Egherni* [The Orphans of the Armenian Genocide]. Los Angeles, CA: Tparan April [Abril Publishers], 1995.

Krieger (pseud. Krikor Gergerian). *Yozgadı Hayasbanutıan Vaveragan Batmutyun.* New York: N.p., 1980.

ENGLISH

Adalian, Rouben Paul. "Comparative Policy and Differential Practice in the Treatment of Minorities in Wartime: The United States Archival Evidence on the Armenians and Greeks in the Ottoman Empire." *Journal of Genocide Research* 3, no. 1 (2001): 31–48.

Ahmad, Feroz. *The Committee of Union and Progress in Turkish Politics, 1908–1914.* Oxford: Clarendon Press, 1969.

Akçam, Taner. *A Shameful Act: The Armenian Genocide and the Question of Turkish Responsibility.* New York: Metropolitan Books, 2006.

———. *From Empire to Republic: Turkish Nationalism and the Armenian Genocide.* London: Zed Publishing, 2004.

———. "Guenter Lewy's *The Armenian Massacres in Ottoman Turkey*." *Genocide Studies and Prevention* 3, no. 1 (April 2008): 111–45.

Aktar, Ayhan. "Homogenizing the Nation; Turkifying the Economy: Turkish Experience of Population Exchange Reconsidered." In *Crossing the Aegean: An Appraisal of the 1923 Compulsory Exchange between Greece and Turkey,* edited by Renée Hirschon, 79–95. New York and Oxford: Berghahn Books, 2003.

Andonian, Aram. *Exile, Trauma and Death: On the Road to Chankiri with Komitas Vartabed.* Translated and edited by Rita Soulahian Kuyumjian. London: Gomidas Institute and Tekeyan Cultural Association, 2010.

———. *The Memoirs of Naim Bey.* 1920. 2nd repr., Newton Square, PA: Armenian Historical Research Association, 1965.

Arai, Masami. "The Genç Kalemler and the Young Turks: A Study in Nationalism." *METU Studies in Developments* 12, nos. 3–4 (1985): 194–244.

Arkun, Aram. "A Preliminary Overview of Armenian-Language Primary Sources Published on the Armenian Genocide." Paper presented at "The State of the Art of Armenian Genocide Research: Historiography, Sources, and Future Directions" conference, Clark University, Worcester, MA, April 2010.

Astourian, Stephan H. "The Road Ahead for Armenian Genocide Studies." Paper presented at "The State of the Art of Armenian Genocide Research: Historiography, Sources, and Future Directions" conference, Clark University, Worcester, MA, April 2010.

Balakian, Grigoris. *Armenian Golgotha: A Memoir of the Armenian Genocide, 1915–1918*. Translated by Peter Balakian and Aris Sevag. New York: Alfred A. Knopf, 2009.

Barton, James L., ed. *"Turkish Atrocities": Statements of American Missionaries on the Destruction of Christian Communities in Ottoman Turkey, 1915–1917*. Ann Arbor, MI: Gomidas Institute, 1998.

Bessel, Richard. "Functionalists vs. Intentionalists: The Debate Twenty Years On or Whatever Happened to Functionalism and Intentionalism?," *German Studies Review* 26, no. 1 (February 2003): 15–20.

Bjørnlund, Matthias. "'A Fate Worse than Dying': Sexual Violence during the Armenian Genocide." In *Brutality and Desire: War and Sexuality in Europe's Twentieth Century*, edited by Dagmar Herzog, 16–58. New York: Palgrave Macmillan, 2009.

———. "The 1914 Cleansing of Aegean Greeks as a Case of Violent Turkification." *Journal of Genocide Research* 1, no. 2 (2006): 41–58.

Bloxham, Donald. *The Great Game of Genocide, Imperialism, Nationalism, and the Destruction of the Ottoman Armenians*. Oxford: Oxford University Press, 2005.

Bookman, Milica Zarkovic. *The Demographic Struggle for Power: The Political Economy of Demographic Engineering in the Modern World*. London: Frank Cass & Co., 1997.

Bora, Tanıl. "Nationalist Discourses in Turkey." In *Symbiotic Antagonisms: Competing Nationalisms in Turkey*, edited by Ayse Kadioglu and Fuat Keyman. Salt Lake City: University of Utah Press, 2011.

Browning, Christopher R. "The Decision-Making Process." In *The Historiography of the Holocaust*, edited by Dan Stone, 173–97. New York: Palgrave Macmillan, 2004.

Chitjian, Hampartzoum Mardiros. *A Hair's Breadth from Death*. London: Taderon Press, 2003.

Dadrian, Vahakn N. "The Armenian Genocide: An Interpretation." In *America and the Armenian Genocide of 1915*, edited by Jay Winter, 52–102. New York: Cambridge University Press, 2003.

———. "Children as Victims of Genocide: The Armenian Case." *Journal of Genocide Research* 5, no. 3 (September 2003): 421–27.

———. "The Convergent Roles of the State and a Governmental Party in the Armenian Genocide." In *Studies in Comparative Genocide*, edited by Levon Chorbajian and George Shirinian, 92–125. London: Macmillan; New York: St. Martin's Press, 1999.

———. "Documentation of the Armenian Genocide in German and Austrian Sources." In *Genocide: A Critical Bibliographic Review*, edited by Israel W. Charny. Vol. 2, 77–125. New York: Facts on File, 1991.

Dadrian, Vahakn N. "Documentation of the Armenian Genocide in Turkish Sources." In *Genocide: A Critical Bibliographic Review*, edited by Israel W. Charny. Vol. 2, 86–138. London: Mansell Publishing; New York: Facts on File, 1991.

———. "Genocide as a Problem of National and International Law: The World War I Armenian Case and Its Contemporary Legal Ramifications." *Yale Journal of International Law* 14, no. 2 (Summer 1989): 221–334.

———. *German Responsibility in the Armenian Genocide: A Review of the Historical Evidence of German Complicity*. Cambridge, MA: Blue Crane Books, 1996.

———. *The History of the Armenian Genocide: Ethnic Conflict from the Balkans to Anatolia to the Caucasus*. Providence, RI: Berghahn Books, 1995.

———. "The Naim-Andonian Documents on the World War I Destruction of Ottoman Armenians: The Anatomy of a Genocide." *International Journal of Middle East Studies* 18, no. 3 (August 1986): 311–36.

———. "Ottoman Archives and Denial of the Armenian Genocide." In *The Armenian Genocide: History, Politics, Ethics*, edited by Richard Hovannisian, 280–310. New York: St. Martin's Press, 1992.

———. "Party Allegiance as a Determinant in the Turkish Military's Involvement in the World War I Armenian Genocide." *Hakirah Journal of Jewish and Ethnic Studies* 1, no. 1 (2003): 57–67.

———. "The Pitfalls of a 'Balanced' Analysis: A Response to Ronald Grigor Suny." *Armenian Forum* 1, no. 2 (Summer 1998): 73–130.

———. "The Role of Turkish Military in the Destruction of Ottoman Armenians." *Journal of Political and Military Sociology* 20, no. 2 (Winter 1992): 257–88.

———. "The Role of Turkish Physicians in the World War I Genocide of Ottoman Armenians." *Holocaust and Genocide Studies* 1, no. 2 (1986): 169–92.

———. *Warrant for Genocide: Key Elements of Turko-Armenian Conflict*. New Brunswick, NJ: Transaction Publishers, 1999.

Davis, Leslie A. *The Slaughterhouse Province: An American Diplomat's Report on the Armenian Genocide, 1915–1917*. Edited by Susan K. Blair. New Rochelle, NY: Aristide D. Caratzas, 1989.

Davison, Roderic H. "The Armenian Crisis, 1912–1914." *American Historical Review* 53, no. 3 (April 1948): 481–505.

Derderian, Katharine. "Common Fate, Different Experience: Gender-Specific Aspects of the Armenian Genocide, 1915–1917." *Holocaust and Genocide Studies* 19, no. 1 (2005): 1–25.

Der Yeghiayan, Zaven. *My Patriarchal Memoirs*. Barrington, RI: Mayreni Publishing, 2002.

Docker, John. "Are Settler-Colonies Inherently Genocidal? Rereading Lemkin." In *Empire, Colony, Genocide: Conquest, Occupation, and Subaltern Resistance in World History*, edited by Dirk Moses, 81–102. New York: Berghahn Books, 2008.

Dündar, Fuat. *Crime of Numbers: The Role of Statistics in the Armenian Question (1878–1918)*. New Brunswick, NJ: Transaction Publishers, 2010.

Ecumenical Patriarchate of Constantinople. *Persecution of the Greeks in Turkey, 1914–1918*. Constantinople [London: Hesperia Press], 1919.

Erickson, Edward. *Ordered to Die: A History of the Ottoman Army in the First World War.* Westport, CT: Greenwood Press, 2001.

Fotiadis, Konstantinos Emm. *The Genocide of the Pontus Greeks by the Turks.* Vol. 13, *Archive Documents of the Ministries of Foreign Affairs of Britain, France, the League of Nations and S.H.A.T.* Thessaloniki: Herodotus, 2004.

Gaunt, David. *Massacres, Resistance, Protectors: Muslim-Christian Relations in Eastern Anatolia during World War I.* Piscataway, NJ: Gorgias Press, 2006.

Ghusein, Faiz el-. *Martyred Armenia*. New York: Tankian, 1975.

Gürün, Kamuran. *The Armenian File: The Myth of Innocence Exposed.* London: K. Rustem and Weidenfeld & Nicolson, 1985; New York: St. Martin's Press, 1986.

Hanioğlu, Şükrü. *A Brief History of the Late Ottoman Empire*. Princeton: Princeton University Press, 2008.

———. *Preparation for a Revolution: The Young Turks, 1902–1908*. Oxford: Oxford University Press, 2001.

———. *The Young Turks in Opposition*. New York: Oxford University Press, 1995.

Hartunian, Abraham H. *Neither to Laugh nor to Weep: An Odyssey of Faith; A Memoir of the Armenian Genocide.* 3rd ed. Belmont, MA: National Association for Armenian Studies and Research, 1999.

Hirschon, Renée, ed. *Crossing the Aegean: An Appraisal of the 1923 Compulsory Exchange between Greece and Turkey.* New York: Berghahn Books, 2003.

Holquist, Paul. "'Information Is the Alpha and Omega of Our Work': Bolshevik Surveillance in Its Pan-European Context." *Journal of Modern History* 69, no. 3 (September 1997): 415–50.

Hovannisian, Richard, ed. *The Armenian Genocide, Cultural and Ethical Legacies.* New Brunswick, NJ: Transaction Publishers, 2007.

———. *The Armenian Genocide: History, Politics, Ethics.* New York: St. Martin's Press, 1992.

———. *Armenian Karin/Erzurum*. Costa Mesa, CA: Mazda Publishers, 2003.

———. *Armenian Van/Vaspurakan*. Costa Mesa, CA: Mazda Publishers, 2000.

———. *Looking Backward, Moving Forward: Confronting the Armenian Genocide.* New Brunswick, NJ: Transaction Publishers, 2003.

———. *Remembrance and Denial.* Detroit, MI: Wayne State University Press, 1998.

Huttenbach, Henry R. "Towards a Conceptual Definition of Genocide." *Journal of Genocide Research* 4, no. 2 (2002): 167–76.

Kaiser, Hilmar. *At the Crossroads of Der Zor: Death, Survival, and Humanitarian Resistance in Aleppo, 1915–1917.* In collaboration with Luther and Nancy Eskijian. Princeton: Gomidas Institute, 2002.

Kaligian, Dikran. *Armenian Organization and Ideology under Ottoman Rule: 1908–1914.* New Brunswick, NJ: Transaction Publishers, 2009.

Karpat, Kemal. *Ottoman Population, 1830–1914: Demographic and Social Characteristics.* Madison: University of Wisconsin Press, 1985.

Kennan, George F. *The Other Balkan Wars: A 1913 Carnegie Endowment Inquiry in Retrospect with a New Introduction and Reflection on the Present Conflict.* Washington, DC: Carnegie Endowment for International Peace; Brookings Institution Publications, 1993.

Kieser, Hans-Lukas. *A Quest for Belonging: Anatolia beyond Empire and Nation (19th–21st Centuries).* Analecta Isisiana: Ottoman and Turkish Studies, 97. Istanbul: Isis, 2007.

Kontogiorgi, Elisabeth. "Forced Migration, Repatriation, Exodus: The Case of Ganos-Chora and Myriophyto-Peristaris Orthodox Communities in Eastern Thrace." *Balkan Studies* 35, no. 1 (1995): 15–45.

Lades, Stephen. *The Exchange of Minorities: Bulgaria, Greece and Turkey.* New York: Macmillan, 1932.

Lemkin, Raphael. *Axis Rule in Occupied Europe.* New York: Carnegie Endowment for International Peace, 1944.

Lewy, Guenter. *The Armenian Massacres in Ottoman Turkey: A Disputed Genocide.* Salt Lake City: University of Utah Press, 2005.

Marashlian, Levon. *Politics and Demography: Armenians, Turks and Kurds in the Ottoman Empire.* Toronto: Zoryan Institute, 1991.

McCarthy, Justin. *Death and Exile: The Ethnic Cleansing of Ottoman Muslims, 1821–1922.* Princeton, NJ: Darwin Press, 1995.

———. *Muslims and Minorities: The Population of Ottoman Anatolia and the End of the Empire.* New York: New York University Press, 1983.

———. *Population History of the Middle East and the Balkans.* Istanbul: Isis Press, 2002.

McCarthy, Justin, and Carolyn McCarthy. *Turks and Armenians: A Manual on the Armenian Question.* Washington, DC: Publication of Committee on Education, Assembly of Turkish American Associations, 1989.

McGarry, John. "'Demographic Engineering': The State-Directed Movement of Ethnic Groups as a Technique of Conflict Regulation." *Ethnic and Racial Studies* 21, no. 4 (July 1998): 613–38.

Miller, Donald E., and Lorna Touryan Miller. *Survivors: An Oral History of the Armenian Genocide.* Berkeley: University of California Press, 1993.

Moranian, Suzanne Elizabeth. "The Armenian Genocide and the American Missionary Relief Effort." In *America and the Armenian Genocide of 1915*, edited by Jay Winter, 146–214. Cambridge: Cambridge University Press, 2003.

———. "The American Missionaries and the Armenian Question: 1915–1927." PhD dissertation, University of Wisconsin–Madison, 1994.

Morgenthau, Henry. *Ambassador Morgenthau's Story*. Garden City, NY: Doubleday, Page & Co., 1918.

———. *United States Diplomacy on the Bosphorus: The Diaries of Ambassador Morgenthau, 1913–1916*. Compiled, edited, and introduced by Ara Sarafian. London: Taderon Press with Gomidas Institute, 2004.

Moses, Dirk. "The Holocaust and Genocide." In *The Historiography of the Holocaust*, edited by Dan Stone, 533–55. New York: Palgrave Macmillan, 2004.

Mourelos, Yannis G. "The 1914 Persecutions and the First Attempt at an Exchange of Minorities between Greece and Turkey." *Balkan Studies* 26, no. 2 (1985): 389–413.

Nalbandian, Louise. *The Armenian Revolutionary Movement: The Development of Armenian Political Parties through the Nineteenth Century*. Berkeley: University of California Press, 1975.

Odian, Yervant. *Accursed Years: My Exile and Return from Der Zor, 1914–1919*. London: Gomidas Institute, 2009.

Orel, Şinasi, and Süreyya Yuca. *The Talat Pasha Telegrams: Historical Fact or Armenian Fiction?* Nicosia: K. Rustem & Brother, 1986.

Papadopoulos, Alexander. *Persecution of the Greeks in Turkey before the European War*. New York: Oxford University Press, 1919.

Riggs, Henry H. *Days of Tragedy in Armenia: Personal Experiences in Harpoot, 1915–1917*. Ann Arbor, MI: Gomidas Institute, 1997.

Safi, Polat. "The Ottoman Special Organization—Teşkilat-ı Mahsusa: A Historical Assessment with Particular Reference to Its Operations against British Occupied Egypt (1914–1916)." Master's thesis, Institute of Economics and Social Sciences, Bilkent University, Ankara, Turkey, September 2006.

Sarafian, Ara. "The Ottoman Archives Debate and the Armenian Genocide." *Armenian Forum* 2, no. 1 (Spring 1999): 35–44.

Sarafian, Sara. "The Absorption of Armenian Women and Children into Muslim Households as a Structural Component of the Armenian Genocide." In *In God's Name: Genocide and Religion in the Twentieth Century*, edited by Omer Bartov and Phyllis Mack, 209–22. New York: Berghahn Books, 2001.

Schabas,William A. *Genocide in International Law*. London: Cambridge University Press, 2000.

Şeker, Nesim. "Demographic Engineering in the Late Ottoman Empire and the Armenians." *Middle Eastern Studies* 43, no. 3 (2007): 46–474.

Semelin, Jacques. *Purify and Destroy: The Political Uses of Massacre and Genocide*. New York: Columbia University Press, 2007.

Shemmassian, Vahram L. "Humanitarian Intervention by the Armenian Prelacy of Aleppo during the First Months of the Genocide." Unpublished manuscript, n.d.

Strauss, Scott. "Contested Meanings and Conflicting Imperatives: A Conceptual Analysis of Genocide." *Journal of Genocide Research* 3, no. 3 (2001): 349–75.

Suny, Ronald Grigor. "Empire and Nation: Armenians, Turks, and the End of the Ottoman Empire." *Armenian Forum* 2 (Summer 1988): 17–51.

Suny, Ronald Grigor, Fatma Müge Göçek, and Norman Naimark, eds. *A Question of Genocide: Armenians and Turks at the End of the Ottoman Empire.* Oxford: Oxford University Press, 2011.

Toynbee, Arnold. *The Western Question in Greece and Turkey: A Study in the Contact of Civilization.* New York: Howard Fertig, 1970.

Üngör, Uğur Ümit. "Geographies of Nationalism and Violence: Rethinking Young Turk 'Social Engineering.'" *European Journal of Turkish Studies* 7 (2008). http://ejts.revues.org/index2583.html.

Winter, Jay, ed. *America and the Armenian Genocide of 1915.* Cambridge: Cambridge University Press, 2003.

Yalman, Ahmet Emin. *Turkey in the World War.* New Haven: Yale University Press, 1930.

Yeghiayan, Vartkes. *British Reports on Ethnic Cleansing in Anatolia, 1919-1922: The Armenian-Greek Section.* Glendale, CA: Center for Armenian Remembrance, 2007.

Yeldan, A. Erinç. "Assessing the Privatization Process in Turkey: Implementation, Politics and Performance Results." *Global Policy Network,* 12 April 2006. http://www.gpn.org/research/privatization/priv_turkey_en.pdf.

Zürcher, Erik. *Turkey: A Modern History.* London: Tauris & Co. Ltd., 2005.

FRENCH

Kévorkian, Raymond, ed. "L'extermination des déportés arméniens ottomans dans les camps de concentration de Syrie-Mésopotamie (1915–1916)." *Revue d'histoire arménienne contemporaine* 2 (1998).

GERMAN

Bihl, Wolf Dieter. *Die Kaukasus-Politik der Mittelmächte. Teil 1: Ihre Basis in der Orient-Politik und ihre Aktionen, 1914–1917.* Vienna, Cologne, and Graz: Böhlau, 1974.

Captanian, Pailadzo. *1915 Der Völkermord an den Armenien: Eine Zeugin berichtet.* Leipzig: Gustav Kiepenheuer, 1993.

Dinkel, Christopher. "Der Einfluss hoher deutscher Offiziere im Osmanischen Reich auf die zum Völkermord and den Armeniern führenden Massnahmen. Ratgeber und/oder Vollzugsgehilfen." Unpublished manuscript, n.d.

Kieser, Hans-Lukas. *Der Verpasste Friede: Mission, Ethnie und Staat in den Ost-provinzen der Türkei, 1939–1938.* Zurich: Chronos Verlag, 2000.

———. *Vorkämpfer der "neuen Türkei": Revolutionäre Bildungseliten am Genfersee (1870–1939).* Zürich: Chronos, 2005.

Kieser, Hans-Lukas, and Dominik J. Schaller, eds. *Der Völkermord an den Armeniern und die Shoah.* Zürich: Chronos Verlag, 2002.

Lepsius, Johannes. *Der Todesgang des Armenischen Volkes: Bericht über das Schicksal des Armenischen Volkes in der Türkei waehrend des Weltkrieges.* Potsdam: Missionshandlung und Verlag, 1919.

Mandelstam, André. *Das Armenische Problem im Lichte des Volker und Menschenrechts.* Berlin: G. Stilke, 1931.

TURKISH

Akçam, Taner. *İnsan Hakları ve Ermeni Sorunu, İttihat ve Terakki'den Kurtuluş Savaşına.* Ankara: İmge Yayınevi, 1999.

———. *1915 Yazıları.* Istanbul: İletişim yayınları, 2010.

———. "Soykırım Suçunda Kasıt Unsuru Konusunda Bazı Notlar." *Birikim* 199 (November 2005): 34–42.

Akhanlı, Doğan, ed. *Talat Paşa Davası Tutanakları.* Istanbul: Belge Yayınları, 2003.

Aktan, Gündüz. "Bir Şey Söyle de." *Radikal,* 22 March 2007.

———. "Rövanş (1)." *Radikal,* 29 November 2005.

Aktar, Ayhan. *Türk Milliyetçiliği, Gayrimüslimler ve Ekonomik Dönüşüm.* Istanbul: İletişim, 2006.

———. *Varlık Vergisi ve Türkleştirme Politikaları.* Istanbul: İletişim Yayınları, 2000.

Aktar, Ayhan, and Abdulhamit Kırmızı. "'Bon Pour L'Orient': Fuat Dündar'ın kitabını deşifre ederken. . . ." *Tarih ve Toplum* 8 (Spring 2009): 157–86.

Alpay, Şahin. "'Soykırım' tezinin zaafları." *Zaman,* 3 September 2005.

Anonymous. "Haver Delal." Unpublished memoir, 1983.

Ara, Masami. *Jön Türk Dönemi Milliyetçiliği.* Istanbul: İletişim Yayınları, 1994.

Artuç, Nevzat. *Cemal Paşa: Askeri ve Siyasi Hayatı.* Ankara: Türk Tarih Kurumu, 2008.

Atay, Falih Rıfkı. *Atatürk'ün Bana Anlattıkları.* Istanbul: Sel Yayınları, 1955.

———. *Zeytindağı.* Istanbul: Bateş A.Ş., 1981.

Atnur, İbrahim Ethem. *Türkiye'de Ermeni Kadınlar ve Çocuklar Meselesi (1915–1923).* Ankara: Babil Yayıncılık, 2005.

Avagyan, Arsen. *Osmanlı İmparatorluğu ve Kemalist Türkiye'nin Devlet-İktidar Sisteminde Çerkezler.* Istanbul: Belge Yayınları, 2004.

Avcıoğlu, Doğan. *Milli Kurtuluş Tarihi.* 3 vols. Istanbul: Tekin Yayınevi, 1987.

Aydemir, Şevket Süreyya. *Makedonya'dan Ortaasya'ya Enver Paşa*. 3 vols. Istanbul: Remzi Kitabevi, 1972–78.

Aydoğan, Erdal. *İttihat ve Terakki'nin Doğu Politikası 1908–1918*. Istanbul: Ötüken Neşriyat, 2005.

Aydoğan, Erdal, and İsmail Eyyüpoğlu. *Bahaeddin Şakir Bey'in Bıraktığı Vesikalara Göre İttihat ve Terakki*. Istanbul: Alternatif Yayınları, 2004.

Babacan, Hasan. *Mehmet Talat Paşa*. Ankara: Türk Tarih Kurumu, 2005.

Bardakçı, Murat. "İşte Kara Kaplı Defterdeki Gerçek." *Hürriyet*, 25 April 2006.

———. "Paşa'ya göre Ermeni sayıları." *Hürriyet*, 26 September 2005.

———. "Savaş Sırasında 93 bin 88 Rum Başka Viláyetlere Nakledildi." *Hürriyet*, 26 April 2006.

———. *Talat Paşa'nın Evrak-ı Metrukesi: Sadrazam Talat Paşa'nın Özle Arşivinde Bulunan Ermeni Tehciri Konusundaki Belgeler ve Hususi Yazışmalar*. Istanbul: Everest, 2008.

Başkatipzade Ragıp Bey. *Tarih-i Hayatım*. Ankara: Kebikeç Yayınları, 1996.

Bayar, Celal. *Ben de Yazdım*. 8 vols. Istanbul: Baha Matbaası, 1967.

Bayur, Yusuf Hikmet. *Türk İnkilabı Tarihi*. 3 vols. Ankara: Türk Tarih Kurumu, 1983.

Behar, Büşra Ersanlı. *İktidar ve Tarih: Türkiye'de "Resim Tarih" Tezinin Oluşumu (1929–1937)*. Istanbul: Afa Yayınları, 1992.

Berberoğlu, Enis. "Dünü unutma yoksa soyulursun." *Hürriyet*, 26 June 1998.

Beşikçi, Mehmet. "Birinci Dünya Savaşı'nda Devlet İktidarı ve İç Güvenlik: Asker Kaçakları Sorunu ve Jandarmanın Yeniden Yapılandırılması." In *Türkiye'de Ordu, Devlet ve Güvenlik Siyaseti*, edited by Evren Balta Paker and İsmet Akça, 147–74. Istanbul: Bilgi Üniversitesi Yayınları, 2010.

Bilgi, Nejdet. *Dr. Mehmed Reşid Şahingiray Hayatı ve Hatıraları*. İzmir: Akademi Kitabevi, 1997.

———. *Ermeni Tehciri ve Boğazlayan Kaymakamı Mehmed Kemal Bey'in Yargılanması*. Ankara: Köksav Yayınları, 1999.

Birinci, Ali. *Hürriyet ve İtilaf Fırkası: II. Meşrutiyet Devrinde İttihat ve Terakki'ye Karşı Çıkanlar*. Istanbul: Dergah Yayınları, 1990.

Bora, Tanıl. *Türk Milliyetçiliğinin Üç Hali*. Istanbul: Birikim, 2009.

Çakmak, Mareşal Fevzi. *Birinci Dünya Savaşında Doğu Cephesi*. Ankara: Genelkurmay Basımevi, 2005.

Çalıka, Hurşit, ed. *Ahmet Rifat Çalıka'nın Anıları*. Istanbul: Privately published, 1992.

Çavdar, Tevfik. *Milli Mücadele Başlarken Sayılarla ". . . Vaziyet ve Manzara-î Umumiye."* Istanbul: Milliyet Yayınları, 1971.

Cengiz, Erdoğan, ed. *Ermeni Komitelerinin Âmâl ve Harekât-ı İhtilâliyesi: İlân-ı Meşrutiyetten Evvel ve Sonra*. Ankara: Başbakanlık Basımevi, 1983.

Çerkez Hasan Amca. "Tehcirin İç Yüzü." *Alemdar*, 19–28 June 1919.

Çetin, Atilla. "TBMM Hükümeti'nin, Osmanlı Devlet Arşivi ve Mülga Sadâret Evrakının Muhafazası Hakkında Aldığı Kararlara Ait Bazı Belgeler." *Tarih Enstitüsü Dergisi Prof. Tayyib Gökbilgin Hatıra Sayısı.* Istanbul: İstanbul Üniversitesi Edebiyat Fakültesi, 1982, 593–610.

Copeaux, Étienne. *Tarih Ders Kitaplarında (1931–1993) Türk Tarih Tezinden Türk-İslam Sentezine.* Istanbul: Tarih Vakfı Yurt Yayınları, 1998.

Criss, Bilge. *İşgal Altında İstanbul.* Istanbul: İletişim, 1983.

Dadrian, Vahakn N. *Ermeni Soykırımında Kurumsal Roller, Toplu Makaleler, Kitap 1.* Istanbul: Belge Yayınları, 2004.

Dadrian, Vahakn N., and Taner Akçam. *"Tehcir ve Taktil," Divan-ı Harbi Örfi Zabıtları, İttihat ve Terakki'nin Yargılanması.* Istanbul: Bilgi Üniversitesi, 2009.

Danişmend, İsmail Hami. *İzahlı Osmanlı Tarihi Kronolojisi.* Istanbul: Sümer Kitapevi, 1961.

Demirel, Muammer. *Birinci Dünya Harbinde Erzurum ve Çevresinde Ermeni Hareketleri (1914–1918).* Ankara: Genelkurmay, 1996.

———. *Ermeniler Hakkında İngiliz Belgeleri (1896–1918) British Documents on Armenians.* Ankara: Yeni Türkiye, 2002.

"Devlet arşivi imha ediliyor; Cumhuriyet tarihi yazılamayacak." *Zaman,* 17 June 2002.

Doğan, Atilla. *Osmanlı Aydınları ve Sosyal Darwinizm.* Istanbul: Bilgi Üniversitesi Yayınları, 2006.

Dündar, Fuat. *İttihat ve Terakki'nin Müslümanları İskan Politikası (1913–1918).* Istanbul: İletişim Yayınları, 2001.

———. *Modern Türkiye'nin Şifresi, İttihat ve Terakki'nin Etnitise Mühendisliği (1913–1918).* Istanbul: İletişim, 2008.

Elden, Ali Fuad. *Birinci Dünya Harbinde Suriye Hatıraları.* Istanbul: Türkiye İş Bankası Kültür Yayınları, 2005.

Gedikli, Fethi. "Osmanlı Devletinin kuruluşunun 700. yılında Osmanlı Arşivlerinin Durumu." *Osmanlı Araştırmaları Vakfı,* www.osmanli.org.tr/web/makaleler/017.asp.

Güler, Ali, and Suat Akgül. *Sorun Olan Ermeniler.* Ankara: Berikan, 2003.

Gürün, Kamuran. *Ermeni Dosyası.* Ankara: Bilgi Yayınevi, 1988.

Habiçoğlu, Bedri. *Kafkasya'dan Anadolu'ya Göçler.* Istanbul: Nart Yayıncılık, 1993.

Halaçoğlu, Ahmet. *Balkan Harbi Sırasında Rumeli'den Türk Göçleri (1912–1913).* Ankara: Türk Tarih Kurumu,1994.

Halaçoğlu, Yusuf. *XVIII. Yüzyılda Osmanlı İmparatorluğu'nun İskan Siyaseti ve Aşiretlerin Yerleştirilmesi.* Ankara: Türk Tarih Kurumu, 1988.

———. *Ermeni Tehciri ve Gerçekler (1914–1918).* Ankara: Türk Tarih Kurumu, 2001.

———. *Sürgünden Soykırıma Ermeni İddiaları.* Istanbul: Babıali Kültür Yayıncılığı, 2007.

"Halep Valisi Celal'in anıları." *Vakit*, 10–13 December 1918.

Hür, Ayşe. "Bu İmha Edilen Kaçıncı Arşiv." *Radikal*, 19 December 2004.

İçimsoy, Oğuz. "Özelleştirme uygulamaları ve özelleştirilen kamu kuruluşlarının arşivleri." Paper presented at the Privatization and Institutional Archives panel discussion, Foundation for the Economic and Social History of Turkey [Türkiye Ekonomik ve Toplumsal Tarih Vakfı], October 1998.

İpek, Nedim. *Rumeli'den Anadolu'ya Türk Göçleri.* Ankara: Türk Tarih Kurumu, 1994.

İslamoğlu, Mustafa. "Şahbabanın Kemikleri Sızlamaz mı?" *Yeni Şafak,* 10 October 1999.

Kadri, Hüseyin Kazım. *Türkiye'nin Çöküşü.* Istanbul: Hikmet Neşriyat, 1992.

Karaca, Taha Niyazi. *Ermeni Sorununun Gelişim Sürecinde Yozgat'ta Türk Ermeni İlişkileri.* Ankara: Türk Tarih Kurumu 2005.

Karay, R. H. *Minelbab İlelmihrab (Mütareke Devri Anıları).* Istanbul: İnkilap Kitabevi, 1992.

Karpat, Kemal. *Osmanlı Nüfusu (1830–1914): Demografik ve Sosyal Özellikleri.* Istanbul: Tarih Vakfı Yayınları, 2003.

Kaymaz, İhsan Şerif. *Musul Sorunu.* Istanbul: Otopsi Yayınları, 2003.

Kocahanoğlu, Osman Selim. *İttihat ve Terakki'nin Sorgulanması ve Yargılanması.* Istanbul: Temel Yayınları, 1998.

Kutay, Cemal. *Birinci Dünya Harbinde Teşkilat-i Mahsusa ve Hayber'de Türk Cengi.* Istanbul: Ercan, 1962.

———. *Etniki Etarya'dan Günümüze, Ege'nin Türk Kalma Savaşı.* Istanbul: Boğaziçi Yayınları, 1980.

Mardin, Şerif. *Jön Türkler ve Siyasi Fikirleri.* Istanbul: İletişim Publications, 1983.

McCarthy, Justin. *Müslümanlar ve Azınlıklar.* Istanbul: İnkilap, 1998.

———. *Ölüm ve Sürgün.* Istanbul: İnkilap, 1998.

Menteşe, Halil. *Osmanlı Mebusan Meclisi Reisi Halil Menteşe'nin Anıları.* Istanbul: Hürriyet Vakfı Yayınları, 1986.

Mil, A. "Umumi Harpte Teşkilat-ı Mahsusa." *Vakit,* 2 February 1933–18 April 1934.

Mutlu, Şamil. *Osmanlı Devletinde Misyoner Okulları.* Istanbul: Gökkubbe, 2005.

Nesimi, Abidin. *Yılların İçinden.* Istanbul: Gözlem Yayınları, 1977.

Orhonlu, Cengiz. *Osmanlı İmparatorluğunda Aşiretlerin İskanı.* Istanbul: Eren, 1987.

Ortaylı, İlber. *İmparatorluğun En Uzun Yüzyılı.* Istanbul: Hil Yayınları, 1983.

———. *Son-Imparatorluk Osmanli.* Istanbul: Timas Yayınları, 2006.

Özdoğan, Günay Göksu. *"Turan"dan "Bozkurt"a: Tek Parti Döneminde Türkçülük.* Istanbul: İletişim Yayınları, 2006.

Özdemir, Hikmet. *Salgın Hastalıklardan Ölümler, 1914–1918.* Ankara: Türk Tarih Kurumu, 2005.

Özdemir, Hikmet, Kemal Çiçek, Ömer Turan, Ramazan Çalık, and Yusuf Halaçoğlu. *Ermeniler: Sürgün ve Göç.* Ankara: Türk Tarih Kurumu, 2004.

Özdemirci, Fahrettin. "Arşivlerimizin Kurumsal Yapılanma Gereksinimleri." Faculty of Languages, History, and Geography, Ankara University, http:// 80.251.40.59/humanity.ankara.edu.tr/odemirci/diger_sayfa_metinleri/fo/ars _kurumsl_yap_grksnm.pdf.

"Osmanlı Arşivi'nin Belgeleri Kâğıt Yapılsın Diye SEKA'ya Gönderildi." *Yeni Şafak,* 17 June 2000.

Öztürk, Kazım. *Türk Parlamento Tarihi: TBMM-II. Dönem, 1923–1927.* Vol. 3. Ankara: TBMM Vakfı Yayınları, No. 3, 1995.

Pamukciyan, Kevork. "Zamanlar, Mekânlar, İnsanlar." *Ermeni Kaynaklarından Tarihe Katkılar.* Vol. 3. Istanbul: Aras Yayıncılık, 2003.

Parmaksızoğlu, İsmet, ed. *Ermeni Komitelerinin İhtilal Hareketleri ve Besledikleri Emeller.* Ankara: DSİ Basım ve Foto, 1981.

Şahin, Necmettin (Sılan). *Said Halim ve Mehmet Talat Paşalar Kabinelerinin Divanı Ali'ye sevkleri hakkında Divaniye Mebusu Fuat Bey merhum tarafından verilen takrir üzerine berayı tahkikat kura isabet eden Beşinci Şube tarafından icra olunan tahkikat ve zabt edilen ifadatı muhtevidir. Meclisi Mebusan, Numara: 521, Devrei İntihabiyye 3, İçtima 5.* Istanbul: Istanbul Meclisi Mebusan Matbaası [1334] 1918.

Sakarya, İhsan. *Belgelerle Ermeni Sorunu.* Ankara: Genel Kurmay Başkanlığı, 1984.

Şakir, Ziya. *Yakın Tarihte Üç Büyük Adam.* Istanbul: Ahmet Sait, 1946.

Samih, Aziz. *Büyük Harpte Kafkas Cephesi Hatıraları.* Ankara: Genel Kurmay Yayınları, 1934.

Sarıhan, Zeki. *Kurtuluş Savaşı Günlüğü: Mondros'tan Erzurum Kongresine,* 4 vols. (vols. 1–3, Ankara: Öğretmen Yayınları, 1986; vol. 4, Ankara: Türk Tarih Kurumu, 1996).

Saydam, Abdullah. *Kırım ve Kafkas Göçleri (1856–1876).* Ankara: Türk Tarih Kurumu, 1997.

Selçuk, İlhan. *Yüzbaşı Selehattin'in Romanı.* Vol. 1. Istanbul: Remzi Kitabevi, 1993.

Şimşir, Bilal. *Rumeli'den Türk Göçleri.* 3 vols. Ankara: Türk Tarih Kurumu, 1988.

Söylemezoğlu, Galip Kemali. *Canlı Tarihler, Galip Kemali Söylemezoğlu Hatıraları, Atina Sefareti (1913–1916).* Istanbul: Türkiye Yayınevi, 1946.

Süslü, Azmi. *Ermeniler ve 1915 Tehcir Olayı.* Van: Yüzüncü Yıl Üniversitesi Rektörlüğü Yayını, Yayın, No. 5, 1990.

Taçalan, Nurdoğan. *Ege'de Kurtuluş Savaşı Başlarken.* Istanbul: Milliyet Yayınları, 1970.

Toprak, Zafer. *Türkiye'de Ekonomi ve Toplum (1908–1950): Milli İktisat-Milli Burjuvazi.* Istanbul: Tarih Vakfı Yurt Yayınları, 1995.

Toros, Taha. *Ali Münif Bey'in Hatıraları.* Istanbul: İsis Yayınları, 1996.

Toros, Taha. "Eski Nafia Nazırı Ali Münif Yegane'in Hatırları, İstibdattan Cumhuriyet'e." *Akşam*, 26 October–21 December 1955.

Tunaya, Tarık Zafer. *Türkiye'de Siyasal Partiler*. 3 vols. Istanbul: Hürriyet Vakfı Yayınları, 1986.

Tunçay, Mete, and Erden Akbulut. *Türkiye Halk İştirakiyun Fırkası (1920–1923)*. Istanbul: Sosyal Tarih Yayınları, 2007.

Tunçel, Harun. "Türkiye'de İsmi Değiştirilen Köyler." *Fırat Üniversitesi Sosyal Bilimler Dergisi* 10, no. 2 (2000): 23–34.

Yalçın, Hüseyin Cahit. *Siyasi Anılar*. Istanbul: Türkiye İş Bankası Kültür Yayınları.

Yalman, Ahmet Emin. *Yakın Tarihte Gördüklerim ve Geçirdiklerim*. Vol. 1, 1888–1918. Istanbul: Yenilik Basımevi, 1970.

Yerasimos, Stefanos. *Milliyetler ve Sınırlar, Balkanlar, Kafkasya ve Orta-Doğu*. Istanbul: İletişim Yayınları, 1994.

Yıldız, Ahmet. *"Ne Mutlu Türküm Diyebilene": Türk Ulusal Kimliğinin Etno-Seküler Sınırları (1919–1938)*. Istanbul: İletişim Yayınları, 2001.

Zürcher, Erik Jan, ed. *İmparatorluktan Cumhuriyete Türkiye'de Etnik Çatışma*. Istanbul: İletişim Yayınları, 2005.

INDEX

Page numbers in italics refer to figures and tables.